"They Can Live in the Desert but Nowhere Else"

Human Rights and Crimes against Humanity

Eric D. Weitz, Series Editor

A list of titles in this series appears at the back of the book.

RONALD GRIGOR SUNY

"They Can Live in the Desert
but Nowhere Else"

A HISTORY *of*

the ARMENIAN

GENOCIDE

PRINCETON UNIVERSITY PRESS
Princeton and Oxford

Armena

My Fellow Traveler Through Life

CONTENTS

ACKNOWLEDGMENTS

I have been fortunate to have friends and colleagues who were willing to read and comment on this book as it progressed from inchoate arguments to a finished manuscript. They include Jeanne Adanır, Ayhan Aktar, Kevork Bardakjian, Donald Bloxham, Yaşar Tolga Cora, Valerie Kivelson, Norman Naimark, Murat Özyüksel, Rolf Hosfeld, Ugur Ümit Üngör, and Eric D. Weitz. Fatma Müge Göçek and Erik Jan Zürcher went through the manuscript meticulously, correcting and commenting on Turkish sources and the nuances of Ottoman history. Likewise Bedross Der Matossian shared his deep knowledge of the Armenian, Ottoman Jewish, and Arab sides of the story. In innumerable ways my colleagues and fellow researchers who participated in the first eight meetings of the Workshop in Armenian-Turkish Scholarship (WATS) are co-authors of this work. They came together when we knew far less about what happened in 1915, and together we searched for why what happened happened. Many of them are far more knowledgeable than I about the intricacies of Armenian, Turkish, and Ottoman history, and their careful readings and reconstructions were essential in the generation of this work. I extend my special gratitude to my extraordinary research assistant at the University of Michigan, Aaron Bekemeyer, who searched through sources and compiled an indispensable chronology of the events before, during, and after the Genocide. His work was supplemented by Adam

Stone, a most reliable fact and footnote checker. I thank the students and audiences who listened to my lectures on the Genocide and sharpened my thinking with their doubts and questions.

Many people and institutions aided in the gestation and completion of this work. My editors, Eric Weitz and Brigitta van Rheinberg, initiated this project by encouraging me to (in fact insisting that I) write this book. They have been supportive throughout this long and difficult exploration. The Armenian Studies Program and the Department of History at the University of Michigan were homes in which I worked with my closest colleagues and friends, and during my sabbatical year (2013–2014) I completed the writing with the generous support of residential fellowships at the Center for Advanced Holocaust Studies of the United States Holocaust Memorial Museum (as Everett and Marian Gordon Fellow), the incomparable American Academy in Berlin (as Anna-Marie Kellen Fellow), and the Kennan Institute of the Wilson Center for Scholars (as a short-term scholar).

While I was writing this book, my daughters, Sevan Siranoush Suni and Anoush Tamar Suni, and I suffered our own tragedy, the loss of our beloved Armena Pearl Marderosian, my wife, their mother, and a woman whom a friend remembered "had no malice in her." It was Armena who insisted the year before she became ill, as if she had a premonition, that we had to make a journey to historic Armenia to see the places—Van, Arapgir, and Diyarbakır—from which our ancestors had come. This book is dedicated, like the work the three of us have done in the years we have gone through without her, to this woman of exceptional generosity and gentleness, positivity, and courage.

This is the story of why, when, and how the Genocide of the Armenians of the Ottoman Empire happened. In cases of mass murder and war, simplification leads to facile accusations of guilt and assumptions of innocence. Appreciating complexity while searching through its thickets to find essential factors leads to understanding. The story told here is of a moment of historical passage, when empires attempted to accommodate themselves to a transforming world in which nations and national states challenged their sources of power and legitimacy. Yet those empires were not ready to give in or give up; they were not prepared to surrender to what later would appear to be irresistible pressures of nationalism, popular empowerment, and regimes based on equality and merit rather than inherited privilege and hierarchy. Looking back from the future the collapse of the Ottoman Empire and the emergence of subject nations appear to be historically inevitable. But for the actors in the last decades of the nineteenth century and the first of the twentieth there were many possible roads that could have been taken. This book investigates those moments of choice when political actors might have acted differently but decided instead to embark on a course that led to devastation and destruction.

The recovery of a difficult past is a challenge to the "assassins of memory," to those who would through distorting sophistries deny or minimize the enormity of a human tragedy.[1] Nations and states have long been in the business of fabricating, sometimes more honestly than at other times, myths and stories of their origins, golden ages, heroic deeds, victories, and triumphs, while eliminating the blemishes of defeats and failures, even mass murders. What appears to be new in our own time is the brazenness of what is claimed, the blatant cynicism of the perpetrators, and their potential reach through mass print and broadcast media, film, and the internet. Historians inevitably have been pulled into this war of images and words. The only weapon against bad history deployed for political or personal vindication is scrupulous investigation that results in evidence-based narration and analysis of what it is possible to know. The proliferation of useable pasts and preferred realities is a challenge to historians. They can take some comfort in the thought that dangers lurk when intellectual constructs stray too far from careful and accurate readings of the world. Reality has a nasty habit of biting back.

Revision of history is constant, even necessary, but in some cases, like that of the fate of the Armenians in the last years of the Ottoman Empire, it has led to the creation of two separate, contradictory narratives that appear to defy reconciliation. Although the literature produced by historians who favor the "Armenian" view and those who support the "Turkish" version actually agrees on many of the basic facts, for decades various authors have emphasized different elements and in general either avoided explanations of the causes of the events or implied an explanation even while not systematically or explicitly elaborating one. The Turkish state and those few historians who reject the notion of genocide have argued that the tragedy was the result of a reasonable and understandable response of a government to a rebellious and seditious population in time of war and mortal danger to the state's survival. *Raison d'état* justified the suppression of rebellion, and mass killing was explained as the unfortunate residue ("collateral damage" in the now fashionable vocabulary) of legitimate efforts to establish order behind the lines. This position, which those who recognize the 1915 Genocide call denialist, might be summarized as follows. There was no genocide, and the Armenians were to blame for it. They were rebellious, seditious subjects who presented a danger to the empire and got what they deserved.[2] Relative peace and harmony had existed in the Ottoman Empire between the state and its religious minorities until outside agitators, usually from the Russian Empire, aroused the nationalist and separatist passions of the Armenians. Still—the denialists claim—despite the existential threat posed by the Armenians and their Russian allies to the survival of the empire, there was no intention or effort by the Young Turk regime to eliminate the Armenians as a people.[3]

On the other side, many historians sympathetic to the Armenians shied away from explanations that might place any responsibility at all on the victims of Turkish policies. Armenian writers and the majority of scholars defended the case that massive deportations and massacres were ordered by and carried out by the Young Turk authorities and that these events constituted the first major genocide of the twentieth century.[4] Because a nuanced account of the background and causes of the Genocide seemed to concede ground to the deniers, Armenian scholars in particular were reluctant to see any rationale in the acts of the Young Turks.[5] Explanation, it was claimed, is rationalization, and rationalization in turn leads to the denialist position of justification. When explanation was offered, it was either an essentialist argument—Turks are the kind of people who employ massacre and systematic killing to maintain their imperial dominance—or related arguments that religion and/or ethnicity were the underlying causes of the killings. Deep, indelible cultural characteristics lay at the bottom of many interpretations.

The most insidious argument spoke of a conflict of two nationalist movements, Turkish and Armenian, over a single contested territory, eastern Anatolia.[6] "For the Turks," wrote the eminent Islamic historian Bernard Lewis,

> the Armenian movement was the deadliest of all threats. From the conquered lands of the Serbs, Bulgars, Albanians, and Greeks, they could, however reluctantly, withdraw, abandoning distant provinces and bringing the Imperial frontier nearer home. But the Armenians, stretching across Turkey-in-Asia from the Caucasian frontier to the Mediterranean coast, lay in the very heart

of the Turkish homeland—and to renounce these lands would have meant not the truncation, but the dissolution of the Turkish state. Turkish and Armenian villages, inextricably mixed, had for centuries lived in neighborly association. Now a desperate struggle between them began—a struggle between two nations for the possession of a single homeland, that ended with the terrible holocaust of 1915, when a million and a half Armenians perished.[7]

In what appeared to be a cool and balanced understanding of why their Ottoman rulers would have used mass violence against a perceived Armenian danger, Lewis placed the Armenians "nearer [the Turkish] home" and "in the very heart of the Turkish homeland," employing language that already assumed the legitimacy and actuality of a Turkish nation-state. In this transparent paragraph Lewis subtly rewrote the history of Anatolia from a land in which Armenians and Kurds were the earlier inhabitants into one in which they become an obstacle to the national aspirations of the Turks, who now could claim Anatolia, rather than Central Asia, as their homeland. His language employed the logic of nationalism as if it had a kind of universal relevance even in political structures that evolved out of and still worked within the logic of empire.

In 1915 the Ottoman Empire was evolving into a more homogeneous Turkic-Muslim state, in large part because of the loss of its Christian-populated territories in the Balkans. Yet it remained a multinational imperial state with large Arab, Kurdish, Jewish, and Christian communities. Already long existing within an international system of powerful nation-states in which an increasingly hegemonic Western conviction that the nation, however defined, was the principal source of political legitimacy, the Ottomans were desperately seeking a road to survival. But Lewis's reading of a notion of ethnic homogeneity as the basis for a national republic of the Kemalist type, which lay in the future, into the moment of Armenian annihilation is ahistorical and anachronistic.

The argument that I make in this book is different: whatever else they were, the Young Turks who carried out the Genocide were never purely Turkish ethnonationalists, never religious fanatics, but remained

Ottoman modernizers in their fundamental self-conception. They were primarily state imperialists, empire preservers, rather than the founders of an ethnic nation-state. There was no thought of giving up the Arab lands that they still controlled, or even eliminating totally their Christian and Jewish subjects, and when opportunity presented itself in 1918 the Young Turks were prepared to move north and east into Caucasia to create buffer states using other Muslim and Christian peoples. On the other hand, over time the Young Turks came to believe that Muslims, particularly Turks, were the appropriate people to rule the empire, that Muslims, particularly Turks, were the most trustworthy supporters of the Ottoman state, and increasingly convinced themselves that egalitarian Ottomanism was a political fantasy. Moreover, the removal of the Armenians, and later the Greeks, laid the basis for the Kemalist state, the current Turkish Republic, and many of the surviving Young Turks were among the founders of the republic. Kemal's ethnonationalism attempted to create an ethnically homogeneous Turkish nation, though ultimately that ambition was thwarted by the millions of Kurds who had lived in eastern Anatolia long before the first Turks arrived and who after 1915 spread to lands formerly held by Armenians.

In their ideal forms nation and empire stand at opposite ends of a political spectrum, but in the actuality of history they influenced, reinforced, and undermined one another at different times and in different ways. Nineteenth-century liberal states were able to compromise and collaborate with imperialism. Even though at home Great Britain, France, Belgium, and the Netherlands enjoyed representative institutions and styled themselves as democracies, they could be (and were) effective (and very often brutal) imperial powers in their overseas empires. "Civilization" in the homeland flourished in parallel with cruel and repressive exploitation of native peoples of Africa, Asia, and the Caribbean. Both the Russian and Ottoman Empires were instances of determined, haphazard, and ultimately futile attempts to modernize and nationalize the empire, to make it at some points more civilly unified and coherent, more *Rossiiskii* (inclusive of all the tsar's subjects) or *Osmanlı* (Ottoman rather than ethnic Turkish), and at other points more ethnically homogeneous, more *Russkii* (ethnic Russian) or *Türk* (ethnic Turk). In neither case was there a clear or even feasible program of creating an ethnonational state like France or the Kemalist Turkish Republic; their projects are better characterized as the creation of "imperial nations" within their empires. The empire was to continue but in a new form appropriate for the modern age, what has been called the age of nationalism and nation-states, but more accurately should be referred to as the age of empires.[8] A succession of modernizing efforts—the Western-oriented Ottoman state–promoted reforms known as the *Tanzimat*, the Hamidian Islamic coalition, and the Young Turks' initial constitutionalism that degenerated into absolutism—followed one another, and non-Turks struggled to find their own place within a tremulous political landscape.

Because the eventual deportations and mass murder of Armenians and the expulsion of Greeks resulted in a relatively homogeneous population of Muslims (Turks, Kurds, Circassians, and others) and the foundation of a Turkish national republic, the history of the last stages of the Ottoman Empire has been subsumed into an organic nationalist narrative, which reads back the emergence of an original, authentic Turkish nation into earlier centuries. The unique moments of attempted imperial regeneration in the *Tanzimat*, Hamidian, and Young Turk periods have as a consequence been effaced. This book is dedicated to reconstructing those moments, which involved new national imaginings of the various peoples of the empire, efforts by state authorities to construct a new kind of empire, and ultimately the destruction of hundreds of thousands of Ottoman Armenians and Assyrians.

In the past decade and a half, certainly since the turn of the twenty-first century, the historiography on the last years of the Ottoman Empire and the Armenian Genocide has made giant strides. The Workshop in Armenian-Turkish Studies (WATS), which first met in 2000 at the University of Chicago amid deep suspicion of the possibility of cooperation of Armenian, Turkish, and Kurdish scholars, pioneered discussion and collaborative work between social scientists of different nationalities and historical schools.[9] Although new forms of denialism have also appeared, the work of Armenian, Turkish, Kurdish, European, and American scholars has created a huge reservoir of documentary materials. A flood of archival documents changed the empirical understanding of what had happened in 1915 and why.[10] Archivally based monographs and brilliantly conceived synthetic studies have made it possible for the first time to understand the Armenian Genocide.[11] As the pioneering Turkish scholar of the Genocide Taner Akçam has summed up, "Taken in their entirety, Ottoman and Western archives jointly confirm that the ruling party CUP did deliberately implement a policy of ethnoreligious homogenization of Anatolia that aimed to destroy the Armenian population."[12] Scholars in Turkey, many of them veterans of WATS, courageously—and against the opposition of their government—held their own conference on "The Ottoman Armenians during the Era of Ottoman Decline" at Bilgi University in Istanbul in September 2005.[13] The backlash against scholarship remained relentless.[14] A principal participant in both WATS and the Bilgi conference, the fearless Turkish Armenian journalist Hrant Dink fell victim to the vicious nationalist attacks on those who championed understanding of the troubled history of these two peoples. On January 19, 2007, a young militant shot and killed him on an Istanbul avenue.

There may be no escape from the political aspects of setting the record straight on any genocide, and the Armenian Genocide more than most other mass killings has been the victim of deliberate, sustained falsification. Historians are embedded in those politics no matter how faithfully they attend to the obligations of their craft. As Turkey and Armenia both construct and reconstruct their historic and present-day identities, they have to deal with the traumas of their twentieth-century emergence. These two countries and their peoples, both at home and in the diaspora, are condemned to live in the present and the future side by side, as they have for half a millennium in the past, their destinies intertwined, their senses of self intimately wrapped up in the other. For historians, who have done so much to construct the pasts with which each nation now lives, the task of reconstruction has become imperative. In a humble way, this book is an effort to create a credible contribution to what honest scholars and journalists, like Hrant Dink, tried (and are trying) to do: tell the story of Armenians, Assyrians, Turks, and Kurds in all its aspects, tragic, heroic, foolish, and well-intended, a story of how people attempted to make a better life for themselves within an empire that itself chose a path that led to the destruction of both the state and millions of its subjects.

WHAT HAPPENED IN 1915

Before turning to a comprehensive explanation of why the Genocide occurred, an excursion that will take us back into the long history of the Armenians and their experiences in the Ottoman Empire, we will look briefly at what happened in 1915. Some 2 million Christian Armenians lived in the Ottoman lands, most of them peasants and townspeople in the six provinces of eastern Anatolia. In an Anatolian population estimated to be between 15 and 17.5 million inhabitants, Armenians were outnumbered by their Muslim neighbors in most locations, though they often lived in homogeneous villages and sections of towns, and occasionally dominated larger rural and urban areas.[15] The most influential and prosperous Armenians lived in the imperial capital, Istanbul (Constantinople), where their visibility made them the target of both official and popular resentment from many Muslims. What has come to be known as the first genocide of the twentieth century had its origins in the aspirations of a small group of Ottoman politicians associated with the Committee of Union and Progress (CUP), popularly referred to as the Young Turks.[16] Both the radicalization of their intentions and the final implementation of their plans occurred in the context of a deepening social and political crisis and the near destruction of the Ottoman state at the hands of external enemies. Having suffered territorial losses in the Balkan Wars (1912–1913) and forced to accept a European-imposed reform in the Armenian provinces, the Young Turks joined the Central Powers— Germany and Austro-Hungary—in 1914 as they waged war against the Entente—Great Britain, France, and Russia—in a desperate effort to restore and strengthen their empire. Armenians precariously straddled the Russian-Ottoman front, and both the Russians and the Ottomans attempted to recruit Armenians in their campaigns against their enemies. Most Ottoman Armenians supported and even fought alongside the

Ottomans against the Russians, while Armenians in Russia, organized into volunteer units, joined the tsarist campaign. In late 1914 and early 1915 massacres of Christians—Armenians and Assyrians—and Muslims occurred in the Caucasus and Persia, where Russians and Ottoman forces faced each other.

In early 1915 the Ottomans lost a major battle on the Caucasian front at Sarıkamış, and important Young Turks attributed the loss to Armenian treachery. In late February to early March 1915 the Young Turk government, led by Talat and Enver, ordered the disarming of Armenian soldiers and their transfer into labor battalions. The first victims of the state were the demobilized Armenian soldiers, who were easily segregated and systematically killed. Thus the muscle of the Armenian communities was removed. Almost immediately the government ordered the deportation of Armenians from cities, towns, and villages in the East, ostensibly as a necessary military measure to ensure the security of the rear. Soon Armenians throughout the country were forced to gather what belongings they could carry or transport and leave their homes at short notice. The exodus of Armenians was haphazard and brutal; irregular forces, local Kurds and Circassians, cut down hundreds of thousands of Christians, as civil and military officials oversaw and facilitated the removal of the empire's Armenian and Assyrian subjects. When some Armenians resisted the encroaching massacres in the city of Van in eastern Anatolia, the Committee of Union and Progress had the leading intellectuals and politicians in Istanbul, several of them deputies to the Ottoman Parliament, arrested and sent from the city. Most of them perished in the next few months. Thus was the brain of the Ottoman Armenian people removed, the intellectual and political leadership and the connective tissue that linked separate communities together. Women, children, and old men in town after town were marched through the valleys and mountains of eastern Anatolia. Missionaries, diplomats, and foreign military officers witnessed the convoys, recorded what they saw, and sent reports home about death marches and killing fields. Survivors reached the deserts of Syria, where they languished in concentration camps; many starved to death, and new massacres occurred.

The causes of the Genocide were both long term and immediate. To understand what happened and why, I explore the lengthy historical trail of events and experiences, the genealogy of attitudes and behaviors. The environment in which Genocide occurred—the imperial appetites of the Great Powers, the fierce competition for land and goods in eastern Anatolia, the aspirations and aims of Armenians, and the ambitions and ideas of the Young Turks—shaped the cognitive and emotional state of the perpetrators (what I call their "affective disposition") that allowed them, indeed in their minds required them, to eliminate whole peoples.[17] In the context of war and invasion a mental and emotional universe developed that included perceived threats, the Manichaean construction of internal enemies, and a pervasive fear that triggered a deadly, pathological response to real and imagined immediate and future dangers. A government had come to believe that among its subject peoples whole "nations" presented an immediate threat to the security of the state. Defense of the empire and of the "Turkish nation" became the rationale for mass murder. Armenians were neither passive nor submissive victims, but the power to decide their fate was largely out of their hands. A "great inequality in agency" existed between Young Turks and their armed agents and the segmented and dispersed Armenians.[18]

The canvas on which the mass deportation and massacre of Armenians and Assyrians took place was a landscape that stretched from Istanbul almost 1,000 miles to the east, beyond the eastern ends of the Ottoman Empire into Persia and the Caucasus. Mountains, valleys, rivers, and deserts were the topographies through which hundreds of thousands of uprooted people moved in convoys guarded by Ottoman soldiers and gendarmes, attacked and slaughtered by the *çetes* (gangs of irregular fighters) of the *Teşkilat-ı Mahsusa* (Special Organization), by Kurds, Turks, and Circassians. Driven to exhaustion, starvation, and suicide, hundreds of thousands, perhaps a million or more, would perish; others would be forced to emigrate or convert to Islam to save their lives. Men died in greater numbers; many women and children were taken into the families of the local Muslims. Tens of thousands of orphans found some refuge in the protection of foreign missionaries. It is estimated conservatively that between 600,000 and 1 million were slaughtered or died on the marches. Other tens of thousands fled to the north, to the relative safety of the Russian Caucasus. Hundreds of thousands of women and children, we now know, were compelled to convert to Islam and survived in the families of Kurds, Turks, and Arabs. By the end of the war 90 percent of the Armenians of the Ottoman Empire were gone, a culture and civilization wiped out never to return. Those who observed the killings, as well as the Allied powers engaged in a war against the Ottomans, repeatedly claimed that they had never witnessed anything like it. The word for what happened had not yet been invented.[19] There was no concept to mark the state-targeted killing of a designated ethnoreligious people. At the time those who needed a word borrowed from the Bible and called it "holocaust." My great-grandparents were among the victims.

SOURCES, NOTES, AND TRANSLITERATION

While writing this book I came to realize that one lifetime was not enough to exhaust the sources and literature on the Armenian Genocide. While not all relevant archives are accessible, the available sources are extraordinarily rich. Thanks to diligent predecessors an abundance of archival documents are either in print or online. In recording the sources in the notes, I have adopted a somewhat unorthodox method in the interest of clarity and accessibility for future scholars. The archival sources that I have read are recorded first in the notes, followed by references to publications where the documents can also be found. If I was not able to see the original or published document and was compelled to rely on the work of other scholars whom I have found to be reliable, I refer first to the source from which I took the information and, if available, then indicate the archival source that the published work used. Given the citation style of various authors, some of these published archival references are not as complete as the ones I myself read. Still, my intention is to give as full a record of the sources as possible in order to facilitate the work of future scholars of the Armenian Genocide and the late Ottoman period.

On transliterating Turkish, Russian, and Armenian words, I have followed a modified Library of Congress system without diacritical marks. Place names in Anatolia are usually given in the modern Turkish version, and places in Russia, the Balkans, the Caucasus, and elsewhere are given in the primary local language. For cities like Istanbul and Izmir the standard English version has been used rather than İstanbul or İzmır, with the capital dotted İ. Armenian words and names have been transliterated as written in today's Eastern Armenian even if the person, place, or word was used primarily in Western Armenian, for example, Grigor Otian rather than Krikor Odian.

"They Can Live in the Desert but Nowhere Else"

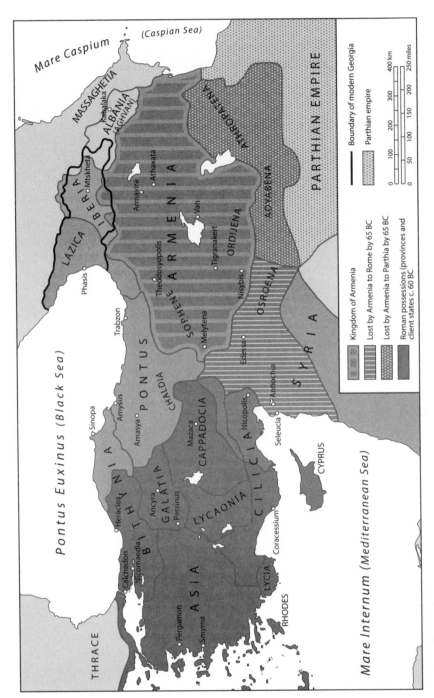

Ancient Armenia

CHAPTER ONE

Empire

TURKS, OTTOMANS, AND THE OTHERS

History, one might argue, is written not only by the victors but also by those who have the greatest access to books, printing, and the means of communication. For most Europeans and Americans the history and images of the Turks of the Ottoman Empire emerged from the tales of Western travelers, resident missionaries, itinerant journalists, and a number of dedicated Orientalist scholars. These images were almost invariably negative, though fascination with the exotic aspects of Ottoman life—harems in particular—sometimes tempered, sometimes reinforced the dominant representations. The most prevalent Western visions of the Middle East, which have been dubbed Orientalism, saw Europe as progressive and dynamic and the Orient as stagnant, underdeveloped, and even deviant from the flow of history as defined by Europeans.[1] Along with lazy Arabs and wild Kurds abided the "Terrible Turk." The prominent Liberal politician William Gladstone, who served as British prime minister four times between 1868 and 1894, wrote a widely read pamphlet, *The Bulgarian Horrors*, in which he graphically depicted the Turks as a threat to Christendom and as a people whose principal quality was unbridled savagery. "They were upon the whole, from the black day when they first entered Europe, the one great anti-human specimen of humanity. Wherever they went, a broad line of blood marked the track behind them; and, as far as their dominion reached, civilization disappeared from view."[2] Professional historians have recently tried to revise these stereotypes, modulating and refining the long history of the Ottomans. Yet the frequent episodes of brutal violence, massacres, ethnic cleansing, and eventually genocide remain indelible parts of that history, neither to be avoided nor left without explanation.

Who were the Turks? The simplest definition of the original Turks is that they were tribes of people who originated in Siberia and Central Asia and spoke one or another Turkic language. Having converted to Islam by the tenth century, Turkish-speaking tribes migrated westward, and in 1071 the Seljuk Turks (named after an earlier chieftain), led by Alp Aslan, defeated the Byzantine army at Manzikert (Malazgirt), near Lake Van, and captured the emperor. Anatolia was then open to further migrations of Turks, who over centuries conquered much of the lands in Asia Minor and the Balkans until in 1453 Mehmed II the Conqueror (1451–1481) took Constantinople and ended the thousand-year Byzantine Empire. The achievements of the Ottomans were extraordinary, at least in the first several hundred years of their imperial rule. A former nomadic people became the founders and rulers of a vast and expanding empire. Their initial political vision was based on an "ever-victorious army" and an "ever-expanding frontier" until repeated defeats by European armies forced a reconsideration of their territorial ambitions.[3] As in the Russian Empire of Peter the Great and Alexander II, defeat in war encouraged the Ottoman rulers to implement reforms in the military, in the bureaucracy, and more broadly in society. By the nineteenth century the Ottomans faced a double challenge: from imperialist competition among the Great Powers and from the rise of an alternative form of legitimacy and statehood—nationalism and the nation-state.

In an age such as ours we take for granted that nations and nation-states are the normal form of human political existence. Yet throughout most of human history the most long-lived and ubiquitous states were in fact great multiethnic, multireligious empires. From ancient Egypt, Assyria, China, and Rome through the last days of imperial rule in the 1970s, empires held sway over much of the globe. And European empires, formed in the eighteenth and nineteenth centuries, ruled most of the non-European world for about one hundred years.

Like other great empires, the Ottoman Empire was a composite state in which the ruling center was distinct from those it ruled. The realm was governed by the imperial dynasty, the Family of Osman (*Al i Osman*), which based its right to rule on the view that its superiority was natural, divinely ordained, and therefore justified. The imperial paradigm was a system in which the Ottoman sultan, by right of conquest and divine sanction, ruled over subjects of various religions and ethnicities in a structure of inequity and subordination that maintained, reinforced, and even produced difference. Two kinds of distinction were institutionalized in the Ottoman Empire in its first centuries: a vertical distinction between the ruling institution and the ordinary subjects of the sultan; and horizontal distinctions among the various religious communities in the empire. The ruling institution, made up of the sultan, his high clergy (the *ulema*), ministers, governors, bureaucrats, and the military, those who served the state (the *askeri*), was separate and above the "flock" (the *reaya*, the ordinary people).[4] Within the *askeri* an elite of *Osmanlı*s arose, those most knowledgeable of the "Ottoman way." The *askeri* paid no taxes, while the *reaya*—the peasants, artisans, merchants, herdsmen, and others—were subject to taxation. From the eighteenth century on, the term *reaya* was applied only to non-Muslims, underlining their inferior status.[5]

Like other traditional empires, the Ottoman realm was organized on the basis of strict distinctions and discriminations that were hierarchical in nature, with advantages and disadvantages ascribed to different persons and peoples according to their official positions and religious beliefs. The various religious and cultural groups of the empire were separate but unequal. Occasionally non-Muslims could rise in government service if they were able to demonstrate the necessary cultural competence of the Ottomans, but they always retained the stigma of difference and implied inferiority. While possessing no rights that limited the power of the sultan, non-Muslims were, nevertheless, respected as different from but subordinate to the ruling Ottoman elite.

In the early modern period, from the sixteenth to the eighteenth centuries, "a society existed . . . where 'difference' instead of 'sameness' was paramount," and there was almost no desire on the part of political leaders to transform difference into sameness.[6] The Ottoman political world was distinct from the Western Enlightenment public sphere of a value-neutral, universalistic ideal in which what is shared is highlighted and the particular, that which is different, becomes a problem to be resolved. In the

Ottoman lands difference was seen as normal and normative, something natural to be accepted.[7] In the early Ottoman centuries discrimination did not necessarily lead to repression. "Persecution of difference," one historian writes, "was not really acceptable. Since Ottoman rulers did not like social disorder, they attempted to fix or freeze the particular, but they did not change it."[8] Because the very distinction of the ruling institution from its subjects, and its superiority, gave it the right to rule over others, it was essential to the legitimacy and justification of the rulers' power that distinctions and hierarchies be maintained. Until the twentieth century sultans did not engage in forced homogenization of the population, though at times they ordered movement (*sürgün*) of specific populations to shore up the security of a borderland or to increase Islamic presence.

Although the empire was by the nineteenth century most often ruled by ethnic Turks, it was not conceived as an ethnic Turkish state but as a multinational Islamic empire, which included Arabs, Kurds, and Circassians, as well as other Muslim, Christian, and Jewish peoples. Those at the top of society had their own language, *Osmanlıca* (Ottoman Turkish), which was used in documents, poetry, and bureaucratic practice. The imperial language was not intelligible to ordinary people, and though it was not used widely as a spoken language, competence in Ottoman Turkish defined those in positions of influence and power from those outside.[9] The governing Ottomans ruled over Sunni and Shi'i Muslims, as well as more heterodox groups like the Alevis, sometimes referred to as *kızılbaş*, and the Yezidis. Ottoman authorities noted that these different sectarian or ethnic groups, even though Islamic in one form or another, might be troublesome to the state. But differences were tolerated, maintained, and even reinforced.

The empire was a kind of negotiated arrangement between the central authorities and the elites of the various peripheries.[10] The Ottoman center did not usually rule the provinces directly but through intermediaries over which they had varying degrees of control. In the eighteenth century the provincial local notables (*ayan*) were the key players in both the economy and governance of the regions and were usually trusted by the populace more than officials sent from the capital.[11] The Ottoman practice of indirect rule had both advantages and disadvantages. The sultans could rely on local agents to keep order, collect taxes, and carry out the empire's policies; but at the same time Istanbul was faced by what political scientists call the principal-agent problem. What was the supreme ruler to do when his local notables went their own way and enriched or empowered themselves, diminishing the reach of the ruler? Particularly difficult to control were the easternmost provinces of Anatolia, what had been historic Armenia and where most of the Ottoman Armenians lived. There Turkish dynasties resisted Istanbul in the early Ottoman period even more than Christian notables did in the Balkans. Sultans granted Kurdish chieftains governorships and broad powers to rule in the lands that bordered Iran and the Arab lands. The enormous province of Diyarbakır, whose ancient walled city housed a large Armenian and Assyrian population, was for centuries a fiercely contested buffer zone between Safavid Iran and the Ottoman lands.[12]

Besides social and geographic differences, the empire involved religious and ethnic distinctions and discriminations as well. Muslims had privileges and rights that non-Muslims did not. Islamic rulers conquered, subordinated, and tolerated the non-Muslim People of the Book, Christians and Jews, who lived under the *dhimma* or *zimma*, the pact of toleration of those living under Islam. Under this pact Christians and Jews could practice their religion, maintain their churches and synagogues, and largely control their own affairs as long as they recognized the superiority of Islam, paid the special poll tax (*cizye*), and obeyed the state authorities. The Christian churches and their hierarchies, like the institutions of the Jews, were part of the imperial structure. For centuries, right up to the 1870s, the sultans ruled over more Christians and Jews than Muslims and were able to do so precisely because they had effective imperial institutions that delegated power to obedient servitors of the regime. Between the Muslims and their non-Muslim fellow subjects the relationship was to be separate and unequal, but protected.[13] The Quran contains verses that both stigmatize non-Muslims and praise the religion of Jews and Christians. While the texts can be taken to justify a variety of attitudes and policies, in different

Istanbul (Constantinople), the Galata Bridge. View from Pera, the European section toward the old city. Felix Bonfils, 1870.

times and places Islam adapted to the social and political environment in which it was practiced.[14]

Islam was the state religion both in the sense of the official religion that legitimized and bound the state to its Muslim peoples and as an actual institution and instrument of the state.[15] Islam was key to justifying the rule of the Ottomans. The sultan was also the caliph, the leader of Sunni Islam. Shared religion linked the ruling elite to the Muslim population of the empire. They spoke in the same vocabulary and ideals. But at the same time Ottoman rulers subordinated religious concerns to the needs of the state. Conflicts arose with Shi'i Muslims, not so much on religious grounds but whenever the Ottomans perceived them as an internal threat to their state.[16] Sultan Süleyman (1520–1566) energetically encouraged the education of religious elites, built magnificent mosques, and established schools and Islamic courts, integrating his empire while making sure that religion was subjugated to the state. The *kadıs* (judges) were instrumental in administering justice and maintaining "a basic moral and cultural unity" in the realm.[17] Both Muslims and non-Muslims took cases to the *kadıs*. Along with the Islamic religious law (sharia, or *şeriat*), the Ottomans promulgated more flexible secular laws (*kanun*), some of which were borrowed from their predecessor, the Byzantine Empire. But Islam spoke to only part of the empire's population, and sometimes not very loudly even to them. Difference coexisted with dissent from the official ideology. Ultimately the empire was marked by dominance without hegemony, that is, rule backed by force without a high degree of acceptance or acquiescence by many. When force weakened or was absent, people went their own way; when force increased, it was often met by resistance.

THE IMPERIAL PARADIGM AND THE NATION-STATE

In the imagination of Ottoman elites their sultan's territories were the Well-Protected Domains (*Memalik-i Mahruse*) and later the Sublime Ottoman State (*Devlet-i Aliye-i Osmaniye*). What the West understood as the Ottoman Empire, or more commonly Turkey, its rulers acknowledged in the nineteenth century as an empire, a great state governed through the offices of the Sublime Porte (*Bab-ı Ali*).[18] The capital lay between what cartographers had designated as Europe and Asia, the border being the narrow strait, the Bosphorus (*Boğaziçi*), and the name of the city changed from Byzantium to Constantinople and finally to Istanbul for Turkish speakers. Each nationality in the city had its own name for the place: the Greeks were content with *Konstantinopoulos*, which came from their language; Armenians shortened it to *Bolis*; and Russians, who had their own claims on the center of Orthodox Christianity, called it simply *Tsargrad*, the city of the emperor. All recognized it as an imperial capital, the hub around which a multicultural society of diverse religions and languages revolved.

As a form of state, empire is quite different from the ideal type of nation-state, which usually aspires to create national communities of

Istanbul (Constantinople), the main street in Pera, the European section.
Collection of Maggie Land Blanck.

homogeneous and legally equal citizens. Empires were almost always
built on principles of hierarchy, inequality, and institutionalized difference—both among peoples and between ruling elites and their subjects.
Indeed, these two state forms—nation-state and empire—stood in tension one with the other in the emerging nineteenth-century discourse of
the nation, just as one of the longest surviving empires, the Ottoman, confronted the prevailing Western conceptions of the nation. A number of
Turkish, Greek, and Armenian thinkers and actors were intrigued by the
particularly modern form of "imagined" political community that came
together in the late eighteenth and early nineteenth centuries around the
notion of bounded territorial sovereignties in which the "people," defined
as members of a nation, provide the legitimacy to the political order.[19]
The implications of nationalism were subversive for many aspects of the
imperial order. For those who could reconceive themselves as nations the
idea of national self-determination provided a new legitimation for separation from the empire. At the same time Westernizing officials within

the ruling Ottoman elites were intrigued by other Western ideas, such as equality under the law, and in the reforms of the *Tanzimat* (Reorganization) period (1839–1878) Ottoman bureaucrats introduced laws and practices that in their application began to undermine the legitimation formulas for the traditional distinctions and hierarchies of empire.

The "discourse of the nation" originated in Europe but spread throughout the colonized world, first manifested in the French Revolution as an expression of state patriotism. Through the nineteenth century nation or nationality increasingly became ethnicized until the "national community" was most often understood to be a cultural community of shared language, religion, and other characteristics with a durable, antique past, shared kinship, common origins, and narratives of progress through time.[20] By the twentieth century such imagined national communities, thought to be products of blood and nature, were the most legitimate basis for the constitution of states, displacing dynasties and challenging alternative formulas for legitimation like conquest, the divine sanction of rulers, and the superiority of certain races. As the idea of what constituted a nation shifted toward ethnic homogeneity and equality, the incompatibility between traditional empire and nation-state widened. Yet for much of the late nineteenth and early twentieth centuries both imperialists and nationalists often sought ways to maintain their pluralistic states as "national empires" within which "imperial nations" might dominate.[21]

Nationalists, most particularly ethnonationalists, viewed their nations as ancient, continuous, and organic—products as much of nature as history. Yet no matter how much they might stress the elements of ethnicity, language, and kinship, nationalists were fervent in their creation (they might say "recovery") of the national past. The writing of history was tightly tied to the emergence of nations and nation-states. The story to be told aimed to make the nation appear as a stable subject moving continuously through time, fulfilling a project over many centuries of coming to self-awareness.[22] For both the great nineteenth-century empires and their subordinated peoples, this powerful rethinking of history in the idiom of the nation had the effect of homogenizing disparate events and processes into a single, progressive narrative so that other ways of understanding experience lost their authority. It was precisely in the context of the dominant discourse of the nation in the twentieth century that once-viable imperial states became increasingly vulnerable to nationalist movements that in turn gained strength from this new sense that states ought to represent, if not coincide, with nations. The longest-lived polities in premodern history, empires operated within a different legitimating paradigm—one based on rights of conquest, divinely ordained rulers, and mandates bestowed through dynastic continuity. The new nationalism was affiliated with the spread of notions of popular sovereignty and of democratic representation of the interests of ordinary people. A fundamental tension arose between inequitable imperial relationships and egalitarian concepts of national democracy. Whereas in empires and ancien régime monarchies rulers benefited from being different from the ruled—German dynasties were enthroned in most European monarchies in the nineteenth century—in nation-states rulers were of the people and often elected by the people.

None of the empire states of the late nineteenth and early twentieth centuries passively accepted inexorable decline or the triumph of the nation-state. The great contiguous state-empires of Eastern Europe and the Middle East—the Russian, Persian, and Ottoman Empires—resisted democratization, fearful that concessions to the people would undermine the dominant imperial elite's right to rule and the hierarchical and inequitable relationship between metropole and periphery in the empire. These modernizing or nationalizing empires attempted to adjust to the new constellation of national states, to modernize their imperial structures and ideological underpinnings. Rather than accepting the caricature of empires as backward and doomed to extinction, imperial modernizers envisioned the empire as a progressive civilizing force leading benighted peoples into a prosperous and secure future. Even Karl Marx and Friedrich Engels, fervent anti-nationalists and anti-imperialists in their own self-conception, accepted the view that the British in India and the Americans in their dealings with Mexicans were engaged in progressive projects of introducing bourgeois civilization.[23] The efforts of these empires, ultimately aborted by the catastrophe of World War I, were attempts at a kind of imperial refurbishing aimed at creating a political community that was multinational or multireligious rather than a single ethnic nation along with a more modern state able to confront the challenges of representation, popular mobilization, and the bureaucratic efficiency of Western nation-states. But they dealt with their internal problems of governance in radically different ways. The Russians tried repression, concession, and Russification, while the Ottomans tried constitutional reform, greater centralization, and the multiculturalist approach known as Ottomanism before turning to the most desperate and disastrous policy, that of physical elimination of designated peoples.[24] Austro-Hungary fell somewhere in between the autocratic empires of the Russians and Ottomans and tried to deal more tolerantly with its constituent peoples, decentralizing the empire and making concessions to the various non-German peoples.

THE *MILLET* SYSTEM

Before they completed the conquest of Anatolia and swept through the Arab territories in the sixteenth century, the Ottomans took over the Balkans, which would become for a long time the heart of their empire. Millions of Balkan and Anatolian Christians were subjects of the sultan. The Ottoman policy of toleration encouraged Jews fleeing from Spain and Portugal after 1492 to settle in the empire. The glory of a great and powerful ruler—an emperor or a sultan—shone, unlike that of a simple prince or king, because he or she occasionally ruled over many lands and peoples.

The key difference between communities in early Ottoman society was religion, rather than ethnicity or language, which took on relevance only later. The procedure by which the Ottomans governed the various non-Muslim peoples of their empire was improvised over centuries, eventually to be referred to as the *millet* system. Systematized only in the nineteenth century, the *millet*s were communities based on religion, rather than on some idea of primal origin, language, or culture. Headed by religious leaders—the Grand Rabbi (after 1835) and the patriarchs of the Greeks and Armenians—the *millet*s were imperial institutions, creations produced by the Ottoman state's policies of recognizing difference and ruling its peoples through intermediaries. The state interfered little in the daily workings of the *millet*s, delegating much authority to the religious head of the *millet*, who in turn had been granted powers by the sultan. Certainly no effort was made to break down the boundaries of these communities and homogenize the population of the empire, or even Anatolia, around a single identity. Unlike the efforts at integrating and homogenizing populations that occurred in the absolute monarchies of Western Europe or, more programmatically in the French state after the revolution of 1789, there was no state project of "making Ottomans" or turning "peasants into Turks" in the Ottoman Empire, at least not before the reform period of the early nineteenth century. Indeed the *millet* system preserved, even produced, difference, and underlined the inferiority of the non-Muslim *millet*s to the dominant Muslims. Rather than engaging in any kind of nation-building project, the early modern Ottomans were involved in an imperial state-building effort that sought at one and the same time to maintain the distinctions of hierarchy between rulers and ruled, Muslim and non-Muslim, without integrating a disparate society into a single, homogeneous whole.[25] Unity in the empire came from the person of the sultan-caliph to whom all peoples, regardless of religion or ethnicity, owed allegiance. The *millet*s were separate but not completely cut off from one another. To many the separateness appeared most important, but in the imperial setting cultures and languages, distinct as they were, shared many elements of a trans-*millet* Ottoman culture. *Millet* institutions, religious differences, and the primary language that the literate read emphasized singularity of identity, but at the same time there was exchange and movement between members of different *millet*s. Multiple identities reflected in bi- and trilingualism were normal in everyday life. Ottoman Armenians spoke Turkish or Kurdish along with Armenian in their daily interactions with their compatriots, neighbors, and the authorities, and many of them used Armenian only in their religious life.

NOMADS AND KURDS

Among the most ancient inhabitants of eastern Anatolia were the Kurds, a traditionally nomadic people with whom the settled Armenians had strained relations and frequent conflicts. Muslim in religion, tribal in social organization, and difficult to integrate into the imperial system, the Kurds were one of the three points of the triangular social ecology that made up eastern Anatolian society: the Ottoman authorities (and their Turkish compatriots); the Armenian peasants, craftsmen, and merchants; and the Kurdish tribesmen. Both nomadic and sedentary by the nineteenth century, Kurds were usually organized into tribes led by *agha*s (powerful lords). At the base of Kurdish society was the household descended from a male ancestor. Marriage was almost always within the tribal group. Clans (groups of households loosely linked to a putative ancestor) and tribes were sometimes grouped into larger tribal federations through the intercession and at the command of the imperial states within which the Kurds lived.[26] The tribes were based on kinship and descent along the male lines, but loyalties were directed to specific leaders rather than to the tribe. Divided by their tribal affiliations, loyalties to kin and leaders, the rugged mountain terrain, and their various dialects, which are related to the Iranian branch of Indo-European languages, Kurds were a fragmented people, difficult to organize, unite, or conquer completely.

The image of Kurds in Western literature derived from the Orientalist sensibilities of travelers. They were said to be "naturally brave and hospitable," yet "in common with many other Asiatic races [to] possess certain rude but strict feelings of honor." Their earlier nobility largely disappeared under the rule of the Turks, and—in the words of one observer—"in most regions they have degenerated into a wild, lawless set of brigands proud, treacherous, and cruel." To complete the picture, writers told of their hatred of the ruling Turks and their contempt for the obsequious Christians, but never failed to mention that among them were "as fine specimens of the human animal as are to be found anywhere—sinewy, agile, and alert, with a steady penetrating eye as cool, cold, and cruel as that of a tiger." Close as they were to nature, they were hardly far removed from animals and "a race of fine possibilities, far superior to the North American Indian, to whom they are often ignorantly compared."[27]

The fierce image of Kurds reflected the observations of outsiders on customs and practices abhorrent to the travelers. Kurds engaged in their own form of summary justice, the blood feud, taking revenge on a member

Kurdish tribesmen. Pascal Sébah, 1873.

of an alien group for a wrong done to a member of its own group. Revenge was a way to restore a balance that had been ruptured. When a Kurdish tribal leader killed a Christian "owned" by another lord, the lord killed two Christians of the tribal leader in revenge. Although the Christians had no role in the murders, rather than killing the actual murderer, revenge was taken against people from the offending group.[28] Such revenge killings were sanctioned by custom and the Quran (2:178): "Believers, retaliation is decreed for you in bloodshed: a freeman for a freeman, a slave for a slave, and a female for a female"—a rule that can be found as well in the Old Testament. In the absence of a mediating state authority conflict was resolved by violence, either between households and tribes or between tribes and higher amalgamations, tribal federations or emirates.

When nomadic Turks moved in waves from Central Asia through Anatolia into the Balkans, and their leaders, like Seljuk and later Osman, settled their followers and founded multiethnic empires, the victors eventually established a tenuous suzerainty over the Kurds. The Ottomans conquered most of the lands inhabited by Kurds by the early sixteenth century, and after a long series of wars a rough frontier separated the Ottoman holdings from those of Safavid Iran. Even after the Ottomans conquered Anatolia and the Arab lands, other nomadic peoples continued to live and move through the Ottoman Empire, most importantly the Türkmens. The Ottomans used the nomads both in their military expeditions and to settle various regions. Sunni Kurds in particular were employed as allies of the state, to police the lands contested by Shi'i Iran and to repress the Alevis, a dissident branch of Islam. Many Kurdish tribal leaders became wealthy and powerful lords in eastern Anatolia. Kurdish emirs ruled in places like Bitlis, southwest of Lake Van, in essentially autonomous emirates. Most Kurds lived in the mountains, while Armenians worked the agricultural plains.[29] Kurdish chieftains subordinated and exploited both Christian and Muslim farmers, taxing them, wintering in their houses, and stabling their flocks in their barns.[30]

Rather than forcibly settling the nomads, the Ottomans at first permitted them to continue their traditional life. Only in the late seventeenth century, after the first major losses of territories to Europeans, did the Ottomans begin to promote sedentarization of nomads in their borderlands.[31] Two centuries later, threatened by Balkan resistance and secession and pressured by the influx of hundreds of thousands of Muslim refugees from the Caucasus and the Balkans, the Ottomans more systematically organized programs of settlement of both refugees and nomads. The refugees were settled among Armenians, Alevis, and Kurds, diluting the concentrated communities of those considered less trustworthy. By the late nineteenth century eastern Anatolia had become both ethnically more diverse and the site of a bitter, often ferocious contest for land and power that pitted Kurds and Turks against Armenians, Assyrians, and Greeks.

Ottoman power emanated from the center, that is, Istanbul, and dissipated as it reached eastward into Anatolia. In the pre-*Tanzimat* period Ottoman officials in the provinces governed through "polite fictions."[32] Gifts were exchanged, bribes were given and taken, and the local authorities would gesture to the suzerainty of the sultan but not interfere with local power holders.[33] Government efforts to centralize the empire met with resistance from local notables who had long run their affairs with little state interference. Urban elites looked with contempt on the backward nomadic and semi-nomadic society in the east. They were suspicious of the remnants of competing, traditional elites and of the odd variety of heterodox religious practices and beliefs in the empire's peripheries.[34] Either visibly or disguised, power was ultimately backed by force, the potential use of violence by the stronger. In Anatolia landlords and tribal chiefs maintained retainers, often no more than hired thugs, to enforce their rule or collect their dues. Politics was the prerogative of the officials, not ordinary people. The very word for politics in Turkish, *siyaset*, in earlier centuries had been synonymous with "death sentence imposed for reasons of state."[35]

The disruption wrought by well-intentioned (from the point of view of state-building) reformers reached over all of eastern Anatolia. Centralization of power and the imposition of taxes were innovations that were anathema to the Kurdish chieftains in the east. Military campaigns that occasionally degenerated into massacres crushed the independent tribal autonomies. A vast territory extending from Bitlis to Mosul, from Diyarbakır to Urmia, was under the rule of the great Kurdish chief Bedirhan Bey, who even minted his own coins. When in 1843 and again in 1846 Nestorian Christians were massacred in Hakkari, the Ottoman government, pressured by Great Britain and France, turned on Bedirhan and drove him into exile in Crete.[36] By 1847 the Ottomans had destroyed the vast Kurdish emirate, but they did not have the troops or personnel to effectively rule the conquered territories. Instead of bringing state order

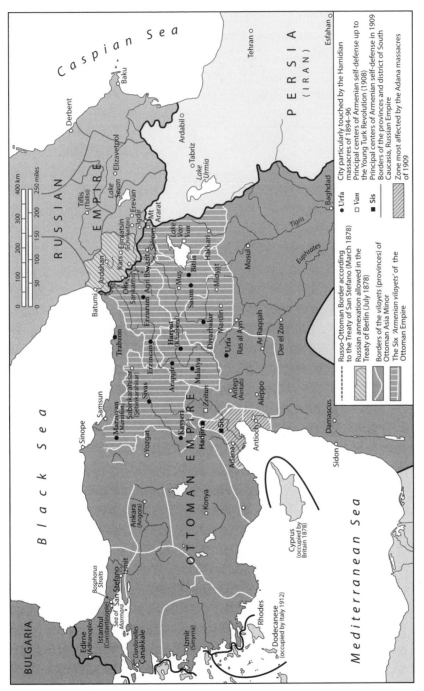

Legend:
- Russo-Ottoman Border according to the Treaty of San Stefano (March 1878)
- Russian annexation allowed in the Treaty of Berlin (July 1878)
- Borders of the *vilayets* (provinces) of Ottoman Asia Minor
- The Six *'Armenian vilayets'* of the Ottoman Empire

- ● Urfa   City particularly touched by the Hamidian massacres of 1894–96
- □ Van   Principal centers of Armenian self-defense up to the Young Turk Revolution (1908)
- ■ Sis   Principal centers of Armenian self-defense in 1909
- Borders of the provinces and district of South Caucasia, Russian Empire
- Zone most affected by the Adana massacres of 1909

Ottoman Empire.

to the region, they initiated a period of Kurdish tribal rivalries. This was centralization without effective administration, state intervention without the rule of law, imposed responsibilities without rights or the practice of impartial justice.[37] Outside the tribal structure, religious authorities, most importantly sheikhs, enjoyed authority because of their association with the divine. In a society riven with conflict, sheikhs played the role of mediator and conciliator. With the breakup of the emirate, some of the sheikhs who replaced the former rulers of "Kurdistan" were particularly zealous members of the Naqshbandi mystic order.[38] These sheikhs feared the inroads made by Western missionaries, tied as they were to European and American powers, and were anxious to prevent domination by the unfaithful.[39] Fervently religious, they viewed the Christian Armenians as "enemy unbelievers."[40]

The distance between those who governed and those who were governed widened for Muslims and non-Muslims as well. At the edges of the empire the local notables—Turkish and Kurdish in particular—tried to maintain a degree of autonomy, sometimes as agents of the state, often as semi-independent exploiters of the local peasants. Benefits were to follow, most importantly the protection of the law and justice from the state, but they rarely reached the non-Muslims or even the poorer Muslims. "It was only with the decline of the Empire," the Ottoman historian Şerif Mardin writes, "that Ottoman officials became plunderers of their own society, and that the relation between officials and the periphery—especially the peasant heavily burdened with taxes—increasingly showed the mark of 'Oriental despotism.'"[41]

The problems of Christian peasants compounded with the Land Code of 1858, which required those working or claiming the land to register their holdings with the state authorities. In theory, the sultan was the owner of all land in the Ottoman Empire, but those who worked the land had the right of usufruct. In 1858 the government granted use of the land to individuals for payment. Communal and shared tenancy rights in the land were eliminated in a move to reduce tribal holdings and to benefit the actual cultivators. Possession soon became full ownership, that is, a kind of private property. In practice, however, registration favored rich and powerful Muslim landlords. Kurdish sheikhs and *agha*s grew wealthy by acquiring land; urban landlords emerged; and peasants lost many of their traditional rights, becoming sharecroppers or hired laborers.[42] Armenians, who had earlier paid taxes only to Bedirhan, found themselves double-taxed, once to local Kurdish landlords and then to the Ottoman state. Since the landlords legally held the land, the Ottoman state backed the landlords when peasants protested. Not only did the suppression of the Kurdish principalities and the land law fail to create order, on the contrary they created "greater anarchy."[43]

Relations between Kurds and Armenians ranged from coexistence and tolerance to the most vicious cruelty. Influential Kurdish tribesmen appropriated land from Armenians when the opportunity arose. A British consul, who like many of his European colleagues took a special interest in the Armenians, reported in the 1870s, "The people in the Armenian provinces suffer under the following provincial evils: Firstly, robbery, exaction, and oppression at the hands of the Kurds. In some parts nomad Kurds make raids on villages, carrying off flocks and herds and other plunder, and sometimes burning what they cannot carry away. In other parts influential Kurdish families parcel out the villages (especially Christian) in their neighborhood among their various members, and regard them as their property. The inhabitants have to pay them black-mail, cultivate their lands, pasture their flocks, and give and do for them anything they may demand."[44] Travelers and diplomats reported that in Van, Bitlis, Diyarbakır, and elsewhere the Kurds held the Armenians in a kind of semi-feudal servitude. Not only did Armenian villagers pay taxes in kind and money to the Kurdish chieftains, but they were also obligated to work a set number of days for the Kurds and to board and feed them in Armenian villages during the winter months. In some areas Kurdish lords bought and sold Armenians like sheep or cattle and seized their land, homes, and women. The Russian vice consul in Van, Tumanskii, wrote in May 1901:

> In Sassun *kaza* [district] there exists an almost feudal dependence of Armenians on the Kurds with all its juridical consequences: each Armenian is assigned to some Kurd and is obligated to labor

for him; Kurds sell their serfs when they need money; if a Kurd kills a serf, the lord [of that serf] takes revenge by killing a serf belonging to the murderer. Some beys have even insisted on the "right of the first night" in Armenian villages.[45]

In the popular culture of Kurds a cult of hospitality existed together with wariness of strangers and even acquaintances. One could not trust a Turk (*Waki khabr a Rumian*); Persians were obese or deceitful (*Waki Ajam k'low a*); Arabs were looked down on: "The Arab is like a fly; the more you shoo him away, the more insistent he becomes" (*Arab waki maish hendi pish dakan hartaina paish*). While the Kurds often had good relations with Assyrians (Nestorian Christians), it was different with the Armenians. "Between us (and Nestorians) there is but a hair's breadth, but between us and the Armenians a mountain" (*Nav byn a ma wa muyeka nav byn a ma wa fellah chiayeka*). Armenians were unclean ("With fingernails like an Armenian [*Nynuk Fellah*]") and untrustworthy. "A watery chestnut, a mongrel, and an Armenian—don't trust any of them" (*Haspe kulla sy e tulla maire fellah lai ma ba owla*).[46] Violence was part of life, and one's honor had to be protected. "It is better to have blood on one's hands than to be in debt" (*Miruf khundar bit qarrdar nabit*). One did not leave the account with one's enemy unsettled. Death was the guest of everyone, and it was better to die than grow old.[47]

The former equilibrium between Muslim and non-Muslim *millet*s was rapidly disappearing in the second half of the nineteenth century. And nowhere was this more starkly evident than in the Armenian provinces. The rise in tension in eastern Anatolia and the resultant resistance and massacres were not only the product of the failure of the traditional Ottoman political structure to adapt to the new requirements of the non-Muslim peoples but also the result of fundamental social changes in eastern Anatolia itself. The mountainous plateau of historic Armenia was an area in which the central government had only intermittent authority. Survival pitted the three main peoples of the east—the Kurdish nomadic leaders, the semi-autonomous Turkish notables of the towns, and the Armenians—against one another. Local Turkish officials ran the towns often with little regard to central authority, and Kurdish beys held much of the countryside under their sway. The fourth contender for power was the Ottoman state itself. In many cases the only way Istanbul could make its will felt was by sending in the army. Though the Porte saw Armenians by the turn of the century as an unruly and subversive element, earlier in the century it had been the Kurds who had repeatedly revolted against the Ottoman state and collaborated with the invading Russians. Only with the campaigns of 1834, 1843, and 1878 were the troops of the sultan able to put down the major Kurdish insurrections. Despite Ottoman incursions, in many areas the Kurdish beys had carved out a de facto autonomy and remained the most powerful authority, ruling over the local Armenian peasants with little interference from Istanbul.

The competition for land was further complicated by the movement into eastern Anatolia of Muslim refugees, first from the Caucasus and later from the Balkans. When tsarist Russia defeated the resistance movement in the North Caucasus, thousands of Muslims were deported or chose to move to Anatolia, where the government welcomed Muslim settlers. In their new homes they were known as Circassians, no matter if their origins and self-descriptions were Cherkess, Adyge, Abkhaz, Kabardin, or Avar. For the next century, as the Ottomans lost territories in the Balkans, Muslims left Europe for the hinterlands of the East. The Ottoman authorities promised them land, and the Armenians felt particularly threatened by these *muhacir*s (refugees) favored by the state. A British consul in Diyarbakır reported on an early wave of immigrants in 1879—Circassians (Cherkess and other North Caucasians) from Russia: "It has been arranged to locate 4,000 Circassian families in this province: most of the heads of the Christian communities have requested my assistance to prevent this arrangement, which is most undesirable in the existing unsettled state of the country. . . . A few days since[,] it became known here that the Government contemplated settling in the Vilayet of Diarbekir 4,000 or 5,000 families of Circassian emigrants. The news created great excitement, as the memories of the former Circassian immigration came to mind, when 40,000 people passed through Diarbekir from the north on their way to the settlement of Ras-el-Ain,

Zeytun, Armenian fortress town. Nubarian Library Collection.

causing great suffering to the population of the country passed through, who had first to support them, and then to suffer from their robberies and other depredations."[48]

The relations of nomads to settled peoples can be illustrated in the heroic story of the mountain town of Zeytun, located in Cilicia, the southeastern corner of Anatolia, which experienced the baleful effects of the modernizing reforms of the Ottoman state. Zeytun had five hundred years earlier been part of an independent Armenian kingdom. The 1,500 households were almost exclusively Armenian, and years before a grateful sultan had granted the Zeytuntsis the privilege of freedom from state taxation and interference from the Ottoman authorities. Zeytun gained a reputation as "freedom-loving," defending its independence, often in alliance with some of the Kurdish or Türkmen tribes in the region. But the *Tanzimat* changed the equation for Zeytun. The modernizing state wanted to end the autonomy of the Cilician peoples. The government decided to settle nearly 30,000 Circassian refugees who had fled from Russia after the Crimean and Caucasian wars in the northern Cilician districts around Zeytun, Maraş, and Hacin (Hadjin).[49] To enforce its new policies the Ottomans sent the military to attack the Armenian towns in 1860 and 1862. The French emperor, Napoleon III, demanded an end to the attack on Zeytun, and though the attacks decreased, the government withdrew the special status of Zeytun, imposed taxes, and installed a governor (*kaymakam*) in the district. Clashes continued between Circassians and Armenians, even as the local nomads were forcibly settled, ending their autonomous existence as well.[50] From the 1860s on, the markers of difference between Muslim and Christian, Armenian and Kurd or Circassian or Turk, took on a new significance as competition for land intensified. That competition pitted Circassian refugees not only against Armenian farmers, but also against newly settled Kurds.

Social relations, as well as relations with the Ottoman state, changed significantly in the 1890s with Sultan Abdülhamid II's formation of the *Hamidiye* regiments made up of loyal Kurdish tribesmen. The creation of this Cossack-like militia served a variety of purposes: extension and securing of central Ottoman state power in the vulnerable borderlands adjacent to the Caucasus and Persia; integration and affiliation of powerful Kurdish tribesmen to the Ottoman state; and the solidification of an Islamic partnership in eastern Anatolia that could act as a restraint and repressor of the Armenians.[51] Just ten years earlier, in 1879–1881, the Ottomans faced a threat from a powerful Kurdish chieftain, Sheikh Ubeydullah, who organized a confederation of tribes to create an autonomous region ruled by his followers. Suppression of insurgents was replaced by a policy of accommodation and integration. The sultan's commander, Zeki Paşa, recruited the best-positioned and potentially most loyal tribes.[52]

In the changing landscape of eastern Anatolia Kurdish tribes had to find their own ways to adjust to and benefit from the transformations that were taking place. Some lived by theft and plunder and deserved the appellation "bandits." Others used their ties to local Ottoman officials or position in the Ottoman paramilitary *Hamidiye* units to advance their own well-being. They preyed on the most vulnerable, often Armenians but poor and vulnerable Muslims as well, and if there were complaints, they reported to the authorities that their victims were actually revolutionaries or terrorists.[53] A British officer reported in 1906 that the *Hamidiye* "make raids on the villages, ill-treat the people, take their cattle and sheep and crops, often killing an odd Armenian as well. These Kurds give as excuse for these raids—if excuse is needed—that the villagers are revolutionaries, or are harbouring revolutionaries, the latter excuse being often true, though quite against the wish of the Armenians."[54]

Intense rivalries kept different Kurdish tribes and clans from cooperating against the state. Local struggles for power and advantage intersected with relations between the state and provincial actors. Some tribal leaders, like Mustafa Paşa of the Miran tribe, were exonerated of murder and massacre because of their connections with Zeki Paşa, the commander of the *Hamidiye*. Mustafa managed to build a semi-autonomous emirate by remaining loyal to the government. Others, like his rivals, the Bedirhan, were part of the radical opposition to Abdülhamid, "concerned as *Ottomans* with the fate of the empire" but convinced that the sultan's policies and the *Hamidiye* were causing more damage than good.[55] They managed to have Mustafa Paşa assassinated in 1902.

However intolerable the lack of governance and justice, Armenians in general bore up under it, except for an occasional revolt such as that at Zeytun in 1862 or at Erzurum in 1882. But in the last third of the nineteenth century, as the population of Muslims and Christians grew, as additional Muslims from the Caucasus and the Balkans settled in the area, and as many Armenians emigrated to Russia, Europe, and America, the competition for the limited agricultural resources of the area intensified. Armenians appealed to but could not rely on the Ottoman state to defend them from the more powerful Muslim landlords, and pressure grew on those Armenians left in Anatolia to protect their endangered position. Undergoverned, subject to the willful violence of the strong, and fiercely contested for possession of the land, eastern Anatolia was by the early twentieth century the vortex of a fierce struggle both between Christians and Muslims and between great rival empires fearful of their competitors' ambitions.

THE "SICK MAN OF EUROPE" TAKES THE CURE

If there is a dominant image of the Ottoman Empire it is one of steady decline, a movement from its original expansion and strength up to the end of the seventeenth century to its pathetic position as the "Sick Man of Europe" by the nineteenth century. Many in power shared this view, as did some of those they ruled. In an age of ruthless international competition, the Ottomans were seen as an imperial victim of Western imperialism, an unfit preindustrial power, backward, weak, and about to collapse. Scholars have both worked within that paradigm of decline and collapse and, in more recent years, criticized it as a Eurocentric, Orientalist reading of a more complex history. To understand the late Ottoman period it is essential to appreciate the different dynamics within and between empires and nation-states; the emerging form of statehood in Europe; the ways in which autocracy differed from European liberalism and constitutionalism, which were becoming increasingly potent in the nineteenth century; and how capitalism affected those great states that straddled Europe and Asia (the Ottoman and the Russian) that came to economic modernity later than those Western European states first transformed by this new mode of production. At the same time these very differences between Europe and the Ottomans enticed and influenced significant members of the Ottoman elite who were prepared to learn from the West, imitate, and adopt what they thought most useful for the empire's survival and prosperity. For some Ottoman bureaucrats Europe looked like a progressive future, a possible way out of backwardness and decline. In order to survive in the competitive nineteenth century, traditionally conceived empires had to find ways to meet the challenge of the increased power and influence of capitalist and industrial Europe. They had to become modern, more like Europe, at least in some aspects. Pressure from Europe combined with the new aspirations of the Christian minorities and the European orientation of a few reforming Ottoman officials to nourish a consensus among a small but influential group of government figures that the institutions of the empire had to be transformed to compete in the age of nationalism and liberalism.

Reforming sultans faced formidable opposition from conservative forces close to the court, most importantly the Janissary corps, household guards who repeatedly protested innovations. In what was called the "Auspicious Incident" in 1826, the reforming Sultan Mahmud II (1808–1839) abolished the Janissaries and launched a far-reaching series of changes in military and governmental policy. A new army was formed, the state's powers increased, and more power flowed from the center out to provinces. The sultan sought to create a unifying sense of a people (*halk*, then a new word for the Ottomans) by appealing to their love for the fatherland (*vatan*), their commitment to Islam, and their appreciation of the vernacular Turkish language.[56] Conceived by its authors, the reforms known as the *Tanzimat* were not so much an imitation of Europe as a return to the glorious days of Sultan Süleyman *Kanuni*. The first great decree that marked the *Tanzimat*—the *Hatt-i Sherif* of Gulhane (1839)—offered a promise of equality to non-Muslims "according to the requirement of the sharia order." This meant that all subjects, no matter their religion, would have equal protection but not equal participation in power or full equal rights. Mahmud II declared, "From now on I do not wish to recognize Muslims outside the mosque, Christians outside the church, or Jews outside the synagogue."[57] In a second great decree—the *Hatt-i Hümayun* (1856)—which was issued under European pressure, equality went further: Muslims and non-Muslims were declared fully equal under the law. All subjects of the sultan would be treated more or less the same, as Ottomans. Since this second law was a significant break with Islamic traditions of inequality between the faithful and the unfaithful, it was met by fierce opposition, particularly outside the capital. For Muslims as the ruling nation (*millet-i hakime*) such unrestricted equality undermined the very principles on which the Islamic state and its idea of justice was based.[58] Not all non-Muslims greeted the law enthusiastically. Equality meant the loss of certain privileges. While Muslims saw the promulgation of the law as "a day to weep and mourn," Greeks were upset that "the state has made us equal with the Jews. We were satisfied with Muslim superiority."[59] Ultimately non-Muslims were dependent on the willingness of the state to carry out its promised reforms. In practice Armenians, Greeks, and Jews remained the victims of unequal treatment and "other doubts and suspicions that emerged increasingly as faith in the viability of the Ottomanist synthesis of nationalities—a synthesis to which the official commitment to egalitarianism was directly linked—began to erode."[60]

Empires in the modern age were caught between maintaining the privileges and distinctions that kept the traditional elites in power and considering reforms along liberal lines that potentially could undermine the old ruling classes and the existing social order. To deal with this imperial dilemma, the reformers of modernizing empires searched for new legitimation formulas that softened the rhetoric of conquest and divine sanction and emphasized the civilizing mission of the imperial metropole, its essential competence in a new project of development. Needing to justify the rule of the traditional elites over peoples who were asserting their own claims to power or even defining themselves as nations, the idea of developing inferior or uncivilized peoples became a dominant source of imperial legitimation and continued well into the twentieth century.[61] Like the overseas empires of the British and French and the contiguous land empire of the Russians, so the Ottomans proposed their own *mission civilisatrice* to bring the peripheries of their realm, the unsettled nomadic peoples, and other benighted subjects into the modern world.

Self-consciously borrowing and reproducing aspects of European nation-states, the reformers aimed to bring the diverse peoples of the empire under a shared identity and greater central state authority. Local identities competed with the attempts by nineteenth-century reformers to bring greater order to the sultan's realm by promoting an inclusive Ottoman designation for all the sultan's subjects.[62] This notion of legal protection of non-Muslims was central to the aims of what came to be known as Ottomanism (*osmanlılık*) and was instituted briefly in the Constitution proclaimed in December 1876. But the ideological umbrella of Ottomanism was broad enough to include under it those who believed that the unity of the empire could be best guaranteed by having the Ottoman Turks rule over the other nationalities. At the center of the Ottoman state and society would be the ethnic Turks; they were the "fundamental element" around which other Islamic peoples would be blended.[63] Over time the empire's ruling elite, though still Ottoman, grew ever more Turkish. Thirty-four of the last thirty-nine grand viziers (prime ministers) of the Ottoman state were Turkish, that is, they were Anatolian or Rumelian Muslims whose mother tongue was Turkish.[64] Ethnicity, rather than religion, became increasingly a marker of identity, and as in nation-states the modernizing empire paid greater attention to the coincidence of ethnicity between those who ruled and those who were ruled. This whole process might be characterized as nationalization or modernization, but what it did first and foremost was upset a rickety traditional order—the imperial paradigm—without replacing it with a stable system.

European and Ottoman non-Muslim liberals applauded the *Tanzimat*'s egalitarian reforms and were frustrated by the government's failure to fulfill its promises. There was a fundamental tension between the differentiation of Muslims and non-Muslims, the latter's subordination to the former, and the liberal universalist principles of equivalency and equality under the law. Conservative officials and men of religion balked at implementing decrees that they saw as subversive of God's intent. Even those reformers who sincerely wanted to enact the reforms found that the state had limited ability to carry them out. Shortly after Abdülhamid II (1876–1909), the last sultan with significant power, came to the throne, *Tanzimat* came to an end. Instead of promulgating reforms, the state made promises without commitment, dragged its feet, and tried the patience of the Western powers. Abdülhamid had his own notion of how to modernize his empire, but it was profoundly different from the egalitarianism of Western liberals or Ottoman minorities. His strategy involved regulation, centralization, and bureaucratic extension of his personal power. He recognized that some form of modernization was essential for the security and future prosperity of his realm. Rules had to be enforced, taxes collected, population censuses carried out (as they were in 1885 and 1907), and borders defended. Nomads were to be settled or recruited into armed military units. The amenities of urban life were to be enhanced, roads built, and promenades laid for leisurely pursuits. Clock towers were built all over the empire that showed European twenty-four-hour time rather than the prayer times of the Quran. Printing presses, newspapers, and vocational schools were promoted. But so was censorship, and police surveillance was enhanced. The sultan promoted the building of railroads and enticed the Germans to engage in projects too expensive and technologically advanced for the Ottomans. The British and the Russians watched these developments with great suspicion and opposed the building of Ottoman railroads, which would only strengthen the empire and Germany's position within it. For Abdülhamid there was no time to lose. Time had to be speeded up.

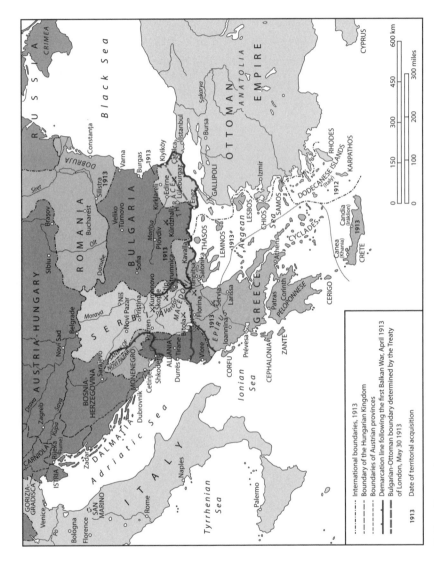

Balkan Peninsula

CHAPTER TWO

Armenians

Maps sometimes tell stories that states would rather forget. No matter what the Ottomans named the region or how they divided it up, mapmakers outside the empire designated the extensive mountainous plateau in eastern Anatolia as Armenia. Six provinces (*vilayets*)—Erzurum, Van, Bitlis, Sivas, Harput (Kharput, Kharberd), Mamuretülaziz, and Diyarbakır—were included as the *Vilayat-ı Sitte*. The name Armenia, like the maps and the linking of the six provinces into one category, was a claim that connected a people and a territory. Contemporaries, both local and foreign, referred to the same area as Kurdistan. As one British observer put it, "It means simply the country inhabited by Kurds, just as Armenia means that inhabited by Armenians. In many parts of Asia Minor the population is mixed, and while the Turks prefer to call such districts Kurdistan, the friends of the Armenians style them Armenia."[1] Both claims were perceived as threats by the Ottoman authorities and as opportunities by outsiders. The territory itself had historically been contested as a transit space of trade from east to west, a strategic highland whose possession gave the holder a military advantage over rivals. But it was also extreme in a number of important ways: extremely hot in summer and cold in winter and extremely difficult to move through swiftly. Impassable roads and rivers that could not be navigated, high mountains as well as brigands and ungoverned tribesmen, made travel precarious. With a good horse one might make a journey of 20 or 30 miles in a day, perhaps without baggage a few hundred miles in a week. But mud and heat, swollen streams, and hostile inhabitants threatened any ambition for speed or even completion of the journey.

What was considered Armenia, and had been home to Armenian kingdoms and principalities for more than 1,000 years, was a huge rectangle of 60,000 square miles, about the size of the U.S. state of Iowa or

Illinois. It was contained within the eastern part of what the ancient Greeks had called Anatolia and modern Westerners called Asia Minor. Anatolia's most stunning lake, the largest in modern Turkey, is Lake Van, near the city that carries its name and encloses the island of Aghtamar with its tenth-century Armenian cathedral, *Surp Khatch* (Holy Cross). The region by the lake was in medieval times the Armenian kingdom of Vaspurakan. North from Van were the Bagratid kingdoms and their principal city, Ani, now a collection of ruins hard against the border with the Armenian Republic. Farther east and north was Gharabagh (Karabakh), the "Black Garden," where the principalities of Siunik maintained their presence long after the conquest of other Armenian states. Far to the south, bordering the Mediterranean was Cilicia, an Armenian diaspora principality, later kingdom, which existed for three hundred years (1080–1375). Much of the plateau on which the Armenians lived lies from 4,000 to 6,000 feet above sea level with mountains ranging above 10,000 feet. Its highest peak—Ararat to Westerners, Massis to Armenians—is almost 17,000 feet high. The Ottoman name for the mountain, Ağır, means "heavy"; the modern Turkish name, Ağrı, means "pain."

WHO ARE THE ARMENIANS?

When people tell the story of their own nation, at least in much of the Old World, they begin in the most ancient times or even with Creation itself. Armenians are one of the fortunate few ethnic or religious groups, like Jews, Georgians, Egyptians, Indians, and the Chinese, that have a long literary pedigree, a collection of texts that tell their story from the dawn of history through the Middle Ages. In the early fifth century CE a cleric named Mesrop, later known as Mashtots and beatified as a saint, created an alphabet to record their language and translate the Bible. Almost immediately his fellow priests and monks began recording what they understood as the prehistory of their people: the eponymous hero Hayk, who defeated the giant Bel and after whom the people—*Hay* in their own language—and their country—*Hayastan*—were named; and their first kings, including Armen after whom outsiders borrowed the name

Armenian. Sometime in the early Middle Ages (the century is disputed) the "father of (Armenian) history (*batmahayr*)," Movses Khorenatsi, wrote a chronicle, which became the foundation of what later would be transformed into a national historical narrative. One thousand years before Mesrop, in the fifth century BCE, the Persian king Darius the Great had the first written mention of Armenia carved into the great rock at Behistun. Both conquerors of the Armenian plateau and Armenian writers themselves chronicled the rulers of their kingdoms and principalities. The clerics who meticulously copied manuscripts and illustrated them with exquisite miniatures were most concerned with the feats of their patron rulers and the glory of the Christian religion. Armenians proudly noted that their king, Trdat, had converted to Christianity before Constantine the Great (again the date is disputed: traditionally 301, it is more likely 314). Therefore Armenia could claim to be the first country to have adopted Christianity, just before the Roman Empire.

Already in the ancient world, before Christianity, Armenians were an identifiable people with their own Iranian-style tribal structure and borrowed paganism. An almost exclusively rural society with minimal state organization, they were ruled by a warrior class, an elite of pagan priests, and a rough kind of kingship. Insofar as there was political organization, it was highly decentralized with great autonomy for the emerging nobles. By the time Rome expanded into eastern Anatolia and Caucasia, in the reign of the king Tigran the Great (95–55 BCE), this basically Iranian culture and society had taken on features of the Hellenic West. Usually fractured among princes and nobles, vulnerable to the great empires and invaders from Arabia and Central Asia, Armenia's unity was fragile and fleeting, its state structures rudimentary. Under Tigran Armenia briefly expanded to unite the whole of eastern Anatolia and parts of Caucasia, a multiethnic empire under the dominance of a prince with connections to both Rome and Parthia. That short-lived polity became in the minds of modern nationalists the basis of a claim to a greater Armenian homeland.

In Roman times trade with distant markets flourished throughout Armenia, and urban life probably took on greater importance, though Armenians still did not have the feature that would stereotype them in

Tigran the Great, King of Armenia (95-55 BCE).

modern times, the character of tradesmen and merchants. Armenians remained largely a peasant population with a small elite of nobles (*na-khararner*) and warriors loosely bound to their king. Even under Tigran, the state authorities had to contend with the persistence of more ancient forms of social organization—the clan loyalties built into the *nakharar* system. These divisions among Armenians were a much more potent determinant in their fate than the relatively weak institution of kingship. A cluster of principalities that fought one another fiercely, the Armenian princes often allied with non-Armenian powers against their fellow Armenians. Arabs patronized the Armenian kings of the Bagratuni family, and Byzantium allied with the Mamikonians, the progeny of St. Vardan.

From the first mentions of Armenia in the ancient Greek and Persian sources, their neighbors recognized Armenians as a distinct people with a collective name and their own language, a branch of the Indo-European family of languages. Although political solidarity was weak among Armenians, there was a commonality of speech, an attachment to territory, and fierce devotion to the national religion, first pagan, later Armenian Christianity. Religion, whether the amalgam of Iranian and Greek deities that formed Armenian paganism or the moderately monophysite Christology that the Armenian Church adopted, was the primary identification of this people, coinciding roughly with the linguistic and territorial community. The Armenian Church accepted only the first three ecumenical councils of the church headed by the Byzantine emperor but broke with Greek Orthodoxy after the Council of Chalcedon (451 CE) insisted on a particular formula of Christ as divine and human. Armenians, Nestorians, and other Eastern Christians maintained their own distinct interpretations of the nature of their Savior. With Christianity the boundaries of their church coincided with the linguistic cultural community. As the easternmost outpost of Christianity, Armenia took on a special role in the preservation of the faith, but rather than fighting for Christianity in general Armenians fought to preserve the unique faith of the Armenians. Even as Armenians turned their cultural face to the West and adopted a universalistic religion, they particularized it, made it their own, and defiantly distinguished themselves from the powerful Greek Orthodox Byzantine Empire to the west. Only later in the Middle Ages, during the Crusades, did Armenians join in a wider movement of pan-Christian defense.

With the invention of the Armenian alphabet in the early fifth century and the translation of the Bible into Armenian, clerical writers elaborated a literary tradition complete with histories, geographies, and philosophical and theological texts that exalted the greatness of this unique people, their heroes and martyrs, their faithfulness, and their sacrifices for Christ. The earliest written works of Armenians testify that they also shared a common myth of descent and history that placed them at the very origin of the human story. Armenian nationalists easily trace back a "national" identity to the "father of (Armenian) history," Movses Khorenatsi, who proudly proclaimed, "Although we are a small country and very restricted in numbers, weak in power, and often subject to another's rule, yet many manly deeds have been performed in our land worthy of being recorded in writing."[2] The clerical writers saw Armenians as a small, isolated people, suffering and being martyred for Christ. From the Battle of Avarayr (451 CE) on, Armenians were ready, in the view of those who wrote their histories, to sacrifice themselves, like the Maccabees of ancient Israel, for

Armenian Minature Painting. Russian National Library.

the greater glory of God. In that battle against the Persians, the Armenians lost their leader, Vardan, later declared a saint, but preserved their right to practice their own religion. The day of the battle, *Vardanants*, when Armenians were martyrs to their faith at the hand of Mazdeist Persians, became a central symbol in the story of national preservation.

Medieval Armenians built thousands of churches and dozens of fortresses, and created a Christian civilization with its own autonomous church that stood between Rome and Byzantium in the West and the Persian Empire to the east. In the seventh century CE Arabs overran Armenia in their first major campaigns to spread the new religion, Islam. But the Arabs did not colonize Armenia. Instead they settled in a few towns where they carried on lucrative trade with the locals and foreign merchants. Four hundred years later the Seljuk Turks delivered a near fatal blow to the Byzantine Empire at the Battle of Manzikert (Malazgirt) (1071) and subjugated the Armenians. The principal Armenian kingdoms, those of the Bagratunis (with their capital at Ani) and the Artsrunis (in

Vaspurakan, present-day Van), fell one after the other, beginning a long period of Armenian dispersion. The last independent Armenian kingdom, the southern diaspora outpost in Cilicia on the Mediterranean, fell in 1375 to the Mamluks of Egypt. A few noble families, led by princes called *meliks*, held out for several hundred more years in the mountains of Gharabagh and Zangezur, in regions known as Syunik, Aghvan, and Artsakh. After the Mongols, Türkmens, and other nomadic peoples came through with great devastating invasions, the Ottoman Turks completed the conquest of Armenia in the fifteenth century, leaving parts of its eastern provinces to the Persians.

DIASPORA AND HOMELAND

For the next five centuries Armenians were divided between those still living in the lands lost to their imperial overlords and those dispersed into other lands, forming colonies and maintaining the traditions of their religion and culture. Over time many local Greeks and Armenians in Anatolia converted to Islam, assimilating into the Turkish and Kurdish population. Others stubbornly held on to their faith and language, while some remained Christian but adapted to the dominant culture and spoke Turkish. Still others moved out of the country altogether. Armenians migrated to Georgia, Crimea, or the Ottoman capital Istanbul, or were forcibly moved by the Persian Shah Abbas I to Isfahan (1604). Armenian merchants and artisans could be found in Moscow, Lvov, Venice, Amsterdam, Cadiz, Calcutta, and Madras. They formed an international network of traders whose distant affairs reached from the Pacific through Eurasia to Western Europe.[3] When Enlightenment Europeans described Armenians in their anthropologies, their image as merchants and tradesmen became the dominant representation. In his Baltic seclusion, the philosopher Immanuel Kant maintained, "Among the Armenians . . . there rules a certain commercial spirit of a peculiar sort; namely, of wandering on foot from the borders of China to the coast of Guinea in order to buy and sell, which indicates the peculiar descent [*Abstamm*] of this reasonable and industrious people, who in a line from northeast to southwest travel through almost the entire extent of the ancient continent and know how to obtain a peaceful reception from all the peoples they encounter, which proves the superiority of their character to the fickle and groveling character of the contemporary Greeks, whose first form can no longer be ascertained."[4]

From the late fourteenth century to the twentieth the major spiritual and political institution for Armenians was the church. The former royalty and nobility of Armenia had largely disappeared, and in their place the clergy became "the de facto representatives of the 'nation.'"[5] But the church was divided among its supreme head, the catholicos at Ejmiatsin, in the Persian (and after 1828 Russian) Empire; rival catholicoi in Sis, Aghtamar, and Gandzasar; and the Ottoman-sanctioned patriarchs in Constantinople and Jerusalem. Still, monasteries continued to transmit the traditions of the Armenians; patriarchs and catholicoi collected taxes, enforced rules, and even imprisoned dissenters. The pervasive infighting and corruption sapped the energy of the church, and Catholic missionaries from the West nibbled away at the Apostolic faithful whom they considered heretics.

In the early modern period energetic church leaders attempted sporadically to interest Western capitals in a crusade to liberate Armenians from their Islamic rulers, the Ottomans and the Persians, but with almost no results. Most of the liberationist activity came from diaspora Armenians, merchants in Persia, Europe, and India, interested in the restoration of an Armenian state. The group of merchant activists in Madras wrote political tracts that shifted the blame for the Armenian condition from their own sinful past onto the despotism of foreign rulers. The adventurous Persian Armenian Joseph Emin (1726–1809), who set out to convince monarchs in Europe to aid him in liberating Armenia, indicted the Armenian clergy for their message of passive acceptance of Muslim rule. The fragmentary nature of these liberationist efforts, the fragility or absence of connection between them, and the different motivations and ambitions of the actors were later woven into a single, coherent narrative of a "national liberation movement."[6] In Soviet Armenian historiography the efforts by the princes of Gharabagh or the self-appointed liberators Emin or Israel Ori were fashioned into a Russian orientation that served as justification for the eventual tsarist conquest of eastern (Persian) Armenia and the inclusion of Caucasian Armenia within the Soviet Union.

By the eighteenth century Armenians in what had been historic Armenia, like their Georgian neighbors to the north, were on the brink of cultural extinction. Both church and merchant leaders perceived a deep crisis for their people. In the Enlightenment circles of Western Europe the eighteenth century was a moment of transition from more traditional understandings of nation to a more modern one. The nature and vocabulary of politics were changing, and theorists were suggesting a new location for the source of sovereign power. With the triumph of the French Revolution of 1789, the idea that divinely sanctioned kings had the right to rule over obedient subjects was repeatedly challenged by new claims that the people constituted as the nation were the true sovereign and had the right to delegate power to government. For the next century other claimants—nobilities, the middle classes, and autocratic monarchs—rejected the pretension of the masses to supreme power. Many in the eighteenth century found it hard to imagine that a nation might exist without a monarch. Emin, like his contemporary, the catholicos Simeon Erevantsi (1763–1780), fretted that without a king, a figure around which the people might assemble, the nation could not survive. He looked with despair on his countrymen, whom he saw as worthy of contempt because they had no solidarity, "no love for one another." "You are without honor, and by the disunion of your nation, all nations insult you; you are contemptible, and without zeal."[7]

Most Armenians were poor peasants who knew little about their past, except the fragments passed down in the oral traditions and the religious messages of the clergy. The work of the philologists, grammarians, and historians who wrote for the small elite who could read and had some interest in rather esoteric intellectual endeavors met with a frustrating silence. In Venice an Armenian Catholic order headed by Father Mkhitar of Sebastia (Sivas) spearheaded efforts to introduce Armenian education, print books in the classical Armenian language (*grabar*), and revive old texts and write new histories of the Armenians. The literary and cultural revivalists of the late eighteenth and early nineteenth centuries, particularly the Mkhitarist monks, saw themselves as cultivating the national spirit through promotion of the language. Father Ghevond Alishan, who himself had never been to historic Armenia, wrote elegiacally about the landscape in which the ruins of ancient churches were the inspiration for a revived national feeling. But even as they promoted enlightenment and borrowed the idiom of the nation from the West, this generation of religious teachers rejected the more radical and democratic aspects of Western and East European nationalism that they observed. Though the mission of the Mkhitarists was spiritual revival, both the Armenian community and the state in the Ottoman Empire frustrated their efforts to convert Armenians to Catholicism. The sultan and the Armenian patriarch collaborated in repressing Armenian Catholics in the empire in the 1820s, and only after the devastating Ottoman defeat at Navarino (1827) and the later Ottoman rapprochement with France did the sultan agree to create a Catholic *millet* (religious community).

The Catholic fathers reached out by opening schools, presenting plays, and providing a model of energy and dedication that inspired succeeding generations of patriots, even as their younger acolytes rejected the original religious (in this case Catholic) impulse of their forefathers.[8] Ironically, the Mkhitarists inspired and even trained people who later became the first secular nationalists, some of whom turned into bitter and outspoken opponents of clerical authority.[9] The evident possibility of being Catholic or Protestant and also being Armenian raised a critical distinction between nation and religion. Mkhitar, the founder of the order, may have claimed that "I sacrifice neither my nation to my religion nor my religion to my nation," but such a statement clearly distinguished between the two.[10] The precise connection (or disconnection) between religion and nationality became the ground on which clerics and secular intellectuals would contest the nature of being Armenian.

NATIONALISM BEFORE THE NATION

The genesis of Armenian nationalism occurred in the diaspora, in far-removed places like the Mkhitarist monasteries in Venice and Vienna or in Madras, where the first Armenian newspaper was published at the end of the eighteenth century. In the years before the nineteenth-century explosion of nationalism, Armenians held a variety of views on what constituted their nation and what ought to be done to make it prosper. The influential catholicos Simeon Erevantsi was concerned about the degeneration of Armenians, their turning away from books and education, which he attributed to their division, their dispersion, and external threats to their faith. His solution was to centralize the Armenians around the see of Ejmiatsin, the Armenian Jerusalem, both to weaken the rival catholicosates and to combat the growing influence of the Catholics. The catholicos, like many other Armenians, believed fervently in the exceptionality of the Armenians and the holy purpose in their preservation. God "loves the Armenian nation," he wrote, "in a special and unique manner among all the Christians and finds it particularly suitable and worthy of his kingdom."[11] Armenians should be suspicious, wrote Simeon, of Catholic books; even their grammars were insidious, like spies penetrating a country. For him being Armenian meant being a member of the Apostolic Church, a view diametrically opposed to that of Mkhitar, who hoped to reconcile his Armenian nationality with his Catholic faith.

Simeon's vision of a church-centered nation contrasted with that of the activist merchants of Madras, who proposed a new Armenian state won through struggle against the Ottomans and the Persians. Armenians did not need a church-centered nation or an absolute monarch, they contended, but an elective republic. When Simeon read what the merchant activists had written, he excommunicated the author of a heretical tract, ordered that the printing press in Madras be closed down, and commanded that all copies of the offending books be burned. For churchmen like Catholicos Simeon all authority came down from God and had been bestowed on Ejmiatsin; for the merchant intellectuals of Madras, however, the nation itself, in its worldly form, was the fountainhead of authority. These two competing notions would be fought out among Armenians (and other peoples as well) for the next century and beyond.

The story of the Armenian reformers is most often told as a tale of revival and recovery of a dormant nation that had existed since primeval times. But historians of nationalism have in recent decades emphasized how much creativity, imagination, and pure invention went into the reconceptualization of the modern nation. A disjointed, fractured history of a dispersed people without a state or even much of a territory in which they constituted a majority was cobbled together as a continuous, organic narrative of origins, heroism, tragedies, and perseverance through adversity. A founding moment in the romantic nationalization of Armenian history was the publication in 1784–1788 of the three-volume history of Armenia by the Mkhitarist monk Mikayel Chamchian, which brought together the medieval historians with a more critical sensitivity to sources. His *Hayots batmutyun* (History of the Armenians) reproduced the myths of Armenian origin and favored where possible Catholics over Apostolic Armenians. Yet his work was the first modern attempt to produce a full history of the Armenians from their origins to the present, integrating disparate events and personalities into an organic narrative. Armenia's primeval beginnings, in line with the accounts of the early medieval historians, were said to go back to Hayk, son of Torgom, grandson of Japheth, son of Noah himself. The ark had landed in the mountains of Urartu, according to the Old Testament. Mount Ararat, the highest peak in Anatolia, was appropriated as the place of that landing and became a national symbol for Armenians. In the Armenian tradition to which Chamchian subscribed, the language spoken by humanity before the confusion of tongues at the Tower of Babel was Armenian. The tall, muscular king of the Armenians, Abgar, was said to have written a letter to Christ, inviting him to come to his kingdom to avoid the wrath of the Israelites. The Bagratid princes and kings of the eighth to eleventh centuries claimed to be of Jewish origin, related to King David, and, thus, linked to God's chosen people. In their own view Armenians were not just one Christian people but the people of the first Christian state, not just converts in the early fourth century but the recipients of the word of God from the apostles Thaddeus and Bartholomew.[12] The Armenian tradition was sustained not only by written works like Chamchian's, but by oral transmission as well. My grandmother, an uneducated woman from Diyarbakır, told me the story of

Armenian as the original human language when I was a child, and only much later did I learn that this tale had long been inscribed in medieval Armenian histories.

ERMENI MILLETI: THE ARMENIANS OF THE OTTOMAN EMPIRE

Armenian history has often been written as that of a separate, coherent nation that stood opposed to the Muslims and the Ottoman state. Yet for hundreds of years Armenians lived in a multinational empire into which they were effectively integrated. They were Ottoman subjects, subordinate to Muslims and the state, but able to make a living and even profit by their association with a powerful polity. The Armenian Church, itself institutionally tied into the Ottoman system of governance, usually preached acceptance of the fate befallen the Armenians; advocated deference toward their rulers and social betters, both Muslim and Armenian; and opposed rebellion of any kind. Yet even as they legitimized the system in which their people lived, clerics remained aware of the special burdens they bore. For Armenian scribes the symbiosis of early Ottoman society was far less benign for the unbeliever (*gavur*) than for the faithful Muslim, and clerical writers, among them Manuel of Garahisar, noted that Armenians had to endure the oppressive rule of the Turks "because of [our] immense sins."[13] Writing in the sixteenth century, a particularly harsh period when Ottoman-Safavid wars raged through eastern Anatolia, the Armenian chronicler Hovhannes Tsaretsi wrote, "Because my sins have become so great, the Ottomans have conquered the Armenian provinces, destroying and laying low all the villages and settlements, and they rule in all places. So heavy was their burden of taxes, that many left their property and their father's legacy. . . . Their oppression spread from generation to generation. Until now we find ourselves under their evil rule. As a consequence, people have left their birthplaces and scattered to all ends of the earth."[14]

A conquered people, Armenians had lost both their political and demographic hegemony over their own historical territory after the fall of the Armenian kingdoms from the eleventh through the fourteenth centuries. Ottoman Armenians understood that they were a subject people, that the ruling elite was Turkish and Islamic, and that even their compatriots who succeeded in society and the state had to adapt to the expectations of the ruling Ottoman elite in order to advance. Discrimination and subordination were woven into the fabric of their lives. The attitude assumed by Muslims was reflected in the words of a Janissary in the late eighteenth century who upbraided his comrades for beating up an old man: "Why did you need to cause a public commotion by whipping [the old man] as if he were an Armenian infidel?!"[15]

Survival as Armenians through the half millennium of Ottoman rule can in part be attributed to the religious and linguistic tenacity of many Armenians (those who did not convert or emigrate) and to the continued efforts of clerics and intellectuals to maintain the Armenian literary tradition. But as we have seen, the *millet* system, the remarkable system of indirect rule through religious communities that the Ottoman government eventually sanctioned, was extraordinarily important in distinguishing and preserving a sense of Armenianness. Along with the discrimination, abuses, and inferiority that Armenians were forced to endure, the *millet* system provided considerable benefits and a degree of cultural and political autonomy. The church remained at the head of the nation; Armenians with commercial and industrial skills were able to climb to the very pinnacle of the Ottoman economic order, but not to the highest rungs of the political hierarchy. This was the domain of Sunni Muslims. The government permitted a variety of educational, charitable, and social institutions to operate, though often with onerous restrictions. Armenians, like Jews and Greeks in the Levant and the Balkans, benefited from the early Ottoman victories over commercial competitors from the West. As the Ottomans drove back the Venetians and other Italian and European powers in the eastern Mediterranean, Christian merchants in the Ottoman realm flourished under the protection of their sultan.[16] Business had less prestige for Muslims and was for centuries largely the purview of Christians and Jews. That would change eventually with the coming of commercial capitalism and industrialization. Without exaggerating the harmony of Turkish-Armenian relations between 1453 and 1878 or neglecting the considerable burdens imposed on non-Muslims, particularly Anatolian peasants, this long period can be seen as one of relatively "benign symbiosis."

Rather than being connected exclusively and in all situations with members of their own *millet*, Armenians lived within and interacted with the multicultural world of the empire. Many of them spoke Turkish, Kurdish, or Arabic along with or rather than Armenian; many, perhaps most, were bi- or trilingual. The last Armenian patriarch of the Ottoman Empire, Zaven Yeghiayan, began life in the late nineteenth century as an Arab-speaking boy in Mosul, and, as he wrote in his memoirs, only later "I learned my own national tongue as though it were a foreign language and, over time I grew to become a proper Armenian. At that time, like many ignorant people, I would confuse nationality and religion, and think that the Armenians were descended from the Hebrews."[17] In the late nineteenth century Armenian literary figures wrote novels in Armeno-Turkish—mostly Turkish words but in Armenian script (*Ermeni harfli*).[18] Arguing that Armenian letters were much easier to learn and read than the Arabic script in which Ottoman Turkish was written, American missionaries published Turkish texts in Armenian script, which Turks then read.[19] Freer of Arabic and Persian words than Ottoman Turkish, the Armeno-Turkish texts used plainspoken Turkish, the vernacular language of ordinary people. Armenians were the first to write, produce, and act in plays in the Ottoman Empire, first in Armenian, then in Turkish (in the Armenian script).[20] Ordinary people of various religions and ethnicities sat next to each other at minstrel performances (*âşık* or *aşuğğ*), at shadow puppet plays (*karagöz*), or while listening to storytellers (*meddah*). Theater was a place where cultures met, and playgoers of various religions worried about the ill-fated lovers on stage and laughed together about the pretentions of Frenchified fops.

Although the Armenian language was of central concern for Armenian nationalists and the church, for most of their countrymen it was an instrument to be used for practical purposes. "Language was not invested with identity in the same way that the modern nation-state invests it," writes Aron Rodrigue. "Distinctions of identity were not automatically coded by language. Language was for communication and religion."[21] Both Turks and Armenians valued the knowledge of more than one language. Armenians said, "As many languages as you know, that is the kind of person you are" (*Kani lezu kides, aynkan mart es*). And Turks likewise believed, "[With] one language [you are only] one person, two languages [makes you] two people" (*Bir dil bir insan, iki dil iki insan*).[22] While the language they spoke in their daily life, their housing, and their foods might differ little from that of their Muslim neighbors, the barriers imposed by different faiths and social standing kept peoples apart. Armenians and other non-Muslims were obliged to observe certain restrictions in the way they dressed. Their social interactions were primarily with people in their own *millet* rather than with those outside with whom they were unlikely to worship or marry or even bathe in the same *hamam* (bathhouse). Members of Ottoman minorities developed social interactions with other non-Muslims or with Europeans resident in the larger cities.[23]

Among the Ottomans religious distinction was foundational to the sense of who one was and to which community one belonged. But religious identities coexisted with other identities: local identities, a sense of place and where one came from, as well as membership in a larger Ottoman world. Armenians were both of the *millet* and cosmopolitan. They could even revel in the differences and singularities of the various cultures and milieus through which they moved. They were able to function within their own community and the wider Ottoman world without ceasing to be either Armenian or Ottoman. But they were never equal to their rulers or well-placed Muslims. Non-Muslims were not permitted to bear arms. Since they were under the protection of the sultan, so the official discourse proclaimed, there was no need for the *gavur* to carry weapons to protect themselves.[24] Non-Muslims performed the occupations considered beneath the faithful—tanning, winemaking, money-changing, and castrating slaves. A non-Muslim was required to dismount from his horse when a Muslim approached. And in the realm of legality and justice non-Muslims often perceived that the authorities favored their co-religionists rather than the People of the Book, Jews and Christians.

Even as Armenians borrowed the idioms of the nation, blending them with their own religious distinctions, religion remained the principal official marker of difference. Catholic and Protestant missionaries in the Ottoman Empire were unable to convert Muslims, who would suffer death if they adopted Christianity (at least up to 1844).[25] They turned their attentions to Armenians and Greeks, but the former proved more susceptible to conversion. In 1859 the Russian consul at Trebizond reported back that the Armenians, "not having a defender among the Christian nations, have been left, with their religious leader, to the arbitrary rule of the Turks. Their faith in their religion is thus weak."[26] The missionaries, primarily American Protestants, were dedicated and zealous believers who saw as their sacred mission bringing the true religion to the heathen and fallen. Even though Armenians were Christians from late antiquity, the evangelical Americans conceived their work as guidance toward enlightenment and salvation. An American missionary half a century later explained how he understood his mission: "Proselytizing was not the object of our labors. But the Gregorian Church had become very corrupt early in its history, its priesthood was ignorant and lax, and the Bible, written in a language which had long been obsolete, was a sealed book to the mass of the people. Baptism and the sacraments were considered the essentials of religion not the living of a holy life. The aim of American missions was to purify the Gregorian Church, educate the priesthood and the people, and, by giving them a Bible translated into modern speech, help them to become Christians in reality as well as in name."[27]

The impact of foreign missionaries on Armenians was enormous.[28] They converted many and created schools that trained a new generation of professionals, particularly teachers. Besides the famous Robert College in Istanbul, there were colleges throughout Anatolia: Anatolia College in Marsovan, Central Turkey College in Antep, Van College in Van, Euphrates College in Harput, and others. They operated with the reluctant permission of the Ottoman state, which suspected that their mission was as political as it was religious. The schools were forcibly closed, their faculty and students deported, in 1915.

Dispersed among three contiguous empires and scattered even farther abroad by their mercantile interests and the oppressive conditions in eastern Anatolia, Armenians were often more divided than united, separated from one another by politics, distance, dialects, and class differences. The wealthier urban Armenians of Istanbul saw themselves as leaders of the *millet*, yet they did little for their fellow Armenians far from the city in eastern Anatolia. The *millet*s themselves included diverse elements. They did not correspond exactly to ethnolinguistic lines. The *Ermeni milleti*, for instance, included not only the Armenians of the national (Apostolic) church, but also Copts, Chaldeans, Ethiopians, Syrian Jacobites, and others, many of whom, along with Armenian Catholics and Protestants, gained their own *millet*s in the early nineteenth century.

In the inequitable relationship of subordination and superordination, with the Muslims on top and the non-Muslims below, the sheer power and confidence of the ruling Muslims worked for centuries to maintain in the Armenians a pattern of personal and social behavior manifested in submissiveness, passivity, and deference to authority. As supplicants, they were seen to act in calculatedly devious and disguised ways. Until the last quarter of the nineteenth century the Armenians worked within the Ottoman system and accepted the burdens of Muslim administration without much protest. Their deferential behavior earned them the title "loyal *millet*" (*millet-i sadıka*) in an age when the Greeks and Slavs of the empire were striving to emancipate themselves through revolutionary action.

The late nineteenth century was marked by ideas of strictly defined races existing in stark difference from one another, an age when science itself proclaimed the actuality of race as a principal definer of human potential. Travelers, missionaries, and government officials fed the public with elaborate images of the national character of the peoples of the Ottoman Empire. Many who journeyed through eastern Anatolia noted the lack of spirit of the provincial Armenians and their renowned intriguing character traits that appeared to distinguish them from the Turks and Kurds. A famous English traveler writing under the pseudonym Mrs. Bishop confessed to "a prejudice against the Armenians." Nevertheless, she found it impossible to "deny that they are the most capable, energetic, enterprising, and pushing race in Western Asia, physically superior, and intellectually acute," therefore capable of being "raised in all respects to our own level." She shared the standard view that though "Oriental," they possessed a remarkable "shrewdness and aptitude for business." "Whatever exists of commercial enterprise in Eastern Asia Minor is almost altogether in their hands."[29] The British traveler and diplomat Mark Sykes provided one of the more extreme characterizations of the Armenians. "Even Jews have their good points," he wrote, "but Armenians have none. His cowardice, his senseless untruthfulness, the depth of his intrigue, even in the most trivial matters, his habit of hoarding, his lack of one manly virtue, his helplessness in danger, his natural and instinctive treachery, together form so vile a character that pity is stifled and judgment unbalanced."[30] One can certainly agree that Sykes's judgment was unbalanced, that he failed to reflect on what life might be like for an unarmed, settled Christian population living among armed, often nomadic Muslims who enjoyed the support of the state.

Unwittingly, those who ran the Ottoman Empire contributed to the making of nations. Before Abdülhamid II Armenians had been considered the most loyal *millet* in the empire; after 1878 the authorities imagined them as subversive, ungrateful subjects of a benevolent state. Both the Ottoman and Russian regimes ascribed an identity to the Armenians, first as loyal and commercially endowed, later as dangerous and disloyal. Imposed identities, along with shared senses of similarity and solidarity within the Armenian community, lessened divisions among Armenians and forged a common sense of belonging to a people worthy of preservation and defense. What began as a message from spiritual leaders, poets, and militants filtered into the consciousness of ordinary men and women. Repression and alienation from the cosmopolitan society in which they had flourished cemented links between Armenians and frayed ties to the Ottoman world.

The discourse of the nation that emerged from Europe emphasized most emphatically two elements: that a people constituted as a nation has the right to rule itself and that it also possesses a right to what it holds to be its homeland, a designated territory from which it originated. Such an understanding would eventually become the most powerful legitimation for state authority and territorial possession. Its very logic, however, reifies and dichotomizes different peoples as distinct, homogeneous nations. In the last years of their empire Ottoman state authorities came to believe that the nationalism of the most radical Armenian leaders reflected the authentic feelings of their collective nation. Therefore reprisals against all, not the few, were necessary. The simple conflation, implicit in the discourse of the nation—that the people possess naturally, essentially, and unproblematically national sentiment if not full consciousness (that is, they always possess the potential to become a full-fledged nation)—opens the way to action against a whole people so distinguished and defined.

THE UNEVEN REACH OF CAPITALISM

The introduction over time of distant markets, wage labor, and the commodification of goods, services, and people, taken together, was the most significant revolutionary transformation in human life in the modern age. Indeed, the spread of capitalist relations of production was fundamental to what characterizes modernity. Karl Marx eloquently anticipated the revolutionary force of the penetration of capitalism in his prescient formulation: "All fixed, fast-frozen relations, with their train of ancient and venerable prejudices and opinions are swept away, all new formed ones become antiquated before they can ossify. All that is solid melts into air, all that is holy is profaned, and man is at last compelled to face with sober senses his real conditions of life and his relations with his kind."[31]

As Marx predicted, capitalism brought with it roiling change, instability, destruction of old ways and worlds, and a cruel confrontation with unforgiving economic demands. The coming of capitalism to the Ottoman Empire was "polarizing and destabilizing."[32] Non-Muslims engaged in the new commerce and industry in the larger cities grew rich, while Muslim officialdom, dependent on the dwindling revenues of the state, grew poor. A Europeanized bourgeoisie visible and distinct in its style, language, and religion stood apart from the Muslim elites and above ordinary Muslims.

Long embedded in the Ottoman commercial economy, non-Muslims adjusted on the whole more rapidly to the possibilities and exigencies of the new economy. While prominent and successful Muslim merchant families flourished in Anatolia and elsewhere, the widespread perception (that extends to historians of the Ottoman Empire today) was that non-Muslims made up the largest and most influential number of owners and operators of industrial and commercial enterprises and stood out as close colleagues of European investors and entrepreneurs. To explain their success in business, contemporaries employed hoary stereotypes of Armenian merchants, Greek traders, and Jewish moneylenders. Europeans held the stereotypic characterizations of ethnic groups to be a true map of the real world and calculated that Greeks, Armenians, and Jews were in fact good merchants and could navigate the intricacies of the Ottoman tax system and internal trade regulations better than either they or the uneducated Muslims could.[33] These prejudices about national character may have contributed to success in business for some, but social factors were far more important. Non-Muslims' prominence in commerce and industry began with their fortuitous base in urban locations and with their ties to the outside world. Christians and Jews, who made up only about 17 percent of the population of Anatolia in 1912, were disproportionately represented in towns and cities. Around 1900 non-Muslims made up 55.9 percent of Istanbul's population, 61.5 percent of Izmir's, 42.8 percent of Trabzon's, and about one-third of the population of Diyarbakır *kaza*, Erzurum, Sivas *kaza*, and Ankara *kaza*.[34] Their international networks, language skills, and prior experience in entrepreneurial practices gave Armenians, Greeks, and Jews an advantage over the less well-educated Muslims. What privileged the non-Muslims was not only the appeal to Europeans to deal with people of their own religion or their presence in cities or their skills at language, but also their marginalization in the Ottoman preindustrial economy. Another factor arose from the fact that agriculture in Anatolia was based on small peasant farms rather than large estates owned by noble landlords. The sheer number of farms and the diversity of products made it impossible for foreign traders to control the

Ottoman agricultural market and instead gave non-Muslim middlemen an important intermediary role to play.

A non-Muslim bourgeoisie, with Western style and tastes, developed in the port cities of the empire.[35] These men of business were competitors with both European merchants and the less well-positioned Muslim entrepreneurs, who were losing out in the nineteenth century to non-Muslims in both foreign and domestic trade. Muslims, on the other hand, were mostly involved in trade within the empire, between towns in the interior and between those towns and the port cities.[36] The non-Muslim commercial bourgeoisie also challenged the state bureaucracy, which had its own economic interests, most importantly extracting what it could from the country's peasants.[37] Muslims, who dominated the empire politically and demographically, began to be subordinated economically and socially to non-Muslims in the work world from the mid-nineteenth century. By the turn of the century only eleven of the forty-two printing plants in the empire were owned by Muslims and twenty-six by non-Muslims; of metal-working plants, twenty were owned by non-Muslims, only one by a Muslim; of the famous Bursa raw silk manufactories, six were owned by Muslims, two by the government, and thirty-three by non-Muslims. At the top of the economic pyramid in the early twentieth century Europeans occupied the most lucrative posts. Besides industrial ownership, Armenians and Greeks held important positions as managers and salaried employees in Western-financed companies, in mining and especially on the railroads. The Anatolian railroad was largely financed and managed by Germans, but middle-rank positions were held, half by Europeans, half by Ottoman Greeks and Armenians. Ottoman Christians also made up the guards and station personnel, while the Muslims held the lower-paid jobs—line workers and cleaners. The occupational division by ethnicity and religion led to frequent complaints. Even the relatively privileged Greek and Armenian employees expressed their discontent that they received less pay for the same jobs as Europeans. "An Armenian stationmaster may have earned twice the wage of a Turkish fireman but it was only a fraction of his European supervisor's salary."[38]

Labor conflict easily took on ethnic and religious dimensions. By the middle of the nineteenth century the porters (*hamallar*) in Ottoman ports were largely Armenian since Muslim porters had been driven out as supporters of the repressed Janissary corps and Greeks because of their independence movement. The same fate befell the Armenian porters after the Bank Ottoman seizure by Armenian revolutionaries in 1896 after which they were replaced by Kurds or drifted away because of excessive taxes. After 1908 Armenians tried to regain their old positions in the ports, but the Muslim porters resisted their reinstatement.[39]

Capitalist production and exchange in the Ottoman ports and towns accelerated with the opening of trade with Great Britain, already established as the pioneer industrial power. The 1838 Treaty of Balta Limanı between the Ottomans and the British opened up Ottoman markets to British and later European trade, ended monopolies on agricultural products, and established common tariffs and taxes for foreign and Ottoman merchants. The door to expanded commercial capitalism was unlocked. At the same time, however, the "income distribution within the empire polarized, impoverishing Muslim guildsmen and peasants."[40]

The reforms of the *Tanzimat* were meant to modernize society and the economy of the empire, but like many programs of reform they were incomplete and led to unintended consequences. As we have seen with Kurds and Armenians in the East, the land reform of 1858 basically reinforced existing social hierarchies based on property, benefiting those with money and power who could register lands and disadvantaging the poor who worked the land. Conflicts over land were at the center of the growing tensions among the different religious and ethnic groups in eastern Anatolia. Registration was adjudicated by the courts, which operated according to Islamic law and favored Muslims. What was fundamentally a matter of economics and embedded differences in political clout was therefore easily ethnicized, interpreted, and understood as a conflict between Turks, Kurds, and Armenians.

Armenian peasants in eastern Anatolia and Cilicia competed with Muslim refugees for the most desired and scarce resort—land. The pressure of new settlers favored by local officials and courts pushed Christian

Hamals by a shop in Trabzon, 1889. Verney Lovett Cameron, 1889.

peasants to petition the government. The Armenian patriarchate counted hundreds of cases of Muslim usurpation of Armenian lands. The state most often supported Muslim claimants, and many Armenians reluctantly moved to the towns or emigrated abroad, further eroding their position in a contested landscape. Yet in the burgeoning market economy some Armenians did well. In some areas, like Cilicia from the 1870s on, Armenians who were prominent in urban trades and crafts, finance, and international commerce used their superior economic position to buy up large landholdings.[41] Once the sultan permitted non-Muslims and foreigners to buy Muslim lands (1858), Armenians and Greeks began purchasing properties that Muslim debtors could no longer pay for. Armenian emigrants to America and Europe sent home their savings and on their return brought new machines and technology to their farms. With Muslim refugees from the Caucasus and the Balkans migrating to Anatolia, and Armenians intent on keeping or expanding their holdings, the intense competition for land pitted Christians against Muslims.

What might have been seen as economic and social competitions were increasingly framed in ethnic and religious terms; what might have been understood as conflicts associated with social standing were seen as one ethnoreligious community against another.[42]

In the last years of the empire, on the eve of World War I, an important British diplomat, Gerald Henry Fitzmaurice, chief dragoman and first secretary at the British embassy in Istanbul, summed up the sustained process of alienation of Armenian lands. He discerned a long-term Ottoman policy of deracinating the Armenians of the empire by systematically usurping their land. "The Turkish Government," he wrote, "after the Treaty of Berlin [1878], realizing that a sense of nationality cannot easily live without a peasantry, and that if it succeeded in uprooting the Armenian peasantry from the soil and driving them into the towns or out of the country, it would in great part rid itself of the Armenians and the Armenian question, condoned and encouraged Kurdish usurpation of Armenian lands."[43] The land policy extended from the Hamidian period (1876–1908) through the years of the Young Turk government (after 1908).

Under both Abdülhamid II and the Young Turks the marketization of the Ottoman economy developed at the same time as the central state reached farther out in the peripheries of the empire. Agriculture was increasingly commercialized, and as the value of land rose powerful people took matters into their own hands and dispossessed defenseless peasants of their land. A wealthy and powerful man would invade a peasant family's land with armed attendants and force the family to move out, with their animals. Notables accumulated land and privatized it according to the Land Code of 1858, often supported by state officials. Such seizures of land hit Muslims as well as non-Muslims, but for Armenians and Greeks the losses were seen as part of an Ottoman policy to weaken the Christians and favor the Muslims. Peasants petitioned the authorities, particularly after the 1908 revolution, but their moral appeals to fairness, justice, and rights seldom succeeded before the raw exercise of physical force. In some cases the authorities returned confiscated land to Armenians, but when they attempted to reclaim it, they were met by Kurds with guns.[44] In eastern Anatolia Armenian and Kurdish peasants deprived of their land either found work as tenants to great landlords or in desperation emigrated from their native villages.

The expansion of trade benefited (and disadvantaged) some *millets* (and even segments within *millets*) more than others. With the Greeks suspect as rebels (and after 1821 possessing their own independent state) and the Ottomans favoring the Armenians as the "loyal *millet*," urban Armenians profited enormously from their association with the Porte. The *amiras* and *sarrafs*, the wealthy money-lenders and bankers who financed the tax-farming system, along with the less affluent *esnafs*, the craftsmen and artisans of the towns, accumulated wealth with which they subsidized schools, hospitals, and philanthropic organizations.[45] Though highly placed, the *amiras* were always vulnerable to the arbitrary power of the sultan, and when reforming officials progressively eliminated the tax-farming system, the wealthy *sarrafs* suffered financially. The Armenian commercial class, particularly in the Europeanized district of Istanbul known as Pera or Galata, sought protection, even citizenship, from the Western embassies and benefited from the various concessions and privileges (the famous capitulations) given reluctantly by the Porte to European powers.

The well-positioned, visible Armenians of the Ottoman capital worked to improve their position in the empire both through pushing for internal political reform and by close cooperation with Europeans. Armenians published the first newspapers in the empire, and between 1830 and the 1870s there were about one hundred different Armenian newspapers, many of them short-lived, in Istanbul.[46] The Armenian merchant and financial families more and more frequently sent their children to be educated abroad or to the new schools set up in Turkey by Catholic and Protestant missionaries. Many Armenians adopted European manners and dress, *alafranga* (in the French or European manner) as it was called. They became visibly distant from the demographically and politically dominant Muslims. Armenians ran the imperial mint, an Armenian was chief architect to the sultan, and Armenians ran the Foreign Correspondence Office of the government. Armenians filled the ranks of the professions; they were the doctors, dentists, lawyers, pharmacists, photographers, and moneychangers. More than a dozen Armenians, backed by the votes of both Christians and Muslims, were elected to the first Ottoman Parliament in 1877.[47] The mid-nineteenth century was marked by a new cultural consciousness or cultural nationalism that celebrated the particular experiences (and sufferings) of Armenians and emphasized the threads that through time bound that ethnoreligious group together. The revival of Armenian literacy, the flourishing consciousness of their shared past, and their interest in promoting a specifically Armenian education and culture were later grandly labeled a renaissance (*Zartonk*) by Armenian writers. As Armenians became visible, upwardly mobile, entrepreneurial, and distinct in their style of life, their very success generated envy and resentment among others. As merchants, shopkeepers, bankers, and professionals who dominated certain professions from dentistry to photography, Armenians stood out in the eyes of some as people with unearned social position, envied status, and undeserved privilege. When some Ottoman Muslims strove to imitate the ways of the West, it seemed as if the Armenians were already halfway there.

Whether considering themselves Turks or Muslims, those who were not Christians felt uncomfortably inferior to the more prosperous and seemingly free people of the Europeanized parts of their cities. This was most evident in Istanbul, where the contrast between Pera and the Islamic parts of the capital was immediately palpable. Turkish speakers sensed condescension from Christian merchants or awkwardness before a well-dressed man or woman wearing a hat. One writer remembered that "all Muslims felt inferior in front of the hat."[48] "If a [European] theater company came to Pera," another observer wrote,

> and . . . if you lived in [the Muslim part] in Istanbul . . . and if you did not have enough money in your purse to rent a carriage . . . then you would have to go from [Muslim] Istanbul's mud covered streets immersed in darkness across the . . . bridge, climb the hills and, half penitent by this time, enter the theater. . . . You were still happy if you enjoyed art for two hours to forget all that trouble, difficulties, your hurt personal pride. But as you returned home

soiled [in mud], staggering in the dark with something twisted within your heart as you thought and as your heart ached about the foreigners, the Greek Rum, Armenians, Jews on the other side of the bridge leading a very pleasant life in their own magnificent mansions, while the Turk on the other side pulled the blanket of his deprived life ... over his head to sleep, only to awaken the following day to see the sun turbid once again. This was the life of the Turk and the degree of the unhappiness and misery felt by the [Muslim Turkish] youth of that time.[49]

TANZIMAT AND ITS DISCONTENTS

In the early nineteenth century the waves of revolutionary changes that had roiled Europe reached the Ottoman Empire. The fallout from the French Revolution, the rise of European nationalism, the inroads of European capitalism and the Industrial Revolution, the expansion of Russia into the Caucasus and British shipping into the Black Sea—all had effects on the internal life of the Ottoman peoples, differentially felt by the various *millet*s. Wealthy Armenians thrived. The Armenian bankers (*sarraf*s) dominated the patriarchate and used their offices to enrich themselves. They chose and dismissed patriarchs at will. Less wealthy artisans (*esnaf*s) resented being left out of communal politics and repeatedly protested their marginalization.

Encouraged by the *Tanzimat* reformers in government and the theorists of the liberal ecumenicalism known as Ottomanism, the more progressive Armenian leaders petitioned and pressured the Porte and tried occasionally to enlist foreign support for reform.[50] An alliance of mutual interest tied progressive bureaucrats and liberal Armenians together in an effort to modernize the empire along European lines. In pursuit of a future within the empire, reformist Armenians sought elimination of the more repressive Ottoman institutions, like tax-farming, and pressed for guarantees of equality under the law, and perhaps autonomy under a Christian governor for the Anatolian provinces. A foreseeable consequence of egalitarian reforms, however, would be to undermine the traditional hierarchical, Muslim-dominated political and social order in which Christians were at a legal disadvantage.

Social tensions between the rich and the not-so-rich tore at the Armenian community and threatened the peace of the Ottoman capital. By the 1840s the influence of the bankers had declined, and an advocate for broadening participation in the running of the community, Matteos Chukhajian, was elected Armenian patriarch of Constantinople (1844–1848). To resolve the disputes within their community Armenians worked out regulations for their *millet*. Councils were set up to aid in the governance of the patriarchate. From an autocratic structure dominated by the wealthiest parishioners, the patriarchate was gradually transformed into a constitutional institution involving the guildsmen as well. Through the 1850s the struggle between the conservative *amiras* and the reformers working in the *Tanzimat* mode continued.[51] A "constitution" was issued in 1860 but suspended soon after until the sultan responded to the pleas of leading Armenians and reluctantly granted a "regulation" (*nizamname*) in 1863 that authorized the formation of a central assembly for the Armenian *millet*. With this decree, which the Armenians called the "national constitution" (*Azgayin sahmanadrutyun*), the *Ermeni milleti* had a formal, institutional structure, one that brought the dominant Constantinopolitan Armenians into greater contact with their Anatolian compatriots and transformed the Armenian patriarchate of Istanbul into a representative body governed by a National Assembly. Although the provinces were greatly underrepresented, the assembly was elected by Armenians from all over the Ottoman Empire and it chose the patriarch, who represented the *millet* before the sultan's government. An Ottoman institution, the Armenian National Assembly consisted of two chambers, the Political and the Religious Councils. The very existence of these institutions, despite the fractious nature of their politics, contributed to the cohesion of Ottoman Armenians, solidifying their collective identification with their co-religionists. The Armenian constitution served as a model for other *millet*s and for the Ottoman Constitution of 1876.[52]

Those within the Armenian National Assembly and the patriarchate of Constantinople who were reform-minded worked hard to bring greater order and rationality to the operation of the *Ermeni milleti*, particularly in the complex hierarchy of the far-flung church. Within the Ottoman Empire the Armenian Apostolic Church had patriarchates in Istanbul and Jerusalem as well as two historic catholicosates, in Sis (Cilicia) and Akhtamar (on Lake Van). The local holders of monasteries and many clerics were unwilling to concede their powers and privileges to the Istanbul patriarchate, which in collaboration with the Ottoman state wanted to subordinate the entire network of churches in the empire to its authority. Division and conflict, personal and political, was rampant. In one case the catholicosate of Akhtamar fell into the hands of a cleric who was implicated in the murder of his predecessor. Pretenders to Armenian religious power were in some cases closely embedded in local networks of power, even involving Kurdish and Türkmen chieftains. And to complicate matters further the catholicos of all Armenians, in Ejmiatsin across the border in the Russian Empire, was also reluctant to grant Istanbul prerogatives that compromised his own position. Reformers were frustrated, but over time the Constantinople patriarchate, with the help of the Ottoman state, established greater authority over the outlying churches. *Tanzimat*, which was intended to modernize an empire, had contradictory effects, simultaneously increasing the power of the imperial center while contributing to the greater consolidation of the Armenian community within the empire and to a sense of an Armenian nation.[53]

While the wealthy Armenians of the capital both influenced the patriarch and controlled the National Assembly that dealt with certain aspects of *millet* affairs, the provinces remained radically underrepresented. A frequent complaint from the east was that Istanbul Armenians, as the leaders of the community, were not fulfilling their obligation to care for the lower orders. This alienation from the center was highlighted by the work of Bishop Mkrtich Khrimian, affectionately known as *Hayrik* (Little Father), in Van, the most Armenian of the towns of eastern Anatolia. Khrimian edited a journal, *Ardziv Vaspurakani* (The Eagle of Vaspurakan [the medieval Armenian name for the Van region]), in 1858, in which he exposed the suffering of his parishioners and spoke vaguely of Armenian self-defense. He emphasized the depth of the historic and cultural connections of Armenians to the high plateau in which they had lived for more than a millennium and a half while at the same time affirming his people's loyalty to the legitimate authority of the sultan.

As patriarch of Constantinople (1869–1873), Khrimian came into conflict with the more conservative forces among the capital's Armenians when he attempted to increase provincial representation in the National Assembly. The activist priest prepared a major report (*Teghekagir Gavara-kan Harstaharuteants*) in 1872, which was discussed and partly revised by the National Assembly.[54] Submitted to the Porte, the report enumerated the abuses of Armenians by provincial authorities and the burdens laid on them—unfair taxes arbitrarily collected; the non-admission of testimony in court by non-Muslims; the "rapes, depredations, and thefts and, above all, murders [that] remain without punishment, or have remained undiscovered"; and the attacks by Kurdish tribesmen on Armenian farmers. Khrimian appealed to the sultan to realize the protections and justice promised in the *Hatti-i Humayun*. As a loyal Ottoman, the patriarch petitioned to his lord, reiterating the fidelity of the Armenians to the sultan. Khrimian contrasted Armenian devotion to the empire with the Kurdish tribesmen who neither paid taxes nor provided armed support to the state. He went so far as to suggest, "Let either the Kurds who continually oppress our nation be disarmed, or let the Armenians be put in a position to protect their life, honour and property against the oppressors." The sultan, he proposed, should introduce a "powerful police" into Anatolia and permit Armenians to join the force.[55] Prominent liberal Armenians, like Grigor Otian, then the president of the National Assembly, supported Khrimian. But neither patriarch nor national assembly could overcome either the Ottoman government's unwillingness to carry out reforms in the provinces or the conservative Armenians' indifference toward the provincial Armenians. In 1873 Khrimian, the most forceful and respected Armenian clergyman in the empire, resigned as patriarch.

The life trajectory of one prominent Ottoman Armenian, Grigor Otian (1834–1887) (Krikor Odian in Western Armenian orthography), illustrates the odyssey of an engaged man who at first was convinced that the future of the Armenians lay within the Ottoman Empire only to be disillusioned in the last decade of his life. Otian was fluent in Ottoman Turkish, as well as classical and spoken Western Armenian. He was the author of a grammar of the local vernacular Armenian. His fortunes rose and fell with the eminent *Tanzimat* grand vizier Midhat Paşa, one of the central figures in the mid-century reform movement and a personal friend. A key advisor and member of the Ottoman State Council, Otian was given the highest rank in the empire's civil service. With the outbreak of the Russo-Turkish War of 1877–1878, he was caught, like many of his compatriots, between his loyalty to the empire and his hopes that the Russians or British would push the sultan to alleviate the condition of the Armenians. He wrote the memorandum that the Armenian delegation presented to the Congress of Berlin. Soon after, Abdülhamid suspended the Ottoman Constitution, deposed and banished Midhat Paşa, and brought the *Tanzimat* to an end. Otian fled to Paris, convinced that he had no future in his homeland. Despite repeated requests by Abdülhamid that he return to Istanbul, Otian chose to remain in exile and died impoverished in France.[56] For an Ottomanist Armenian like Otian the coming to power of Abdülhamid was the moment when his country abandoned him and his people.

The contradictions in the *Tanzimat*'s egalitarian reforms were evident in the regime's attempt to recruit Christians for the Ottoman army. The exclusive right of Muslims to bear arms had reinforced the inferior social position of Christians. Given the option after the Crimean War (1853–1856) of serving or paying a tax to avoid recruitment, Christians preferred to pay rather than serve. Most Christians were not interested in the hard life of the soldier or the risks of death in battle. Many Muslims, on the other hand, were wary of arming Armenians and Greeks and reluctant to promote Christians into the officer corps. They regarded bearing arms as a privilege of the faithful not to be entrusted to the untrustworthy.[57] Abdülhamid II, who would reverse many of the gains of the *Tanzimat*, was opposed to arming Christians, whom he characterized as disloyal and linked to the European powers. "Requiring military service from the non-Muslims is merely a pipe dream that would be like suicide for us," he said. "If we the Turks who are the dominant nation agree to do

military service under equal conditions with the people among our subjects from different religions and sects, we would be sure to find ourselves
in a bad situation. . . . We are right to be anxious about this because the
Christians within our empire have always united with the Great Powers
and worked against us."[58]

CHAPTER THREE

Nation

SPEAKING NATIONAL

In the vision of ethnonationalists multinational empires were doomed, and the future belonged to ethnically homogeneous states. Nationalists rejected the multilingual cosmopolitanism of empires, seeing the loss of a primary national language as national death. Often when nationalists looked at the ethnically and religiously diverse world they saw "opposed national communities . . . separated by unbridgeable gulfs."[1] The organization of schools by nationalists was in part an effort to institutionalize and promote ethnonational differences between the peoples of the empire. Teachers would become the "organic intellectuals" of the nation, the promoters of national ideas and ideals.[2] But in the mid- and late nineteenth century the triumph of exclusive ethnonationalism or separatist nationalism was neither foreordained nor inevitable. Ottoman Armenians were torn between those who sought a life within the empire, accommodating themselves to the cosmopolitan imperial setting, and those radicals influenced by Caucasian Armenians and Western nationalisms who were intrigued by possibilities of greater self-rule. The nationalization of Armenians occurred, not in isolation or primarily from within, but in synergy with and in response to the developing discourses of liberalism and the nation in Europe and the nationalisms of other peoples, most notably the French and the Greeks. National separatist movements of the Ottoman peoples of the Balkans, along with the Western imperialist incursions into and repeated defeats of the Ottoman Empire, contributed to a general sense of Ottoman decline that stimulated Westernizing bureaucrats to attempt to reform the empire and Europeanized Christians to consider either separating from the empire or, in the case of most activist Armenians, to petition for internal reform along more liberal lines. As potent as the message of the nationalists was, especially among the young, for most Armenians daily life was more concerned with making a living, tending their farms and businesses, and caring for their families. Politics and the state were usually far away, except when it was time to pay taxes.

Their long literary tradition and established presence in the highlands of eastern Anatolia and southern Caucasia made it easy for Armenians to identify the rough location of a homeland. But Armenians were scattered and lived among Muslims who in most regions constituted the majority of the population. Dispersion and the intermixing of peoples made the notion of a coherent and contiguous Armenian homeland problematic. Where that territory was exactly, what its extent and boundaries ought to be, was contested. For Armenian intellectuals and many foreigners Armenia was basically associated with the eastern Anatolian highlands, eventually with the six Armenian *vilayet*s. This was popularly called the *Erkir* (the Country), the homeland. How it ought to be governed, what degree of independence and sovereignty it should enjoy, were issues that both divided Armenians and frightened the Muslims and other Christians among whom they lived.[3]

Appropriately for a dispersed people faced by three imperial authorities—Ottoman, Russian, and Persian—the nationalism of many Armenian thinkers was not primarily territorial. Neither the clergy nor the powerful conservatives in the capital, who benefited from their privileged positions within Ottoman society and close to the state, were interested in creating a territorial nation. Some early Armenian nationalists, like Stepanos Nazariants, entertained the concept of a non-territorial nationalism, a cultural connection based on language and historical experience but forgoing claims to a specific and limited territory. That conception, however, fell away in the late nineteenth century as nationalists affirmed the importance of a distinct Armenian territory even though Armenians were scattered throughout the empire and living among and beside Muslims.

Rather than a separate Armenian state, almost all Ottoman Armenians, particularly the church and the Ottomanized Armenian elite, hoped for improved existence within the empire instituted by reform from above by their "benevolent government." The view of most Armenian leaders coincided with that of the *Tanzimat* decree that asserted that the "present crisis results from the defective dispensation of justice, and from members of the public administration erecting into law the arbitrary dictates of their own will."[4] The more liberal and radical elements, among both Caucasian and Ottoman Armenians, increasingly turned their attention to the poverty and oppression suffered by the Armenian peasantry in the eastern provinces. A sense of a fatherland (*hayrenik*) developed among Armenian writers, and a distinction was drawn between *azgasirutyun* (love of nation), which heightened the sense of a cultural nation beyond a specific territory, and *hayrenasirutyun* (love of fatherland), with emphasis on the people in Armenia (*Hayastantsiner*). Students of Khrimian, like Bishop Garegin Srvantstiants, who had long complained about the distance of Constantinople Armenians from the fatherland, and Arsen Tokhmakhian, who later turned to revolution, celebrated the Armenians of historic Armenia who had "preserved the faith and suffered because of it."[5] Intellectuals promoted writing in the vernacular Armenian language (*ashkharabar*) rather than the classical language (*grabar*) still employed by the church. Srvantstiants organized the publication of the Armenian oral epic *Sasuntsi David* (David of Sasun), which served as an inspiration for young radicals. Imbued with a deeply populist nationalism, centered on the peasants of eastern Anatolia, Armenian intellectuals traveled as teachers to the East in an effort characterized as *depi Hayastan* (to Armenia). Although many clerics and the Armenian Church hierarchy advocated caution and patience, churchmen like Khrimian and Srvantstiants contributed to the growing agitation and resistance among young Armenians. The government responded by removing prominent teachers, like Mkrtich Portukalian in Van and Martiros Sareyan in Muş, from their home provinces and exiling Khrimian to Jerusalem.

Ordinary Armenians turned to their spiritual leaders and pleaded with them to intercede with the Ottoman authorities to redress their grievances. Their appeals repeatedly failed. A number of notable Armenians made overtures to the Russians and the British, hoping that the Great Powers might pressure the sultan to alleviate the conditions of the Armenians of the East. The Armenians of Charsanjak, who likened themselves to the "people of Israel," pleaded to Catholicos Gevorg IV in 1867 that they were "living in a state of captivity." Burdened by myriad taxes and fees to their *agha*s (overlords), "those who resist, refuse, or delay are put in chains and have to face bastinado, the sword, or the rifle." The villagers had sent petitions to the Armenian patriarch and the Ottoman vizier in Istanbul but received no reply. "The *agha*s have sucked our blood like leeches and there is no possibility of reconciliation.... We are informing Your Holiness that sooner or later an incident will provoke our inhabitants to action and no one will be able to stop it then.... This is our final request."[6] When appeals to the Ottoman state and to foreign powers failed, the last resort for desperate Armenians, particularly young men, would be resistance and revolution.

Armenians appealed, not only to their church hierarchy in the Russian Empire but to the tsarist state as well. In 1872 merchants in Van requested that the Russian government send a consul to their city to guarantee "the safety of trade routes and protection of religion, lives, and goods of the downtrodden Christian people of Vaspurakan."[7] Four years later the Armenian merchants of Van suffered a devastating fire that wiped out almost one hundred Armenian shops. Many suspected that the blaze was the result of arson. Armed Kurds and soldiers pillaged shops, while the authorities stood by. Muslim butcher and grocery shops were untouched.[8] That same year when Europeans interceded on the behalf of Bulgarians who had suffered massacres at the hands of the Ottomans, the Armenians of Istanbul made their own plea to Catholicos Gevorg IV.

> We are sure that if the Europeans become aware of the terrible pains suffered by the Armenians, they will feel sympathy for us as well and will spare our people further agony.... We suffer incessantly day and night, under the heavy torture of the Turkish regional commanders, tax collectors, landlords, and other tyrants. They ridicule our priests in public and offend the decency of our women and the honor of our maidens. They slaughter our young and old men and scorn our holy altars and sacred vessels of our churches. Woe on us! What misfortunes haven't befallen on our people.

They asked the catholicos "to be bold and to deliver our message to the Christian nations, so that they may find a remedy for the sufferings of an ancient nation."[9]

With the failure of reform—the end of *Tanzimat*, the withdrawal of the Ottoman Constitution in 1878, the steady replacement of Ottomanism with policies preferential to Muslims—and in the face of European disinterest in the fate of the Armenians through the 1880s, the situation of the Ottoman Armenians began to deteriorate rapidly. Increasingly Ottoman authorities interpreted any manifestation of cultural revival or resistance by non-Muslims, however individual or local, as an act of national rebellion. The government restricted the powers of the Armenian National Assembly, accepting only reports (*takrirler*) dealing with churches and monasteries. Armenian journals from Russia were banned. The state prohibited all forms of national expression, forbidding the word *Hayastan* (Armenia in Armenian) in print as well as the sale and possession of pictures of the last Armenian king, Levon V, who had lost his throne five centuries earlier. Instead of seeing them as the "loyal *millet*," Ottoman officials and Muslim intellectuals began to look on Armenians as unruly, subversive, alien elements who consorted with foreign powers. The conservative Islamic clergy, long alienated by the Frenchified reformist bureaucrats among Muslims, were offended by the behavior and wealth of the most visible Armenians, those merchants who lived in the capital, particularly those in Europeanized districts of the capital, like Pera, who affected Western manners or even took foreign citizenship. A highly placed Ottoman observer noted the resentment of religious Muslims toward the effects of the *Tanzimat*: "Many among the people of Islam began complaining thus: 'Today we lost our sacred national rights [*hukuk-i mukaddese-i milliyyem-izi*] which were earned with our ancestors' blood. The Muslim community [*millet-i islamiyye*], while it used to be the ruling religious community [*millet-i hâkime*], has [now] been deprived of such a sacred right. For the people of Islam, this is a day to weep and mourn.'"[10]

At the end of the nineteenth century and the beginning of the twentieth, attitudes toward Armenians by Turks, and vice versa, were shifting. A Turkish journalist later remembered his childhood "wars" in the Balkans where Muslim children on one hilltop flung stones with their slingshots at Christian children on another hilltop. For hours they fought "as if we were in a national war and continued until we were able to chase the infidel children away. As the enemy withdrew from the war, we spread out onto the mountains with yells, gathered crocuses, and returned to town like heroes who had won wars." While still children, animosity toward Christians was instilled, and "since we did not know any better, we regarded the Christian children who were infidels as the enemy. They were not [yet] Greeks and we were not [yet] Turkish. Then society was divided into two as Christian and Muslim."[11]

The elevation of the word *Türk* into a proud, national designation occurred quite rapidly. A Turkish novelist recalled, "In our childhood, Turk meant vulgar and wild (*kaba ve yabani*). We were of the community of Islam and Ottoman. In the books explaining the principles of Islam (*ilmihal*), our principal lesson [to learn] was that religion and nationality was one and the same. The word fatherland (*vatan*) was forbidden. . . . We had been subjects of the Sultan. At the end of the school week, we lined up and shouted 'long live our sultan!'"[12] At the same time the Armenians had themselves changed dramatically in the four middle decades of the nineteenth century. The increase in social communication among Armenians had fostered a powerful sense of secular nationality among many Armenians. Influenced by Western ideas, Armenian intellectuals had developed a new interest in the Armenian past, and instead of conceiving themselves solely as part of a religious community, more and more Armenians began to acquire a Western sense of nationality, a feeling of kinship with Christian Europe, and a growing alienation from the Muslim peoples among whom they lived. The depth or spread of this new national consciousness should not be exaggerated. Certainly more potent in the larger cities and in localities where Armenian or missionary schools helped to shape new ways of thinking, Armenian nationalist ideas spread slowly into eastern Anatolia. Equally if not more influential in shaping Armenian attitudes in the late nineteenth century than the positive images created by Armenian and foreign intellectuals was the negative experience of poor Armenians at the hands of their Muslim overlords.

Social differentiation among *millet*s and the resultant tensions existed throughout the nineteenth century, but the frames in which they were given meaning changed. Ottoman Westernizers recognized that the Muslims were the least prepared of the *millet*s to adopt Western ways and would require the state to assist their progress. To religious Muslims, the visibility of better-off Armenians in the capital and towns appeared as an intolerable reversal of the traditional Muslim-*dhimmi* hierarchy that, in turn, generated resentments toward Christians. The inferior status of Muslims in the industrial and commercial world only intensified the sense of exploitation at the hands of Armenians and foreigners. Anxiety about status, xenophobia, and general insecurity about the impersonal transformations of modern life combined to create resentments toward and anxieties about the Armenians.[13] After 1878, and particularly after the turn of the century, Turkish patriots constructed Armenians as disloyal subjects suspiciously sympathetic to Europeans.

ACROSS THE BORDER: THE ARMENIANS OF TSARIST RUSSIA

As a population living in three contiguous empires as well as in dispersion throughout the Middle East and Europe, Armenians in the Ottoman and Persian Empires were influenced by their compatriots living in the more Europeanized cities of the Russian Empire. In 1828 the Russian army took the Persian khanate of Erevan (which nearly a century later would become the capital of independent Armenia) and established a new frontier on the Arax River. The local Armenian notables, led by Archbishop Nerses Astarakatsi, aided the Russian army under General Paskevich, and Tsar Nicholas I personally expressed his gratitude to Nerses for his loyalty.[14] "The Russian troops who entered Persia during the last war," General Lazar Lazarev reported, "were treated as family members by the Armenians."[15] Almost immediately Paskevich received requests from Armenians and Greeks in Persia to be resettled within the territory conquered by the Russians. After the brief Russian occupation of Erzurum, thousands of Armenians and Assyrians followed the tsar's army across the border and settled in Russian Caucasia.[16] At this euphoric moment Russia was seen as the liberator of Christians who had endured life under Muslim monarchs. Russian officials promised a more lawful regime to the Armenians than they had experienced in Persia or Turkey, and indeed tsarist rule proved less harsh and arbitrary than that of the authorities in the Islamic empires. Backward as Caucasian Armenia was, it benefited from both the physical security offered by the Russian presence and gradual, uneven economic development. Most Armenians in Caucasia, like their compatriots across the borders in the Persian and Ottoman lands, were peasants, often dominated by Muslim landlords. Erevan province, which leading Armenians had hoped would be granted autonomy by the tsar, developed more slowly than its neighboring provinces, and the small city of Erevan housed a Muslim majority until the turn of the twentieth century.[17]

Crossing the high Caucasus and moving north into Russia, young Armenians and Georgians made contact with European learning. The enlightened viceroy of the Caucasus, Prince Mikhail Vorontsov, established a European theater in Tiflis, and the culture of the Continent filtered into the city. Those who aspired to Western civilization could listen to Italian opera, dress in the latest Parisian fashions, and visit the newly opened library to read the latest works from Russia and Western Europe.[18] Tiflis (Tbilisi) rivaled Istanbul as an Armenian cultural capital. Theaters played the comedies of Gabriel Sundukian, who skewered the pretenses of the Armenian bourgeoisie and celebrated the simple *kinto*s, the street peddlers. Newspapers in Russian, Georgian, Armenian, and Azeri reflected the cosmopolitan mix of peoples in this "Paris of the Caucasus."

Armenian businessmen had long had a presence in Tiflis and Baku, the major cities of Caucasia, and through the nineteenth century they flourished as a wealthy and politically important part of society. Armenians were instrumental in the development of the oil industry of Baku, which until the early twentieth century was the largest producer of oil in the world. The mayors of Tiflis were almost always Armenian; Armenians were well represented in the municipal councils of Tiflis and Baku; and until the last decades of the century Russian authorities allowed Armenian religious freedom and cultural and educational development. While the Armenian Apostolic Church remained important, the Armenian bourgeoisie possessed the resources and energy to offer an alternative leadership to the community.

The center of the Armenian Church, Ejmiatsin, was now in Russian territory, and the tsarist government soon came to an agreement with the church. In 1836 Emperor Nicholas I issued a decree (the *Polozhenie*) governing relations between the state and the Armenian Church. The church was to refrain from political affairs and subordinate itself to the ultimate power of the tsar. But at the same time the Armenian Church was given considerable autonomy, in contrast to the Georgian Orthodox Church, which had lost its independence after the Russian annexation. The decree guaranteed the Armenian Church the security of its considerable properties, granted freedom of worship to Armenians, freed the clergy from taxation, and gave the church power over Armenian religious schools (though their curriculum had to be approved by the Holy Synod of the Russian Orthodox Church and communicated to the Ministry of Interior). For nearly fifty years the state interfered minimally in Armenian affairs, perceiving little threat to its interests, and the church often used the policing powers of the state to enforce its decisions among the Armenian people—a classic example of indirect imperial rule.

While for many Armenians the coming of the Russians represented a liberation from centuries of Muslim dominance and the opening of channels to European enlightenment, the positive aspects of Russia's entry into Caucasian affairs were tempered by the kind of "civilization" that Russians brought with them—a mixture of militarism, autocracy, bureaucratic insensitivity to cultural specificity, and obscurantism that tried to limit the influence of European ideas. Russian rule, thus, had a contradictory effect on the Armenians. For many it opened roads to the West, taught new ways of thinking, and expanded the expectations of what the future could hold. At the same time, the full power of the Russian state was directed to creating a conservative mentality, support for the status quo, and acceptance of Armenian subordination to Russian authority. Still, the incorporation into Russia, and the easier contact with Europe, created a receptive environment for the work of a small number of Armenian intellectuals determined to create a shared sense of nationality among their people. As in the Ottoman Empire, so in Russia, the cultural and political aspirations of the young Armenian intelligentsia increasingly came into conflict with the traditional clerical authorities and the Armenian business elite. Building on the work of the Mkhitarist scholars of Venice and Vienna, Armenian intellectuals in Russia, almost simultaneously with those in Istanbul and Izmir, began to work out the notion of an Armenian nation as a secular ethnic community rather than a religious people. Armenian clerics, however, like Catholicos Simeon a generation earlier, saw the upstart intellectuals and European-style nationalism as an affront to tradition and their authority.

What is most often described as the national cultural awakening or the modern Armenian renaissance was, in fact, not a spontaneous release of a deep-seated Armenian spirit, but the product of hard political and intellectual work by Armenian scholars, teachers, and political activists. The road to emancipation, it was thought, ran through education, the building of schools, and the training of a new generation. Before the nineteenth century what passed for education for Armenians was in the hands of the church. The aim of such teaching was to train clerics for service and to preserve the literary monuments of classical Armenian culture. Caucasian Armenians, however, had no schools before the Russian annexations, and the first schools established by the government—a noble *uchilishche* (school) and an orthodox seminary, both in Tiflis—were alien to most Armenians. As new subjects of the tsar, Armenians began establishing schools in Russia half a century before similar schools in the Ottoman Empire. Young priests and university-educated lay instructors, like the writer Khachatur Abovian (1805–1848), worked to stretch the boundaries of education and introduce Western literature, the latest science, and a demythologized history. Students were pulled in one direction by the rigid traditional instruction of most of the higher clergy and in another by the younger *kahananer* (married priests) and lay teachers.

The young men coming out of Armenian Church schools and Russian state schools went on to university in Moscow, St. Petersburg, and Dorpat (now Tartu, Estonia), as well as in Europe (Heidelberg, Berlin, and Jena). Unlike their Armenian compatriots from Ottoman Turkey, who were much more likely to be trained in France and Italy and imbibe the Mkhitarist influences of the Catholic monks in Venice and Vienna, the Armenian intellectuals of Russia came under Russian and German teachings. Idealist philosophy and the accompanying idea of nationality as the soul of a people made a considerable impact on the thinking of these students. But like their contemporaries in Turkey, these intellectuals were vitally interested in the burning cultural issue of the day—the creation of a living Armenian literary language. Eastern Armenians spoke a dialect peppered with Georgian and Russian words, while Erevantsis, Gharabaghtsis, and Crimean Armenians often had trouble understanding one another. Almost all books, as well as the first Armenian newspaper in Russia—*Kovkas* (Caucasus) (Tiflis, 1846–1847)—were printed in *grabar*, the classical Armenian language used by the church. The Westernizing intellectuals with their commitment to spreading education and culture wanted to base the new standard literary language on one or another of the spoken dialects (*ashkharhabar*). The most powerful advocate of *ashkharhabar* was the teacher-writer Khachatur Abovian, who in the early 1840s wrote the first novel using the Erevan dialect, which was soon accepted as the literary standard of Eastern Armenian. This work, *Verk Hayastani* (Wounds of Armenia), was a patriotic attack on the effects of Russian rule on Armenia and did not spare the conservative clergy. The Russian censors removed a telling passage from the first edition in 1858 in which Abovian warned his readers that if they spoke Armenian the Russians would punish them. Prophetically Abovian foresaw his own end. In 1848, the year of revolutions in Europe, the young writer disappeared. Some say he was killed by the tsarist authorities; others, also with little hard information, claim he was exiled to Siberia.

The shift in Armenian identity from primarily religious to primarily ethnic was neither quick nor ever complete. From the cluster of elements that Armenians considered central to their collective identity—church, language, customs, ancestors, places of origin—nineteenth-century secular intellectuals argued for the importance of ethnicity and language as the proper sources of the nation. Setting themselves against the dominance of the conservative Armenian Church, lay intellectuals, in both Russia and Turkey, shifted to an anticlerical, secular nationalism by the fourth decade of the nineteenth century. No longer willing to discuss cultural and political issues in the language of martyrdom and sin, eastern Armenians like the novelist Abovian, the journalist Mikayel Nalbandian, and later the poet Rafael Patkanian, the novelist Raffi, and the journalist Grigor Artsruni, articulated a new, radical vision of the historic Armenian nation.

The claims of the secular patriots were a challenge to the most sacred of Armenian traditions and an attempt to create new ones. Sacrifice and dedication to the idea of a more secular Armenian nation remained central to their inspiration. Enlightenment continued to be a major concern, not the light of God, however, but of Western learning, modern science, the ideals of the French Revolution and the Russian intelligentsia, and the visions of revolution, freedom, democracy, and its radical cousin, socialism. The revolutionary nationalists rejected one of the most common and unquestioned views of Armenian history: that the church was the institution that held the Armenians together through their long and troubled passage. In the late 1870s Raffi deployed the newly coined Armenian word *azgutyun* (nationality) and proclaimed, "The idea of nationality is established not by religion but rather by [a nationality's] *racial characteristics*, among which language occupies the first place, which is and always remains the base for the preservation of the nation." To the church's exclusionary idea of Armenianness, Raffi opened the door to fellow ethnics of different religious persuasions: "Whether he is a Catholic, a Protestant or an Apostolic, the Armenian always remains an Armenian on account of the fact that he or she shares the same racial characteristics, speaks with the same language, belongs to the same *dohm* [clan]."[19]

The gaze of the radical poets, writers, and journalists who came of age in the mid-nineteenth century was directed toward the Ottoman Empire. That was where Armenians suffered the most and where they believed a revival was most needed. Raffi has the poet asking Lake Van to tell him, "Shall Armenia, that was once a garden, / Always be a thorny desert gray? . . . / Is a glad day coming when a banner / Shall on Ararat its folds expand, / And from every side Armenian pilgrims / Hasten to their beauteous fatherland?" In Patkanian's poem "The Tears of Arax," the river laments that the "filthy Turk or Persian" lives along her shores and that Armenians are scattered. "My own Armenian nation / Is banished far away; / A Godless, barbarous people / Dwells on my banks today." He urges his fellow Armenians to "march forth / To battle, without fear; / And, if the worst befall us, / Facing the foe like men, / Win back in death our glory, / And sleep in silence then!"[20] In his famous poem "*Nor Tari*" (New Year) Patkanian wishes that the new year will end Armenia's sorrows, that the country will breathe free. He hopes that "Armenia [will] stand on its feet," and "half-ruined Karin [Erzurum] [will] be our capital" above which the Armenian flag will fly.[21]

The novels of Raffi, particularly *Khent* (The Fool) published in 1880, had their loyal readers both in Caucasia and across the border in the Ottoman and Persian lands.[22] In this work an Armenian tries to incite a rebellion against the Ottomans. Russian censors worried about the effect of this book, which "has had such great success among the Armenian intellectuals of Transcaucasia. . . . Since the ideas in this book do not agree with our policy, I suggest that we stop the spreading of this work among the Transcaucasian Armenians."[23] The Russian vice consul at Van, a city in eastern Anatolia not far from the border of Russia and heavily populated by Armenians, wrote to his superiors in 1880 that nationalism was spreading among the Armenians, influenced by the "Araratian Society." He worried particularly because most of its leaders as well as their funding came from Russian Armenians in the Caucasus. "The Armenian activities here are pro-Russian in nature. The Turkish government is aware of this and has begun strict measures to restrict contacts between Turkish and Russian Armenians."[24]

Writers like Raffi and Patkanian, along with journalists like the prolific editor of *Mshak* (Cultivator), Grigor Artsruni, created an international public conversation among Armenians about Armenians. They described the fate of a single people divided into three empires and sharing common problems. The self-narration by Armenian nationalists of the Armenian experience in the Ottoman Empire was of a people conquered by foreign invaders, made captive in their own ancient land, and oppressed by unjust and cruel rulers, yet all the while maintaining their essential Armenian religious culture and yearning to be free. As with other nationalist constructions, Armenian writers emphasized the continuity of their nation moving through time, overcoming adversities, martyred for the faith, and victimized by a government imposed on them. As historians and novelists melded discrete and unconnected events into a coherent story that was almost always about the nation, they implied that empire was an illegitimate and archaic polity that prevented the full expression of the nation's aspirations. Writers translated the resistance of Christian Armenians, led by Vardan Mamikonian, against the Mazdeist Persians in the fifth century into a defense of nation and fatherland, rendering the story less about religious martyrdom and salvation after death and more about national resurrection in this life.

What had been burdensome in the past became intolerable in the present. The arbitrary rule of Islamic conquerors became impossible to justify. In the new paradigm of liberalism and national self-determination the Ottoman Empire was marked by social lawlessness and a predatory state that thwarted the "natural laws" of economic competition. The very creation of a coherent national narrative that effaced the complexities of interethnic coexistence within the empire and stigmatized the kind of cosmopolitan adjustment to imperial life in which the Armenian merchants had flourished and Armenian Christianity had maintained its authority reinforced the sense of difference between Turks and Armenians. Distance between peoples increased, borders between them hardened, and sharing in the commonalties of Ottoman culture and life became suspect in the minds of radical nationalists. By the late nineteenth century the nationalists narrated the past and present through the prism of the nation, and in their own affective disposition Armenians felt themselves as innocent victims who at the same time were morally, intellectually, and culturally superior to the ruling Turks and Kurds. Resistance by the local Armenians (sometimes in alliance with non-Armenians) of Zeytun in Cilicia to protect tax exemptions granted more than two hundred years earlier by the seventeenth-century sultan Murad IV were scripted in a more modern idiom of rights and national oppression.[25] The local was turned into the all-national. Social bandits and brigands, like Avo near Van or Arabo and Micho near Taron, became rebels and freedom-fighters.[26]

RUSSIAN REACTION

Up to the 1880s Armenian aspirations and Russian state interests seemed to coincide. Although Armenian peasants had to endure landlords and state officials who perpetuated their inferior status and economic backwardness, the Armenian middle class and many professionals believed that their welfare was best served by working within the tsarist system. Russian protection made commerce possible; security for property provided an incentive for industry. Russian education and access to Europe seemed to promise a future of greater enlightenment and culture. During the Crimean War (1853–1856), when Russia stood alone against the Ottoman Empire and most of the European powers, Armenians in Russia supported the tsar against the Ottomans. Though Caucasian Armenians were not placed under any military obligation until 1887, during both the Crimean War and the Russo-Turkish War of 1877–1878 they formed volunteer units to fight against the enemies of the Russian state. A Russian-Armenian general, Vasilii Bebutov, emerged as a hero of the Crimean War, as did the young Armenian officer Mikhail Loris-Melikov (1826–1888), who went on to become the tsar's minister of interior.

On November 15 (27), 1855, the Ottomans surrendered Kars, the major fortified town in eastern Anatolia that centuries before had been the center of an Armenian kingdom. It was apparent to many Armenians that Russian arms were their best hope for bringing their compatriots in the Ottoman Empire under a more modern, less repressive regime. Russia, however, was forced to cede Kars back to Turkey in the Treaty of Paris (1856). Two decades later, when Russia and Turkey again went to war, Armenian generals once more participated in the fighting. Arshak Ter-Gukasov led the Russian armies that occupied old Bayazet and Alashkert (Eleşkirt), where local Armenians joyfully greeted the Russian troops. Kars was taken once again, this time by General Hovhannes Lazarev, and Armenian volunteers fought alongside Russians in the battles for Ardahan and Erzurum. The Russian Armenian press praised Russia's efforts to liberate the Armenians of the Ottoman Empire, and a general consensus developed among educated Armenians that Armenia's most effective ally was tsarist Russia. In 1878 the Russo-Ottoman border was redrawn, and Kars and Ardahan were annexed to the Russian Empire. By this act more than 100,000 Armenians were added to the empire's population. To the Ottoman authorities not only were the Russians seen as a dangerous and avaricious enemy, but Armenians were increasingly perceived as a threat to the integrity of their empire.

As Russia put itself forward as the true champion of the oppressed Turkish Armenians, pro-Russian feelings ran high among Armenians. In the last years of the reign of Alexander II (1855–1881) a zenith of Armeno-Russian collaboration was reached. When Russian revolutionaries threatened the stability of his empire, the emperor turned to Count Loris-Melikov to head the Russian government and establish order. Generally perceived as a liberal, at least in the Russian context, Loris-Melikov was able to carry out a number of political reforms while simultaneously tracking down the radicals who opposed autocracy. But on the very day of his greatest triumph (March 1, 1881), hours after the tsar signed a draft for a consultative assembly to advise the autocrat, Loris-Melikov suffered his greatest defeat. Terrorists threw a bomb at the emperor's carriage and mortally wounded Alexander. Within a few weeks the new tsar, Alexander III (1881–1894), dismissed his Armenian minister after his advisors warned him that Loris-Melikov was not a "true Russian." The era of reform was over. An age of reaction began.

The removal of Loris-Melikov, an Armenian completely acculturated into Russian imperial culture, marked the beginning of the end of Armenian identification with the empire. In the last two decades of the nineteenth century the Russian government turned against the Armenians, as state officials began to see them as a potential danger to the empire. The conflict between the tsar and his Armenian subjects had its origins in the long developmental process that Armenians had undergone since 1801. Parallel to what occurred to their Ottoman compatriots, the very success of middle-class Armenians in establishing themselves as the dominant class in urban Transcaucasia made them visible targets for the social and ethnic resentments of other nationalities and the Russian government. The powerful and ambitious merchants and industrialists that came to head the Russian-Armenian communities rivaled businessmen from other nationalities, pushed aside the traditional Georgian landed nobility, and became an almost unchallengeable political and economic force in the major cities of Caucasia. At the same time, in both Russia and Turkey, a well-educated Westernized intelligentsia, often the children of the bourgeoisie, had formulated a sense of nationality and promoted the teaching of the Armenian language and the national cultural heritage. These developments had occurred earlier and more rapidly among Armenians than among Georgians, Azerbaijanis, or Ottoman Turks. Social and cultural differences between Armenians and their neighbors became more apparent during the nineteenth century, as each national intelligentsia emphasized the distinctiveness of its people. Once Armenians became a subject of international concern, they appeared to the conservative governments of both the Russian and Ottoman Empires to be a subversive force. Neither the Romanovs nor the Ottomans were prepared to give in to nationalisms that might dismantle their multinational empires. Armenians, who straddled the border between the Orthodox Christian and Sunni Muslim states, had become a problem, a disruptive element that potentially could aspire to create a separate state of its own.

Like the contemporary regime of Abdülhamid II, so Alexander III set out to increase the strength, unity, and uniformity of its vast realm by issuing laws and regulations to improve the central administration's control over the peripheries of the empire. To the non-Russian nationalities this process was seen negatively as Russification, and the leaders of ethnic communities resisted to the best of their ability the whittling away of their privileges and local powers. The government, on the other hand, believed that the elimination of different legal systems and enclaves of local autonomy was essential for Russia's ability to govern itself effectively and defend itself from foreign threats. The imperial government welcomed what might be called "spontaneous Russification," the more or less voluntary acculturation or assimilation of non-Russians into the

Russian-speaking cultural community. Many Armenians in the tolerant years of Alexander II had adopted Russian endings for their names, sent their children to Russian schools, and adopted the mannerisms of their Russian overlords. From their end the government promoted administrative Russification, the introduction of Russian institutions, laws, and bureaucratic practices in the ethnic areas. The entire first two-thirds of the nineteenth century had witnessed the steady replacement of Georgian and Armenian laws and customs by the norms of Russian bureaucratic absolutism. Much more noxious for the Armenians was the forced yet haphazard cultural and linguistic Russification that was attempted in the last two reigns, those of Alexander III and Nicholas II (1894–1917).

Both of these tsars, father and son, were dedicated to a vision of autocracy that was rapidly becoming unsustainable. Both were committed anti-Semites, loathed the Poles, whom they considered disloyal, and listened attentively to advisors who preached a chauvinistic vision of "Russian principles, Russian strength, Russian people." Both were suspicious of Armenians. Russian was to be the state language, and the teaching of other languages was to be curtailed. Although this policy of cultural and linguistic Russification was applied neither consistently by the central government nor with conviction by local authorities, the periodic, fitful implementation of laws aimed against the ethnic minorities created in their wake a powerful opposition to autocracy. Ironically, the very policy of forced cultural Russification resulted in a stronger identification with one's own nationality.

In 1885 the zealous governor of the Caucasus, Prince A. M. Dondukov-Korsakov, ordered all Armenian parish schools closed and their replacement by Russian schools. The Caucasian authorities believed that nationalism and a revolutionary spirit, "patriotism and populism," were rampant among Armenian students and had to be eradicated. Five hundred schools, attended by 20,000 pupils and employing 900 teachers, were shut down. Almost immediately the Armenians organized secret schools. A year later the government decided to reopen the Armenian schools, but their staffs were purged and stricter state surveillance over teachers was established. This unilateral abrogation of the earlier agreement with the Armenian Church (the *Polozhenie* of 1836) and the callous treatment of the educational system run by the church had a galvanizing effect on the Russian Armenian communities. The Russophilia prevalent among Armenians rapidly evaporated. Elements within the church grew more hostile to the Russian state. Young Armenian intellectuals emerged from the school crisis more nationalist and more radical. Within a few years many of the veterans of this struggle became involved in the formation of the first Armenian revolutionary organizations within Russia. Provoked initially by tsarist Armenophobia, Armenian radicals from the Caucasus soon turned their gaze to their even more severely repressed brethren across the border in the Ottoman Empire.

DIASPORA IN PERSIA

From earliest times Armenians were a mobile people. They established communities from India to Amsterdam. Many assimilated into the dominant population, notably those who emigrated to Poland and Eastern Europe and converted to Catholicism. Armenians in the Persian Empire may be considered a diaspora since the major community, those living in Nor Julfa, a suburb of the Isfahan, had been forcibly brought to that place by Shah Abbas I from the Ararat plain. Christians in a Shi'i Islamic state, they carved out a space in which they survived, even at times thrived, for centuries. They were treated as an inferior religious minority without the same rights and privileges as Muslims. Yet within a short time Armenians identified with the land in which they lived, and they maintained dual loyalties both to their own Christian community and to the Islamic empire. Many Armenians, however, did not learn or use the Persian language but preferred to communicate exclusively in Eastern Armenian.

When the Russian armies took the Persian lands in the South Caucasus, many Armenians decided to emigrate to the conquered territories in order to live under a Christian government. Others, however, preferred to stay in their ancestral homes, tend the orchards and gardens of their families, and remain loyal to their Persian overlords. The Persian government accused the Russians of forcing Armenians to emigrate, but the Russians denied that they had compelled Armenians to leave.[27] By the early twentieth century, and probably earlier, when Iranian Armenians used terms like "our fatherland" and "our country" they were referring to Iran.[28] Kept apart and remaining distinct from the Muslim majority, even as they worked to fit into Persian society, Armenians "became acculturated rather than fully assimilated."[29] Two related identities competed for primacy: an inward-looking Christian Armenian identity and a broader Iranian allegiance. During the period of the Iranian Constitutional Revolution (1905–1907), Muslim Iranian intellectuals reconfigured their idea of Iran from a Muslim Shi'i nation to the "nation of Iran," an idea that "especially appealed to Iranian-Armenians as an ethnically and religiously distinguishable minority who sought to partake of the benefits of being incorporated into the Iranian 'self' rather than to endure and sustain the consequences of 'otherness.'"[30] The idea of Iran as a geographical space in which different nations (*millat*) could live together proved to be more inclusive in its understanding of nation than the vision of a Turkic nation formulated by nationalist Turkish intellectuals after the Young Turk Revolution of 1908. Persia's Armenians would also suffer in the years of Ottoman massacres, but the bulk of them would be untouched and survive. Other diaspora communities became the last refuge of Ottoman Armenians. Deeply affected by the fate of their compatriots, the diaspora became the place of national continuity and memory.

NATIONALISM AND REVOLUTION

Nationalism is a radical simplification that divides what formerly had been complexly interwoven. The cosmopolitan subjects of imperial societies were required by full-blown nationalists to give their primary loyalty to their nation, usually to the exclusion of any other or to the empire. Lines were drawn more clearly between peoples, and nationalists policed the boundaries of the ethnic community, deciding what rules applied, what conventions were to be observed, which traditions were authentic and which were not. As we have seen, the empires within which the diverse communities lived contributed inadvertently to the consolidation of nationalist discontent by repressing cultural expression. An unintentional collaboration between imperial overlords and nationalist oppositionists reinforced the defining lines of difference that made conflict and violence more likely and cosmopolitan coexistence increasingly more difficult.

Although Armenians did not turn to revolutionary activity in any significant numbers until the very end of the nineteenth century, the intellectual influences of the first generation of Armenian "enlighteners," with their emphasis on Western learning and the idea of the nation, had led many young Armenians to question the principles of the traditional order. Reason and science were considered preferable to faith and obedience to custom. Nationality seemed a more compelling principle on which to build a state than loyalty to a foreign dynasty. Though there were grave risks in questioning the religious and political authorities in Russia, some committed individuals were prepared to follow the examples of Russian radicals, like Aleksandr Herzen and Nikolai Chernyshevskii, or Armenian martyrs to the cause of liberation, like Mikayel Nalbandian.

In the 1870s and 1880s the most influential tendency among educated Armenians was not revolutionary politics but the liberalism represented by the newspaper *Mshak* (Cultivator). Edited for twenty years (1872–1892) by the popular and influential Grigor Artsruni, *Mshak* promoted a pro-Russian attitude among Armenians, advocated economic development along capitalist lines, and polemicized against the newly fashionable doctrines of socialism. Reform rather than revolution was the preferred way to improve Armenian life in Russia. While Russian radical youth turned to peasant socialism (populism, or *narodnichestvo*), their Armenian contemporaries for the most part remained liberal and committed to gradual reform. But some young Armenians, inspired by the romantic nationalism found in Raffi's novels, began to search for new ways to serve their people.

For Russian Armenians the turn to revolutionary struggle was actually a commitment to the liberation of Armenians in Turkey, not of those in Russia. This led in the 1880s and 1890s to an organizational separation of radical Armenians from Russian and Georgian revolutionaries. Whereas the Armenians were nationalists and were willing to fight alone against their Turkish enemies, the Russians and Georgians were more often socialists and resolved to join in a multinational effort against

Russian autocracy. By the 1880s a significant minority of young Armenians, many of them from Russian Caucasia, conceived of revolution as the only means to protect and promote the Armenians. The patriarch of Constantinople informed a Russian officer that "the situation is so desperate that he would not rule out an armed insurrection." He himself had been approached with "the idea of a revolt," a plan that he rejected but that "a small group of zealots" might carry out.[31] Both Christian and Turkish activists opposed the "Bloody Sultan" and saw the restoration of the 1876 Constitution as a principal political goal.

Distressed by the plight of their countrymen, Armenian radicals turned toward self-defense, the formation of revolutionary political parties and the organization of political actions that would encourage Western or Russian intervention into Ottoman affairs. For the young nationalists revolution was the only effective response to the impossibility of significant reforms coming from the state. The activist teacher Mkrtich Portugalian in Van encouraged and organized young people before being arrested in 1885 for "assembly without permit." Exiled to Marseilles, Portugalian published a periodical, *Armenia*, which inspired some back in Van to contemplate establishing a sovereign Armenia through revolution. They adopted the name *Armenakan* and have been dubbed by historians the first Armenian political party in the Ottoman Empire. Two Armenakans tried to smuggle arms from Salmas in Persia to Van but were killed by the Ottoman police in 1889. The next year an ill-equipped army of Caucasian Armenians, led by Sarkis Gugunian, attempted to cross the Russian border to defend Armenians. They were driven back by Ottoman troops only to fall into the hands of Cossacks, who arrested them. Influenced by European nationalism and Russian populism, the revolutionaries found it extremely difficult to activate the Ottoman Armenian peasantry, their chosen constituency.[32] Isolated attempts at smuggling arms, propagandizing students, or organizing protests (Erzurum in June 1890, Kum Kapı in Istanbul a month later) failed to gain much popular support. But in the imagination of historians the tens, sometimes hundreds, of people in small, scattered groups were seen as a movement, with all the attendant connotations of coherence, coordination, and progress.

On both sides of the Ottoman-Russian frontier autocratic governments increasingly viewed Armenians, particularly the well-educated, as
subversive elements. Both states patrolled the frontier to prevent the revolutionary virus from infecting their own country and the other. Repression led to further resistance. The Russian government's closure of Armenian schools in 1885 mobilized large numbers of students, and a number
of Caucasian radicals traveled in 1886 to Geneva, where they formally
established a revolutionary party and published the first issue of its newspaper, *Hnchak* (Bell), in November 1887. Socialist but not specifically
Marxist, the Hnchak party was led by the charismatic Avetis Nazarbekian
and his wife, Maro Vardanian. They advocated an independent, socialist
Armenia. Their means was armed struggle. First, Ottoman Armenians,
those living in the historic Armenian homeland, would be liberated, and
that movement would inspire the liberation of Russian and Persian Armenians. From the three a federated republic would be formed, which
would be a first step forward to socialism. In their party's program the
Hnchaks outlined their reasons for the use of terror:

> The purpose of terror is to protect the people, when it is subject
> to persecution, to raise its spirit, to inspire and elevate a revo-
> lutionary disposition among them, to show daring on behalf of
> the people protesting against the government, and thus to main-
> tain the faith of the people toward the task on hand, to shake the
> power of the government, to abase its reputation of being pow-
> erful, to create extreme fear [in its ranks]. The means to achieve
> these goals are: to annihilate the worst Turkish and Armenian
> personalities within the government, to annihilate the spies and
> the traitors.[33]

Meanwhile in South Caucasia other Armenian young people, equally
inspired by Russian populism, were forming their own revolutionary organization. Kristapor Mikayelian and his friends founded *Eritasard Hayastan* (Young Armenia) and began organizing other revolutionary circles in Turkey and Persia. In 1890 the Hnchaks and the Caucasian radicals

founded a common organization in Tiflis—the *Hay Heghapokhaganneri Dashnaktsutyun* (Armenian Revolutionaries' Federation). But within a year the more strictly socialist Hnchaks left the party.

Historians critical of or hostile to the Armenian radicals and their aspirations have tended to homogenize the diverse views and practices of Armenian revolutionaries into a single, monolithic, anti-Ottoman and anti-Turkish program. The actual history of the oppositional intelligentsia, however, tells a more complex story of contestation and conflict over goals, strategies, and tactics. By the mid-1890s the Hnchaks were themselves split between radicals led by Nazarbekian and moderates who rejected socialism and moved toward liberalism. Some Hnchaks favored an independent Armenian state, while others were content with a degree of autonomy within the Ottoman Empire. The Hnchak leader Stepanos Sapah-Gulian declared that "the very moderate desires and the short-term goals put forward by the Armenian nation and the Armenians' fighting forces have never stood in opposition to the real, permanent interests of Turkey considered as a state. What the Armenians are demanding today is not in any way intended to weaken or paralyze Turkey, to dismember and, ultimately, destroy it, to pulverize the Turkish people and, on its ruins, reestablish the Home of the Armenians."[34] But another editorial a year later in the same newspaper, *Hnchak*, explained that the party could not cooperate with the Turkish opposition because of profound differences about the future shape of the Ottoman state. "The Young Turks like to say that they want to propel the country by peaceful means down an evolutionary path toward a purely internal revolution of all state functions and all laws. But they do not for a moment consider giving up an inch of the state."[35]

Once the Hnchak party split over strategic goals, the Dashnaks emerged as the leading political party among Armenians in all three empires, Ottoman, Persian, and Russian, a position it held for the next three decades. Their members divided between those who favored a nationalist message and those for whom a socialist orientation was paramount; some preferred to work primarily in Russia and others focused on the *Erkir* (the Country, i.e., Ottoman Armenia). In general the Dashnaktsutyun subordinated the social question to the national. Concerned that Armenian survival was at stake if some action was not taken soon, their first declaration rang with such phrases as "this is not the time to wait." The Dashnak manifesto called on the whole nation, young and old, rich and poor, even the clergy, to unite in the fight for national liberation. The Dashnaks did not see themselves as the representatives of any single group or class but as the revolutionary vanguard of the entire nation. Thinking pragmatically about the power of the empires in which Armenians lived, Dashnaks called for *azad Hayastan* (Free Armenia), a liberated people benefiting from political reforms, but not for an independent state. Their more limited goals and more practical program made them the foremost leaders of the Armenian revolutionary opposition.

The Russian police believed that the idea of revolution had penetrated all the classes of Armenian society, the wealthy as well as the poor. Even the catholicos was suspect. No longer was the tsarist regime interested in supporting the Armenians against the Ottoman Empire. The Russian police intercepted collections of money in support of the liberation movement in Turkey. Censors prohibited the use of the words "Armenian people" or "Armenian nation." The government encouraged notoriously chauvinist anti-Armenian journalists. Leading Georgian poets took up their pens to draw vicious portraits of Armenians. Fears of revolutionaries were combined with fears of foreigners and hatred of the bourgeoisie into a single murky image of the Armenians as a pariah nation isolated within the Russian Empire.

Most Armenians stood aloof from the activities of the revolutionaries, until the tsarist government itself provoked the great majority of the Russian Armenian community to abandon its passivity and support their movement. The Armenophobe governor of the Caucasus, Prince Grigorii Golitsyn, launched a campaign against Armenian educational and charitable institutions. When in 1903 Nicholas II ordered the confiscation of Armenian Church properties by the state, this violation of the *Polozhenie* of 1836 created precisely the kind of revolutionary sympathies that the government sought to prevent. Armenians of all classes marched in solemn processions to protest the confiscation. Demonstrations turned violent. Rocks were thrown. Shots were fired. People were wounded and killed. Catholicos Mkrtich I, the former Khrimian *Hayrik*, refused to accept the new law. Insurrection broke out in Baku, coinciding with economic strikes by workers throughout Caucasia. In October Hnchaks wounded Governor-General Golitsyn. Tsarist officials reported to their superiors that a revolutionary situation had been created in Transcaucasia. As Armenians of all political persuasions turned against the Russian government, the Dashnaktsutyun decided to take upon itself the self-defense of Caucasian Armenians. For the first time the major Armenian political party devoted a significant portion of its manpower to the fight in Russia. Workers were now prompted to join in strikes and demonstrations. Terror was directed at tsarist officials who were considered anti-Armenian.

At the same time that Armenian revolutionary activity increased, a general revolutionary crisis shook the tsarist empire. On January 9, 1905, the soldiers of the tsar fired on a peaceful demonstration of workers in St. Petersburg, killing dozens. "Bloody Sunday," as that event was thereafter known, precipitated a year of violence—mutinies, general strikes, and peasant uprisings. For Armenians the lines of battle soon became ethnic and religious. The killing of an Armenian soldier by a Muslim in Baku led to a revenge murder, which then exploded into Armenian-Muslim clashes and pogroms. All of Caucasia was intricately mixed, with Muslims, then known as Tatars (today's Azerbaijanis), and Armenians living in the same towns or neighboring villages. Fearing what the other side might do, Armenians and Muslims fought each other in the streets, both sides massacring the innocent and helpless. Muslim clergy urged their faithful to defend the tsarist order. The police and army usually stood aside. With the tsarist order in Caucasia in danger of collapse, Nicholas II responded to the urgings of his more liberal advisors and decided to make concessions to the opposition. He appointed a new viceroy of the Caucasus, Count Illarion Vorontsov-Dashkov, a man considered a friend of the Armenians. The government returned church properties to the Armenian Church.

The last twelve years of the tsarist regime (1905–1917) may be viewed as a constitutional experiment that ultimately failed. Responding to the massive resistance throughout the country, Nicholas issued a manifesto promising all the people of the empire civil rights and the establishment of a representative legislature, the Duma. The tsar had been forced to limit his absolute powers, but he remained unwilling to make the deep political and social reforms demanded by the liberal and radical elements in Russia. Once the revolutionary wave receded, Nicholas resisted any further reforms and used his police and army to crush the revolutionaries. Hundreds of Dashnaks were put on trial in 1912, but the skillful defense by renowned lawyers like Aleksandr Kerenskii (later prime minister of Russia in 1917) and Pavl Miliukov (foreign minister in 1917) resulted in light sentences and acquittals for many.

Forced into a semi-legal existence in Russia, the Dashnaks, nevertheless, maintained much of their authority in the eyes of the peasants and workers and remained the most influential Armenian political activists among Armenians. Persecuted by the tsarist government, the Dashnaktsutyun turned its attention back to the Ottoman Armenians. As Europe moved toward World War I, the image of Russia as a potential savior for Armenians was dimmed and tarnished. Across the Arax River, Ottoman Armenians looked warily at the Russian state: was it a potential savior or simply another unpredictable imperial master?

CHAPTER FOUR

Great Powers

For the Great Powers of Europe Armenia was a problem, but even more so were the Armenians: a Christian people living in an Islamic empire increasingly suffering under the rule of the "Terrible Turk." Far from the centers of "civilization," Armenians represented for many an outpost of Christian culture. Humanitarian sentiments mixed with cool strategic interests to involve Britain, Russia, France, Austria, and others in the cause of Armenian protection. The German Empire professed a kind of official neutrality or indifference toward the Armenians as they worked to cultivate good relations with the Ottomans. Americans were concerned about beleaguered Christians since Protestant missionaries and enterprising merchants were engaged with the Christian subjects of the sultan. Yet the international involvement of Europe was not only ineffective in changing the Ottoman treatment of non-Muslims but ultimately proved disastrous for the Armenians. Great Power attempts to force the Ottomans to ameliorate their treatment of Christian peoples intensified Ottoman suspicions of the Armenians and were fundamental in ultimately convincing their leaders to seek a "final solution" to the Armenian Question.

In the nineteenth, and even more in the early twentieth, century the Ottoman Empire was the object of the ambitions of the European Great Powers. Whoever dominated the empire, and particularly its capital Istanbul and the Straits that connected the Black Sea with the Mediterranean, would have a colossal advantage over the other imperial powers. The principal adversaries were Russia and Great Britain. When tsarist Russia forcibly intervened in domestic Ottoman affairs in favor of the Orthodox Christians, Britain rallied a coalition to preserve the territorial integrity of the empire. Britain and France fought the Crimean War (1854–1856) on behalf of the Ottomans and forced Russia to back down. When Russia reemerged after its defeat in 1856 to challenge the Ottomans again in

1877–1878, it was Britain, along with Bismarck's Germany, that limited its claims to Ottoman territory and rights. Great Britain took upon itself the difficult task of both supporting the integrity of the Ottoman Empire and demanding significant reforms to protect its Christian subjects. It promoted economic liberalism and free trade at the same time as it insisted on special privileges—the infamous capitulations—that effectively advantaged the Europeans in trade with the Ottomans. Britain's principal interest was to block Russian advances and influence in the empire, particularly in eastern Anatolia. To gain British protection the sultans had to give up full sovereignty in their realm.

Before Europe was involved in Armenian problems, the Great Powers took up the cause of the Christian peoples of the Balkans. Russia had actively supported the independence movement of the Greeks in the 1820s, and other powers had responded to Ottoman mistreatment of Serbs and Bulgarians. The infamous Ottoman massacre of some 20,000 to 25,000 Greeks on the island of Chios in 1822 had enormous reverberations throughout France, inspiring a painting by Eugene Delacroix and a story by Victor Hugo. Another major crisis erupted in 1876 when the Ottomans brutally put down a rebellion by Bulgarians. Both Chios and Bulgaria demonstrated that the Ottomans repressed insurrection by massively retaliating with massacres that slaughtered both rebels and civilians. The Bulgarian massacres shocked the British and Russians in particular, and the prominent politician William Gladstone's widely read pamphlet, *The Bulgarian Horrors and the Question of the East*, inflamed anti-Turkish feeling among the broader public. The Ottoman government itself was in disarray; two sultans were deposed in the year before Abdülhamid II took the throne (1876).

As European representatives convened in Istanbul to discuss the future of the empire, the new sultan, in a masterstroke instigated by his advisor, Midhat Paşa, promulgated a Constitution, a paper promise of far-reaching institutional changes. He created an Ottoman Parliament in which non-Muslim deputies, Christians and Jews, were overrepresented. Although the Constitution did not limit seriously the powers of the sultan or guarantee fundamental rights like freedom of assembly or organization of political parties, at least there was now a forum for expressing the views of educated society. Russia, however, was not placated by the declaration of a Constitution, and on April 24, 1877, Alexander II declared, "The Porte has remained immovable in its categorical refusal of every effectual guarantee for the security of its Christian subjects. . . . Turkey, by its refusal, places us under the necessity of having recourse to arms."[1] The Russo-Turkish War of 1877–1878 was short and decisive. Hundreds of thousands of Ottoman soldiers, all of them Muslim (since only Muslims were eligible to serve as soldiers), were killed. Russians quickly advanced within striking distance of Istanbul in the west and Erzurum in the east.

Ottoman Armenians were caught between their loyalty to the imperial government and their desire for reforms promoted by the Europeans. On the eve of the crisis that would lead to war, the Armenian National Assembly prepared a report on the despoilments suffered by provincial Armenians. In their view Armenians were loyal Ottomans who sought justice from the new sultan, and their message to their ruler emphasized their continuing fidelity to the empire. "The Armenians have always within the limits set before them spontaneously rendered every service to the Ottoman Empire; in one word, the Armenians seek their future in the prosperity and welfare of this empire, and concession of their demands will benefit not only themselves, but the country, in accordance with the good intentions of our august Sovereign."[2] At the beginning of the war, the Armenian patriarch of Constantinople, Nerses Varjabedian, cautioned his flock not to support the Russians but to remain loyal to the sultan. Armenian deputies in the Ottoman Parliament loudly proclaimed their devotion to the empire and their distrust of the Russians who claimed to be defending the Christians of the empire. They blamed the difficulties that Armenians experienced in the East on corrupt officials or on Kurds and Circassians, not on the central state. Russian rule, they asserted, would be far worse than the tolerant dominion of the sultan.[3] The Armenian National Assembly went as far as to call for allowing Armenians to serve in the Ottoman military, though the patriarch opposed such a measure.[4] Armenian deputies in the Ottoman Parliament thought of themselves as Ottomans, representatives of their multiethnic constituents, yet as the war progressed, they increasingly acted as spokesmen for the Armenian community. "As deputies, the non-Muslim could not totally shed their sectarian identity," writes the historian Roderic Davison, "however much they might feel and act as Osmanlis. They had, in effect, a dual character, and in a sense they still represented their *millets*."[5]

Armenians in the East were generally in favor of the Russian advance. The wealthy Pasdermajian family in Erzurum, a city that Armenians called by its ancient name *Karin*, entertained the Russian Armenian General Loris-Melikov in their Green Room during the Russian occupation of the city and presented him with a milky white Arabian stallion as a gift to the tsarevich Alexander Alexandrovich (the future Alexander III).[6] The Armenian National Assembly in Istanbul decided to send a delegation to the Russian commander, Grand Duke Nicholas, at Edirne (Adrianople) to petition for protection, and urged the patriarch of Constantinople to influence the Russian negotiators. Fearing that the Russians would back Armenian claims to land and territory, Kurds in both the Ottoman and Persian Empires took matters into their own hands, massacring thousands of Armenians and destroying dozens of Armenian villages in June and July 1877.[7] The governors of Van and Diyarbakır admitted to a British representative that they were afraid to constrain the Muslim perpetrators when the empire was engaged in a "titanic struggle" with Russia.[8]

Flush with victory, the Russians in March 1878 imposed the harsh Treaty of San Stefano on the Ottomans and forced them to give up most of their Balkan territories. Serbia, Montenegro, and Rumania became independent states; Bulgaria was granted autonomy under a Christian prince; and Bosnia-Herzegovina became an Austrian protectorate. Russia gained territory in Caucasia: the towns of Batumi, Kars, and Ardahan, with the surrounding villages. Article 16 of the treaty compelled the Sublime Porte to carry out "the improvements and reforms demanded by local requirements in the provinces inhabited by the Armenians, and to guarantee their security from the Kurds and Circassians."[9] The Russians would continue to occupy the region until the reforms went into effect.

The Russians had won the war, but they were about to lose the peace. The Treaty of San Stefano did not hold, for it was too advantageous to the

Russians to be acceptable to the other European powers. The Ottomans found a firm supporter in Great Britain, at least for a few more years, and on June 4, 1878, secretly signed the infamous Cyprus Convention by which the British received the island of Cyprus in exchange for a pledge to fight against Russia should the tsar attempt to keep his conquests in eastern Anatolia.[10] Given the intense feelings of the British public, the Armenians were not to be abandoned. The sultan had to pledge once again to introduce reforms acceptable to the British. Internationally isolated, Tsar Alexander II agreed to send his representatives to a Congress in Berlin, convened by the "honest broker," German Chancellor Otto von Bismarck, to work out a definitive treaty between Russia and the Ottoman Empire.

In a desperate attempt not to be left out, Istanbul Armenians sent a delegation headed by the former patriarch, Khrimian *Hayrik*, to put forth the Armenian concerns. Such appeals to the Great Powers and to an international public sphere were not novel: individual Jews and groups of Jews had appealed to the Congress of Vienna in 1815 to secure rights, and Jews also made their way to the Congress of Berlin.[11] The Armenian leadership was inspired by the formation in 1861 of an autonomous regional government in Lebanon, which had been granted a Christian governor and ethnically proportional representation of Muslims and Christians in a local council.[12] Khrimian's proposal included a map indicating the provinces (the six *vilayet*s) to be included in the reform and estimates of the Armenian population, claimed to number about 2 million, that is, almost two-thirds of those living in eastern Anatolia.[13] Consultative councils made up of equal numbers of Muslims and Armenians were to be set up to report on conditions in the provinces, and the sultan would appoint Armenians as governors. Those to be represented in the new institutions and the subsidized schools would be the settled population; the nomadic Kurds were not included in the proposed reforms.[14]

The powers at the Congress of Berlin paid no attention to the Armenians and rewrote the Treaty of San Stefano, reducing Russia's territorial and political gains. Article 61 of the Treaty of Berlin called for reform but without any mention of a timetable or Russian military presence to ensure compliance. The Armenian delegation in Berlin plaintively complained but to no avail. "Although much more oppressed than other Christian populations," the Armenians had "caused no trouble to the Ottoman government . . . yet being a Christian nation, it had hoped to find in our century the same protection afforded to the other Christian nations," which included "the right of living its life and of being governed on its ancestral land by Armenian officials." Khrimian returned to Istanbul empty handed. He soon told his congregation that the other powers had placed a tasty "dish of liberty" on the table in Berlin, but they all used an iron ladle (*erkate sherep*) with which to taste the *harissa*.[15] The Armenians had only a paper spoon, which collapsed as soon as it was used.[16] The implication to many was that Armenians would be taken seriously only when they too had an iron ladle, that is, when they took up the armed struggle for their freedom.[17] The Armenian patriarch, however, attempted to interpret in the most positive light the new role taken by Britain as the principal protector of the Ottoman state.

The Congress of Berlin was the last major meeting of the Concert of Europe, for the Great Powers soon divided into antagonistic alliances. But the Treaty of Berlin had two important effects for Armenians. First, it forced the removal of Russian troops from eastern Anatolia, inhibiting the Russians from being the sole effective arbitrators of the future of the Ottoman Armenians. Second, the Armenian Question, which had been the thin edge of Russia's wedge into Ottoman affairs, was transformed into an international issue, a matter of concern (should they choose to be concerned) of all the Great Powers. The Armenians became an instrument that could be used by European states to intervene in the internal affairs of the sultan's realm. They were a category distinct from other Ottoman peoples, possessing a special status and international visibility that even with the subsequent neglect by Europe isolated them as a special problem for the Ottoman government. These overtures to the Great Powers, along with the Western styles affected by some wealthy Armenians, conspired to create in the minds of many Turks an image of an alien population within an Islamic empire, foreigners in what each side considered their own homeland.

Great Britain worked with the Porte to implement some kind of protection for Anatolian Armenians, but the obstacles proved intractable. There were no reliable statistics as to the ethnic and religious breakdown of the population. Each community exaggerated its numbers and reduced those of the other. Various estimates in the last decades of the nineteenth century put the Armenians anywhere from more than 15 percent of the population in the six provinces to more than 46 percent.[18] Armenians argued that the Kurds, Circassians, and other nomads, who did not pay taxes and were not subject to conscription, should be excluded from representation. They were "itinerant and idle peoples who live at the expense of the peasantry."[19] Rumors spread that Armenians would be given an independent state. A Kurdish sheikh, Ubaydullah, told an Ottoman official that he would never permit "an independent [Armenian] state in Van" or allow the Nestorians (Syriac Christians) "to hoist the British flag and declare themselves British subjects."[20] He organized a rebellion against the Ottomans in 1879 with the aim of forming an independent Kurdistan, but was defeated. Kurds who had been armed during the war with the Russians failed to surrender their weapons back to the government, and incidents of violence increased precipitously.

Even though the situation in the East deteriorated rapidly, the Armenian Question receded from the attention of Europe for the next decade and a half. Britain, which had inserted itself into this conflict, sent military consuls to the Armenian provinces for a few years. European complaints that there was "no evidence to prove that any amelioration ha[d] been effected" were met by the sultan's claims that he was indeed implementing reforms and that the demands from abroad were unreasonable.[21] The attention of Western governments faded, but the European public did not forget. There was something abnormal and unacceptable in the minds of many Europeans of a vulnerable Christian people being ruled by what they considered a despotic Islamic empire. In the journals and newspapers of the day Ottoman Christians were at one and the same time depicted as oppressed and potentially civilizable, therefore on both accounts deserving support. For the British especially, Armenians were not "outsiders within Europe" but "a kind of civilised outsider in the eastern world, a part of Europe which had been displaced."[22] British writers envisioned Armenians as a dispersed or dismembered nation, not simply Christian but in the British imagination a cradle of civilization facing barbarism. Looking eastward, British observers concluded that centuries of Turkish rule had corrupted the Armenians, whose degeneration was evident in everything from their fabled skills as cheats to their inferior hygiene. Armenians were in a sorry state but worthy and capable of redemption. Because these unfortunates lived in and were products of the East, their road to recovery required intervention by real, unspoiled Europeans like the British, who would have to protect and promote the Armenians. By its concern for Armenians, Britain enhanced its own self-generated role as defender of civilization. London was prepared to become the absent voice of the mute Orient in a humanitarian version of an imperial mission. British compassion was tempered by the ambiguity that was felt toward a distant and degenerate people, but when news arrived of atrocities against Armenians in 1894–1896, British Armenophiles were galvanized. The images of innocent Christians and savage Turks that the earlier Greek atrocities and "Bulgarian Horrors" had done much to form were once again confirmed.[23]

In the United States as well, social reformers took up the Armenian cause. Some of them, like William Lloyd Garrison Jr., scions of the abolitionist movement of earlier decades, joined with the poet Alice Stone Blackwell, Julia Ward Howe, the author of "The Battle Hymn of the Republic," and leading politicians to issue humanitarian appeals to what they took to be the conscience of Protestant America. The missionary impulse combined with genuine outrage at the suffering of an ancient Christian people at the hands of Muslims. Rather than based in abstract ideas of human rights, which would in the future be concerned with the pains endured by any and all human beings simply because they were human, late nineteenth-century humanitarianism was directed toward those victims who shared a common religion with Christian America. Ideas of race and civilization similar to those that inspired Western imperialist extensions into Asia and Africa mixed with convictions about the true faith and the road to salvation. The founder of the American Red Cross, Clara Barton, undertook her own hazardous trip to the killing fields of eastern Anatolia in the spring of 1896. That same year the Republican Party platform of William McKinley spoke of the "deep sympathy" that the massacres in Armenia aroused in the American people, along with their interest in aiding the Cubans against Spain and annexing Hawaii.[24] Along with the flag and the sword, the Bible was a weapon of imperial expansion.

In the last quarter of the nineteenth century both the reading public and diplomats in European capitals found a ready image to personify the Ottoman Empire and its treatment of the Armenians: that of the new sultan, Abdülhamid II. In the face of military defeat, Abdülhamid came to the throne in a coup, deposing his half brother. From his portrait he appears a grim, wary young man, his fez and Western coat testifying to his ambition to modernize his empire. His idea of the modern was order, stability, and centralized power. He loved opera and carpentry, making much of his furniture in the Yıldız Palace. At first liberals within the empire and foreign supporters of the Ottomans, like British Prime Minister Benjamin Disraeli, believed that the sultan was interested in Western-style reforms like some of his *Tanzimat*-period predecessors. But when Ottoman parliamentary deputies criticized the sultan's handling of the war with Russia, Abdülhamid abrogated the Constitution and gathered the threads of power into his own hands, reducing the influence of the high officials of the Supreme Porte. Suspicious of others (some claim he was paranoid), fearful of assassination and the activities of revolutionaries (both Armenian and Balkan), Abdülhamid built up a network of spies to report on those both close to and far from him. "For a quarter century," wrote a British diplomat, "the empire was ruled through espionage."[25]

Historians have softened the picture of Abdülhamid II and depicted him as a ruler dedicated to modernizing his empire. The distinguished diplomatic historian William Langer, for example, wrote in 1935: "Whether Abdul Hamid deserves the black reputation that has been pinned to him is a matter of debate. If he was 'the bloody assassin' and the 'Red Sultan' to most people, he was the hard-working, conscientious, much harassed but personally charming ruler to others." But the dark sides of his character are not easily erased from his portrait. The sultan felt particularly threatened by the Armenians and believed they were in league with the other revolutionaries: the Young Turks, the Greeks, and the Macedonians. He feared his own army and particularly the navy, which had played a key role in the overthrow of his uncle, Sultan Abdülaziz. Some contemporaries believed "that Abdul Hamid was the victim of what we moderns call a persecution complex. He was terrified, and for that reason surrounded himself not only with high walls, but with all sorts of dubious characters, especially spies and delators who justified their existence by bringing ever more alarming reports."[26]

A "shrewd tactician," the sultan skillfully played off one religious community and one European state against another, desperate as he was to prevent the dismemberment of his empire.[27] Abdülhamid was determined to counter "the disruptive forces of liberalism, nationalism and constitutionalism" by promoting the traditional, Islamic aspects of his realm.[28] He was upset by what he perceived as a European double standard, which condemned Ottoman violence against insurgent subjects. "We are accused in Europe," he complained, "of being savages and fanatics. . . . [Yet] unlike the Czar I have abstained till now from stirring up a crusade and profiting from religious fanaticism, but the day may come when I can no longer curb the rights and indignation of my people at seeing their co-religionists butchered in Bulgaria and Armenia."[29] Suspicious of Britain, Abdülhamid cultivated a new relationship with the young German emperor, Wilhelm II, whom he elaborately feted on the kaiser's visit to Istanbul in 1889. The sultan found sentiment in favor of his anti-reform, anti-Western stance among conservative and religious elements. Ottoman society proved to be resistant to the reform legislation, and for several decades no serious opposition to the sultan's patriarchal rule was generated among the Turkish population. The sultan himself was frank about his strategic choice: "I made a mistake wishing to content myself with the example of my father, Abdul Mecid, who sought to carry out reforms by persuading the people and creating liberal institutions. From now on, I shall follow the example of my grandfather, Sultan Mahmud. Like him, I understand that it is not possible to move the peoples whom God has placed under my protection by any means other than force."[30]

The horizons for Armenians changed radically with the Russo-Turkish War of 1877–1878, the coming to power of Abdülhamid II, his abrogation of the Ottoman Constitution in 1877, and the turn toward a more accommodating policy with the Kurds that eventually involved repression of the Armenians in the 1890s. The sultan was deeply disturbed that his ascension to power was greeted by the insatiable appetites of the European powers and what he considered the treachery of one of his subject peoples. In the sultan's mind, the Armenians' treachery and Europe's meddling in the empire were intimately linked. He began to curtail the rights of the Armenian patriarchate, restrict what earlier rulers had granted in the Armenian "regulation" (*nizamname*), and even jailed some Armenian clerics. The perennial divisions and conflicts among Armenian clerics played into the hands of the sultan. The claimant to the catholicosate of Sis in southeastern Anatolia wanted to wriggle free of the regulations imposed on him by the Istanbul patriarch. In conversation with Abdülhamid, the Armenian cleric warned the sultan that the patriarch "was little more than an untrustworthy Russian agent." Playing into the sultan's suspicions of the Armenians, Sis was allowed to report directly to the Porte rather than through the patriarchate.[31]

Abdülhamid imposed stricter control on Armenian schools and textbooks, as well as the missionary schools whose pupils were mainly Armenians.[32] Priests were harassed, their residences searched, and on occasion they were arrested. As the government with which the church had worked turned against the Armenian clergy, the authority of the patriarch and his priests diminished in the eyes of many.[33] State employment was restricted to those who had studied in official state schools, effectively eliminating non-Muslims from the bureaucracy. The government shifted provincial boundaries to ensure a Muslim majority in every *vilayet*. Kurdish or Turkish districts were attached to Armenian areas so that Christians would not form a majority. The sultan's lack of trust was reflected in efforts to reduce employment of Armenians on the railroads being built with German help throughout the empire. A memorandum from the sultan's administration noted that "in consideration of the necessity that all persons employed in the public services should be trustworthy and dependable, which is a necessity that has now gained in urgency, it has been decided that all people of the Armenian nation and all those hailing from Van and Bitlis," employed in the stations between Haydarpaşa and İzmit, should be investigated and all untrustworthy elements should be sent back to their hometowns.[34]

In an empire that after 1878 because of the loss of lands in the Balkans had become more Muslim and was now primarily based in Asia rather than Europe, Abdülhamid deployed a conservative Islam as his state ideology. He took up the title "caliph" of all Muslims, even though that designation had long been discarded. His solution to the imperial crisis was "to redefine Ottomanism and give it a Muslim coloring." "The state could theoretically survive the loss of parts of some provinces to Christian nationalist movements," writes the historian M. Şükrü Hanioğlu, "but if the Muslims of the empire—who by 1900 accounted for three-quarters of the population—were to split along ethnic lines, the Ottoman polity was doomed."[35] A visible and concrete sign of this Islamic unity policy was the sultan's decision in 1900 to begin the construction of the Hijaz Railway from Damascus to Mecca, a line built solely with Ottoman resources with a holy purpose, to facilitate the way for Muslims from around the world to make the *hadj*.[36] The new emphasis on Islam as a unifying creed frightened the British, who ruled over millions of Muslims in India. London worked surreptitiously in the Arab lands to undermine Ottoman influence, raising the specter of a pan-Islamic menace. At the same time a rival, the German kaiser, declared himself the champion of the world's Muslims.

In November 1890 Abdülhamid institutionalized an alliance with the Sunni Muslim peoples of his realm by creating the *Hamidiye* regiments, similar to the Cossacks in Russia and made up primarily of loyal Kurds. Organized into official irregular armed regiments, Kurdish villagers were trained by Turkish *yuzbashis* (officers) from the regular army and given special uniforms and access to arms.[37] Though the Kurds had been much more of a threat to Ottoman unity than the Armenians in years past, Abdülhamid backed these fellow Muslims against Christian Armenians, whom he considered the more disruptive element and one linked to his enemies abroad. He established schools in the capital to

Hamidiye Cavalry. Harry Finnis Blosse Lynch, *Armenia: Travels and Studies, Vol. 1* (London 1901).

train the children of the Kurdish and Arab elites. In this way Abdülhamid attempted to secure Kurdish loyalty and at the same time create a force to extend state power to the Russian and Iranian borders of the empire.[38] If the observations of a British military attaché traveling through the *vilayet* of Diyarbakır are accurate, the sultan's task was formidable.

People of all stations and religions "spoke with bitter curses of the 'Osmanlis.' Kurds, Arabs, Armenians, Jacobites, Chaldeans, all hate the dominant race." On the other hand, he continued, "None, however, seem like the Turks, to possess the spirit or aspiration to rule, they long only to be free from the yoke that oppresses them."[39] Formed to keep order and reinforce the presence of the state in the East, according to a historian of the institution, the *Hamidiye* "actually further antagonized the Armenian population and exacerbated the very conflict the organization was designed to quell."[40]

The harsh equilibrium that had existed between Kurds, Turks, and Armenians in eastern Anatolia faltered in the 1880s and then collapsed in the 1890s. Armenian intellectuals and revolutionaries played a role in bringing Armenian acquiescence and acceptance of the existing order to an end, as did foreign travelers, Western diplomats, and increased contact with the outside world. Abdülhamid's strategic decision to align the Ottoman state with the Kurds and back them against the Armenians was the final precipitating factor. A fierce, uneven struggle began in the 1890s between the autocratic state and the Armenian revolutionary committees.

If one accepts the sociologist Max Weber's definition of the state—the institution that holds the monopoly of legitimate violence—then at the turn of the twentieth century the Ottoman state did not function effectively in the eastern reaches of Anatolia. There *Hamidiye* units, Muslim refugees, and Kurdish and Türkmen tribes all competed with the regular army and police. In this context some Armenians decided that they had no alternative but to organize for self-defense. Inspired by the Bulgarian struggle for independence and frustrated by the failure of Europeans to come to the aid of supplicant Armenians, young radicals decided that organization, agitation, and resistance were required to push the Ottoman government to improve the condition of the Armenians. Against their conscious intentions, the Great Powers at the Congress of Berlin had sanctioned nationalist struggle as an effective means to European recognition of a people's right to political freedom. It had worked in the Balkans, why not in other parts of the Ottoman Empire?

THE HAMIDIAN MASSACRES, 1894–1896

After the losses it suffered in the Russo-Turkish War of 1877–1878—much of the Balkans, parts of eastern Anatolia, and Cyprus—the Ottoman Empire steadily shed other territories in the next two decades. In 1881 France made Tunisia its colony; the next year the British secured their dominance over Egypt, guaranteeing a safe route to their Indian possessions; and three years later the Bulgarians became the protectors of Eastern Rumelia.[41] The empire's external vulnerability was more than matched by its internal instability: economic and fiscal crises, the integration of more than 800,000 Muslim refugees from the Balkans, and resistance from indigenous peoples. In the 1890s the regime faced threats from Macedonian and Armenian revolutionaries and an uprising of the Greeks of Crete. The very instability and insecurity felt by the regime drove it to extreme and vicious policies against its opponents. When ordinary subjects of the sultan refused to give in to exactions by powerful local lords and resisted kidnappings, forced conversions, or seizures of land, these acts were seen as insurrection in the eyes of the state. Following the pattern of massive retaliation that had marked Chios in 1822 and Bulgaria in 1876, the Ottomans repeatedly launched indiscriminate massacres of largely defenseless people.[42] Officials and officers justified such measures as necessary to preserve the empire and its traditional order.[43] An empire built through military conquest and resting largely on coercion rather than consent required, in the minds of many of its rulers, prophylactic violence to maintain order and serve as an example to others to forgo rebellion. Instead of instituting reform leading to greater autonomy and justice for his subjects, Abdülhamid chose repression. Whatever the difficulties the empire faced, bad governing only made things worse. Abdülhamid's repressive policies blackened the image of the empire, which Europeans considered "barbaric," and its ruler, who was soon depicted in the international press and in popular caricatures as the "Bloody Sultan." Eventually his own people would dub his reign as the period of despotism (*istibdad*).

Abdülhamit II (1876-1909).

Following the Congress of Berlin the Ottoman Empire had been on probation, its very existence to be determined by its behavior toward its Christian minorities and the continued tolerance of the Great Powers.[44] From the 1880s Britain's support for the Ottomans declined and Germany's increased. France and Germany became fierce competitors for investment and influence in the empire. European tolerance of Ottoman behavior, however, was severely tested in the mid-1890s. What became known later as the Hamidian massacres took place against the background of decades of tension between the local Armenian peasants and the Kurds in eastern Anatolia. Armenians had the choice of remaining the silent victims of the Kurds and state injustice, petitioning the authorities for protection, or organizing their own self-defense. They did all three.

The urban Armenian elites, particularly the clergy and the wealthy business class, generally opposed the revolutionary parties. The Armenian Church tried to work with the government. Patriarch Ashikian petitioned the Porte in 1890 to stem the violence against Armenians in the East.[45] He received no redress. Popular Armenian attitudes toward the radicals were marked by ambivalence. A well-placed Armenian told a longtime British resident in the country, "We admit the movement is a hopeless one, but what can we say to our poor countrymen at Yuzgat [Yozgat] and elsewhere when they tell us 'Better die once than die a thousand deaths such as we die daily under the present oppression'?"[46] Only with great difficulty did the radicals, always a tiny minority among Armenians, convince some of the more self-reliant of their countrymen, like those of Sasun and Zeytun, to resist Kurdish taxation and impositions.

In the summer of 1894 Ottoman officials, suspecting that revolutionaries had stored arms and ammunition in the Armenian cathedral of Erzurum, raided the sanctuary, desecrating the building and inflaming the local Armenians. No weapons were found, but protests led to clashes, and about fifteen Armenians were killed, others wounded. The crowds turned on several houses of foreigners and missionaries.[47] To protest the violence against Armenians, the Hnchak party held a demonstration in Kumkapı, the Istanbul neighborhood that housed the Armenian patriarchate, in July 1890.[48] A number of armed Hnchaks disrupted Mass in the patriarch's church and demanded that Patriarch Ashikian join them in a demonstration. The patriarch refused but was forced into his carriage and into the protest. Government soldiers surrounded the demonstrators, freeing the patriarch and arresting the leaders of the demonstration. The patriarch denounced the protestors, exposing the divide between the church and the radicals. Four years later the revolutionaries attempted to assassinate him.[49]

Incidents flared up throughout Anatolia without warning. In December 1893 in the central Anatolian town of Yozgat someone cut the telegraph wires. In their investigations the police roughed up villagers, abducted women, and seized a priest, tied his hands, and "dragged him along for several days through ten or eleven other villages in the hopes of scaring the people into denouncing the perpetrators of the damage done to the telegraph lines." Armenians gathered in the church to draw up a petition to the provincial governor, but fearing an outbreak of violence between Armenians and Muslims, the governor sent an army officer to the church and himself urged Muslims not to be alarmed. A British consular report tells what happened next:

> The commotion caused among the Mussulmans by the Christian assemblage roused greater fear among the Armenians, and they would not obey the orders of the Governor to disperse, thereupon a Turkish soldier—possibly with the intention of merely frightening them into obedience—fired off his gun, hitting an Armenian in the leg. Thinking this was the commencement of a general attack on them, the Armenians fired back and wounded about ten Turks, of whom three have since died. One Armenian was killed, but only two or three were wounded. The Turks withdrew soon afterwards, but the Armenians remained for some time at the church, and for several days did not leave their houses or open their shops, as they feared Turkish reprisals.[50]

Violence continued into early 1894. The authorities considered the Armenians to be "in a state of rebellion," and the government declared martial law in the *sanjak* of Yozgat. Churches were searched; the Muslims believed that Armenians hid weapons in their churches. Armenians were accused of various crimes. A petition by Protestant and Gregorian Armenians to the British embassy stated, "The local authorities made it their business to saddle the Armenians with every crime and offense that occurred in the district." Police and officials molested Christians, and dozens of Armenians were sentenced to death or long prison terms. It was rumored that seven Turks were also hanged.[51]

Farther south and east, Sasun was a semi-autonomous region in which Armenians largely ran their own affairs but under the overlordship of Kurdish tribal chiefs. Here Armenians were armed and had not paid taxes to the central government since the 1860s, though they were obligated to pay the *hafir*, a protection tax, to the Kurdish chieftains.[52] The Armenian revolutionary, Mihran Tamatian, a Hnchak from Istanbul, arrived in the fall of 1891 to teach the local Armenians self-defense. The activists, who numbered about ten, clashed with Kurds the following summer, and early in 1893 Tamatian was arrested. A few months later, in the summer of 1893, some three or four thousand Kurdish tribesmen entered the *kaza* of Sasun and attacked the Armenians in the mixed village of Talori. The Turkish *mutassarif*, the governor of the *sancak* of Guendj, arrived with his troops and arrested several Armenians but no Kurds. The soldiers then plundered the Armenians, and the *mutassarif* told the authorities at Bitlis that the Armenians were in revolt. The villagers retreated into the mountains for several months, returning only the next spring. Still, they refused to pay the taxes levied by the governor of Bitlis because of the state's failure to protect them from the Kurds. This led to a second visit by the army.

Encouraged by Hnchak party activists, the Sasuntsis held off the Kurdish forces sent by the official head (*kaymakam*) of the *kaza* of Kulp. Negotiations broke down when the governor arrested some Armenian leaders, and the crowd beat him. When once again it was reported that the Armenians were in rebellion, regular Ottoman troops, along with *Hamidiye* troops, were brought in to crush the "insurrection."[53] Instead of restoring order, the army indiscriminately massacred men, women, and children. For three weeks, in August and September, "the Armenians were absolutely hunted like wild beasts, being killed wherever they were met," wrote the British commissioner sent later to investigate.[54] About nine hundred people were slaughtered. The British investigator surmised that the brutal killings occurred "because the Turkish authorities were unable to brook the feeling of independence which had survived among the Armenians of that district."[55] Even more ominously, the local Turks feared that the Armenians "were plotting against the Empire and the Turkish element in the population."[56]

The Sasun massacres reopened the Armenian Question. A Commission of Inquiry was set up. Retired Prime Minister Gladstone used his eighty-fifth birthday as an opportunity to call for the strongest possible action to prevent further atrocities. The foreign secretary, Lord Kimberley, was appalled to learn that Abdülhamid had conferred a medal of honor on Zeki Paşa, the officer who oversaw the Talori killings. This affront to the Great Powers was proof enough, he concluded, "that the Sultan himself is the author of the merciless measures against the Armenians."[57] A high Ottoman official, former foreign minister, and grand vizier, Said Paşa, fled in fear of his life to the British embassy in Istanbul and reported that Abdülhamid had told him that "the Armenian question must be settled not by reform but by blood." At first Said did not understand what His Majesty meant. "I thought he referred to war with a foreign Power, but I find that he meant massacre."[58]

The Sasun events began a cycle of killing, by both state authorities and local Kurds, which is best explained by what might be called an "ecology of violence." Three elements came together in the last quarter of the nineteenth century that resulted in a toxic conjuncture that exploded into plunder, resistance, and massacre. First, the old equilibrium with Kurds ruling over local Armenians who submitted to their authority steadily broke down in the second half of the century. Second, the state's ambition to establish its own authority over eastern Anatolia did not produce a monopoly of power in the hands of Ottoman officials but instead contributed to an increase in rivalry with traditional authorities, greater disorder, and violence. The state was nearly bankrupt, having lost the wealth produced by the Balkans. Soldiers were not paid for months. Third, Armenians were no longer willing to be ruled and taxed in the ways they had been in the past. Their resistance led to clashes with Kurds and Turks, and both local and state militaries indiscriminately killed men, women, and children. What might have been contained locally was interpreted from above as rebellion against the state. What began as a tax revolt escalated into a major confrontation between the three peoples living in the region.

A solution to the plight of the Armenians was exceedingly difficult. The fact that they were a majority in but a few districts in the six *vilayets* meant that realistically no independent Armenian state could be formed that would not include millions of Muslims. Almost all Armenians recognized the demographic dilemma in which they existed and were willing to live within the Ottoman Empire—but with guarantees of protection and justice. A feasible solution to the problems in the region was some form of autonomy or a protectorate by Europeans, but the Great Powers feared that one or another of them would become overly influential in the region, and the Ottomans persistently resisted such an infringement on their sovereignty. The Russian government was wary of the creation of an autonomous Armenia within the Ottoman Empire since it might attract the loyalties of their own Caucasian Armenians, of whom tsarist officials were increasingly suspicious. When Khrimian *Hayrik*, the catholicos of the Armenians, traveled to St. Petersburg in early 1895 to plead to the tsar for relief of the Ottoman Armenians' miseries, Nicholas II refused to grant him an audience. When monarchs and foreign ministers considered the balance of power, they concluded that there should be no serious change in the status quo. That left the option of imposing reforms on the recalcitrant Ottomans. Provoked by the events in Sasun, Britain, France, and Russia worked out a "Project of Reforms for the Eastern Provinces of Asia Minor" and presented them to the Porte on May 11, 1895. Local governors (*vali*) were to be approved by the Great Powers, and Armenians were to be given better protection and compensation for their losses. A high commissioner and a Commission of Control were to supervise the implementation of the reforms.

To the sultan the proposed reforms were anathema. The precedent of autonomy leading to independence in the Balkans loomed like a specter. The Ottomans saw an even greater danger in what they believed the Armenians were up to. As one official recorded, "[T]he Armenian affair is not like the Bulgarian or Serbian affairs, because it has arisen in Anatolia which is the crucible of Ottoman power."[59] Once Abdülhamid refused to agree to the reforms, Britain alone of the Great Powers might have acted to pressure the sultan to capitulate. Public opinion favored intervention, and Queen Victoria was very sympathetic to the Armenians. The prime minister and foreign secretary, Lord Salisbury, was so disgusted by

the Porte that he broached the possibility with Russia of breaking up
the Ottoman Empire and parceling out pieces to the European powers.
But when Salisbury approached the Russians about enforcement, Foreign Minister Prince Aleksei Lobanov-Rostovskii informed him, "Russia would certainly not join in any coercive measures."[60] By this time the
earlier positive attitude of Russian authorities toward Armenians had
soured into suspicion of Armenians as a subversive element threatening
the Russian as well as the Ottoman Empire. Tsarist Russia, the country
that had been the greatest foe of the Ottomans, no longer banked on the
Armenians but saw another possible ally in the Kurds.[61] The tables had
completely turned. Great Britain, the Ottomans' traditional defender
against the encroachments of Moscow, was less committed to Istanbul
since they had built the Suez Canal, had taken dominion over Egypt, and
had a more secure route to India. In the mid-1890s Russia protected the
integrity of the Ottoman Empire while London proposed partition. Armenians remained pawns in this "Great Game."[62]

In late September 1895 the Hnchaks notified the Porte that they
planned a peaceful demonstration to protest the repression of the Armenians in the very center of Istanbul's old city, at the Bab-ı Ali (the great
gate, the Porte). During Mass at the Armenian cathedral in Kumkapı,
about twenty Armenian women who had traveled from Van, Bitlis, and
Erzurum presented the patriarch with a petition outlining the suffering
of Anatolian Armenians and pleaded with him to organize a mass march
to the Porte to ask for reforms. The patriarch implored the congregation
not to violate the law by demonstrating. Rely instead, he pleaded, on his
intercession with the state. The crowd shouted, "We have had enough; we
have made up our minds, and we want liberty or death!" As the marchers
filed out, they were met by police; shots were fired from both sides. Sixty
Armenians and Turks were killed. In the evening Muslim theological
students, known as *softa*s, ran through the streets wielding heavy sticks,
attacking whomever they thought was Armenian. This time, organized
by the revolutionaries, some demonstrators returned fire. An Ottoman
major who ordered his men to shoot was himself shot, whereupon the
police waded into the crowd, killing indiscriminately.[63]

For the first time foreigners in the capital witnessed the killing of Armenians. Appalled by the audacity of the Armenians, who in their view had provoked the violence, some defended the sultan. The American minister plenipotentiary to the Porte, Alexander Watkins Terrell, who referred to Abdülhamid as "the ablest sovereign in Europe," later reported how the sultan graciously praised the talents of the Armenians who were protected and who thrived in the empire.[64] On the other hand, a British observer, Canon Malcolm MacColl, defended the Armenian demonstrations as understandable resistance to Hamidian repression. In his view the sultan aimed to "kill the aspirations of the Armenians by a reign of terror, by the death and expatriation of their leaders and educators and by the confiscation of books, thus driving them back into the barbarism which comes of ignorance and helplessness under the dominion of armed force: there you have in a nutshell the explanation of the Sultan's dealings with the Armenians for the last few years. Their demonstration was quite legal and quite pacific."[65]

The Europeans feared that the violence would reach their countrymen living in the empire. This was enough for the Triple Alliance (Germany, Austria, and Italy) to bring its own weight to bear on the Ottoman government. Pressured by Europe, the sultan finally agreed to yet another European-imposed reform on October 17, 1895, though he kept the agreement secret. The crisis did not abate, however. In the next months the British contemplated sending their fleet into the Dardanelles, the first of the two narrow straits that controlled passage from the Mediterranean to the Black Sea. Russia had long had its own interests in controlling the Straits; Austria too involved itself until Germany and France deterred their rival powers from any precipitous moves. Britain's willingness to coerce the sultan faltered before the concerted efforts of Russia, France, Germany, and Austria to prevent any scramble for the spoils of the Ottoman Empire.

The massacres of Armenians continued. Sasun was followed by resistance at Zeytun, and clashes occurred in Trabzon, Erzurum, Arapgir, Bayburt, Bitlis, Urfa, and Diyarbakır. George White, the American president of Anatolia College in Marsovan, described what he witnessed in November 1895.

I . . . saw our neighbors running out to join the mob, each with a gun or a sword in his hands. A little later I . . . heard shots come, ping, ping, against the walls of the little room where we stood together looking out. Through a crack in one of our gates I saw a woman lying in the street, slashed and hacked and just at the point of death. . . . The Armenian shops in the market, where the Armenians were the shop keeping class in a city of 25,000 or more people, were virtually all picked as clean as a bone. . . . Armenians to the number of about 125 were killed. . . . The government was in full control throughout.[66]

The mobs that turned on Armenians killed them while calling them "infidel" (*gavur*), "pigs," or "dogs." Armenians responded with their own epithets, "dogs" being a favorite. In Erzincan a British diplomat reported, "The massacres and pillaging commenced at about half-past 9 and lasted till 1 in the morning, the pillaging, however, continuing till the evening. The number of Armenians killed was over 200, whilst about 400 were wounded. All the shops except twenty-three were wrecked. Order was ultimately restored by the efforts of Zeki Pasha, who also took steps for the recovery of the stolen goods, a considerable quantity of which was brought back and deposited in the Armenian church pending its redistribution; notwithstanding this, the ruin of the Armenian community is complete, and the misery great."[67]

Christianity as well as signs of class and culture marked Armenians for killing. The Turkish nationalist Ahmed Rıza, one of the founders of the Young Turks' revolutionary Committee of Union and Progress, explained in his own understanding why anti-Christian atrocities occurred: "This may seem exaggerated, but the fact is that, in our country, there is no comparison between the fate of the Ottoman Christians and that of the Muslims. The Christians are far happier, or, if one prefers, less wretched. . . . If Christians are the preferred targets of looting, the reason is that they enjoy greater wealth and material comfort than the Muslims and that, either out of fear or suspicion of the victor, they generally keep their doors shut."[68] Many Armenians made the pragmatic choice to save themselves by assimilating and converting to Islam. They insisted on the sincerity of their decision. "We converted of our own free will," wrote the Armenians of Köyulhisar in Sivas province, their statement written in Turkish in Armenian letters. "Our identity papers state that we are Armenians, but in our hearts and our dress we are Muslims. . . . In short, may the state hang us if it pleases, we are willing and we will not turn our back on Islam."[69] When two thousand Kurds attacked the town of Divriği in Sivas *vilayet*, killing at least twenty-three Armenians, some five hundred Armenians petitioned through their village elders to convert to Islam, the men to be circumcised. Istanbul responded cautiously and recommended that the conversions be postponed until peace was restored. The government did not want more attention turned to the Armenians, fearful of the effect on foreign powers. The Armenian patriarch protested to the government that the conversions were forced by fear and could not be considered voluntary. He pleaded to the Porte to take "rapid and effective measures" to guarantee the safety of Armenians who returned to their faith.[70] Tens of thousands of Armenians were being killed. The indiscriminate violence disturbed some local officials. The governor of Sivas wrote, "If the Kurds do not listen to reason, it will be necessary to use armed force against them."[71]

Massacres and abductions of Christian women were particularly savage in Diyarbakır. The town was the center of a huge province of the same name and housed a cosmopolitan population made up half of Christians and slightly less Muslims. The Christians were divided into different denominations with the Armenians the largest group in the city. Besides Apostolic Armenians and Orthodox Greeks, there were Catholic and Protestant Armenians, Assyrians (Syriacs), and Greeks. Close to the Armenians, but a distinct religious community of its own, the people known as Assyrians or Syriacs included a number of Christian groups who spoke dialects of Aramaic, the ancient Semitic language that Jesus spoke. In the Ottoman lands Assyrian Christians were divided into Syrian Orthodox (*Süryani*, also known as Jacobites), Nestorians (*Nesturi*), and Catholic Nestorians (Chaldeans, *Keldani*). Armenians referred to all of these groups as *Aisor* or *Ashur*. The Syriac Orthodox Christians were part of the

Ermeni milleti, but in the nineteenth century the Catholic Syriacs were attached to the Catholic *millet* along with Armenian, Greek, and other Catholics. Tensions had developed between Armenians and Assyrians over the latter's wish to have their own *millet* and disputes over church properties in Jerusalem.[72] Yet the relations between the two communities were generally extremely close, indeed fatally so, for Syriacs would be condemned to the same fate as Armenians in the 1890s and again in 1915.[73] As members of the *Ermeni milleti* are often confused with Armenians, most Assyrians had faced hostility and repression from local Kurdish tribesmen throughout the nineteenth century.[74]

The Muslims in the city were Kurdish speakers, but identified themselves as Ottomans or Muslims. The designation "Kurds" was reserved for the nomads and tribesmen in the countryside. Muslims in both town and province were disturbed by the relative success of local Armenians. A historian of Diyarbakır has summarized the accumulating resentments felt by Muslims against Armenians as the "natural" order of Muslim as rulers and Christians as subjects appeared to be reversed.

> Every small change in a Christian's behavior became a possible source of irritation, and Muslims began feeling discriminated against. It appears that by 1895, whatever the Armenians did in Diyarbekir was offensive in Muslim eyes. Armenians were accused of monopolizing import/export trade. They built a clock tower that was higher than a minaret. When a cholera epidemic broke out, it was said that more Muslims than Armenians fell victim.[75]

During Ramadan two notorious officials spread rumors that the sultan himself had ordered the massacre of all Christians. The events in Sasun and Istanbul reverberated in Diyarbakır, and hostility toward Armenians grew palpably more intense. When a new governor (*vali*), Mehmed Enis Paşa, known to be hostile to Christians, was appointed early in October 1895, local Armenians protested, blocking streets, ringing church bells for three days and nights, and sending a telegram to the patriarch in Istanbul protesting the church's support for the *vali*. Such a protest was quite unprecedented and demonstrated a new political awakening, perhaps stimulated by radical activists. When news arrived that the sultan had accepted the reforms imposed by the Europeans, local Muslims were enraged by rumors that the "six Armenian *vilayets*" had been granted to the Armenians for a "separate kingdom."[76] They began to arm themselves. Anti-Christian notables in the region actively incited people to take revenge on the Armenians.

Only the intervention of authorities to prevent a bloody clash might have avoided violence. Instead the police chief insulted Armenians who aired their complaints to him, and the *vali* clearly sided with those hostile to the Christians. Both Christians and Muslims anticipated trouble and prepared to defend themselves. The local Islamic judge (*kadi*), "pale and trembling," feared that the town would be turned into "another Damascus," a reference to the anti-Maronite massacres in 1860.[77] On November 1 shots rang out during and after Muslim afternoon prayers. Pillaging, in which prominent Muslims participated, began, and soon the main market was on fire. Hundreds of shops were consumed by the blaze. The next day Muslim gangs broke into Christian houses, killing some and carrying off women and children. The Christians fled to the compounds of the French missionaries and the consulate, which in turn were attacked by mobs. The French consul there frantically telegrammed his ambassador: "The city is engulfed in fire and blood. Save us."[78] Only on the third day did the *vali* intervene and call a halt to the pogroms.[79]

In a remarkable telegram, sent to the sultan the day after the killings, important Muslim public figures in Diyarbakır expressed their anxiety about the reforms leading to Armenian autonomy or independence. "The effort to separate these six provinces from our Ottoman homeland has overwhelmed us all with sorrow and turned every Islamic house into an abode of lament." They went on to reveal their resentment at the exalted position of many Armenians and their fear that they were aiming at taking further advantage of the Muslims. "It is clear that the Armenians live under much happier conditions than the Muslims and are not as destitute and pitiful as they claim but, in reality, in this area own many places of work and have capital. Feeling discontented with their current advantages they will surely strive passionately to acquire still more privileges and to realize other unnecessary benefits that are contrary to Islamic law." Their language reflected their loyalty to the empire and caliphate but also the Young Turk opposition to Abdülhamid. For these men the situation was intolerable, and they declared that they would take action. "We also want justice. The intention of the Armenian traitors is to break the holy bond between Muslims in this region, people who are the bravest and most loyal subjects of the State and the Grand Caliphate. We cannot tolerate such actions.... We proclaim unanimously that we will spoil, with our blood, the lines and the pages of the privileges, which will be given to the Armenians."[80]

Within the city between 300 and 1,200 Armenians were killed, along with some 70 to 200 Muslims.[81] Thousands lost their homes and businesses. Kurds had taken more than 500 women and girls, many forcibly converted to Islam, apparently with the connivance of the *vali*, Enis Paşa. While the tribal Kurds of the countryside were kept out of the city of Diyarbakır, they pillaged, plundered, killed, and kidnapped Christians in the outlying villages and towns of the province. Yet as violent as Kurds were in the countryside and Muslims were in the town, the Kurds of the local *Hamidiye* did not join the pogroms. They were under the powerful Kurdish tribal leader Milli İbrahim Paşa, a man of the old empire, a tribal leader whose imperial mode of politics involved recognition and acceptance of ethnic and religious differences. When Kurdish tribesmen surrounded Viranşehir and began plundering Christian shops, İbrahim Paşa ordered his troops to protect the local Christians. Vulnerable Armenians in Mardin, Urfa, and Siverek responded by moving to the protected Viranşehir.[82] Instead of devastating repression, the rule of İbrahim Paşa meant protection of those different and subordinate.[83] Twenty years later, however, during the Genocide of 1915, his Milli tribe, under the command of his son, participated in the mass killings of Armenians and Assyrians.[84]

With little relief after the massacres, and fearing a recurrence, Armenians began leaving the city they called *Tigranakert*, which they believed, erroneously, had been founded by their ancient king, Tigran. Azniv Tashjian never forgot the death of her sister, her throat slit, left to die in a pit, eventually to succumb to infection when the wound was wrapped in soiled rags. She carried the story to America, where she fled with her family after the massacres. There she, my maternal grandmother, repeated the tale, but only rarely.

In his official report (*fezleke*) to Istanbul the *vali* Enis Paşa blamed the disturbances on the Armenians, who had initiated the violence for no apparent reason and were "eager for rebellion" (*ihtilalcuyane*).[85] The dragoman of the British embassy, Gerald Fitzmaurice, carried out his own investigations and reported that a Muslim mob had surged through the city, crying, "Our Padisha has ordered that the Armenians be massacred, and that no Christians are to be left in the country." While the crowd killed at will, "the Ottoman official and reserve soldiers who had turned up in early December stood aside."[86] The outrages against women troubled the foreigners in the town as well as the Ottoman official sent to investigate the events. He eventually threw up his hands when the sultan refused to punish the perpetrators, and Istanbul ignored European demands that Enis Paşa be replaced.[87] In the aftermath of the massacres Diyarbakır was a ruined landscape of destroyed or abandoned houses and people left without work or sustenance. However involved the authorities were in the initial massacres, either instigating them or failing to prevent their spread, officials sent by the sultan prevented Kurds from restarting the killing a few weeks later. Half-heartedly a few personnel changes were made, a desultory implication of the promised reforms. A difficult year passed, and finally in November 1896 Enis Paşa was removed as governor.

Moving on from Diyarbakır to Urfa near the Persian border, Fitzmaurice discovered that eight thousand Armenians had been murdered in two days. More than two thousand had died in the cathedral, trapped there after it was set on fire.[88] The Ottomans blamed Armenian revolutionaries for provoking the massacres, but the British ambassador rejected that scenario. "The charge against the Armenians of having been the first to offer provocation," he reported to Lord Salisbury, "cannot be sustained."[89]

In the spring of 1896 the conflict moved to Zeytun. In the words of a British diplomat, "The Armenians of Zeitoun and the neighbouring villages, like the Sasunlis, are mountaineers, and more formidable than most of their race." Fearing an attack, the villagers overran the Turkish garrison in the citadel, killed all the soldiers, and held off retaliatory strikes for months. Ambassadors offered to mediate the standoff of Turks and Armenians in Zeytun. Consuls arrived in the area in late January 1896. A Mr. Barnham telegraphed what he saw: "This afternoon I visited the Zeitoun river and saw the bodies of the Turkish soldiers who were killed by the Zeitounlis. One of them admitted yesterday that 230 had been massacred. In many cases they are tied hand to hand, their heads split open by axes, or they are killed by sword cuts or shots, and in some cases their hands and feet cut off. One of the Turkish authorities told me that a zaptieh had his eyes cut out, filled with gunpowder, and his head blown to pieces."[90] Weary and ragged, the Zeytuntsis agreed to give up their weapons and were amnestied. Their safety was to be guaranteed by the Great Powers, and a Christian *kaymakam* was to be appointed in Zeytun. The agreement was almost immediately broken by the government, which appointed a Turk to the post of *kaymakam*. Protests by the diplomats had no effect.

In June members of the three Armenian revolutionary parties—the Dashnaks, the Hnchaks, and the Armenakans—fought Kurds in Van. The British consul negotiated a cease-fire and safe passage for the combatants, but as they moved toward the border they were attacked by Kurds and Turks, their ranks decimated. Farther on Persian Kurds set upon them, killing most of them and cutting off their ears as trophies.[91] When the Armenian patriarch, Matdeos II (Izmirlian), condemned the massacres, the sultan responded by exiling him to Jerusalem. He would not return to Istanbul until after the 1908 Young Turk Revolution.

In town after town—Amasia, Aintab, Caesarea, Malatya, Maraş, Mardin, and Muş—and in countless villages killing continued. At Marsovan, a British diplomat wrote,

> At 7 o'clock Turkish—about noon—a Turk rushed into the Pasha Jami Mosque shouting that the Armenian Committee was advancing to the attack. The Mussulmans rushed from the mosques, and, at the same time, just as if a signal had been given, the villagers swarmed into the town from the surrounding country, and the whole mass bore down upon the market-place with

shouts of "Kill the Kiafir, loot his goods." The soldiers joined in the attack, and assisted the mob to dispatch the Armenians. The whole market was pillaged with the exception of three shops belonging to Greek Rayahs, the only Greeks in the market, which were protected by the troops. Men and women were killed like sheep after refusing to accept the Mahommedan faith, which was offered them as their only alternative. The doors of closed shops were broken in, the inmates murdered, and the wares dragged out and carried off. Even the iron doors of the Bedestan, or covered bazaar, were smashed with axes, and the whole of it pillaged—"not a needle was left." A young Turk of rank was seen meanwhile encouraging the rabble, and shouting to them to make the most of their time.[92]

In Harput Kurds from Dersim entered the towns and began killing Armenians, pillaging and then burning their houses. The local Turks joined in. Missionaries tried to help the victims, hiding hundreds in one of the school buildings. The Circassian commandant of gendarmerie tried to stop the violence, but neither he, the governor, nor the mufti was able to suppress the crowds.[93] In Sivas Kurds carried off Armenian women. Of the two thousand Armenians in Gürün previous to the massacre, only five hundred survived. "The dead lay about in heaps for days poisoning the air; there was no possibility of interring them. The majority of the survivors are homeless and penniless; famine is staring them in the face; they are begging their bread."[94]

Both government officials and ordinary people were deeply suspicious of Armenians, their fears exacerbated by the activities of the revolutionaries. Even though the Muslims far outnumbered Armenians almost everywhere, each side anticipated violence from the other. Both Armenians and Muslims saw the other through an emotional veil, an affective disposition that interpreted any untoward movement as a threat. Almost any spark could set off a massacre. When out of fear Armenian merchants closed their shops, Muslims took this to be a sign of preparation for conflict. When a band of "unknown brigands" attacked and killed a Turkish

officer near Kemakh in August 1895, the authorities declared the crime
to have been committed by Armenians. Soldiers sent to apprehend the
bandits plundered villages, "committing all kinds of outrages."[95] A month
later a band of Armenians attacked a hated Turkish judge from Karahisar.
The judge was carried "off to the mountains, where he was tortured and
his body cut to pieces." Revolutionaries decimated the soldiers sent to
capture the Armenians, and a second force of twenty-eight Circassians
was deployed to deal with them. An armed band of about thirty to forty
Armenians operated near Sivas, causing "much excitement among the
Mussulman population."[96]

Whether for reasons of state interests or humanitarian feelings, the
European states read with alarm the reports of the massacres. Here was
a case when *Realpolitik*—the need to preserve the Ottoman Empire—
and the concerns for fellow Christians collided. Diplomats in Istanbul
repeatedly "drew his Highness' serious attention to the gravity of the
situation in the provinces." The grand vizier assured them that the authorities "were doing their best to restore order, and had sent orders to
the Moslems in all parts of the Empire not to resort to vengeance, but to
keep quiet. His Highness was fully alive to the dangers which threaten
the Ottoman Empire if the present state of affairs was allowed to continue, but he maintained that the Armenians had been the aggressors in
every instance, acting under orders from the Armenian Societies, and that
they did everything to provoke the Mussulmans to violence in the hope
of forcing the foreign Powers to intervene. It was with the Armenians,
therefore, that the responsibility for the disturbances lay."[97]

Among the Ottoman elite, the diplomatic corps, and Armenians,
opponents of the revolutionaries saw outside agitators as the instigators
of violence. Ottoman reports repeatedly blamed Armenians for the massacres. From Arapgir they claimed that Armenians set fire to a mosque
and attacked the Muslim quarter. Incendiary bombs were discovered in
the homes of Armenians.[98] The discontent, even despair, of Armenian
villagers, however, existed before the revolutionaries arrived. Their frustration with the depredations of the Kurds and their conviction that no
real justice was available from the government made them receptive to the

message of the radicals. Militants from the various parties provided guidance, coordination, encouragement, and, when they were able, arms to the peasants. In the uneven struggle against the armed Muslims, unarmed Armenians looked to these strangers crossing over from Russia for protection. Villagers clandestinely supported the fighters with food, shelter, and information. What to the Ottomans appeared to be insurrection and to the Armenians self-defense was an unbalanced, unequal, uncivil war that degenerated into indiscriminate and brutal massacres of largely unarmed, unprotected Armenians.

BANK OTTOMAN

The Dashnaks issued a protest in the name of the "Armenian people," warning that "the patience of down-trodden nations has its limits." The next day the party declared, "The time of diplomatic play is passed." On August 26, 1896, a small group of Armenian revolutionaries, led by Papken Suni, escalated the tension by seizing the Bank Ottoman in the Galata district of Istanbul. Inspired by the Russian populists, the young Armenian radicals were desperate idealists who feared that inaction would lead to annihilation of their people. In their collective note delivered to foreign embassies, they declared, "The blood shed by our 100,000 martyrs gives us the right to demand liberty. . . . We mourn in advance the loss of all those, whether foreigners or natives, who may be the victims of fate in the general alarm. . . . We shall die, we know, but the revolution which has penetrated to the marrow of the Armenian nation will continue to threaten the throne of the Sultan so long as we have not obtained our rights as men, so long as a single Armenian remains."[99]

One of the men who seized the bank, Garegin Pasdermajian, better known by his *nom de guerre* Armen Garo, was a twenty-four-year-old student of agriculture in Nancy, France, when he learned of the Hnchak activities and the massacres in Zeytun. He and a few of his fellow students wrote to the Hnchak headquarters in London but were brushed off. They received a more positive reply from *Droshak* (Flag), the Dashnak newspaper in Geneva. After meeting with the Dashnaks, they were dispatched first to Cyprus and then to Istanbul, where the planning was already under way to seize the bank. The Dashnaks considered three different actions: an expedition to relieve Zeytun; organizing armed groups in Persia to retaliate against hostile Kurds; or "an act of revenge in Constantinople."[100] Garo arrived by ship in early August and met with his co-conspirators. Their aim was to force the hand of the Great Powers to land troops in the Ottoman capital by holding the 150 European officers of the bank hostage. Simultaneous with the seizure of the bank there was to be a raid on a military barracks in Samatia across the Golden Horn and the assassination of the grand vizier, Sadrazam, on the Galata Bridge. Bomb throwers would be placed at Galatasaray and on Pera Street to prevent soldiers from advancing on the bank. Hundreds of bombs were prepared, but the actual raid was haphazard and disastrous. Dressed as *hamals* (porters), the conspirators carried heavy bags that appeared to contain coins into the bank. But they were discovered by guards, and their commander, Papken Siuni, and two others were killed immediately. Garo took command of the dozen and a half outmanned survivors who made it into the bank. Soldiers fired into the bank for hours while the Armenians tried to close the great doors. Several defenders were blown to bits by their own bombs. One wounded man begged to be shot, and another reluctantly ended his misery. Untrained and not accustomed to using weapons, many of the men were unknown to their leader, who barked out orders in Armenian. One young man with a revolver in each hand answered in Turkish, "*Baron, ben Ermenice bilmem, Türkçe söyle*" (Mister, I don't know Armenian, say it in Turkish). Garo suspected the fellow might be a Turk until reassured by another.[101]

The employees of the bank huddled on the second floor, frightened by those they suspected were bank robbers. Garo tried to convince them that they were Armenian revolutionaries who would do them no harm unless their demands were not met or an attack were launched on the bank. If attacked, the band of revolutionaries would detonate their bombs, blow up the bank, and die with their hostages. Negotiators were dispatched with the demands that the massacres come to an end; that reforms to protect Armenians be enacted; that Armenian political prisoners be released; and that the patriarch, thought to be too friendly to the palace, be dismissed. From inside the insurgents could hear the howls of the mob outside, incensed by the bank seizure. Massacres of Istanbul Armenians had begun. A huge crowd wielding swords, sticks, and axes tried to smash their way into the bank, chopping at the doors. Garo ordered his men to drop some twenty bombs on them, killing and wounding many, the rest scattering over bodies, the wounded reaching out and pleading not to be left behind.[102]

At one in the morning, twelve hours after they had first entered the bank, the rebels were called to the window to meet with the Russian representative, M. Maximov, the designated envoy of the Great Powers. For two hours Garo and Maximov argued about the terms. The Russian arranged safe passage for the surviving revolutionaries to a British ship in the harbor, with a promise that the massacres would cease, political prisoners would be released, and reforms would be enacted.[103] When Garo and his men emerged from the bank, Maximov was shocked to see only seventeen rebels, not the two hundred that the Ottomans had claimed were inside the bank. "Allow me, once again, to shake your hand," he said to Garo. "The coup was masterfully executed." At least that is how Armen Garo remembered the conversation years later. The rebels were escorted through the streets of Istanbul to the yacht of Sir Edgar Vincent, the director of the Bank Ottoman, and from there by French ship they were taken to Marseilles.

Crowds of Turks rampaged through the streets, targeting Armenians, killing about five to six thousand of the two hundred thousand Armenian residents of the city. They struck ferociously at the poorest of the Armenians, the *hamal*s, rather than the middle-class merchants. The police and army stood by and watched as the killing went on until the evening of August 27. A Kurdish intellectual and his friends came upon some Armenians in a carpet store; they killed them all and took the bodies in carriages to Saray Burnu and threw them into the sea where the current was strongest. Summing up his feelings, he said, Armenians "were like rabid dogs attacking the family that fed them."[104] In the ensuing months thousands of Armenians were forced to leave Istanbul, making their way with few resources to other parts of Anatolia.

Britain's ambassador to the Porte, Sir Philip Currie, a man usually supportive of the Ottoman government, was shocked by the bloodshed that followed. "The last few days have enabled me to realize what St Bartholomew's Day was like, and the sights I have witnessed have made a most profound impression upon me.... The awful cold-blooded barbarity of the mob, which was deliberately organized and armed by the Turkish Government, makes one forget the provocation which the Turks undoubtedly received, and long for the punishment of the real author of these abominations."[105] The European ambassadors in Istanbul reacted quickly. They sent a strong note to Abdülhamid demanding an immediate end to the massacres, "an unheard-of state of things, which is calculated to bring about the most disastrous consequences for Your Majesty's Empire."[106] The killings stopped immediately.

Having risked their lives and lost comrades in their desperate effort to raise awareness of the Armenian massacres, Garo and the survivors of the raid, feeling deceived by the Europeans, bitterly contemplated the failure of their mission.[107] At the time, and later, there were those who blamed the massacre on the Armenian revolutionaries, absolving the Turks of the primary blame. In what he evidently considered a neutral and balanced view, Ardern G. Hume-Beaman, an English "expert on things oriental," wrote at the time, "It is all very well to call [Abdülhamid] the 'Great Assassin,' but from the Moslem point of view he was very fairly justified in killing any number of rebellious infidels who were being supported by combined Europe in what he and every Turk considered as a plot against the realm. The Turks retorted on the English especially, that we used to blow Moslems from the muzzles of our guns and burn whole villages and mosques in India for an insult offered to one of our officials, and were they not to make an example of these Armenian dogs?"[108]

In the aftermath of the Bank Ottoman seizure much of Europe lost sympathy for the Armenians as victims of the "Terrible Turks." In France the Hnchaks were dismayed by the actions of their Dashnak rivals and questioned the motives for their action, which they considered a sign of political immaturity. Hnchaks organized public meetings to stem the anti-Armenian feelings, inviting prominent French intellectuals like the historians Ernest Lavisse and Anatole Leroy-Beaulieu and politicians like the socialist leader Jean Jaurès to speak out in protest against the Ottoman excesses.[109]

For most observers in the West and in Russia the real author of the Armenian massacres was the sultan himself. When British consuls in eastern Anatolia complained to the sultan about the excessive force used against the Armenians, Abdülhamid replied to Sir Philip Currie, the British ambassador:

> the Armenians, who for their own purposes invent these stories against the Government, and finding that they receive encouragement from British officials, are emboldened to proceed to open acts of rebellion, which the Government is perfectly justified in suppressing by every means in its power. . . . His Imperial Majesty treated the Armenians with justice and moderation, and, as long as they behaved properly, all toleration would be shown to them, but he had given orders that when they took to revolt or to brigandage the authorities were to deal with them as they dealt with the authorities.[110]

In his later memoirs Abdülhamid further sketched his private feelings about the Armenians, gendering them as womanly and cowardly.

> Although it is impossible to deny that the Armenians dwelling in our eastern provinces are a great many times well founded in their complaints, it is fitting to say also that they exaggerate. Armenians look as if they are crying for a pain they don't feel at all. Hiding behind the great powers, they are a nation [*millet*] who raise an outcry for the smallest of causes and are cowardly and coy like a woman. Just to the contrary, Kurds are strong and quarrelsome. . . . In these regions [*buralarda*] the Kurds have always been considered as the gentlemen and the Armenians the male servants.[111]

The sultan's explanations for the violence of the mid-1890s followed a pattern of explanation that denied indigenous causes or governmental responsibility for massacre. Rather blame was placed on the victims themselves and on foreign powers. In her study of the development of Turkish denialism, the historical sociologist Fatma Müge Göçek maintains, "during this phase of Ottoman rule, the Ottoman ethical framework gave precedence to the preservation of the sultan's dynasty. Since the sultan's rule was legitimated through the delivery of justice to all his subjects, rather than acknowledge the failure in such delivery to his Armenian subjects through the reforms of 1839, 1856 and 1876, the sultan instead blamed the intervention of the Great Powers in the affairs of the empire thereby claiming that the Armenian unrest and ensuing massacres had foreign origins. The denial of the domestic origins of the violence against the Armenians thus comprised the first stage of denial."[112]

When *The New York Times* reported the burning of five Armenian villages and the rendering of five thousand Armenians homeless in the late summer of 1895, the newspaper noted that "the Turkish authorities," responding to an attack on Turkish gendarmes by a "band of brigands," decided "without making any inquiry," that "the assailants were Armenian revolutionaries from Kemakh, who intended to release exalted Armenians who are still in prison at Kars." The headline of the brief article read "Another Armenian Holocaust," the first instance of the use of that biblical term to refer to mass killing of Armenians.[113]

The Hamidian massacres were designed to pacify a troubled region; repress a people, the Armenians, considered seditious and insurrectionary; and forge ties of mutual advantage between the state and the Kurdish tribesmen. A few years before the massacres, Abdülhamid had mused that the British, French, and Russians had benefited from the activities of missionaries since "religious influence is then transformed into political leverage." His government, however, could not restrain the Christian missionaries because that would bring down the wrath of the Europeans on the Porte. To avoid "the vexing interventions of the three powers' ambassadors," the "only way to fight against them is to increase the Islamic population and spread the belief in the Holiest of Faiths."[114] The methods used were not simply those of conventional policing or even military suppression but also involved the unleashing and encouragement of irregular forces and ordinary people to take matters into their own hands and launch massive killing indiscriminately on a designated population—men, women, and children alike. The contradictions inherent in an Islamic state, ostensibly dedicated to protection of the People of the Book, and the mass killing of innocents were borne out in the speeches of Sadeddin Paşa, the officer whom Abdülhamid sent to the eastern provinces in early 1895. When he spoke to Muslims, he urged them to refrain from mistreating Christians. "My co-religionists! Our exalted prophet [Muhammad] decrees 'he who tortures Christians or Jews cannot find comfort in heaven. . . .' Likewise the Ottoman sultan abided by these principles and offered the same protection for six hundred years." In the modern age, "the age of communication," he warned, "the whole world learns what is happening even in remote places in half an hour." He reassured his audience that the sultan had not and would not "give in to the Armenians. . . . There is no truth to the news you have heard that the Armenians have been granted a principality. In this province [Van], there are three Muslims for every Armenian. How is it possible for one Armenian to dominate three Muslims?"[115] But when he spoke to the Armenians in the East, Sadeddin Paşa warned them that they were "traveling down a wrong path, with the danger of death awaiting" them. As the representative of the Ottoman state, he told them, "Give up, do not deviate from the path you have been following for the last four centuries; do not part from loyalty. You will regret it. And regrets after the fact would be of no use." Armenians, he added, were no match for Kurds. "Do not plunge into any rash acts. If you do, you will find yourselves alone with the Kurds. . . . Kurds are warriors, Armenians [are] cowards from birth. In addition, one can guess where the Armenians' lack of familiarity with arms will lead."[116]

While there was both spontaneous violence at the village and city level and organized Kurdish attacks, the bulk of the killing in the mid-1890s was the result of government troops and the crowds they licensed to kill. When the massacres ended, it was estimated that some 100,000 to 300,000 Armenians had lost their lives. No one knows for sure. The American clergyman and journalist George Hughes Hepworth, who traveled to eastern Anatolia after the massacres on assignment from the sultan to report on them, wrote, "Neither [the sultan] nor anyone else knows how many were killed during these massacres, for accuracy is impossible. The Armenians cannot be safely trusted because their terror makes multiplication easy. The Turkish officials cannot be trusted, for since all Europe was infuriated their business was to minimize the affair."[117]

Europe was shocked once again. The emperor of Germany, Wilhelm II, who had earlier befriended Abdülhamid and would later as well, exclaimed, "The Sultan must be deposed."[118] The British too entertained such thoughts, but within weeks the passions generated by the massacres in Istanbul dissipated. Most of Europe still preferred keeping the Ottoman Empire intact rather than dividing it up. The Russians briefly considered sending its fleet to take control of the northern end of the Bosphorus, but ultimately the tsar decided not to act unilaterally. All the powers agreed that if the Porte did not initiate reforms they were prepared to use force. Finally, in February 1897, after months of deliberations, the ambassadors in Istanbul finished yet another reform plan, which ran to sixty-four pages. But they never submitted it to the sultan, for a crisis over the island of Crete led to a brief Greco-Ottoman war and superseded their concern for the Armenians.

Blame for the mass killing of Armenians in the mid-1890s must fall on the highest levels of the state. The sultan himself had encouraged and supported anti-Christian, particularly anti-Armenian, propaganda. In some places, like Urfa, the fierce hostility toward Armenians was generated by fears that these particular Christians presented a danger to Islam and to the authority of the ruling Muslims. The ease with which the religious students, the *softas*, could be mobilized testifies to the fervor and fear of the future that drove the faithful. Yet in other places religion was not a primary motivating force. Simple greed or lust accounted for atrocities. In Istanbul most of the killing took place in the prosperous Europeanized Pera district, and hundreds of shops were looted. At the same time that merchants and the wealthy were attacked, most of the victims were simple porters, the ubiquitous and more vulnerable *hamals*.[119] Since the authorities intervened reluctantly and late, allowing "popular justice" to take its course and then rarely punished those who tormented Armenians, the permissiveness of the state not only allowed but contributed to the escalation of violence. Individual cruelty, even sadism, ran free without restraint. In some places, like Samsun, the local governor would not permit attacks on Armenians, and none occurred.[120] "Religious fanaticism probably played a smaller part in the massacres than is generally supposed," the British embassy memorandum of December 1896 pointed out. "After the massacres the Moslems were generally ready to fraternize with the surviving Christians, whom they treated good-humouredly as people who had had a severe lesson and might be expected to behave better in the future." Pessimistically, fatalistically, it concluded, "It is impossible to improve the condition of the Christians under a Moslem Government in Turkey, except within the limitations of what is really the fundamental law of the Empire, viz., that Moslems are a privileged aristocracy superior to Christians."[121]

In later years, after the Genocide of 1915, many read the Hamidian massacres as the first stage of a series of massacres that would culminate in genocide. A number of historians believe that a policy of eliminating the Armenians already existed in the minds of Hamidian officials. Others view the Hamidian model of imperial rule as leading inevitably to the genocide that lay ahead.[122] On closer examination, however, the Hamidian killings were not genocidal but a kind of "exemplary repression," demonstrating to the sultan's subjects what the consequences of resistance and rebellion would be. Unlike the Genocide of 1915–1916, the 1894–1896 massacres were not intended to eliminate the sultan's Armenian subjects but rather to restore the old equilibrium in inter-ethnic relations, an imperial settlement in which the subject peoples would accept the dominance of the Ottoman Muslim elite with little overt questioning. That equilibrium, however, had already been upset by four factors: the European intervention that internationalized the Armenian Question; the Armenians' appeals to the Europeans for assistance in reforming the empire; the sultan's own policies of centralization and bureaucratization; and the sultan's strategic alliance with Muslim

Kurds against Christian Armenians. At the same time the program to support the in-migration of Muslims (*muhacir*) from the Caucasus and the Balkans changed the demographic balance in the region in favor of the Muslims. "Now, thanks to the wise measures taken by Your Majesty," one provincial governor wrote to the sultan, "Muslims are a majority everywhere."[123] Abdülhamid's pro-Islamic policy, institutionalized in the irregular *Hamidiye* units of armed Kurds, undermined the customary system of imperial rule as much as did the emerging new vision of nationality borrowed from the West.[124] The exercise of massacre, which culminated in the mass killings of 1894–1896, was a means of maintaining the decaying status quo as the preferred alternative to reform and concessions to the Armenians.[125]

Difference need not lead to conflict, and conflict need not lead to killing, mass murder, or genocide. But markers of difference define the lines along which such conflict or killing might take place. The lines are not given by nature but are constructed in culture and experience. Armenians developed over time ideas about Turks and Kurds, and they about Armenians, all against the background of the enforced and religiously sanctioned superiority of Muslims and the inferiority of the *gavur* (unbeliever). Armenians and other non-Muslims were referred to as *gavur* (*kafir* in Arabic), a potent word that connoted a miscreant or ingrate, who did not appreciate the good done to him or her by those better off.[126] In the folk expressions and sayings of common people, the *gavur* was by nature disloyal, avaricious, and not to be trusted. "Good done to a *gavur* brings no good in return." Friendship with such people was impossible, even dangerous.[127] But such stereotypes and essentialized characterizations of others had long been commonplace. They did not of necessity lead to conflict, violence, or genocide.

Armenians had no state of their own like the Greeks that might protest their treatment; they did not constitute a large percentage of the population like the Kurds and Arabs. They were unprotected, relatively weak, and thus the easiest and most vulnerable group on which social, ethnic, and religious grievances might be concentrated. By encouraging the anti-Armenian hostility of the Muslims, the state created an

Armenian scapegoat that could be blamed for the defeats and failures of the Ottoman government. Shifting responsibility and guilt onto others was (and still is) a potent tool of governing, usually used by weak or threatened states. The Ottomans maintained the social system in eastern Anatolia by violence, now state violence, and rejected the claims of their Armenian subjects for a more just relationship. Abdülhamid and his supporters elaborated a rhetoric justifying massacres as strategically necessary and as legitimate means to preserve the integrity of the state. Those who participated in the massacres—whether out of resentment, rage, religious fervor, personal greed, conviction that the Armenians were a threat to their traditional values or the state, or a combination of these motivations—did so largely with impunity. The authorities punished few if any perpetrators of the violence and rendered justice to few of the victims. A pattern of permitting violence and justifying it in the name of religion or state security was established. No right of popular resistance was recognized, and all acts of protest, resistance, or rebellion were seen as the result of the artificial intervention of outside agitators. Moreover, the view developed that not Turks or Kurds but the Armenians themselves were responsible for the disaster that befell them and that explanation would be repeated in the 1909 massacres in Adana and again in the Genocide of 1915. One Turkish official told an American investigator at the time of the Hamidian atrocities, "I assert that the Armenians have brought the calamity on themselves by their ambition for autonomy."[128]

Even more pernicious was a tendency to view Armenians as outsiders rather than legitimate members of society, a disposition to construct the Armenians as a threat to what was normal, familiar, sacred, or treasured. Long treated as different, the *dhimmi* were easily identified, marginalized, and mistreated. Through the nineteenth century they became objects of suspicion, placed outside the law and the protection of the state. At moments of vulnerability or sensing danger people could easily turn on those enemies living among them whose very religion, education, and way of life were believed to tie them to foreign enemies. During the early years of Abdülhamid's reign the Armenians ceased being considered the "loyal *millet*" and increasingly were perceived as alien to the empire, foreigners within the imperial body, outsiders. They had become a problem.

These attitudes and beliefs at the top of the state were not simply cognitive conclusions but were heavily inflected with and by emotions. Deep sentiments like resentment, fear, anger, and hatred were integral to the mental universe of those constructing the Armenians as foreign, deceptive, and treacherous. The emotional world—or affective disposition—involves certain proclivities to belief, perception, and behavior, the context in which certain actions are likely to occur and other choices are not made. Conceptually affective disposition bridges the space between structural and environmental influences and human action. Rather than structures, environmental conditions, or experience determining motivation for action, it is within the affective disposition that particular meanings are created, and it is on the basis of those understandings that people are propelled to act on their feelings and convictions.

The sultan believed that his state's security required the further Islamization of the empire. According to his private secretary, Abdülhamid believed that the Ottomans should no longer "stick splinters in our own flesh by welcoming sectarians [*sectateurs*] of alien religions. Within the limits of our State, we can tolerate but members of our own nation [*people*] and believers [*sectateurs*] in our own faith. We must see to reinforcing the Turkish element." Abdülhamid worried about the flow of Muslim refugees from the Balkans, which weakened Istanbul's hold on Ottoman Europe, Rumelia. "We must reinforce as much as possible the Muslim element in Rumelia, and quite especially in Anatolia; first of all, what we have to do is to assimilate to us the Kurds."[129] Armenians, on the other hand, were a recalcitrant group, difficult to control or convert, and in the views of the authorities not to be trusted.

State authorities, foreign observers, and the revolutionaries themselves exaggerated the influence and effectiveness of the Armenian revolutionary committees. The activities of Armenian revolutionaries frightened the American missionary Cyrus Hamlin, one of the founders of the famous Robert College on the Bosphorus. In December 1893 he published a short article in *The Congregationist*, which would prove formative in what would later be known as the provocation thesis, that is, the argument that the Armenians provoked the Ottomans deliberately and therefore deserved what befell them. Hamlin reported a conversation with a "very intelligent Armenian gentleman, who speaks fluently and correctly English as well as Armenian, and is an eloquent defender of the revolution." The Armenian assured Hamlin that the Ottoman Armenians had "the strongest hopes of preparing the way for Russia's entrance to Asia Minor to take possession." This would be accomplished by Hnchak bands, which "will watch their opportunities to kill Turks and Kurds, set fire to their villages and then make their escape into the mountains. The enraged Moslems will then rise and fall upon the defenseless Armenians and slaughter them with such barbarities that Russia will enter in the name of humanity and Christian civilization and take possession." Shocked, Hamlin "denounced the scheme as atrocious and infernal beyond anything ever known." "We Armenians are determined to be free," the Armenian responded. "Europe listened to the Bulgarian horrors and made Bulgaria free. She will listen to our cry when it goes up in the shrieks and blood of millions of women and children." Hamlin pointed out that "your people do not want Russian protection. They prefer Turkey, bad as she is." "Yes," he replied, "and for such stupidity they will have to suffer."[130]

In a letter published a year later in the *New York Herald* (December 20, 1894), Hamlin again raised the issue of Armenian revolutionaries. But here, in words less often reproduced, he stressed that the Ottoman government had no reason to fear such a movement for it "knows well that there is no place in the Empire where one thousand or even one hundred Armenians could assemble with hostile intent. And besides they have no arms, and they are not accustomed to their use. They would be lambs in the midst of wolves." He went on to point out that "[t]he plots of the revolutionists were harmless as to any effective force, but were very pernicious in arousing fanaticism. The fact that a few hairbrained young men in foreign lands had plotted a revolution was sufficient reason in the view of Moslem fanaticism for devoting the whole race to destruction. It was this which I feared and it is this which has happened."[131]

"The change produced in Ottoman feeling was enormous," wrote the British diplomat Charles Eliot, who served in Turkey in the mid-1890s. "The Turks had formerly regarded the Armenians as the best kind of Giaour—harmless, serviceable, comfortable infidels, whom one could not expect to meet in heaven but who were very useful here below. But it now appeared that this was not the case." Armenians appeared "as seditious as Greeks and Bulgarians; they had secret committees and revolutionary printing-presses; they were probably arming and conspiring to massacre good Moslems." Eliot concluded "that the fears of the Turks, however unfounded we may think them, were wide-spread and quite genuine."[132]

Fear of the Armenians was greatly exaggerated. While radicals struggled to convince villagers of the Armenian cause and threatened businessmen who refused to contribute to their movement, the number of militants remained small and their ranks divided. Armenian nationalists were forced to rely on handfuls of activists, many from Persia and Russia. Yet a few determined men or women, daring to strike out at established authority, unafraid of losing their lives and willing to kill others, were able to shatter the normal, oppressive tranquility of social order, frighten their powerful opponents, and inspire others to follow them. Their efforts at "propaganda of the deed," spectacular activities like terrorist attacks or the seizure of the Imperial Bank Ottoman, however, proved counterproductive. The Bank Ottoman seizure was followed by riots and massacres in the city that left five to six thousand Armenians dead, and Europeans failed to come to the aid of the victims. After losing their leader and several of their men, all the Dashnaks gained was public notoriety and safe passage to Europe.

The events of the 1894–1896 left the Armenians of the Ottoman Empire exposed and more vulnerable than ever. The American clergyman George Hughes Hepworth feared the worst: "[D]uring my travels in Armenia I have become more and more deeply convinced that the future of the Armenians is extremely clouded. It may be that the hand of the

Turks will be held back through fear of Europe, but I am sure that the object of the Turk is extermination, and that he will pursue that end if the opportunity offers. He has already come very near to its accomplishment, for the Armenians of to-day are an impoverished people, hopeless and in despair."[133]

Sympathy for the plight of the Armenians was widespread in the international public sphere, but humanitarian sentiments rarely led to meaningful action.[134] In Germany, the Protestant vicar Johannes Lepsius took up the Armenian cause, collected information on the Hamidian massacres, and in September 1896 published a scathing report in his book *Armenien und Europa* (Armenia and Europe). French and English translations made him an international public figure, a credible reporter on the atrocities that had taken place in Anatolia. The media spread the stories of Turkish atrocities and Armenian suffering throughout the world. International humanitarianism mobilized its forces. Religious groups, the peace movement, and the Socialist International expressed outrage at what had happened and sympathy for the Armenians. Volunteers collected money for Armenian refugees and orphans. Dreyfusards launched the journal *Pro Arménia* with an editorial board of leftist luminaries. The eminent French politician Georges Clemenceau contributed the foreword to a book of eyewitness accounts of the massacres.[135] Americans organized "Armenian Sundays" across the nation.[136] Theodore Roosevelt, who like many Americans considered European diplomacy to be perfidious and unwilling to do its "duty to humanity," saw himself as a champion of the oppressed Armenians. After he became president he told a friend, "As for the Armenians in Turkey, if I could get this people to back me I really think I should be tempted to go into a crusade against the Turk."[137] The United States supported its Protestant missions and schools in the Ottoman Empire and readily naturalized Armenians who converted, making them American citizens and giving them protection of the U.S. government, including immunity from Ottoman courts, but there was no serious move to intervene further into Ottoman politics. The Porte protested, demanding that the 1830 treaty with the United States be amended, but Protestants, like Roberts College President

George Washburn, convinced politicians at home to prevent any change in the treaty.[138]

With the end of the massacres Abdülhamid stabilized his regime. In some ways he was in a stronger position than in his first two decades in power. Many Kurds were allies and organized in the *Hamidiye* regiments; Armenians pulled back from revolutionary activity and either rebuilt their lives in the ruined landscape or (like my maternal grandmother's family) emigrated. Abdülhamid found unexpected political support from outside. The German kaiser favored the Ottoman Empire in his expansionist program of *Weltpolitik* (World Policy). Concerned about the "Slavic" menace from the East, he shared with the sultan a sense of danger from Russia.[139] Wilhelm II visited Istanbul in 1898 and met privately with the sultan, who impressed him with the trappings of his autocratic office. By drawing close to the sultan, whom he privately referred to as a scoundrel (*Schurke*), the kaiser expanded his influence in the East, defying the British and French sway over the Middle East. The kaiser's "civilizing mission" extended not only to Germany's eastern borderlands but to the Muslim world as well. Wilhelm declared in Damascus that he was the eternal friend of 300 million Muslims, and the Germans sealed their friendship with the Ottomans with an agreement engaging the Germans to build the Berlin to Baghdad railroad.[140]

The Hamidian regime did more to incite than to modulate the mutual suspicions of Turks, Kurds, and Armenians. A *vali* or *kaymakam* in a province or town could choose to either ameliorate conditions and forestall clashes or play to the fears of his constituents and promote violence. An American physician and missionary, Clarence D. Ussher, noted how on the eve of the 1908 Young Turk coup, the *vali* of Van echoed "his royal master, Abdul Hamid, in character and methods. He used every means in his power to incite the Armenians to revolt in order to have a pretext for massacring them. But, Ussher reported, many Armenians were unhappy with the "constant endeavor of the revolutionists . . . to draw the attention of Europe to the Armenians and the way in which they were treated by the Ottoman Government." Deeply religious, the peasants in particular rejected "the infidel propaganda conducted by some of [the revolutionary] leaders" and "finally compelled them to abandon it. This propaganda had filled the Turks with horror and had, no doubt, not a little to do with enabling the intriguing Vali to arouse their hostility to Armenians generally."[141] Indeed a spark set off a conflagration, and one hundred Armenian merchants in Van were massacred, their bodies thrown into the lake.

State security has a logic of its own. In a world where protection of state authority and the existing social order is estimated to overrule the welfare of the subjects of the state, resistance is regarded as criminal behavior. Almost any resistance is treated as rebellion and seen as a declaration of war against the authority of the state. Rather than normal politics of negotiation and compromise, both sides invoke the logic of war—rendering the enemy incapable of effective resistance, acting preemptively to prevent expected danger. Criminal or insurrectionary acts of individuals or small groups are treated as acts by a whole people. Yet even that logic places limits on the punishment of those not directly involved, the wanton killing of the innocent, and the indiscriminate slaughter of noncombatants, women and children whose only guilt is their ethnic or religious kinship with the initial perpetrators of violence. That form of retribution, collective punishment, would in time be considered a violation of the laws of war and the Geneva Conventions. A line has been crossed when either rebels or the state target noncombatants, and a different moral verdict must be pronounced.

The Hamidian system lasted thirty years. It was characterized by incomplete attempts at centralization, along with empowerment of regional elites and lawless exploitation of the most vulnerable ordinary subjects, tempered by periodic resort to mass violence by the state and its agents. The very cruelty, injustice, and arbitrariness of Hamidian rule produced dissent, opposition, and resistance—eventually leading to the overthrow of the sultan. Despite what Abdülhamid and his officials imagined, the most immediate threat to the sultan came not from a scattered, repressed Christian people but from determined Turkish oppositionists increasingly alienated from the regime. Turks, Kurds, and Armenians were prepared to resist the "Bloody Sultan," and influenced by the Armenian revolutionary committees, Young Turks turned toward more radical solutions to stem the empire's decline. Organizing against Abdülhamid, the Turkish oppositionists promised another road to the empire's future: through constitutionalism, revival of the *Tanzimat*, and equality of all the sultan's subjects in a common effort to create a modern state.

CHAPTER FIVE

Revolution

DEBUT OF THE ARMENIAN REVOLUTIONARIES

Beginning in the 1890s and continuing through the first decade of the twentieth century, up to the Young Turk Revolution of 1908, a veritable war existed between the Ottoman state and a militant opposition to the sultan's regime. Up to the coup that would limit his power and eventually overthrow him, Abdülhamid II faced the threat of various revolutionary movements—the Macedonian, the Armenian, and the Young Turk, as well as other nascent nationalist and sometimes separatist stirrings among Arabs, Albanians, Circassians, and Kurds. Reflecting a widespread belief in the efficacy of revolutionary violence, young people in particular took up guns, knives, and bombs to incite ordinary men and women to resist state repression at the turn of the twentieth century. Europe and the Ottoman Empire lived with a generalized fear of "anarchists," who targeted prominent politicians and heads of state.[1] Inspired by Russian revolutionaries, Macedonian radicals launched an armed uprising against the imperial regime in 1903. Twenty thousand rebels faced 200,000 Ottoman soldiers. Defeated, with thousands killed and hundreds of villages burned, the Macedonians nevertheless continued their terrorist campaigns.[2] The rivalries between Christians and Muslims, and between Orthodox Greeks and Orthodox Bulgarians, as well as the armed resistance by thousands of Albanians, kept the Balkans unstable and presented constant problems for Istanbul. On the eve of World War I the various Balkan states went to war with Turkey and one another, and almost all of the Ottoman holdings in Europe were lost.

Although Armenians organized revolutionary committees, local defense of Armenian villagers, and individual acts of terrorism, they did not mobilize large numbers of their countrymen in frontal attacks on the

Ottoman state as did the Macedonians, the Albanians, the Kurds, and, eventually, the Young Turks. What the Armenians lacked in numbers, they more than made up for in the determination and ferocity of their resistance, qualities that inspired both admiration and fear within the Turkish opposition. Much of Armenian violence, with the exception of the spectacular seizure of the Bank Ottoman in 1896 and individual assassinations, was conceived as self-defense against the rapacious extortions of Kurdish tribesmen. Terror was deployed for a variety of purposes: to protect and defend, to revenge injustices, to inspire the victimized Armenian peasants to resist, to convince the sultan to implement reforms, and to pressure Europe to fulfill its promises.

Hnchaks and Dashnaks alike advocated individual terrorism as a tactic, both against those who abused their countrymen and against fellow Armenians in order to extract revenue or eliminate collaborators. They required wealthy Armenians to contribute to the party or face reprisals. The bourgeois of the towns were reluctant to aid the revolutionaries who threatened the comfortable equilibrium that they maintained with the Ottomans.[3] What a Dashnak historian calls "demonstrative activities and propaganda" in 1894–1896 involved assassinations of Armenians "who served the Sultan and the Turkish government," among them a "spy," a police chief, a defrocked celibate priest, and a surgeon.[4] In July 1895 two men brutally murdered a prominent Protestant Armenian, Kuyumcu Garabet, near his church in the town of Marsovan. The killers stabbed Garabet seventeen times, ripping open his abdomen. One was captured soon after and turned out to be a member of an Armenian revolutionary committee that had concluded that the jeweler Garabet was a traitor who had been reporting to the authorities on the political activity of Armenians. Two weeks later a second Armenian was assassinated in a similarly sanguinary manner. Two hundred Armenians were arrested and questioned. A fire broke out mysteriously in a new Turkish school. Muslims gathered in mosques and talked about massacring the Christians, but the crackdown on the Armenians appeared sufficient to prevent further violence.[5]

For the Armenian revolutionaries "terrorist" was not a word of disapprobation but characterized a warrior hero prepared if necessary to become a martyr (*martyros* or *nahadak*). Young militants modeled themselves on the ancient hero Vardan Mamikonian, the martyr to the Christian faith in the fifth century, and the novelist Raffi invoked the image of Vardan in several of his popular works.[6] Even as they used rhetoric that originated in the church, the revolutionaries challenged the established clerical and bourgeois authorities and laid a bold claim to represent and even lead the whole of the Armenian nation. Their sacrifice was for the Armenian people, not Christianity. Emotionally and strategically they were driven by a sense of urgency that Armenians would soon cease to exist as a people if brave men were not prepared to sacrifice themselves. For some there could be no cooperation with the oppressors, the Turks and Kurds, and any violation by those who ruled the country had to be avenged; for others the only rational choice was to ally with the potentially progressive elements among the Muslims and together fight Hamidian reaction.

In the summer of 1897 the Dashnaks attacked the Sublime Porte with bombs, but their attempt to arouse concern for Armenians (as reported by a Dashnak historian) "did not achieve the expected results and was unsuccessful as an act of propaganda."[7] Individuals transported arms from the Caucasus and Persia into the Ottoman Empire, and Hnchaks and Dashnak party members either initiated or participated in a few battles with Kurdish or Ottoman forces. The largest operation, the Khanasor Expedition, involved 253 guerrillas. Before the attack their leaders posed before a banner with skull and crossed bones and the word *vrezh* (revenge) on it. Fierce in their demeanor, armed with long rifles, daggers, and bandoleers of ammunition across their chests, they were model *fedayi*, those who sacrifice. The fighters crossed over from Persia and attacked a Kurdish tribe, the Mazriks, slaughtering nearly all the adult men. Kurds counterattacked, pursuing the Armenians toward Persia and killing twenty of them.[8]

Throughout Anatolia the Armenian revolutionaries formed committees (*komitener*), which were admired and imitated by the Turkish radicals opposed to Abdülhamid's regime. Within Ottoman territory the Dashnaks were most successful in organizing peasants in the Van and Muş-Sasun regions. In the aftermath of the Hamidian massacres of 1894–1896, Dashnak leaders were discouraged by the failure of their campaigns to achieve the necessary response from the European powers. For the next five years they curtailed revolutionary activity while supporting and even participating in the Macedonian resistance.[9] Secret negotiations between the Dashnaks and the Hamidian regime were carried out through the intermediation of prominent Armenians loyal to the sultan, Artin Paşa Dadian; his son, Diran Bey Dadian; and his nephew, Drtad Bey Dadian, who spent eight months in Geneva seeking an end to Dashnak terrorism. The Dadians' mission failed, and the Armenian revolutionaries looked to the nascent Turkish opposition to Abdülhamid—the Young Turks as they were known—as possible partners in their campaign to change the Hamidian regime.[10]

At first the Dashnaks were skeptical of "the seriousness of [the Young Turks'] desire for reform," not having seen in the past twenty years "this party attempt to protest the crowned murderer's unexampled injustices and outrageous crimes in *active* form." A failed attempt at a coup d'état in 1896 against the sultan led to arrests and the suppression of the Turkish radicals. Just before the turn of the century, the Dashnaks sensed a more militant mood within the Turkish opposition. "Today, however, we are happy to be able to point out that groups which . . . have split off from this movement are professing more radical ideas . . . [and] have invited us to show our solidarity with them. . . . If, today, there exists a degree of national antagonism between Ottoman Turks and Ottoman Armenians, the blame for it lies primarily with the government. We are convinced that, in future, once acceptable political conditions have been brought about in Turkey, our two nations will continue to live in peace and harmony and will, united in a common effort, make their way toward the highest form of civilization."[11]

Cooperation was possible between Armenian and Turkish opponents of the sultan as long as the Armenians made it clear that they did not desire separation from the Ottoman Empire and an independent state. At their Fourth World Congress in Vienna in 1907, the Dashnaks adopted the slogan "Oppressed of all nations, unite!" The goal of their struggle was to establish democratic federations in both Russia and the Ottoman Empire. There was no call for separation or independence for the Armenians. They affirmed their socialist platform, linking their

Andtranik Ozanian (1865–1927), Armenian revolutionary and commander of volunteers against the Ottoman Empire. The New Armenia Pub. Co. (1920).

movement with the most determined radical movements in Europe. For most Dashnaks, however, socialism remained a rhetorical cover behind which the national struggle was fought.[12] The Dashnaks' terrorist committee continued assassinations of dissident or separatist activists. Several important party notables fell victim to internal bloodletting.

The persistent tensions and frequent disputes between Muslims and Armenians could without warning flare up into armed clashes. In the mountain town of Sasun, near Muş, where Hamidian massacres had occurred ten years earlier, Armenian revolutionaries organized armed bands to defend the region from marauding Kurds. In 1901 and again in 1904 *fedayi* led by the intrepid Andranik Ozanian fought with Ottoman soldiers near Muş. Holed up in *Arakelots* (Holy Apostles) Monastery, about fifty men resisted thousands of Ottomans for several weeks, finally slipping away in small groups. A little more than two years later ten thousand Ottoman soldiers and about six to seven thousand Kurdish irregulars surrounded some two hundred Armenian guerrillas. Unarmed villagers joined the resistance. The *fedayi* Kevork Chavush, a local fighter known as the "Lion of the Mountains" (*Sareru aslan*), launched a preemptive strike against some Kurdish villages in January 1904. The Ottoman forces rallied and counterattacked some months later, only to be routed by the guerrillas. After bringing in artillery, the army drove the rebels and thousands of villagers into the mountains. In the aftermath thousands of Armenians were massacred, and forty-five villages razed.[13] The Armenian catholicos, Khrimian, pleaded with the Russian tsar, Nicholas II, to intercede with other Great Powers to pressure the Porte to stop the atrocities.[14] Two leaders of the rebellion, Andranik and Serop, also wrote to the European diplomats to clarify that the aim of the rebels was reform, not "any interference with the territorial integrity of the Ottoman Empire, or at any form of political separation. Armenians claim no sovereignty over the races living with them; they simply claim such administrative reforms as will protect their persons and property from the attacks of the local authorities, from Turks and from Kurds."[15]

Desperately impatient, Armenian revolutionaries were significantly more militant and willing to use violence against the Hamidian regime than many of the Young Turks. One of the founders of the Dashnaktsutyun, Kristapor Mikayelian, dedicated himself to carrying out a plan to assassinate Abdülhamid. Other attempts by Greek conspirators and the Young Turks had failed. Mikayelian's elaborate plot centered on exploding multiple bombs near the reclusive sultan's carriage as he emerged from the palace for the ritual of Friday prayers. Such a dramatic assassination would make visible to Europeans the determination of the Armenians and demonstrate the vulnerability of the Ottoman state. But while testing bombs in Bulgaria, Mikayelian and a young comrade were themselves blown up. The Dashnaks went ahead with their plan, and on July 21, 1905, the carriage wired with explosives exploded, killing twenty-eight bystanders and guards and wounding another fifty-six. The sultan, how-ever, delayed in conversation with the Sheik-ul-Islam, was unhurt and demonstratively drove his own carriage to the safety of his palace. Once again the Armenian revolutionaries had failed to achieve their principal goals. The sultan lived; the Dashnaks' secret networks were discovered; and, though some Turkish revolutionaries praised the bombing, many Muslims opposed to Abdülhamid were appalled by the Armenians' plans to unleash a wave of revolutionary violence.[16] Innocent people died, and the prestige and power of the regime did not suffer particularly from this demonstrative act. Europeans indicated that they admired the courage and resilience of the sultan.

THE YOUNG TURKS AND THE MODERNIZING EMPIRE

In the second half of the nineteenth century Turkic intellectuals, in both the Ottoman and Russian Empires, aroused interest in a new conception of a Turkish nation. Responding to the works of European Orientalists who discussed an original Turkic or Turanian race, men like Ismail Gasprinskii in Crimea, Mirza Fethali Akhundov in South Caucasia, and Huseynizade bey Ali from Baku attempted to teach pride in being Turkish and speak-ing a Turkic language. Identification with a supranational community of Turks distinguished the race or nation of the Turks from the multinational Ottoman state.[17] Yet inherent in that identification with the Turkic was a confusion about the boundaries of the nation and the location and limits of the fatherland (*vatan*). Was the homeland of the Ottomans the Balkans or Anatolia or the somewhat mystical Turan of Central Asia?

The roots of Kemalist Turkish nationalism may be traced back into the late Ottoman period, yet before 1908 Turkish nationalist ideas were confined almost exclusively to a small number of intellectuals and radical oppositionists. Allegiance to the nation of Turks was quite weak in the late Ottoman Empire. The first intellectual opponents to the regime of Abdülhamid were more Ottomanist than nationalist, that is, favoring a cosmopolitan, multinational society within a modern form of the impe-rial state. In 1889 a number of students at the military medical school in

Istanbul organized the first oppositional group, the Committee of Ottoman Union (*İttihad-ı Osmani Cemiyeti*). Among Ottomans multiple identifications competed, such as religion, ethnicity, empire, or subnational communities, like tribes, clans, or regions. An ambiguity about what constituted the nation thwarted (or at least delayed) the development of a strong and coherent nationalism among Ottoman Turks.

The word *Türk*, which referred to the lower classes of rural Anatolia, was in the nineteenth century contrasted to *Osmanlı* (Ottoman), a term usually reserved for the ruling elite. Islam also had a far more positive valence among ordinary Muslims than identification with being Turkish. There were signs of change, however, in the last quarter of the nineteenth century, and the shift came from the top down. The Ottoman Constitution of 1876 established Ottoman Turkish (*Osmanlıca*) as the official state language and required members of government and Parliament to know it. At the turn of the century Young Turk nationalists, like Ahmed Rıza, began to substitute the word *Türk* for "Ottoman."[18] Turkish nationalist ideas rivaled the ecumenical Ottomanist views that remained dominant among the first generation of Young Turk intellectuals. Rival visions of the future, however, led to tensions between the dominant Turks and the non-Turkish *millet*s, particularly the Armenians, and over time reduced the Young Turks' commitment to Ottomanism. However slight the influence of Turkism was in the Ottoman twilight, such ideas grew in the years before, during, and after World War I to become fundamental to the ideology of the future Turkish Republic.

Yet before World War I, the Ottoman Turkish opposition was marked more by shared anxieties than by clear programmatic positions. As one writer put it, "In reality, the Young Turks did not have a common view but common 'worries' that the Ottoman Empire was drifting towards an inescapable fall."[19] A participant in the movement against Abdülhamid remembered, "We woke up each day with a news which discouraged us, filled us with despair and which was revolting to us. A dark cloud followed upon the heels of the morning sun which appeared in the horizon. Fires erupted here and there in the country; before the Cretan uprising could be suppressed, Kurdish, Albanian and Armenian movements came to the open. The accursed rushed from place to place in the horizon, starting fires everywhere. The Turks were rushed to wherever it went, and attempts were made to put out the fires with their blood."[20]

The Young Turk opposition to Abdülhamid was not tightly bound by a single ideology. Its ranks included revolutionaries and gradualists, religious critics and militant secularists, constitutionalist opponents of autocracy and even non-Muslim federalists. Turn-of-the-century Turkish revolutionaries, including some who would later lead the Kemalist movement, grew out of an intellectual milieu that exalted science, rejected religion, and borrowed freely from Western sociology. Influenced by the ideas of Charles Darwin, Claude Bernard, Ludwig Buchner, and even the crowd studies and phrenology of Gustave Le Bon (who set out to prove that intellectuals have larger craniums by doing research in Parisian millinery shops), "the Young Turk ideology was originally 'scientific,' materialist, social Darwinist, elitist, and vehemently antireligious; it did not favor representative government."[21] Neither liberals nor constitutionalists, the Young Turks were étatists who saw themselves as continuing the modernizing projects of the *Tanzimat* reformers—Mustafa Reşid Paşa, Mustafa Fazıl Paşa, and Midhat Paşa—and the work of the Young Ottomans.[22] Earlier, Ottoman Westernizers had hoped to secure Western technology without succumbing to Western culture, somehow to preserve Islam but make the empire technologically and militarily competitive with the West. Reform had always come from above, from Westernizing statesmen and bureaucrats, a response to a sense that the empire had to change or collapse. The Young Turks shared those values, but steadily added new elements of Turkism to their imperial étatism.

WORKING TOGETHER SEPARATELY: YOUNG TURKS AND ARMENIAN REVOLUTIONARIES

The fledgling Turkish and Armenian revolutionary movements found refuge outside the Ottoman lands, in Tiflis, Geneva, and Paris. While the Hamidian massacres raged in Anatolia, Turkish radicals, among them Ahmed Rıza, met with their Armenian counterparts in Paris, appalled by the regime's treatment of Ottoman subjects. Even as a Turkish nationalist, Rıza believed that the Hamidian massacres of Armenians "flew in the face of the traditions of Islamicism and the precepts of the Koran." Directing his criticism at Abdülhamid, he proposed, "We wish to see the sultan surrounded by counselors who are steeped in both Muslim precepts and the ideas of order and progress."[23] Even though the Turkish oppositionists were more moderate and more willing to compromise with the imperial state than were the Armenians, the Armenian and Turkish activists worked together on occasion. Despite their suspicions of each other, in 1899 they sent a joint delegation, headed by Rıza, to the Hague Peace Conference.[24]

The tensions within the Young Turk movement between Ottomanists and Turkish nationalists erupted at the First Congress of the Ottoman Opposition, which opened in Paris on February 4, 1902, and was attended by Armenian representatives. The nationalist minority at the Congress, led by Ahmed Rıza, categorically rejected foreign intervention and any special arrangements for the Armenians in the six eastern Anatolian *vilayet*s. The liberal majority, led by Prince Sabahaddin, a nephew of the sultan, favored such concessions as a basis for an Armenian-Turkish alliance. When the majority came out in favor of mediation by the Great Powers to implement the treaties that the absolutist regime refused to execute, the minority essentially broke with the rest of the movement. Efforts by the majority to appease the minority failed. The Armenian delegates submitted a declaration that the Armenian committees were ready to collaborate with the Ottoman liberals to transform the present regime; that outside common action, the committees would continue their own efforts with the understanding that their actions were directed against the present regime and not against "the unity and the organic existence of Turkey," and that their particular actions would be directed toward implementation of Article 61 of the Treaty of Berlin and the memorandum of May 11, 1895, and its annex.[25]

Given their mutual reservations, collaboration between the Armenians and the fragmented Turkish opposition was always tense. The Armenian activists could conceive of working together only if special reforms in the East guaranteed by Europe were implemented. For many Turks this was an outrageous demand. As İsmail Kemal, a member of the majority, put it: "I recognize you not as an independent element but as Ottomans. You have rights as Ottomans. [However,] you do not have the right to bargain with us and make offers as if you were [representatives of a] state."[26] In response to this statement, the Armenians walked out of the Congress. Soon after, however, the Armenians sent a letter to Sabahaddin stating that they "were ready to participate in all efforts to overthrow the present regime" and that "they did not oppose the establishment of a constitutional central administration that would execute" special reforms for the six provinces. The Dashnaks and the majority of the Young Turks at the Congress came together, and the Young Turks even agreed that an Armenian was to sit on their central committee.[27] The Hnchaks, however, who had reunited their party after a six-year schism, refused either to attend the Paris Congress or to give up their goal of an independent Armenian state.[28] Cooperation with the Young Turks meant that Armenians would have to agree with the Turkish opposition that the territorial integrity of the Ottoman state was inviolable.

Ominously for the Armenians, however, it was not the Ottomanist majority, but the nationalist minority, at the Congress that actually represented the more powerful, even dominant, tendency in most of the Young Turk committees and newspapers. In the first decade of the twentieth century the ground eroded under the Ottomanist orientation. Sabahaddin and the liberals were committed to a multinational society that recognized both equality and difference among the *millet*s. His secretary reported that the prince said, "We and the minorities have lived separately. We have thought separately. Nothing has ever succeeded in bringing our social perspectives closer together. Since we are the ones who have marched on their lands and conquered them, it is now incumbent on us to soften their hearts. Our duty and our interests alike require that we do so."[29] Sabahaddin opposed Armenian terrorism, however: "Our Armenian compatriots, instead of pursuing a propaganda of the deed, would be acting in a way much more favorable to their interests if they pursued a propaganda of ideas in Turkish circles."[30] His moderate, inclusive policies infuriated his more nationalist compatriots, who saw them as ranging from "elastic, vague and obscure" to treacherously akin to the views of the Armenians. The radical doctors Bahaeddin Şakir and Nazım accused the prince of being "a British agent" who "approved of the program of the Armenians, who want to leave us." To finish him off, they brought up the fact that he was Georgian, not a pure Turk.[31]

Over time most Turkish activists gravitated to a more nationalist position in which the superiority of the ethnic Turks (already implicit in Ottomanism itself) and their privileged position within the state were more explicitly underlined.[32] The Turkish nationalists clustered around the Ottoman Committee for Union and Progress (*İttihat ve Terakki Cemiyeti*) and built a network of local committees committed to a Turkist vision.[33] The Tatar intellectual Yusuf Akçura (1876–1935) proposed in 1904 that instead of Ottomanism or pan-Islamism, Turks should "pursue a Turkish nationalism based on race."[34] Young Turk literati, like Ziya Gökalp (1876–1924), were infatuated with notions of progress, of a future in which the Turkish race would experience a new life (*Yeni Hayat*) and develop "new men" (*yeni insanlar*) who would be free of the corruptions ("alcohol and dissipation") of "rotten, sick, putrid" Europe.[35] The conception of a Turkish nation extended far beyond the Ottoman Turks or Anatolian Turks to a pan-Turkic ideal celebrating the ties between all the Turkic peoples stretching from Anatolia through the Caucasus to Central Asia. This was expressed most vividly in Ziya Gökalp's famous poem "Turan": "The fatherland for Turks is not Turkey, nor yet Turkestan, / The fatherland is a vast and eternal land: Turan!"[36] Many of the Turanists argued for a purified Ottoman Turkish language, freed of Arabic and Persian words, that would serve as the language of this Turkic nation and as the official language for the non-Turkic peoples of the empire.

Turkish nationalism, pan-Turanism, pan-Islam, and Ottomanism were all part of a complex, confusing discussion among Turkish intellectuals about the future of the Ottoman state and the nation. Uncomfortable with the supranational ideal of Ottomanism, the Turkish nationalists criticized the thrust of the universalism of the *Tanzimat* reforms. Gökalp tried to clarify the differences. "If the aim of Ottomanism (*Osmanlılık*) was a *state*," he wrote, "all the subjects would actually be members of this state. But if the aim was to construct a new *nation* whose language was the Ottoman language (*Osmanlıca*), the new nation would be a Turkish nation, since the Ottoman language was no other than Turkish."[37]

Despite their suspicions, Turkish oppositionists met with the Armenian radicals secretly to work out some form of coordinated activity. Dr. Şakir's close confidant, Diran Kelekian, the Armenian editor of the Istanbul Turkish-language daily newspaper *Sabah* (Morning), tried to persuade the young physician that only a liberal solution, a decentralized empire, would attract the non-Muslims. "The non-Muslim subjects are ready to become Ottomans, because they hope that by preserving their nationality and making their nationality a component of Ottomanness they would become Ottomans. Becoming Christian Turks by gradually forgetting their racial [origins], however, would not be found beneficial."[38] Already in dialogue with the Dashnaks, leading CUP members, including Şakir, Rıza, and Dr. Nazım, met several times in the summer of 1906 with representatives of the Hnchak party. Stepanos Sapah-Gulian sensed that the Young Turks feared an imminent collapse of the empire and had concluded that they needed to come to an agreement with the Armenians. But the negotiators were unable to agree on fundamental issues: Armenian territorial autonomy or independence, the future of Turks and Kurds in Armenia, and how far-reaching reforms might go beyond the 1876 Midhat Constitution.[39] When the Dashnaks met in a long, drawn-out Congress that lasted from late February to early May 1907, many delegates were wary of joining in common cause with the Young Turks. Only after one hundred sessions did the majority vote for "solidarity among the oppositional groups in Turkey." Their public pronouncements repeatedly declared the party's opposition to secession and its commitment to equal rights for all peoples in the empire.[40]

In 1907, on the joint initiative of Armenian revolutionaries and the CUP, a second Congress of Ottoman oppositionists was held in Paris. This gathering, chaired in turn by Prince Sabahaddin, Ahmed Rıza, and the Dashnak Aknuni (Khachatur Malumian), was the high point of

Armenian-Young Turk cooperation in the pre-revolutionary period. The Hnchaks again refused to attend, but the Paris-based CUP and Dashnaks decided to form a joint committee to organize propaganda work.[41] A number of Young Turks had come to accept that violence was required to overthrow the Hamidian regime. Following what Armenian revolutionaries had initiated in the 1890s, they turned to political assassinations of officials, officers, and muftis loyal to the sultan. The principal organizer of the killings was an obscure telegraph operator in Salonika, Talat Bey (1874–1921). He and fellow Freemasons formed the Ottoman Liberty Society (*Osmanlı Hurriyet Cemiyeti*) in 1906. Military officers upset with foreign intervention in Ottoman Macedonia joined the secret organization, among them the handsome, flamboyant officer Enver Bey (1881–1922).[42] They recruited men, including criminals, to form irregular armed bands.[43] At one stroke an intellectual movement gained military muscle. Men with arms backed up the thoughts and plans of secular reformers. Toning down their Turkism tactically and taking on a veneer of Ottomanism to appeal to the diverse peoples then in rebellion in Macedonia, the revolutionaries became active in the Macedonian resistance to Istanbul. After a visit from Dr. Nazım to Salonika in the spring of 1907 they joined forces with the Paris-based radicals and renamed themselves the Ottoman Committee of Progress and Union (*Osmanlı Terakki ve İttihat Cemiyeti*). This organization would after 1908 become the leading political committee in the empire, the Committee of Union and Progress (*Osmanlı İttihat ve Terakki Cemiyeti*), or CUP.

Fearing that the Europeans or the sultan were about to preempt their action against the imperial authorities, and convinced that the tsar and the British monarch had conspired to separate Macedonia from the empire, the Young Turks precipitated military mutinies, organized demonstrations for the restoration of the Constitution, and threatened to march on Istanbul. In July 1908 Abdülhamid capitulated, restored the Constitution of 1876, and allowed a new Parliament to convene. Without a mass movement or widespread expressions of discontent, a revolution ended the autocracy of Abdülhamid and brought a somewhat constitutionalist government to power. What looked like a liberal restoration or

Greek Lithograph celebrating the restoration of the Ottoman constitution, 1908.
Sotirios Christisdis 1908.

a revolution was in actuality a coup d'état by a small group of military
officers and civilian activists in the Balkans. There was no popular uprising. As Hanioğlu concludes, "Rather, it was a well-planned military
insurrection, conceived and executed in Macedonia by a conspiratorial
organization whose leadership harbored a quintessentially conservative
aim: to seize control of the empire and save it from collapse."[44]

YOUNG TURKS IN AND OUT OF POWER (1908–1909)

Only after the insurrection had taken place did people all over the empire come out in support of the revolution. Ottoman Armenians and
other minorities joyfully greeted the restoration of the liberal Constitution, hopeful that the new government would provide a political mecha-
nism for peaceful development within the framework of a representative

parliamentary system. People marched through Istanbul, Izmir, Jerusalem, Damascus, and other cities and towns, praising the sultan, whom they thanked for restoring the Constitution.[45] The revolution was more a restoration than a radical turning point in Ottoman political life. The sultan's power was reduced, though his continued presence gave a degree of legitimacy to the new men in power. A Chamber of Deputies, in which non-Muslims were well represented, was chosen in quite transparent elections. Prisoners were released. Exiled figures—most importantly for the Armenians, the deposed patriarch of Constantinople, Madteos III Izmiriliyan, the writer Grigor Zohrap (1861–1915), and the liberal Prince Sabahaddin—were allowed to return to their homes, to great rejoicing of their followers.[46] Workers expressed their pent-up frustrations in a series of strikes, and peasants petitioned the government for redress of their grievances, most importantly directed at the perennial problem of arbitrary taxation and illegal land seizures by local notables and tribal chiefs. Security improved throughout the country; for a time Kurdish landlords ceased their seizures of peasant lands. The Russian consul at Bitlis wired his government eight months after the revolution: "During the past few months, due to the new government's policy, the Kurds have been unrecognisable. They have stopped their looting and killing in the Armenian vilayets, something which is difficult to expect from them."[47] In town after town crowds of people forced the dismissal of Hamidian officials who were replaced by men loyal to the new regime.[48]

Society woke up. Dozens of newspapers appeared; socialists, feminists, and democrats all expressed their hopes for a freer, more just society. Women appeared more frequently in public, at concerts and at the theater, and women's education became more available. Protestant missionaries, whom the Hamidian regime had viewed suspiciously, were permitted to speak at Young Turk clubs as "pioneers of progress."[49] In their celebrations, ringing of church bells, and waving of flags, Armenians became more visible to the Muslim public. In the eyes of the more traditional Turks and Kurds the public display and new confidence of the Christians was confusing, offensive, and even frightening. The revolution opened up a lively public sphere fed by the appearance of newspapers and journals, social clubs, and political organizations. Town criers (*tellallar*) brought the news to far-off places and to the vast majority who could not read.

The empire's subjects mobilized themselves or were stimulated by party activists, and issues of foreign policy, especially perceived threats to the state, energized protests and boycotts. When Austro-Hungary took advantage of the transfer of power in Istanbul by annexing Bosnia-Herzegovina, and the Bulgarians followed by declaring independence and seizing Eastern Rumelia (Thrace), crowds including Armenians and Greeks as well as Muslims, poured into the streets in patriotic protest. Merchants and port workers boycotted those foreigners who had compromised Ottoman sovereignty, and children shouted at people wearing Austrian-made fezzes to tear them off.[50] Although they had opened the door to public expression, the Young Turks feared that the populace could mobilize in ways threatening to the regime. After all, they had read Gustave Le Bon and his warnings about the pathologies of *la foule* (the crowd). Even as they permitted protests and demonstrations, the Young Turks attempted to manipulate them by organizing official, orderly public meetings.[51]

The Armenians of Istanbul carried out their own mini-revolution in 1908. Influential Armenians and party leaders demanded the resignation of the Patriarch Maghakia Ormanian, who had served from 1896 and was considered an ally and supporter of the hated Abdülhamid. A man of great erudition and the author of the authoritative history of the Armenian Church, Ormanian had accumulated enormous power in his hands after the sultan closed down the elected Armenian National Assembly. Crowds followed the patriarch's carriage, accusing him of stealing 30,000 gold pieces from the patriarchate's treasury, and humiliated him before setting him free. The former patriarch Madteos Izmirlian was reelected as head of the church in the empire, and the National Assembly was reinstated.[52] In his enthusiasm for the new order Zohrap declared in Turkish to a crowd of 50,000 in Taksim Square, "Our common religion is freedom."[53]

The 1908 revolution proclaimed a new era for the empire, a progressive step into a European-style modernity based on constitutionalism, equality, fraternity, and personal freedom. The Ottomanist program proposed a shared citizenship made up of diverse peoples united in their allegiance to the empire. Still the visions of many Young Turks and those of the non-Muslim minorities differed considerably. Ottomanism in the eyes of many Turks meant assimilation of ethnic differences, the establishment of Ottoman Turkish as the lingua franca of the empire, a centralized state apparatus, and the end of the distinct privileges of the various *millet*s. For the minorities, on the other hand, Ottomanism meant recognition of their separate identities and languages, the preservation of their privileges in the *millet* system, and decentralization of the empire.[54] When prominent Young Turks spoke of the Turks as the *millet-i hâkime* (the ruling nation), such statements exposed the difference between an empire based on a superior and dominant people ruling over subordinate peoples and an egalitarian multinational state in which all peoples would have their rights and distinctions accepted and recognized. Freedom and equality for all in practice meant the loss of privileges for some.

Working within the embryonic constitutionalist order, Armenian politicians faced a dangerous dilemma: their future depended on the good will and policies of the Young Turks. An American missionary describing the vulnerability of Armenians remembered Jesus' words to his apostles: "Behold, I send you forth as sheep in the midst of wolves: be ye therefore wise as serpents and harmless as doves."[55] As an editorial in an Armenian paper noted, "The majority of the nation is in agreement that reforming the condition of the Armenians of Turkey is dependent on the reform of Turkey." Armenians had to refrain from "shouting 'Armenian,' or . . . talk[ing] about independent Armenia." Nothing should be done or said that would incite bitterness against Armenians or "incite the people of the *ancien regime*."[56] The Dashnaktsutyun, which now was able to operate openly, dissolved their armed *fedayi* bands, gave up underground activity in both "Constitutionalist Turkey and Iran," and even closed down their influential journal, *Pro Armenia*, which promoted the Armenian cause in Europe.[57] While some Armenians took advantage of the new legalities and armed themselves for self-defense, given their full commitment to an Ottomanist vision, the Dashnaks used the podium of the Parliament to express their commitment to a more democratic state.

In September 1908 the Dashnaks recognized officially the territorial integrity of the empire but called for administrative autonomy for the Armenian regions. Their ten-point "Platform" (December 1908) came out in favor of "Turkish Armenia [as] an inalienable part of the empire, reorganized in accordance with the principle of decentralization."[58] What the Armenians could not accept was the Turkish nationalist program of assimilation that they identified with the Ahmed Rıza wing of the Young Turks. The Dashnak newspaper *Droshak* editorialized: "Union," as conceived by Rıza, "simply means assimilation. [The Young Turks] wish to do what great nations with a high level of civilization have not succeeded in doing with ethnic minorities down to the present day. They think it has suddenly become possible . . . for the Ottoman Empire to assimilate, at least, the other ethnic groups, although these groups have a centuries-old cultural heritage and are, collectively, at an incomparably higher intellectual level; they think the Empire will at last dissolve them in the predominant Turkish."[59]

The commitment of the Armenian parties to the territorial integrity of the empire did not shield Armenians from accusations of separatism and subversion. No matter what policies Armenians adopted or what positions they proclaimed, suspicions ran high among Muslims about their ultimate goals. The Young Turks sought ways to work with the Armenian political parties but did not trust them. Talat asked a Hnchak leader about the Dashnaktsutyun, a party that proudly proclaimed itself the "Armenian Revolutionary Federation": "Has anyone ever seen the government of a country authorize the existence of a party calling itself 'revolutionary'?"[60] Armenians remained cautiously optimistic about the revolution's potential for significant change but remained doubtful and wary about the intentions of the Young Turks. Many Armenians supported the Prince Sabahaddin wing of the Young Turk movement, hopeful that the liberals would carry the day, but it was the CUP that swept the first elections held in the empire in thirty years, taking 160 of the 288 seats. Armenians fielded their own candidates, often in collaboration with the CUP, in the chaotic, haphazard electoral campaigns, and various Armenian parties fought each other in Armenian districts. Disappointed that only fourteen Armenians were elected to Parliament, instead of the hoped-for thirty, Armenians nevertheless were prepared to operate within the constitutional system. Their leaders worked through Parliament on issues of general concern to the empire. Their principal spokesman in the chamber, the writer Grigor Zohrap, told an interviewer that the Armenian deputies wanted "above all to work toward the general welfare of the Empire. The particular interests of the Armenian nation come afterwards."[61] Other elected Armenian parliamentary deputies included the Dashnak activist Vahan Papazian and the veteran of the Bank Ottoman raid, Armen Garo.[62] For the next four years the Dashnaktsutyun was effectively a political ally of the *İttihat ve Terakki Cemiyeti*, wagering that together they would create a liberal, lawful state.

Even the militant Hnchak party, consistently dubious about the ultimate aims and attitudes of the Young Turks, moderated its position after 1908. The following year they declared that they would work within the constitutional structure and abjure revolution. Unlike the Dashnaks, rather than side politically with the CUP, the Hnchaks remained in the opposition. Still more moderate Armenians, many of them former "reformed" Hnchaks, formed a new, liberal party, the Armenian Constitutional Democratic Party (*Hay Sahmanadrakan Ramkavar Kusaktsutyun*), which hoped to push the empire further toward democracy.[63] The liberals, supported by moderates and people of property, rejected the idea of separation and independence for the Armenians, as did the socialists, and pushed for reforms: the abolition of the *Hamidiye* regiments, the end to Kurdish and Turkish exploitation and abuse of Armenian peasants, the return of seized land, and improved judicial institutions.

Serious divisions prevented the Ottoman Armenians from presenting a united front in the political arena. Dashnaks and Hnchaks competed for support; the church remained suspicious of and even hostile to the radical political parties, which to it represented socialism and atheism. Catholic and Protestant Armenians maintained some distance and distinction from Apostolic Armenians, and the peasants of Anatolia complained about the indifference or condescension of the urban middle and upper classes. In the aftermath of the Young Turk Revolution peasants were faced with hunger and even famine in some districts of the East. Yet tens of thousands of Armenians who had emigrated or been forced off their lands returned to their native villages.[64] Complaints continued to come into Istanbul about the kidnapping of young girls and forced marriages. Armenians took advantage of the new freedom to inform their political representatives, church officials, and the Ottoman authorities that they continued to experience violence at the hands of Turks and Kurds. Muslims complained that Armenians were exploiting the opportunities offered after 1908 to punish Kurds and others who committed offenses against Armenians. In Van a Dashnak *fedayi* killed a Kurdish chief who had murdered his brother and kidnapped his sister-in-law and niece, which served only to increase local Muslim anger at Armenians.[65] The parties supplied villagers with arms to defend themselves, which gave greater confidence to Armenians and fed the fears of Muslims. The Young Turks, who had promised to deal with the predations of Kurds on Armenians, were stymied by their own political pragmatism. Any concession to Armenians would alienate the Kurds. A simple solution was to abdicate responsibility and do nothing.

Neither the Young Turks nor the Armenians in Istanbul could easily estimate the degree of support for their political movements in eastern Anatolia. Dashnak historians claim that the party's support was greatest in the regions of Van, Sasun, Dersim, Erzincan, and the plain of Muş. Sometimes only a handful of activists moved among the villagers, some of whom were grateful for their presence, others who feared that the militants only stirred up trouble for which the locals would later suffer.[66] When the *fedayis* learned about the coup against Abdülhamid, they came down from their mountain hideouts and were greeted like conquering heroes by Armenians and Turkish officials alike. Some Dashnak fighters turned to legal work, building schools and spreading their message; others drifted away, upset that their leaders in Istanbul had demanded that they disarm.[67]

The first half decade after the 1908 revolution was a period of constant governmental crisis and violent turnover. In the decade that the Young Turks dominated the Ottoman state twelve different cabinets were formed and replaced. Despite its paramount role in the revolution and its dominant majority in Parliament, the CUP did not enter the sultan's government but influenced policies from without. Its central committee remained far from the capital, in Salonika, and promoted its views from behind the scenes. The CUP considered the liberal Turkish opposition to be a major enemy and worked assiduously to blacken the reputation of Prince Sabahaddin. The committee did not shed its conspiratorial, secretive nature; it refused to publish the names of the central committee members; and it operated without transparency, without much public knowledge of its activities, when it issued orders to its agents or supporters in the government. Their Congresses were held in secret, and they dealt harshly with opponents, even murdering journalists.[68] Behind closed doors activists like Dr. Şakır and Dr. Nazım played key roles, fostering the Turkish nationalist line. No single figure, however, dominated, and the committee was careful to take decisions collectively.[69] Even as the political party that the committee headed grew to hundreds of thousands of loosely affiliated members, the flow of decisions went down from a small core group in the central committee to the local committees.

Ruling a fragile, threatened multinational empire required flexibility and adaptability toward the constituent peoples. With different orientations toward different constituencies, the Young Turks had no overriding consensus, let alone unanimity, on policy toward their non-Turkish subjects. They had several competing "imagined communities" in mind for the future Ottoman Empire. For some there was still a commitment to the supranational ideas of Ottomanism; for others a Turkish nationalist program was paramount. When dealing with the large Arab population, the Young Turks used Islamic appeals to "safeguard the unity and continuity of what was left of the empire. Islam became the pillar of the supranational ideology of Ottomanism, with religion imparting a new sense of homogeneity and solidarity."[70] Young Turk ideology, insofar as it hung together, was a soup of various ideas and orientations—or better, a stew of undigested ingredients: some idea of primordial Turks, dreams of the mystical Turan from which they originally came as well as of a new proposed homeland in Anatolia, and even an Ottomanist vision of a multicultural empire.[71] Both adherents and opponents were able to seek and find something that reflected their sympathies or hostilities. Fundamental to the Young Turk temperament was its commitment to preservation of the empire, which required modernization and greater unity. As étatist modernizers, the Young Turks imbibed what appeared to be a feature of European success. The lesson learned was that greater ethnic solidarity among Turks, however defined, and Muslims was essential to Ottoman survival.[72] An important part of their imperial project was to solidify the role of Turkish language, and of Turks particularly, in the governance of the empire.

After 1908 Turkish nationalist intellectuals flourished, putting out occasional newspapers or journals—*Türk Derneği* (Turkish Society), *Genç Kalemler* (Young Pens), *Türk Yurdu* (Turkish Homeland), and *Türk Ocağı* (Turkish Hearth)—and organizing patriotic societies. The Young Turk government passed resolutions reaffirming Turkish as the official language of the empire, requiring all state correspondence to be carried on in Turkish, and establishing Turkish as the language for teaching in elementary and higher education, with local languages to be taught in secondary schools. Non-Turks saw the promotion of Turkish as a deliberate program of Turkification and an erosion of the program of Ottomanism.[73] Such policies challenged the advantages that the non-Muslims had gained from their intimate association with the European states. Not only Greeks and Armenians, but Arabs as well, resisted some of the modernizing programs of the CUP that at one and the same time attempted to universalize rules and obligations for all peoples of the empire and threatened to undermine the traditional privileges and autonomies enjoyed under the *millet* system. Many influential leaders of the non-Muslim *millet*s were suspicious even of the initially liberal program of the Young Turks, fearing that a civil order without ethnic distinctions would cost them their privileged status. Powerful Greek and Armenian clergy opposed the laws that would have eliminated their separate (and usually superior) educational institutions and the exemption of non-Muslims from the military draft. Even though not bearing arms was a sign of inferiority, non-Muslims preferred, when they could afford it, to pay the *bedel* (exemption payment) and opt out of service. If they had to serve, they demanded that they serve in their own ethnoreligious units, but the Young Turks opposed forming such national units.[74] The German ambassador to Istanbul, Baron Adolf Marschall von Biberstein, noted the contradiction in the position of the Ottoman Christians. "Up until now the Christians in the Turkish Empire have played the role of helots who groaned under Turkish oppression and wanted nothing other than equal rights. Now that the equality of all races and religions [has been] constitutionally guaranteed, they cry for their old privileges."[75]

The primary goal of the Young Turks was to restore full sovereignty to the Ottoman state, thus ending the privileges of foreign powers within the empire. Increasingly the appeals of multiculturalism faded before those of Turkish homogeneity. As his influence and power in both party and government grew, Talat became convinced that social, political, and cultural equality among the peoples of the empire was an impossible utopia. As early as a secret Congress in Salonika in November 1910, he told his fellow CUP members, "According to the constitution, there is to be perfect equality between Muslims and non-believers. You know and feel yourselves that that is absolutely impossible: both the sharia and our history stand in the way of such equality. Hundreds of thousands of believers rebel at the thought; however—this is the interesting point—it also runs counter to the feelings of the unbelievers. They do not want to become Osmanlis; all the means set in motion to develop a sentiment of Osmanliism have proved unsuccessful and will remain so for a long time to come. . . . There can be no question of equality until the day when the Ottomanization of all groups is an accomplished fact. That is a long, arduous task."[76] Left unclear in his statement was what he meant by complete Ottomanization: was it a full civic acceptance of the empire with its diversity or, more likely as implied by his rejection of "perfect equality," was it a program of Turkification? He might even have imagined civic equality in an empire based primarily on Ottoman Turkish language and social norms.

Like earlier Ottoman governments the Young Turks were forced to bargain with the centrifugal forces in the empire, most immediately the powerful local and provincial elites. They soon made deals with those ready to become their allies and carry out their policies. The Kurds were

indifferent, even hostile, to the new order, which threatened their authority and diminished the aura of their sultan and caliph. In Diyarbakır,
for example, the Young Turks backed one tribal group, the city-based
Pirinççizades (relatives of Ziya Gökalp), against the formerly powerful
Hamidian chieftain Milli İbrahim Paşa. Another important family, the
Cemilpaşazades, opposed the Pirinççizades and the CUP. The opening
of the public sphere after 1908 allowed the formation of Kurdish political
and intellectual organizations and wider expression of Kurdish nationalist ideas. The revolution provided both opportunity and anxiety: opportunity to act in the interest of one's family or "nation" and anxiety that
one's privileges and status held in the old regime would be threatened.[77]

ADANA, APRIL 1909

Change came too rapidly and too radically for many, particularly the
more religiously conservative. Resentment grew from liberals and non-
Muslims that a small group was running things too exclusively. Early in
1909 the grand vizier, Kamil Paşa, who had gravitated toward the liberals, responded to Armenian suggestions and offered a bill to the Parliament to create a committee of inquiry to look into the problems of
eastern Anatolia and suggest reforms. The Armenian deputies spoke up
in support of the bill but met stiff resistance from others. Ultimately the
Ottoman Parliament took no action, and neither government nor Parliament seriously addressed the question of order and security in the eastern
reaches of Anatolia. Indecision and inaction only intensified the tensions
within the population.

The heavy-handed practices of the CUP—slander, manipulation of
elections, and even murder—engendered opposition throughout political society. Expressing the fierce determination of his party, Enver declared, "All the heads dreaming of sharing power must be crushed . . . we
have to be harsher than Nero as far as ensuring domestic peace is concerned."[78] The prominent editor of an oppositional newspaper, Hasan
Fehmi, who had written critically about CUP, was assassinated while
walking on the Galata Bridge. This event galvanized disparate opponents

of the CUP—liberals, low-ranking soldiers and officers, and popular religious organizations. Six days later, on April 12, 1909, an army mutiny in the capital was accompanied by crowds of religious protestors who called for the restoration of the sultan's powers and the religious law, *şeriat*. The cabinet resigned, replaced by the sultan's appointees, and Young Turks fled the city. Some twenty Unionists were killed. Talat hid in the home of the Dashnak leader Aknuni; his comrade, Halil Bey, in Zohrap's home; and Dr. Nazım in the Dashnak militant Azarig's. Insurgents broke into the Parliament building where the Armenian deputy Bedros Halajian, a member of the CUP, confronted them and defied them to shoot him.[79] The Dashnaks and other political organizations issued a proclamation defending the Constitution. Young Armenians came out to defend Armenian neighborhoods in the capital. From Salonika, the original source of Young Turk support, the Action Army (*Hareket Ordusu*) advanced on Istanbul, and by April 23 it had entered the city and reestablished the revolutionary authorities. Balkan Christians—Macedonians, Bulgarians, and others—joined in the liberation of the capital, demonstrating that non-Muslims were loyal to the constitutional revolution.[80] Dashnaks worked with the Action Army to secure the city. The CUP deposed Abdülhamid and installed a new sultan, Mehmet V, brother of the deposed Abdülhamid, but his power was severely curtailed and dependent on the CUP. The victorious CUP turned on the opposition, executing the leaders of the coup and many of the insurgents. Shaken by the mutiny, which came to be known as the "March 31 Events" (*Otuzbir Mart Olayları*), the CUP pushed through legislation that limited individual and group rights. All subjects regardless of religion were now obligated to serve in the armed forces.

Far to the east, in various Anatolian and Arab towns, riots broke out. They were quickly brought under control in most of the towns, but in the Cilician town of Adana on the Mediterranean, social tensions arising from competition for land and work and the accumulating resentments and fears of Muslims erupted in the killing of Armenians. In many ways these massacres were an unintended consequence of the new freedom. Armenians in Adana and elsewhere had become bolder, organized demonstrations, published leaflets and newspapers, and bought and sold arms.[81] At the same time that Armenians became more visible and active, the Young Turks were establishing their own infrastructure throughout Anatolia, setting up their committees and replacing officials of the old regime. A vicious political struggle developed between those supporting the CUP and those favoring the old notables of the town. Adana was particularly vulnerable, for it was an economic hub to which migrant workers flowed from the towns of the eastern provinces, complicating the ethnic makeup of the city. Almost half the city was Christian (30,000 Armenians among them). A microcosm of the Ottoman industrial and agricultural economy, Adana housed thousands of Muslim migrant laborers, half as many Armenian migrant workers, in a world dominated at the top by foreign and Christian (Greek and Armenian) textile plants. Muslims were less advantaged economically and resented the privileges and power manifested by the Christians.[82]

Tensions and fear of imminent massacres grew in the first year of the revolution. The young Bishop Mushegh Seropian urged Armenians to arm themselves—not against the government—but "to fulfill their duties toward the country and constitution . . . [as] a means for self-defense against an unfortunate attack, until the constitutional government comes to their aid."[83] Local authorities considered the activist bishop an instigator who favored restoration of the medieval kingdom of Cilician Armenia and had him banished to Cairo. The charges were absurd, as a perceptive British diplomat noted, but the commander of the French fleet in the Mediterranean reported the accusations as verifiable facts.[84]

Even before the April coup in Istanbul, sparks capable of igniting conflict flew. In a fight between an Armenian and a Turk, the Armenian killed the Turk and escaped to Cyprus. People prepared for a struggle. The *vali* of Adana telegraphed to Istanbul that he feared violence would soon break out. The Ministry of Interior answered, "The financial institutions along with foreign buildings should be protected and peace should be preserved."[85] That particular formulation appeared ominous to many Armenians. As Grigor Zohrap would later tell the Parliament, the telegram "did not say 'Kill the Armenians,' but 'restore order,'" a phrase that had been used by the Hamidian regime; its true meaning was well known in state circles.

When news of the coup in Istanbul reached Adana, armed men poured into the streets with axes, swords, and cudgels. Armenian merchants closed their shops, which only further incited the crowds, which feared that the Armenians were preparing to attack. Armenians fled to the Armenian quarter and prepared for a siege. The attack soon came, and for three days Muslims beat and killed Armenians, setting fire to the Armenian quarter. The Armenians returned fire, and Muslims died in the ensuing carnage. Running short of ammunition, the Armenians called on the government for help. The *vali* brought Armenian and Muslim notables together, and the first wave of violence ended.

A week passed. The Turkish-language media and a prominent CUP leader spewed forth the view that the killings and the fires were caused by the Armenians, who planned a revolt to create their kingdom of Cilicia. The press blamed Bishop Mushegh and the Hnchak party for inciting violence in order to provoke Europe into intervening in the empire. The local CUP newspaper, *İtidal* (Moderation), concluded that the Armenians "were the reason of their own destruction, the Turks, and of the country."[86] Rumors spread, and word of mouth raised fear of another attack. On April 25, to the relief of the Armenians, government soldiers arrived. But when shots were fired at the soldiers' tents, the local commander claimed that they had been fired on by Armenians and ordered an attack.[87] For the next two days soldiers and local armed *başibozuk*s (unpaid irregular forces) ferociously attacked the Armenian quarter, setting fire to churches and schools in which local Armenians had taken refuge. The authorities offered no protection, as the killing turned exceptionally brutal. Local agitators and clerics fed the anger of the Muslims with tales of the Armenian destruction of Adana.

A Catholic priest, Father Rigal, witnessed the horrors and, as he reported, heard "the piercing cries of the unfortunates felled by the bullets and, still louder, the savage cries of the men busy slitting people's throats; the wrenching appeals of a throng of people in a circle of flames as their tormentors prepare to burn them alive . . . the sinister gangs running past, laden down with booty . . . these hordes of butchers who trample corpses underfoot, stab them full of holes, smash in skulls with their gun butts and then, the supreme insult, spit on their victims."[88] Men and women were hacked to pieces or burned alive; boys circumcised, then shot; children killed before their parents' eyes; women violated as their men were dying.[89] Bodies were thrown into wells. This wave of violence was far greater than the first. Not only were the Ottoman soldiers unwilling to protect Armenians or keep order, but they were also seen arming civilians who participated in the massacres.[90]

Many foreigners—missionaries, teachers, factory owners and employees, and diplomats—worked to save Armenians. The British consul in Mersin, Lieutenant Colonel Charles Doughty-Wylie, directly intervened in the fighting in an effort to bring it to a halt, first in Mersin and then in Adana. British, German, Italian, and French warships sailed to the port town of Mersin but stood by and offered no significant help to the victims.

A dauntless American missionary, Rose Lambert, had come to the remote mountain town of Hadjin (Haçin) ten years earlier to care for orphans from the Hamidian massacres. Hadjin was a town of about 20,000, almost exclusively Armenian. Some 3,500 feet above sea level, surrounded by mountains that rise higher, it was a natural fortress with only three roads providing entry. In her vivid memoir Lampert noted that with the proclamation of the new regime in 1908 Muslims grew increasingly anxious about their loss of status and the new freedom given the Armenians. For many it was unbearable that Christians and Muslims were to be equal or that Christians could now bear arms. When news of the Adana events reached the Hadjin region Armenians withdrew into the town as Muslim villagers moved into the hills surrounding the town. Fear gripped people on both sides. Neither Turks nor Armenians were able to anticipate what the other might do; both believed the other was determined to kill them. For weeks each side fired sporadically at the other. The Muslims set fire to part of the town. Ottoman soldiers arrived, only to begin aiding the attackers. The fighting concluded when a regiment led by a determined officer broke the siege, scattered the villagers, and restored order.

While the Armenians of the town managed to hold off the Muslim attackers, those in the villages in the plains below were far less fortunate. Whole villages were wiped out and most of the men killed. Remembering what horrors she had witnessed and heard about, Lambert lamented, "Space will not permit me to write in detail of the many who were crucified, thrown into the river, killed with swords and axes, burned by the thousands in the churches or in their homes, and of the many who were tortured and killed in such hideous and awful ways that dare not be repeated, but it is estimated that in the vilayet of Adana between twenty and thirty thousand were slain and months later the plain was still strewn with their bones."[91] The word "holocaust," originally a Greek term for the complete burning of an animal sacrifice, was used here for the first time in the twentieth century to describe the mass killings of a defenseless population. The April events came to be known as the "Cilician Vespers."[92]

Courts-martial were held to assess who was guilty of the riots and massacres in Cilicia. Local Ottoman officials propagated the story of rebellious Armenians. Doughty-Wyllie testified, "Every Turk in the town is fully persuaded that the Armenians set light to their own houses, with, I suppose, the idea of bringing about foreign interference. They tell gruesome stories of Armenian atrocities on Moslems, such as poisoning the wells with dead bodies, the burning alive of wounded men, atrocities on women and the like. It is true that some wounded and corpses have been burned, that many bodies have been thrown into wells, and that very many outrages have been committed, but I cannot think myself that many of these have been done by Armenians, who are always in the minority. There have, of course, been exceptions."[93]

The heads of Adana's Christian communities defended their actions, declaring their fealty to the Constitution. "As true Ottomans, our desires and aims were to defend the Constitution, to render it always services and be counted its partisans. We strongly protest against all idea of a rising which is attributed to us, we never revolted and never even thought of it, being faithful and submissive subjects, we became victims of the jealousy and the intrigues of some partisans of the old regime, and of certain fanatics."[94] In a declaration (*takrir*) to the Ottoman Parliament the Christian "Spiritual Heads of Adana" gave their own interpretation of the causes of the massacres: "The only thing that could have brought these misfortunes upon us Christians, we suppose would be, our religion first, our tendency for progress, our excessive joy during the proclamation of the Constitution, but these things are not faults."[95] Both Turkish perpetrators and victimized Armenians were arrested and punished. The Adana *vali* Cevad Bey and others derelict in their duty or complicit in the events were merely suspended from office for a while. The French minister to Istanbul, Pichon, was appalled at the injustice:

> Six Armenians were just hanged in Adana by order of the court martial, together with nine Muslims, for provoking massacres. Thus the court martial has largely adopted the version of events put forward by the Adana authorities, who wanted to pin the blame for the catastrophe on the Armenians. We protest against this injustice, as a result of which six representatives of the cruelly mistreated Armenian population were punished along with representatives of the Muslim authors of the massacres.... The director of Adana's Turkish newspaper *İtidal*, who personally participated in the massacre and, since then, has published dangerously slanderous articles against the Armenians, has not been disturbed in any way and is pursuing his campaign.[96]

The Ottomans estimated officially that more than 5,000 Armenians and nearly 2,000 Muslims had been killed in the town of Adana alone, but witnesses and historians calculate the number of victims far higher, somewhere between 20,000 and 25,000 people in the whole region. Greeks were generally not touched by the mobs, but Armenians in towns nearby—Mersin, Hadjin, Tarsus, Alexandretta, Antioch, and others— also suffered. The Istanbul government punished those it considered responsible for the massacres, fifty Muslims and six Armenians, but their guilt was more by association than from their actual role. In some places the *vali* or *kaymakam* kept order and prevented any killing, demonstrating by counterexample that massacres that occurred were in large part the fault of officials who either instigated them or failed to take the necessary action to avoid them. The official governmental Enquiry Commission ordered by Istanbul found the Adana *vali*, Cevad Bey, egregiously negligent and therefore responsible for the subsequent horrors.[97]

The parliamentary commission sent to Adana to investigate the causes of the "holocaust" was enveloped in controversy, but the commissioner Hakob Babikian, himself a member of the Salonika Young Turk committee, reported that the tales of Armenian initiation and calls for a Cilician kingdom were completely false. He told an interviewer that, sadly, in Turkish society there was a tendency not to acknowledge what Muslims had done and to see observations by foreigners as attacks on Muslims.[98] Fellow deputy Zohrap, speaking in Parliament, echoed that thought: "The government remains faithful to the long-standing tradition of denying the facts, as in the case of the Adana events; for a long time, it refused to acknowledge the number of victims, although official information later confirmed it." As he spoke, Zohrap was pulled down from the podium by Young Turk deputies and roughly manhandled.[99] A few months later the grand vizier, Hilmi Paşa, exonerated Armenians of the charges of insurrection in Adana and recognized that those Armenians who had engaged in revolutionary activity during the Hamidian period aimed solely "to achieve emancipation from the unbearable harassment and misdeeds of a despotic government."[100]

The ruins of Adana stood like monuments to destruction, stark facades bereft of interior spaces. The once-prosperous Armenian community, which more than a decade before had escaped the Hamidian massacres, was now devastated and would never again regain its economic and social position. These massacres differed from those of 1894–1896 in that neither Abdülhamid nor the central government played a direct role. Rather local officials, intellectuals, and clerics inflamed the inchoate fears of the Muslims who, anticipating some action by the Armenians, preemptively launched brutal attacks on them. Even though the Young Turks in Istanbul were not involved, influential adherents of the CUP in Adana incited people to riot and soldiers affiliated with the CUP participated in the massacres. Adana was more like an urban riot

Adana after the massacres, 1909.

that degenerated into a pogrom rather than a state-initiated mass killing. Underlying the ferocity of the bloodletting were the hostile emotions of fear and anger directed against Armenians suspected of ambitions to dominate Muslim lands and peoples.[101] The affective disposition of the instigators and the crowds, with its tightly twisted strands of fear, anger, resentment, and anxiety about possible futures, had already been present in its embryonic form in the Hamidian massacres, articulated by the highest circles of the state, and would grow following Adana as the myth that Armenians caused their own destruction continued to fester through the nascent public sphere.

CHAPTER SIX

Counterrevolution

POWER AND OPPOSITION

The events of 1909 were in a true sense a counterrevolution. The trend from the April events to the end of Young Turk rule was toward greater authoritarianism and eventually one-party dictatorship. Restored to power, the Committee of Union and Progress remained a government without a secure social base. Suspicious of the common people as well as their elected representatives in the Parliament, the Young Turks in power acted neither as liberals nor democrats. They claimed to rule in the name of the people, and they maintained the democratic facade of Parliaments and elections even as they established an authoritarian government. Interested in holding on to power (as all politicians are) and preserving the empire, they had to work out how that might be accomplished. What ideological formulations might be used to win support and provide legitimacy to the government was a contested question never completely resolved. The former postal clerk Talat became minister of interior in August 1909 and skillfully increased the CUP's influence within the government. A huge, bulky man with large hands, thick wrists, and an imposing manner, Talat impressed by his enormous size and strength. He played a key role in purging the state bureaucracy of older officials, replacing them with CUP loyalists. Armenians were pleased by Talat's appointment because he had "long been a key point of contact" between the Dashnaks and the CUP.[1] But their government was fragile and insecure. The party's hold on the state ultimately relied on its ties to the army. Whoever could quickly mobilize a military unit was able to pave a path to power.

The Armenians were stunned by the tragedy in Adana, and many began to doubt the sincerity of the Young Turks. The Armenian deputy Zohrap feared that "the Turk has not matured enough for constitutional

Mehmet Talat Paşa (1874–1921), Ottoman minister of Interior and Grand Vizier, principal architect of the Armenian Genocide, 1915–1916.

order."[2] With few other options, however, the Dashnaks decided to continue their cooperation with the CUP. While some Armenian politicians moved away from the CUP, the Dashnaks signed an agreement on August 20, 1909, with the CUP to defend the Constitution and preserve "the sacred Ottoman fatherland from separation and division."[3] Dashnaks considered the CUP to be the most progressive element among the Ottomans, dedicated to constitutionalism and the rule of law. Even the Armenian party most suspicious of the Young Turks, the Hnchak party, affirmed in July 1909 that it would work exclusively within the law.[4] The alternatives to the CUP—religious conservatives or supporters of the Hamidian regime—were far worse.

Armenians could not expect much help from Europe. Russia was rounding up Armenian revolutionaries in the Caucasus and organizing a mass trial. The British held to their longtime policy of opposing any Russian expansion into Anatolia while urging the Ottomans to consider reforms to aid the Armenians. The Armenian Question, for London, was an internal Ottoman matter. British Foreign Secretary Sir Edward Grey turned down the idea that Britain ought to warn the Young Turks that any repetition of the Adana massacres would lead to Great Power intervention. "[S]uch a declaration," he wrote, "might be a direct incitement to the Armenians to create disturbances which might provoke retaliation on the part of the Turks in the shape of massacres with a view to bring about the intervention of the Powers on behalf of the Armenians."[5]

Eastern Anatolia became an even more contested region: the Ottomans feared losing it to Armenians, Kurds, or the Russians. The Kurds and the Armenians were locked in a deadly embrace, rivals for land and power in a territory that both thought rightly belonged to them. The Russian government secretly encouraged Kurds to rebel against the Ottomans, thus weakening the state's control over eastern Anatolia, and several important Kurdish chieftains worked closely with the tsar's agents.[6] The Young Turks were inconsistent in their policies toward Kurds, at times reining them in and at other times allowing them to continue their attacks on Armenians. The Hamidian regiments were not dismantled, as Armenians had hoped, but reorganized as "tribal regiments" playing essentially the same role.

A key concern of the Armenian politicians was the land question, the dispossession of Armenian peasants from their farms, and the migration of the villagers into towns, cities, or out of the country. Return of confiscated properties was a serious matter of dispute between the Dashnaks and the CUP. The Armenian National Assembly set up a Commission of Usurped Lands, which analyzed 135 reports presented to the Ottoman governments from 1890 to 1910 and found 7,000 cases of illegal land seizures in 35 districts (*sancaks*) of the eastern provinces. This amounted, the commission concluded, to 741,000 hectares of Armenian lands confiscated in 20 years and the estimated emigration in the preceding 40 years of 100,000 Armenians.[7] The percentage of Armenians living in the eastern provinces declined in the three and a half decades from the Treaty of

Berlin to World War I. The influx of Muslims from the Caucasus and the Balkans increased the pressure on the poorest and most vulnerable Armenians. Kurdish lords used coercion, cash, and credit to extract land from the poor, Muslim as well as Armenian.

When they first came to power, the Young Turks attempted (and to a degree succeeded) in stemming the land seizures, but they were not forceful enough in the provinces (or willing enough) to restore lost properties to their rightful owners. A relatively weak government, constantly threatened by domestic and foreign opponents, saw little advantage in antagonizing Muslim landlords. The man in charge of the land question, Talat, was most reluctant to deal with the issue administratively and handed it over to the courts. The courts, however, were notoriously corrupt, usually favored Muslims, and were too costly and too slow for poor peasants. Tensions rose over the failure of the government to evict Muslim refugees who had been settled on Armenian and Kurdish lands during the Hamidian period. Some Muslims saw Armenian efforts to regain what had been taken from them as an affront to the "natural" order of Muslim privilege and superiority. Ordinary Kurds who had suffered losses at the hands of Kurdish lords followed the Armenian example and petitioned the state for return of their properties. The government's failure to deal with the land problem and redress Armenian grievances soured the sympathies of the Armenian political elite toward the Young Turks.[8] Armenians interpreted the "failure to settle the usurped lands question . . . as evidence of bad faith on the part of the Committee [of Union and Progress], and of their secret intention to persist in the old methods of breaking up the peasantry."[9]

The brief respite from violence that many Armenian villages and towns had experienced after 1908 faded fast. Kurds in the Khuyt region defied the local governor's efforts to recruit soldiers, turned on Armenians, and managed to escape punishment when Istanbul restrained the provincial authorities from taking action against the rebels.[10] The post-1908 liberalization encouraged Armenians to plead their case with the government, but the more visible the Armenians became the more exposed they were to the hostilities of others. Even foreign observers shared the disdain for the Armenians' raising disruptive issues. A British report noted, "The Armenians seem to possess in an eminent degree the art of making enemies, and competent observers are of opinion that a notable demoralization of the national character in these regions was produced by the lavish distribution of relief after the massacres of 1896. This decadence has been still further accentuated since the restoration of the constitution, and mainly by the pernicious influence of the Tashnakists [Dashnaks] and the Armenian refugees from the Caucasus."[11]

After 1909 anti-Armenian and anti-Greek sentiments grew among Ottoman Muslims as well, both in the top leadership of the CUP and among ordinary people. The ongoing crisis over Crete and the Aegean Islands kept hostilities between Greeks and Turks simmering. The assertion of increased Greek control over Crete in 1910 and the election of the Cretan politician Eleftherios Venizelos as prime minister of Greece sparked outrage among Muslims and boycotts of Greek businesses. Although some leaders called for boycotts only of foreign Greek (*Yunanlı*) enterprises, Ottoman Greeks (*Rum*) were also targeted. The government tried to stop the boycotts, but port workers and activists carried them out anyway. The government in Athens angrily blamed the Istanbul authorities for being too weak to stop the boycotts, while accusing them of being their backstage organizers. Protests that had earlier been directed against foreign interests were now being directed against non-Muslim Ottoman subjects. The evolving affective disposition demonizing Armenians and Greeks conflated hostility toward foreigners with the antagonism felt toward "alien" Ottomans.[12]

Each year witnessed a steady deterioration in the attitudes of Muslims toward Greeks and Armenians, and of Christians toward the dominant *millet*.[13] When the journalist Ahmed Şerif toured the eastern provinces he observed how much better educated and industrious Armenians were than Turks. Disappointed in his own people, he called on Turks to reassert themselves in Ottoman society.[14] The Ottoman official Ahmet Hilmi Kalaç visited a village school near Kayseri. He noted that the teaching was in Armenian and the pages of the only primer in Turkish had not yet been cut. "In order to change the frigid atmosphere that ensued, the teacher tried to get the students to sing a song. They started to sing a song in Armenian. 'Don't they know [one] in Turkish?' I asked. The instructor separated a group among the more senior students. They sang, shouting out one of the popular freedom songs of the time. In the verses, they kept substituting the word 'Armenian' for 'Ottoman' stating 'we are the bravest of the brave; we are Armenians.' The children had no idea what they were singing, and the instructor kept changing color [from embarrassment]." Kalaç sadly concluded, "In those days there was not much that could be done other than leaving the Armenians alone, only preventing them when they took offensive action."[15]

The Armenian Hnchak activist Stepanos Sapah-Gulian traveled through the eastern provinces of Anatolia in the late spring and summer of 1911 and found that CUP clubs, which were supposed to be open to Greeks and Armenians, were exclusively Turkish. The schools set up by the CUP were teaching their students to say they were Turks rather than Ottomans. In Amasia people were boycotting Armenian merchants. In Sivas the situation was particularly tense. Armenians made plans to patrol their neighborhoods and markets, especially at night. Armenians complained about endless shakedowns by Turkish officers and notables. They were often told that "the Constitution will not suffice to free you from our clutches; you are our merchandise; we will treat you as our needs dictate."[16] The mutual suspicions between Turks and Armenians were revealed when cattle began to die in Sivas province. An Armenian veterinarian, Dağavaryan Efendi, found a cure for the disease in Lebanon and inoculated the cattle of the Sivas Armenians. Muslims soon noted that their cattle continued to die while the Armenians' thrived. A Muslim deputy to the Parliament from Sivas complained to Talat about the differential treatment and the gap between educated Armenians and the local Muslims.[17]

Armenian political leaders protested against the turn toward nationalism among Turks, their cultivation of the Kurds, who had been largely indifferent if not hostile to the reforms of the Young Turks, and their flagrant neglect of their own initial constitutional impulses. Turkish writers referred to the Ottoman territory as "Turkish land."[18] A movement to develop an autarchic Ottoman economy, the *Milli İktisat* (National Economy), aimed at abolition of the capitulations, the encouragement of native industry and local entrepreneurs. Pamphlets in Turkish extolling the idea of the "National Economy" increasingly referred not to a cosmopolitan Ottoman economy but one that was Islamized or Turkified. The tone of the pamphlets was ferocious. Non-Muslims were "sucking the blood of Muslims," and as cited in a report by the acting British consul-general in Smyrna, the unsuspecting, soporific Muslims were the victims of voracious Christians. "The Christians, profiting from our ignorance, have now for ages been taking our place and taking away our rights. These vipers whom we are nourishing have been sucking out all the life-blood of the nation. They are the parasitical worms eating into our flesh whom we must destroy and do away with. It is time we freed ourselves from these individuals, by all means lawful and unlawful."[19] More than forty Armenian merchants in Bandırma sent a telegram to the Ministry of Interior complaining that their customers had been beaten by Muslim boycotters, their merchandise destroyed, while the authorities looked on with indifference.[20]

Grigor Zohrap rose in Parliament to decry the continued abuse of Armenians. He regretted that the Constitution had become "an empty shell."[21] Opposition to the CUP grew among Ottoman Muslims as well in the next few years, and in early 1911, after being implicated in a financial scandal, Talat resigned from the government. He remained influential, however, as head of the CUP's parliamentary delegation. In November 1911 an alliance of non-Muslim liberals and other opponents of the CUP united in the Party of Freedom and Understanding (*Hurriyet ve İtilaf Firkasi*). The Young Turks were in disarray, disunited, and unable to agree on policies. The Dashnaks openly expressed their discontent with the CUP. At their Sixth World Congress, held in Istanbul in the summer of 1911, the delegates noted "with sorrow that, despite a series of hopeful initiatives, in the three years of constitutional rule the government's policies not only haven't created an improved life for, and reconciliation between, peoples of all religions and races; but they have generally given way to creating distrust between peoples and the denial of national rights." The

Grigor Zohrap (1861–1915), Armenian writer and parliamentary deputy, murdered during the Armenian Genocide.

resolution regretted the "right-wing elements" that have gained influence in the CUP. If steps were not taken to remedy the situation, the Congress resolved, the Dashnaks and their parliamentary deputies would have to "struggle against the government's anti-Armenian policy, using all legal means as circumstances demand."[22]

With the liberal alliance (*İtilaf*) opposing them and new elections for Parliament looming in early 1912, the CUP remained interested in an electoral alliance with the Dashnaks. The committee obtained an agreement from the Dashnaks to curb the activities of the Persian Armenian revolutionary, Ephrem Khan, a key figure in the Iranian constitutionalist resolution. Impressed by the Dashnaktsutyun's transnational network, the CUP signed an agreement with the Dashnaks early in 1912, but the Dashnaks kept the pact secret.[23] The Hnchaks sided with the *İtilaf*, which promised decentralization of the empire and proportional representation in Parliament for non-Muslims. In turn the Hnchaks reaffirmed their commitment to the territorial integrity of the empire, its opposition to separatism, and its defense of equal rights for all nations.[24] The CUP brazenly manipulated the elections, and what would soon be known as the "big stick" (*sopalı seçim*) election, because of their heavy-handed tactics, resulted in a huge CUP victory and the near elimination of the liberals in the Parliament. The party failed to fulfill its obligations to the Armenians. Only ten Armenian deputies were elected. The Dashnaks, disappointed and hurt by what many saw as treachery by the CUP, were divided as to whether to continue to collaborate with the CUP or break off relations.

The defeated *İtilaf* refused to concede power to the CUP and took advantage of a military mutiny to force the CUP cabinet to resign in July and dismiss the Parliament. Executive power replaced legislative. This "coup" by the liberals brought the Sabahaddin wing of the reformist movement into power. Non-Muslims were appointed to high government posts, among them Gabriel Noradounghian, an Armenian who briefly served as foreign minister of the Ottoman Empire.[25] Seriously weakened, the CUP retreated to the sidelines; some members went underground. The disarray at the political center of the country only increased the potential for violence in the East. When Kurdish tribesmen attacked Armenian villages in Van province, armed Armenians resisted, killing Kurds.[26] Murders of prominent Armenians took place in Diyarbakır, Sığırt, and Van. Armenians marched in protest. After being mistreated, a few young Armenians serving in the Ottoman army deserted and turned to brigandage in Hadjin. To prevent further interethnic violence, the government replaced governors in Van and Bitlis. Armenians were encouraged by this gesture, as was a clerk in the British Foreign Office, who wrote, "No previous Turkish Government has ever shown such good intentions as regards Armenia." Another "very good move" followed when the *Sheikh-ul-Islam* instructed his senior clerics in the East to work to prevent crimes against Armenians, which were "contrary to the precepts of holy law."[27]

CATASTROPHE IN THE BALKANS

As Europe drifted through the last decade before World War I, the Ottoman government—as we have seen—experienced a series of political and military defeats: the annexation of Bosnia-Herzegovina by Austro-Hungary in 1908, the subsequent declaration of independence by Bulgaria, the merger of Crete with Greece, revolts in Albania in 1910–1912 and in Yemen, and losses to Italy in Libya (1911). The remaining Ottoman holdings in the Balkans were inhabited by more than 6 million people, two-thirds of them Christian, one-third Muslim. The reformist strategies of the Young Turks had failed to convince the Great Powers to support the empire's claims to sovereignty in its European lands. Sensing the weakness of their imperial sovereign, the Balkan Christian states—Montenegro, Serbia, Bulgaria, and Greece—allied in October 1912 and turned on the Ottomans. Ostensibly the war began over demands for reforms in Macedonia but ended with the quick and brutal defeat of the Ottoman army and the establishment of Albania as an independent state. Armenians found themselves on both sides of the front lines. Some four thousand lived in the ancient Ottoman capital, Edirne (Adrianople). Armenians in the Balkan Christian states sided with their governments against the Ottomans, and the Armenian militants Andranik and Garegin Nzhdeh organized several hundred Armenian volunteers to fight alongside the Bulgarians against the Ottomans. Important Armenian spokesmen joined rallies and spoke in favor of defending the Ottoman fatherland, and Armenians fought together with the imperial forces.[28] Rumors spread that Armenians had massacred Turks, but the minister of war, Nazım Paşa, issued a statement praising the conduct of Armenian soldiers.[29]

The wars were extraordinarily vicious. Each state wanted to cleanse land for its own people, and Greeks and Bulgarians murdered civilians of the other nationality (fellow Orthodox Christians) "like sparrows," burning their villages and gouging out their eyes while they were still alive.[30] Even though Muslim Albanians were among those who resisted the Ottomans, the bulk of those fighting the empire and taking vengeance on ordinary Muslims were Christians. Soon Balkan Muslims were trudging

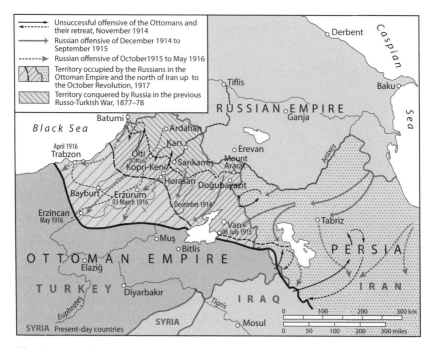

The Caucasian Front.

eastward into the empire, on to Anatolia, telling tales of atrocities suffered by Balkan "Turks."

The Ottomans faced the armies of four separate states—Greece, Serbia, Bulgaria, and Montenegro—as well as Albanians who sought independence from the empire.[31] The Bulgarian capture (March 26, 1913) of the fortified town of Edirne after a five-month siege was a stunning defeat for Istanbul and forced the Ottomans to sign a humiliating peace. When the Balkan states turned on each other, ganging up on Bulgaria, a second war broke out. The Ottomans managed to retake Edirne (July 23) without firing a shot, but in the course of the two Balkan Wars (1912–1913)

Istanbul lost almost all of the Ottoman territory in Europe, the lands that they referred to as *Rumeli*. Salonika, the very city from which the Young Turks emerged and where they had held their Congresses, was lost, eventually to Greece.[32] The Balkans had been the core of the Ottoman Empire for half a millennium. As hundreds of thousands of Balkan Muslims were forced to migrate from Europe into Anatolia, the lands to the east, contested by Turks, Kurds, and Armenians, took on a new importance in the eyes of the Ottoman leaders and Turkish intellectuals, who reimagined Anatolia as the heartland of the Turks. To deal with the migrants a new agency—the Office of Tribal and Immigrant Settlement (*Dahiliye Nezareti İskan-ı Aşair ve Muhacir'in Müdürıyeti*, or IAMM)—was created within the Ministry of Interior in May 1913. This office would play a key role in the demographic reengineering of Anatolia in the next half decade, moving *muhacir*s (refugees) to Anatolia, shifting Muslims (most often Kurds) from one place to another to avoid concentrations of non-Turks, settling nomads, and physically removing Armenians.

The massive displacement of Muslims from the Balkans, their migration eastward into Anatolia, brought with it stories of loss, humiliation, and violence perpetrated against Muslims. Pamphlets and books, illustrated with gruesome pictures of slaughtered Muslims, related horrific tales of atrocities by Christians against Muslims, and depicted rape, bayonetting of children, and crucifixion of Muslims. Many of the stories told of humiliation of the better-off and better-educated at the hands of people of lower status.[33] What Bulgarian Christians might have done to Turks in the Balkans bled over to calls for revenge against Christians within the empire. The Turkish-language press vehemently attacked Armenians and threatened boycotts and even massacres.[34]

Defeat and the loss of territories deemed the patrimony of the Ottomans had a devastating emotional impact on the Young Turk leaders. They attributed their losses to the treachery of Christians, a trope that became dominant in the stories of the nationalist writer Ömer Seyfeddin, himself a participant and prisoner-of-war during the Balkan conflict.[35] A militant Turkist, Seyfeddin begrudgingly admired the elemental nationalism of the Balkan Christians and hoped that Turks would

respond to their instinctual essences of family and nation. He was convinced that nations were engaged in a Darwinian struggle for survival,
and in such a brutal conflict of one against all the artificial notion of cosmopolitan Ottomanism was harmful. In his story "The Bomb," Seyfeddin tells a tale of savage Bulgarian *komitaciler* (revolutionaries) who decapitate a Muslim and torture his wife to extort money. In another story,
the young boy Primo, son of a mixed marriage, ultimately responds to his
authentic Turkish nature. Seyfeddin noted that Turks had come out of
Asia and conquered, educated, and civilized a large part of Europe, only
to become the victims of their former subjects determined to destroy
them.[36] Tales of atrocities committed by Greeks and Bulgarians against
Balkan Muslims fueled hostility toward Christians in what was left of
the empire. Ottoman commanders defeated in the Balkans claimed that
Christians betrayed them and assisted the enemy armies.[37] The influential CUP member Dr. Nazım reported to the British consul in Izmir that
"the nation" was filled with "the sentiment of hatred."[38] Despair—that
is, loss of hope in an acceptable future—colored the emotional world of
the defeated. Loss mixed with an urge to revenge that loss. "I watched
the fall of a vast empire like the collapse of an old mansion," remembered a young witness, "without comprehending a thing, moaning with
great suffering as if I had been caught under its wreck. A nation was
disintegrating, sinking into the darkness of history. . . . All we could do
was . . . protest [to no avail] . . . sing bitter marches and shout 'vengeance,
vengeance.' . . . If we the Turks did not save ourselves by escaping this
collapsing building, we would have remained under the wreckage. That
would have been the end of our life as a nation."[39] A principal leader of
the CUP, who directed the Red Crescent in Edirne during the war, Dr.
Bahaeddin Şakir, and his colleagues "cried for the lost pieces of the fatherland, for the army that lost its honor, for the [Muslim Turkish] populace trodden over by the enemy, and for our virtues that had become
stained."[40] Enver, disoriented by the expulsion from "those plains and
plateaus irrigated by the blood of our ancestors," lamented that the Turks
had "to leave to yesterday's servants those open spaces where the Turkish
frontier warriors once rode their horses; to depart from our mosques,

tombs, religious lodges, bridges and castles. To be expelled from the Balkans into Anatolia is something a person cannot bear. I am willing to give the rest of my life in order get vengeance from the Greeks, Bulgarians and Montenegrins."[41] Talat cried, his wife reported, for the first time in her memory on the "saddest day in his life . . . when Adrianople fell to the enemy."[42]

The theme of revenge, the urge to set right the wrongs that had been done against Muslims and Turks, ran through the memories of those who had suffered in the Balkan Wars. What they held as "sacred soil" was slipping from their hands. The empire appeared to be on an irreversible decline. "My whole spirit, my entire being screams vengeance! vengeance!" a veteran of the war declared. "If there is not an iota of affection in the heart of the century to be moved and saddened by blood and cruelty. . . . Then pity be upon us as Turks, as Ottomans if we do not scream Vengeance! Vengeance!"[43] Enver's anger at the Balkan humiliations festered even when he became one of the three most powerful men in the empire. In a letter to his wife, he revealed his inability to come to terms with "the savagery the enemy has inflicted . . . a stone's throw from Istanbul." If she only knew what he knew, she "would understand the things that enter the heads of poor Muslims far away. But our anger is strengthening: revenge, revenge, revenge; there is no other word."[44]

A casualty of the Balkan wars was the ecumenical vision of the Ottomanists, the idea of a multinational, religiously diverse empire of equal subjects. Even other Muslims, like the Arabs, were not trustworthy enough to keep the empire intact.[45] Turks had to rely on themselves. "Experience shows that only the Turks can protect the country's interests," wrote Ahmet Ağaoğlu, a member of the CUP.[46] While some intellectuals and politicians, like speaker of the Parliament Halil Bey, spoke of irredentist visions to retake the Balkans, and some proposed a vast Turanian empire extending through the Caucasus into Central Asia, others directed their eyes to what was increasingly being seen as the homeland (*vatan*) of the Turks, Anatolia. Now that the Balkans had been lost, Turks had to rely on Anatolia. In 1913 Naci İsmail proposed a Turkey for Turks in Anatolia (*Anadolu'da Türkiye*), rejecting Ottomanist politics

(*Osmanlı siyaseti*) as "Armenian politics" (*Ermeni siyaseti*). Previsioning what would become Kemalism after the war, a prominent Turkist, Naci İsmail, proclaimed, "One government [means] one nation" (*bir hükümet, bir milletdir*). There was no place here for Armenians, Greeks, or even Kurds.[47]

The most important leaders of the Young Turks were natives of Rumeli; they were veterans of the struggle to keep Macedonia, Bulgaria, and Albania within the Ottoman Empire. The losses of these territories were personally traumatic. When they turned their gaze to Anatolia, however, they continued to see the situation in that land, largely unknown to them, through eyes that had witnessed the losses in the Balkans. Both western Anatolia, where large Greek populations lived relatively harmoniously among Muslims, and eastern Anatolia, with its complex mix of Kurds, Turks, Armenians, and Assyrians, differed culturally and socially from the Balkans. Yet the sociological images the desperate leaders of the empire had of the varied lands over which they ruled had already been deeply influenced by their experiences in Rumelia.[48]

Perhaps the most brutal statement on the program desired by the most nationalist of the Young Turks was reported by the liberal Ottomanist journal, *Mecheroutiette*, published in French in France. Quoting Dr. Nazım, the author wrote that this high-ranking member of the CUP had declared, "The pretensions of the various nationalities are a capital source of annoyance for us. We hold linguistic, historical and ethnic aspirations in abhorrence. This and that group will have to disappear. There should be only one nation on our soil, the Ottoman nation, and only one language, Turkish." Nazım went on to propose that the Young Turks would first defeat the Albanians, "who think they are invincible," and having shed Muslim blood, "let the *gavur*s [unbelievers] beware." "The first Christian to move a muscle will see his family, house and village smashed to smithereens. Europe will not dare raise its voice to protest or accuse us of torturing Christians because our first bullets will have been expended on Muslim Albanians."[49]

For Turkish nationalists, both intellectuals like Ahmed Ağaoğlu and Ziya Gökalp and Young Turk officials and officers like Talat and Enver, saving the empire went along with strengthening the Turkish nation within the empire. Nationalism and imperialism were conjoined: within the boundaries of the state the Turkish and Islamic peoples would be favored and their demographic weight increased; outside the boundaries Turks and Muslims would be mobilized to join the Ottoman dream of a great Turanian or Islamic state. Those who did not fit in would either assimilate or emigrate, remain subordinate to the ruling metropolitan nation or be physically eliminated. How the empire would be modernized within the competitive constellation of more homogeneous imperialist nation-states was a decision that would have to be made. The choice was neither fatally predetermined nor purely circumstantial; ultimately it was a choice—a choice that would seal the fate of non-Muslims of the empire as well as lay out the path for Turkish history for the next century and beyond.

ON THE EVE OF THE GREAT WAR

As the Ottomans suffered setbacks in the first Balkan War the Europeans demanded that the Muslim city of Edirne, the earlier capital of the empire and only 150 miles from Istanbul, be handed over to Bulgaria. The Ottoman government of Kamil Paşa appeared about to concede to these demands when on January 22, 1913, a group of Young Turk officers, led by Lieutenant-Colonel Enver Bey and Talat, raided the Sublime Porte and forced the grand vizier to resign at gunpoint "at the demand of the people and the armed forces."[50] They killed Minister of War Nazım Paşa and a few of his associates. Seizing power in the midst of a war that the empire was losing, the new government failed to stave off the Bulgarian capture of Edirne and was forced to bring the first Balkan War to an end in March. When the Bulgarians fell out with the Serbs and Greeks, the Ottomans launched their own campaign to retake Edirne. The Bulgarians retreated, and Enver marched into the city proudly declaring himself (in a reference to Murad I, who had initially taken the city in the fourteenth century) the "Second Conqueror of Edirne." In a series of treaties the Young Turks established a new border for what was left of their European possessions.

For the next five years, fateful for all Armenians, the CUP was supreme. The most influential leaders were the triumvirate—Minister of War Enver Paşa, Minister of Interior Talat Paşa, and Minister of the Navy Cemal Paşa. The three men held different views and varying degrees of power. Enver, a diminutive man of fine features and impeccable uniforms, controlled the army. He had risen from rather humble origins as had his fellow conspirators, but married into the imperial family. His sway over the military was challenged by Cemal, who remained less influential than either of the other two top ministers. Talat was closest to the party regulars and was skilled in political maneuvering among the top leaders of the CUP. Their forcible seizure of power, at a moment of danger to the empire, meant that for the triumvirate and their supporters preservation of the imperial state was more important than the original goal of their 1908 revolution, the restoration of and rule through the Constitution. As Der Matossian puts it, "For them, constitutionalism was only a means to an end: to maintain the integrity of a centralized Ottoman Empire."[51]

From the 1913 coup forward the CUP operated as a single-party state, placing its people in all the important positions in the government. They reinvented themselves as an open political party, though without abolishing their secret apparatus. The powers of Parliament were curtailed, and those of the Council of Ministers enhanced. Censorship was implemented, and opposition parties were rendered powerless. The German ambassador to Istanbul, Hans Freiherr von Wangenheim, applauded these centralizing measures, the turn "from a true parliamentary system to a monarchical-constitutional system of governance." The empire's creeping authoritarianism appeared to be approaching a form of government similar to that of the Wilhelmian *Reich*.[52] Enver relied on his Special Organization (*Teşkilat-ı Mahsusa*), a band of volunteer officials who were prepared to carry out the dirty jobs of assassination or terror against *gavur*s.[53] Controlling much of the means of communication and a formidable network of party committees, the CUP handily won the election of 1913–1914 since they were the only party running. The Armenians ran their candidates in the lists of the İttihadists (CUP); they demanded

January 1913, Coup d'état in Istanbul; the murder of Minister of War Nazim Paşa.

Enver Paşa (1881–1922) and Cemal Paşa (1872–1922) visiting the Dome of the Rome in Jerusalem, 1916.

eighteen seats but had to settle for thirteen, four or five of which had to be CUP members and most of the others approved by the Unionists.[54]

As part of their efforts to bring their empire into the twentieth century, the Young Turks dedicated enormous resources to creating a strong army and a competitive navy. At the request of the Ottoman government the kaiser sent General Otto Liman von Sanders to Istanbul to supervise reform of the military. The British, French, and Russians saw Liman's appointment to head the Ottoman army as a turn toward a German orientation, even though the commander of the Ottoman navy was none other than British Admiral Arthur Limpus.[55] The Russian foreign minister,

Sergei Sazonov, rattled sabers, upset that the Ottomans might improve their military prowess. But his government was not prepared to go to war over this issue. The crisis over Liman subsided quickly once the general was promoted to marshal in the Ottoman army and removed from actual command of its forces.[56]

As radically ethnonationalist as some of the Turkish intellectuals had become on the eve of the war, pragmatism and opportunity kept the options for the empire's future fluid. Various visions competed even as the lines of defining differences among Ottoman subjects sharpened. The men who came to power in January 1913 shared the ideas expressed in the Turkish nationalist journals.[57] They stood between empire and an ethnonational state, in favor of a more Muslim, more Turkish empire but never moving completely toward the future Kemalist vision of a Turkey for the Turks. They believed that in the Darwinian world of nation-states their modern empire had to be more Turkish, more Islamic, and less multicultural. Their strategic vision was formed within a mental world in which foreign and domestic enemies had been linked. In the affective disposition of leading and ordinary Turks the possibility of extraordinary violence toward disloyal Christians became ever more rational and justifiable. Influential Turks were convinced that the only available future for their state and nation was to reform the empire along more ethnically and religiously homogeneous lines and either render the non-Muslims impotent or in some way eliminate them from the future empire.

The masterminds of the coup considered a number of strategies to deal with their beleaguered empire. Three-quarters of a million Greek Christians lived along the Aegean coast, and the city of Izmir (Smyrna) was largely Christian. The Young Turks made secret plans to encourage emigration to Greece or move the Greeks inland.[58] The CUP organized boycotts of Greek businesses, and by May–June 1914, 150,000 Greeks were forcibly moved to Greece.[59] Later, during the war, other tens of thousands would be moved eastward into the interior of western Anatolia. The triumvirate believed its most serious threats, however, were farther east, not only from the Armenian Question but from Kurdish insurgents.

A major rebellion broke out near Bitlis, another north of Lake Van, still another in northern Iraq, and later others in and around the towns of Jezire, Midyat, and Hasankeyf. Large armies were deployed, and in May 1914 twelve Kurdish leaders were executed in Bitlis.[60] Rebel Kurds tried to secure support from local Armenians and more pacific Kurds. The Christians proclaimed their loyalty to the Ottoman state, which in turn armed Armenians to fight Kurds.[61]

Facing armed resistance from rebellious Kurdish tribesmen who were supported by the Russians, the Young Turks remained concerned with what they perceived as the Armenian threat, the imagined internal conspiracy that Europeans could potentially use as a wedge to splinter the empire. The complexity of the situation in the East was illustrated in the British ambassador's communiqué to the foreign secretary in which he noted that local Ottoman authorities displayed "commendable energy" to control the Kurds, but at the same time these "spurts . . . are usually followed by relapses into virtual acquiescence in the state of lawlessness which has really come to be looked upon as the normal condition of Eastern Anatolia. It would appear that no stable state of security can be looked for . . . until a Kurd who has killed an Armenian is looked upon and dealt with as a 'murderer' and not as a man who has simply 'killed an Armenian.'"[62] About the same time government regulars joined together with five hundred Dashnak fighters to suppress the Kurdish Gravi tribe located between Van and Başkale. Many Armenians, however, were so discouraged by the ongoing insecurities that they decided to emigrate rather than resist, leaving villages and towns depleted of Armenians.[63]

Tensions between Kurds and Armenians rose in an arc from Cilicia to Van to Erzurum. The governor (*vali*) of Diyarbakır reported that the local Muslims were upset by rumors that the Armenians and Kurds would receive greater autonomy.[64] The Armenian patriarch appealed to the grand vizier to stop further deterioration in the situation of the Armenians and circulated his appeal to the British, French, and Russian ambassadors. "The unfortunate outcome of this war [in the Balkans]," he wrote, "added a thirst for revenge to a centuries-old hatred. From one end of

Anatolia to the other, a threat of massacre gathered over their heads. They became hostages in the Muslims' hands. If these massacres did not occur, it was due solely to the fact that the Armenians, albeit victims of the most reprehensible crimes, refrained even from demanding justice, for fear that their attitude might be interpreted as a provocation. . . . The government's action, which is such as to suggest that the Armenians are always ready to take up arms, only whips up the hatred of the fanatical masses."[65] He addressed his own government with a dire prediction. "This situation suggests that the Armenians no longer have the right to live in the Ottoman Empire. This state of affairs can only lead to the annihilation of the Armenian element in the above-mentioned regions; the government's multiple assurances about the adoption of measures to preserve the honor, life and property of our countrymen have had no effect, and as there is nothing to add to the supplications, complains and protests to which I have already drawn attention, it only remains for me to appeal, with an eye to the future destiny [of] the Armenian people—excluded from society—to the conscience and sense of responsibility of the Ottoman state and people, as well as the pity of the civilized world."[66] The grand vizier brushed aside the patriarch's petition and answered that strong measures had been taken to pursue "the bandits and criminals," that is, the Kurdish bands threatening "public order."[67]

The triangular relationship between Armenians, Kurds, and Turks was fraught with tensions, but at the same time the parties negotiated their differences within the conflict-ridden environment. Murder cases in Van, for example, were adjudicated, occasionally with Armenians ending up on the winning side. The local governor of Van, Tahsin Bey, wanted to impress on the Armenians that his government differed from that of the former sultan and was honestly attempting to pursue a program of improvement. He told a local Armenian official, "We, Young Turks, want to vow to the entire world that there is a sharp difference between the previous [Hamidian] and the current rule. We can govern the country with a European understanding and we, showing a just and impartial attitude, can also satisfy the minorities and establish strong cooperation with them. You [Armenians] with your current attitude encourage contrary currents which are at odds with such cooperation, and [your] eyes are always turned towards the Great Powers."[68]

Kurdish tribal leaders spoke openly of killing Armenians and appropriating their property. The Russian consul in Erzurum reported in April 1913 that a Kurdish *agha*, without hesitation, before an audience that included Armenians, addressed his fellow Kurds complaining that they had been too tolerant of the Armenians, that all their troubles stemmed from those people, and advised them to prepare for massacres of Armenians and the seizure of their properties.[69] A month later the viceroy of the Caucasus, Vorontsov-Dashkov, wrote to Sazonov, the Russian foreign minister, "The situation of the Turkish Armenians is truly becoming critical, and they, perhaps not without reason, are fearful that in the nearest future they will experience an even more terrible time than they have lived through up to now."[70] Russian Consul Adamov in Erzurum feared that Muslims were preparing for a massacre of Armenians and awaited only a signal from Istanbul. Russia, he advised, must act soon or would lose the sympathies of the Armenians who looked to it for protection.[71]

Armenian anxiety at their increasing vulnerability was reflected in a prescient editorial in the official Hnchak newspaper, which reported, "When the least occasion offers . . . Turkish nationalism, which, today, has the government of the country in its grip, will, without hesitation, ruthlessly massacre the Armenians, as a historical *necessity*. And, this time, it will massacre them more mercilessly than in 1895–1896, more violently than during the Catastrophe of Adana." The representatives of Turkish nationalism, it went on, "have no desire whatsoever to accept the idea of the existence, development and vitality of the Armenian people."[72] In desperation, convinced that the Young Turks aimed at annihilation of the Armenians, the Seventh General Congress of the Hnchak party, held in Constanza, Rumania, in September 1913, resolved to take up "violent revolutionary tactics" once again "as the only way to foil the Unionists' criminal plans." The decision, however, was far from unanimous, and Hnchaks within the empire opposed this move toward revolution. Minister of Interior Talat and his colleagues were upset by the open letter that the Hnchaks sent to European governments condemning the turn toward tyranny in Istanbul.[73] A secret agent embedded within the Hnchak party hierarchy, Artur Esayan (Arshavir Sahakian), reported to Talat that the Hnchaks intended to assassinate him. Arrests were carried out.[74]

Armenian politics remained fractious even as the threats to their community intensified. Even though they had announced publicly in August 1912 that their alliance with the CUP had been terminated, the Dashnaks continued to search for ways to work with the Young Turks. Suspicions ran high on both sides. The Dashnaks were divided as to whether the party should organize a national liberation movement to inspire the Europeans to take their demands seriously. But lacking sufficient armed fighters, the party resolved once again not to provoke the Ottomans but to work within the framework of the Constitution and the empire.[75] Yet in November 1913 the party bureau decided that they had to respond to Kurdish killings in kind. Terror would be deployed against *beys* and *aghas* who used violence against Armenians, and any land seized from Armenians would be reappropriated by force.[76] Armenians in the diaspora, scattered through Europe and America, would have to take up the *Haykakan Tat* (the Armenian Cause) and increase the visibility of Armenians in European public opinion.[77] An editorial in the party's principal journal, *Droshak*, regretted the alliance with the CUP but saw no alternative. "Constitutional Turkey has . . . with greater deceitfulness and more methodically . . . been sucking the blood of the Armenian people like a vampire for the past four years . . . and we, naïve as we were and blinded by illusion, insensibly drew closer, a step at a time, to this fatal abyss." Despairingly, the editorial concluded, "Today we are confronted with a cruel, frightening dilemma. At stake is the very existence of the Armenian people: it will either secure real assurances of its survival as a nation or must prepare to disappear under the ruins of Turkey, like a sacrificial victim. There is no half-way solution, no half-way exit."[78] Although they had disbanded their *fedayi* units, the Dashnaks intensified efforts to arm ordinary Armenians.[79] The preferred weapon of choice was the easily concealed Mauser pistol.[80] While students and workers contributed the funds needed to purchase weapons, the party's militant tactics met opposition from wealthier Armenians.[81] In an ever more precarious environment Armenian political activists pursued three tracks at once: working within the constitutional system, armed defense of their compatriots, and renewed appeals to the European powers to pressure the Ottoman government to introduce reforms in eastern Anatolia.

Ottoman Armenians had refrained from appeals to Europe since the 1908 revolution, but their frustration with the Young Turks had reached a breaking point. The increasingly volatile situation in the eastern provinces convinced the community's leaders that they had to put pressure on their government. When at the conclusion of the Balkan Wars the ambassadors of the European powers met in London to work out the borders of the Balkan states, Armenians in both Russia and Istanbul decided to organize their own efforts for meaningful reform in eastern Anatolia. Late in December 1912 the Armenian National Assembly met secretly in the Ottoman capital to create a Security Commission and an Exploitation Commission to work out a reform plan. Zohrap and others held conversations with Russian diplomats. Behind the scenes the Dashnak party, in both the Ottoman and Romanov Empires, was deeply committed to the effort, but the Ottoman Armenians primarily worked through appeals to their own government.[82] Meanwhile, the catholicos in Ejmiatsin, Kevork V, discussed the issue with the viceroy of the Caucasus and formed a delegation in Paris to formulate and advocate the Armenian position on reforms. He appointed an eminent diplomat, Boghos Nubar, head of the delegation. Approved by the Russian government, the delegation promoted the plan for Armenian autonomy under a European commissioner, with equal representation of Christians and Muslims in all military and administrative offices.

Russia's multiple interests in the fate of the Ottoman Empire involved not only its Christian and Slavic subjects but also the question of the Straits. Fifty percent of all Russian exports were shipped through the Bosphorus and the Dardanelles, 90 percent of its grain.[83] For centuries Russian rulers had dreamed and plotted to "recover" Constantinople and bring it into the Orthodox Russian Empire, but Europe had repeatedly frustrated that ambition. Both Russia and its Armenians wanted a reformed Armenia under some European supervision but were not prepared to go as far as a Russian protectorate or Russian occupation.[84] Nubar assured the Europeans that rather than autonomy, which was impracticable at the present time, the Armenians sought the establishment of an administration capable of protecting their lives and property.[85] He worked secretly with the Armenian patriarch in Istanbul and the leading figures of the Armenian Political Council. "It was important to keep the Patriarchate's collaboration with Boghos Nubar Pasha as secret as possible from the government," Patriarch Zaven remembered, "given that the latter was ill-disposed toward the Armenians and convinced that the Armenians served the interests of foreign powers—especially those of Russia."[86]

For the European powers preservation of the Ottoman Empire was more desirable than partition, which would mean dominance of the various parts by one power or another. The sultans had borrowed heavily from the Europeans, and their public debt was being administered by a European authority. For the empire to survive, the Great Powers were convinced that reform in the Armenian provinces was vital. Consensus was difficult, however, because the Great Powers were seriously divided diplomatically. The Triple Alliance of Germany, Austria, and Italy faced the Triple Entente of Britain, France, and Russia. In 1907 Russia and Britain had agreed to establish two spheres of influence in Persia, with Russia dominating the northern regions. On the question of the future of the Ottoman Empire and the Armenians, Britain found itself trying to balance its relationship with its latest ally, Russia, with its commitment to the grander Concert of Europe, which required consultation with all the Great Powers.

The defeats in the Balkan Wars left Istanbul extraordinarily vulnerable to whatever Europe planned for its future. In late October 1912 European ships anchored off Istanbul as their governments considered occupying the city and other parts of the empire.[87] To the surprise of many the CUP government decided in April 1913 to adopt a new tactic in dealing with the wearying Armenian Question. Eastern Anatolia was a major security problem for the empire, poorly administered and subject to the potential appetites of other states. The Young Turks recognized that something had to be done, and rather than wait for the Great Powers to impose a harsh reform on the Ottomans, the Porte turned to the British and requested that they support inspectors for various offices and the gendarmerie. London decided not to act unilaterally and to consult with the other European states. Russian Foreign Minister Sazonov voiced his objection to being forced to play second fiddle to Britain. In response the British agreed to have the whole matter discussed in a conference of ambassadors in Istanbul.

The European Great Powers argued for the next half year about sending European agents to the Armenian provinces. Neither Armenian representatives nor Ottoman officials were invited to the negotiations. The Great Powers agreed that the Ottoman Empire should neither be partitioned nor divided into spheres of influence. The Russians submitted a reform plan in June, which called for the consolidation of the six eastern *vilayets* into an Armenian province to be administered by a Christian governor-general approved by the Great Powers and Istanbul as well as a Chamber of Deputies made up equally of Muslims and Christians. Britain was not prepared to accept Russia's "Mandelshtam Plan" for Armenian autonomy under a Christian governor-general.[88] Sidelined, Germany was suspicious of both the British, whom they feared would gain a foothold within the Ottoman bureaucracy, and the Russians, whom they suspected wanted simply to annex the Armenian provinces. Germany was concerned that its huge investment in the Baghdad railroad, which ran through eastern Anatolia, would be jeopardized by Russian intrusions. "The Russian bear wants Armenian honey," wrote *Deutsch-Asiatische Gesellschaft*.[89]

The Russians were prepared to go to war if there was another outbreak of Armenian massacres, but after months of maneuvering, Russia and Germany resolved in September 1913 that two inspector-generals would be appointed for two different parts of eastern Anatolia to supervise the implementation of reforms. Trabzon, Erzurum, and Sivas would be in one sector, while the rest of "Armenia" would be in the other. No single united "Armenia" would be established. Elected councils consisting of equal numbers of Muslims and Christians would be established to aid in the governing of the regions. There was no mention in the agreement of returning confiscated lands to their former owners or to ending the settlement of refugees (*muhacirler*) from the Balkans in the east. There was no mention of Armenia or Armenians.

Turkish nationalists were distressed by the idea of foreign inspectors. In their view the "Turkish heartland," the last refuge of the Turkish nation, was threatened. The nationalist newspapers *Tanin* (Echo) and *Jeune Turk* (Young Turk) wrote about a new European crusade humiliating the empire at a moment when it needed to recover. The triumvirate stiffened its opposition to foreigners as administrators of parts of its territory. The British ambassador, Sir Louis Mallet, tried to convince the Porte that the Europeans' proposal, with some modifications, was more advantageous than having a single European power dominate eastern Anatolia. He told his own government that they should rely on Talat, "who is a man of great courage and force of character." Perhaps Talat's recent visit to the eastern *vilayet*s would have some positive results if Europe did not provoke Istanbul to adopt a more extreme policy.[90] To the British embassy it appeared as if relations between the Armenians and the government were improving. The British vice consul in Van reported that the Armenians were "above all" a commercial race interested primarily in economics not politics. Ottoman good will and investment in roads, railroads, and motorboats on Lake Van would greatly improve the situation. He worried, however, that the Dashnaks had secretly supplied Mauser pistols to some in the city who were carrying them openly to signal that they could "hold their own" should the need arise.[91]

The Armenian National Assembly had elected a new patriarch to replace Hovhannes Arsharuni, whom influential men felt "did not discriminate as to where he went and with whom he associated himself. He took part in family entertainment, spent time in pharmacies and barbershops, and went into proper as well as improper places."[92] With tensions increasing between government and community, the Assembly decided to elect a younger man, one from the provinces who knew the life of ordinary Armenians, and was unconnected to the parties and factions in the capital.[93] In his triumphal passage from Diyarbakır to Istanbul, Bishop Zaven Yeghiayan was feted in town after town not only by Armenians but also by Ottoman governors. Military parades were held, and the Ministry of Interior ordered a ship to carry him from Trabzon to the capital.[94]

Shrewdly the patriarch-designate turned down a similar offer of a ship from the Russian consul, a gesture that "left a very good impression on the [Ottoman] government."[95] When the patriarch was ushered in to meet the sultan, Mehmet V simply said *"memnun oldum"* (Pleased to meet you), after which an official conferred a prestigious decoration on the new patriarch, "at the time considered a sign of extraordinary sympathy toward [him]." Like his predecessors Patriarch Zaven emphasized (once again) the loyalty of the Armenians to the empire.[96]

The Young Turks resisted the imposition of inspectors and tried to convince the Armenians to give up on this issue. A CUP participant in the discussions with the Dashnaks acknowledged that the Ottomans wanted "to turn [the Dashnaks] around from the dangerous road they had set upon." Yet, he went on, "it was not possible to convince these dreamers."[97] The military governor of Istanbul, Ahmed Cemal, dined with the Dashnak leaders on the island of Prinkipo (Büyükada) in the Marmara Sea in June. He warned his Armenian interlocutors that they were making a serious error working with the Russians on the reform. "At stake," he told them, "is the territorial integrity of Turkey, which has become imprudently endangered as a result of your action." He blamed the government's failure to implement reforms on the acute economic difficulties the country faced. "The Armenians should have understood this rather than backing us up against the wall."[98]

In December 1913, Minister of the Navy Cemal called the Dashnak leader Vartkes to meet with him and told him that the Armenians should not insist on "European controls," which were likely to lead to three or four hundred thousand Armenians massacred. That in turn would result in Russian intervention and occupation. When Vartkes asked why Cemal was telling him this, he replied, "So that you go tell your people to come to their senses." Two prominent Dashnaks, Armen Garo and "Little Sarkis," told CUP representatives that massacres would require them to resume revolutionary activities in Istanbul. "[T]hose responsible will not escape us," they warned. To calm the waters, the CUP representatives swore that Cemal "had spoken foolishly, without authorization."[99] Other CUP officials held a quite different view about the possibility of working with the Armenians. That same month Ömer Naci, a key member of the CUP's highest leadership, indicated that it was his "personal conviction, upon my investigations, that ungrounded misunderstandings [regarding the true intentions of Armenians] stem from not being closely familiar with the spirit and mindset of the leading intellectual circles of the Armenians. Because I personally know that the leaders of Armenian political parties—for instance the most organized of them, the leaders of the Armenian Revolutionary Federation are convinced that so long as the cultural identity and national rights of the Armenian people are respected, the ultimate objective of the Armenian community should be to remain as a loyal Ottoman constituency."[100] These two distinct and contradictory visions of the Armenians battled one another in the mindset of the leading Young Turks.

The Ottoman government agreed extremely reluctantly, in principle, to the plan to install European inspectors in the eastern *vilayets*. After several more months of haggling over details, the agreement was signed on February 8, 1914, to the great pleasure of the Armenians. Overoptimistically, the Russian chargé d'affaires in Istanbul, wrote, "The act of February 8 marks, without any doubt, the dawn of a new and happier era in the history of the Armenian people!"[101] Other foreign diplomats saw it as the first step to the eventual economic and political partitioning of Anatolia into spheres of influence. A British military attaché in Istanbul warned that the reform would "set all the provinces on fire" and "open the way for massacres throughout the country."[102] The CUP leaders hated the imposition of inspectors in Anatolia, and Cemal Paşa later recalled in his memoirs that one of the reasons for the empire going to war was to rid itself of this reform.[103] Remembering how similar reforms in the Balkans had ended in independence for the Christians there, Talat referred to the European reform as a major impetus for removing the Armenians from compact settlement in Anatolia. He reported to the grand vizier on May 26, 1915, after the deportations were under way, "it has been seen through bitter experience that reforms and organizations that are created under foreign influence and pressure have led to the dividing and partition of the Ottoman homeland"; therefore, the government and army were considering "how to prepare and implement the means for eliminating this trouble [*gaile*]."[104] By trouble, he meant the Armenian "problem."

For the first time in decades the European powers had come together in agreement on the Armenian Question and were prepared to implement a reform package. In May a Norwegian, Major Nicolai Hoff, and a Dutchman, Louis Constant Westenenk, formerly a regional administrator in the Dutch East Indies, were commissioned as the European inspectors. Armenian party leaders briefed the appointed inspectors, hopeful that an era of reform had finally begun. The inspectors cooled their heels in the prestigious Tokatliyan Hotel in Pera while the minister of interior delayed the final composition of their staff. Talat would not agree to have Armen Garo, the hero of the Bank Ottoman seizure, serve as one of Hoff's assistants. Garo and Vramian met with Talat, who not long before had told Garo, "[A]s time goes on, we are drifting further apart, and the day may come when we will no longer understand each other's language." The meeting went badly, with both sides throwing bitter accusations at each other. Talat likened himself to Bismarck, the architect of the modern German Empire. Garo challenged the minister's grandiose plans to assimilate the Kurds and "empty Armenia of Armenians, so that you will be rid of the Armenian question once and for all." He warned, "We will not allow you that much time to realize your plans. Our national consciousness is so far advanced that we will prefer to demolish this great edifice called the Ottoman Empire, rather than permit you to see Armenia without Armenians. . . . We will not permit you to drive our working people out of our ancient land, for the benefit of nomadic Kurds and *Muhajirs* from Rumeli."[105] Turning red in the face, Talat suddenly rose and, claiming to have another appointment, abruptly left.

The reform agreement was a rather good solution to a seemingly intractable problem. The Ottomans were offered a minimum of foreign intervention, which was designed to alleviate the Armenian problem and thereby keep the European states from more aggressive interference in the empire. Russia was held at bay, and the Armenians could hope for better living conditions in the future. Since none of the Great Powers wanted partition or war over the Armenian Question, they could take some solace in the fact that the crisis over the Armenians had led to neither. That place in history would be left to Sarajevo. One inspector, Major Hoff, made his way to the East and spent a short time in Van, but the Porte soon had him recalled. When he reached Istanbul, the Armenian parliamentary deputy Vartkes Seringulian quipped, "You have reformed Armenia, *inshallah*, and now you are back."[106] Ottoman troops were mobilizing. Westenenk never made the journey.[107] The Great War had begun.

The history of the Armenians from ancient to modern times has been a story of a people living in and between different empires. By the early twentieth century the ambitions of Russian, Persian, and Ottoman imperial leaders increased the stakes for all three empires and the Armenians living on the various sides of the frontiers. The Ottoman and Russian Empires in particular were modernizing and, to an extent, nationalizing empires; that is, they increasingly conceived of their security and their future survival as demanding a greater reliance on the core nationality in their respective realms. Both the Romanov and the Ottoman governments were convinced that their states required the presence of loyal servitors— Russians for the tsarist empire; Muslims or, even better, Turks, for the Ottomans—along their vulnerable frontiers. Armenians were not merely inconvenient because of their geographic location, they were a disturbing, potentially treacherous element whose loyalty to the state was highly suspect—for both the Russians and the Ottomans. Assurances by Armenians of their fidelity to their overlords were of no avail. In the affective dispositions of important officials, the Armenians could not be trusted. Many highly placed Russians saw them as subversive revolutionaries; on the eve of World War I tsarist hostility toward Armenian intellectuals and activists culminated in the arrest and massive trial of five hundred Dashnaks. The Ottoman authorities considered Armenians to be Russophiles and separatists. Armenians were themselves ambivalent about their imperial masters. Most Ottoman Armenians would have preferred the Ottoman Empire if a reformed state guaranteed their safety and prosperity. Others saw Russia as a savior, a Christian empire preferable to the Ottomans. In the hope that European intervention would improve their lot, Armenians appealed to the Western powers, but these overtures only served to antagonize the Ottomans and irritate the Russians.

Four choices were possible for the empire after 1908. The first was reform as desired by the European Great Powers and the Armenians, which would fulfill the original constitutional agenda of an Ottomanist state. The Ottoman state might have moved from the imperial paradigm of discrimination and legal inequities to a multinational state with a single, civil, multinational nation of Ottoman citizens. A second was to transform the state into an Islamic empire, allying Turks with Kurds and Arabs, subordinating the non-Muslims. A third, and the one desired by many Young Turks, was to remain an empire dominated by Turks, again subordinating the non-Turks, and perhaps expanding eastward to integrate other Turkic peoples into a Turanian empire. The fourth solution, like the first, would be to cease to be an empire altogether but to become an ethnonational state of the Turks, to expel or assimilate non-Turks. The Kemalists made this choice after the defeat in World War I with the formation of the Turkish Republic. Not yet clearly envisioned before and during the war by the principal state actors, this last option would require the dismemberment of the empire state, the loss of the Arab territories, and the physical removal from Anatolia or forceful assimilation of millions of Armenians, Greeks, and Kurds.

Although the Ottomanist option remained part of the official rhetoric up to World War I, most of the influential Young Turk theorists and activists by 1914 had long abandoned this liberal multicultural approach for more intensive Turkification. To several key leaders the pan-Turanian form of Turkic nationalism seemed to offer the most effective alternative for preserving the empire and the political hegemony of the Turks. Yet even after the coup of 1913 the three Paşas, Enver, Talat, and Cemal, never completely agreed on a clear ideological orientation and wavered among Ottomanism, the pan-Turanian form of Turkish nationalism, and pan-Islam.[108] The Young Turks moved toward a hybrid solution: preservation of as much of the empire as they were able to sustain, while making that empire more secure by increasing the number of Turks and reducing the population of Christians. "Speaking for myself," Cemal Paşa wrote, "I am primarily an Ottoman, but I do not forget that I am a Turk, and nothing can shake my belief that the Turkish Race is the foundation stone of the Ottoman Empire.... In its origins the Ottoman Empire is a Turkish creation."[109] How that demographic reduction would be achieved was decided ultimately in the crucible of war, but already in the years leading up to the war a few determined militants among the Young Turks considered and openly spoke about the most extreme form of extermination.

CHAPTER SEVEN

War

What was then known as the "Great War" was a catastrophe for all the peoples of the Ottoman Empire and most completely for the Armenians and Assyrians. Of the more than 20 million subjects of the sultan, perhaps as many as 5 million would perish as a consequence of the CUP's decision to join what was for them a war not of necessity but of choice. Most of the victims were civilians. Eighteen percent of Anatolian Muslims would die, the casualties of battle, famine, disease, and governmental disorganization. About 90 percent of the Armenians would be gone by the end of the war—deported, massacred, forcibly converted to Islam, or exiled beyond the borders of the new Turkey. The Young Turks entered the war to save, even enhance, their empire, only to preside over its demise. The war laid the foundations for the empire's successor, the national state created by a Turkish nationalist movement, by ethnically cleansing what would now become the heartland of Turks and mobilizing millions of ordinary Muslims to fight for their fatherland. "In Turkey's collective memory today," a historian of the Ottoman war writes, "the Ottomans lost the First World War; the Turks won it."[1]

The Ottoman Empire fought from 1914 to 1918 on nine different fronts, from the Dardanelles and the Balkans to Palestine and Arabia to the Caucasus and Persia. More than 3 million Ottomans, mostly Turks, were conscripted to fight the war against the Entente. An estimated 771,844 were killed, more than half by disease. The mortality rate reached 25 percent.[2] Only Serbia would suffer the loss of a higher percentage of its population than the Ottomans. The war blurred the distinctions between civilians and the military. Violence would be visited on all citizens in this total war. Civil society would suffer enormously, while the state's power would be extended into society in unprecedented ways. The gross domestic product in Turkey in the 1920s was half the prewar level.[3] The urban populations of the region would not recover until the 1950s. Millions of people would be moved, either conscripted or forcibly deported by their government. Every tenth person in the Ottoman Empire would become a displaced person in the years of war.[4] Hundreds of thousands would be slaughtered as a consequence of state policy, and hundreds of thousands more would be forcibly converted to Islam, losing their original identity as Christians. In the twelve years from 1912 to 1924, the non-Muslim population in Ottoman Asia Minor fell from roughly 20 percent to 2 percent.[5]

In the capitals of Europe the war was greeted enthusiastically, particularly by young men, the very people who would most suffer at the front. Workers and socialists demonstrated against war in Berlin, Paris, and St. Petersburg, but the passions accompanying nation, state, and empire combined with fear of the foreigner to inspire people to follow their kaiser, president, or tsar and join up. Only a few radical parties, like most of Russian Social Democracy and militant Bulgarian Marxists, opposed the war. The common language of the time spoke of a war of races, Teuton versus Slav, and of a clash of civilizations, Western Enlightenment against Eastern barbarism. War had its own compelling logic of submitting others to overwhelming force, winner take all, and total destruction of the enemy. The Great War was not simply a clash of armies in the field but a total war in which civilians would suffer as much if not more than combatants. As Germans crossed into Belgium, Russians into Austrian Galicia, and Ottomans into Persia and the Caucasus, distinctions were blurred between men with arms and unarmed women and children. Europe, the self-described epitome of civilization, descended into savagery, and governments casually transgressed traditional limits on what states might do in the name of self-defense. German newspapers proclaimed, *"Not kennt kein Gebot und kein Verbot"* (Urgency knows neither law nor obstacles).[6] The slaughter of tens of thousands of the enemy required in the minds of the perpetrators that measures be taken to prevent effective retaliation. To assure that today's victims did not take revenge tomorrow even greater brutality would be required.

As European states propelled one another into a ferocious and fratri-cidal war in 1914, the Young Turks became convinced that the survival of their empire required two related policies: an effective alliance with one or more of the Great Powers; and mobilization, indeed militarization, of Ottoman society in order to deal with the disruptive internal divisions that both weakened the state and provided opportunities for foreign actors to intervene in the empire's internal affairs. In an age when the imperialist states of Europe controlled more than three-quarters of the globe, the Ottoman Empire was fair game for the last round of the New Imperialism. The Young Turks' foreign policy was intimately related to their domestic difficulties, their inability to find a solution to the discon-tents of their constituent peoples. War, it was thought by some, might provide an opportunity to free the empire from the aggressive appetites of the Great Powers and to effect a final solution to the seemingly insa-tiable aspirations of the empire's remaining non-Muslims. Ottomanism and European-style reforms had been tried, the young militants in power thought, but they had not strengthened the empire. Enver's recapture of Edirne in 1913 seemed to confirm that a strong military could repair what diplomacy had failed to achieve. War and the creation of a truly sovereign state were necessary, and independence and security could be accomplished through a German alliance and war.[7]

High German and Austrian officials also considered the problem of loyalties within the Ottoman Empire. In the fall of 1914 an Austrian of-ficer and Orientalist, Victor Pietschmann, wrote up a report for German generals serving in the Ottoman army, pointing out the logistical and strategic liabilities presented by the Anatolian Armenians in the coming Ottoman campaign against Russia in the Caucasus. "In case of a campaign against Russia, the Turks will have to cross lands inhabited by a people, the majority of whom have been deeply influenced by the enemy, who has planted the seeds of hatred and revenge in them, turning them into another enemy, and what is more the Turks will have to run this campaign with units made up of the sons of those people."[8] Such strategic thinking involving demographic disposition of whole peoples had become a stan-dard part of military planning as Europe moved toward war.

REMOVAL OF THE GREEKS

War was constantly lurking in Europe in the half decade before the Great War. In 1914 the Ottomans came to the doorstep of another war with Greece over the disposition of the Aegean islands of Chios, Mytilene, and Limnos. Populated by Greeks but close to the shores of Anatolia, the islands, which the Greeks had seized in the Second Balkan War, were seen by the Ottomans as potential strategic threats to the mainland. Europe rebuffed Istanbul and granted Greece full sovereignty over the islands, one more humiliating blow for the Young Turks. Greece and the Ottoman Empire moved closer to war. Athens was concerned about the imminent delivery to the Ottomans of two British-built dreadnoughts, giant ships that would alter the balance of power in the Aegean in favor of the Ottomans. The ships were in part financed by public subscription, a sign of the growing national pride and support for modernization from ordinary Ottomans.

Large numbers of Orthodox Christians lived in the towns and villages on the Aegean coast, most importantly in and around the cosmopolitan port of Izmir (Smyrna). Talat was convinced that these Ottoman Greeks (*Rum*), supported as they were by a foreign state, compromised the security of the empire. He and his colleagues discussed removal of the Greeks, Orthodox by religion but often Turkish-speaking, from the vulnerable western provinces, an ethnic cleansing to be carried out by intimidation and violence by ordinary Muslims secretly backed by the government. Local militias expelled them from their homes and sequestered their property, even while Talat assured the Europeans that all measures were being taken to protect local Christians. In the beautiful seaside town of Foça, armed men attacked the local Greeks on June 12, 1914, killing about fifty.[9] Not far away at the village of Saraköy the Greeks defended themselves until they ran out of ammunition and were slaughtered.[10] At the same time Talat negotiated with Greece, Rumania, and Russia about population exchanges of Christians and Muslims.[11]

The American ambassador to the Ottoman Empire, Henry Morgenthau, who fervently believed that the Germans skillfully manipulated the Young Turk regime, was convinced that it was the Germans who suggested to the Turks that the Anatolian Greeks living on the Aegean littoral be "moved from the seashore" for military reasons.[12] Back home the American press castigated the Ottomans for the violence against Christians, which they saw as confirmation of the savagery that accompanied Islam. The Ottoman ambassador to Washington, Rüstem Bey, was so incensed by the criticism of his country and countrymen that he issued a brusque statement that spotlighted the imperial brutalities that Americans and Europeans had committed. If Christians had been killed by his government, it was not because of religion, he claimed, but because they were rebels conspiring with foreign powers. "Supposing... that the negroes were discovered to be engaged in a conspiracy with the Japanese to facilitate the invasion, of the United States by the latter, how many of them would be left alive to tell the tale?"[13]

The removal of more than one hundred thousand Greeks from the Mediterranean littoral to the Greek islands or the interior of Anatolia, Morgenthau reported, "were bona-fide deportations; that is, the Greek inhabitants were actually removed to new places and were not subjected to wholesale massacre."[14] Later, in early 1915, after the Ottoman government entered the war, Greeks in Thrace, along the Sea of Marmara, the Dardanelles, the Bosphorus, and the Black Sea coast, numbering several more hundreds of thousands, were deported to the interior of Anatolia, but again they were not "subject to general massacre as were the Armenians."[15]

Istanbul did not want war with Greece, then neutral and ruled by a pro-German king. Prime Minister Venizelos informed the German ambassador in Athens that in the event of a war between Turkey and the Entente, Greece would without question remain neutral if two conditions were met: the Ottomans would not move against the Greek islands in the Aegean; and the Ottomans would cease deporting its Greek subjects.[16] The Young Turks agreed, and Talat commanded the governors throughout the empire to cease the "attacks on or oppression of Greeks." Talat promised the Germans that the Greeks would henceforth be treated with the utmost tolerance and restraint. However suspicious they were of their Greek subjects, the Young Turks stopped the ethnic cleansing of Ottoman

Greeks for short-term pragmatic reasons, in concert with their German allies.[17] When the Ottoman leaders carried out deportations of Greeks, they did so for primarily strategic reasons, a prophylactic measure in preparation for war, not unlike the actions taken toward foreign subjects in Istanbul and Jews in Palestine. Ottoman Greeks were inconveniently located and therefore when it was convenient had to be moved. Although the Greeks were Christians, the Young Turks did not imagine them to be as treacherous and threatening as the Armenians, who were depicted as subversive elements who were secretly planning (and in some cases were said to carry out) a massive insurrection against the Ottoman state to aid the Russians and their allies. There would be no Greek genocide, but, according to Talat's own figures, more than 93,000 Ottoman Greeks were forcibly moved from their homes to other parts of the empire by the end of the war and another 164,000 emigrated under duress to Greece.[18] The more than 200,000 Greek Christians who became refugees were seen by some as retaliation for the 400,000 Muslim refugees uprooted by the Balkan Wars.[19] Muslims fleeing from the Balkans were settled in emptied Greek villages.[20] When the Ottoman Greek representative to Parliament from Aydın, Emmanouil Emmanouilidis *efendi*, asked Talat why *muhacirs* were being settled in Greek villages, forcing the local Greeks to leave, the minister of interior replied, "It was not necessary to choose the Greek villages to settle the *muhacirs*. If we need empty lands, there are many stretching from Üsküdar, all the way to the Gulf of Basra." But, he continued, if they were sent to the deserts, they would die of hunger.[21] Those deserts would later become the last refuge of deported Armenians.[22]

THE MANEUVERS OF AUGUST

Istanbul was gearing for war. The conflict with Greece was avoided, but the Young Turks anticipated a more general conflagration. European diplomats were more convinced than ever that after the Ottoman defeats in the Balkan Wars partition of the empire's remaining territories was not far off. The Ottomans interpreted the arrival of German warships in the Mediterranean as a sign of friendship and protection, but in the thinking of the Germans they were there for the eventual breakup of the empire.[23] The Ottomans desperately sought allies but were divided about which side to join—the Triple Alliance or the Entente. On the eve of the war the Young Turks fished in the troubled waters of international diplomacy to see if the Entente powers would be interested in an alliance, but no convincing offers came from Britain or Russia. Members of the government engaged in individual diplomatic forays. Enver negotiated with Rumania, and Talat made a trip to the Crimea to see Tsar Nicholas II and Sazonov. Both Enver and Talat lied to their counterparts about what proposals had been made to them by other powers and what agreements they had signed.[24] Germany appeared most attractive to many in high positions in Istanbul because it had not been involved in the piecemeal picking away of Ottoman territories like Britain, France, Italy, Russia, and Austro-Hungary had been. Germany's interests in the empire were largely financial, especially the protection of its investment in the railroads it was building in the Near East.[25] The German ambassador to Istanbul, Baron Hans Freiherr von Wangenheim, opposed an alliance with the Ottomans, whom he considered militarily unable to stand up to the Russians. The Ottoman leaders threatened that if Germany did not ally with them, they would be forced to join the Entente. Emperor Wilhelm II fervently desired an alliance with the Ottomans and saw himself as the protector of the world's Muslims. His grandiose schemes were tempered by the Foreign Ministry, which tacked between a commitment to preserve the empire's territorial integrity (since it was unlikely to get much of a share of the spoils) and plans for a protectorate over the whole Near East. Still, to the Young Turks Germany was their ally of choice since their principal enemy remained Russia, a country with which the Ottomans had already fought twelve wars.

When the "July Crisis" broke out after the assassination of the Austrian heir apparent, Franz Ferdinand, in Sarajevo (June 28, 1914), both the Austrians and the German kaiser strongly pushed for allying the Triple Alliance with the Ottomans. On August 2, a secret treaty was signed. Publicly, Istanbul announced its policy of armed neutrality, but the Russians quickly learned that the Ottomans and Germans had signed an agreement. The Germans urged the Young Turks to enter the war as soon as possible, but Enver and Talat were in no hurry to fight and delayed active engagement in the expanding conflict for several more months. When two German battleships found refuge in Ottoman waters, passing through the Straits into the Black Sea, Enver declared the two ships to be the property of the Ottoman navy. A confrontation with the tsar's fleet was anticipated.

The same day that the Young Turks concluded a secret alliance with Germany, Talat ordered provincial governors to prepare to mobilize the population for war. "[W]hatever steps and measures are necessary for war and an attack on us must be undertaken right now and reports submitted regularly."[26] Enver followed with a telegram to Fourth Army headquarters in Baghdad: "War with England is now within the realm of possibilities. Contact [the local Arab leaders]. Since such a war would be a holy war [*böyle bir harb mukaddes olacağına*] ... it will definitely be pertinent to rally the Muslim population ... invite everyone to come to the state's defense in this war" in which "Muslims will rise up" and "end Christian rule over Muslim peoples."[27]

Even after signing the alliance with Germany, for the next several weeks in August the leading Young Turks continued to flirt with allying with the Russians. Russia's ambassador to Istanbul, Mikhail Giers, and the Russian military attaché in Istanbul, Major-General Maksim Leontiev, strongly favored such an alliance. Giers advised that the Ottoman Empire be kept neutral until "that point in time when circumstances permit our own firm entrance into the Straits."[28] He wrote to Foreign Minister Sazonov, "the historic moment has finally arrived in which we have the opportunity to make the Ottoman Empire submit to us."[29] The French foreign minister, Gaston Doumergue, and his associates noted Ottoman fears of Russian intentions to take the Straits and suggested an Entente guarantee of Ottoman territorial integrity to "calm" them. No matter what they promised now, Doumergue thought, the allies could solve "the Straits question in line with our thinking at war's end." Other French diplomats argued that it might "be more advantageous for us to include Turkey on the side of our enemies and in that way to finish her off."[30]

Enver told General Leontiev that if the Russians accepted the Ottoman proposal to ally, he would tell the German officers in the empire that "without a minute's hesitation: now you are our enemies, and I ask you to leave." He explained, "[I have] only Ottoman interests" in mind.[31] The Ottomans wanted promises that Russia would guarantee their territorial integrity and not support the efforts of Armenian nationalists in Anatolia. Sazonov, however, was hesitant to make the necessary concessions and insisted that the Armenian reform project, already agreed to by the Great Powers, be implemented. To woo the Ottomans away from Germany the Entente powers issued a note in mid-August promising to guarantee Ottoman territorial integrity in exchange for neutrality and demobilization.[32] At the same time Russia augmented its troops in the Caucasus, preparing for an eventual war with the Ottomans by maintaining "the closest of relations with the Armenians and Kurds." The Russian army was to prepare "the rapid transportation of weapons and provisions across the [Ottoman-Russian] border and for the distribution of these among the population on the other side of the border." Within weeks the decision was taken in St. Petersburg "to prepare a rebellion of the Armenians, Assyrians, and Kurds" in the event of war with the Ottomans.[33] Russia, however, would not provoke war with the Ottomans, even though they anticipated its imminent outbreak. "[F]rom a political point of view," wrote Sazonov, "which is shared by France and England, it is very important that a war against Turkey, if it proves unavoidable, is caused by Turkey itself."[34]

Neither continued neutrality nor the alliance with Russia and the Entente came to pass. Istanbul went to war as an ally of the Triple Alliance. Had the choices of a few highly placed men in Istanbul and St. Petersburg been calculated differently, had the Ottomans joined with the Entente, the outcome of the war and therefore the history of the twentieth century would have been different.[35] The fate of millions of people hung on the notes passed between envoys and their superiors. Had Ottoman and Russian decisions been different, had the Ottomans and their allies been able to proceed with the agreed-upon reforms in Anatolia, in all likelihood there would have been no Armenian Genocide.[36] Decisions and timing were everything. As one historian of the Genocide has written, "If the war, for instance, had started one or two years later, allowing enough time for partial implementation of the reform plan, with its proportional representation of Christians in the gendarme force in the eastern provinces where Armenians mostly resided, it is very possible that the persecution, forced deportation and extermination of Ottoman Armenians would not have been viewed as easy an option, at least in that area."[37] As overdetermined as the Armenian Genocide appears in retrospect, there was nothing inevitable about the decisions and the consequences of the decisions that the Young Turks took in the late winter of 1915.

Ambassador Morgenthau noted that the Ottoman government was divided about the German alliance and the war. Talat told Morgenthau in late October 1914 that Turkey would join the war on Germany's side because he was convinced that Germany would win and take revenge on the Turks if they did not help.[38] Analyzing "the whole situation most dispassionately," Talat declared that "the only guide to action should be cold-blooded policy." "Russia is our greatest enemy," he continued, "and we are afraid of her. If now, while Germany is attacking Russia, we can give her a good strong kick, and so make her powerless to injure us for some time, it is Turkey's duty to administer that kick!"[39]

The Germans urged the Ottomans to enter the war as soon as possible and tantalized them with dreams of expansion. Admiral Eduard von Capelle, deputy navy secretary, told the Ottoman military attaché in Berlin, "Turkey has a future in the Caucasus and its surroundings. If we are successful, these [regions] will be yours."[40] A few weeks later Enver requested the delivery of four thousand rifles to be used to arm Caucasian Muslims for an insurrection against the Russians. He emphasized his commitment to the cause of pan-Islamism, a favorite interest of the German emperor.[41] As Germany's major ally, Austro-Hungary, suffered colossal losses in September in its war with Serbia and against the Russians in Galicia, and the Young Turks continued to hesitate entering the war, German Ambassador Wangenheim warned them that if they waited until victory before joining the war, the Ottomans would not share in the spoils.[42] By early October the top leaders in Istanbul gave in to pressure from Berlin and prepared to enter the war. Enver met with his confidant, the German diplomat Hans Humann, and assured him that he had mobilized an army of more than 300,000 men along with labor battalions (*amele taburları*), into which "all the unreliables: Greeks, Armenians, etc.," would be put. Enver believed the war would "advance the people's national identity," just as it had in Germany, where he witnessed "the tireless willingness of all to sacrifice, commitment of the whole person to the fatherland." For Enver such an identity was "indispensable." In his opinion the "Balkan war was lost at the time mainly because everyone thought of himself, no one of the fatherland."[43] Both Germany and the Ottomans would have benefited from continuation of armed neutrality, as Ambassador Wangenheim advocated, but those far from the scene in Berlin insisted on the Ottomans entering the war immediately.[44]

In September Istanbul announced the abrogation of the capitulations, the special privileges awarded to European commerce within the empire. The Armenian reform project was quietly discarded. On October 29, the German admiral Wilhelm Souchon, commanding a joint German-Ottoman fleet, attacked and sank two Russian ships in the Black Sea. Without written orders from Istanbul, but with a clear understanding that leading cabinet officials approved, Souchon went on and bombarded the Russian fortress-city of Sevastopol. Souchon and Enver reported that it was the Russians who attacked the Ottomans, and that myth became a powerful recruiting tool in mobilizing popular support for the war.[45] But in fact the attack was a deliberate move by Berlin and a small number of high officials in Istanbul—Enver, Talat, and Cemal—to start a war with Russia. Grand Vizier Said Halim Paşa and Finance Minister Cavid Bey opposed the action. The four non-ethnic Turks in the cabinet resigned in protest, among them the Armenian Oskan Effendi (Vosgan Mardigian). Ambassador Morgenthau met with Talat that day, and the minister seemed resigned: "Well, Wangenheim, Enver, and I prefer that war should come now."[46] Russia and Britain immediately retaliated. Russian troops crossed the border into Erzurum province. On November 10 the Ottomans officially declared war on Russia and its allies.

DILEMMA OF THE DAMNED

What would evolve into genocide began haphazardly in policies designed both to rearrange the demographic topography of Anatolia and to prepare for the war with Russia and its European allies. For the Young Turks the war was conceived as a transformative, revolutionary opportunity, a moment to gamble in order to save their empire and make it more secure. How that might be accomplished was influenced and shaped by their own understanding of what they desired, who their friends were, and who had to be eliminated in order to realize their emerging vision. As they worked out their jerrybuilt design of the future empire and improvised the means to achieve it, the party leaders consolidated their hold over the state. When Enver became minister of war in January 1914, he immediately purged the army of hundreds of officers, solidifying the military's loyalty to himself and the CUP. The Ministry of Interior under Talat took command of the Ottoman gendarmerie. To realize their ambitions in the East the Young Turks organized a second secret organization, a new Special Organization (*Teşkilat-ı Mahsusa*) similar in aims to an already existing paramilitary and working eventually in tandem with the original organization.[47] Headed by Dr. Şakir and Dr. Nazım, along with Atıf Bey and Rıza Bey, the organization was financed and supplied by the Ministry of War but in cooperation with other parts of the government and under the direct supervision of the party. Formed initially for covert action in Russian Caucasia and Persia, the new *Teşkilat-ı Mahsusa* recruited tribesmen—Circassians, Kurds, and others—as well as prisoners, criminals, and bandits for its ranks. Prisons were emptied on orders of the government. More than ten thousand imprisoned criminals, many of them convicted of murder, were given a new role as fighters in the squadrons of the Special Organization. By fighting for the fatherland these former "people without honor" (*namussuz*) became respectable (*namuslu*).[48] Referred to as *çetes* (gangs, guerrillas), these specially recruited fighters were available to the Young Turks independently of the regular army and could be used for actions against designated civilians.[49]

As the CUP leaders in Istanbul promoted the idea that the Armenians were disloyal and a threat to their security, disturbances broke out in distant parts of Anatolia. In May 1914 Muslims and Christians clashed in the bazaar and center of Diyarbakır and again in August Muslims looted Christian shops while the local police looked the other way.[50] The British vice consul in Diyarbakır, Thomas Mgrdichian, met late in August with the Kurdish parliamentary deputy Feyzi Pirinççizade in his home, who ominously told him that "if the Armenians insisted on their foolish game, they would ultimately pay a high price for it. Russia, France, and Great Britain cannot help them, and cannot and will not be able to save them, while Turkey is in a position, free and capable to do whatever she wants in the matter, without either Austria or Germany ever saying a word of protest about it."[51] As if fulfilling Feyzi's prophecy, a huge fire broke out in August, destroying primarily Armenian shops in the Diyarbakır bazaar. The Armenians were convinced Feyzi Bey had deliberately set the fire on instructions from the Committee of Union and Progress.[52]

Ordinary Turks echoed the elite's suspicions of Armenians. When the cleric Grigoris Balakian arrived in the port of Istanbul in September 1914, the chief of the customs house inspectors praised what he took to be his pro-German feelings and advised that he try to convince his compatriots to "renounce their love for Russia. They have gone to such extremes in their affinity and love for the Russians, French, and English, that on the day that the Russians win, the Armenians smile . . . but when the Russians have been defeated, they are sad. This much sincerity will cause them much trouble later on."[53] Balakian despaired that the Armenians were not sufficiently aware of the dangers they faced. "[G]iving way to our feelings," he wrote, "we threw ourselves as a nation blindly into a precipitous adventure."[54]

Yet despite the growing consensus among Turks that Armenians were disloyal, key figures in eastern Anatolia dissented from the prevailing view. The *vali* in Van, Tahsin Bey, informed his government that "neither before the general mobilization nor after has there been a single person from the Armenian population who has immigrated to Russia [or] Iran or fled [their home]. Among the local Armenians there are neither thoughts of revolt nor even opposition to the government.... On the contrary, among the Dashnaks one can see [an attitude of] vocal support for and assistance vis-à-vis the government in regard to the general mobilization and the war." The Armenians "in the private clubs in which the younger Armenian merchants and leaders meet," however, say that "they do not want the Russians to be defeated by the Germans" since the effort to carry out the "Armenian Reforms can [only] go forward if Russia were to become dominant in Europe."[55] Similarly Mustafa Bey in Bitlis reported that in "an honorable display of patriotism" the Dashnaks in Muş urged Armenians to join the army. Hnchaks and the Armenian Church held back, however, and "prevented [the Armenians] from fulfilling their national duty" until it became clear that it was in the Armenian interest "to fully comply with the government's directives."[56] Sabit Bey, the *vali* of Memüretülaziz, likewise saw no need to form a militia solely reserved for the Muslims.[57]

The violence escalating in the fall of 1914 troubled Armenian leaders throughout the empire, but they were caught on the horns of a dilemma. Neither their own government nor the Entente offered much help. Optimistic activists saw the war as an opportunity; a Russian victory would promote the interests of the Ottoman Armenians. But more pessimistic leaders feared that open support of the Russians would bring disaster on the vulnerable. The ambivalence of many Armenians—questioning whether they should continue to rely on their Ottoman overlords or throw in their lot with the Russians—was clear in the actions of a prominent Dashnak, Hovhannes Kachaznuni, who was sent from Van by his party comrades to the Caucasus to persuade his compatriots to cease recruiting volunteer units supporting the Russian campaign against the Ottomans. Shortly after reaching Tiflis, Kachaznuni himself joined the volunteers.[58] The patriarch sent his own man to Tiflis to convince the Armenians in Russia to act with "great caution"; his representative reported back that the atmosphere in Tiflis was euphoric about the war. Armenian "volunteers were signing up to 'fight against the Turks and liberate Turkish Armenia.'"[59] Caucasian Armenians, and a handful of Ottoman Armenian defectors, actively supported the Russian war effort in opposition to what the leading Armenian political parties and politicians on the Ottoman side advocated.[60]

The defection of a few Armenian revolutionaries like Kachaznuni and Armen Garo, who were joined by Armenian deserters, confirmed in the imagination of already suspicious Young Turks that Armenians as a whole were potential internal enemies of the state. Within the affective disposition of important Ottoman leaders, shared by overwhelming numbers of Ottoman Muslims, the Armenians represented a palpable threat to their future existence. Whereas the Europeans saw the Armenians as victims, the Ottomans saw themselves as victims, of both Europe and the treacherous Armenians. Despite the fact that Armenians were serving in the Ottoman army and their political parties and the church had urged loyal participation in the defense of the empire, the Young Turk leaders were convinced that all Armenians were potentially disloyal and likely to be pro-Russian; therefore measures had to be taken to neutralize them. The war was an opportunity to eliminate any future threat from the Armenians. Without Armenians in Anatolia there was no Armenian Question, no pretext for Europe to dismember the empire.

On the eve of the war the Ottoman public sphere narrowed, as one after another political institution was shuttered. On July 4 the Armenian National Assembly, the institution that ran the affairs of the *Ermeni milleti* and had been reinstated in 1908 thirty years after Abdülhamid II had suspended it, was closed down.[61] A month later, on August 3, just days after the war in Europe broke out, the Ottoman Parliament was recessed. General military mobilization was announced. The CUP and the Ministry of War discussed what needed to be done with the non-Turks located in strategically vulnerable places.[62] In the view of the military and civilian authorities mobilization for war allowed, indeed required, the arrest, dispersion, and even execution of enemies of the state. Having effectively eliminated the Ottoman liberal opposition, the government turned on the Hnchak party, the Armenian organization they considered most dangerous. On July 16, 1914, twenty of the principal leaders of the party in Istanbul were arrested, followed by the roundup of another one hundred activists. Those still free considered dissolving their legal organization and going [...] involved in a consp[...] still active in Istanbul tried to defend them [...] suspicions directed at them. Their efforts failed, and the government effectively destroyed their painstakingly constructed networks.[63]

When the Dashnaks gathered in a Congress in Erzurum (August 2–14), Şakir and his associate Naci Bey arrived as emissaries from the Special Organization and met for three days with several Dashnak leaders to discuss joint action. The Unionists asked what the Armenians would do in the event of a Russian invasion. The unequivocal answer was that they would defend the Ottoman Empire. The Unionists then proposed that in the event of war with Russia the Dashnaks help the *Teşkilat-ı Mahsusa* destabilize the rear of the Russian army. Şakir claimed that Georgian and Russian Muslims had already approved such plans. In return for Armenian aid he promised an autonomous state for the Armenians that would include Russian Armenia and several *sancak*s of the *vilayet*s of Erzurum, Van, and Tiflis. The Dashnaks answered that Caucasian Armenians were no longer as confident of Ottoman reform and constitutionalism as they had been at the time of the Young Turk Revolution. The Russian government, moreover, had made overtures to the Armenians, improving their relations. In any case, the Dashnaks could not accept Şakir's offer to stir up Russian Armenian rebellion, and the party affirmed its neutrality: Russian Armenians would fight for tsarist Russia and Ottoman Armenians would fight for the Ottoman Empire. The Dashnaks were committed to have Ottoman Armenians join the army, and their compatriots would pay the special taxes dedicated to the war effort.[64] Şakir reported the Dashnaks' rejection of the offer, and the CUP secretary general wrote back in coded response: "Beyond a doubt, the Armenians are not inclined to collaborate with us. [See to it] that our orientation is kept secret from them."[65] On September 6 Talat ordered his security apparatus to follow the local leaderships of Armenian political parties.[66] Şakir hatched a plot to murder the key Dashnak delegates returning to Russia, but it failed.[67]

The signs that the war would have ominous consequences for Armenians were evident to those who looked for them. As they sailed to apazian, "You can be sure that they're going to do something to us."[68] Sensing danger, but with increasingly less room to maneuver, important Dashnaks clung to the slim reed of hope that their loyalty would persuade their Young Turk allies of the past not to harm the Armenians. The Dashnaks rejected a suggestion from the French prime minister that the party "help the Entente."[69] Armenians in Russia were about to join the war effort against the Ottomans, but important Ottoman Armenians were not particularly attracted to Russia. The prominent Dashnak Simon Vratsian thought it childishly naïve of Armenians to rely on the Russians, who "have set out to conquer the Armenians' lands and their hearts will not grieve if Armenian blood once again flows abundantly here and there."[70] Bishop Grigoris Balakian was dismayed that no one grasped the gravity and believed that as long as their "beloved Talaat was interior minister, no danger faced them."[71] When asked by the patriarch to serve as prelate in the eastern Anatolian city of Erzincan, not far from where the Ottomans would engage the Russians, Balakian declined the appointment. The priest who went in his place, Sahak *vartapet* Odabashian, was murdered on the way to take up his post. The patriarch protested "this first martyrdom" to the government but received no response.[72]

Through the last months of 1914 Talat steadily implemented anti-Armenian measures. He ordered increased surveillance of Armenian political leaders, told his provincial agents to watch Armenians for potential espionage and pro-Russian activity, and prohibited communications involving Armenian nationalism. As anti-Armenian violence increased in the frontier areas, the minister of interior had all remaining Armenian policemen dismissed.[73] Those Armenians who contemplated their future in the Ottoman Empire came to realize that international politics, geography, and the ambitions of their own government conspired against them.[74] Ottoman Armenians had become hostages of the Ottoman state, driven outside the law, and their erstwhile protectors in Europe were no longer in a position to aid them. Their sympathies and interests probably lay more with the Entente, but their country was joining the Triple

Alliance, which would give the government a free hand to deal with its internal problems.

THE HOME FRONT

The fate of the Armenians was directly tied to the social disintegration and political radicalization of the Ottoman leaders that accelerated with the coming of war. The mobilization for war was chaotic, and its effects would be felt long after the defeat of the empire.[75] Out of a population of about 25 million people, almost 3 million men were conscripted into the armed forces; all fit males between the ages of twenty and forty-five regardless of religion were drafted. All social and economic resources would be required to win the war. As part of mobilization the government requisitioned supplies from merchants. This policy quickly turned into a license for plundering goods from Armenians and Greeks in particular, but the widespread corruption and arbitrariness of the confiscations and the collection of war taxes affected nearly everyone.[76] The army demanded the use of people's animals and vehicles on which their livelihood depended. People resisted and hid their animals, and the military forcibly entered their houses and barns to find them.[77] "Under the heading of 'military goods,'" an Armenian reported, "so much was taken from the people that we will not be mistaken if we say that half of the people will not even have enough for their daily nourishment in winter."[78] The American Protestant missionary Henry H. Riggs, born in Turkey, fluent in both Turkish and Armenian, traveled the road from Arapgir to Egin (Agn) and witnessed the devastating effects wrought by the chaotic mobilization. "At every village where I stopped I found homes desolate, and suffering was beginning to be keen because the breadwinners had gone to the front. Armenians and Moslems alike shared in this hardship, and a bond of sympathy was everywhere manifest between the two races. And this in spite of the fact that for the Moslems this was a Holy War, while the Armenians were being forced to fight in defense of all that they loathed and feared in the Turkish government. Yet all were suffering together, and neighbors became more neighborly under the stress of the common anxiety and the common hardships."[79]

The mass mobilization of young men for service, known to the Ottomans as *seferberlik*, produced fear and anxiety among the recruits who did not know what to expect and had frightening images of military service.[80] The state was not prepared to carry out such a massive war effort, and recruits were poorly treated, housed in mosque yards, where they pleaded for help from civilians. In Syria where massive starvation occurred in 1915–1916 largely because of the British naval blockade, *seferberlik* took on the meaning of famine. One out of seven inhabitants died there by the end of the war.[81] This was the destination to which the Young Turks consigned their deported Armenian subjects.

The call-up of men for military service was not popular, and even though turnout was high at first, desertion soon became a major problem. The Armenian prelate of Şabinkarahisar, a small town in the Giresun mountains inland from the Black Sea, wrote to the patriarch late in September 1914: "We exhorted our people to fulfill their duty toward the fatherland, and the people hurried to respond to the call that they were hearing. But when they met an unfriendly and unsympathetic reception, many among them considered it preferable to flee. This unfriendly attitude toward the Armenians is demonstrated every day in our city and the surrounding Armenian-inhabited villages, where confiscations and forced labor are being implemented with the utmost severity."[82] Young men who refused to be conscripted into the army were rounded up by force and threatened with capital punishment. By the end of the war between 300,000 and 500,000 Ottoman soldiers deserted, one out of six conscripted. Fourteen percent of all soldiers mobilized suffered from dysentery and typhus, as well as other diseases.[83] Conscription was haphazard and indiscriminate and emptied towns and villages of needed skills and labor. The army did not have adequate uniforms, footwear, or provisions. Soldiers were paid late if at all. The poor rail connections forced soldiers to march hundreds of miles, sometimes without proper food or equipment.[84] As they moved through towns and villages emptied of men, they forced their way into homes for the night, helped themselves to food and supplies, and took advantage of the women. Particularly vulnerable, the wives, mothers, and sisters of soldiers were dishonored, sometimes forced into prostitution. Caught between their duty at the front and protection of their families, soldiers deserted, only to become themselves perpetrators of violence against unprotected women.[85]

The policies and practices of provisioning a huge army eliminated the distance and distinction between the war front and the home front. The state that had been distant encroached on the daily life of its subjects in new and painful ways.[86] The wealthy and some special groups of peoples, many non-Muslims, were permitted to pay a military exemption tax and avoid conscription. This policy stoked resentment among those in the ranks who could not afford the exemption payment. In the economy of shortages and great need corruption was endemic. Those who could afford to pay bribes avoided the worst confiscations of their goods and animals.

The recruitment of non-Muslims had been state policy since 1909, a part of the secular modernization program and Ottomanism of the Young Turks. When the empire entered the war, the Ottoman army was multinational. Most Greeks opted out, but Armenians and Jews were conscripted and more than 26 percent of recruits were Arabs.[87] Turkish commanders considered Arab units less war-worthy than Turkish units, and Kurdish regiments were thought most undependable of all.[88] The growing mistrust of Christians, however, made it difficult for Armenians, Assyrians, and Greeks to serve alongside Muslims. In Diyarbakır, for instance, two thousand young Armenians called up by the army refused to serve and escaped to the roofs of the town's dwellings. They set up markets and a network to supply their needs. Their resistance lasted from June 1914 until January 1915, when they finally submitted and were drafted into the Ottoman labor battalions and dispersed throughout the empire.[89] Already in October 1914 many non-Muslims were transferred or recruited directly into the dreaded labor battalions.

Armenian men were caught between their leaders who urged them to join the army and the wanton discrimination, ill treatment, and suspicions they met from the recruiters. The prelate of Erzurum wrote in September, "The Armenians have been and will be upright. Everybody has responded to the call to military duty, in person or by paying the exemption fee. They are taking every precaution not to invite even the slightest suspicion upon themselves. These things are well known to the Turks and the İttihad and government circles, but it seems to me that *they wish to create pretexts to show the Armenians as untrustworthy.* What these imaginary pretexts may lead to it is impossible to foresee, but certainly they do not promise a prosperous future."[90] Rumors spread that the Dashnaks had armed themselves (which was legal under the Constitution) with the aim of attacking Muslim villages. The perceived threat of Armenian çetes (irregulars) overwhelmed signs of Armenian loyalty, and any incident of Armenians killing Turks (as occurred near Muş) only confirmed the disposition to see Armenians as internal enemies.[91] For the Armenians the government was the principal cause of "irregularity and mischief . . . provoking and arming the dark forces against the Armenians."[92] Armenian officials reported back to the patriarchate that exaggerated reports of a "fictional uprising attributed to the Armenians" were being transmitted to Istanbul.[93]

RUSSIA ON THE CAUCASIAN FRONT

In 1914 the image of the Russian military was of a steamroller that by its very size and strength could overwhelm its enemies. Potentially the tsar could mobilize some 12 to 15 million men. But behind the facade of enormous force Russia was far more vulnerable than appeared. The Russian Empire's major concern was its western front, the colossal struggle it was undertaking with the German and Austrian Empires.[94] St. Petersburg would have preferred the Ottomans to stay out of the war, and while some officials and officers harbored visions of annexing Armenia, the government's policy was basically defensive rather than offensive.[95] Russia wanted reform in the "Armenian provinces," not annexation.[96]

Two days after the Ottoman attack, the tsar informed his subjects, "It is with complete serenity and the assistance of God that Russia takes on the appearance of this new enemy, this ancient oppressor of the Christian faith and all Slavic nations. . . . Together with all Russian nations, we believe without fail that Turkey's reckless intervention in the present conflict will only accelerate her submission to fate and open up Russia's path towards the realization of the historic task of her ancestors along the shores of the Black Sea."[97] Once it became clear, however, that a front would open in the south, the Russians rapidly built up their forces in the Caucasus. As an ally of the British, Russia no longer had to keep large armies in Central Asia as part of the "Great Game" between the two empires. Troops from Turkestan and Siberia, Transcaspia and the Transbaikal, were deployed to Caucasia. One hundred and fifty thousand reservists were called up.[98] Even though part of the Caucasian army had to be moved to the eastern front after the disastrous defeat by the Germans at Tannenberg, a formidable army faced the Ottomans in the Caucasus, commanded formally by Viceroy Vorontsov-Dashkov and more immediately by his adjutant, General Aleksandr Mishlaevskii, a former military historian who specialized in the period of Peter the Great.[99] The talented General Nikolai Iudenich served as chief-of-staff. On the Caucasian front, unlike Russia's western front, the war would be waged as a "war of movement" (*Bewegungskrieg*) rather than a "war of position" (*Stellungskrieg*).[100]

Both the Russians and the Ottomans wanted to use Armenians on both sides of the frontier against their enemies, pawns in their own titanic struggle. Except for the few who defected from the Ottomans to the Russians at the beginning of the war, most Armenians stayed loyal to their home empire. "Russian Armenians"—those living in the Caucasus and particularly in the cosmopolitan city of Tiflis—were generally enthusiastic about the Russian war effort against the Ottomans. Hampartsum Arakelian, the editor of the leading Armenian newspaper, *Mshak*, saw participation in the war as a patriotic duty, as both an Armenian and a Russian subject. "Only Russian forces," he wrote, "can secure the liberation of much-suffered Armenia and end the martyrdom of the Turkish Armenian community."[101] The leading writers among the Caucasian Armenians encouraged their countrymen to take advantage of this historic moment. Sofia Daniel-Bek rhapsodized, "We are standing against our centuries-long, historic enemy, who has, like a leech, sucked Armenians' blood, destroyed Armenians' home, trampled Armenians' honor. We are standing against our sworn enemy. Full of fiery revenge and limitless anger. The moment of vengeance has arrived."[102] A few months later an editorial in the Tiflis Dashnak newspaper *Horizon* declared proudly that Armenians who in the past had been extremely cautious were "walking tall as they take to the [war] stage."[103]

There were cautionary notes as well. The Marxist author David Ter-Danielian, who wrote under the pseudonym "D. Ananun" (Anonymous), was critical of the rush to war. He emphasized the differences between the political development of Armenians in the two empires and castigated the arrogance of Russian Armenians who persistently looked down on their Ottoman compatriots as victims who might be sacrificed. Close to the Hnchaks, Ananun warned the Dashnaks, "The politics of incitement, which might open the door of disaster for Armenians, must be avoided."[104] Other Armenians, like the cleric Grigoris Balakian, then a student in Berlin, worried that organizing volunteers in Russia was "an extremely dangerous development likely only to irritate the İttihad government and lead to grave consequences for the more than two million Armenians living in the Turkish empire."[105]

Russian state policy shifted on the eve of the war from relative hostility toward its own Armenians to an effort to attract them to the cause of the Entente. On August 5, 1914, the Ejmiatsin catholicos, Gevorg V, wrote to Viceroy Vorontsov-Dashkov that he doubted the sincerity of the current Ottoman government to carry out the promised reforms of the Armenian provinces. He asked the viceroy to convey to the emperor the fidelity of the Armenian community of Russia to the tsar and his empire, "as well as the attachment and sympathy without doubt [*sans faille*] of the Armenians of Turkey. Defend equally along with the tsar the hope that nourishes the Armenians of Turkey."[106] A month later, on September 2, Vorontsov-Dashkov requested that the catholicos use his authority "to have our Armenians join with those found on the other side of the frontier." The viceroy would inform them "what they must do in case of a Turkish-Russian war; I will instruct them as to the nature of their missions and demand that they carry out their duty."[107] The tsar made a grand promise to the catholicos that "a brilliant future awaited the Armenians," for once the war was concluded "the Armenian question will be resolved in accordance with Armenian expectations." Of course, this depended on Armenian loyalty to Russia, and

Nicholas warned the Armenians not to follow the Bulgarian example and turn away from their Russian benefactors.[108]

In August Vorontsov-Dashkov negotiated with prominent Russian Armenians, including the mayor of Tiflis, Alexandr Khatisian, to organize volunteer battalions of Armenians, some of them former Ottoman subjects.[109] Several thousand young men responded to the call. Four battalions were formed under the overall command of the legendary *fedayi* Andranik, born in the Ottoman Empire but already a veteran of the Balkan Wars where he had fought against the Ottomans. Among his sub-commanders was the former deputy to the Ottoman Parliament and leader of the Bank Ottoman seizure, Armen Garo, who had disobeyed the instructions of the Ottoman Dashnak party and defected to the Russians. These units were distinct and visible, not an integral part of the Russian army. The fact that subjects of the sultan, however few in number, were fighting on the Russian side offended the Ottomans and confirmed their suspicions of the Armenians. To those who saw the Armenians as traitors it did not matter that far more Ottoman Armenians joined the Ottoman army and fought against Russia until they were disarmed and sent to serve in labor battalions. Or that the formation of Armenian volunteer battalions in Russia matched what the Ottomans were doing on the other side of the frontier with the *Teşkilat-ı Mahsusa*, organizing Muslims to foment rebellion in Russia territories.

The Russians organized Christians in Persia into volunteer militias to defend the region against anticipated Ottoman forays. Christian villages in which Assyrians outnumbered Armenians were scattered in the plains near the town of Urmia, which became the headquarters of the militias. A Russian expert on Iran, then a diplomat in Persia, Vladimir Minorskii, opposed the militarization of the borderlands, fearing that "the measures we are currently planning will bring us no military advantage whatsoever and will serve only to unleash just reprisals upon the Christians and their supporters."[110]

The first phase of what would become genocide began as early as May 1914 when Ottoman agents penetrated the Russian borderlands and attempted to incite Muslim peasants to revolt.[111] As Ottoman troops moved into Ajara in December, they slaughtered Russian Armenians.[112] When Russian forces returned to the region, they also looted and marauded, and the correspondent for the *Manchester Guardian* reported that General Vladimir Liakhov "accused the Moslem natives of treachery, and sent his Cossacks from Batum with orders to kill every native at sight, and burn every village and every mosque. And very efficiently had they performed their task, for as we passed up the Chorokh valley to Artvin not a single habitable dwelling or a single living creature did we see."[113] While Russian authorities sanctioned some of the violence, lower-level commanders and ordinary soldiers acted on their own, raping, pillaging, and murdering ordinary civilians.[114] Suspecting the Muslim Ajars of disloyalty, the Russians decided to deport Georgian Muslims away from the borderlands.[115] Ajars were killed in the deportations, but the Russians generally refrained from systematic massacres or widespread arbitrary killing. The campaign to deport Ajars continued until September 10, 1915, when the authorities called a halt to it. The Russian government's campaign to nationalize the empire and combat "enemy aliens" was brutal at times, particularly in Galicia where the state targeted Jews for deportation, but unlike the treatment of Armenians and Assyrians in the Ottoman lands, it never metastasized into mass murder and genocide.[116] Russians distinguished their Muslim subjects from more loyal Christians, but their hostility was not as deep. They neither perceived Muslims as severe a threat as Ottoman Muslims felt toward Armenians and Assyrians nor did they descend to the kind of systematic savagery carried out across the frontier.

WAR WITHOUT DECLARATION: THE EASTERN BORDERLANDS

The Caucasian front was the longest front for the Ottomans and the most difficult to defend and supply.[117] The Ottoman-Russian border stretched 280 miles, but the zone of fighting extended twice that distance, deep into Ottoman territory and Persia. The lands between Russia, Persia, and the Ottoman Empire were a frontier region with porous borders. The Ottoman Third Army faced its traditional enemy, Russia, in an expanse of rough mountainous terrain lacking railways or adequate roads.

The climate was severe in winter and would contribute to the Ottomans' greatest defeat in the war. Caucasia, nevertheless, was a principal goal of the regime, for it was where the Ottomans had lost territory to the Russians in 1877–1878 and where their ambitions for strategic security were founded on finding Muslim allies across the border. If the faithful of Azerbaijan and Daghestan could be rallied to the Ottoman cause, the possibility arose that small buffer states would in the future stand between the Romanov and the Ottoman Empires.

The Young Turks' most important agent in the east, Bahaeddin Şakir, traveled to Erzurum, where he set up "councils" (*encümen*) for the *Teşkilat-ı Mahsusa* and organized a "Revolutionary Association for Caucasia." Local grievances combined with instigation by imperial agents on both sides to incite brutal mutual massacres. The irregular forces of the Special Organization, some around Trebizond under the command of the Ministry of War, others around Erzurum under Talat's Ministry of Interior, were active in the Caucasian regions that had been Ottoman until annexed by the Russians in 1878. The Germans set up their own headquarters in Erzurum to coordinate their activities in the Caucasus and Persia. Plans were made to infiltrate Russian territory and blow up the Baku-Batumi oil pipeline, as well as recruit Caucasian Muslims to fight against the Russians.[118] An ambitious officer, Max von Scheubner-Richter, became vice consul in the city, essentially an outpost for gathering information on the frontier region and recruiting men to fight the Russians.

Istanbul had decided not to tolerate compact non-Muslim populations anywhere near its vulnerable frontiers. In a telegram dated August 28, 1914, Talat's Ministry of Interior threatened that "those non-Muslim individuals who cross the border without a passport in hand [are to be] arrested and those found to be attempting to bring across weapons and ammunition are to be summarily executed."[119] In mid-September Talat signaled one of his agents by telegram that the *Teşkilat-ı Mahsusa* should instigate rebellion within neutral Persia.[120] Not far from the Persian border, in Van, the French vice consul, Barth de Sandfort, reported that a printed proclamation was circulating in Persian Azerbaijan, the region populated by Turkic speakers, calling on Muslims to show "Islamic solidarity in order to drive the enemy from our land."[121]

The Ottomans wooed Sunni Kurds and Turkic-speaking "Azerbaijanis" to their side and lumped the Assyrians in with the Armenians as enemies of the Ottoman state. When Ottoman Assyrians refused to be mobilized into the Ottoman army, the authorities requisitioned their property and set fire to their villages. Many fled to Persia. Since the Russians occupied much of northern Persia, gangs of recent recruits launched attacks on their troops and the Assyrians across the Persian border, looting Christian villages.[122] On the very eve of the declaration of war, on October 26, 1914, Talat ordered the deportation of the Assyrians from the border regions controlled by his government westward into central Anatolia. "The Nestorians," he explained, "have always remained suspect to the government due to their predisposition to be influenced by foreigners and become a channel and an instrument. Because of the operations and activities in Iran, the concern of the government over Nestorians has increased, particularly about those who are found along our border with Iran. The government's lack of trust of them results in their chastisement—their deportation and expulsion from their locations to suitable provinces such as Ankara and Konya."[123] The Assyrians had thought of the violence they were enduring as a continuation of the familiar brutalities suffered before the war, but this mass deportation was an unprecedented innovation. Assyrians were to be dispersed among myriad villages, submerged into a sea of Turkish-speaking Muslims. Rather than resettlement, this policy was aimed to destroy a distinct culture.[124]

The thirteenth Russo-Ottoman War began along the Persian and Caucasian borders. In late August and early September, before war had been officially declared, the fighting in the borderlands of the East was largely the task of the *Teşkilat-ı Mahsusa*. Ottoman troops attacked villages and moved toward the city of Urmia. Assyrian and Armenian volunteers fought alongside the Russians.[125] When the Russians fell back to Urmia, they exposed the Christian villages of the plain. Two missionaries witnessed the attack on Urmia by Kurdish and Turkish troops under the command of Turkish officers. "After having descended in the plain of Urmia the Turco-Kurds burned all the Christian villages which they encountered on their way, such as Anhar, Alwatshe and massacred the columns of refugees."[126] Another witness reported that Nestorian and Armenian villages "were ruthlessly wiped out after the Russian retreat."[127]

The Ottoman campaign in Persia rapidly degenerated into chaotic slaughter as the front between the Ottomans and Russians moved back and forth. The *Teşkilat-ı Mahsusa* carried out massacres in Pertus and Yörük, near Ardanuç and Olti.[128] When the Ottomans retook the cities of Saray and Başkale from the Russians, they exacted reprisals on the local Christians, whom they considered collaborators. In the first week of December, gendarmes and *Hamidiye* units "pillaged and burned the Armenian houses, killed all of the men and left their cadavers in the street, captured the beautiful girls, and abandoned the women and children without food or shelter.... The Armenians of the villages of Paz, Arak, Piss, Alanian, Alas, Soran, Rasoulan, and Avak were ... conducted to a place where all were massacred."[129] The victims were primarily men. A woman watched as her husband and sons were tortured to death.

> They were beaten from all sides and ordered to become Muslims, but they refused. Before my eyes Hurshid Bey shot my sons with a pistol. As I saw what happened, I tried to protect my husband, but Hurshid Bey kicked me in the face knocking out two teeth. Then he shot my husband with six bullets. The corpses of the dead, even that of my husband, were left lying in the road. We were not allowed to bury the dead. Hurshid Bey ordered that the corpses be smeared in excrement. In the following four days the dogs ate the corpses. Then Hurshid Bey ordered that the corpses be thrown in the latrine, where even the cross of the village church got thrown. Then Hurshid had the whole village burned and twelve people killed.... 150 women and girls were forced to become the wives of Hurshid Bey's relatives.[130]

At the same time that the Ottomans were fostering rebellion among Georgian Muslims and Turkic peoples across the border in Russia and Persia, the Russians set out to stir up revolts among Armenians and Kurds in the Ottoman lands. The Ottomans were well aware of the Armenian battalions on the Russian side and feared their infiltration into Anatolia, where they might join up with Armenian deserters from the Ottoman army.[131] Armenian volunteer forces preceded the primary attack of the Russian army when in early December the battalion commanded by Armen Garo pushed some of the peripheral Ottoman forces between Beyazıd and Manzikert toward the west. The Ottomans reported that the Armenian troops massacred Muslims unable to withdraw with the Ottoman army in the course of the next two weeks. *Teşkilat-ı Mahsusa* took Ardahan on December 29 and moved up toward Batumi through Ajara, the region populated by Georgian Muslims. In town after town they called out Christian men and shot them. Massacres followed. Fleeing Armenians told the Russians what had happened, and Cossacks retaliated with their own massacres. Russian units aided by Armenian volunteers thwarted any further advance, and the Ottomans pulled back. When the Russians retook Ardahan in early January, they too engaged in pillage of the market, burned the Muslim quarter, and killed any Turks they encountered.[132] Savagery by one side incited savagery on the other, and the efforts by General Zubov to stop the Muslim-Armenian bloodletting in Kars went unheeded.

Once again leaving the Christians in Persia undefended, the Russians pulled back from Urmia and Salmas, retreating from Persia altogether in early January. Abandoning their animals and property, Armenians and Assyrians who were able trekked through the snow and mud for seven days to reach the Russian border. Men who served in the volunteer militias were separated from their families, which were left behind.[133] The Russians counted nearly 50,000 Armenian and more than 8,000 Assyrian refugees by the end of January.[134]

To most observers the reports of massacres of Armenians were particularly alarming because of the memory of what had happened years before, fear of what might occur, and the evident scale of the killings. "On the first of the month," the German consul in Erzurum reported to his ambassador, "three Turkish irregulars visited a distinguished priest in the village of Osni on the Erzurum plateau, where they ate and slept. The next morning they forced him to accompany them to the edge of the village, where he was shot to death with a shotgun." Consul Schwarz observed, "The Armenian population maintains that the Turkish party 'İttihad' instigates this movement. It is a matter of fact that Turkish officers do not see eye to eye with the Armenians and reproach them with being friendly to Russia and helping Russian troops to get into Turkish territory. Even with the Turkish population, as one can see from certain symptoms, the old hatred is rising again." Erzurum Armenians anticipated a new round of massacres. Ambassador Wangenheim reported to Chancellor Bethmann Hollweg on the "Turkish excesses against Armenians," which he urged the grand vizier to stop. "But the Grand Vizier pointed out that these incidents did not occur without Armenian provocation; as proof he pointed out that Armenians are openly taking sides against the Turkish cause in the war, and he mentioned that the Bulgarian Armenians sent a troop of volunteers to Russia."[135]

TOTAL WAR

With rumors and accusations spreading that Armenian soldiers were deserting, prominent Armenians met in Istanbul with the patriarch and decided he should send a circular to the provinces urging Armenians everywhere to declare their fidelity to the empire and maintain good relations with the government and the CUP.[136] "[Our] people should be exhorted," the patriarch's circular declared, "from the church pulpit and on other occasions, in writing and orally, to fulfill their obligations toward the Ottoman fatherland with complete sincerity, just like they have done for centuries."[137] As a gesture of good will, the Istanbul Armenians promised to found a field hospital at the expense of the Armenian nation. The patriarch met with Petros Halajian, a member of the CUP and a government minister, and requested he inform his party comrades that the Armenians of the empire would fulfill their duties.[138]

The Young Turks wanted more from the Armenians. Once again they tested the waters, sending emissaries to Erzurum and Van to determine whether the Armenians would agree to instigate an uprising in the

Russian South Caucasus. Once again the offer was rejected. With violence directed against Armenians increasing, prominent Armenians met with Cevdet, the *vali* of Van, to air their grievances, but Cevdet turned on them and accused them of misconstruing the situation. He wrote to Talat ominously, "I believe that the Armenians will be a problem."[139]

The descent into total war was accelerating. A few weeks after the entry of the Ottomans into the war, the state and religious authorities issued a *fetva* (legal opinion) declaring the struggle with Britain, France, Russia, Serbia, and Montenegro to be a jihad. The term *cihad* in Turkish can be variously interpreted as a great personal struggle against one's urges or a campaign against infidels.[140] To the West jihad meant a "holy war" directed at mobilizing Muslims against Christians. The Ottomans had occasionally declared various conflicts in the past *cihad*—several wars against Russia (though not the Crimean War, the Russo-Turkish War of 1877, or the Balkan Wars). The declaration was meant to mobilize Muslims, particularly the Arabs, who were being courted by Britain to revolt against their colonial overlords. As caliph, Sultan Mehmed V also appealed to the Shi'i of Iran and to Muslim subjects in the colonies of the Entente powers, most importantly in Egypt and India.[141] The major Shi'i clerics in the Ottoman cities of Najaf and Qerbala followed with their own *fatwa* of *cihad*.[142] At the same time the proclamation of *cihad* excluded the non-Muslims of the empire and placed them in the anomalous position of being recruited to fight for the Ottoman cause while that cause was proclaimed a struggle against much of Christian Europe with whom many Armenians and Greeks identified.[143]

To inspire people to fight for the empire was a difficult task after the long series of Ottoman defeats culminating in the Balkan Wars. The call for jihad was meant to inspire people through their faith. Although the Young Turk leaders themselves were not deeply pious—many were even hostile to Islam—they were prepared to use religious appeals instrumentally to mobilize ordinary people. Foreign observers were convinced that anti-Christian sentiments were fundamental to Islam, and some went as far as American Ambassador Morgenthau to hold that violence was inscribed in Islam.[144] On November 14 mobs attacked several foreign stores in Istanbul—the Bon Marché, an Austrian shop advertising "English clothes" for sale, as well as the Armenian-owned Tokatlian's, "the most important restaurant in Constantinople."[145] "That was the extent of the 'Holy War'!"[146] The Armenian satirist Ervant Otian had a similar memory of the declaration of jihad:

> Afterwards, a vast procession, which included all Turkish workers—nutsellers, porters, coachmen, butchers and so forth—paraded through the streets to the ear-splitting accompaniment of drums and pipes (*davoul zourna*). This motley crowd, preceded by strangely dressed men with savage faces waving naked swords in the air, flowed over the Galata bridge and headed towards Pera to demonstrate their enmity outside the Russian, French and British embassies. The demonstrators weren't satisfied with all this and, in the late afternoon, attacked the Tokatlian Café, smashing windows, destroying the furnishings and utensils, dinner services and ornaments, and severely beating several Christian customers who happened to be there. The announcement of the holy war ended with this savage act.

Yet, Otian notes, "proclamations of holy war, the ensuing events and the Turks' anti-Christian demonstrations that were repeated nearly every day in one form or another, began to worry Constantinople's inhabitants, especially the Armenians towards whom a special hatred seemed to be expressed."[147]

Istanbul was desperate to find ways to reach the public and inspire them to fight and die for the empire. Literacy was low, particularly outside the cities. Probably less than one out of ten could read, perhaps half the people in Istanbul but only about 3 to 4 percent in the eastern Anatolian towns of Van or Hakkari.[148] Poems, folktales, and songs, many of them laments, took up what the printed page could not.[149] The government presented the war as a struggle to recover lost lands in the Balkans and the Caucasus, as an opportunity to take revenge on those who had despoiled their patrimony, and as the necessary self-defense of the fatherland against the aggression of the British and the Russians.[150] The Ottomans presented

themselves as the victims of certain malevolent European powers that attacked the Ottomans on the Black Sea and in the Caucasus. The theme
of restoring a sovereign and no-longer dependent empire was mixed with
the need to defend Islam and wreak revenge for recent losses. All these
threads came together in the celebration of the ordinary Ottoman soldier, "Little Mehmet" (*Mehmetçik*), who embodied state patriotism with
religious dedication, obedience, and loyalty to his superiors.[151] *Mehmetçik*
was a Turk more than he was an Ottoman; non-Muslims and even Arabs
were excluded.[152] In a well-known story written in 1915, Turkish soldiers
ready to be martyred sang, "The Turk's blood has drenched this land;
my mother gave birth to me for this day."[153] The enemies of the empire
were not only foreign states but devious, untrustworthy, stealthy internal
elements as well, people connected to foreign states and waiting for an
opportunity to turn on the Turks. Having lost the Balkans and believing
that their last stronghold was Anatolia, the Young Turks felt that the war
for that homeland required the elimination, one way or another, of the
Christians, an action that they justified as self-defense.

SARIKAMIŞ

Once officially in the war, the Ottomans came under attack from different margins of their empire. The British took Basra at the southern end
of Mesopotamia in late November as the Russians began their moves out
of Caucasia. The first Russian probe across the border was a disaster, and
Enver was encouraged to launch a major campaign on the Caucasian
front. He decided to repeat the enormously successful German maneuver
at Tannenberg and encircle the Russian army headquarters near the town
of Sarıkamış, an outpost that had been taken by the Russians three decades earlier. Winter was approaching, and the Ottoman Third Army was
not properly equipped. The geography was suitable for a defensive stance,
but not for offensive operations.[154] His local commander and German allies warned Enver of the difficulties of a winter campaign in the rough
terrain around Sarıkamış, but he was determined to strike a decisive blow
against Russia. The Russians, however, had significant advantages. They

Russian troops at the battle of Sarıkamış, December 1914–January 1915.

had extended their railroad line from Tiflis to Aleksandropol and on to Kars and Sarıkamış, integrating the former Ottoman territories into their empire, while the Ottomans had done little building of their rail infrastructure on the other side of the border. Abdülhamid had agreed in 1900 to allow only the Ottomans or the Russians to build a railroad along the Black Sea; since the Ottomans were ultimately unable to construct the line, and the Russians decided not to build in Ottoman territory, Russia essentially prevented the railroad from being built. The last station in northern Anatolia was in Ankara, 700 miles west of Erzurum, the headquarters of the Third Army. In eastern Anatolia the only means of transport was by draft animals, by oxcarts, or by foot. Supplying an army in the East would become even more difficult once the Russians established their control of the Black Sea in the middle of 1915.

Enver took personal command of the army in the East. The fighting raged for almost a month, from late December into mid-January. At first Enver was dramatically successful. The Ottomans moved closer to Sarıkamış, and the Russians were about to pull back when General Iudenich decided to make a stand. The Ottoman troops were not prepared for the harsh winter in the Anatolian highlands; they had marched for days through deep snow, and thousands froze to death. Early in 1915 the Russians, accompanied by Armenian volunteer units, pushed the Ottoman army back. A disastrous defeat followed. The Ottomans lost more than 45,000 men killed; thousands more deserted or were taken prisoner. The Russians lost about 28,000 killed or wounded.[155] Enver left his army on January 8 for Istanbul, congratulating them on their "performance, which he claimed, rivaled the glorious days of the early Ottoman Empire."[156] A Turkish military historian refers to Enver's loss as "the self-inflicted defeat of the Ottoman III Army at the Sarıkamış Offensive."[157]

At the same time as the disaster at Sarıkamış, a general panic gripped Istanbul. It was feared that the city would fall to the Bulgarians, who might join the war on the side of the Entente, or to the British, who were rumored to be about to break through the Dardanelles. Talat, Ambassador Morgenthau reported, "was the picture of desolation and defeat" in early 1915 as the thunder of the British guns at the Straits seemed "to spell doom."[158] There was fear of revolution in the city, and posters denounced the minister of interior. The prefect of police, Bedri Bey, rounded up unemployed young men and expelled them from the capital. The Young Turk leaders planned to burn down the city if the British broke through, a wanton act that shocked Morgenthau. "There are not six men in the Committee of Union and Progress," Talat told him, "who care for anything that is old. We all like new things."[159] The authority of the CUP, Morgenthau estimated, "throughout the empire was exceedingly tenuous." British troops landed and took ancient Ottoman forts at the mouth of the Straits of the Dardanelles in mid-February. At the moment when the Allied fleet attempted to move through the Dardanelles and reach the Sea of Marmara on March 18, the Ottoman state "was on the brink of dissolution." "Among the subject races the spirit of revolt was rapidly spreading," Morgenthau wrote. "The Greeks and the Armenians would also have welcomed an opportunity to strengthen the hands of the Allies."[160]

But the Allies did not break through; the Germans and Turks held them off, and the fleet pulled back. The panic continued for another month. Leading Armenians were arrested in Istanbul on April 24, and when on the next day the Allies landed troops at Gallipoli in another futile campaign, the Young Turks responded by rounding up foreigners to use as hostages placed among the Muslim villages in the Gallipoli region. The police even briefly arrested the prominent lawyer and commentator on Ottoman affairs Sir Edwin Pears, a forty-year resident of the Ottoman capital. The panic only subsided once Bulgaria joined the Central Powers (October 14, 1915) and the Ottomans gained a direct rail line to Germany.[161]

Toward the end of January Enver, who as commander was largely responsible for the Sarıkamış disaster, returned from the front, unsure of his reception by the public. The "generalissimo" told the Armenian patriarch that he avoided captivity during the battle only because an Armenian, Sergeant Major Hovhannes, executed an "unauthorized maneuver."[162] Once back in Istanbul Enver ordered that no negative news about the losses at Sarıkamış be reported. Even parliamentary deputies and the cabinet ministers were not told what had happened. Disinformation was widely spread. Addressing Parliament, Enver spoke of a great victory, but even strict censorship could not prevent deserters and survivors of the battle from spreading the truth. The German advisors to the Ottomans were well aware of the disaster in the East. Enver and his closest associates framed the story of the battle in their own way, and the prevailing view placed Armenian treachery at the center of the narrative. Given the attitudes and sentiments that many Muslims had toward Armenians, they became a convenient excuse for Ottoman losses, an available scapegoat.

Sarıkamış marked the end of the first phase—the sporadic massacres and deportations along the Caucasian front and in Persia—of what would metastasize into genocide. Enver's disastrous defeat was the prelude to the "final solution" of the Armenian Question. The Russians posed a real danger to the Ottomans, just at the moment that Allied forces were about to attack at Gallipoli in the west. Fear turned into anxiety, a generalized fear without a specific object, fear of an unpredictable future. Anger at perceived betrayal metamorphosed into hatred of those who by their nature were devious and treacherous. Their very existence undermined the empire and the Turkish nation. Enver took two hundred "Russian" Armenians as hostage from Olti and imprisoned them in Erzurum. He had thirty Armenians from Ardahan, another territory that had been Russian since 1878, hanged before the Istanbul Gate in Erzurum.[163]

The violence was random, and the *çete*s of the *Teşkilat-ı Mahsusa* even turned on fellow Muslims. The army demanded the disbandment of the irregular units or their integration into the regular army. The main danger, however, was seen to be the Armenians. In this moment of defeat and desperation, the triumvirate in Istanbul decided to demobilize the Armenian soldiers and other non-Muslims in the Ottoman army, disarm them, and move them into labor battalions.[164] On February 25 the Ottoman General Staff released Enver's Directive 8682 on "Increased Security Precautions," which called for the removal of all ethnic Armenian soldiers and officers from command posts and headquarters staffs. The directive went on to accuse the Armenian patriarchate of transmitting military secrets and locations to the Russians.[165] While some Armenians continued to serve as soldiers, doctors, and translators well into 1916, their humiliating demotion convinced many non-Muslims to desert rather than shovel garbage, push wheelbarrows, and dig ditches.[166] Whether Armenian soldiers had served loyally and risked their lives or been conscripted reluctantly and were ready to desert after what they had experienced was unimportant to Talat, Enver, and their closest associates. This new, cleansed army, emptied of its "unreliable" elements, would be able to do things that the ethnically and religiously mixed army could not.

Dispatches from the East repeatedly spoke of Armenian treachery, rebellion, and the potential threat to Ottoman supply lines. Any incident of Armenian resistance, any discovery of a cache of arms, was transformed into a vision of a coordinated widespread Armenian insurrection.[167] When the British ship HMS *Doris* shelled the Syrian coast, blew up a bridge, and took several Armenians on board, Ottomans perceived an immediate threat to their rail connections along the southern coast. On the suggestion of the commander of the Fourth Army, Cemal Paşa, who had suffered a defeat in Suez at the hands of the British in the first months of 1915, Talat ordered the removal of Armenians from the area of Dörtyol, an important rail connection.[168] On March 2 he informed the authorities in Adana that the "plan for the Armenians of Dörtyol to be sent to the areas assigned to them" had been accepted in order "not to permit the manifestation of an environment that will result in revolt and rebellion." Actions were to be taken "extremely forcefully and speedily in those areas where Armenian operations and activities have increased, and to suppress each occurrence in the place where it has occurred, by means of effective and definitive measures."[169]

What evolved rapidly into genocide began as sporadic massacres that following a colossal defeat resulted in political panic, despair, and a thirst for vengeance. Rationalized at the time and later as a military necessity, framed by the imperial ambitions and distressed perceptions of the Ottoman leaders, demobilization of soldiers and particular deportations of Armenians and Assyrians quickly turned into a massive attack on entire peoples, a systematic program of murder and pillage. Deportations ostensibly taken for military reasons rapidly radicalized monstrously into an opportunity to rid Anatolia once and for all of those peoples perceived to be an imminent existential threat to the future of the empire.

CHAPTER EIGHT

Removal

The story sounds as if it should begin, "once upon a time." But this is not a fairy tale but a report related by a credible witness, the priest Grigoris Balakian.

> A high-ranking Turkish official in Adana had a close relationship with a wealthy Armenian who held an official position in that city and enjoyed respect and influence in local European circles. One day in the beginning of February 1915 the former invited the latter to meet with him, and said to him in confidence: "A new storm is about to break upon the Armenians so I hope that you will save yourself." The horrified Armenian merchant asked, "What can I do to save myself?" The Turkish official answered tersely, "Go to Mersin, get on a steamship, and escape to Europe. . . . don't waste time by saying, 'Let me save my wealth.' Believe me, later you will be sorry."[1]

Learning that deportations of whole families were planned, the merchant fled with his family. Before leaving Adana he warned the Armenian catholicos of Cilicia, Sahag II Khabayan, who in turn confirmed the story in a conversation with one of the three supreme leaders of the empire, Cemal Paşa, who was passing through Adana as commander of the Syrian and Palestinian front. Cemal claimed to have attempted to moderate the program of wholesale deportation of Armenians and limit it to writers, intellectuals, and political leaders, but he had failed to convince his colleagues. Sahag sent a courier to inform the patriarch in Istanbul of what he had learned. The Armenian patriarch conferred with the German ambassador and told the courier that he had been assured that there would be no massacres. Armenians, he said, should "steer clear of provocative actions, busy themselves with their daily work, and obey government orders and instructions."[2]

RADICALIZATION

Sometime after the disastrous defeat at Sarıkamış, but before either the major Gallipoli landings or the resistance of the Armenians at Van, a small cabal of Young Turk leaders decided that the Armenians had to be deported from areas near the military fronts. Assessing the catastrophic loss in the east, the key Young Turk agent in the region, Bahaeddin Şakir, returned to Istanbul from his six-month stay in Erzurum and reported to the party leaders that the internal enemy was as dangerous as the foreign.[3] In his memoir the Young Turk Arif Cemil, who worked with Şakir, justified what was about to take place: "[N]umerous documents that were discovered [plainly showed] that the domestic enemies who had organized inside the country were preparing to attack our army from the rear. After Dr. Bahaeddin Şakir had brought all this to the attention of the *İttihad*'s Central Committee in Istanbul, the Committee worked together with him on defining the measures to be taken; thanks to them, the Turkish army avoided a great danger. The result of their collaboration was the deportation law."[4]

Şakir's central role in moving toward massive deportations and massacres is both undeniable and obscure. An account by Hüseyin Cahit Yalçın, a journalist sympathetic to Şakir, noted that Bahaeddin Shakir's role in the deportations "was not dissected or illuminated even at our most intimate [CUP] meetings. I do not have a clear, absolute opinion, but from a word used when other issues were being discussed, a thought that leaked out, jests that could not be contained, in summary, from all the fine and slight clues, according to the guess that strongly manifested itself in me, he was the greatest motivator and creator of the deportation business." Şakir laid the groundwork in his travels in the eastern provinces and "dragged along with him some of his influential friends in government." Yalçın added, "because of [these actions], when there comes one day the need to rejuvenate Şakir's memory, the eastern provinces will bare their chests to his statue in gratitude."[5]

The decision that "the deportation of the Armenians was necessary for the sake of our national ideals" was taken after serious and prolonged deliberation in the central committee of the CUP, sometime at the end of March or beginning of April 1915.[6] Without elaborately working out what they were about to do or considering the consequences of undertaking such a massive displacement of population in time of war, the Young Turks moved step by inexorable step to ever more radical implementation of their security policies. "A reading of Ottoman archival materials," writes the historian Taner Akçam, "suggests that these early measures, such as the disarming of Armenian recruits in the Ottoman Third Army and their transfer to labor battalions, the searching of Armenian villages for weapons, and the staging of raids against these villages to appropriate food and other necessities for the war effort, might have been temporary measures rather than the first steps of a predetermined plan."[7] Each step the government took made matters worse, creating the conditions for resistance and for individuals and groups to take matters into their own hands. Intelligence reports from the East spoke excitedly about weapons caches, severed telegraph lines, and sporadic killing by Armenians. Such reports fed the mood in Istanbul about Armenian treachery and confirmed what the Young Turks already believed. They discounted contrary reports that Armenians were pacific and loyal, with a few exceptions, or that much of the trouble was the result of disorderly mobilization and the high number of deserters, or were simply part of the "undeclared war in the Caucasus between the Ottoman Empire and Russia."[8] The anxieties of the Young Turks about the Armenians, their fears of insurrection, their exaggeration of the threat from "Armenian gangs," not only accelerated a process leading toward genocide but created the conditions that made genocide less and less avoidable.

By the spring of 1915 the second phase of what was fast developing into genocide was under way. The first effects of the new policy touched the Armenian men serving in military labor battalions.[9] Described by one historian as "sitting ducks," these men had already been separated, disarmed, and marked as unreliable. Kept under guard, they were taken in groups, sometimes one hundred at a time, to deserted places where they were shot or bayonetted, often by irregular forces or Kurdish bands. Skilled Armenian workers or engineers employed in the building of the Baghdad Railroad were often exempted, sometimes protected by their German employers, until most of them too were finished off in 1916.[10] The commander of the Caucasian front, Vehip Paşa, was enraged that "his" Armenians toiling on road repair were removed and killed, and he called for court-martial of those implicated. Many Armenian soldiers, at least for a while, evaded death by converting to Islam, but tens, if not hundreds, of thousands of others were murdered.[11]

After Sarıkamış the remnants of Enver's Third Army, as well as deserting soldiers, filtered into villages, living off and preying on the inhabitants. With them came typhus, which devastated both soldiers and civilians. The American consul-general George Horton reported from the Aegean port of Izmir [Smyrna] on February 4 that "lawless Turkish bands are appearing in increasing numbers in [Smyrna] district and are spreading a reign of terror among the Christians of all races." It was not clear if the bands were deserters or *komitaci*s (political agents) sent out by the Young Turk Committee, "which is really the government or the power behind it, to terrify and drive out the Christians."[12] Gangs destroyed the village of Piruk in the *kaza* of Suşehir. In Erzurum two soldiers killed a prominent Armenian banker, Setrak Pastermajian, the brother of the parliamentary deputy Armen Garo, who had defected to the Russians.[13] In mid-February eight hundred Armenians were sent from Salmas in Persia toward neighboring villages where they were tortured, mutilated, and then killed and thrown into wells and cisterns.[14]

The Young Turk leaders suspended the Ottoman Parliament on March 1, and a forum where protests might have been heard was silenced.[15] In the next weeks British and French ships attacked the Dardanelles. Armenians living on the Gallipoli peninsula were moved, eventually ending up in Syria. The Russian consul in Persia, Pavl Vvedenskii, reported that the Ottomans had executed more than seven hundred Assyrian and Armenian Christians between the Chaldean town of Khosrowa and the Armenian town of Dilman. He noted headless corpses and bodies crushed under rocks from fallen walls.[16] "I have investigated twenty villages," he wrote. "Everywhere there is complete ruin and devastation. Churches, schools and libraries have only walls [standing]. Icons and sacred items are lying in the mud, torn and riddled with bullets. Some churches were transformed into stables or supply rooms for food or plunder. The villages are full of corpses of the poor victims of massacres, which were carried out by Turks and Kurds everywhere. . . . The corpses bear the marks of cruel killing with axes, daggers and blunt objects."[17] So brutal were these executions that the Ottoman high commander was stunned by what was referred to as an "unfortunate incident" caused by undisciplined troops and wild volunteers.[18] In the middle of the month when the Russians were about to return to Salmas, the retreating Ottomans "secured the names of all Christians by a ruse, pretending that all who registered would be protected." An American Presbyterian missionary, F. N. Jessup, related what happened next: "Then they gathered all the men into one place and carried them out in companies of about twenty-five, each to be shot down in cold blood. Others were tied with their heads sticking through the rungs of a ladder and decapitated, others hacked to pieces or mutilated before death. In this way practically every Christian man remaining in Salmas was massacred. You can imagine the fate of girls and women."[19]

Even as the panic over the potential Allied breakthrough in the Dardanelles subsided, the plans for dealing with the Armenians matured. The journalist Hüseyin Cahit Yalçın listened carefully to Enver's analysis as the two of them toured the Dardanelles in March. "When he talked about the events at the Caucasian front," Yalçın remembered, Enver "recounted the difficulties the army faced, the damage it suffered and the danger it fell into. In their attempt to hit the Turkish army from the rear, the rebelling Armenian committees attacked supply lines, killed the wounded, spied for the enemy, in short created a catastrophe for the Turkish army." Enver indicated that "he believed in the necessity to uproot all the Armenians in the Eastern provinces and send them elsewhere. When he saw me hesitate in front of the scope and difficulty of this endeavor, he explicated as if to respond to a question I had in my mind, but could not express. . . . 'Nothing will happen to these Armenians, and provisions will be made to settle them in places where they will not produce any harm.'"[20]

The operation of deportations, followed by mass killing that appeared to be out of the control of the government, was organized on two distinct but related tracks: through official government channels and through an alternative network of party and personal communications. "There are certain secrets that I learned in my most recent, brief service in the [İzzet Paşa] cabinet that didn't survive more than 25–30 days," wrote Reşit Akif Paşa just after the World War ended. "Among these I came across one peculiar thing. This deportation order was given openly and in official fashion by the Interior Ministry, and communicated to the provinces. But after this official order [was given], the inauspicious order was circulated by the Central Committee to all parties so that the armed gangs [*çete*] could hastily complete their cursed task. With that, the armed gangs then took over and the barbaric massacres then began to take place."[21] Later during the trials of the Young Turks held in 1919, former Ankara Governor Mazhar Bey testified, "I acted as if I did not understand the orders concerning the deportation of Armenians that I received from the interior minister in Istanbul. As you know, other provinces had already completed their deportation operations that I had not yet begun. [Then] Atıf Bey arrived. . . . He orally relayed to me the order regarding the killing and annihilation of the Armenians. I told him 'No, Atıf Bey, I am the governor, I'm not a bandit. I cannot do it. I will get up from the [governor's] chair and you can come and do it.'"[22]

Through March 1915 sporadic violence and massacres broke out in different parts of Anatolia and Persia. War, hunger, and dislocated populations tore asunder the threadbare fabric of Ottoman society. No particular direction or clear intention was apparent; local grievances that had accumulated for decades combined with a novel permissiveness granted by war to incite brutalities of extreme viciousness. Order and the norms of civil life broke down steadily throughout Anatolia in early 1915. In Sivas Turks accused Armenians of having poisoned the bread served to the army. All the Armenian bakers and some soldiers were jailed. The bread was tested on some dogs, and it was said that several dogs died. But an investigation exonerated the Armenians, and "the matter was buried, with a public announcement to the effect that the municipality had poisoned the dogs to get rid of them."[23]

REBELLION AT ZEYTUN

In the historically resistant region of Zeytun Muslim refugees from the Balkans, resentful and angry because of their suffering in and after the recent wars, moved in and settled among the local Armenians.[24] With the call for military mobilization young Muslims about to be recruited flowed into Zeytun, which had been designated a conscription center. Deserters turned to banditry, and clashes occurred between townspeople and newcomers.[25] Many Zeytun Armenian young men refused to join the Ottoman army, despite the urging of their political leaders. Tensions were high in the region, and Armenians in the diaspora sought to exploit them and organize a rebellion in Cilicia against the empire. Boghos Nubar in Paris and others contemplated an Allied landing on the coast, which would inspire a rebellion by Zeytuntsis and others. Local Armenians opposed such an adventure, and the Allies never agreed to the plan. The desperate situation in Zeytun inspired others to think of rebellion, but after the church authorities preached patience and caution, most Armenian leaders gave up the idea of resistance. The Cilician catholicos Sahak II cautioned the Zeytuntsis to refrain from rebellion, and even though Armenians in Zeytun were themselves divided, the majority of the 20,000 inhabitants opposed insurrection.[26] Some Armenian notables reported the activity of younger radicals to the Ottoman authorities, who arrested and tortured Armenians suspected of disloyalty; some were beaten to death.[27]

The first deportations of civilian Armenians began in March. On the twelfth the Cilician town of Dörtyol was emptied of Armenians; many of the men disappeared into the labor battalions. The Armenians did not resist. Three who tried to flee were shot. An Armenian working for the German consulate in Adana was impressed by the discipline shown by the military during the arrests, which "took place without misdeeds or excesses," probably because "the Turks allied themselves with the Germans. They would disapprove of any brutal and unjust act and prevent it from happening."[28]

As reports filtered in that Christian soldiers were being disarmed and placed in labor battalions, deserters became bandits and bandits became rebels. On March 13 the army moved into Zeytun ostensibly looking for deserters.[29] A few dozen resisters holed up in the St. Astuatsatsin (St. Mary) monastery but failed to inspire the Armenian populace. No aid came from other parts of Cilicia. Ottoman troops took the monastery on March 26, 1915, and burned it to the ground. The rebels fled into the mountains as the soldiers raided the town, searched houses, rounded up deserters, and arrested suspects. The loyalist Armenian notables were arrested along with rebels; many of them were eventually deported, some hanged. Beginning on April 8 and continuing into May, the town was nearly emptied, with only a few hundred families remaining. Some 22,000 Zeytuntsis, almost all women and children, were sent westward; many ended up in Konya.[30] Few provisions were made for the deportees once they arrived.[31] Thousands starved or weakened by hunger died from disease. On April 24 Talat issued a new order: there were too many Armenians in Konya; they should be sent to the southeast, to Aleppo, Der el Zor in the Syrian desert, and Urfa. In early May Talat ordered that Zeytun be completely emptied of Armenians. Almost immediately their houses were turned over to Muslim refugees, many of them from Bosnia.[32] What had been a minor rebellion by a handful of deserters, an action opposed by the majority of Zeytuntsis, became in 1915 the catalyst for a massive expulsion of the Armenians from the region, a step forward toward the elimination of a whole people.[33]

PRELUDE TO GENOCIDE: VAN

Throughout eastern Anatolia relations between Muslims and Armenians rapidly deteriorated through late 1914 and early 1915. West of Lake Van the region of Muş, inhabited by Kurds and Armenians, had fallen into anarchy by the end of 1914. The Dashnak parliamentary deputy Vahan Papazian arrived in December and tried to mediate with the local authorities to prevent collapse and rebellion. Kurds attacked Armenians, and Armenians contemplated withdrawing south into the mountains of Sasun for protection. Two Dashnaks, Ruben Ter Minassian and Koriun, fearing that some Kurdish gendarmes whom they had fed and housed planned to murder them, trapped them in a stable and set it on fire. Papazian and other activists fled into the mountains.[34] Nearby in Bitlis several young Armenian men were arrested and hanged, the same day as resistance in the eastern Anatolian city of Van began.

Lying at the foot of a towering rock formation, Van was inhabited long before Armenians arrived. The great citadel at Tushba, the capital of the Urartian Empire, was built there in the ninth century BCE. Van became the capital of the ancient and medieval Armenian states of Vaspurakan, which for centuries were ruled by the princely Artsruni family. On islands within the great Lake Van and on its shores devout Armenians built severe stone churches. The most famous, *Surb Khach* (Holy Cross), adorned with iconic reliefs, stands to this day like a sentinel on the island of Aghtamar. The intrepid traveler H. F. B. Lynch visited Van at the turn of the century and reported that an Armenian proverb proclaimed, "Van in this world and paradise in the next."[35] Turks had their own view of Van, expressed in song, "*Dünyada Van, Ahrette iman*" (Van in this world, faith in the afterlife).[36] Rising in the old city of Van was a great rocky outcrop from which the ruins of the venerable citadel overlooked the town. At the base of the towering rock was the old walled city with churches and mosques sharing the crowded space with bazaars and houses primarily inhabited by Armenians. Beyond the walled city was the suburban district of Aigestan, the garden city, with vineyards and orchards, which stretched eastward for 4 miles; here too Armenians dominated. Another 10 miles east across the plain rose Mount Varag on which the medieval Armenians had built the venerable monastery Varagavank (*Yedi Kilise* in Turkish). The Van *vilayet* housed the largest and most compact population of Armenians in Anatolia; nowhere else in the empire were Armenians a majority of the inhabitants. Some 450 towns and villages dotted the sparsely populated province, inhabited by between 110,000 and 200,000 Armenians.[37]

In the months leading up to the war the local Armenian nationalists, the Dashnaks, were a principal political force in the region, closely allied with the relatively enlightened governor, Tahsin Bey (Hasan Tahsin Uzer).[38] The American physician and missionary Clarence Ussher testified that the Dashnak leaders Arshak Vramian, a member of the Ottoman

Parliament, Aram Manukian, and Nigol Mikaielian, known as *Ishkhan* (Prince), "did all in their power to keep the peace throughout these months when the political situation was exceedingly complicated and the tension extreme. They knew themselves to be living in a powder magazine where the smallest spark would cause an all-destructive explosion. An act of most justifiable self-defense might prove such a spark. So they told the Armenians to submit to anything rather than to antagonize the Government; to submit to the burning of two or three villages, the murder of a dozen men, without attempts at retaliation which would give the Turks some excuse for a general massacre."[39] The Dashnaks aided the authorities in mobilizing Armenians for the army, even though the call-up was disorganized and disruptive. Men were dragged to the drafting center straight from church irrespective of age or service worthiness. Commerce and the harvest came to a halt, and tensions rose as news of the massacres of Armenians in Persia filtered into the town along with refugees.

These were not the only ominous signs that a tempest approached. Istanbul recalled Hoff, one of the European inspectors assigned to carry out the Armenian reforms, to the capital shortly after he had reached Van. A local Dashnak leader in Bayazid was murdered, and three important Hnchaks were arrested for allegedly plotting against the regime. On November 21 the authorities expelled all French missionaries from the city now that France and the Ottoman Empire were at war. American missionaries remained, along with other foreigners like Dr. Ussher, who witnessed the unfolding events. The *vali* Tahsin Bey at first resisted Şakir's plans and testified to the loyalty of the Armenians, but as governor he carried out the order from Talat that Armenians working in government in the eastern provinces of Erzurum, Van, and Bitlis be dismissed.[40]

In towns and villages around the city Armenians clashed with irregular forces. When a telegraph cable was cut, the authorities suspected Armenians were preparing for an insurrection. Armenians organized self-defense units, even as the Dashnaks attempted to prevent confrontations. A friend of Tahsin Bey and well-known to the minister of interior, the parliamentary deputy Vramian, wrote to Talat, concerned that the government was turning against its Armenian subjects: "An anti-Christian policy will not help save the country. . . . The government must cease to consider the Armenian elements in the empire as enemies. If the government is at present incapable of guaranteeing the Armenian people the exercise of its sacred rights—its life, honor, religion and property—then it ought to authorize them to defend those rights by itself."[41] On January 26, 1915, Vramian wrote to Cevdet Bey, who soon would become governor of Van, and noted how relations between Armenians and the authorities had deteriorated since the war began. "Both sides—the government against the Armenian, the Armenian against the government—are distrustful to each other. Yet, it was not long ago—only a couple of months back, during Tahsin Bey's term—that [Ottoman] officials and the Armenian political organization [the Dashnaks] used to meet one another and emphasize their sincere cooperation. Leaving aside many [other] examples, we should not forget the passionate demonstration [in support of Ottoman military conscription]" organized by Aram "with drum and fife" under the auspices of the Dashnaktsutyun. But once the war broke out the mistrust grew exponentially.[42]

Tahsin Bey was transferred to Erzurum, and on March 15, 1915, the new *vali* of Van arrived in the city and was greeted ceremoniously by officials, local dignitaries, and both Manukian and Vramian. Cevdet Bey was Enver's brother-in-law and had recently been involved in the massacres of Armenians and Assyrians in Persia. He arrived in the city with thousands of Circassian and Kurdish troops and soon secured the loyalty of local tribesmen and the gendarmerie. Smartly dressed, with a trimmed Ottoman-style mustache, he met with Vramian, whom he knew well, for several hours shortly after settling in the city.[43] Cevdet demanded that another four thousand young Armenians be mobilized. Knowing that they would be sent to labor battalions, the Armenians hesitated. The Dashnaks held discussions with the *vali*, but early in April several Dashnaks were arrested in a neighboring town. When Ishkhan went with a delegation to secure their release, he and his mates were attacked by Circassian irregulars and killed. Deputy Vramian was arrested and soon after murdered.

Rumors spread that Cevdet had nicknamed his guard the "butcher battalion" (*Kasab taburu*) and was proud of the "clean sweep [he had made] with the Armenians and Assyrians in Iranian Azerbaijan. We must do the same with the Armenians of Van." A Chaldean bishop heard Cevdet brag that he had cleansed the Christians from the country of Başkale and Saray and would like to do the same from Van and its surroundings.[44] Cevdet ordered his "butcher's battalion" to launch massacres in villages around the city. Ussher remembered that he was with Cevdet when the colonel of the *Kasab taburu,* "composed of Turkish convicts, entered and said, 'You sent for me.'" "Yes," replied Cevdet. "'Go to Shadakh and wipe out its people.' And turning to me he said savagely, 'I won't leave one, not one so high,' holding his hand below the height of his knee."[45]

Crowds claiming to be carrying out the orders of the governor began killing Armenians. The authorities demanded that the Armenians give up their arms, but obeying that order seemed to the inhabitants of Van to be suicidal. Gangs attacked village after village. The men were systematically killed, the women and children often simply abducted. Thousands fled into the mountains, or to the Varag monastery, or, if they could make it, to Van itself. The last major Dashnak leader in the city, Aram Manukian, organized the fortification of the Aigestan quarter as some 15,000 Armenian peasants from neighboring villagers made their way there. Cevdet's troops surrounded Aigestan, which was cut off from the walled city. The two Armenian refuges were unable to communicate with one another. On April 20 the Ottoman forces attacked the barricaded Armenians.[46]

The next day the Venezuelan soldier-of-fortune Rafaël de Nogales arrived in Van to bolster the Ottoman effort to dislodge the Armenians. Despite his working against the Armenians and having strong prejudices about all the religious and ethnic groups in the empire, de Nogales witnessed and reported on the atrocities of 1915.[47] In his romanticized picaresque account of his daring exploits and narrow escapes, even when appalled at the horrors visited on Christians, he insisted that the Armenians brought their destruction on themselves, both in 1894–1896 and in 1915–1916. As a soldier he at the same time affirmed, there "can be no doubt that the Turk, in spite of all his defects, is the first soldier and first gentleman of the Orient."[48] On the other hand, he believed Armenians represented "in spite of their grave defects, a civilizing nucleus." "Had the

Armenians been more prudent and less ambitious, they would probably control Turkey today."[49]

On his way to Van de Nogales "stumbled, near El-Aghlat, upon mutilated Armenian corpses strewing the length of the road. One hour later columns of smoke surged up from the opposite shore of the lake, indicating the sites where the cities and hamlets of Van were being devoured by flame."[50] When he was awakened in a town outside Van by shots being fired, he soon learned that "the civil authorities themselves" supported by the Kurds were "attacking and sacking the Armenian quarter." De Nogales approached the official head of the town, who was directing the orgy. "He astounded me by replying that he was doing nothing more than carry out an unequivocal order emanating from the Governor-General of the province . . . *to exterminate all Armenian males of twelve years of age and over*." The killing went on for an hour and a half, and de Nogales managed to rescue seven Armenians, the only survivors. He turned them over to the *kaymakam*, who promised to protect them *başim üzerinde* ("upon my head" [under his own guarantee]).[51] Later that evening he had them killed, their bodies thrown into the lake along with forty-three others who had managed to hide during the massacre. On the ship that de Nogales took to cross Lake Van, two of the four Armenians on board disappeared during the night. "The civil authorities of the Sultan," he mused, "kill noiselessly and preferably by night, like vampires." Passing Aghtamar, the only Armenians he saw were the corpses of the bishop and the monks; gendarmes had slain them.[52]

In the town of Artamid, de Nogales witnessed another massacre. "Pursued by Kurdish bullets, which felled them by the dozens, the Armenians ran hither and thither like frightened rabbits, and not a few of them sat upon the ground, stupefied, awaiting death like sheep bound to the sacrificial altar, without making the slightest attempt to save themselves. Only a small group of young men kept defending themselves desperately, their backs to a wall, until overcome at last by sheer exhaustion, they fell one after another under the cutlasses and bullets of the Kurds, who used the sword whenever possible in order to keep from wasting cartridges."[53]

While the Armenians within Van, dug in behind trenches, withstood Cevdet's siege, the *vali* sent his forces to massacre the villages outside the city. Cevdet was desperate to end the siege as the Russian army was moving ever closer to Van from the north. Early in May he proposed an amnesty to the besieged Armenians, threatening that Ottoman artillery was on its way and would reduce the city to rubble. The Armenians in turn proposed that they be permitted to leave the city for Persia, and that the *vali* accompany them to guarantee safe conduct. De Nogales suggested he go instead, but Cevdet refused to allow him to go. Cevdet wanted a pretext for getting the Armenians to leave the city, "so that he might have them slain on the way."[54] The negotiations collapsed, and the siege continued. Cevdet brought Armenian women and children from the surrounding villages to the city and sent them toward the Armenian defenders. He intended to have them taken in by the Armenians, increasing the chances that starvation would induce surrender. The Armenians refused entry to the villagers, and de Nogales reported in shock that "instead of gathering in those unfortunates, the Armenians were shooting them down, wounding some and killing others."[55]

Refugees swelled the numbers huddled in town and the Varag monastery. Many found sanctuary in the American compound under Dr. Ussher's care.[56] The compound was relatively safe until May 14, when suddenly the Ottoman forces began shelling it. But this was their final gesture, and they abandoned the city as the Russian army approached. When Ussher and his associates ventured out to see what was left of Van, they came upon "Armenian houses whose occupants had not succeeded in fleeing to the Armenian lines of defense before the siege and there were many of these, very many in the heart of the Turkish quarters discovered there Armenians with their throats cut, and wells filled with mutilated bodies. And all Armenian prisoners and Russian prisoners of war had been killed before the Turks fled."[57]

When the Russians swept through Van province, they estimated that their soldiers came upon some 55,000 corpses, which they burned as they moved forward. The dead accounted for about 50 percent of the Armenians in the Van region. Some villages managed to defend themselves.

In others Armenians were untouched because the local Kurdish chieftain rejected the orders that came down from Van.[58] There was a degree of choice on the part of local officials, rather than blindly obeying orders from above, that determined whether tens of thousands of Armenians and Assyrians would live or die.

On Tuesday, May 18, Armenian units attached to the Russian army were the first to enter Van, surprised to find that the siege had ended. The next day Russian troops arrived, and the Armenians handed the keys to the city and the citadel to the Russian commander. He appointed Aram Manukian governor of the province, the first Armenian supreme authority in the region in more than half a millennium. His government would last only until July. Aram's first orders allowed Armenians to loot Muslim houses and to burn them down so that the owners could not return to them.[59] The burning was called *talan*, a word taken from Arabic and used in Turkish, Kurdish, and Armenian to mean "plundering." Armenian shops were also looted by Armenians, and the pillage soon spread to the countryside. Armenians took their own revenge, "searching the city for hidden Turks, of whom they found quite a number, especially in a rather distant gypsy quarter. The men they put to death; the women and children they spared." Ussher claimed, "Armenians showed themselves far more humane than the Turks." Yet "they did not comport themselves in a manner worthy of the splendid spirit they had manifested during the siege. They burned and murdered; the spirit of loot took possession of them, driving out every other thought. Work, everything else, was neglected. The leaders closed their eyes to what was going on. Our protests were in vain for two or three days until the first madness passed. We remembered what they had had to endure from the Turks all their lives. Much of this loot was only recovered plunder. And many would not injure a Moslem and restrained others, because, they said, 'We are Christians.'"[60]

Aram's government was made up largely of Dashnaks, though some Hnchaks and Ramkavars were included. Ramkavar leaders opposed the revengeful looting and burning, but a kind of craze seized many of the Armenian inhabitants. Locals were upset that Russian Armenians dominated the new Armenian administration.[61] Accusations that some officials had profited from the looting undermined the confidence of some in the government. Andranik, who kept his battalion outside the city, tried to rally Van Armenians to fight for the liberation of other cities, especially Bitlis and Muş, but with no success. The Vanetsis were interested primarily in their own town, and some fighters from the city deserted their units to return to their homes and relatives. Disagreements divided the locals from their liberators.[62] The Dashnak newspaper *Ashkhatank* (Work) criticized corrupt officials and the venality of some Armenians, claiming that such behavior was the result of living in the Muslim empire for centuries.[63]

The Armenians set about rebuilding their homes, but not in the walled city, which the Ottomans had relentlessly shelled. To this day that part of Van has not been rebuilt; a new city was founded nearby, and the old city left buried under mounds of dirt and rubble. Aram's government excluded Muslims from their councils but worked with Assyrians and Yezidis. Kurds particularly were seen as hostile. Cossacks and Armenian volunteers slaughtered Kurdish villagers, retaliating and taking revenge for the similar slaughters that had devastated Armenian villagers. Aram was aware that the Russians supported Kurds, and different aims divided the Armenians and the Russians. Killing was part of an effort to eliminate a Kurdish presence in what Armenians hoped would be a regained homeland. In late June the Russians ordered the Armenian administration to allow Kurds who were loyal to Russia to return to their villages and to protect them from further abuses. Aram protested, declaring that the Kurds were a threat to the Armenians, but the Russian general stood fast. Most Kurds, however, did not take up the Russian offer and remained in their mountain retreats.

By summer the Russians had been stopped by Cevdet at Bitlis and began their withdrawal from Van. On July 17, 1915, the Russian military ordered all Armenians to abandon Van. For a few hours Armenians hesitated, fearing a Russian plot to cleanse the region of Armenians, but the threatened approach of the Ottoman forces convinced them to retreat with the Russians. Tens of thousands of Armenians, as well as the last Americans in the city, walked the nearly 200 miles to the relative safety of the Caucasus, but along the way at least one-third of them perished in attacks by Kurds. A few weeks later Cevdet Bey took the city with a small force. When the Russians made their second advance to Van in September, they found the city deserted, an "Armenia without Armenians."

For the Armenians Van was a moment of resistance, the "defense of Van" against the government that seemed determined to annihilate them. For the local Muslims and the Ottoman authorities Van was an uprising, the insurrection that they had long suspected the Armenians had intended to launch. A month later, from his new post in Erzurum, the former *vali* of Van, Tahsin Bey, castigated the policy chosen by his government. "Rather than deporting the Armenians in the middle of a war, I suggest for my part, that they be maintained in their present situation until further notice and not be spurred to revolt by the illegitimate use of force." He was convinced that "[t]here would have been no revolt at Van if we had not ourselves created, with our own hands, by using force, this impossible situation from which we are incapable of extricating ourselves, and also the difficult position in which we have put our army on the eastern front. After enduring this painful experience and its deadly consequences, we are, I fear, making the mistake of putting our army in an untenable situation," and then referred to an Arabic saying, "like someone who has poked out her own eye while trying to apply mascara to her eyelids."[64]

The German ambassador in Istanbul had a quite different response to what had happened in Van. When the German consul Dr. Eugen Büge in Adana and Max Scheubner-Richter in Erzurum wrote to Wangenheim that the Ottoman government appeared to be moving toward "partial extermination of the Armenians," the ambassador responded, "As regrettable and, in many respects, also detrimental to our interests as the persecution of the Armenian population is, however, the most recent events in the border provinces, such as the revolt in Van and other procedures in the country's interior, do in fact justify the severe measures taken by the authorities. The Imperial Embassy is, therefore, not in a position to prevent these measures for the time being."[65] However, as he learned more about the extent of the deportations and the accompanying violence, the ambassador realized that the expulsions of Armenians were "being carried out ruthlessly." Talat had said "that the Porte is intent on taking advantage of the World War in order to make a clean sweep of internal enemies—the indigenous Christians—without being hindered in doing so by diplomatic intervention from other countries." Wangenheim went on to note what the Armenian patriarch had told a German official: "Deportation is just as bad as massacring, and it would not be surprising if the Armenians finally retaliated, even if they had no chance of succeeding, 'like a tormented animal that turns against its tormentors.'"[66]

Apologists argue that Armenian insurrection required repression in the name of state security. But there was no significant Armenian threat until the locals were provoked. No sizable uprising occurred, except in isolated efforts to defend a town or village that was under attack. Armed resistance remained local and uncoordinated with other locations. Even though permitted since 1908 to carry arms, most Armenians were in fact unarmed and hardly able to mount a rebellion of any size against the army, police, and irregular forces.[67]

THE AMBASSADOR'S WITNESS

The United States was neutral in 1915, staying out of the World War for another two years. Its ambassador in Istanbul, Henry Morgenthau, was uniquely positioned to observe what was happening to the Armenians, both as an accredited diplomat and as a personal friend of the highest officials in the Ottoman government. In his dispatches to the Department of State, his personal diary, and a subsequent memoir, Morgenthau provided informed and insightful reports on the thinking of the Young Turk leaders.[68] As a contemporary witness Morgenthau's account influenced generations of readers, including historians, and in many ways created the template through which the Genocide has been understood. As remarkable as his recording was, it needs to be seen critically as the testimony of a man of his own time with all the attendant prejudices of the early twentieth century, as well as appreciated as the view of a sensitive and engaged observer.

American ambassador to the Ottoman Empire (1913–1916), Henry Morgenthau (1856–1946).

Morgenthau's memoir was written in the last year of World War I, a time of intense passion about the enemies of the Allied powers. In many ways the book is more anti-German than anti-Turkish. For Morgenthau the major instigation of the Genocide came from the principal enemy of the Allies, Imperial Germany. In answer to an inquiry by Morgenthau about his plans to publish a book, President Woodrow Wilson wrote on November 27, 1917, to encourage him to write his "full exposition of some of the principal lines of German intrigue."[69] In his preface to the work, dated a month before the armistice, Morgenthau went as far as to begin: "By this time the American people have probably become convinced that the Germans deliberately planned the conquest of the world," which he labels "the greatest crime in modern history."[70] While hardly the propaganda piece that his critics have claimed, the memoir reveals the mind and experience of an American official who held the essentialist views of national character that determined the understanding of human motivation in those years. He often uses "the Turk" in the singular to describe Turkish attitudes, mentalities, and emotions, further homogenizing, naturalizing, and essentializing nationality, as if a shared national character dictated the beliefs and behaviors of millions of Turks. A keen observer, privileged in his access to power, the ambassador, nevertheless, read the strange world to which he had been assigned with passionate preferences that distanced him from those whom he observed.

The ambassador knew little about Armenians before he arrived in Istanbul. He wrote to his wife that he had received the Armenian patriarch and through translators learned that Armenians "are like vassals to the Kurds who pounce down on them from their mountain fastnesses whenever they need anything and when one of the Kurd chiefs hears of or sees a nice Armenian girl or bride or wife—and likes her, he unhesitatingly takes her away and puts her in his house." As he sat with the Armenians, smoking cigarettes, sipping coffee, and discussing religion, he noted that "there has been considerable intermarrying with Jews and that by this time there is a decided strain of Jewish blood in them. I asked about this because they all look like Jews and have the same characteristics, the same stubborn adherence to their past and religion and a strong race pride."[71]

Morgenthau achieved an extraordinary intimacy with Enver and Talat, not only dining and riding with them in the Belgrade forest, but also at the same time confronting them with naïve frankness about his objections to their policies. His subtle, rounded portraits of these men probed their psychology in a desperate attempt to comprehend their actions. For Morgenthau, the driving motivation of the leading Young Turks was no longer reform but "an insatiable lust for personal power."[72]

The hulking figure of Talat, broad-backed with an iron grip, was particularly intriguing to Morgenthau. Talat "went from one emotion to another as lightly as a child; I would find him fierce and unyielding one day, and uproariously good-natured and accommodating the next."[73] He had risen from humble origins, beginning as a mailman and later a telegraph operator, and, according to Morgenthau, Talat was rumored neither to be an ethnic Turk nor inspired by Islam or any religion.[74] "I hate all priests, rabbis, and hodjas," he told the ambassador.[75] By the time Morgenthau befriended him, Talat had become disillusioned about the possibility of reform in the Ottoman Empire. "I have been greatly disappointed at the failure of the Turks to appreciate democratic institutions. I hoped for it once, and I worked hard for it—but they were not prepared for it."[76] Talat, like all the Turkish leaders—according to Morgenthau—was motivated primarily by fear, most particularly, fear of Russia, the most serious threat to the empire's territorial integrity. This fear of Russia drove the Ottomans "into the arms of Germany."[77]

Morgenthau carefully distinguished Enver from Talat. A much more diminutive figure, Enver was suave, elegant, audacious, and fond of luxury, in contrast to the plain-living Talat. Enver was Germany's principal supporter in Istanbul, and once he became minister of war in January 1914, he helped pave the way for the empire to ally itself with the Germans. The third member of the triumvirate, Cemal Pasha, was a sincere pan-Turkist. "He despised the subject peoples of the Ottoman country—Arabs, Greeks, Armenians, Circassians, Jews," the ambassador noted. "[I]t was his determination to Turkify the whole empire."[78]

Morgenthau's text is replete with indelible characteristics of "the Turk." "Psychologically primitive," the Turk is essentially "a bully and a coward; he is brave as a lion when things are going his way, but cringing, abject, and nerveless when reverses are overwhelming him."[79] The Ottomans reverted in the war years to an older ancestral type: "the basic fact underlying the Turkish mentality is its utter contempt for all other races. A fairly insane pride is the element that largely explains this strange human species. The common term applied by the Turk to the Christian is 'dog' . . . he actually looks upon his European neighbor as far less worthy of consideration than his own domestic animals."[80] Yet there are also positive qualities. Besides a "keen sense of humour," "one of the most conspicuous traits in the Turkish character" is "its tendency to compromise and to bargain."[81] "So far as I can discover," Morgenthau informed his readers, "the Ottoman Turks had only one great quality, that of military genius." But, lest we forget their most essential qualities, he continued, "[s]uch graces of civilization as the Turk has acquired in five centuries have practically all been taken from the subject peoples whom he so greatly despises."[82] Non-Turks were subjects without rights, "merely chattels, which may be permitted to live when they promote the interest of their masters, but which may be pitilessly destroyed when they have ceased to be useful." The most primitive qualities of the Turk modified over centuries, but after the failure of the democratic revolution there was "an atavistic reversion to the original Turk."[83]

While many historians have explained the deportations and massacres of the Armenians as the perverse product of Turkish nationalism or patriotic dedication to the Ottoman Empire, Morgenthau reported, to the contrary, that he observed no popular enthusiasm for the European war.[84] Patriotism, he repeated several times, was alien to "the Turk." There was support for a war against Greece to win back the Aegean islands, and ordinary Turks subscribed to a fund to buy battleships from Britain to strengthen the Ottoman navy. But, writes Morgenthau, "[t]he Turkish people have little spontaneous patriotism or any enthusiasm of any kind."[85] In a letter to President Wilson, Morgenthau reflected, "The majority of the Turks, within one week after entering the war, realized and admitted their error in doing so, irrespective of the attitude of some of the members of the Cabinet. They have ever since been anxious for peace and look to you as the Peacemaker."[86]

Resorting to his foundational notions of the Turkish character, Morgenthau was repeatedly appalled by the willingness of the Turks to resort to violence, which he related to their emotional volatility. "The Turks, like most primitive peoples," Morgenthau confidently claimed, "wear their emotions on the surface, and with them the transition from exultation to despair is a rapid one."[87] When Talat heard that the English had bombarded the Dardanelles and killed two Turks, he exploded to Morgenthau: "We intend to kill three Christians for every Moslem killed."[88] Measuring Talat's emotions and waiting for the right moment to make his requests, the ambassador noted that "Talat had shown several moods in this interview;

he had been by turns sulky, good-natured, savage, and complaisant. He also had a keen sense of humour, greatly loved a joke and a funny story."[89] The ambassador, who in his own representation was the epitome of decorum, politesse, and civilization, was on many but not all occasions proud to be able to tame or manipulate the Ottoman leader.

As he pondered why a government would order hundreds of thousands of its subjects from their homes, force them to march until they fell, and be massacred while defenseless, Morgenthau elaborated a number of possible causes for the deportations. Several of his conclusions became foundational for Western and Armenian historiography of the Genocide. He begins with the nationalist perspective that the Young Turks were committed to a Turkified empire and adopted the policy of Abdülhamid II. "Their passion for Turkifying the nation seemed to demand logically the extermination of all Christians—Greeks, Syrians, and Armenians."[90] The error of past Muslim conquerors had been that they had not obliterated the Christians, "a fatal error of statesmanship" that "explained all the woes from which Turkey has suffered in modern times."[91] The war presented an opportunity because Russia, France, and Britain could no longer stand in the way as they had during Abdülhamid's reign. "Thus, for the first time in two centuries the Turks, in 1915, had their Christian populations utterly at their mercy. The time had finally come to make Turkey exclusively the country of the Turks."[92]

Morgenthau proposed that nationalist ambitions combined with elemental fears to drive the Young Turks to mass murder. Already in January and February, Ambassador Morgenthau received "fragmentary reports" of killings of Armenians, but he regarded them as repetitions of the kinds of repression common in the East.[93] Talat and Enver dismissed such reports "as wild exaggerations."[94] In a later, extended conversation—this one without Morgenthau's Armenian dragoman present—Talat spoke more frankly, admitting that the government had taken a firm decision to deal with what they considered Armenian treachery:

> I have asked you to come today . . . so that I can explain our position on the whole Armenian subject. We base our objections

to the Armenians on three distinct grounds. In the first place, they have enriched themselves at the expense of the Turks. In the second place, they are determined to domineer over us and to establish a separate state. In the third place, they have openly encouraged our enemies. They have assisted the Russians in the Caucasus and our failure there is largely explained by their actions. We have therefore come to the irrevocable decision that we shall make them powerless before this war is ended.[95]

Talat's argument revealed the basic emotional outlook that had evolved among Ottoman leaders since Abdülhamid: resentment at the Armenians' success at the expense of Turks; anxiety about a future in which the Muslim-*dhimmi* order would be reversed with the *gavur* on top and the Muslim below; anger at the betrayal at the Armenians, their affiliation with the Russians; and fear that Armenians favored by Europe were the thin edge of the wedge to bring down the empire. When Morgenthau attempted point by point to refute Talat's argument, the minister interrupted, "It is no use for you to argue . . . we have already disposed of three quarters of the Armenians; there are none at all left in Bitlis, Van, and Erzeroum. The hatred between the Turks and the Armenians is now so intense that we have got to finish with them. If we don't, they will plan their revenge." Fear and anger had degenerated into hatred, the powerful sense that it is not what the other has done but the fundamental nature of that other that is a threat. Anger at some action might be excused, accepted, or ignored; it dissipates over time. But hatred of the essential character of another means that that other must be eliminated as it poses an existential threat to the desired future. At one of their meetings Talat told Morgenthau, "No Armenian . . . can be our friend after what we have done to them."[96]

On August 3, 1915, Morgenthau wrote in his diary of his meeting with Talat: "He gave me the impression that Talat is the one who desires to crush the poor Armenians."[97] Talat reportedly told friends with pride, "I have accomplished more toward solving the Armenian problem in three months than Abdul Hamid accomplished in thirty years."[98] To the ambassador he confirmed "that our Armenian policy is absolutely fixed and that nothing can change it. We will not have the Armenians anywhere in Anatolia. They can live in the desert but nowhere else."[99] In despair, Morgenthau told Talat, "You are making a terrible mistake," and repeated that three times. "Yes, we may make mistakes," Talat replied, "'but'—and he firmly closed his lips and shook his head—'we never regret.'"[100]

APRIL 24, 1915

The Young Turks stirred anti-Armenian feelings in Istanbul with news of the trial of the imprisoned Hnchaks accused of sedition, separatism, and assassination plots that ran through May and June 1915. Articles appeared in the nationalist journal *Tanin* sensationalizing what was called "The Grand Conspiracy."[101] While the evidence against those who had languished in jail for nearly a year was tainted and the accusations exaggerated, the judges treated the indicted with respect. The presiding judge, Hurşit Bey, regretted that he had to pass the most severe sentence on these Armenian "patriots." "The attributes of history in our reality," he pronounced, "are arranged in such a way that what constitutes 'patriotism' for one is viewed as destructive treason by the other. . . . What great deeds vigorous individuals like you could have accomplished, if the ideal of a common welfare had been pursued under one banner. . . . What benefits could have been borne from a mutual understanding that eluded [us], the other end of which is sad and dark."[102] The spokesman for the accused, Paramaz (Matteos Sargsian), was then permitted to address the court and exposed the limits of the professed Ottomanist vision of the court. He and his doomed comrades, he avowed, had fought "for the happiness of this poor country" and sacrificed "to make the brotherhood between Turks and Armenians a reality." But those ruling the country "deliberately pursued [the goal] of exterminating us, forgetting that the liquidation of the Armenians is tantamount to the destruction of Turkey." He went on: "You began massacring us when, one day, we decided to assume a position that would allow us our self-respect. You excluded us from the protection of the law when we sought to benefit from the rights granted by Midhat's truncated constitution. Among the groups making up Turkey, we were the most dedicated and productive, and we were the ones you forced to suffer the most. Even today, brandishing the charge that we seek to create an independent Armenia, you want to crush us." The court condemned twenty of the accused to death for treason and separatism, and early in the morning of June 15, 1915, they were hanged secretly in the courtyard of the Ministry of War.[103]

The events at Zeytun and Van accelerated Young Turk plans to disarm and deport the Armenians and to decapitate the "nation" by eliminating its leadership. Early in April, as news filtered into the capital of the atrocities occurring in the East, the Armenian patriarch, Zaven Ter Yeghiayan, called in Petros Halajian, an Armenian member of the Committee of Union and Progress, to intercede with his party comrades to "spare our people." Halajian reported back that Talat had assured him that no massacres would take place in the countryside because the government would not give its consent.[104] At the same time, however, the minister ordered that more moderate Ottoman officials in the provinces be replaced. Patriarch Zaven made continual efforts to intervene with Talat, who repeatedly evaded his entreaties. When the patriarch finally met him on April 21, Talat assured him the government "did not have any particular policy regarding the Armenians." The minister was troubled by the widespread desertion of soldiers "running away with their weapons."[105] A day later a decree was issued requiring the civilian population to give up their arms within five days.

On April 23 the Armenian National Assembly met to discuss what might be done to convince the government to rethink its malicious policy toward Armenians. The Dashnak parliamentary deputy from Erzurum, Vartkes Serengulian, explained why Armenian soldiers feared giving up their weapons. He believed that they deserted not to go over to the enemy but to protect themselves. Zohrap was charged with writing up "a sincere memorandum" to the government, expressing the loyalty of the Armenians. The next day, April 24, the patriarch went to see Talat, who emerged from his office and shocked the priest by declaring that Vartkes had told him, "If the Turkish army returns from the Caucasus front, we will shoot it in the back!" The stunned cleric replied simply, "Vartkes is not our Nation's representative."[106]

Hüseyin Cahit Yalçın told a quite different story about Talat and Vartkes in a memoir written twenty years later. The two men had long been friends, and Vartkes went to see Talat to ask about rumors that the Armenian committee leaders were about to be arrested. Talat told him, "Now it is our turn, Vartakes [*sic.*]. You know that you have caused great troubles in this land." The minister alluded to the reforms forced on the Ottomans by the Russians and how the Armenians imagined they would eventually be brought into the Russian Empire. "This is politics, Vartakes. This is our turn, and, now it is we who are strong. We are going to do what is necessary for the interests of *Türklük* [Turkishness]." Vartkes pleaded that he now was married, with a child. Talat took pity and told him to leave the city immediately. "Go. Leave now, don't wait even a minute."[107]

On the evening of April 23 and into the next morning the police arrested several hundred leading Armenians in Istanbul, including parliament deputies and intimates of Talat. The arrests appeared to begin with a raid on the offices of the Dashnak newspaper, *Azatamart* (Freedom Battle). Anyone who might have provided organization or resistance was picked up. Besides Armenian members of Parliament, bishops, doctors, lawyers, journalists, and writers were taken from their homes to prison.[108] The patriarch and others hid those who had escaped the initial roundup. Armenians in the city were stunned and confused: Were only the Dashnaks being arrested? Why was the ethnomusicologist Father Komitas picked up? The writer Ervant Otian, who edited the Armenian newspaper *Zhamanak* (Time), realized that the dragnet would soon pull him in and went into hiding. He was arrested five months later.[109]

On April 24, 1915, Talat sent the following telegram to the High Command of the Ottoman army, calling for the most radical measures to deal with the Armenians.

It has become clear once again with the latest revolts which have occurred at Zeytun and Bitlis, at Sivas and Van, that the Armenian committees, which for a long time have been trying to establish an autonomous administration with their revolutionary political structure in the Ottoman territories, dare to act against us immediately following the [Ottoman] declaration of war with the cooperation of the Dashnaks of Russia, and that the Ottoman Armenians have decided to launch a revolt with all their forces following the weakening of the [Ottoman] army [and thus] to take perfidious actions against the existence of the [Ottoman] fatherland and its future. With the discovery of bombs in Kayseri, Sivas, and in other provinces as well as publications, and, the formation of volunteer [Armenian] regiments within the Russian army against the Ottoman state, it has become evident that the Armenian committees, which have their centers in Europe as well as the adjective "revolutionary" in their names and attack the Ottoman land in the company of the Russian army, are assembled under the authority of their chiefs, who have Ottoman origins, to menace the rear of the Ottoman Army and to obtain with all means possible their ultimate goal, autonomy.

Since, he went on, the Ottoman state "cannot tolerate any longer the existence of the [Armenian] committees, which constitute the sources of conspiracy," Talat had "made the necessary preparations" to abolish the Armenian political organizations,

> those of Nubar [Boghos Nubar Paşa] as well as those of the Hnchaks and the Dashnaks—in the capital and in the provinces; to confiscate all the documents found to prevent their destruction; to arrest immediately the leaders and members of the committees as well as the other Armenian notables known to the forces of Ottoman security and judged harmful [to the state]; to collect all Armenian suspects whose continued residence in their current homes is judged to be detrimental; to begin to search for arms in suspicious places in the company of the military and in coordination with local commanders; to take the detainees before military tribunals after the inspection of the captured documents.

With the permission and approval of the military, he concluded, "these directives will be given [to the regional authorities] to do what is necessary."[110]

With the soldiers disarmed and the intellectuals and politicians under guard, the muscle and mind of the Ottoman Armenians had been effectively eliminated. The mass arrests on April 24 marked a radically new phase in the Ottoman program to deal with their Armenian subjects. From disarmament and sporadic massacres, a systematic campaign of removing hundreds of thousands of people from their homes began. The ultimate intent of the government was still unclear, both to the targeted victims and to provincial officials. Confusion reigned. A few people were returned to Istanbul, and the ultimate destination of the deportees had yet to be determined. Some were marched westward, others to the east. What was clear was that without adequate planning, infrastructure, or organization, deportation of hundreds of thousands of people meant the physical destruction of communities, families, and individuals.

In his laconic diary entry, Morgenthau related that he had dinner with Talat that Saturday evening, April 24: "We asked him about Armenians and he admitted that they had arrested a great many of them. He said he wants them to leave the city. They intend to put them among Turks in the interior where they can do no harm." Talat went on to comment that Zionists were also "mischievous and that it is their duty to get rid of them" as well. Morgenthau concluded that Talat "is evidently as much afraid of internal trouble as the war, and they have made up their mind to crush all possible attempts at revolution."[111] That same day, Talat ordered the closure of Armenian political organizations and forbade any travel documents be given to Armenians suspected by the government or involved in politics.[112] More ominously, he ordered that the convoys of Armenians already expelled from Iskenderun (Alexandretta), Dörtyol, Adana, Hadjin, Zeytun, and Sis be redirected away from their original westward destinations in central Anatolia (which "would result in a concentration of Armenians there, and in their cooperating with local Armenians after a while") and instead sent southeast to the deserts of Syria, to Aleppo, Der Zor, and Urfa.[113] The historical sociologist Michael Mann writes, "This was a decisive change. They might have been expected to survive at Konia, but they would likely die in the Syrian desert."[114]

When Morgenthau brought up the issue of the arrests of prominent Armenians in the capital, Talat resorted to his usual argument that the government was acting in self-defense, that the Armenians in Van "had already shown their abilities as revolutionists," and that Armenian leaders in Istanbul "were corresponding with the Russians, and he had every reason to fear that they would start an insurrection against the Central Government."[115] When Morgenthau reported to Talat that Armenians had been killed in Konya, Talat asked, "Are *they* Americans?" "They are not to be trusted," he went on. "[B]esides, what we do with them does not concern the United States.... As to your Armenians, we don't give a rap for the future! We live only in the present!"[116] He repeatedly asked for money earmarked by Americans for Armenian relief to be given to the Turks, who also needed aid "as badly as they do."[117] He requested that the insurance premiums due to Armenians from American companies be paid to the Turks since the Armenians no longer had any need for them.[118]

Talat was explicit in his exculpatory explanations to Morgenthau about the decision to arrest the Armenian leaders. "These people ... refused to disarm when we told them," Talat explained to Morgenthau. "They opposed us at Van and at Zeitoun, and they helped the Russians. There is only one way in which we can defend ourselves against them in the future, and that is just to deport them." When Morgenthau protested that that was not a reason for "destroying a whole race" or "making innocent women and children suffer," Talat simply added, "Those things are inevitable."[119]

The independent-minded priest Balakian, who was arrested in the initial April arrests and ultimately survived the deportations, believed that the arrests were made according to names on an Armenian blacklist "compiled with the help of Armenian traitors, particularly Artin Megerdichian, who worked with the neighborhood İttihad clubs." Balakian and others were taken across the Marmara Sea to the magnificent Haydar Paşa Station from which they were moved by train to the rail station of Sincan Köy near Ankara, on the way to Ayaş. There more than sixty names were read out and the group divided. Among those who departed that night were editors of the major Armenian newspapers, leading revolutionaries, teachers, actors, the poet Siamonto (Atom Yarjanian), a tailor, and an umbrella salesman.[120] Taken off in carriages, most of them were tortured and killed soon after in the valleys outside the future capital of Turkey. The Caucasian Armenian Khachatur Malumian, who wrote for the Dashnak press under the name "Aknuni," was a close friend of Talat and continued to believe that he and his compatriots would be isolated for a while and then released. But when he was taken away at Ayaş, he shouted to those left behind that he did not mind being murdered because as a man he was destined to die anyway. "But," he added, "it hurts me that we were tricked by these rascals."[121] At another point of separation someone watching those taken away muttered, "The bastards chose the crème de la crème among us to put down."[122] Balakian and the others, fearful of what lay ahead, were taken east of Ankara to the town of Çankırı. In his carriage Balakian comforted the musicologist and collector of folk songs Father Komitas, who "seemed mentally unstable. He thought the trees were bandits on the attack and continually hid his head under the hem of my overcoat, like a fearful partridge. He begged me to say a blessing for him ("The Savior") in the hope it would calm him."[123]

Those Armenian leaders still at liberty were confused as to the extent of the government's intentions. The patriarch convened a rump session of the National Assembly to make yet another appeal to the government. Authored by Grigor Zohrap, who had not yet been arrested, it called for "mild and forgiving policies, rather than severe and repressive ones; this is how we ask the government to treat the Nation, at least out of respect for the memory of the thousands of Armenian soldiers who spilled their blood for the defense of the Ottoman fatherland."[124] When they presented the appeal to Grand Vizier Said Halim, he answered that the government still had confidence in the Armenians but had "decided purely for the security of the country" to drive "the partisans from the city and neutraliz[e] them." Stores of arms had been discovered that the government was convinced were to be used against the state. Both the patriarch and Zohrap rejected the charges of Armenian disloyalty, but to no avail. When they met with Talat later that day, the minister reiterated, "All those Armenians who either through the pen, their words, or their work have endeavored or may endeavor in the future to build an Armenia, are considered the enemies of the state, and, in times such as these, they have to be dispersed."[125] He admitted that some innocent people had been caught in the roundup—"for instance, Abraham Pasha's cook, who is a poor man"—but these *measures [were] implemented only against party members. It is certain that we do not have evidence of any serious movement against the state,* but for the tranquility and the safety of the country, we have decided to disperse all party members and to dissolve all political parties. . . . [W]e will send back non-party members."[126] Indeed, some unfortunates, like Father Komitas and a number of physicians, were returned to Istanbul. The fragile musician, however, suffered a mental breakdown from which he never recovered.

Integrated as Armenians were in Ottoman society, with many of their prominent politicians and intellectuals in close contact with the highest authorities of the state, comprehending what was about to befall the Armenians proved nearly impossible. Fearful of Ottoman intentions, the imprisoned intellectuals from Istanbul who were held in an armory in Çankırı were briefly relieved when they were allowed out of their prison to live in town. Relaxing and hopeful that soon he would be returned to the capital, Diran Kelegian, who had edited the Turkish-language newspaper *Sabah* (Morning), called on the local *mutasarrif,* Asaf, a former pupil of his. Out of deference and respect to his teacher, Asaf showed him the decoded text of a telegram he had received from Istanbul: "Telegraph us immediately as to how many Armenians have already died and how many are left alive—Talat." Incredulous, Kelegian asked what this meant. Asaf answered with a sarcastic laugh, "This simply means, 'How many have you already massacred and how many are still alive.' Because there has been neither earthquake nor flood, nor any other natural disaster by which people would die en masse."[127] A talented journalist whose pen might be used against the CUP, a man once convinced that a constitutionalist solution was possible in the Ottoman Empire but no longer able to believe in the Ottomanist project, Kelegian was soon after killed on a bridge over the Halys River.[128]

Vartkes and Grigor Zohrap were spared arrest on April 24, and though offered the opportunity to escape they stayed in the city. Zohrap continued to plead for the Armenians and challenged Talat that someday he would have to "justify his crimes." Talat replied that there was no one who could bring him to account. Zohrap asserted that as a member of Parliament he would demand it. Several days later Zohrap went to the *Cercle d'Orient* club where he and Talat played cards together as if the Ottomanist connections between Armenians and Muslims were still intact.[129] The next day Zohrab was arrested along with Vartkes. The intellectuals and politicians who had been exiled from Istanbul on April 24 and afterward were moved progressively eastward. Small groups were taken away and never seen again. On August 26, near Ankara, several of the most prominent of the Istanbul Armenians were murdered, among them the poet Daniel Varuzhan and the parliamentary deputy Zohrap. According to one account, Circassian irregulars took the victims from their carriages, ordered their police escorts to leave, and "nailed them to the ground with iron stakes that were a meter long. They proceeded to pluck all the hairs out of Archimandrite Ardavaz's beard, and after administering various tortures they cut off his head. Then they beheaded everyone else. Finally they stripped them naked and cut off their limbs."[130] Later, Cemal Paşa, whose relationship with Armenians swung from friendship to hostility, had the murderer Serezli Çerkez Ahmet, who had already participated in massacres of Armenians in Van, Urfa, Diyarbakır, and Aleppo, courtmartialed and hanged in Damascus on September 30, 1915.

In the months following the April 24 events, villages, towns, and cities were emptied of Armenians. Deportations began in late April from Erzurum, considered a frontline city, and the patriarch, assured by German diplomats, interpreted this as a wartime measure to remove non-Muslims from the proximity of the front.[131] The same night that Istanbul Armenian leaders were arrested, two hundred were seized in Erzurum. Thirty prominent Armenians were sent to Erzincan and murdered on the way. Some four to five hundred others were kept in the central prison of

Erzincan, where they were tortured and interrogated about hidden arm caches and plans to revolt.[132]

A systematic deportation of the remaining Armenians from Erzurum began in May, against the will of the *vali* but at the request of the army. The Russians launched their second major campaign in Anatolia on May 6, moving down the Tortun Valley toward Erzurum. The German vice consul, Max Scheubner-Richter, reported to his ambassador that there was no resistance or rebellion from Erzurum Armenians. The men had already been drafted; those who wanted to join the Russians fled long ago, and the latest deportations affected only women and children. Women threw themselves and their children in the path of the consul's horse's path and begged for help. "The sight of these poor, moaning people filled me with pity," he wrote, "and it was embarrassing—but even more embarrassing for me was the feeling of not being able to help." The consul feared the worst and concluded: "I cannot rule out the possibility that this relocation and the government's measures—which must (or are meant to!) result in the economic ruin and the partial extermination of the Armenians—could drive the Armenians to an act of desperation, even if this is without hope of success, which would then naturally lead to a general slaughter. Should such an act not be carried out, the local Armenians would thus prove that they are the most obsequious and peaceable subjects of Turkey."[133]

In fact there was no significant resistance by Erzurum Armenians. Tens of thousands were driven under guard into the wilderness. Survivors reported later that the caravans were looted, individuals murdered, others taken into Muslim families and forced to convert. Most children under age five were to be spared for adoption by Muslims. Some women leaped into the Euphrates rather than surrender to their captors. Kurdish women attacked the Armenians with knives, calling for money and searching the corpses for valuables. People were marched through the Kemah gorges along the Euphrates, a long passage with the turbulent river on one side and insurmountable cliffs on the others that soon became a sanguinary killing field. The irregulars of the *çete*s bayonetted the men, threw bodies in the river, and raped women, some of whom managed to pull their attackers to death in the river. Most of the killing was done by local Kurds and the irregular forces sanctioned by the authorities.[134]

Through April, May, and June, the principal reason given for arresting, deporting, or killing Armenians was because of desertion and rebellion, the two connected intimately with the underlying apprehension that the Armenians were fundamentally disloyal and prepared to aid the Russians given the chance. Deportation descending into massacre was rationalized as a military necessity. The massacres were no longer simply spontaneous or local but part of an overall plan to reduce the Armenians to impotence, to make any resistance impossible, and to Islamize eastern Anatolia as much as possible. For Ottoman officers and officials state security and defense of the Muslim population made any excess in treating Christians reasonable and justified.

CHAPTER NINE

Genocide

War allowed a greater degree of arbitrariness and permissiveness in dealing with ordinary people. Once the fighting started, the state requisitioned goods and animals, drafted men into the armed forces, and deported and even killed those it considered traitors. Whatever loyalties Armenians held toward the Ottoman state became unsustainable when exile and massacre became the new norm. The Ottoman authorities drove otherwise loyal, neutral, or passive Armenians out of the imperial fold into a netherworld of resisters and outlaws. The Young Turks compounded the "Armenian problem," made enemies of former friends, and expended enormous resources to render the Armenians impotent. Their own project of modernizing and securing the empire was undercut by their ambition to make Anatolia safe from Christians. Any restraint from religion, from the precepts of Islam to protect the People of the Book, was eliminated. The Armenian patriarch was told that in the distant past a particularly "savage and fanatical" sultan "had given orders for all Christians to be put to the sword. When the Sheikh-ul Islam of the time heard about this, he immediately presented himself to the Sultan and declared that the Sultan's order went against the religion of Islam, and he succeeded in persuading the Sultan to rescind that savage order." The patriarch tried the same tactic with the current Sheikh-ul Islam, but Musa Kyazim, a middle-aged "fanatic İttihadist . . . declared his incompetence for such an intervention" and "responded mockingly: 'Such things would happen in older times.'"[1]

Fear and a profound sense of insecurity compounded by the defeats in the winter of 1915 and the threats from Allied forces had combined into a toxic perception of all Armenians as an internal subversive force allied to the Russians. The war presented a unique opportunity to eliminate this long-term existential threat to the empire and the plans of the

Young Turks for a more Turkified empire. Reason (strategic advantage) and emotion (fear, a sense of future danger) as well as humiliation at the hands of Armenians and a sense of betrayal conspired together to generate plans for mass deportation and massacre.

Telegrams from Istanbul and the provinces, rumors and bulletins by officers and officials, told of Armenian treachery and insurrection. There was no revolt, however, no organized uprising, no coordinated Armenian insurrection led by the remnants of the Armenian political parties. The purported rebellion was a fiction concocted and spread largely by military communiqués. Isolated incidents were synthesized into a general resistance by Armenians, a revolutionary movement said at times to number tens of thousands of rebels who suddenly, mysteriously, appeared sometime after Sarıkamış. Reading those reports convinced people that Armenians indeed were dangerous rebels. The terms "uprising" and "revolt" were used whenever there were clashes between the army and military deserters or bandits, Muslim and non-Muslim. In actuality, the clashes were between armed men, on one side government and irregular troops, on the other desperate victims or hungry deserters, with little or no support from the general population. Later testimony at the trial of Ottoman officials after the war revealed that elaborate and dramatic stories of insurrection had been fabricated and transmitted. Of his commander, Kamil Paşa, the retired officer Pertev Paşa testified: "When submitting his reports, he would exaggerate minor events and blame the Armenians for any defeats [that our forces suffered]."[2] After carefully reading through the military documents in the Ottoman archives, Taner Akçam concluded that "the allegations of an Armenian revolt in the documents . . . have no basis in reality but were deliberately fabricated."[3]

Three distinct authorities operated in eastern Anatolia through 1915 and into 1916: the army High Command, the local Ottoman authorities, and the party committees of the CUP and their "responsible secretaries."[4] Civilian authorities carried out the operations of the deportations, but ultimate initiation and instigation came from the party and the military. "The committee carried on a disastrous alternative government," wrote the German vice consul in Erzurum, "and often thwarts the government's perhaps well-meant intentions, such as for example regarding the re-settlement of the Armenians. The brusque measures used here and the massacres are no doubt due to the activity of these committee members, whose influence appears to be quite great."[5] Şakir set up a special deportation committee in Erzurum, which established the lists of those to be deported.[6] From Istanbul the central committee of the İttihadist party used its secret networks to circulate its orders.[7] The principal architect of the destruction of the Armenians, Talat, managed the deportations through his private channels. As Ambassador Morgenthau remembered, and Talat's wife, Hayriye Talat (Bafalı), later revealed, the minister had his own private telegraph installed in his home. From there he was able to communicate through the night with his regional agents.[8]

Organized by civilian officials, the deportations and much of the actual killing were done by local Kurds and the irregular forces organized by the CUP. The Ottoman Third Army was occupied with the invasion of the Russians and was ordered not to interfere with the deportations. Soldiers who attacked the disarmed Armenians in labor battalions were subject to courts-martial and punished.[9] Still, the Ottoman army was supreme over the region where the first deportations and massacres took place, and Mahmud Kamil Paşa, the commander of the Third Army, declared that the Armenians were "sowing discord in the army's rear" and were a serious threat to the Russian campaign.[10] He informed the government that in order "to preserve the life and existence of our nation, it has become necessary—if distressing—to punish with full severity and deport those who have revolted [and] . . . to mercilessly extirpate, down to the last man, all traitors who are conducting armed revolt against the government."[11]

Local government officials, like the *vali* Tahsin Bey, might be wary of the efficacy of deporting or destroying the Armenians, but since Kamil Paşa vigorously advocated deportation, they followed orders and coordinated the expulsions.[12] In an attempt to ameliorate the devastation of the deportees, German Vice Consul Scheubner-Richter traveled the 70 miles north from Erzurum to meet with Mahmud Kamil Paşa, who justified the deportations as "military measures." The vice consul bluntly told the commander, "This general deportation is nothing but a massacre. . . . Due to the lack of means of transportation, hardly half will reach their destinations." Kamil tried to cut off the conversation. "They will be dispersed in the interior and settled among Mohammedans." Scheubner-Richter insisted, "No uprising is expected from the local Armenians. So far the deported have been the old men, women and children. Are you going to claim this too is for military reasons?" Kamil then inadvertently revealed that the state's plans reached far beyond military necessity, to the elimination of a distinct ethnoreligious community and culture: "Armenians who convert to Islam will not be deported."[13]

On May 26 Enver sent a note to Talat explaining that it had been decided verbally to send the Armenians of the East to remote places in the south but to ensure that they made up not more than one-tenth of the population of tribesmen and Muslims in any settlement. No Armenian village was to have more than fifty houses, and no deported Armenian family was to change its place of habitation either to travel or to resettle elsewhere.[14] Talat followed up immediately with a note to the Council of Ministers that the Armenians who were hindering the operations of the army were to be sent southward to Mosul and Der el Zor, to the south and southeastern parts of Aleppo province and Syria. "This measure," he wrote, "is judged necessary for the foundational interests of the State."[15] The next day, May 27, the government promulgated the infamous "temporary law on military measures against opponents of the government in time of war," which granted the army extraordinary powers to use force and "to transfer and settle—individually or as a whole—the inhabitants of a village and a town into other location[s]" whenever they suspected anyone of treason or espionage.[16] Article 1 authorized all commanders of the army, the army corps, and the divisions and their deputies and detached [*müstakil*] local commanders "to immediately interfere in the most severe way in order to make arrests to pacify the situation and to annihilate the attacks and resistance from the very foundation if they are faced in one way or other [by] any opposition, armed resistance and attacks by the population."[17] Three days later the property of the Armenians was ordered distributed among the Muslim tribes and refugees.[18] The government thus solved two "problems" with one stroke: the removal of their perceived Armenian threat and the settlement of hundreds of thousands of Muslim nomads and refugees.

Genocide involves not only physical destruction of a people—although that is its fundamental definition—but also its cultural annihilation. The identity of Armenians for the Ottomans was not as indelibly fixed as the identity of Jews would be in the racist imagination of the Nazis. Still, the collective stereotypes of Armenians as grasping and mercenary, subversive and disloyal, turned them into an alien and unsympathetic category that then had to be eliminated.[19] Talat informed the officials at Der el Zor on June 23 that Armenians were not only to be widely dispersed but that no Armenian schools should be created. Pupils were to be educated solely in Ottoman state schools, that is, in Turkish. Armenian villages were to be set five hours distant from one another, and none of them should be situated on high points that would permit defense or resistance.[20] The possibility of revived communal presence was to be reduced to an absolute minimum. Moreover, anyone disobeying the orders sent out from Istanbul was to be punished. A few weeks later, on July 10, Kamil Paşa tightened the regime's grip in the East with an infamous telegram that ordered that any Muslims who had given shelter to Armenians in their homes were to be punished. "Since this is a violation of government orders, heads of household who shelter or protect Armenians are to be executed in front of their houses and it is imperative that their houses be burned down." He instructed his subordinates, "See to it that no as yet undeported Armenian remains behind and inform us of the action you have taken. Converted Armenians must also be sent away."[21]

Under the strain of the war and the enormous effort to eliminate Armenians, the unity of the Young Turk leadership weakened. Talat used his own agents to carry out his policy of extermination and worked around the ostensible ruler of Syria, his old colleague, Cemal Paşa, who was more reluctant to massacre Armenians. Although Cemal had used his enormous power to punish Arab nationalists, hanging many of them, and gained a reputation as a particularly bloody despot, he was not prepared to go as far as Talat, Enver, Şakir, and Nazım in destroying Armenians. It

appeared that Cemal thought that the deported Armenians would lessen
the weight of the Arabs in the economy and perhaps ameliorate extreme
Arab nationalism.[22] Seeing an opportunity to save their compatriots, Armenians in the diaspora, most notably the Dashnak activist Dr. Zavriev,
corresponded with Boghos Nubar and foreign diplomats to suggest that
Cemal, who was known to be estranged from Talat, might be convinced
to break with Istanbul. If the Allies were willing to grant Cemal power
over the Middle East and guarantee the territorial integrity of Ottoman
holdings in Asia, he might be turned from an enemy into an ally. Ultimately nothing came of these bizarre plans about which the Russians were
most enthusiastic but key British and French politicians were dubious.

DESCENT INTO BARBARITY

The peripatetic de Nogales managed to extricate himself from Van and
the clutches of Cevdet, whom he believed planned to have him murdered
rather than leave alive a Christian witness to what he had done to Armenians. He made his way to the headquarters of his superior officer, Halil
Bey, a man whom he reviled as an incompetent soldier who "cost Turkey
very dear" and who used mass killing of Christians as a tool of war.[23] The
Venezuelan freebooter was thoroughly disgusted by the massacres of the
Christians, and he asked to be relieved of his post.[24] He made his way to
Siirt in Bitlis *vilayet*, where in mid-June on a tranquil day he came upon
a pastoral scene shattered by a hillside covered by thousands of nude
and bleeding corpses. Bodies with throats slashed were being attacked
by flocks of vultures "while the scavenger dogs struck sharp teeth into
the entrails of beings still palpitating with the breath of life." When he
entered the city, he learned that Cevdet Bey had ordered the massacre
and then had moved on to Bitlis to carry out even more massive killing.
The "Angel of Destruction for the Armenians of the eastern provinces,"
Cevdet carried out orders of Halil Bey, who took revenge on the Armenians for what he took to be "the moral and material aid they had lent
the Russians" during the conquest of the province of Van.[25] The brutality
licensed by those in authority was contagious. De Nogales excused the

Armenian victims, 1915.

regular army, both "Ottoman and Muscovite [which] respected and protected the prisoners captured from the other side," but "the Cossacks and
the Armenian *comitadchis*, like our Kurd guerillas, killed without mercy
all the enemy wounded and defenseless that fell into their hands."[26]

What de Nogales had seen and heard was the systematic destruction
of thousands of Armenians and Assyrians in dozens of villages as Halil
and Cevdet marched toward Bitlis.[27] The pattern would be repeated
over and over again. After the men were gathered together and shot, the
women were offered to the local Kurds; those not killed or converted
were marched away, usually to be murdered later. Halil ominously noted
that de Nogales "had been the only Christian . . . in the army to witness
things that should never have been witnessed by any Christian."[28]

Halil Bey, who was the uncle of Enver and a divisional commander
in the Ottoman Third Army, survived the war, escaped imprisonment by
the British when they occupied Istanbul, and died in 1957 after writing

his memoirs. Halil wrote proudly, "The Armenian nation, which I had tried to annihilate to the last member of it, because it tried to erase my country from history as prisoners of the enemy in the most horrible and painful days of my homeland, the Armenian nation, which I want to re-store its peace and luxury, because today it takes shelter under the virtue of the Turkish nation." He was prepared to help Armenians if they re-mained "loyal to the Turkish homeland," if they betrayed "the Turks and the Turkish homeland, I will order my forces which surround all your country and I won't leave even a single breathing Armenian all over the earth. Come to your senses."[29]

Savagery had become commonplace; indifference to mutilation had become normal; and viciousness spread like spilled blood, covering a wider and wider landscape. Callous killing was not only permitted but encour-aged, and the few who held back because of moral or religious restraint could themselves be sacrificed. Tucked into a valley southwest of Lake Van, with houses tightly packed on the slopes of a natural amphitheater, the town of Bitlis had been home to a medieval Armenian kingdom, and for six hundred years, from the thirteenth to the early nineteenth centuries, the center of a Kurdish emirate. Armenians made up a large minority of the town's inhabitants until their annihilation in June 1915. When news reached Bitlis on April 20 of the Van resistance, the *vali*, Mustafa Abdül-halik [Renda], Talat's brother-in-law, ordered the arrest of "the cream of the youth of [Armenian] Bitlis" and marched them through the streets in shackles to the curses of the local Muslims. They were hanged outside the city, their bodies left for two weeks and then devoured by dogs.[30] Two months later small groups of men were arrested, among them Khachik Vartanian, the respected pastor of the Armenian Protestant Church. A few families resisted the police with what arms they had. Gendarmes escorted many of the men outside the city, where they were killed and their bodies burned. Three days later, on June 25, Cevdet arrived with his "butcher's battalion." Leading Dashnaks were tortured and hanged. Armenian nota-bles were imprisoned and forced to pay heavy indemnities. In some places Armenians were herded into barns and burned; elsewhere women were used as prostitutes to serve Ottoman soldiers until they contracted vene-real disease and were poisoned. Children who had managed to hide were hunted down and drowned in a river or thrown into pits.[31] By the end of the month all but a dozen Armenians had been eliminated from Bitlis. Estimates placed the number of Armenian victims in Bitlis *vilayet* at 15,000.[32]

The destruction on the plain of Muş to the northeast of Bitlis was many-fold worse. Here more than 141,000 Armenians lived in 234 towns and villages. Most of the able-bodied men had been conscripted a year before, leaving the Christians of the region defenseless. As in other provinces, the cleansing of the villages preceded the evacuation of the major town. From July 9 to 14 the plains were emptied of Armenians; many fled southward into the mountains of Sasun, others to the Russian lines in the north. After the bishop and about one hundred others were arrested and shot, the Ottomans shelled the Armenian neighborhoods of the city of Muş. Soldiers and the irregulars in the *çete*s broke down doors and killed defenders with bayonets and axes. Looters rampaged through the devastated houses.[33] As the Russian army moved forward, some 80,000 Muslims fled to Bitlis.[34] What had been an Ottoman town peopled by Muslims and Christians—the ancestral home of the American Armenian writer William Saroyan—became a Turkish and Kurdish town.

By the summer of 1915 the Ottomans were at war, not only with the Russians, British, French, Australians, and New Zealanders, but also with their own Armenian and Assyrian subjects, at least those who managed to defend themselves before being slaughtered. The sanctuary of the mountain retreat of Sasun to the south of Muş had resisted incursions of Turks and Kurds throughout its history, but in 1915 it faced the formidable army of Kamil Paşa. From mid-July to early August tens of thousands of Armenians held off the assault of the Ottoman troops, but hunger and lack of ammunition forced the defenders to attempt to break out and reach the Russian lines about 25 miles from Muş. Several thousand succeeded, but most of those huddled in the mountains were cut down or deported.[35]

Most of the Armenians in Bitlis and Muş were killed in their home *vilayet*; relatively few were deported. Credit and blame for the killing falls on the highest command of the Ottoman forces, as well as the obedient *vali*, Mustafa Abdülhalik, a man whom his superior, Vehib Paşa, believed to be "resolute, caring, brave, charitable, and human, devoted, patriotic, and religious." Vehib, who would command the Third Army from March 1916, was appalled by this "example of atrocity of a kind never before seen in the history of Islam." Nevertheless, he exonerated Abdülhalik, "a man without fault and endowed with civic virtues" who "was not able to put a stop to these events, which I shall never be able to approve."[36]

In the Black Sea port city of Trabzon, the home of Pontic Greeks as well as Armenians, Turks, Laz, Abkhaz, Ajars, and other Muslim and Christian peoples, the Armenians felt particularly vulnerable when in November 1914 Russian ships bombarded the city. They attempted to demonstrate their loyalty, but the local *vali*, Cemal Azmi, a high-ranking original member of the CUP, was determined to eliminate them one way or another. The local prelate, Kevork Turian, was arrested and murdered, and boatloads of Armenians were taken by ship out to sea and drowned. Children were poisoned in the Red Crescent Hospital.[37] Some 15,000 Armenians were deported in convoys from the city and its surroundings. They were attacked by the thugs of the *cete*s, pillaged, or slaughtered as they moved south. The American consul in the port of Samsun reported that "groups of Armenian males" were massacred by peasants; women and children would soon be "dying of hunger or despair, a horrible massacre reminiscent of the period in which they rid Constantinople of its dogs and left them all on a island to die!"[38] The deportees from Samsun and Marsovan were moved through the beautiful river town of Amasia, and along with the local Armenians driven toward Tokat, some of the men separated from the others, tied together, and clubbed to death. "If Turkey is, in general, not up to scratch in matters of organization and talent," the consul wrote, "this time, when it was a question of massacres, theft, and so on, it showed nicely coordinated, nicely accelerated savoir-faire in swiftly expediting hundreds of thousands of creatures to the next world."[39]

DIYARBAKIR

The ancient walled city Diyarbakır was ruled by a fiercely loyal CUP member, Dr. Mehmed Reşid, one of the founders of the movement. A dedicated Turkish nationalist, although a Circassian himself, the product of the Military Medical School that had produced patriotic modernizers committed to imperial and Turkish survival, Dr. Reşid was obsessed with "those who harass the fatherland from within . . . who ruin our country, exploit our villages, and cause our enemies to insult our religion and our nation."[40] His anti-Christian enmity, rooted in his modernizing ambitions and security concerns for the empire, extended to the Ottoman Greeks as well as the Armenians, and he worked on the eve of the war to expel the Greeks from western Anatolia. He was appointed *vali* in Diyarbakır in March 1915 to replace the relatively tolerant Halil (Kapancı) Bey, who in Reşid's opinion had thrown "the affairs of the government into great chaos, and reduced the state's hold to zero."[41] Reşid arrived in the city with thirty to fifty special forces made up of Circassians and augmented them with recruits from the local prison. With this armed strength he set out to destroy the Christian population of the *vilayet*.[42] He rooted out more mild officials and in their place appointed CUP militants.[43] The American consul in Aleppo, Jesse Jackson, informed the embassy on April 25 that the ancient walled city of Diyarbakır was experiencing a "perfect reign of terror." By that time hundreds of prominent Christians had been judged disloyal and imprisoned. Almost two dozen had been beaten to death, others bastinadoed.[44]

Dr. Reşid enthusiastically reported to Talat how he had orchestrated "the pursuit of deserters . . . with utmost severity." Churches of Armenians and Assyrians had been searched; caches of arms had been found, deserters apprehended, and the most important Christian leaders detained.[45] He personally supervised killing or sent his trusted agents to Mardin, Midyat, and other towns to carry out his orders. He told Muslim notables, "The time has come to save Turkey from its national enemies, that is, the Christians. We must be clear that the states of Europe will not protest or punish us, since Germany is on our side and helps and supports us."[46] He had the town crier announce that all Christians had to turn over all shooting weapons that they possessed within twenty-four hours to the commander of the gendarmes. The search for arms served as the principal excuse for arrests and mass killing.[47] When he received the "temporary law" of May 27, 1915, ordering the deportation of the Armenians, Reşid complained that there were no instructions on how to carry out the expulsions or which Armenians to deport. At first he deported only the men but then was ordered to send all Armenians into exile. With inadequate troops and no planning or provisions, the governor relied on Circassian gendarmes, decommissioned soldiers from the Balkan Wars, and local recruits from the peasantry and *esnaf* (artisan) class. Reşid related that thousands of Armenians deported from Bitlis, Harput, and Trabzon passed through Diyarbakir province, whence looters and pillagers attacked them, following the Armenians for days to pick up what they could. Like Talat, he claimed that an orderly deportation was impossible, particularly in the face of angry and frightened Muslims.[48]

The leading Armenians met to discuss whether they should organize resistance or trust the Ottoman authorities. When a particularly eminent figure, a member of the Ottoman provincial council, threatened anyone who decided for resistance, the matter was dropped.[49] With no organized defense, the Christian elite of Diyarbakır were arrested on May 11, ostensibly to prevent a rebellion. Many were tortured, others killed, still others sent to Mosul.[50] The torture was exceptionally cruel, as the Armenian who served as British vice consul reported: "Hagop Bozo and some of his associates were shoed and compelled to run like horses. They drove red-hot horse shoes in the breast of Mihran Bastajian and his associates. They forced some others to put their heads under big presses, and then by turning the handles they crushed the heads to pieces. Others they mutilated or pulled their nails out with pincers. . . . Others were flayed alive." The Armenian bishop was dragged through the streets, and in front of a crowd was doused with gasoline and set afire. The flames were quenched before he died, and he was thrown into the stables of the municipal hospital where the American missionary, Dr. Floyd Smith, found him dying in agony.[51]

The *vali* convinced the Kurdish tribes outside the city to carry out their "religious duties and obligations."[52] He conspired with the Kurdish Parliament deputy Pirinççizâde Aziz Feyzi to employ a well-known outlaw, Ömer, to murder Armenians. Short and dark with a pockmarked face, Ömer wore "a big turban on his head around which hung many coloured silk insignias to show that he was a Kurdish chief. . . . He presented a picture of a portable armoury, being armed with a Mauser rifle, two revolvers, a sword, a dagger, a *yataghan* [*yatağan*, a single-edged knife] and carrying with him an enormous amount of bullets and cartridges."[53] Reşid arranged to have 635 "elite" Armenians of the city sent on 23 rafts down the Tigris. When the rafts reached a secluded gorge, Ömer's men attacked, killed, and stripped them.[54] Armenians in the town witnessed the clothes and goods of the victims being sold in the bazaar.[55] For his efforts—more precisely because he did not share the loot—Ömer was himself killed on Reşid's orders.[56]

Some weeks after the initial massacres, Rafael de Nogales ventured into Diyarbakır on his way to Aleppo. In mid-June the bazaars were almost deserted, their tapestry, leather goods, and woolen industries "practically paralyzed." He lodged with Mehmed-Asım Bey, the gendarme commander who had carried out the massacres. He proudly showed de Nogales photographs of the arms he had seized. The peripatetic soldier was not impressed by the motley collection of fowling-pieces and a few army guns. He was convinced that "this ostentatious collection of elements of war was nothing more nor less than the work of Mehmed-Asım Bey himself, in his attempt to mislead and impress the public." Armenians, he realized, possessed firearms; one could not survive in the region without them. Indeed the possession of weapons was legal and had been authorized by the Young Turks.[57] De Nogales called on Dr. Reşid, who intimated that "in regard to the extermination of the Armenians of his *vilayet*, he had merely obeyed superior orders; so that the responsibility for the massacres perpetrated there should rest not with him, but with his chief," Talat Bey. As de Nogales remembered, the order had come in a circular telegram "containing a scant three words: '*Yar—Vur—Oldur*,' meaning, 'Burn, demolish, kill.'"[58] To the soldier of fortune Dr. Reşid was worse than the despised Cevdet: "panther though he showed himself to be, [Cevdet] never ceased being a valiant soldier as well, even to a certain degree generous with his foes; while [Dr. Reşid] was merely a hyena, who killed without ever risking his own life."[59]

Occasionally when particular atrocities attracted the attention of foreigners, Talat made gestures that appeared to be aimed at protecting

Armenians or preventing the worst excesses by the local population "naturally, to the extent that it is possible." Local people along the routes of deportation, he telegraphed, "should never become involved in this [operation], and absolutely no place or possibility must be given for such incidents to arise that would produce clashes between the various communities and would simultaneously look very bad to the outside world."[60] Pressured by the Germans, Talat reined in the zealous Reşid, complaining that the governor was persecuting Christians indiscriminately rather than simply targeting Armenians.[61] The German vice consul in Mosul reported to his embassy that he was told by the former *mutasarrıf* of Mardin that Reşid in Diyarbakır was "causing havoc like an eager bloodhound amongst the Christians of his Vilayets. Also just recently in Mardin he allowed seven hundred Christians, mostly Armenians and including the Armenian Bishop to be slaughtered like sheep in one night near the city. They had been gathered together by the Gendarmerie sent especially from Diyarbekir. Reshid Bey continued with this bloody deed against the innocent whose numbers have surpassed two thousand, confirmed today by the Muetessarif."[62] German concern about the massacres in Diyarbakır and Mardin resulted two days later in a telegram from Talat scolding Reşid for his indiscriminate killing of Christians: "It has recently been reported that massacres of Armenians and Christians without distinction as to sect have been organized within the province, and that in Mardin, for example, some seven hundred people from among the Armenians and other Christian inhabitants were recently taken outside of the city at night and, with due authorization, slaughtered like sheep by those individuals who had been brought from Diyarbakir, and that the total of those killed to date in these massacres is estimated at two thousand persons, and that there are fears that, if a speedy and definite end is not put to this then persons, and the Muslim inhabitants of neighboring provinces, will rise up and engage in a general slaughter of Christians." Talat considered it inappropriate "that the disciplinary and administrative measures adopted with regard to the Armenians be extended to the other Christians." He ordered Reşid to stop the indiscriminate anti-Christian measures that were "very detrimental to the country."[63] In August Talat sent telegrams to the eastern provinces ordering that Armenian Catholics and Protestants not be deported.[64] The minister's careful distinction between those who should and those who should not be deported or massacred implied that some, namely those of the *Ermeni milleti*, were fair game.

No judicial action, however, was taken against Reşid at the time, although he was transferred to Ankara and ordered to send the money, jewels, and goods of deported or murdered Armenians that he had seized to the capital.[65] But Dr. Reşid was one of those who did not get away. At the war's end he was arrested and imprisoned in the maximum-security Bekirağa prison along with others suspected of atrocities.[66] After a successful escape, he went into hiding and wrote an exculpatory memoir. When discovered, he committed suicide. Reşid justified what he had done to the Christians as the acts of a faithful state servant, who operated in conditions of state weakness and disorganization. Much of the random looting and killing, he claimed, was by ordinary people whom the authorities could not control. When Reşid turned the homes of exiled Armenians over to Muslims, they destroyed the houses in a mad search for hidden wealth.[67] He combined his medical distancing from the patient with his fervent feelings for the fatherland. "Either they us, or we them. . . . Faced with the necessity of having to choose, I did not hesitate for long. My Turkishness triumphed over my identity as a doctor. . . . The Armenian bandits were a load of harmful microbes that had afflicted the body of the fatherland. Was it not the duty of the doctor to kill the microbes?"[68] He later confessed that his conscience bothered him, but what he had done was not for personal glory or enrichment but because he believed "that we were on the point of losing the fatherland. . . . I overcame my hesitations and I risked [everything] boldly."[69] His boldness included having Armenians and Assyrians imprisoned in the dungeons of Dara, the ancient Persian settlement hewn from rock outside Mardin, and ordering the murder of hundreds of infants, who were thrown off the arched stone bridge outside of Diyarbakır.[70] Reşid's friend, Halil Edib, in Mardin congratulated Dr. Reşid for ridding the province of 120,000 Christians: "I kiss your hands, you who have gained us the six [eastern] provinces and you have opened to us access to Turkestan and to the Caucasus."[71]

RUSSIA AND THE ARMENIANS

With their own government set on destroying them individually and as a nation, many Armenians understood that their salvation lay in a Russian advance into eastern Anatolia. Those who were able fled to the Russian lines and on to the Caucasus. Faced by the prospect of acquiring and ruling a vast and troubled territory, the tsarist government reaffirmed its policy in Armenia. Rather than proposing annexation and colonization of Armenia—an accusation leveled at the time and later by historians—the Russian Foreign Ministry reworked the reform plan of 1914 into its own "Basic Principles for the Future Ordering of Armenia," which proposed stronger supervision of the region by a European governor-general. Maintaining essentially the 1914 reform agreement with more vigorous oversight, Russia remained committed to reforms and Ottoman authority over eastern Anatolia rather than division among the Great Powers. In July 1915 Foreign Minister Sazonov informed Ambassador Benckendorff in London that "the formation of an autonomous Armenia under the sovereignty of the Sultan and under the tripartite protectorate of Russia, France, and England would be the natural result of the longstanding favorable attitude not only of Russia, but of its Allies as well, toward the Turkish Armenians."[72] The Russians were cautious about annexation, and only when in 1916 their allies concluded the Sykes-Picot Agreement dividing up the Ottoman lands did Petrograd somewhat reluctantly consider annexations in Anatolia.

Relieved by his nephew, the tsar, as commander-in-chief of the Russian Imperial Army, Grand Duke Nikolai Nikolaevich arrived at his new post as viceroy of the Caucasus in the fall of 1915. The grand duke considered his predecessor, Vorontsov-Dashkov, to have been too "pro-Armenian," and he set out to redress Russian policy in a more balanced way, taking into greater consideration the desires of Kurds. Nikolai Nikolaevich immediately revived the military campaign in Anatolia. The "Iudenich Offensive" in eastern Anatolia and the "Baratov Expedition" into western Persia both met with success. In early 1916 the Russians took Erzurum, Rize, Bitlis, and Trabzon, followed not long after by Erzincan.

Exhaustion of the Russian forces and renewed resistance by the Otto-
mans brought their advance to a halt before taking Harput or Diyarbakır.
The Ottomans had lost most of northeastern Anatolia by the time the
Russian Revolution nullified the tsarist army's advances. The progress of
Russian arms in 1916 encouraged certain officials in Russia, particularly
those in the Ministry of Agriculture, to consider "colonization," that is,
agricultural settlement of the devastated lands depleted of Armenians.
With the capture of Erzurum in February 1916, Minister of Agriculture
Aleksandr Naumov warned that land should be protected from grasping
speculators who would take advantage of the absence of the former pos-
sessors.[73] The Ministry's agents proposed that productive agriculturalists,
Armenians and Russians, be given land. By increasing the wealth of the
region and settling Russians, the security of the borderlands would be
ensured. Ultimately, however, the viceroy of the Caucasus, Grand Duke
Nikolai Nikolaevich, and the military did not sign off on the elaborate
and ambitious plans of the Ministry of Agriculture.

Foreign Minister Sazonov wrote to the grand duke advocating an
ethnically nonpartisan policy in Anatolia. Neither autonomy for the Armenians nor their replacement by Muslims was desirable. "It seems to me
that the best outcome for us in ordering the reconquered areas of Turkey
would be to be especially firm in following the principles of legality, justice, and an entirely nonpartisan relation to all the diverse elements of
the region, not setting one against the other and nor providing exclusive
protection to any one particular nationality [*narodnost'*] at the expense
of another." Other officials attempted to convince the viceroy to be more
pro-Kurdish. "If one is to view [the Ottoman slaughter of the Armenians]
not from a humanitarian, but from a political point of view," one of the
grand duke's secret agents wrote, "and as an already accomplished fact—
one for which the Armenians bear the blame—one must say that there is
this positive side: Turkey has left us an Armenia without Armenians."[74]
Russian officials did not accept such extreme views, and the grand duke
agreed.[75] Essentially Russian policy remained occupation not annexation
and colonization until the fall of the tsar in February 1917 eliminated Russia as a serious player in historic Armenia. After the Bolshevik takeover of

power in Petrograd in October 1917, the Russian occupation turned into a spontaneous withdrawal. The Ottomans would retake the eastern provinces—this time denuded of most of their Christian subjects.[76]

GERMANY AND THE ARMENIANS

The question of German involvement in the Armenian Genocide has divided historians. A case has been made for German participation, even instigation. Others argue that the Germans had little influence on the Ottomans, who did what they intended in any case.[77] The evidence favors the view that the German government knew what was occurring but did almost nothing to prevent deportations and mass killing, and deliberately maintained a relative silence on the elimination of the Ottoman Armenians. Germany was the one European power that might have been able to ameliorate the conditions of the Armenians. The best word to describe the German role is complicity (*Mitschuld* in German) rather than initiation, participation, or responsibility. Talat was sensitive to German official and public opinion and occasionally adjusted his policies to placate them. But German diplomats and officers did not intervene forcefully to stop the Armenian deportations and massacres. They had the military power but not the political will to stop the massacres.

Indeed German officers and civilians serving with the Ottomans shared their views that Armenians were a real threat to the war effort. Most of the information about the Armenian insurrection came from the Ottomans, and they believed it. Two nurses in Erzurum, Norwegian Thora Wedel-Jarlsberg and German Eva Elvers, told Johann Heinrich Mordtmann, the German consul general in Istanbul, that "the Armenians themselves were to blame for the misfortune which had befallen them; the two associations, Dashnaktsutiun and Hintschak, which had systematically worked on and terrorised the Armenian population for years, were mainly to blame. The Turkish government was completely right to take action against these dangerous elements." They were repulsed and indignant, however, over the killing of innocent women and children.[78] The liberal intellectual Ernst Jäckh, the head of the German-Turkish

Friendship Society, traveled in Anatolia and the Balkans in the fall of 1915 and reported back approvingly that Enver had secured the country against an Armenian revolution in the army's rear. Jäckh reminded opponents that the participation of "the Turks" in the war was the key to victory.[79]

Back in Berlin the General Staff did not agree that Ottoman Armenians were a danger, but neither the High Command nor the kaiser and his government were willing to antagonize their Ottoman allies. What they desired most was a strong and stable Ottoman ally, not the destruction of the Christians. For many Germans in the government and the army Armenians were a problem rather than—as they were for many German Protestants—Christian brethren. Uncomfortable with the radicalism and violence of the Ottoman government's policy, which was wreaking havoc with the Ottoman economy, Germans officials saw Armenians as the "Jews of the Orient," who took advantage of the poor Muslims but at the same time were essential to the smooth running of commerce and production. While "all Orientals are involved in intrigues," the "Armenians and Greeks are masters of the trade," an earlier German ambassador reported. "The economic activity, which elsewhere the Jews perform, namely the exploitation of the poorer, popular classes through usury and similar manipulations, is here performed exclusively by Armenians and Greeks."[80] Germans preferred to work with ethnic Turks, and as far as the Armenian Question was concerned, it was best to keep silent.

German missionaries, medical personnel, officers, and diplomats knew what was being done to the Armenians. Ambassador Wangenheim, already suffering from the illness that would prove fatal some months later, informed the German chancellor, Theobold von Bethmann Hollweg, as early as July 7 that "the way in which the relocation is being carried out shows that the government is indeed pursuing its purpose of eradicating the Armenian race from the Turkish Empire."[81] He enclosed the mild protest made to the Porte a few days earlier, largely to absolve the Germans of any responsibility in the massacres. Wangenheim accepted the initial Ottoman rationale for the deportations—that they had been dictated by military necessities—but he was upset that the mass expulsions "include without distinction the guilty and the innocent" and "are accompanied by acts of violence, such as massacres and plundering."[82] Convinced that there had been an "Armenian conspiracy," the ambassador feared most "that our enemies will later accuse us of being accomplices. With the help of my reports, we will be in a position to prove to the hostile world at an appropriate time, in particular through the press, that we have always expressly condemned the exaggerated measures of the Turkish government and even more so the excesses of local official bodies."[83]

At the end of August Talat informed the German ambassador, "*La question arménienne n'existe plus*" (The Armenian question no longer exists).[84] Wangenheim died on October 25 and was buried in the park of the German embassy's summer residency in Tarabya overlooking the Bosphorus. His successors, Prince Ernst zu Hohenlohe-Langenburg and Paul Wolff-Metternich, attempted to reverse the German position and protested more vigorously to stop the massacres. However, the Ottoman government's overall policy toward the Armenians did not change as a result of the German complaints. On September 25 the German special ambassador Hohenlohe-Langenburg noted that the Sublime Porte has gone back on its assurances that it would be more humane in carrying out the deportations. His consuls in Adana and Aleppo confirmed that the authorities were starving the deportees.[85]

One of the most devastating admissions about the atrocities against Armenians came from Lieutenant Colonel August Stange, a German who served as a commander of one of the units of the *Teşkilat-ı Mahsusa* from the end of 1914 through the summer of 1915. "[H]undreds of thousands have simply been murdered," he wrote, and the "military reasons are only secondarily behind the evacuation." What he witnessed was the working out of "a long-held plan fundamentally to weaken, if not to destroy, the Armenian people . . . decided on and well organized in Constantinople by the Young Turk Committee using the army and voluntary bands with members of the CUP present at the localities."[86]

The head of a German parliamentary delegation, Matthias Erzberger, a Center Party member of the Reichstag, met with Talat and Enver and urged them to put an end to the forced conversions and persecutions of

Armenians. Erzberger saw no distinction between deportation and massacre and informed his Foreign Ministry that those being deported were perishing. "The people are driven like herds of animals for weeks and months to their destination and only in the rarest cases has the necessary food been provided for. Thus, these poor people fall prey in huge numbers to hunger and disease. Once they reach their destination they do not remain there, either, but are driven to a new destination and from here to another one, thus never having a chance to rest.... Hunger and threats drive them into the hands of the Turks. The children then become Turkish on their own or, as so-called 'war orphans,' they are made into Turks by the authorities."[87]

German consuls in the field believed "that the deportations mean the intended destruction of all Armenians in Turkey" and reported that a Turkish official had told them, "We want an Armenia without Armenians." "This is the principle on which the government acted and still acts, the implementation of which has caused perhaps 4/5 of the entire Armenian population, including women and children, to be deported from its residences in Asia Minor and sent marching to Mesopotamia and Syria, mainly on foot. As far as is generally known here, only three towns have been completely excluded from this: namely, Constantinople, Smyrna and Aleppo."[88]

Of the Young Turks Ambassador Wolff-Metternich angrily wrote, "From a clique that proclaims *liberté, droit civil pour tous*, constitution and slaughters hundreds of thousands of innocent people I do not expect much."[89] He met with the president of the Parliament, Halil Bey (Menteşe), who claimed he disapproved of the "Armenian persecutions" but said he was powerless before the triumvirate at the head of the state. Like Wangenheim, Wolff-Metternich was concerned that the Germans not be blamed for the massacres.[90] He presented his case to Enver and Cemal "in an exceedingly sharp language." But, he concluded, "protests are useless, and Turkish denials that no more deportations are to be undertaken are worthless."[91] When Wolff-Metternich met with Talat, whom he believed to be the "brain behind the deportation of the Armenians," the minister, who had just returned from Anatolia, claimed to have taken extensive measures to feed the deported Armenian families. Crimes committed against Armenian property and person, Talat told him, would be severely punished. Measures, however, had to be taken against the conspirators. "Only the deportation of the whole could ensure security." Wolff-Metternich mentioned a "peculiar opinion" expressed by Talat, that "we [the Germans], in a similar situation, would have acted in the same way to eradicate a revolutionary movement in Germany with force." The ambassador objected, pointing out "that the innocent should not be hurt when pursuing the guilty, and that only those found guilty of crimes should be punished."[92]

Germany had much to gain from the Ottoman alliance. As long as the Ottomans fought against the Russians and British, they held down hundreds of thousands of Allied troops that might have been thrown against the Germans. Because the Germans were latecomers to the imperialist scramble for colonies, their ambitions for *Weltmacht* could be enhanced in the Ottoman Middle East—if the Central Powers won the war.[93] When Ambassador Wolff-Metternich suggested to his government that it would have to "inspire fear in the Turkish government" to make it change its policies vis-à-vis Armenians, the German chancellor, Bethmann Hollweg, made clear what German priorities were: "The proposed public reprimand of an ally in the course of a war would be an act which is unprecedented in history. Our only aim is to keep Turkey on our side until the end of the war, no matter whether as a result Armenians do perish or not. If the war continues much longer, we will need the Turks even more."[94] German voices supporting the Armenians were effectively ignored or silenced. Upset with Wolff-Metternich's protests, Berlin acceded to the Young Turks' request to have him recalled, and after serving less than eleven months, he left Istanbul in October 1916. The liberal German politician Gustav Stressemann, later a Nobel Prize laureate, sneered at Wolff-Metternich's support for the Armenians and wondered "whether Herr von Metternich was the ambassador of the German Empire or the ambassador of the Armenians?"[95] Wolff-Metternich's successor, Richard von Kühlmann, arrived in Istanbul the next month and vigorously supported Ottoman policy. He considered Talat to be "the strong man that

Germans always felt the empire needed."[96] After an American request to the Germans that they do something to alleviate the situation of the Armenians, there was some discussion about deporting Armenians to Germany, where there was a labor shortage. The highest-ranking German officer in the empire, Liman Von Sanders, however, opposed the idea, which he thought "would raise the distrust of the Turks and, thus, cause political damage." At the same time he took measures to have deportations from Izmir stopped.[97] Back home in Germany, the government issued guidelines to the press that explicitly stated that "it is best to keep silent about the Armenian question."[98]

THE AMERICAN AMBASSADOR AND THE MINISTER OF WAR

As more and more evidence came into the American embassy that Armenians were being deported and murdered, Ambassador Morgenthau requested a meeting with Enver, who proved to be extraordinarily frank about what was happening. He reiterated the standard argument. "The Armenians had a fair warning," he claimed, "of what would happen to them in case they joined our enemies. Three months ago I sent for the Armenian Patriarch and I told him that if the Armenians attempted to start a revolution or to assist the Russians, I would be unable to prevent mischief from happening to them. My warning produced no effect and the Armenians started a revolution and helped the Russians. You know what happened at Van." He appealed to the sense of military necessity that he expected the ambassador to share. "You must understand that we are now fighting for our lives at the Dardanelles and that we are sacrificing thousands of men. While we are engaged in such a struggle as this, we cannot permit people in our own country to attack us in the back." He claimed that he had the greatest admiration for the intelligence and industry of the Armenians, and would have liked nothing better than to see them as a real part of the nation. But when they allied with the empire's enemies, they had to be destroyed.[99]

Enver combined an argument that action against Armenians was a justified response to rebellion in time of war with the larger claim that the government had to act preemptorily to prevent future, anticipated insurrections. "We now have this country in our absolute control and we can easily revenge ourselves on any revolutionists. . . . The great trouble with the Armenians is that they are separatists. They are determined to have a kingdom of their own, and they have allowed themselves to be fooled by the Russians." Enver understood the strength of a revolutionary movement: their own movement had taken power when "there were only two hundred of us. . . . It is our experience with revolutions which makes us fear the Armenians. If two hundred Turks could overturn the Government, then a few hundred bright, educated Armenians could do the same thing. We have therefore deliberately adopted the plan of scattering them so that they can do us no harm."[100]

Enver's remarks revealed that behind the genocidal killings was a deep sense of insecurity and an awareness that his government was vulnerable. The minister's views on the Armenians had radicalized over time. Whether he actually believed in the Armenian danger, convinced himself that all measures must be taken to eradicate a potential internal threat, or used that scenario to accomplish more far-reaching plans to Turkify Anatolia cannot be conclusively determined, but given the mental and emotional universe that had developed among the Young Turks it appears that all of these elements were present and reinforced one another. The German naval attaché Lieutenant Commander Hans von Humann, "a rabid anti-Semite and enthusiastic expansionist," who had been raised in the Ottoman Empire and was a close friend of Enver, told the ambassador of Enver's hesitance about the deportation of the Armenians: "At first Enver wanted to treat the Armenians with the utmost moderation, and four months ago he insisted that they be given another opportunity to demonstrate their loyalty. But after what they did at Van, he had to yield to the army, which had been insisting all along that it should protect its rear. The Committee decided upon the deportations and Enver reluctantly agreed."[101] Humann agreed with Talat and Enver, repeating Talat's words justifying the deportations in "order to be better allies for you, that is, without the weakness of an internal enemy." Expressing his commitment to *Realpolitik*, the attaché told his naval superiors in Berlin that "because of their conspiracy with the Russians, the Armenians are being more or less annihilated. This is hard, but useful."[102]

Morgenthau was convinced that Talat, rather than Enver, had been the more determined to rid the empire of the Armenian threat.[103] Other Young Turk leaders held quite similar views. Foreign Minister Halil Bey "regarded the elimination of this race with utmost good humour."[104] Morgenthau observed the anxieties of the most powerful men in the state and read them through the lens of his ethnic stereotypes. If the Germans were the cool, calculating men driven by *Realpolitik*, the Turks were driven by fear, "the only emotion which really actuates the Turk." He viewed them as a unique people who neither hated nor loved, who had no lasting animosities or affections. "They only fear. And naturally they attribute to others the motives which regulate their own conduct."[105] That fear was understandable, given the precarious position of the empire in the deadly power struggle in Europe, the internal instability of the country, and the threat from Russia. The sense of imminent danger was easily transferred to the Armenians, who were perceived as internal allies of a rapacious foreign power.[106]

Ambassador Morgenthau decided to resign his post in the spring of 1916. He was discrete in public about what the Ottomans were doing to Armenians, but in an interview he declared that "one of the main reasons for his resignation as ambassador to Turkey [was] his great desire to make known to the people of the United States some of the conditions in the Turkish empire, especially as they affect the long suffering Armenians. He wanted to assist in the raising of funds for Armenian relief and to make known in a tactful way to the Turkish authorities the thoughts of the American public on the conditions in that land." "In my childhood," Morgenthau said, "I cried over 'Uncle Tom's Cabin,' and wept at the way the Negroes were sold into slavery. Later on I read 'Evangeline' and my heart went out to the poor woman and her lover; but all of these things are nothing compared to what went on in Turkey under my own eyes. I do not want to give too many harrowing pictures and it will not be wise for me to go much into details, but I will say that I have been requested to state that most of the stories that have reached the United States are founded on facts."[107]

VOICES OF PROTEST

In Germany the loudest voices raised about the Armenian massacres came from Protestant clergy, but the government pressured the media enough that such dissenters were barely heard.[108] The activist Armenophilic clergyman Dr. Johannes Lepsius, already famous for his protests against the Hamidian massacres twenty years earlier, convinced the German Foreign Office to sponsor a trip for him to Anatolia to encourage Armenians to join the war effort. By the time the energetic pastor reached Istanbul in July 1915, massacres and the Russian withdrawal from Van rendered his mission meaningless. He decided that his new task was to inform his countrymen of what was happening to the Ottoman Armenians. The government opposed his efforts, but Lepsius managed to distribute more than 20,000 copies of his book, *Bericht über die Lage des armenischen Volkes in der Türkei* (Report on the Situation of the Armenian People in Turkey), before the strict censorship in Germany caught up with him.[109] The left Social Democrat Karl Liebknecht broke the silence and referred in the Reichstag to Lepsius's evidence of atrocities perpetrated by Germany's ally. He asked whether the government was aware that "hundreds of thousands of Armenians in the allied Turkish empire have been expelled and massacred" and what steps the government had taken "to bring about the necessary atonement, to create a humane future for the rest of the Armenian population in Turkey, and to prevent similar atrocities from happening again."[110] The Foreign Office was so annoyed with Lepsius, who "continuously cause[d] the Imperial Government grave inconvenience with his Armenian propaganda," that it tried to deny him visas and even while he was resting at a bathing resort on the coast in the Netherlands tried to induce indirectly the Dutch government to deport Lepsius to Germany "for military reasons."[111]

In Istanbul the Armenian Patriarch Zaven not only continued through the spring and summer of 1915 to petition the Ottoman authorities and plead with them to stop the massacres but wrote secret letters to Bishop Ghevont Turian of Bulgaria, then still a neutral state, which he wanted conveyed to the catholicos in Echmiadzin and to Boghos Nubar and the Armenian National Delegation in Paris. "The Ottoman government's

Armenian patriarch of Constantinople (1913–1922), Zaven Ter Yeghiayan (1868–1947). Bibliotheque Nationale de France.

plan," he testified, "is 'Armenia without Armenians' and it has already started to settle Muslims on Armenian lands and in their houses." He had heard that the waters of the Euphrates were full of corpses and that those that marched on were condemned to die in the desert. "This is a plan to completely exterminate the Armenians.... If Armenians abroad are unable to move the conscience of the neutral states, very few of the one and a half million Armenians will be left within a few months. It is inevitable that they will perish."[112]

As Europe became aware of atrocities, Russia pressured its allies, Great Britain and France, to issue a statement condemning what the Russians called "crimes against humanity" and holding the Ottoman government and its agents responsible for these crimes. The document issued on May 24, 1915, was the first international text to use this language.[113] Allied diplomacy, however, had little effect on the Ottomans while they were at war with the Entente. Three days after the Allied declaration, the Ottomans promulgated a law legitimizing the deportations for "security and military interests." Winston Churchill, who until recently had served as first lord of the admiralty, offered on October 20, 1915, "a proposal to use mustard gas in a final attempt to break through the Turkish defenses" at Gallipoli in retaliation "for the massacres of Armenians as well as the killing of many British soldiers after they had tried to surrender." His proposal to massively kill Ottoman Muslims was rejected by cabinet officers, however, because it would arouse discontent among the Muslims of India and Egypt.[114]

Few Ottoman voices openly protested the Armenian deportations. A notable exception was Ahmed Rıza, a founder of the Young Turk movement and the early leader of its nationalist, vociferously anti-Armenian wing. As a member of the Ottoman Senate (*Meclis-i Ayan*), which was allowed to reconvene late in September 1915, Rıza demanded that the government explain its policy toward the Armenians. "[T]hey are wandering in the mountains at this very moment, in a state of misery and bafflement. I appeal to the sense of mercy and justice of the government to either send them back to their towns or settle them wherever it is that they have been deported, before the winter makes itself felt." Other deputies denounced Rıza's intervention, complaining that he should not "pester the government with questions related to internal affairs" at such an "important and delicate time."[115] A week later Rıza rose again, appalled at the confiscation of Armenian properties that had been legitimized by the "Abandoned Properties Law" adopted on September 26, 1915. "It is also not legal to classify the goods mentioned by the law as abandoned goods because the Armenian owners of these goods did not abandon them willingly, they were exiled, expelled forcefully. . . . If this law is enforced, these people will have been tyrannized once more." He appealed to the Unionists' commitment to constitutionalism but to no avail. The forced confiscations were unlawful, atrocious: "Grab my arm, eject me from my village, then sell my goods and properties, such a thing can never be permissible. Neither the conscience of the Ottomans nor the law can allow it."[116]

CONVOYS AND CONCENTRATION CAMPS

From May through November 1915 almost all Armenians in eastern Anatolia were forcibly driven from their homes, the men usually taken off and killed outside the town, the women and children marched in groups toward the southeast. Here and there a local administrator resisted the orders to deport the Armenians. In Adana, where thousands had been killed in 1909, Catholicos Sahak protested the deportations and the moderate governor relented. Talat then sent his second-in-command, Ali Münîf (Yeğena), to the city to enforce the orders to remove the Armenians.[117] Sahak was exiled to Jerusalem. In Ankara the local governor Hasan Mazhar also refused to carry out the deportation order. Having convinced himself that Armenians were no danger, he had prominent Turks sign a petition to Talat affirming that they had no suspicions about the Armenians. The minister again sent his own agent, thirty-year-old Atıf Kamçıl, a native of Salonica, to replace the recalcitrant governor and enforce the policy of deportation. Ankara had a large and wealthy community of Armenian Catholics, who had kept aloof from nationalist politics. Atıf had caravans of dispossessed Armenians sent out of the city, where they were attacked by *çete*s and ruthlessly slaughtered with axes.[118] Far to the south, several regional officials in Diyarbakır *vilayet* refused to carry out Dr. Reşid's orders to exterminate Christians. Not only were they dismissed, but several of them—most notably Hilmi Bey, the *mutassarif* of Mardin—were murdered on the *vali*'s orders.[119]

The more militant Young Turks carried out the deportations and killings with greater determination. The term that officials used to describe the "cleansing" of the Armenians was *paklayalım* (let's purge).[120] In Sivas *vilayet* the local *vali*, thirty-two-year-old Ahmed Muammer Bey,

Convoy of Armenian deportees guarded by Ottoman soldiers, 1915. From the collection of Project SAVE Armenian Photograph Archives. Photographed by an anonymous German traveler.

was a Young Turk zealot ready and eager to carry out the orders from Istanbul and enrich himself in the process. Sivas, known to the Armenians as *Sebastia*, was a wealthy province with a million inhabitants including more than 200,000 Armenians and 100,000 Greeks and Assyrians. It housed the beautiful riverside town of Amasia and the educational center Marsovan, with its esteemed Anatolia College. Its troubles began ominously on New Year's Day, 1915, with the murder of the newly appointed prelate, Sahak Odabashian. Following the Ottoman defeat at Sarıkamış thousands of Third Army soldiers and Russian prisoners-of-war flooded into the province, followed a month later by çetes. Deserters, many of them Armenian, were imprisoned. Typhus raged. Early in March Armenian notables were arrested. Others followed until about five thousand were languishing in the Sivas central prison. They were held until the convoys of Armenians were sent off at the end of June and into July. The murder of the men took place in gorges outside the city. As a caravan of women and children from Marsovan, Amasia, and Tokat passed through Sarı Kışla, it was "stopped in front of the government building, all boys and girls were taken from their mothers and led into rooms; the caravan was forced to continue on its way. Announcements were made in the surrounding villages for everyone to come and choose from these children."[121] Some valued artisans and doctors survived the devastation of the Sivas Armenians for some time longer. Five thousand young men in the labor battalions were kept working until they were systematically massacred in July 1916.[122]

Convoys of dispossessed Armenians, marched from the north and west, moved through the *vilayet* of Mamuretülaziz, which the local American consul, Leslie A. Davis, soon labeled the "Slaughterhouse Province."[123] The twin towns of Mezreh, the provincial capital on the plain (today's Elazığ) and Harput on the mountain above, were centers not only of Armenian culture and learning (at the famous Euphrates College) but also of vigorous missionary activity. Here Danish, German, and American Protestants, inspired by the tragedies of the 1890s to aid the Ottoman Christians, ran hospitals and schools. In 1915 they became vivid witnesses to the devastation of those among whom they worked. The pious and dedicated Danish nurse Maria Jacobsen had come to eastern Anatolia to "serve the Lord with gladness."[124] With the general mobilization for war in 1914 the local authorities took advantage of the extraordinary situation to confiscate goods and buildings, punish those who did not report for duty, and send off the new recruits toward Erzurum and the Russian front. Chaos and confusion became the norm.[125] "People sit and cry all around," Jacobson wrote. "When you meet them in the street (I mean the women) you see their unhappy faces—full of worry and sorrow—and they say to me, 'What will become of us? Have you any news from the front? My sons are also there. They will never return.'"[126] Despair and a sense of helplessness nourished passivity and loss of will. The missionaries intervened where and when they could, to save prisoners or heal the sick and wounded, but by May 1915 their Armenian teachers were being arrested and flogged. Rumors of a planned general massacre spread.[127] Soldiers surrounded Harput and drove the people out. Eight hundred boys and men were roped together and taken to Khanköy. As a surviving witness, Melcon Lulejian, related: "Just before evening an order was given to the soldiers to shoot—and this was followed by a hail of bullets. But they ran out of ammunition before everyone was killed, so they began slashing with the small axes they carry in their belts, and with bayonets." Melcon felt the rope binding him loosen and he ran off with others into the night; he was the only one who found refuge in the missionaries' hospital in Mezreh.[128]

Reverend Henry Riggs was shocked by the viciousness with which the deportations were carried out. Relations between ordinary Muslims and Armenians had not been hostile in Harput. "As for the feelings of the Moslem population, I saw no evidence whatever during the early months of 1915 that they suspected or feared their Armenian neighbors.... The attack on the Armenian people, which soon developed into a systematic attempt to exterminate the race, was a cold-blooded, unprovoked, deliberate act, planned and carried out without popular approval, by the military masters of Turkey."[129] The Muslims had to be inflamed, writes Riggs, and he heard the *vali* tell fabricated stories "to arouse resentment in the hearts of Turks present."[130] Arrests, searches, and torture were sufficient to create a case against Armenians. The tactic appeared to work. "The friendly attitude of the Moslems underwent a marked change. Suspicion took the place of confidence, as many common people were persuaded of the reality of the charges brought against the imprisoned Armenians."[131] The idea of an uprising of the Armenians, he concluded, "was under the circumstances absolutely absurd," but government officials made a great show of arming Muslim civilians to prevent it.[132]

As Armenians tried to sell what they could before deportation, Turks bought up property and possessions at absurdly low prices. Some Muslims, however, refused to enrich themselves at the expense of the suffering victims. They looked on the Armenian goods as *haram* (forbidden), something cursed rather than blessed. Others willingly took over the houses abandoned by Armenians.[133] As a Christian, Jacobsen lamented for her co-religionists and what they had lost. "How different everything has become in the last year, and it appears now that all our work has been completely destroyed. Instead of the clean, intelligent, and enlightened Armenian people, there has now come an ignorant and completely uncivilized people."[134]

Extermination went along with deportation, a deliberate policy to reduce the Armenians to impotence. Bahaeddin Şakir wrote to the CUP secretary in Harput, inquiring, "[H]ave the Armenians who have been dispatched from there been liquidated [*tasfiye ol-*]; have those detrimental and dangerous persons, whom you reported to have been exiled and sent off, been exterminated [*imha edil*] or simply sent off into exile somewhere else. Please be explicit in your report, brother."[135] The caravans of refugees faced torture, interminable forced marches, disease, hunger, and thirst. Women and girls were raped; the sick were left behind to die.[136]

The train lines extended south to Aleppo, and eastward they stopped at Ras al Ayn, a collection of mud huts, before continuing on to the sandy white city of Mardin. Strategically important stretches of the line had yet to be completed—the tunnels through the Taurus and Amanos mountain ranges—and thousands of Armenian workers and engineers toiled at finishing the tunnels and tracks. While they worked, tens of thousands of their countrymen were driven either by train, by cart, or on foot along the rail line. Stations became concentration camps. Forty thousand Armenians were camped at Katma by October, and the next month 50,000 were ordered to move on to Ras al Ayn.[137] The German marshal advising the Ottoman army, Liman von Sanders, demanded that people who were aiding the military, who were working on the railroads, or who were needed for medical assistance, should not be arrested or deported without his permission.[138] For some time the Armenian rail workers were exempted from deportation, but by July orders came from Istanbul to move them to Aleppo province and farther east. The engineer Winkler, in charge of the construction, tried to prevent the deportation, but the *vali* insisted on obeying his orders, even though exiling the workers would delay completing the rail line. The Germans pleaded with the authorities not to remove Armenian engineers and white-collar employees, and here they were more successful. Many survived, thanks to men like Winkler and despite the efforts of the German Lieutenant-Colonel Böttrich, head of the railway department of the Ottoman General Staff, who not only supported the deportations but also personally signed a deportation order.[139] When German railway officials gathered incriminating evidence about the Ottoman atrocities, Cemal Paşa, commander of the Fourth Army and virtual dictator of the Syrian provinces, ordered that photographing Armenians should be considered espionage. The evidence collection continued secretly, and men like the intrepid German medic Armin Wegner compiled a fragile visual record of the death marches.[140]

As tens of thousands of deportees reached the Syrian desert towns, concentration camps were hastily, haphazardly set up in Tel-Abiad, Ras al Ayn, Mamureh, Katma, and Aleppo. These camps, however, were not intended to be places of refuge. They were way stations toward extermination. They were death camps. "The government is providing no shelter whatsoever for these collection camps," German diplomats reported. "The more wealthy among the deportees have a small tent with them, the poorer ones are having to make do with improvised roofs made of mats, bedding, etc." Little food or fuel was provided. There were no latrines and very little water available.[141] Two Arab officers informed the British of massacres secretly ordered in Ras al Ayn, where some 12,000 Armenians were concentrated under the guardianship of hundreds of Kurds. "These Kurds were called Gendarmes, but were in reality mere butchers; bands of them were publicly ordered to take parties of Armenians of both sexes to various destinations, but had secret instructions to destroy the males, children and old women, and dispose of the young women among the villagers of the Urfa plain. These Kurds always returned after absence of 3 or 4 days on such expeditions. . . . Two sayings were common among the common soldiers: 'Ras-ul-Ain is a shambles' and 'No man can ever think of woman's body except as a matter of horror instead of attraction, after Ras-ul-Ain.'"[142]

The camps were strung along the Euphrates, ending in the town of Der el Zor, which lies deep in the Syrian desert on the right bank of the Euphrates. Early in 1916, sometime after the fall of Erzurum to the Russians, the government in Istanbul ordered the liquidation of the camps. Cevdet, who had served as *vali* in Van, was sent as governor to Adana. In March the camps north of Aleppo were closed, the deported Armenians sent farther south, many never reaching their destination. The Armenians huddled in Ras al Ayn were forced to march on. The last stop of the caravans of deportees from Anatolia was usually Der el Zor. Its name reverberates today with the final solution of the Armenian Question.

When the Armenians first arrived in Der el Zor, the *vali* of the province was Ali Suad Bey, who attempted in some ways "to soften their ills." August Bernau, a German working in the region for an American oil company, considered the governor to be a "man of courage," praised by the refugees. Ali Suad considered the Armenians to be people who might settle and develop the remote, desolate land to which they had been exiled. Some, indeed, even began "a small trade and would have been happy to remain in this town." The authorities soon recalled Ali Suad and replaced him with Salih Zeki Bey, a man "remarkable for his inhumanity and cruelty."[143] When the new governor saw that the Armenians were flourishing, that they had essentially "created a veritable Armenia, and the market was largely in their hands," he took drastic measures. Orphans were thrown out of the orphanages; torture and hangings became the norm. "Girls raped or delivered to Arabs of the surrounding villages, for their pleasure or their service, children drowned in the river; neither the weak, nor the innocent were spared."[144] Zeki was determined to liquidate all the Armenian men but was thwarted by military authorities who needed them for construction work. Eventually he was able to have many of them killed and to send off twenty-one convoys of Armenians.[145]

Bodies lined the road along with the debris of migration: "wagons left behind because the livestock pulling them have died; broken wagons, remnants of clothes and scraps which will no longer hang on a person's body, animal corpses and human corpses in every stage of decomposition. Thank goodness that nature's scavengers make short shrift of removing these carcasses." The German diplomat who recorded this wreckage went on to describe Der el Zor itself.

The entrance alone immediately displays the settlers' main occupation: burying the dead, dull brooding, laborious, sick, half-dead movement. Der-el-Zor itself is not an ugly city, with lovely, wide streets. Previously 14000 inhabitants, presently 25–30000. There are no organisational arrangements for the huge, accumulated mass of people. There is insufficient food (for hours the bakers have no bread), a steam-driven mill clacks insufficiently day and night, a shortage of bread and vegetables was determined. 3 hospitals are crowded with over a thousand sick people. 1 local doctor, 1 government doctor, pharmacy almost empty. The local doctor just left town for a few days on a business trip. The mortality rate is 150–200 persons per day (in the words of the local doctor). Only in this way is it possible that thousands of settlers can still be brought in. A large camp above and below the town. On the left bank of the river next to the pontoon bridge masses of dying people have been camped in huts made of foliage typical for this area. They are the forgotten whose only liberator is death.[146]

The more fortunate Armenians found refugee in the Syrian city of Hama, at least for a while. Ervant Otian found a clean, comfortable bed, free from lice, for the first time in the months since being driven from Istanbul.[147] After an Armenian denounced him to the police as a counterfeiter, Otian was rearrested and sent to Der el Zor.[148] Much depended on the will and intentions of local authorities. A German teacher described the deported Armenians who had managed to reach Aleppo: "If you walk into the courtyard you have the impression of walking into a lunatic asylum. If you bring them food, you notice that they have forgotten how to eat. Their stomachs, weakened by months of hunger, are no longer able to absorb any food. If you give them bread, they put it aside indifferently. They lie there quietly and wait for death." Local Muslims were incredulous that their government was responsible for these brutalities. Both Turks and Arabs disapproved of what they were witnessing.[149] A German railroad official noted, "A Mohammedan sheikh, a respected personality in Aleppo, said in my presence, 'When people speak of how the Armenians are treated, I'm ashamed to be a Turk.' Clearly, such people were the exception to the rule, but it's interesting to note their existence nonetheless."[150]

The extermination of the Armenians had a catastrophic effect on the whole of Anatolian society and economy. While some Muslims benefited from the seizure of property and goods of Armenians—a most "primitive accumulation of capital"—many others suffered from the removal of productive farmers and craftsmen, pharmacists, doctors, and merchants. Disease and famine followed in the wake of the deportations, claiming victims without regard to religion or race. The exorbitant economic costs and social dislocations of the Genocide affected Muslims as well as Christians and Jews. In July 1915 the commander of the Ottoman Third Army, Mahmud Kamil, was forced to request reassignment of soldiers to agricultural labor since "all Muslims have been conscripted and the Armenians in their entirety [*kamilen*] been deported." He accurately predicted that the region would fall into "dearth and famine" and the army would be without supplies.[151] Nevertheless, the government of the Young Turks pushed on in its determination to reengineer the demography of Anatolia. Talat kept himself closely informed about the process of the removals. On July 20 he requested that his regional governors provide "two compiled lists containing the figures for existing [population], both earlier and currently, on the basis of the [respective] nationalities of the population in the various towns and villages."[152]

The reports of witnesses flowed westward. By August the evidence of mass murder, rape, seizure of children, and forced conversion was overwhelming. American missionary families described trains filled with deportees. "The refugee trains were made up of cattle trucks and the faces of little children looked out beseechingly from behind the bars. The side doors were open and we could plainly see old men and old women, young mothers with small babies, men, women and children, all huddled together like cattle."[153] On August 29, 1915, three days after the killing of the parliamentary deputy Grigor Zohrap, Talat telegraphed to the authorities in Ankara, "The Armenian question in the eastern provinces has been resolved. There's no need to sully the nation and the government['s] [honor] with further atrocities [*fuzuli mezalım*]."[154]

When the convoys of Armenians were moving through Anatolia, the head of the Armenian Church in the Ottoman Empire, Patriarch Zaven Yeghiayan, tried to meet with Talat, but the minister would no longer see him. Zaven turned to other ministers to make his futile appeals. He consoled himself by remembering the Turkish proverb: "The drowning man will wrap his arms even around a snake."[155] Pirizade İbrahim Bey, the minister of justice and religious affairs, claimed not to have any information or knowledge of massacres. Even though he stated that the Armenians had done much against the government, he insisted that a state would be "out of its mind to exterminate one of the peoples on its land, and our State is not so *ahmak* [foolish] as that.... The government does not wish to be deprived of its citizens, especially when they are useful ones."[156] The patriarch received a similar response from Grand Vizier Said Halim Paşa, who saw the deportations as a precautionary measure. When Talat on September 19 finally consented to meet with the patriarch, he reiterated the standard line about the Armenians. "We knew about the decisions they had taken, that for as long as the Ottoman Army was not defeated, they would assume a waiting stance, and, in the event of [the army's] defeat, they would stage a revolution. They also decided to help Russia. Every day they were piling weapons, bombs, etc., everywhere, but we kept silent and did not undertake searches, so as not to cause internal disturbances." But when the Armenians collaborated with the enemy, and the Ottomans lost part of their country, "we could no longer remain silent." The patriarch weakly protested that such acts were the work of a few men and a whole nation should not be punished for their offenses. Armenians did not expect such a blow "by a person [Talat] they loved most." "I used to love the Armenians," Talat replied, "because I considered them an element useful to the country. But the opposite turned out to be the case. Naturally, I love the fatherland more than I love the Armenians." The patriarch lamented that he no longer had any churches or clergymen. "It was established that many of the Prelates were *khayin* [*hain*, treacherous]," said Talat, who soon fell silent, a sign that the interview was over.[157]

RESISTANCE AND SURVIVAL

Even as news of massacres spread through Anatolia, few Armenians organized effective resistance. As Ottoman subjects integrated into webs of village and city life, it was hard for them to imagine that this time, instead of sporadic and limited violence, a systemic extermination was under way. Most Armenians clung to the conviction that their best defense was to prove their loyalty to the state, and only in a few isolated places did the inhabitants take a stand against the authorities. Anticipating that their turn would come soon, the inhabitants of Şabinkarahisar decided to resist deportation. When their prelate was summoned by the *vali*, beaten nearly senseless, and then murdered, the Armenians in the town barricaded their neighborhoods. From mid-June until mid-July a few hundred defenders kept the Ottoman forces at bay, but ultimately running out of food and ammunition, they succumbed. The victors shot all males over the age of fifteen.[158]

The most dramatic and famous resistance to deportation occurred in the *sancak* of Antakya (ancient Antioch) in Adana *vilayet*, near the Mediterranean. Some 4,200 villagers withdrew to the mountain of Moses, Musa Dağ, where they held off Ottoman troops from the end of July until they were rescued by the French navy in September.[159] The reporting of these events resonated in Europe, and the Czech-German writer Franz Werfel made the incident the subject of the dramatic novel *The Forty Days of Musa Dagh*.

Resistance was the aftereffect of persecution, not, as the authorities contended, the result of prior opposition to the government. The city of Urfa, Reverend F. H. Leslie reported to the American consul Jackson in Aleppo, "is not a revolutionary center and never has been. The people here have always been loyal to the Government and have never resisted, not even when they were butchered like sheep. Why the local Government persists in persecuting a population that has always had a good record for loyalty is very strange."[160] On August 19 an Armenian deserter in Urfa shot at Turkish authorities investigating his home, and the consequences were devastating for the whole town. As the police carried out their search, three shots rang out, killing a policeman, a gendarme, and a soldier. News spread that the infidels were attacking Muslims and that the faithful should arm themselves. A mob stormed Armenian homes and shops. At least 250 Armenians and Assyrians perished in this first round of killing. Mkrtich Yotneghparian organized his compatriots in an effort to defend their community. About two thousand fighters held out for twenty-five days.[161] "The Armenian Quarter," the German consul at Aleppo reported, "almost half the entire town, is extremely well situated for defence purposes on a hill which has many caves." The local Armenians fortified and armed themselves; they occupied the American mission, captured the missionary, and used the barricaded compound as a fortress. Thousands of Ottoman troops were sent to break the resistance.[162] Most defenders were killed, or like Yotneghparian, who shot himself in the head, committed suicide. Deportations soon followed.[163] Celal Bey, the one-time governor of Aleppo province, removed because of his opposition to the deportations, remarked on the Urfa resistance, "Each human has the right to live. A kicked wolf will bite. The Armenians will defend themselves."[164]

The images and myths around Armenian resistance range from unprovoked insurrection by fierce and savage warriors to essentialist stereotypes of Armenians as cowardly, "womanly," and docile who only in the direst circumstances defended themselves. The American consul Leslie Davis, whose vivid reports of massacres in the "Slaughterhouse Province" depicted mass killing in gruesome detail, reverted to racial simplifications to explain what he saw as the passivity of the Armenians. In his report to his ambassador, Davis asserted that Armenians lacked moral and religious principles; that they were a debased race without heroism or self-sacrifice. "On the contrary mothers have given their daughters to the lowest and vilest Turks to save their own lives; to change their religion is a matter of little importance to most of the people; lying and trickery and an inordinate love of money are besetting sins of almost all, even while they stand in the very shadow of death. . . . Absolute truthfulness is almost unknown among the members of this race. Money is sought at any price, even at the risk of their lives. . . . From every point of view the race is one that cannot be admired, although it is one to be pitied."[165] Such were the views of a professional American diplomat, who condemned the killing of Armenians at the same time as he casually accepted the prevalent stereotypes of that "race."

By the late summer of 1915 hundreds of thousands of Armenians and Assyrians had died on the convoys, cut down as they moved toward the deserts of Syria. Hundreds of thousands of others survived, however. Some were artisans or officers whom the Ottomans needed for the war effort or simple necessities. Armenians in the cities of Edirne, Istanbul, and Izmir, located in the westernmost regions of the empire, were largely exempted from deportation. Only those considered security risks, like members of political parties, were sent from the cities. Some Armenians converted to Islam to save themselves.[166] The government's policy on conversion shifted in line with its security concerns. On June 22, 1915, Talat ordered that all conversions, individual or collective, be accepted, but the converts had to be dispersed throughout the province or county in which they lived. Three weeks later the policy was changed. Requests for conversion were now considered suspect; converts might be exempted from deportation after security investigations and if they were needed by the state. As the demographic historian Fuat Dündar writes, "the important point to Talat Pasha was not loyalty to Islam, but rather to the state."[167] Since annihilation of a people was not solely a matter of mass killing, not only of the physical destruction of their homes and removal of their possessions, but also of elimination of their culture and religion, forced or necessitated conversion was part of the same process.

There were also instances of collaboration between Armenians and their persecutors. Most Armenians were not deported from Izmir. Here the *vali* requested that the Armenians point out who the most dangerous persons in their community were so that they could be expelled. The Armenian bishop agreed, and a box was placed in the cathedral where people could anonymously denounce those considered subversive. About thirty names were delivered to the *vali*, and the rest of the Armenian community was spared.[168]

Armenians fortunate enough to find themselves under the protection of foreigners might survive. Pressure from the Austrian and German embassies prevented deportation of Catholic Armenian families from Ankara for a while, and on August 19, 1915, Talat exempted Protestant and Catholic Armenians from exile.[169] Still, if Catholic and Protestant Armenians were considered suspect or lived in an area with too many Armenians, they might be deported. Reverend Riggs and others certified to the

Ottoman authorities who was in fact a Protestant and might be saved.[170] A few were adopted. Good relations with officers or soldiers would sometimes be rewarded with kindness. Officials looked the other way at times when bribes were paid. Richer Armenians did better than the poorer, able to pay bribes or travel by horse or donkey. Most remarkable was the case of those who escaped to the remote mountainous district of Dersim (present-day Tunceli). The Kurds of Dersim, some of whom were descendants of or related to Armenian tribes, were fiercely independent of the Ottoman state, preserving their freedom from taxation and conscription. Religiously eclectic, with strong Alevi ties, the Dersim Kurds helped Armenians flee from Harput and, after sheltering them, assisted them in moving north beyond the Russian lines. The secret passage over the Euphrates into the mountains was costly, and the Kurds profited from the desperation of the Armenians. Reverend Riggs, who clandestinely paid for the flight of many, trusted the "Dersim Kurd," whom he considered "little else than an impulsive child . . . a very amiable animal" who possessed "the instinct of the noble savage . . . to save rather than wantonly to destroy this neighbor against whom he has no grudge."[171]

The Young Turks feared that Armenians and Kurds might ally, and some Kurds repeated rumors that once the government dealt with the Armenians it would turn on the Kurds.[172] Istanbul notified the governors of Van, Bitlis, and Erzurum as early as March 1915 of the danger of Kurdish-Armenian joint action.[173] Istanbul was aware that "thousands of Armenians had taken refuge" in Dersim and "were sustaining themselves." Armenians "who were profiting from the situation were daring to revolt" and were attempting "to take advantage of the well known propensity of Kurds to pillage and revolt." The authorities suggested that since Kurds and Armenians had established a close, almost familial, relationship, it was essential that the locals request *Teşkilat-ı Mahsusa* to take "the necessary steps."[174]

Survival was haphazard, a matter of accident or luck. Most Armenians did not resist, hoping that they would survive by obeying the authorities, not imagining that arbitrary and massive killing was occurring daily. Considered outside the law and no longer protected by the state,

Armenians were designated targets of the deportation and dispossession policies of the government and of the predatory ambitions of anyone willing to steal or kill. Railroad workers were protected, and their German bosses often intervened to prevent their deportation. But eventually most Armenians, engineers as well as manual laborers, were exiled. Conversion was no guarantee. A native of the Black Sea port of Samsun reported that while performing his military service in Çarşamba he heard that the local Armenians decided to temporarily convert to Islam. The government at first accepted this, and official formalities were completed, but then—at the beginning of July—all the Armenians were uprooted and sent toward Mosul. Overweight people and the elderly who could not keep up remained by the wayside; mothers abandoned their infants; children up to the age of ten or eleven, as well as the beautiful women and teenage girls, were handed over to Muslims.[175] Children not adopted were not spared. An orphanage in Harput sheltered seven hundred children under the care of Armenian women. The governor announced, "We are raising our own enemies!" and shut down the orphanage, loaded the orphans and the caretakers into carts, and sent them toward Malatya. Later it was reported that they had been thrown into the Euphrates.[176] Other children were brought to Istanbul and became servants in Muslim households.[177]

END OF THE LINE

Officers, officials, and ordinary people participated in mass killing, plunder, and rape for myriad reasons, from sadism to personal profiteering to fulfillment of duty.[178] The *kaymakam* of Tel Abiad in the Syrian desert watched with indifference as people died around him. He told a German engineer, "My heart is not as sensitive as that of the Europeans; it doesn't bother me to watch these people dying." The same engineer, a Herr Bastendorff, reported that the supervisor over the Armenians in Ras ul Ain "even declared in the presence of our doctor Farah, that it always gave him great pleasure to deflower Armean girls under the age of 12 years." The director of emigrants, Şükri Bey, told him, "The final result must be the

Iconic photograph of Armenians during the Genocide of 1915–1916. Armin T. Wegner.

extermination of the Armenian race. It is the continual battle between the Muslims and the Armenians that is now being finally fought. The weaker of the two must be the one to go." [179]

In Istanbul Talat was most concerned about Armenians who might escape the deportations and questioned his subordinates in the provinces in detail about the number of Armenians deported, who had hidden themselves, taken to the hills, or been protected by civil or police officials. On November 17 the Ministry of Interior sent "top secret" cables to a number of provincial authorities requesting that they write up "in a highly secret manner and forward [to the Ministry] lists of the wealth, education, social status of the Christians in these regions, as well as the prominent or influential members of their communities." [180]

The ancient city of Aleppo (Halep), with its walled city and the famous Baron Hotel owned by the Mazlumian family, was a gathering place for deported Armenians. Many came there so weak that they moved no farther. Death and disease were rampant. Others hid in the city to avoid being moved farther into the desert settlements or concentration camps. The American consul, Jesse Jackson, and the German consul, Dr. Walter Rössler, aided the Armenians as best they could with the help of Swiss and American missionaries. Orphanages were set up to take in abandoned Armenian children. The Mazlumian brothers and other Armenians secretly set up their own networks to provide money and comfort, while some intellectuals shared the Baron Hotel with officers of the Fourth Army.[181] When the number of Armenians exceeded the percentage limitations that the Young Turk government had placed on concentration of Armenians, Istanbul insisted that the local authorities move the Armenians farther south and east. The *vali* of Aleppo province, Celal Bey, opposed the deportations of Armenians and was soon replaced by a more zealous Young Turk, Mustafa Abdülhalik, the brother-in-law of Talat. Transferred to Konya, Celal lamented that he "was like a man standing by a river without any means of rescue. But instead of water, the river flowed with blood and thousands of innocent children, blameless old men, helpless women and strong young people all on their way to destruction. Those I could seize with my hands I saved; the others, I assume, floated downstream, never to return."[182]

In the spring and summer of 1916 an orgy of killing took place; tens if not hundreds of thousands of the deported Armenians were slaughtered along the Euphrates and in Der el Zor. On July 19, 1916, Talat telegraphed the authorities in Der el Zor: "Forbidding harmful Armenian people from congregating along military routes and the immediate deportation of the latter to the interior are appropriate." Ten days later he affirmed that "congregation" of Armenians "in the river basin of the Euphrates and at the military route is going to be dangerous for military transport."[183] A year earlier Talat "had ordered Armenians deported to Der Zor for military reasons; one year later, he ordered Armenians deported *away* from Der Zor, again for military reasons."[184] Zeki recruited Chechen gangs, some of them veterans of killings in the camp of Ras al Ayn, to carry out massacres. Zeki's men effectively and brutally cleansed the area of Armenians from July to December 1916. The only survivors took refugee in Bedouin, Arab, or Turkish homes.[185]

Given that the government was determined that Armenians would nowhere in the empire constitute more than 5 or 10 percent of the population, the same was to be true in Der el Zor. The deported priest Grigoris Balakian befriended the Turkish commandant of his convoy, who told him "no other caravans have passed through this portion of the road to Der Zor. . . . 'Don't be a fool, thinking that the Armenians exiled to Der Zor and the surrounding deserts will be left alive. They too will eventually *be killed*.'"[186] What deportations did not achieve, starvation did. "One woman cut off her hair to sell it for bread," reported an Armenian nurse. "I saw how a woman ate the dried blood of a dead animal on the street. Up to now they all ate grass, but that has also dried up in the meantime. . . . One mother threw herself into the Euphrates after she had watched her child die of starvation, a father too."[187]

Consular reports, the accounts passed on by the Armenian patriarch thanks to clandestine Armenian networks, and the testimony of missionaries kept people who needed or wanted to know informed about what was happening to the Armenians. Talat was determined to dam this flow of information. He wired his brother-in-law, the *vali* of Aleppo, "to convince foreigners traveling in that area that the sole purpose of this deportation is to change people's places of residence. For this reason, it is important, for the time being, to exhibit tactful behavior in order to preserve the forms, and to apply the known methods only in localities where they are appropriate. To this end, I firmly recommend that you arrest people who reveal information or conduct investigations and bring them, on other pretexts, before a court-martial."[188]

The American consul Jackson estimated that of the 300,000 Armenians sent to Der el Zor, their numbers had been reduced by September 1916 "to about 12,000 by death from illness and starvation." These few survivors were then slaughtered.[189] "The second great wave of massacres in Der Zor, Syria," writes Taner Akçam, "during the summer of 1916, seems to have been motivated primarily by demographic anxieties, along with security concerns."[190] The two motives had never been far apart; indeed, the second flowed from the first. The radical ethnic homogenization of the Ottoman East was approaching completion. The principal threat to the Turkish nation and the Ottoman state, the Armenians, had effectively been eliminated.

CHAPTER TEN

Orphaned Nation

While Armenians were still moving into exile and dying in the mountains and deserts, the European powers took the opportunity to work out their own division of the Near East. In January 1916 Britain and France signed the infamous Sykes-Picot Agreement, dividing up the Ottoman Empire's eastern holdings. The Young Turks, however, did not yet imagine that the days of their empire's existence were numbered. That same month Enver Paşa ordered that all Armenian, Greek, and Bulgarian place names—villages, towns, cities, provinces, mountains, and rivers—be given Turkish names.[1] Some Turkification had already occurred. Zeytun, for example, had first become Yeni Şehir and later Süleymanlı.[2] Talat decreed that Armenian businesses confiscated during the deportations were to be eventually turned over to Muslims, "honourable leaders and the elite . . . to allow tradesmen and agriculturalists to participate in its dividends. . . . The growth of entrepreneurship in the minds of Muslim people needs to be monitored, and this endeavour and the results of its implementation needs to be reported to the Ministry step by step."[3] Pressure increased to convert surviving Armenians to Islam. Children particularly were accepted as Muslims, and those who refused were thrown out of the available orphanages and left to die. Those men in the labor battalions who had not yet been killed were converted to Islam.[4] Armenians in Istanbul resisted conversion, but in the East tens of thousands chose survival over faith.[5]

Through 1916 Talat's Ministry remained concerned about how many Armenians had survived the deportations and where they were. Cables from Istanbul requested information on the number of Armenians in the province, how many of the local Armenians had been spared deportation and left in place, how many had come from other regions and been temporarily left in the province, and how many were still on the roads, traveling to other areas. Deportees were not permitted to travel or settle in any place other than to those to which they had been directed. If Armenians returned to their hometowns, "Gather up as many of those individuals who have returned as possible and send them off even further away, and inform [the capital] of the number of persons [sent]." Muslim refugees were directed to occupy the abandoned houses and lands of the Armenians. Other Armenian buildings might be used for prisons where needed.[6] While he closely supervised the movements of the Armenians, Talat continued to make excuses for the horrors visited on them. He told a Berlin journalist, "The Armenian deportation was a military necessity. While being deported to Mesopotamia they were attacked by the Kurds on the way and partly massacred. . . . The Government had ordered their deportation to [Der Zor]. Unhappily, bad officials into whose hands the execution of these orders had been committed went into unreasonable excesses in doing their duty." At this point in the interview, Talat "paused a moment, passed his hand over his eyes as if he wished to drive away a bad vision, and then continued: 'We are not savages. The reports of these tragic events have caused me more than one sleepless night.'"[7]

Far more fair-minded an assessment of motives and purposes behind the Armenian Genocide was given by Max von Scheubner-Richter, the former vice consul in Erzurum, whose extraordinary and contradictory career took him from being critic of the Armenian massacres and supporter of Lepsius to membership in the embryonic Nazi Party. In December 1916 he gave his own evaluation of the "master plan" of the Young Turks, based on his conversations with "leading Turkish personalities." He was convinced that the Young Turks intended to build a purely Muslim, pan-Turkish empire. "Those inhabitants who are neither Mohammedan nor Turkish should be made to become so by force or, if that is not possible, annihilated. . . . The first item on their programme was the execution of the Armenians." The pretext for the deportations was a "supposed prepared revolution of the Dashnak Party," but "local unrest and self-protection measures on the part of the Armenians were exaggerated and taken as an excuse to justify the evacuation of the Armenians from endangered border districts. At the instigation of the committee [of

Union and Progress], the Armenians were murdered along the way by Kurd and Turkish gangs, in places also by gendarmes." The Young Turks considered "revenge against the Arabs . . . but the presently unfavourable military situation made it apparent that this was not yet the right moment."[8] Scheubner-Richter became famous, not for his resistance to Ottoman atrocities, but when in 1923 he marched arm-in-arm with Adolf Hitler during the Munich "Beer Hall Putsch." Scheubner-Richter was shot in the lung and killed immediately; as he fell, he pulled Hitler down with him, dislocating Hitler's shoulder. He probably saved the future dictator's life when a second volley was fired.

The Genocide of the Armenians can be said to have ended by late January 1917. Mass starvation continued, as well as sporadic killing. Refugees died, and fighting between Armenians, Turks, and Kurds went on until the early 1920s, but the intentional massacre of Armenians and Assyrians by the Ottoman state gradually ceased. On January 22 Talat was elevated to grand vizier of the Ottoman Empire. Among his first acts was the ordering of the Greeks of Samsun to be deported to the interior of Anatolia. In a ferocious speech justifying the removal of the Armenians, he once again stated the central argument for the deportations, while denying any intention to physically annihilate the Armenians: "Every government has the right to defend itself against those who stage armed revolts." Weapons and explosives had been found all over Anatolia, primarily hidden in monasteries and churches, he claimed.[9]

Talat assured his German allies that he was reversing his policies toward non-Muslims.[10] Ambassador Kuehlmann informed his chancellor that Talat "confirmed to me in person that he plans to take a new line on all questions concerning the nationality policy."[11] The Germans remained suspicious about Talat's sincerity.[12] Repression, starvation, and massacres did not end. In the ravaged landscape of Anatolia and the Middle East and the continuing chaos of the war, men with guns and ordinary people with knives and axes settled old scores. Driven by personal viciousness and encouraged by officials, killing, often on a mass scale, continued. When the Ottoman army took back Erzincan in February 1917, several thousand Armenian survivors who had returned to the city in the spring of 1916 fled northeast with the Russians. As the Ottomans captured Trabzon and Erzurum in March, and Van and Kars in April, the scene was repeated and massacres followed. In the months following the October 1917 revolution in Petrograd, Russian soldiers "voted with their feet" and deserted the Caucasian front en masse. Ottoman armies swept into the Caucasus after the Treaty of Brest-Litovsk (March 1918), were briefly stopped by Armenian forces at Sardarabad, but wheeled around Erevan, the capital of the newly formed Armenian state, and drove on to Baku, the oil center on the Caspian. The local revolutionaries fled the city, and the Ottomans stood by while Azerbaijanis, taking revenge for the crushing of a Muslim rebellion in March, slaughtered some 20,000 Armenians in September 1918, many of them refugees from Anatolia.[13]

As the Russians retreated from northern Persia in the spring of 1918, the only defenders of the local Christians were Armenian and Assyrian fighters. Local Kurds and the invading Ottoman army attacked Christians. A bloody struggle pitted the Sixth Army against local forces; villagers were slaughtered, Armenians by Muslims and Muslims by Armenians. Already the hero of songs and legends, the Armenian General Andranik, a *fedayi* since the beginning of the century and the commander of one of the Armenian volunteer units from 1914 until 1916 when the Russians disbanded them, defied orders from the fledgling Armenian government (which he did not recognize) and carried out his own campaigns, which involved wanton killing of civilians, in Persia, Anatolia, and the Caucasus.[14]

Even as it curtailed its comprehensive destruction of its Armenian subjects, the Ottoman government sought to justify what it had done. A campaign of denial that would flourish for the next century produced its first documentary collection in November 1917. Entitled "The Revolutionary Targets and Machinations of the Armenian Committees Before and After the Constitution," the collection included documents detailing the activities of Armenian revolutionaries, their nationalist propaganda, and preparation for armed revolts.[15] Most of what is contained in this volume had been collected by Abdülhamid II's interior minister in the 1890s to justify the 1894–1896 massacres of Armenians.[16] A German diplomat, Johann Heinrich von Bernstorff, noted that the collection was "one-sided" and "tendentious," yet he was convinced "when looking through this material one cannot avoid coming to the conclusion that the machinations of the Armenian Committees have been gravely irritating the Turkish government for a long time, and that they justified the repressive measures taken during the war. How far the government overstepped the boundary to self-defence and/or how far it was also swayed by other motives, is another matter."[17]

When Talat a few years after he fled Istanbul turned to his own accounting of the Genocide in his memoirs, posthumously published, he acknowledged that the deportations, which he saw as an "obligation," a requirement "to secure the safety of [the] army and its citizens," had been accompanied by excesses. The already existing hatred between Armenians and Muslims led to abuse by officials, and "in many places people took preventive measures into their own hands and innocent people were molested." He "confessed" that the government should have done more to prevent atrocities. Instead, the government simply gave in to the "Turkish elements" who "were shortsighted, fanatical, and yet sincere in their belief. The public encouraged them, and they had the general approval behind them. They were numerous and strong." If the state had tried to punish them, that would "have aroused great discontent among the people, who favored their acts. An endeavor to arrest and to punish all those promoters would have created anarchy in Anatolia at a time when we greatly needed unity. It would have been dangerous to divide the nation into two camps, when we needed strength to fight outside enemies."[18]

While the Ottoman authorities shifted responsibility from the government to ordinary people and blamed the Armenians for their own destruction, the German Reichstag deputy Maximilian Pfeiffer argued that the Armenian Question came to exist only due to British meddling in Ottoman affairs. "England awakened in them the thought of national independence. Through the British embassy in Constantinople, it sent bombs and all sorts of other means to the Armenians whom it had won over for this purpose, enabling them to revolt. The persecution of the

Armenians by Turkey dates back to that time."[19] Officials and allies distributed blame where they were able, just not on the Young Turks themselves. These justifications and rationalizations had their origins in the reign of Abdülhamid II. That narrative radicalized after the Young Turk Revolution, particularly during and after the Balkan Wars. When the Young Turks fell, it was challenged by a counternarrative that blamed the atrocities on the small core of CUP leaders, only to be revived in the postwar years when Armenians were not only rendered guilty of their own destruction but were themselves seen as perpetrators of massacres of Muslims. The death of tens of thousands of Turks during the years of transition from empire to nation-state became central to what Fatma Müge Göçek has called the "Republican narrative," which would be deployed repeatedly to refute Armenian claims that they had been the victims of a genocide.[20]

Even as the war came to an end, important German officials reiterated the discredited defense of the deportations. The former German secretary of state, Arthur Zimmermann, explained that the Ottomans had not been unfriendly toward the Armenians, but "the general revolution in the province of Van . . . consequently led to the issuing of the Turkish deportation orders. However, originally the Turkish rulers neither intended nor foresaw that the execution of the resettlement measures would lead to the destruction of a large proportion of the Armenian people. The definitely deplorable course that things took seems understandable, to a certain extent, if one takes into consideration the primitiveness of internal Turkish conditions, the overall lack of organisation, roads, means of transport, the minimal influence of the central government over the more distant provinces and, finally, the racial and religious conflicts."[21] The German consul in Trabzon had an even less generous estimation of the Armenians: "Anyone who knows the Orient will agree with me that the Armenians are blessed with hardly a trait that humans find attractive. Despite this, the excesses that took place during their deportation—the mass murders of the men, numerous rapes of women and children, and theft of their possessions cannot be condemned severely enough. . . . [T]he Turkish government was at least not unhappy about the attacks against the Armenians that led to their almost complete annihilation in East Anatolia, and still holds this opinion today."[22]

By October it was clear that Turkey had lost the war and had to surrender. Talat and his cabinet were compelled to resign on October 8, 1918. The new government decreed that Armenians were permitted to return to their homes.[23] On October 30 the Mudros Armistice was signed and the Ottomans withdrew from the war. The mood in Istanbul was one of relief that the devastating war was over. The war had not been popular and the losses had been colossal. Armenians and Greeks were ecstatic that the Allies were triumphant.[24] Within two weeks World War I ended with the defeat of the Central Powers, and British, French, and Italian troops occupied Istanbul. They would stay almost five years, until late September 1923. Suddenly the world changed for Turks, Germans, and Armenians. The Armenians were seen as allies of the Allies and treated as beneficiaries of their victory. British Foreign Minister Lord Curzon described the defeated Ottoman Empire as "a culprit awaiting sentence."[25] The British were determined to fulfill their promise of May 24, 1915, to bring the perpetrators of "crimes against humanity" to justice. The defeated Germans were also at the mercy of the Entente powers and were looking for ways to enhance their position in the coming negotiations. The new authorities in Berlin asked Lepsius, "the well-known friend of the Armenians," to publish exculpatory documents that would show that Germany was not responsible for the Armenian atrocities.[26]

INVESTIGATIONS AND TRIALS

The formerly powerful Young Turks were now fugitives. With the help of the German military, seven of the top CUP leaders secretly boarded a captured Russian destroyer and fled first to Sevastopol on December 3, 1918, eventually making their way to Berlin. Talat, Enver, and Cemal were joined by Bahaeddin Şakir and Mehmet Nazım, as well as by the chief of the Police Directorate and Public Security, Osman Bedri, and Cemal Azmi, the governor known as the "butcher of Trabzon."[27] Former colleagues and opponents in the Ottoman Parliament decreed that the guilty perpetrators should be returned to face charges. Investigations began, but the German government refused to surrender their former allies. "Talaat stuck with us faithfully," German Foreign Minister Wilhelm Solf declared, "and our country remains open to him."[28] The CUP dissolved itself and took on a new party name, *Teceddüt Fırkası* (Party of Renovation), but continued its existence and activities in a new guise.[29] A popular new discourse emerged: "the Turkish nation was not responsible for perpetrating the widespread carnage but ... a few adventurers from Salonica had committed these crimes, and now that they had fled, the matter was closed." Back in Istanbul the priest Balakian witnessed, "All the Turkish papers expressed this view; all refused to acknowledge responsibility, writing: 'We are innocent; we weren't the ones committing those crimes. It was those who've fled; those accursed ones destroyed our fatherland, reducing the country to ruin. And now they've fled, abandoning the poor innocent people to their fate.'"[30]

The years 1918 to 1923 in what was still the Ottoman Empire were momentous times of state collapse, Allied occupation of Istanbul, Greco-Turkish and Armeno-Turkish Wars, the nationalist resistance under Mustafa Kemal in eastern and central Anatolia (what the Turks call *Kurtuluş Savaşı* [War of Liberation]), and the resurgence of a Turkish national state, legitimized in 1923 by the Treaty of Lausanne. That treaty would not mention the Armenians or the Genocide, but in the first years after the World War Ottoman authorities and occupying powers paid great attention to the question of the Armenians. Many exiled Armenians returned to the capital, optimistic that the Allies would help their people recover. Defended by the Allied occupation, Istanbul Armenians confidently attempted to reestablish their civil and cultural life. Armenian newspapers appeared, clubs were organized, concerts were held and plays were performed. Many women living in Muslim families and orphans in Muslim households, in orphanages, or in hiding—at least those who could be found—rejoined the Armenian community.[31] Armenians who were seen to have collaborated with the Young Turks were declared "traitors," and revolutionaries made plans to assassinate them.

The Ottoman Parliament, rendered impotent during the war, resumed more regular meetings, and a number of Armenian deputies, all
of them elected as members of the Committee of Union and Progress,
brought up the issue of the deportations and massacres. Ahmed Rıza,
who had opposed Talat and raised objections to the Armenian deportations, spoke about how Armenians "were savagely [*vahşiyane*] murdered"
as part of an "official [*resmen*]" policy carried out by the state (*devlet eli
ile*).[32] The Temporary Law of Deportation of May 27, 1915, which had
given the removals a gloss of legitimacy, was rescinded. A commission
was created to gather evidence from the CUP and provincial authorities, and CUP offices were raided and documents confiscated. As early as
November and December 1918 investigations of the crimes of the Young
Turk government and the Armenian atrocities began. Military tribunals
were sent up, and in the first months of 1919 about three hundred prominent CUP members, military officers, and government officials were
arrested.[33] Beginning in February 1919 with the opening in Istanbul of
the trial of the Yozgat officials, some fifteen trials examined the events
of 1915–1916.[34]

Living under occupation and anxious to improve the Turkish image
as the Allies met in Paris to establish the postwar order, the Ottoman
government under Grand Vizier Damad Ferid Paşa recognized the crimes
against Armenians and attempted to negotiate with their representatives.
Ferid met an old colleague, the former Ottoman Minister of Foreign Affairs Gabriel Noradounghian, in Paris to talk about a Turkish rapprochement with the Armenians. "You don't know what mischief [the Young
Turks] wrought upon the Armenians," Ferid told him. "If I were to begin
telling you . . ." Noradounghian interrupted: "I know, I know, and much
better than you could know." With such widespread knowledge of the
Ottoman atrocities, there was no room for rapprochement. "Don't tell
me I have come for nothing," the grand vizier inquired. "I am afraid that's
the way it is," his former colleague replied. "We merely groped for old
memories to talk about for a little while," Noradoungian recalled, "and I
bid him farewell."[35]

The reality and horror of the Armenian Genocide was public knowledge, and the postwar Ottoman governments not only acknowledged what had happened but moved to indict and punish the major perpetrators. Yet the trials occurred against the background of Allied occupation of Istanbul and the growing nationalist movement in Anatolia. In early April the court condemned the lieutenant governor in Yozgat, Kemal Bey, to death, and sentenced the commander of the gendarmerie, Tevfik Bey, to fifteen years at hard labor. Kemal was hanged, but his funeral turned into a demonstration. The British high commissioner, Admiral Somerset Arthur Gough-Calthorpe, commented that "the perpetrator of crimes, the nature of which would send a shudder through any civilized community, was treated as a hero and martyr among Moslems; but then, his victims were Christians."[36] Only two other perpetrators were executed, one from Erzincan, the other from Bayburt. Fifteen others were condemned to death in absentia, among them Talat, Enver, Cemal Paşa, Dr. Nazım, Baheddin Şakir, and Cemal Azmi, the Trabzon governor who had supervised the drowning of Christians. The courts-martial also condemned to death Mustafa Kemal and more than one hundred other adherents of the nationalist resistance.[37] The press printed stories of atrocities and the proceedings of the trials. If one searched one could have found the indicting statement of Vehib Paşa, who bluntly revealed a major mastermind of the massacres in the East. "[T]he killing and liquidation of the Armenians, as well as the plundering and seizure of their property," he testified, "was the result of the decisions of the CUP Central Committee, and . . . the person who outfitted, commanded, and brought into service these butchers of humanity within the Third Army's zone [of operation] was Bahaeddin Şakir. . . . [T]he government heads submitted to the orders and instructions of Dr. Bahaeddin Şakir Bey . . . the entirety of the human tragedy within the Third Army['s zone], and all the crimes and evil deeds came about and were manifested under the direction of Bahaeddin Şakir, who in one place would summon friends freed from prison sentences, in another gendarmes with bloodstained hands and bloodshot eyes . . . and so on."[38]

After the fragile government of Damad Ferid Paşa released forty-one prominent prisoners in May, the British moved sixty-seven of the accused to Malta, where the trials continued until larger considerations of international politics convinced the Allies to give up the prosecution of Ottoman officials. The nationalists under Kemal moved from strength to strength, and the Ottoman government in Istanbul appeared weak and dependent on the British. Investigations of the perpetrators ceased, and one by one the trials against the Young Turks came to an end, with most of the defendants set free and those imprisoned on Malta released.[39]

While Istanbul lived under foreign occupation, nationalist resistance to the fragmentation of the empire gained momentum in Anatolia under the popular officer Mustafa Kemal. The Allies considered the nationalist insurgency to be a plot by the Unionists to return to power. The nationalists, on the other hand, were careful to deny any connection to the former governing party, and this view of a clear separation between the CUP and the Kemalists prevailed as the dominant interpretation in Turkish republican historiography. In fact, the links between the Young Turks and the Kemalists were tight. The CUP helped initiate the nationalist movement in Anatolia, and many Young Turks joined the Kemalist ranks.[40]

In May 1919 the Greek army landed at Izmir on the Aegean coast and moved inexorably westward. Taking advantage of Ottoman weakness and with the approval of the Allies, the Greeks were determined to "recover" lands lost to the Turks five hundred years before. The invasion increased public support for the Turkish national resistance. The nationalists, dedicated to the notion that Anatolia ought to belong to the Turks, opened their first Congress in Erzurum on July 24, 1919, the anniversary of the Young Turk Revolution. They brought together representatives of the eastern *vilayet*s ironically (or perhaps symbolically) in the abandoned Armenian Sanasarian *Varzharan* (High School). The delegates affirmed that these provinces would remain within the Ottoman Empire and that no special privileges would be granted to Armenians or Greeks. A second Congress was held in Sivas in early September, extending the commitment to preserve Turkish sovereignty over all of Anatolia and Rumelia. In his speech Kemal mentioned the Armenians only once but made reference only to their aggression, not to the massacres. "In the East the Armenians have begun their preparations to expand their state up to the banks of the Kızılırmak and even now their genocidal [*sic*] policy has started to reach our borders."[41] Former Unionists heavily populated the Sivas Congress as it called for self-determination and legitimized the struggle against efforts to establish Greek or Armenian power in Anatolia.

At the end of the month, with the crisis between Anatolia and Istanbul intensifying, Grand Vizier Ferid resigned. A pro-nationalist government came to power, and the nationalists swept the elections in October. The new Parliament in Istanbul, which also opposed the occupation, adopted the basic features of the Erzurum and Sivas program as the "National Pact" (*Misak-ı Milli*). As nationalist as the movement was—that is, dedicated to the preservation of a Muslim Turkish nation—it was at the same time committed to maintaining the Ottoman Empire. Only later, as the result of the takeover of the movement by Kemal and the radicals was a republic proclaimed.[42] In the new Turkey envisioned by the nationalist movement there was no space and little future for Armenians. Those Armenians who made their way back from exile to their homes found them occupied by Muslims, many of them refugees themselves. Clashes occurred. Thousands of Armenians returned to Cilicia under French protection, but it was only a matter of time before they would have to abandon their recovered homes.

Kemal was a skillful politician, able to rally supporters and deal ruthlessly with his enemies. He spoke in December 1919 about the dual danger facing the Turks: from the Allied powers and the non-Muslim minorities. He made it clear that the Armenians were responsible for their fate. "Whatever has befallen the non-Muslim elements living in our country, is the result of the policies of separatism they pursued in a savage manner, when they allowed themselves to be made tools of foreign intrigues and abused their privileges. There are probably many reasons and excuses for the undesired events that have taken place in Turkey. And I want definitely to say that these events are on a level far removed from the many forms of oppression which are committed in the states of Europe without any excuse."[43]

In 1919–1920 Kemal outmaneuvered those Unionists who opposed his growing power within the nationalist movement. The irrepressibly adventurous Enver Paşa allied himself with the Bolsheviks and attempted to reach Anatolia to challenge Kemal, but one by one Kemal eliminated those opposed to his dominance. The leaders of the fledgling Turkish Communist movement under Mustafa Suphi were mysteriously drowned in the Black Sea. Enver turned his attention to Central Asia, and there he perished in a battle with the Communists in June 1922. Kemal's hand was strengthened by his supporters' victories over the Armenians and the Greeks. The Kemalists fought the French occupiers around the city of Maraş in Cilicia, a town to which Armenian refugees had flocked thinking the Allies would protect them. Armenians fought alongside Algerians and Senegalese in the French forces. When in February 1920 the French precipitously pulled out, the Turks moved in and massacred some five to twelve thousand Armenians.[44] The defeat of the Greeks in September 1921 at the Sakarya River, only 50 miles from Ankara, was a turning point in the Turkish resistance to the Allies. Aided by recognition from the Soviet government as a fellow anti-imperialist and his military victories, Kemal secured his position as the preeminent leader of the national resistance.[45]

In response to the upsurge of the nationalists, the British clamped down hard on Istanbul in March 1920, taking control of the city in an efficient military operation. They dissolved the elected Parliament. By 1920 two rival Ottoman governments confronted one another: the Allied-imposed government of the restored Ferid in Istanbul and Kemal's Grand National Assembly in Ankara. The Allies moved ahead with their plans to divide and rule Turkey. On August 10, in the exhibition hall of the famous French porcelain factory, the Allies signed the Treaty of Sèvres, which effectively would have fractured the empire into European zones of influence and established a large, independent Armenian state in the east. Galvanized by the Greek invasion and Sèvres, the Kemalists mobilized Turks and Kurds to fight for the empire's sovereign independence. Ferid's second cabinet fell in October 1920, replaced by the pro-Ankara government of Tevik Paşa.

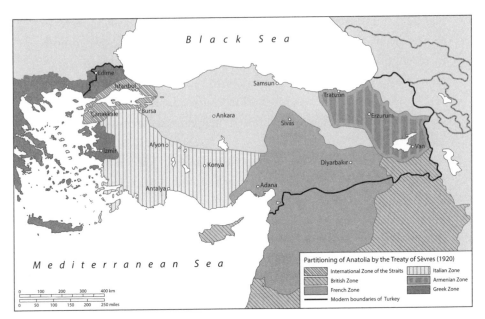

Partitioning of Anatolia.

The Treaty of Sèvres was never implemented, but it remains to the present day a specter in both the Armenian and Turkish imaginations. For Armenians it represents a dream unfulfilled, the end of their vain hope that President Woodrow Wilson would use his considerable powers to create a large Armenian state in eastern Anatolia. For Turks Sèvres is a nightmare, a "complex," the perpetual fear that Turkey might be divided up by its foreign or domestic enemies.

The Allies gave up the fight against the nationalists even as Armenians under arms attempted to take territory for their newly independent state centered around Erevan. Eastern Anatolia was once again a battleground, this time between Armenians left abandoned by their allies and the increasingly powerful Turkish nationalists collaborating in their anti-imperialist struggle with Soviet Russia. Armenians took revenge on those who had decimated the Ottoman Armenians, massacring as they had been massacred. These killings, a numerical fraction compared to those who perished in the Genocide, nevertheless, were motivated both by revenge for the victims of 1915–1916 and as an effort to cleanse the region of Muslims. Over time the years 1918–1920 would be conflated with 1915–1916, chronology and motivation confused, and those who would deny or relativize the Genocide limited their gaze to the post–World War bloodletting.

Kemal's army drove the Greeks from Smyrna, known to the Turks as *Gavur Izmir* (Infidel Izmir), in early September 1922, and the Greek and Armenian quarters of the city were destroyed by fire. Tens of thousands, perhaps as many as four hundred thousand, Christians fled from the city; tens of thousands more perished in the occupation and fire.[46] The Turkish War of Independence came to an end a month later with the armistice signed on October 11, 1922, at Mudanya. On November 1, 1922, Kemal's Grand National Assembly abolished the sultanate, removing its rival government. The Treaty of Lausanne (July 24, 1923) eliminated Sèvres. Kemal's troops entered Istanbul on October 6, 1923, and a few weeks later the Republic of Turkey was declared with Ankara its capital.

A STREET IN CHARLOTTENBURG

Talat, Nazım, Baheddin Şakir, Cemal Azmi, and other Young Turks lived in secret but comfortable exile in postwar Berlin. The Germans were willing to protect their former allies but were concerned about negative impressions that exposing their own involvement in the Armenian deportations and massacres might generate. The Foreign Office attempted to use Lepsius's indictment against the Ottomans to exculpate the German government. But the book contained information that implicated Germans as well as Ottomans. By publishing the book, the diplomats argued, "we would be supplying our enemies with weapons against our former friends. This does not serve justice." They told Lepsius, "[Y]our naturally biased criticism of Germany's position, as is made clear in the book, will be dangerous for us, because the entire world will become aware of it, while our reply would be more or less swept under the carpet."[47] Lepsius's findings, however, could not be manipulated. The *New York Tribune* reported,

> No more powerful indictment of Turkey's crimes in Armenia appeared during the war than that presented by a German writer, Dr. Johannes Lepsius, chairman of the German Orient Mission and the German-Armenian Society. Dr. Lepsius has investigated the Armenian persecutions on the spot and incorporated his findings in a report entitled, *"Die Lage des Armenischen Volkes in der Türkei,"* published secretly at Potsdam in 1916. Dr. Lepsius expressly corroborates the testimony of American consuls and missionaries and endorses the report published by the Bryce committee. He charges the responsibility for the Armenian horrors outright to the Turkish government, declaring that the extermination of the Armenian nation was decided upon at Constantinople as a matter of policy.[48]

Berlin was a haven for the fugitive Unionists. Talat lived with his wife in comfort in an apartment in Charlottenburg, not far away from Şakir. They remained closely involved in politics, particularly with the nationalists in Anatolia. Living under false names, they were in contact with both their embassy and the German government. They were careful and secretive about their movements in the city. Several assassinations by Armenian revolutionaries had already occurred—of two Azerbaijani officials who had been involved in the 1918 massacres of Armenians in Baku and of an Armenian collaborator in Istanbul. On March 15, 1921, Talat left his apartment at 4 Hardenbergstrasse and, swinging his cane, walked down the street toward the zoo. Talat was unaware that an Armenian student sent by the Dashnaktsutyun along with others to assassinate major Ottoman perpetrators of the Genocide had been living nearby and carefully following his movements. Soghomon Tehlirian was not yet twenty-four years old. He suffered from seizures that he claimed were related to what he had witnessed in the massacres of 1915 in Erzincan. He had been stalking Talat, and when from his apartment he saw the tall, stout figure pass his window, he decided to act. Tehlirian walked parallel to Talat on the other side of Hardenbergstrasse, then crossed over and faced his prey to make sure of his identity. Talat passed by, and Tehlirian shot a single bullet into the back of his head. Talat fell face first into a pool of his own blood.[49] Tehlirian threw away his German-made 9mm automatic pistol and ran down Fasanenstrasse. A woman fainted, a witness pursued him, and a crowd apprehended and began beating him. In his broken German, Tehlirian shouted, "Me Armenian, him Turkish, no harm for Germany! Let me go, it's nothing to do with you." Rescued by bystanders, the assassin was taken to the nearby Charlottenburg police station. It was Talat's close collaborator, Şakir, who a few hours later identified the body as the former grand vizier of the Ottoman Empire. Some days later the German Turcophiles organized an elaborate funeral for Talat. At the graveside Jäckh praised him as a "statesman of great stature," a "Turkish Bismarck."[50] Tehlirian, immediately a hero to the Armenian cause, was indicted and put on trial in a Berlin courtroom.[51]

The trial took two days and provided sensational reading for the European public. When questioned about the murder, Tehlirian maintained that a vision of his mother compelled him to kill Talat. Witnesses testified to his fragility, epileptic episodes and emotional seizures, and depressed mood induced by what he had lived through. A survivor of the Genocide told her tale of the deportation of Armenians from Erzurum. The court was incredulous. "A gendarme came and wanted me as his woman," she said. "Those who did not obey were pierced with bayonets and had their legs torn apart. They even crushed the pelvic bones of pregnant women, took out the fetuses and threw them away." She was interrupted by a commotion in the courtroom. "I swear this is true," she went on. The presiding justice asked, "Is all this really true? You are not imagining it?" The witness replied, "What I have said is the truth. In reality, it was much more horrible than it is possible for me to relate."[52]

The venerable Dr. Lepsius, then a sixty-two-year-old veteran of the Armenian Question, was brought in to corroborate the evidence on what had taken place in 1915. He placed Talat—the "very soul" of the annihilations—at the center of their planning and execution.[53] He estimated that approximately 1,400,000 Armenians had been deported of which "only ten percent reached their destination; the remaining ninety percent were killed, except for women and girls who were sold by the gendarmes or were abducted by the Kurds or died of exhaustion and hunger."[54] As a patriot, he defended his own government, asserting that Germany "pursued a benevolent and prudent policy with reference to the Armenian Question."[55] Lepsius was followed by General Liman von Sanders, who also denied any German involvement in the deportations and massacres. "As far as I know, the German government did whatever it could at the time, conditions permitting, to help the Armenians." Von Sanders personally had refused to "remove all Jews and Armenians from the German officers' staff" because they were needed as interpreters. "Very often," he added, "we received such nonsensical orders."[56] Bishop Balakian related his story of the marches and his escape. "When we came to the bloodiest city, Yozghat [Yozgat], we saw a couple hundred skulls of women and young girls located four hours distance from the town." He asked the accompanying police captain if only men were being killed and was told, "If we only killed men and not the women and children, then 50 years from now we would have a couple of million Armenians." The captain noted that 14,000 men from Yozgat and surrounding villages had been slaughtered and their bodies dropped into wells. He personally had given orders for a further 40,000 Armenians to be killed.[57]

A witness not called, Walter Rössler, the German consul in Aleppo from 1910 to 1918, recorded his own thoughts during the trial. Still a diplomat on active duty, Rössler noted that if asked to testify, "I would not be able to avoid expressing my conviction that Talaat Pasha is, in fact, one of those Turkish statesmen who wanted the Armenians to be annihilated and carried this out according to plan." He was prepared to confirm that the controversial collection of documents on the massacres collected by Aram Andonian, which he found tendentious, were, "in all probability, genuine." "I would also have to testify that a remark made to me by the Commissioner of Deportations [Şükrü Kaya], who was sent from Constantinople to Aleppo, was actually made, 'You do not understand what we want: we want an Armenia without Armenians.'"[58] The German Foreign Office refused to allow Rössler to testify.[59]

In their closing arguments, the defense attorneys refuted the prosecution's contention that Tehlirian had committed a premeditated murder and that Talat's role in the massacres was not clear. Tehlirian, they argued, had acted with diminished mental capacity because of the trauma he suffered. He had not been completely responsible for his actions. With Talat as much on trial as Tehlirian, the defense declared, "Tehlirian is the avenger of his people, of the one million Armenians who were killed."[60] As the assassin picked up his revolver and descended to the street, he "descends as the representative of justice versus brute force. He descends as the representative of humanity versus inhumanity."[61] The jury retired, deliberated for an hour, and declared Tehlirian not guilty of having intentionally killed Talat.

Other assassinations followed Talat's. On December 6, 1921, a Dashnak assassin, Arshavir Shiragian, killed Said Halim Paşa in Rome. On April 17, 1922, Shiragian and his comrades struck down Şakir and Cemal Azmi in Berlin. A few weeks later Enver died in battle with the Bolsheviks, and rumors proliferated that he had been killed by an Armenian. On July 21, 1922, Cemal Paşa was killed in Tiflis, slain by a Dashnak. By this time it was clear that these "executions" were neither spontaneous nor disconnected. In fact, they were the result of careful planning by the Dashnaktsutyun and a special unit under Armen Garo, a coordinated conspiracy, appropriately named "Operation Nemesis."

Tehlirian's trial and acquittal reverberated through the public sphere. The facts of the Genocide were recognized. Revenge appeared justified, but individuals carrying out retribution was a dubious principle for those concerned with the law and justice. A young law student in Lviv, then part of Poland, considered the consequences. Raphael Lemkin was concerned that "Tehlirian had appointed himself as the executioner of the conscience of mankind." In his private notes, he worried, "Yet can anybody appoint himself to carry out justice? Won't this kind of justice tend to be ruled by emotions and degenerate into caricature? At this moment the murder perpetrated upon an innocent people held a greater significance for me. To be sure, I still had no definitive answers, but I had the certain feeling that the world had to promulgate a law against this form of racially or religiously motivated murder.... Sovereignty, I believed, cannot be misunderstood as the right to kill millions of innocent human beings."[62]

Generations after the Armenian Genocide, even before the word itself had been conjured, ordinary people spoke to their children of the "starving Armenians." They were the reminders of a tragedy that had not yet found its name, the dimensions of which were deployed to measure lesser tragedies. The Genocide was the holocaust before the Holocaust. When he was planning his invasion of Poland in 1939, and advising his officers to forget the boundaries of humane behavior, Adolf Hitler told them, "Who, after all, speaks today of the annihilation of the Armenians?"[63] The mass killing of the Armenians was known but little spoken of in the late 1930s; it remained, however, a memory of human devastation against which others might be compared, "the international standard for horror."[64] The Nazis banned the most popular account of the Genocide, Franz Werfel's *The Forty Days of Musa Dagh*, and the Kemalist government of the Republic of Turkey pressured MGM studios not to make a commercial film of the book.[65] Armenians were not only starving or being fed by relief organizations in the Middle East and Soviet Armenia; not only were the survivors living in orphanages or refuge camps, but the Armenian nation itself had been orphaned—a people without most of their historic homeland and the civilization that had constituted their heritage up to 1915. A few years after the Genocide they were abandoned by most of their former friends.

By the end of the war 90 percent of Ottoman Armenians were gone, killed, deported to the deserts of Syria, or refugees in the Caucasus or Middle East. The number of dead is staggering—somewhere between 600,000 and 1 million killed in the more conservative estimates—and the event shocked European and American opinion. In the early 1940s when he invented the word "genocide," the jurist Raphael Lemkin applied it to two twentieth-century events: the Turkish deportation and massacres of the Armenians in 1915 and the German annihilation of

American Committee for Relief in the Near East Poster by William Gunning King, 1917.

Europe's Jews. The Armenian Genocide was a central event in the last stages of the dissolution of the Ottoman Empire and the foundational crime that along with the ethnic cleansing and population exchanges of the Anatolian Greeks made possible the formation of an ethnonational Turkish republic.

Thinking about the Unthinkable: Genocide

The very word "genocide" conjures images of the most horrendous crimes committed by states against designated peoples. So powerful is the term itself—as a concept in international law, a claim by governments of their own victimization, and a powerful source of national identification—that the term "genocide" has been extended to involve almost all instances of mass killing in our world. While some historians, journalists, and jurists have defined "genocide" so narrowly that the term can be applied only in the case of intended total destruction, as in the Jewish Holocaust, others have stretched it so broadly that any mass killing or even ethnic cleansing—the expulsion of the Greeks from Anatolia or Palestinian Arabs from Mandate Palestine, the Ukrainian *Holodomor* (Death Famine), or Stalin's Great Purges—becomes a genocide. Sadly it seems that nowadays in order to be a full-fledged nation-state one not only needs a flag, a national anthem, and an opera house, but also a genocide. Such a broad usage makes it impossible to single out those instances of state-initiated violence that qualify in a clear way with the original meaning of genocide, the killing of a people, and that can be analyzed comparatively as to their etiology and effects. In this work I employ the word "genocide" in a specific way to designate what in German is called *Völkermord*, the murder of a people, and in Turkish *soykırım* or Armenian *tseghaspanutyun* (killing of an ethnicity or, in an older understanding, race).

Mass murder in and of itself does not a genocide make. Although legal definitions do not capture the full range of historical examples, there is utility in restricting the term "genocide" to what might more accurately be referred to as "ethnocide," that is, the deliberate attempt to eliminate a designated group defined by the cultural characteristics—language, imagined biological origins (race), religion—that have historically bound them together as a community and appear to distinguish that people from

others.[1] While other forms of mass killing—war, massacres, induced fam-
ines, the Great Purges—involve death on a horrendous scale, the motivations and intentions of the perpetrators are different enough from those
of ethnocides that they require distinct explanations. Genocide is not the
murder of people but the murder of a people.

In his first publication using the term he had coined, the lawyer
Raphael Lemkin explained, "The practice of extermination of nations
and ethnic groups as carried out by the invaders [the Nazis] is called by
the author 'genocide,' a term deriving from the Greek word *genos* (tribe,
race) and the Latin *cide* (by way of analogy, see homicide, fratricide)."[2]
As difficult as it is to discern, intentionality is key as the starting point,
and death is the result of the intention to eliminate or render impotent.
Genocide, thus, is "ethnically inspired violence" but should be distinguished from ethnic cleansing, which may entail killing but more immediately involves displacement and deportation, the physical moving of a
distinct population.[3] Ethnic cleansing—whether the American Indians
or Australian aborigines; Chechens, Kalmyks, Crimean Tatars, Volga
Germans, and other Soviet peoples; Palestinians or Kurds—is accompanied by loss of life, and killing is often an instrument to force people
to move. The physical removal of people because one wants the land but
not the people on it is closely related to genocide but may or may not
require mass murder. The imperial ambitions of Europeans and the subsequent settler colonialism, beginning immediately after the discovery
of the Americas in the fifteenth century and continuing into the twenty-
first, resulted in horrendous violence and forced movements of peoples,
brutal precedents to the policies carried out by the Young Turks and the
Nazis. Ethnic cleansing and genocide bleed into one another, points on
a tragic real-world spectrum, but they are usefully kept distinct for ana-
lytical purposes.

The genocidal elimination need not be total, but it should render
the "people" impotent, politically and possibly culturally. Few modern
mass killings or even genocides have resulted in the total liquidation of
a people, and both the Armenian and Jewish genocides resulted in new
states being formed and populated with survivors and their descendants.

Raphael Lemkin (1900–1959), the Polish Jewish lawyer who coined the word "geno-cide" in 1943, and drafted the United Nations Convention on Genocide in 1948. UN photo.

But the mass of Armenians never returned to the historic homeland in Anatolia that they had inhabited for three thousand years, and the Jews, while hardly totally erased, never reconstituted the vibrant Yiddish culture that they had evolved over many centuries in Central and Eastern Europe. Those genocides had results; they were genocidal in the physical, political, and cultural senses.

In both historical and more publicistic writing, the term "genocide" has been used rather promiscuously to apply to mass repression of political opponents, real or imagined. When the Genocide Convention was being debated at the United Nations in the late 1940s, the Soviet representatives strenuously held out against extending the term to political killings, which would of necessity have included Stalin's purges, the millions lost in dekulakization, the Ukrainian *Holodomor*, the deadly settlement of Kazakhs, and the deportations of North Caucasians and other peoples during World War II. The American delegates also resisted any language in the convention that might be turned toward examination of racial segregation and the violence perpetrated against African Americans during the era of Jim Crow.[4] In the interests of unanimity, political, social, and economic groups were not included in the protections of the convention that was adopted by the United Nations on December 9, 1948.

Although on moral grounds one form of mass killing is as reprehensible as another, the framers of the convention may have done historians and political scientists a favor by limiting the definition. In article 2 of the United Nations Convention on the Prevention and Punishment of the Crime of Genocide (December 9, 1948), "genocide means any of the following acts committed with intent to destroy, in whole or in part, a national, ethnic, racial or religious group, as such: a) Killing members of the group; b) Causing serious bodily or mental harm to members of the group; c) Deliberately inflicting on the group conditions of life calculated to bring about its physical destruction in whole or in part; d) Imposing measures intended to prevent births within the group; e) Forcibly transferring children of the group to another group." A capacious definition, the UN's conception has become standard and widely accepted, even as it is contested.

Because mass killings vary so greatly in origin, perpetrator, intention, scale, and intended outcome, no explanation can cover all or even most of the cases. Too many dependent variables make it impossible to come up with the principal causal factors. Stalin's intentions and actions during the Ukrainian famine, no matter what sensationalist claims are made by nationalists and anti-Communists, were not the extermination of the Ukrainian people but were related perversely to the collectivization campaign, the destruction of any form of resistance to the dictates of the ruling party, and the absurdly high targets for requisitioning grain. Incompetence and callousness were as much culprits as fear of potential resistance, anger at the failure to deliver grain, and deep-seated hostility toward peasants and nationalists.[5] Like the Irish Famine of 1845–1852, the Bengal Famine of 1943, and the Chinese Famine of 1958–1961, so in Ukraine the government was culpable in the deaths of millions. It is understandable that such horrific occurrences should be thought of as genocidal in both scope and intention, given that the foreseeable consequences of state policy resulted in mass death. But since they were not directed at the extermination of a definite ethnic, religious, or cultural group, a different set of explanations is required, as is necessary for the Great Purges, the Gulag, and the ethnic cleansing of the "small peoples" of the Soviet Union. The value of the term "genocide" in the public sphere may be moral condemnation, but for historians and social scientists its salience stems, not simply from establishing a category, but from the explanatory potential of that category. Historians must ask the questions "when genocide?" and "why genocide?"

HOW MANY ARMENIANS?

The principal architect of the Armenian deportations, Minister of Interior Talat Paşa, compiled his own record book calculating the number and location of the Ottoman Armenians. Not trusting the official Ottoman count of 1,300,000, Talat estimated that the more accurate number was 1,500,000.[6] This number fell between the official Ottoman figure of 1,251,785, and the figure given by the Armenian patriarchate of 1,915,858. The demographic historian Fuat Dündar holds that 1,500,000 is the best and most reliable number of Ottoman Armenians on the eve of the Genocide that we have.[7]

Dündar calculates that about 281,000 Armenians were permitted to remain in Anatolia and Rumelia, largely in Istanbul (100,000), Aydın (21,000), Edirne (25,000), and Konya (10,000), along with some 75,000 Catholic and Protestant Armenians, artisans, families of soldiers, and some 50,000 converted women and children.[8] He estimates that around 300,000 Armenians survived the deportation and the settlement areas. Another 255,000 fled abroad, primarily to Russia. He concludes that 836,000 Ottoman Armenians survived the Genocide and by the end of the war in 1918 approximately 664,000 had perished.[9] Taner Akçam also uses the numbers given in Talat's "black book," where the minister of interior counted 924,158 Armenians deported. Since Talat had not included more than a dozen locations in his calculations, Akçam estimates the total number of Armenians deported to have been closer to 1,200,000, a figure that corresponds to the early estimates of Arnold Toynbee (1,200,000) and Johannes Lepsius (1,300,000).[10] Raymond Kévorkian has used the statistics gathered by the Armenian patriarchate of Istanbul, now housed in the St. James Monastery in Jerusalem, and estimates that there were just under 2,000,000 Armenians in the Ottoman lands on the eve of World War I.[11] His detailed account in *The Armenian Genocide, A Complete History* concludes that 850,000 Armenians were deported in 1915–1916, of whom 300,000 had perished by the winter of 1915–1916; 500,000 survived until the last round of massacres in the winter and spring of 1916. "[B]y late 1916 the number of those who had perished exceeded 600,000."[12] People continued to die from hunger, disease, and arbitrary and sporadic violence.

Further losses occurred in the half decade after the war when Armenians fought the nationalist Turks and were driven out of Cilicia, Izmir, and elsewhere. The twentieth century had not yet witnessed such a colossal loss of life directed at a particular people by a government. Mass killing of this magnitude made the unthinkable thinkable, and the political engineers that emerged from the Great War were able to calculate higher human costs as their population policies reshaped whole societies.

WHY GENOCIDE?

The purpose of the Genocide was to eliminate the perceived threat of the Armenians within the Ottoman Empire by reducing their numbers and scattering them in isolated, distant places. The destruction of the *Ermeni milleti* was carried out in three different but related ways: dispersion, massacre, and assimilation by conversion to Islam. A perfectly rational (and rationalist) explanation, then, for the Genocide appears to be adequate: a strategic goal to secure the empire by elimination of an existential threat to the state and the Turkish (or Islamic) people. But before the strategic goal and the rational choices of instruments to be used can be considered, it is necessary to explain how the existential threat was imagined;

how the Armenian and Assyrian enemy was historically and culturally constructed; and what cognitive and emotional processes shaped the affective disposition of the perpetrators that compelled them to carry out massive uprooting and murder of specifically targeted peoples and to believe that such actions were justified.

The argument in this book begins, not with primordial nations inevitably confronting one another and contesting sovereignty over a disputed land, but with the accelerating construction of different ethnoreligious communities within the complex context of an empire with its possibilities of multiple and hybrid identities and coexistence. The hierarchies, inequities, institutionalized differences, and repressions that characterized imperial life and rule had for centuries allowed people of different religions, cultures, and languages to live together. Armenians and others acquiesced to their position in the imperial hierarchy and even developed some affection for the polity in which they lived. Shared experiences as Ottomans in some cases led to material prosperity and cultural hybridity, but always under conditions of insecurity and often capricious governance. The imperial paradigm met its greatest challenges from what might be lumped together under the concept of "progress," that is, the technological and industrial advancement of the capitalist West, which rendered the Ottoman Empire relatively backward in the internationally competitive marketplace, as well as the differentiated and unequal development of the various peoples of the Ottoman realm. Religion, language, and culture distinguished the *millets*—the Muslim, Armenian, Greek, Catholic, Protestant, Assyrian, and Jewish—one from another, yet members of all of them could aspire to be Ottoman and participate in the cultural, social, and even political life of the empire without ever achieving full equality with the ruling institution.

From abroad two powerful influences shaped the evolution of the various Ottoman peoples: the increasingly hegemonic discourse of the nation, which redefined the nature of political communities and legitimized culture as the basis of sovereignty and possession of a homeland; and the imperial ambitions of European powers, which repeatedly intervened in Ottoman politics, hiving off parts of the empire's territory, hollowing out the sultan's sovereignty, and insisting on protection of his Christian subjects. Migration of some peoples out of the empire and others into it; competition over land, particularly in eastern Anatolia; Armenian resistance to old forms of "feudal" subjugation to the Kurds—all contributed to structural and dynamic influences that generated a mental world of opposition and hostility among the *millets*.

Determined to save their empire, the Young Turks came to power at a moment of radical disintegration of their state, threatened in their minds by both the Great Powers and the non-Turkic peoples (not only by Balkan Christians, Armenians, and Greeks, but also by Muslim Kurds, Albanians, and Arabs). Their nation within that empire was still in the process of being imagined, effectively neither Ottoman, Islamic, nor ethnically Turkish. Nation lay in the future, and the turn of the century was a period of intense and passionate debate about the nature of Turkish national formation. How would the community be conceived: as a nation of ethnic Turks, with Turks defined as a race or a linguistic group; or as a supranation of Ottomans of various religions, ethnicities, and languages, perhaps with Turks (however defined) as the dominant group; or in the minds of some, as a pan-Turkic or pan-Islamic community that stretched into the Caucasus and Central Asia or into the Arab lands to include people of the same linguistic family or religion? What was clear to those Young Turks who eventually won the political contest by 1914 was that Turks would dominate in one way or another, and that this imperial community would not be one of civic equality. It would, in other words, neither be an ethnically homogeneous nation-state like the paradigmatic states of Western Europe nor a multinational state of diverse peoples equal under the law. It would remain an empire with some peoples dominant over others.[13] For one of the most radical of the Turkish nationalists, Ziya Gökalp, "The people is like a garden. We are supposed to be its gardeners! First the bad shoots are to be cut. And then the scion is to be grafted."[14]

There was no simple binary of nation and empire, certainly not in the age of the discourse of the nation. Empires attempted to become more national but remained structurally and discursively hierarchical, inequitable, and at some level committed to maintaining, even producing, differences between rulers and ruled. At the same time "nations precisely because they had a deeper urge to uniformity than empires did in many ways [become] more imperial in their behavior toward minorities and adjacent communities."[15] The Young Turks, however Ottomanist they were in their inception, became over time national imperialists prepared to take the most desperate and drastic measures to homogenize their state while promoting some peoples over others and annihilating still others.

On the motives and aims of the Young Turks, as well as the timing of their decision to deport the Armenians, some scholars have claimed that massacres of dissident minorities were a consistent Turkish practice. They argue that the Hamidian massacres of the 1890s and the killing of Armenians in Adana in 1909 were precursors of the Genocide, which in turn was a premeditated event planned before the World War. Others have argued (as I have in this book) that the earlier massacres were discrete events different in kind from the Genocide of 1915 and that the Genocide was a largely contingent event that occurred in a moment of radicalization following the catastrophic defeat at Sarıkamış in the winter of 1914–1915.[16] The contention that the Genocide was planned long in advance and realized a consistent Turkish policy of extermination harkens back to the essential notion of the "terrible Turk," an irredeemable enemy of Christians and European civilization, and is similar to the debate in Holocaust scholarship between "intentionalists" and "structuralists."[17] But even those who want to disaggregate the episodes of Ottoman state violence against Armenians agree that the earlier massacres reflected a propensity for violent repression. Repeated official justifications based on security requirements, as well as the inconsistent and ineffective responses by the European powers, served only to open the way for future episodes of violent repression of peoples thought to be rebellious.

The story told here argues that the Genocide was not planned long in advance but was a reaction to a moment of crisis that grew more radical over time. The Genocide should be distinguished from the earlier episodes of conservative restoration of order by repression or urban ethnic violence. Though there were similarities with the brutal policies of massacre and deportation that earlier regimes used to keep order, the very scale of the Armenian Genocide and its intended effects—to rid eastern Anatolia of a whole people—make it a far more radical, indeed revolutionary, transformation of the imperial setup. The story here is that the Genocide was neither religiously motivated nor a struggle between two contending nationalisms, one of which destroyed the other, but rather the pathological response of desperate leaders who sought security against a people they had both constructed as enemies and driven into radical opposition to the regime under which they had lived for centuries.

While an anti-Armenian disposition existed and grew more virulent within the Ottoman elite long before the war, and some extremists contemplated radical solutions to the Armenian Question, particularly after the Balkan Wars, the World War not only presented an opportunity for carrying out the most revolutionary program against the Armenians, but provided the particular conjuncture that convinced the Young Turk triumvirate to deploy ethnic cleansing and genocide against the Armenians. The moment at which disposition became action occurred after the outbreak of war when the leaders' fear that their rule was in peril focused on the Armenians as the wedge that the Russians and other powers could use to pry apart their empire. The European-imposed reform program of 1914 was the immediate manifestation of the Ottomans' fears that their sovereignty over their realm was being compromised and that the European support of the Armenians presented a danger to their state's future.

Had there been no World War there would have been no genocide, not only because there would have been no "fog of war" to cover up the events but because the radical sense of endangerment among Turks would not have been as acute. Without the war there would have been less motivation for a revolutionary solution and more political opportunities for negotiation and compromise. On the eve of the Ottoman declaration of war on Russia, the government engaged in negotiations with the leading Armenian political party, the Dashnaktsutyun, to secure their support in subverting the Russian Empire from within using Russian Armenians. The Dashnaks sensibly refused, precipitating the conclusion on the part of Şakir and others that Armenians were treacherous internal enemies. Young

Turks considered a variety of political options short of genocide, but the inner core of the CUP resolved on the most radical and destructive resolution to the Armenian Question. When it came, the Armenian Genocide was the result of long-term, deep-seated elite and popular hatreds, resentments, and fears intensified by war and defeat—an affective disposition in which Armenians were perceived as irredeemable enemies of Muslims—that in turn shaped the Committee of Union and Progress's strategic considerations as to the most effective ways to save the empire. As spring approached in 1915, the governing few believed that the circumstances were propitious to remove the Armenians. Parliament had been suspended; the state appeared to be at risk from the British navy and Russian armies; and the Armenians could be linked to the Russian advance as collaborators.

The overly capacious term "nationalism" has been promiscuously used to explain almost everything. In this book I disaggregate different forms of national vision. Various imagined national communities overlapped, competed, and succeeded one another in the roughly one hundred years from *Tanzimat* to Kemalism. In late Ottoman history the efforts of Ottomanist reformers to shape an Ottoman national community might be considered a form of ecumenical or civic nationalism. That effort can be contrasted with Sultan Abdülhamid II's project to link Kurds and Turks together in a new national synthesis, a form of Islamic nationality. At the turn of the twentieth century genuine Turkic ethnic nationalists proposed a greater infusion of Turkic elements into state governance and social arrangements, including the foundation of a Turkic-Muslim national economy. Meanwhile Balkan Christian peoples, and Muslim Albanians, expressed their own nationalist aspirations to realize what they believed to be their historical right to nationhood and territorial independence. The Young Turks, humiliated by defeat by Christians in the Balkan Wars, adopted a more radical nationalist rhetoric of revenge and Turkication/Islamization of the population, yet all the while attempting to maintain a multinational empire that included the Arab Middle East and parts of Caucasia. Finally, the Kemalists adopted a form of organic, integral ethnonationalism, based on European models, to forge through state action a homogeneous Turkish nation stretching from Rumelia through Anatolia.

War and social disintegration, the invasion of the Russians and the British, and the defection of some Armenians to the Russian side moved the leaders of the Ottoman state to embark on the most vicious form of securitization and social engineering: the massive deportation and massacre of hundreds of thousands of their Armenian and Assyrian subjects.[18] Ziya Gökalp, who like so many others saw the Genocide as necessary or even forced on the Ottomans, could with confidence write, "There was no Armenian massacre, there was a Turkish-Armenian arrangement. They stabbed us in the back, we stabbed them back."[19] In the view of militant Young Turks and their defenders what was done had to be done in the name of national security, and so a kind of lawful lawlessness was permitted.

The choice of genocide was not inevitable. Predicated on long-standing and ever more extreme affective dispositions and attitudes that had demonized the Armenians as a threat that needed to be dealt with, the ultimate choice was made by specific leaders at a particular historical conjuncture when the threat seemed to them most palpable. The Young Turks' sense of their own vulnerability—combined with resentment at what they took to be Armenians' privileged status, Armenian dominance over Muslims in some spheres of life, and the preference of many Armenians for Christian Russia—fed a fantasy that the Armenians presented an existential threat to Turks. Threat is a perception, in this case the perception that one of the empire's subject peoples was as great a danger as invading armies. Threat must be understood not only as an immediate menace but as perception of future peril.

Reversing an older image of ethnic violence as bubbling up from the masses below, this book locates the initiative and initiation of the Armenian Genocide in the highest levels of the state. The decisions, permission, and encouragement of a few in power provoked and stoked emotional resonance below. It turns out that a few killers can cause enormous destruction. Thugs, sadists, fanatics, and opportunists can with modern weaponry (or even with axes, clubs, and daggers) slaughter thousands with little more than acquiescence from the surrounding population.[20] They in turn can inspire or let loose the rage of thousands of others who will carry out even greater destruction. Genocide in particular is an event of mass killing, with massive numbers of victims but not necessarily of massive numbers of killers. The thugs, set loose by the political elite, create a climate of violence that radicalizes a population, renders political moderates less relevant, and convinces people of the need to support the more extremist leaders. The context of war, with its added burdens and accompanying social disintegration, hardens hostile group identities, "making it rational to fear the other group and see its members as dangerous threats."[21] Added to that, thugs and ordinary people use the opportunities offered by state-permitted lawlessness to settle other accounts with neighbors, take revenge, or simply grab what they can.[22]

Some of the killers in 1915 simply obeyed orders; others were motivated by much more mundane feelings than duty or considered ideological preferences. Social and economic inequalities when combined with ethnic and religious distinctions bred resentment toward those who received more than they deserved from those who had received less. Fear of the other and the future, anger at what had been done to oneself and one's compatriots, simple ambition and careerism all could be found among those who murdered Armenians. Fear, anger, and resentment escalated into hatred, the emotion that saw the other as the essential cause of one's own misery. Hatred required that the other be eliminated.[23] Violence then begat violence and counter-violence. Killing became familiar and justifiable for reasons of self-defense. A cumulative radicalization moved inexorably forward: sporadic, uncoordinated massacres along the eastern frontier gave way to planned deportations, first from frontline areas and then throughout the empire; deportations were accompanied with massacres and death marches; finally, at the end of the road, those who had reached the deserts were starved to death or brutally murdered.

Within the Ottoman imaginary Armenians became the victims of both their success within the *millet* system and their exposure as religiously marked, largely unarmed subjects. Armenians tried but were unable to dispel the perception that they were alien to the Ottomans and a menace that when given an opportunity would reveal its real intent. Like their Muslim overlords and neighbors, Armenians imagined the future by remembering the past.[24] But different Armenians interpreted their experiences over centuries of life under Ottoman rule differently. Many middle- and upper-class Armenians successfully adapted to and integrated into Ottoman society, even though they lived with considerable uncertainty about their security. Villagers and townspeople in the East knew firsthand the harsh treatment at the hands of nomads and Kurdish chieftains, the unpredictability of violence, and the unreliability of Ottoman justice. Their most recent experiences were of mass killing—in the Hamidian massacres of the 1890s and in Adana and Hadjin in 1909. Young political activists, many of them from Russian Caucasia, moved between optimism that they would be able to protect their vulnerable compatriots and pessimism about their ability to organize and mobilize them. Most Ottoman Armenians remained loyal to the empire of their birth but hoped in vain for reforms and protection from their state or European sympathizers. Their emotional world was colored by vulnerability, uncertainty, and mistrust tinged with condescension directed at other Ottoman peoples.

The multitude of determining factors—the overdetermination of what would ultimately be genocide—combined to form an affective disposition both at the top of Ottoman society, among the rulers in the Hamidian period and the Young Turk opposition, and among ordinary Muslims that targeted the Armenians particularly and envisioned them as foreign, subversive, devious, and, eventually, an existential threat to the unity and security of the empire and the Muslims within it. Homophily—preference for those like oneself ("birds of a feather flock together")—fed into a greater sense of security, while xenophobia—fear of the foreign—smoldered when the awareness of material and physical dangers intensified. The two worked together to distance the "we" from the "other." The Balkan Wars of 1912–1913 exacerbated and intensified hatred of Christians in general and heightened feelings of vengeance against those who had humiliated and tormented Balkan Muslims. The imposition of the 1914 reforms, which established European inspectors in the Armenian provinces, was a final blow to Ottoman pride and a confirmation of the treacherous connection between Europe and the Armenians.

The catalytic moment that triggered the most brutal response to anxiety about the future came with the World War. There was no blueprint for genocide elaborated before or even in the early months of war, but the disposition to dispose of the Armenians had already been forming in the decade before Sarajevo. The Armenian Genocide was both the result of increasingly radical attitudes of Turkish national imperialists and was triggered by the events of 1914–1915: the imposition of the European reform plan; the breakdown of CUP-Armenian relations when the Dashnaks refused to instigate rebellion among Caucasian Armenians; the colossal losses at Sarıkamış; and the rapid reconstruction of Armenians as an imminent internal danger. Those who perpetrated genocide operated within their own delusional rationality.[25] The Young Turks acted on fears and resentments that had been generated over time and directed their efforts to resolve their anxieties by dealing with those they perceived to threaten their survival—not with their external enemies but an internal enemy they saw allied to the Entente—the Armenians. What to denialists and their sympathizers appears to be a rational and justified strategic choice to eliminate a rebellious and seditious population, in this account is seen as the outcome of the Young Turk leaders' pathological construction of the Armenian enemy.[26] The actions that the Young Turks decided on were based in an emotional disposition that led to distorted interpretations of social reality and exaggerated estimations of threats.[27] The conviction that Armenians desired to form an independent state was a fantasy of the Young Turks and a few Armenian extremists. The great majority of Armenians had been willing to live within the Ottoman Empire if their lives and property could be secured. They clung to the belief that a future was possible within the empire long after some like Grigoris Balakian thought reasonable. Still, they had been socialized as Ottomans; this was their home and what they knew. Only when their own government once again turned them into pariahs did some of them defect or resist.

The Armenian Genocide, along with the killing of Assyrians and the expulsion of the Anatolian Greeks, laid the ground for the more homogeneous nation-state that arose from the ashes of the empire. Like many other states, including Australia, Israel, and the United States, the emergence of the Republic of Turkey involved the removal and subordination of native peoples who had lived on its territory prior to its founding. The connection between ethnic cleansing or genocide and the legitimacy of the national state underlies the desperate efforts to deny or distort the history of the nation and the state's genesis. Coming to terms with that history, on the other hand, can have the salutary effect of questioning continued policies of ethnic homogenization and the refusal to recognize the claims and rights of those peoples, minorities, or diasporas—Aborigines, native Americans, Kurds, Palestinians, Assyrians, or Armenians—who refuse to disappear.

A Bibliographical Discussion

In many ways a few key works defined the landscape on which the earliest writing on the Armenian Genocide was conceptualized. As indicated in this book, the themes laid out in the American ambassador Henry Morgenthau's memoir remain among the most powerful elements constituting both the narrative of the Genocide and its explanation up to the present time. A few other memoirs and documents appeared sporadically in the years after the Great War, yet little distanced reflection or scholarly attention was paid to the massacres of the Armenians and Assyrians for almost fifty years after the events. The controversial and disputed "Andonian documents" first appeared in *The Memoirs of Naim Bey: Official Documents Relating to the Deportation and Massacres of Armenians* (1920) and were purported to include telegrams from Talat. Turkish scholars have disputed their authenticity, and the Dutch historian Erik-Jan Zürcher also questions their provenance, though he states that other documents corroborate the documents' claim of CUP initiation and involvement in the killings.[1] The most thorough defense of the documents' authenticity is by Vahakn Dadrian.[2] What was written in the first half century reflected either the suffering of those who had endured the deportations and survived or political pleading for appropriate recognition of Armenian losses and recompense in the form of territory or reparations. Armenian political parties, particularly the Armenian Revolutionary Federation (Dashnaktsutyun), worked to keep the plight of dispersed Armenians before the public, and the image of "starving Armenians" was familiar in American and European media. The major powers, however, lost interest in the Armenian Question after the Treaty of Lausanne (1923), which by recognizing the Republic of Turkey and failing to mention the Armenians or to enforce minority protections on the Kemalist state, essentially confirmed the effectiveness of deportations or even murderous ethnic cleansing as a potential solution to population problems. The only existing Armenian political presence, the Armenian Soviet Socialist Republic, did not actively promote awareness of the Genocide until after 1965, and Western governments had few reasons to deal with this vexed matter. In the new Republic of Turkey there was a cold silence about the events of the late Ottoman period beyond the heroic nationalist narrative of Kemalist resistance to foreign aggression. Yet the Armenian Question was not easily laid to rest. The assassination of Talat in Berlin in March 1921 by Solomon Tehlirian, the ensuing trial and acquittal of the assassin, and the killing of Bahaeddin Şakir by Dashnaks in April 1922, Cemal in Tiflis in July, and other perpetrators of Armenian atrocities kept the fate of Ottoman Armenians alive in the headlines—for a while. In November 1933 the renowned writer Franz Werfel (1890–1945) published his epic novel *Die vierzig Tage des Musa Dagh* (*The Forty Days of Musa Dagh*), about the courageous but doomed resistance of Armenian villagers during the Genocide. Enormously popular, the Nazis deemed the novel "undesirable," and Werfel, an Austrian Jew, fled to France after the *Anschluss* and later to the United States. When MGM Studios announced plans to make a film of the novel, the Turkish government applied pressure through the U.S. State Department and succeeded in stopping production.[3]

During the Cold War Turkey decisively joined the anti-Communist camp, and the Republic of Turkey was widely hailed as a model of secular modernization and a staunch ally of the West. A pro-Turkish account by the Princeton professor Lewis Thomas praised the "civilizing" efforts of the Turkish state in its treatment of the Kurds and its forging of an effective anti-Communist democracy.[4] In Turkey a former official in Talat's Ministry of Interior and a CUP member, Esat Uras, compiled a collection of documents purporting to demonstrate Armenian culpability in their own destruction.[5] Armenian diaspora activists at the time appeared more concerned with the conflicts over attitudes toward Soviet Armenia and divisions in the Armenian Church than with a politics centered on 1915.[6]

Interest in the Holocaust, the Armenian Genocide, and genocide as a field of study more generally began to emerge in the 1960s and subsequent decades. "Holocaust consciousness" moved from primarily a Jewish concern into the broader public with the trial of Adolf Eichmann in 1961, Hannah Arendt's controversial *Eichmann in Jerusalem* (1963), and the growing connection made between the tragedy in Europe and the survival of the state of Israel. The very term "holocaust," which earlier had been applied (by David Lloyd-George, for example) to the Armenian massacres, now was nearly exclusively (and with a capital "H") used for the Nazi killing of the Jews.[7] With the fiftieth anniversary of the Armenian deportations in 1965, commemorations were held around the world, none more striking than the demonstrations in Erevan that demanded "*mer hogher*" (our lands) and led, first, to the removal of the local Communist party secretary and, later, to the building of an official monument to the Genocide at Tsiternakaberd.[8] Armenian "genocide consciousness" fed on the persistent and ever more aggressive denial by the Turkish government and sponsored spokesmen, including some with academic credentials, that the deportations and massacres had been ordered by the Young Turk government in an attempt to exterminate one of the peoples of the Ottoman Empire. Actions of Armenian terrorists from 1973 into the early 1980s brought the issue to public attention, but scholarship lagged far behind the agitated public consciousness. Out of the political and historiographical struggles of the 1970s came the first serious work by historians in the late 1970s and through the 1980s. Richard G. Hovannisian's 1978 bibliography of sources on *The Armenian Holocaust* demonstrated both the availability of primary sources for anyone who cared to learn about 1915 as well as the thinness, indeed absence, of academic historical research on the topic.[9] In those years one had to turn to the French physician Yves Ternon, who moved from his studies of Nazi medical atrocities to the Genocide.[10] As a small number of Armenian scholars, notably Richard Hovannisian, Vahakn Dadrian, and Levon Marashlian, as well as a few non-Armenians like Robert Jay Lifton, Leo Kuper, Ternon, and Tessa Hofmann, began to write about an Armenian genocide, a defense of the Turks by Heath Lowry, Stanford Shaw, and Justin McCarthy led to clashes over such basic questions as the number of victims, the role and responsibility of the Committee of Union and

Progress, and whether 1915 should be considered an asymmetrical civil war or intentional, state-directed extermination of a designated people, that is, genocide. At the same time a number of Holocaust scholars, seeking to preserve the "uniqueness" of the Jewish exterminations, rejected the suggestion of equivalence between the Armenian and Jewish genocides. As the historian Peter Novick reports, "Lucy Dawidowicz (quite falsely) accused the Armenians of 'turn[ing] the subject into a vulgar contest about who suffered more.' She added that while Turks had 'a rational reason' for killing Armenians, the Germans had no rational reason for killing Jews."[11]

Armenians were upset at the reduction of the Armenian presence in Washington's United States Holocaust Memorial Museum and by the Israeli government's attempt to close down an international genocide conference in Tel Aviv in 1982 after the Turkish government protested the discussion of the Armenian case. Prominent American Jews, including Elie Wiesel, Alan Dershowitz, and Arthur Hertzberg, withdrew from the conference, but the organizer, Israel W. Charny, went ahead with the meeting.[12] Several American Armenian scholars, however, refused to attend as well, in protest over the Israeli invasion of Lebanon that was taking place as the conference held its sessions. As one state after another officially recognized 1915 as a genocide, the United States and Israel soon became the two most notable exceptions, along with Turkey. Activists in Europe and North America organized a series of campaigns to pressure the holdout states toward genocide recognition.

Two years after the crisis over the Tel Aviv conference, the Permanent Peoples' Tribunal, a civil society organization founded four years earlier (1979) by the Italian senator Lelio Basso, held a "trial" examining the Armenian massacres to determine if it constituted a genocide. Meeting in Paris from April 13 to 16, 1984, the jury heard the accounts of scholars—among them Hovannisian, Jirair Libaridian, Christopher Walker, Hofmann, Ternon, and Dickran Kouymjian—and examined the arguments of the Turkish government and its supporters. In its verdict the Tribunal determined that the "extermination of the Armenian population groups through deportation and massacre constitutes a crime of genocide.... [T]he Young Turk government is guilty of this genocide, with regard to the acts perpetrated between 1915 and 1917; the Armenian genocide is also an 'international crime' for which the Turkish state must assume responsibility, without using the pretext of any discontinuity in the existence of the state to elude that responsibility."[13] By the late 1980s, at long last, the first serious academic scholarship in the West on the fate of the Armenians began to appear in essays, collected volumes, and comparative studies. A new field of genocide studies legitimized serious attention to an event that had been all but erased from historians' memory.[14] Still, much of the energy spent in these debates centered on whether a genocide had taken place.

Even as new works appeared, the Turkish official state denial had set the boundaries of the discussion to the neglect of important issues of interpretation and explanation. Much of the early literature did not deal explicitly with questions of causation. An important intervention by the political scientist Robert Melson labeled the denialist viewpoint appropriately the provocation thesis, that is, outside agitators provoked the Armenians within the Ottoman Empire and upset the relative harmony between peoples that had existed for many centuries. The Ottoman government's response to Armenian rebellion was measured and justified, in this view, and therefore it was the Armenians who brought on their own destruction.[15] As a form of explanation the provocation thesis remained on the political-ideological level and made no effort to probe the negative features of the Ottoman social and political order. No discussion was offered to explain why the overwhelming majority of Armenians acquiesced to Turkish rule and did not participate in rebellion. Nor was any explanation besides greed and ambition given to explain Armenian resistance. Like other conservative views of social discontent and revolution, arguments such as those put forth by Western historians from William L. Langer to Stanford Shaw and Turkish apologists like the former Foreign Ministry official Salahi R. Sonyel, repressed peoples had no right to resistance.[16]

Scholarship on the late Ottoman Empire and the fate of the Armenians burgeoned in the 1990s and 2000s. Historians of the Ottoman

Empire often treated the imperial history as one primarily of the Muslims, particularly Turks, but in time a broader, multinational history began to emerge that integrated the stories of the non-Muslims into the tapestry of the empire.[17] A pioneer in the study of the Armenian Genocide, the historical sociologist Vahakn N. Dadrian, made a major, if controversial, contribution to knowledge of 1915 in his synthetic volume, *The History of the Armenian Genocide*, arguing that the Genocide resulted from religious conflict and a Turkish culture of violence.[18] The beautifully written popular history of poet-memoirist Peter Balakian reproduced in evocative detail the horrors of what happened to the Ottoman Armenians, though his narrative only hinted at a causal argument and did not attempt a sustained explanation of why genocide happened.[19] Bernard Lewis made the classical statement explaining the Genocide as the result of conflicting nationalisms.[20] The argument from nationalism has dominated much of the subsequent historiography on the Genocide. In an anthology edited by Hovannisian, Robert Melson, R. Hrair Dekmejian, Hovannisian and Leo Kuper explain the Genocide as largely the result of Turkish nationalist ideology and the political ambitions of the İttihadist leaders.[21] An important (regrettably unpublished) contribution to the local study of the Genocide was written by Stephan H. Astourian, the author of major articles on the causes, development, and aftermath of 1915.[22] Exceptional work, indispensable to establish the truth about the often-obscured events of 1915, was carried out by two giants among researchers and analysts, Raymond Kévorkian and Wolfgang Gust, who collected the relevant documents that laid the indisputable foundation of facts of genocide.[23]

Perhaps most extraordinary of all, beginning with the former Turkish activist Taner Akçam, a few scholars of Turkish and Kurdish origin explored the blank spots of their own history.[24] Even while writing under the restraints imposed by the denialist state, scholars in Turkey and of Turkish, Kurdish, and Armenian origins used the available access to the archives and elevated the writing on the tragedies of the late Ottoman Empire to new levels of professional authority.[25] The formation of the Workshop for Armenian-Turkish Scholarship (WATS) brought together for the first time Turkish, Armenian, and other historians, sociologists, political scientists, and anthropologists in a common discussion of 1915, its causes and aftermath.[26] Once the static produced by denial was reduced, scholars were able to focus on the relevant but contested questions of why and when genocide occurred and who initiated it. Comparison with other genocides yielded important insights.[27] Among the principal volumes on the Armenian Genocide that benefited from engagement with and intimate acquaintance with Holocaust literature are works by the British historian Donald Bloxham.[28] Taking an international and comparative approach, Bloxham centers responsibility for genocide on choices made by state leaders, which were shaped by "perpetrator ideology," "the most important element in genocide," and seeks to explain not only mass killing but also the continued denial of it. Turkish nationalism, which he sees as "the ideology of the CUP," "alone could translate its agenda into mass expropriation and murder of Christians."[29] His analysis employs the notion of "cumulative radicalization," first used by the German historian Hans Mommsen to analyze the Holocaust. In a grand comparative study of ethnic cleansing and modern mass killing, the historical sociologist Michael Mann suggests a combination of ideological, economic, military, and political power as important ingredients in mass violence.[30] When, for example, an immanent ideology that reinforces already-formed social identities combines with a transcendent ideology that seeks to move beyond existing social organization, this toxic mix of ideological power increases the likelihood of violence. Both interstate warfare and the overlapping of ethnicity with economic inequality increase the likelihood of civil and ethnic conflict. Turning to the Armenian Genocide, Mann rejects the view that Turkish governments had a consistent, long-term genocidal intent. Like Bloxham, he emphasizes the radicalization of Turkish policies from the "exemplary repression" of Abdülhamid II through the encouragement and then forced application of Turkification, on to deportation (ethnic cleansing) and finally organized mass killing, genocide.

One hundred years after the Young Turk government decided to deport and massacre hundreds of thousands of Armenians and Assyrians the controversies over the Genocide still rage, but the balance has shifted dramatically and conclusively toward the view that the Ottoman government conceived, initiated, and implemented deliberate acts of ethnic cleansing and mass murder targeted at specific ethnoreligious communities. Although a handful of "scholars" continue to reject the argument that a genocide occurred or to rationalize the actions of the Ottomans as a necessary, indeed understandable, policy directed at national security, new generations of researchers continue to establish what happened and why. Neo-denialist accounts occasionally appear, but step by agonizing step more accurate accounts and plausible explanations are being generated by the present generation of historians, sociologists, anthropologists, political scientists, and their emerging graduate students.

NOTES

INTRODUCTION

1. Pierre Vidal-Naquet, *Les assassins de la mémoire* (Paris: La Découverte, *1987*)

2. The political scientist Robert Melson has called this argument the provocation thesis. See his *Revolution and Genocide: On the Origins of the Armenian Genocide and the Holocaust* (Chicago: University of Chicago Press, *1992*), and idem, "A Theoretical Inquiry into the Armenian Massacres of *1894–1986*," *Comparative Studies in Society and History 24 (1982): 481–509*). *Besides Turkish official historians, the few active defenders of the provocation thesis, or the notion of an Armenian-Turkish civil war, include Stanford J. Shaw and Ezel Kural Shaw, History of the Ottoman Empire and Modern Turkey (Cambridge: Cambridge University Press, 1977); Justin McCarthy, Muslims and Minorities: The Population of Ottoman Anatolia and the End of the Empire (New York: New York University Press, 1983), and idem, Turks and Armenians: A Manual on the Armenian Question (Washington, DC: Committee on Education, Assembly of Turkish American Associations, 1989); and Heath Lowry, The Story Behind Ambassador Morgenthau's Story (Istanbul: Isis, 1990).*

3. In the past ten years a more sophisticated neo-denialism has emerged, which elaborates the argument that the Armenians were involved in insurrectionary activity that necessitated a counterinsurgency response from the Young Turk government. A number of authors have worked with Professor M. Hakan Yavuz and published works with the University of Utah Press. While there are differences in emphasis and interpretation among their works, these writers are to a large degree sympathetic to the defensive attitudes of Turkish government and military officials, favor evidence and accounts exculpatory of the Young Turk policies, and emphatically reject the notion of genocidal intention. See, for example, Gunther Lewy, *The*

Armenian Massacres in Ottoman Turkey: A Disputed Genocide (Salt Lake City: University of Utah Press, 2005); Sean McMeekin, The Berlin-Baghdad Express: The Ottoman Empire and Germany's Bid for World Power (Cambridge, MA: The Belknap Press of Harvard University Press, 2010); idem, The Russian Origins of the First World War (Cambridge, MA: The Belknap Press of Harvard University Press, 2011), pp. 141–193; Edward J. Erickson, Ottomans and Armenians: A Study in Counterinsurgency (New York: Palgrave Macmillan, 2013); and M. Hakan Yavuz, "Orientalism, the 'Terrible Turk' and Genocide," *Middle East Critique* 23, no. 2 (2014): 111–126.

4. See the pioneering work of Vahakn Dadrian, mostly importantly, *The History of the Armenian Genocide: Ethnic Conflict from the Balkans to Anatolia to the Caucasus (Providence, RI: Berghahn, 1995),* and idem, *Warrant for Genocide: Key Elements of Turko-Armenian Conflict (New Brunswick, NJ: Transaction, 1999);* and Peter Balakian, *Black Dog of Fate, A Memoir* (New York: Basic, 1997; 2nd ed., 2009), and idem, *The Burning Tigris: The Armenian Genocide and America's Response* (New York: HarperCollins, 2003). For a critical review of Dadrian's *The History of the Armenian Genocide,* see Ronald Grigor Suny, in *Slavic Review* 55, no. 3 *(Fall 1996): 676–677.*

5. Genocide with a capital "G" will be used in this book to refer to the Armenian Genocide of 1915, while genocide with a lowercase "g" refers to the phenomenon more generally. This usage is consistent with the now conventional employment of Holocaust with a capital "H" to refer to the genocide of the Jews by the Nazis.

6. For a discussion of explanations that overemphasize religion or nationalism, see Ronald Grigor Suny, "Writing Genocide: The Fate of the Ottoman Armenians," in *A Question of Genocide: Armenians and Turks at the End of the Ottoman Empire,* ed. *Ronald Grigor Suny, Fatma Müge Göçek,* and Norman M. Naimark (New York: Oxford University Press, 2011), pp. 15–41.

7. Bernard Lewis, *The Emergence of Modern Turkey (Oxford: Oxford University Press, 1961; 2nd ed., 1968), p. 356. Lewis would later amend his sentence about the Armenian losses in the subsequent French translation of his book: "and thus a desperate struggle broke out between them, a struggle between two nations for the possession of a single homeland which ended with the terrible slaughter of 1915, when a million and a half Armenians perished, according to certain evaluations, as well as an unknown number of Turks." Lewis, Islam et laïcité: La naissance de la Turquie moderne (Paris: Fayard, 1988), p. 312; cited by Yves Ternon, "Freedom and Responsibility of the Historian: The 'Lewis Affair,'" in Remembrance and Denial: The Case of the Armenian Genocide, ed. Richard G. Hovannisian (Detroit: Wayne State University Press, 1999), p. 243.*

8. For a full discussion of the persistence and power of nineteenth-century empires, see Jürgen Osterhammel, *The Transformation of the World: A Global History of the Nineteenth Century, trans. Patrick Camiller (Princeton, NJ: Princeton University Press, 2014), pp. 392–468.*

9. For an account of the Workshop in Armenian-Turkish Scholarship, see Ronald Grigor Suny, "Truth in Telling: Reconciling Realities in the Genocide of the Ottoman Armenians," *American Historical Review 114, no. 4 (October 2009): 930–946.*

10. See, for example, Ara Sarafian (comp.), *United States Official Documents on the Armenian Genocide, Vols. I–III (Watertown, MA: The Armenian Review, 1993–1996); Raymond Kévorkian, The Armenian Genocide: A Complete History (London: I. B. Tauris, 2011); and Wolfgang Gust (ed.), The Armenian Genocide: Evidence from the German Foreign Office Archives, 1915–1916 (New York: Berghahn, 2014).*

11. Among the works that can be cited are Donald Bloxham, *The Great Game of Genocide: Imperialism, Nationalism, and the Destruction of the Ottoman Armenians (Oxford: Oxford University Press, 2005); David Gaunt, Massacres, Resistance, Protectors: Muslim-Christian Relations in Eastern Anatolia During World War I (Piscataway, NJ: Gorgias, 2006); Hans-Lukas Kieser and Dominik J. Schaller (eds.), Der Völkermord an den Armeniern und die Shoah / The Armenian Genocide and the Shoah (Zurich: Chronos, 2002); Michael Mann, The Dark Side of Democracy: Explaining Ethnic Cleansing (Cambridge: Cambridge University Press, 2005); Norman M. Naimark, Fires of Hatred: Ethnic Cleansing in Twentieth-Century Europe (Cambridge, MA: Harvard University Press, 2001); Benjamin Valentino, Final Solutions: Mass Killing and Genocide in the Twentieth Century (Ithaca, NY: Cornell University Press, 2004); Taner Akçam, From Empire to Republic: Turkish Nationalism and the Armenian Genocide (London: Zed, 2004); idem, A Shameful Act: The Armenian Genocide and the Question of Turkish Responsibility* (New York: Henry Holt, 2006); idem, *The Young Turks' Crime Against Humanity: The Armenian Genocide and Ethnic Cleansing in the Ottoman Empire* (Princeton, NJ: Princeton University Press, 2013); and the essays in Suny, Göçek, and Naimark (eds.), *A Question of Genocide.*

12. Akçam, *The Young Turks' Crime Against Humanity, p. xxiii.*

13. For an informative account of the Bilgi conference, see http://www.armenia pedia.org/wiki/Conference:_Ottoman_Armenians_During_the_Decline_of _the_Empire. I thank Jeanne Adanır for this information.

14. Bedross Der Matossian, "Venturing Into the Minefield: Turkish Liberal Historiography and the Armenian Genocide," in *The Armenian Genocide: Cultural and Ethnical Legacies, ed. Richard G. Hovannisian (New Brunswick, NJ: Transaction, 2007), pp. 369–388.*

15. Akçam, *The Young Turks' Crime Against Humanity, pp. 30–31; Kemal Karpat, Ottoman Population, 1830–1914: Demographic and Social Characteristics (Madison: University of Wisconsin Press, 1985), p. 190; McCarthy, Muslims and Minorities, p. 110.*

16. In the past few decades scholars have designated other early twentieth-century mass killings as genocides, arguing that the first genocide of the twentieth century occurred in German South-West Africa in 1904–1907, when the German military

suppressed revolts of the Herero and Nama peoples with massive deportation, killing, and imprisonment. See Isabel V. Hull, *Absolute Destruction: Military Culture and the Practices of War in Imperial Germany (Ithaca, NY: Cornell University Press, 2005), pp. 7–90.*

17. The literature on emotions and politics in sociology, anthropology, history, and political science has grown exponentially in the past decades, particularly pertaining to ethnic and civil violence. For a representative and influential treatment, see Roger D. Petersen, *Understanding Ethnic Violence: Fear, Hatred, and Resentment in Twentieth-Century Eastern Europe (Cambridge: Cambridge University Press, 2002).*

18. In his reply to an article on 1915 by Turkish Foreign Minister Ahmet Davutoğlu, the historian Gerard J. Libaridian writes, "It is difficult to imagine a 'shared history' that does not take into consideration the great inequality of agency that existed. A shared history does indeed exist, but it is not a history of equals between the Ottoman imperial state and its Armenian subjects." "Commentary on FM Davutoğlu's TPQ Article on the Armenian Issue," http://www.turkishpolicy.com/article/989/commentary-on-fm-davutoglus-article-on-the-armenian-issue/, p. 7.

19. In a fragment omitted from the published version of *Minima Moralia, Theodor Adorno observed that "what the Nazis did to the Jews was unspeakable: language had no word for it." And yet, "a term needed to be found if the victims...were to be spared the curse of having no thoughts turned unto them. So in English the concept of genocide was coined." As a result, Adorno continues, "the unspeakable was made, for the sake of protest, commensurable." "Messages in a Bottle," New Left Review, no. 200 (July–August 1993): 6; Geoff Dyer, The Missing of the Somme (London: Phoenix, 1994), p. 123. I thank Warren Breckman for this citation.*

CHAPTER ONE: Empire

1. The key text on Western images of the East is Edward Said, *Orientalism* (New York: Random House, 1978, 1997).

2. W. E. Gladstone, *Bulgarian Horrors and the Question of the East* (New York: Lovell, Adam, and Wesson, 1876), p. 9.

3. Virginia Aksan, "Ottoman Political Writing, 1768–1808," *International Journal of Middle Eastern Studies* 25, no. 1 (1993): 54–59.

4. For the early Ottoman state, see Halil Inalcik, *The Ottoman Empire: The Classical Age 1300–1600* (New York: Praeger, 1973), especially pp. 65–118.

5. Roderic Davison, "Nationalism as an Ottoman Problem and the Ottoman Response," in *Nationalism in a Non-National State,* ed. William W. Haddad and William Ochsenwald (Columbus: Ohio State University Press, 1977), p. 36; Stephan Astourian, "Testing World-Systems Theory, Cilicia (1830s–1890s): Armenian-Turkish Polarization and the Ideology of Modern Ottoman Historiography" (Ph.D. diss., University of California at Los Angeles, 1996), p. 367.

6. Aron Rodrigue, "Difference and Tolerance in the Ottoman Empire: Interview by Nancy Reynolds," *Stanford Humanities Review* 5, no. 1 (1995): 82.

7. For a fundamental investigation into the policies toward Ottoman non-Muslims, see the collection of important articles edited by Benjamin Braude and Bernard Lewis (eds.), *Christians and Jews in the Ottoman Empire: The Functioning of a Plural Society, Volume I: The Central Lands* (New York: Holmes and Meier, 1982).

8. Rodrigue, "Difference and Tolerance," p. 85.

9. M. Şükrü Hanioğlu, *A Brief History of the Late Ottoman Empire* (Princeton, NJ: Princeton University Press, 2008), p. 35.

10. This argument is at the center of the imperial model suggested in Karen Barkey, *Empire of Difference: The Ottomans in Comparative Perspective* (Cambridge: Cambridge University Press, 2008), pp. 1–27.

11. Fikret Adanır, "Semi-autonomous Provincial Forces in the Balkans and Anatolia," in *The Cambridge History of Turkey, vol. III, The Later Ottoman Empire, 1603–1839*, ed. Suraiya N. Faroqhi (Cambridge: Cambridge University Press, 2006), p. 172.

12. Barkey, *Empire of Difference*, pp. 86–93.

13. Karen Barkey, "Islam and Toleration: Studying the Ottoman Imperial Model," *International Journal of Politics, Culture, and Society* 19, nos. 1–2 (December 2005): 16.

14. For elaboration on the different forms of Islam in Morocco, Indonesia, and the early Ottoman Empire, see Clifford Geertz, *Islam Observed* (Chicago: University of Chicago Press, 1968), and Barkey, "Islam and Toleration," pp. 5–19.

15. Barkey, *Empire of Difference*, pp. 104–108.

16. Barkey, "Islam and Toleration," p. 10, n. 2.

17. Ibid., pp. 11–12.

18. Mustafa Aksakal, *The Ottoman Road to War in 1914: The Ottoman Empire and the First World War* (Cambridge: Cambridge University Press, 2008), p. x.

19. For discussion of the nation as "imagined community," see Benedict Anderson, *Imagined Communities: Reflections on the Origin and Spread of Nationalism* (London: Verso, 1983).

20. Eric J. Hobsbawm, *Nations and Nationalism Since 1780: Programme, Myth, Reality* (Cambridge: Cambridge University Press, 1990); Etienne Balibar, "The Nation Form: History and Ideology," in Etienne Balibar and Immanuel Wallerstein, *Race, Nation, Class: Ambiguous Identities* (London: Verso, 1991), pp. 86–106.

21. See, for example, the various paths taken by European nationalists and state builders in Matthew P. Fitzpatrick (ed.), *Liberal Imperialism in Europe* (New York: Palgrave Macmillan, 2012). The liberal nationalist Lajos Kossuth, a pioneer of Hungarian nationhood, toured his country in 1848 advocating a Danubian Confederation in which Magyars would constitute the ruling nation (ibid., pp. 1–2).

22. See, for example, Balibar, "The Nation Form"; Anderson, *Imagined Communities*.

23. On Marx and Engels, see Neil A. Martin, "Marxism, Nationalism and Russia," *Journal of the History of Ideas* 29, no. 2 (1968): 239–242; Anthony Brewer, *Marxist Theories of Imperialism: A Critical Survey* (London: Routledge, 2002); and Kevin Anderson, *Marx at the Margins: On Nationalism, Ethnicity and Non-Western Societies* (Chicago: University of Chicago Press, 2010).

24. The fundamental problem faced by empires in the nineteenth and twentieth centuries was governing the diversity of their realms. Developing thoughts of David Laitin and Richard Lachmann, Karen Barkey claims, "There are at least four different strategies that empires have exhibited toward ethnic and religious communities: toleration, persecution, assimilation, and expulsion." Barkey, *Empire of Difference*, p. 21, n. 39. The Ottomans would try all four.

25. While distinguishing the earlier centuries, where toleration and discrimination were largely free from persecution, from the nineteenth century, Aron Rodrigue carefully treads the fine line between romanticizing Ottoman practices and reading the pre-modern experience in light of the later nationalist conceptualizations. Yet in emphasizing the element of tolerance, he, like Braude and Lewis, focuses less on the effects of discriminatory power on non-Muslims.

26. Maarten Martinus Van Bruinessen, *Agha, Shaikh and State: On the Social and Political Organization of Kurdistan* (London: Zed, 1992), pp. 39–58. References here are to the 1978 edition of his dissertation.

27. These examples of the stereotyping of the Kurds are from Frederick Davis Greene, *The Armenian Crisis in Turkey: The Massacre of 1894, Its Antecedents and Significance* (New York: G. P. Putnam's Sons, 1895), pp. 49–50, 52.

28. Van Bruinessen, *Agha, Shaikh and State*, p. 61; J. G. Taylor, "Travels in Kurdistan, with notices of the sources of the eastern and western Tigris, and ancient ruins in their neighbourhood," *Journal of the Royal Geographical Society* 35 (1865): 51.

29. Van Bruinessen, *Agha, Shaikh and State*, pp. 189–208. A major source for eastern Anatolia in the seventeenth century is the travel accounts by Evliya Chelebi (1611–c. 1682), *Seyahatnamei* (10 vols., various editions and translations).

30. Van Bruinessen, *Agha, Shaikh and State*, pp. 119–122. For an early history and analysis of Armenian-Kurdish relations, see K. Sasuni, *Kiurt azgayin sharzhumnere ev Hai-Krtakan haraberutyunnere* (Beirut: Hamazgayin, 1969; originally published, 1981).

31. Reşat Kasaba, "Do States Always Favor Stasis? The Changing Status of Tribes in the Ottoman Empire," in *Boundaries and Belonging: States and Societies in the Struggle to Shape Identities and Local Practices*, ed. Joel S. Migdal (Cambridge: Cambridge University Press, 2004), pp. 27–48.

32. Selim Deringil, "'They Live in a State of Nomadism and Savagery': The Late Ottoman Empire and the Post-Colonial Debate," *Comparative Study of Social and History* 45, no. 2 (April 2003): 338.

33. Ibid.

34. Şerif Mardin, "Center-Periphery Relations: A Key to Turkish Politics," *Daedalus* 102, no. 1 (Winter 1973): 170–171. "Thus, in the more general, ecological sense, the center and the periphery were two very loosely related worlds. This aspect of Ottoman society, together with social fragmentation, set up one of the primary problems of the Ottoman establishment: the confrontation between the Sultan and his officials on the one hand, and the highly segmented structure of Ottoman Anatolia on the other" (p. 171).

35. Ibid., p. 173.

36. Gaunt, *Massacres*, pp. 31–32; Van Bruinessen, *Agha, Shaikh and State*, pp. 222–227. In this book Nestorians, along with Chaldeans and other Syriac denominations, will be referred to as Assyrians.

37. Wadie Jwaideh, *The Kurdish National Movement: Its Origins and Development* (Syracuse, NY: Syracuse University Press, 2006), pp. 62–75.

38. The Naqshbandi is a major order of Sunni Sufism that traces its genealogy back to Muhammad, the founder of Islam.

39. Van Bruinessen, *Agha, Shaikh and State*, pp. 295–296.

40. Stephan Astourian, "On the Genealogy of the Armenian-Turkish Conflict: Sultan Abdülhamid, and the Armenian Massacres," *Journal of the Society for Armenian Studies* 21 (2012): 183.

41. Mardin, "Center-Periphery Relations," p. 174.

42. Van Bruinessen, *Agha, Shaikh and State*, pp. 229–233, 296. See also Oya Gözel, "The Implementation of the Ottoman Land Code of 1858 in Eastern Anatolia" (master's thesis, Middle East Technical University, 2007), etd.lib.metu.edu.tr /upload/12608323/index.pdf.

43. *British Documents on Ottoman Armenians, I* (1856–1880), ed. Bilal N. Simsir (Ankara: Türk Tarih Kurumu, 1982); Elke Hartmann, "The Central State in the Borderlands: Ottoman Eastern Anatolia in the Late Nineteenth Century," in *Shatterzone of Empires: Coexistence and Violence in the German, Habsburg, Russian, and Ottoman Borderlands*, ed. Omer Bartov and Eric D. Weitz (Bloomington: Indiana University Press, 2013), p. 179.

44. Cited in Gözel, "The Implementation of the Ottoman Land Code of 1858," p. 71; "Inclosure 9 in No 326, Report by Captain Clayton," in Simsir (ed.), *British Documents on Ottoman Armenians, I*, p. 651.

45. Cited in Mikhail Semenovich Lazarev, *Kurdskii vopros (1891–1917)* (Moscow: Nauka, 1972), p. 40; Arkhiv Vnesnoi politiki Rossii, f. "Politarkhiv," 1901 g., d. 711, ll. 36, 45, report from May 4, 1901.

46. Edward Noel, "The Character of the Kurds as Illustrated by Their Proverbs and Popular Sayings," *Bulletin of the School of Oriental Studies* 1, no. 4 (1920): 89–90.

47. Ibid., pp. 79–82, 87–88.

48. Cited in Gözel, "The Implementation of the Ottoman Land Code of 1858," p. 109; "No. 144, Major Trotter, R. E., to the Marquis of Salisbury, Diarbekir, January 17, 1879, F.O. 424/80," in Simsir (ed.), *British Documents on Ottoman Armenians, I*, p. 304.

49. Stephan H. Astourian, "The Silence of the Land: Agrarian Relations, Ethnicity, and Power," in Suny et al. (eds.), *A Question of Genocide*, p. 72; H. M. Poghosian, *Zeytuni Patmutyune 1409–1921 TT* (Erevan: Hayastan, 1969), pp. 161–162; and Aghassi [Garapet Tour-Sarkissian], *Zeïtoun: Depuis les origines jusqu'à l'insurrection de 1895*, trans. Archag Tchobanian (Paris: Mercure de France, 1898), p. 108.

50. Astourian, "On the Genealogy of the Armenian-Turkish Conflict," pp. 177–180.

51. Janet Klein, *The Margins of Empire: Kurdish Militias in the Ottoman Tribal Zone* (Stanford, CA: Stanford University Press, 2011), pp. 4–5, 20.

52. *Paşa* (Pasha in English) is the Turkish word for a high military officer corresponding to the Western "general." The Turkish letter ş used throughout this book is equivalent to the English sound "sh."

53. Janet Klein, "State, Tribe, Dynasty, and the Contest over Diyarbekir," in Jongerden and Verheij (eds.), *Social Relations in Ottoman Diyarbekir*, p. 161.

54. "Report on the Armenian Position in the Van Vilayet, enclosed with Dickson to Baclay," no. 4, Van, September 24, 1906, Foreign Office 424/210; cited in Klein, "State, Tribe, Dynasty, and the Contest over Diyarbekir," p. 149, n. 103.

55. Klein, "State, Tribe, Dynasty, and the Contest over Diyarbekir," p. 169.

56. Şerif Mardin, *Religion, Society, and Modernity in Turkey* (Syracuse, NY: Syracuse University Press, 2006), pp. 128–130.

57. Cited in Hanioğlu, *A Brief History of the Ottoman Empire*, p. 74.

58. Hartmann, "The Central State in the Borderlands," p. 175.

59. Hanioğlu, *A Brief History of the Ottoman Empire*, p. 75.

60. Carter V. Findley, "The Acid Test of Ottomanism: The Acceptance of Non-Muslims in the Late Ottoman Bureaucracy," in Braude and Lewis (eds.), *Christians and Jews, I*, pp. 363–364.

61. See Frederick Cooper and Randall Packard, "Introduction," in *International Development and the Social Sciences: Essays on the History and Politics of Knowledge*, ed. Frederick Cooper and Randall Packard (Berkeley: University of California Press, 1997), pp. 1–41.

62. "Ottomanism was mainly a literary tradition in that the intellectuals who espoused it rarely went farther than authoring theoretical articles about the need for a conception of Ottoman citizenship." Uğur Ümit Üngör, *The Making of Modern Turkey: Nation and State in Eastern Anatolia, 1913–1950* (Oxford: Oxford University Press, 2011), pp. 26–27.

63. Deringil, "'They Live in a State of Nomadism and Savagery,'" p. 328.

64. Ibid., p. 338.

CHAPTER TWO: Armenians

1. Odysseus [Sir Charles Norton Eliot], *Turkey in Europe* (London: Edward Arnold, 1908), p. 384.

2. Robert W. Thomson, *Moses Khorenats'i: History of the Armenians* (Cambridge, MA: Harvard University Press, 1978; Ann Arbor: Caravan Books, 2006), pp. 66–67.

3. See Philip Curtin, *Cross-Cultural Trade in World History* (Cambridge: Cambridge University Press, 1984), pp. 182–206, and Sebouh Aslanian, *From the Indian Ocean to the Mediterranean: The Global Trade Networks of Armenian Merchants from New Julfa* (Berkeley: University of California Press, 2011).

4. Immanuel Kant, *Anthropology from a Pragmatic Point of View*, trans. and intro. Mary J. Gregor(Carbondale: Southern Illinois University Press, 1978), p. 236. My thanks to Samuel Weeks for finding this quotation.

5. Sebouh Aslanian, "Dispersion History and the Polycentric Nation: The Role of Simeon Yerevantsi's *Girk* or *Koči Partavčar* in the 18th Century National Revival," *Bibliotheque d'Arménologie Bazmavep*, no. 39 (Venice: S. Lazarus, 2004), p. 14.

6. I have explored the fragmented earlier self-images of Armenians in the introduction to my *Looking Toward Ararat: Armenia in Modern History* (Bloomington: Indiana University Press, 1993), pp. 1–11. See also Razmik Panossian, *The Armenians: From Kings and Priests to Merchants and Commissars* (New York: Columbia University Press, 2006).

7. *The Life and Adventures of Joseph Emin, An Armenian, Written in English by Himself* (London, 1792; 2nd ed., ed. Amy Apcar, Calcutta: Baptist Mission Press, 1918), p. 112.

8. Kevork Bardakjian, *The Mekhitarist Contributions to Armenian Culture and Scholarship* (Cambridge, MA: Harvard College Library, 1976).

9. For an account of the development of the first secular intellectuals among Armenians, see Ronald Grigor Suny, "The Emergence of the Armenian Patriotic Intelligentsia in Russia," in *Looking Toward Ararat*, pp. 52–62.

10. James Etmekjian, *The French Influence on the Western Armenian Renaissance* (New York: Twayne, 1964), p. 72.

11. Cited in Aslanian, "Dispersion History," p. 58.

12. An English translation of the abbreviated version of Chamchian's history is available: Father Michael Chamich, *History of Armenia From B.C. 2247 to the Year of Christ 1780, or 1299 of the Armenian Era*, trans. Johannes Avdall (Calcutta: Bishop's College Press, 1827).

13. *Mair tsutsak hayeren dzeragrats matendaranin Mekhitariants I Venetik* 1 (1914): 321; cited in Gerard Libaridian, "The Ideology of Armenian Liberation: The Development of Armenian Political Movement Before the Revolutionary Movement (1639–1885)" (Ph.D. diss., University of California at Los Angeles, 1987), p. 31.

14. Quoted in M. K. Zulalian, *Armeniia v pervoi polovine XVI v.* (Moscow, 1971), p. 37.

15. Cited in Fatma Müge Göçek, *Denial of Violence: Ottoman Past, Turkish Present, and Collective Violence Against the Armenians, 1789–2009* (New York: Oxford University Press, 2014), p. 77; Cabi Ömer Efendi, *Cabi Tarihi—Tarih-i Sultan Selim-i Salis ve Mahmud-u Sani (Cabi Chronicle: The History of [Sultans] Selim III and Mahmud I)* (Ankara: TTK, 2003), vol. II, pp. 803–806.

16. Frederic C. Lane, *Venice, A Maritime Republic* (Baltimore: Johns Hopkins University Press, 1973), p. 300.

17. Zaven Der Yeghiayan [Armenian patriarch of Constantinople, 1913–1922], *My Patriarchal Memoirs*, trans. Ared Misirliyan, ed. Vatche Ghazarian (Barrington, RI: Mayreni, 2002), p. 19.

18. Murat Cankara, "Rethinking Ottoman Cross-cultural Encounters: Turks and the Armenian Alphabet," unpublished manuscript, p. 3.

19. Ibid., pp. 8–10.

20. Börte Sagaster, "The Role of Turcophone Armenians as Literary Innovators and Mediators of Culture in the Early Days of Modern Turkish Literature," in *Between Religion and Language: Turkish-Speaking Christians, Jews and Greek-Speaking Muslims and Catholics in the Ottoman Empire*, ed. Evangelia Balta and Mehmet Ölmez (Istanbul: Eren, 2011), pp. 108–109.

21. Rodrigue, "Difference and Tolerance," pp. 6–7.

22. Mentioned in Nora Cherishian Lessersohn, "'Local Cosmopolitanism' in Late Ottoman Provincial Society: Recovering Armenian Complexity through Hovhannes Cherishian's (1886–1967) Memoir," unpublished manuscript.

23. Fatma Müge Göçek, *Rise of the Bourgeoisie, Demise of Empire: Ottoman Westernization and Social Change* (New York: Oxford University Press, 1996), p. 35.

24. I am grateful to Fatma Müge Göçek for this insight.

25. Selim Deringil, "'The Armenian Question is Finally Closed': Mass Conversions of Armenians in Anatolia during the Hamidian Massacres of 1895–1897," *Comparative Studies in Society and History* 51, no. 2 (2009): 347. Even after 1844 "apostasy was still seen by the Muslim general population as a moral sin, and many an Armenian [who had converted to Islam] was deterred from apostasy by a fear that his Muslim neighbors might well take the law into their own hands, as in fact often occurred."

26. George Bournoutian (trans. and commentary), *Russia and the Armenians of Transcaucasia, 1797–1889: A Documentary Record* (Costa Mesa, CA: Mazda, 1998), p. 421.

27. Clarence D. Ussher, *An American Physician in Turkey: A Narrative of Adventures in Peace and War* (Boston: Houghton Mifflin, 1917; reprinted, London, 2002), p. 79; Kévorkian, *The Armenian Genocide*, p. 319.

28. Jeremy Salt, *Imperialism, Evangelism, and the Ottoman Armenians, 1878–1896* (London: Frank Cass, 1993), pp. 30–39.

29. Mrs. Bishop [Isabella L. Bird], *Journeys in Persia and Kurdistan*, 2 vols. (London: John Murray, 1891), vol. II, p. 336.

30. Mark Sykes, *Through Five Turkish Provinces* (London: Bickers and Son, 1900), p. 80; see also Robert Adelson, *Mark Sykes, Portrait of an Amateur* (London: Jonathan Cape Ltd., 1975), p. 65.

31. Karl Marx, *The Communist Manifesto*, chapter 1.

32. Fatma Müge Göcek and Murat Özyüksel, "The Ottoman Empire's Negotiation of Western Liberal Imperialism," in Fitzpatrick (ed.), *Liberal Imperialism in Europe*, p. 193.

33. On the non-Muslim bourgeoisie, see Y. Doğan Çetınkaya, *The Young Turks and the Boycott Movement: Nationalism, Protest and the Working Classes in the Formation of Modern Turkey* (London: I. B. Tauris, 2014), pp. 13–20.

34. Justin McCarthy, "Foundations of the Turkish Republic: Social and Economic Change," *Middle Eastern Studies* 19, no. 2 (April 1983): 139–151. The figures for the *kaza* (district) are lower than the non-Muslim figure for the town would be because of the larger representation of Muslims in the surrounding peasantry.

35. Bedross Der Matossian, "The Armenian Commercial Houses and Merchant Networks in the 19th Century Ottoman Empire," *Turcica* (2007): 147–174.

36. See the study of the Muslim Nemlizade family of Trabzon as an example of an important Muslim merchant network: Yaşar Tolga Cora, "A Muslim Great Merchant (*Tüccar*) Family in the Late Ottoman Empire: A Case Study of the Nemlizades, 1860–1930," *International Journal of Turkish Studies* 19, nos. 1–2 (2013): 1–29.

37. Fatma Müge Göçek argues that the Ottoman bourgeoisie was divided between a commercial non-Muslim element and a Muslim bureaucratic element. The non-Muslims lacked political power, while the Muslim elite interested in state reform lacked independent economic resources. *Rise of the Bourgeoisie*, pp. 138–139, *passim*.

38. Donald Quataert, *Social Disintegration and Popular Resistance in the Ottoman Empire, 1881–1908* (New York: New York University Press, 1983), p. 79.

39. Çetinkaya, *The Young Turks and the Boycott Movement*, pp. 58–71.

40. Göcek and Özyüksel, "The Ottoman Empire's Negotiation of Western Liberal Imperialism," p. 197.

41. Astourian, "Testing World-Systems Theory, Cilicia (1830s–1890s)," pp. 552–563. See also Donald Quataert, "The Commercialization of Agriculture in Ottoman Turkey, 1800–1914," *International Journal of Turkish Studies* 1, no. 2 (Autumn 1980): 38–55.

42. This insightful point was conveyed to me in the research and writing of the young scholar Dzovinar Derderian.

43. Cited in Astourian, "The Silence of the Land," p. 65; Great Britain, Foreign Office, Confidential Print, Turkey, *Further Correspondence respecting the Affairs of Asiatic Turkey and Arabia*, FO 424, Volume 239, Document 321 (hereafter FO424/239/32), enclosure by Fitzmaurice, annexed to a report by Marling to Sir Edward Grey (Constantinople, 27 August 1913), pp. 346–347.

44. Nilay Özok-Gündoğan, "A 'Peripheral' Approach to the 1908 Revolution in the Ottoman Empire: Land Disputes in Peasant Petitions in Post-Revolutionary Diyarbekir," in *Social Relations in Ottoman Diyarbekir, 1870–1915*, ed. Joost Jongerden and Jelle Verheij (Leiden: Brill, 2012), pp. 210–212.

45. Hagop Barsoumian, "Economic Role of the Armenian Amira Class in the Ottoman Empire," *The Armenian Review* 31 (March 1979): 310–316. See also the publication of his dissertation, idem, *The Armenian Amira Class of Istanbul* (Yerevan: American University of Armenia, 2007).

46. Elke Hartmann, "The 'Loyal Nation' and Its Deputies: The Armenians in the First Ottoman Parliament," in *The First Ottoman Experiment in Democracy*, ed. Christoph Herzog and Malek Sharif (Würzburg: Ergon Verlag, 2010), p. 208.

47. Ibid., pp. 187–190.

48. Göçek, *Denial of Violence*, p. 117; Falih Rıfkı Atay, *Batış Yılları* (Istanbul: Bateş, 1999), pp. 14–15, 18–19.

49. Göçek, *Denial of Violence*, p. 119; Halid Ziya Uşakıgil, *Kırk Yıl: Anılar* (Istanbul: İnkılap, 1987), pp. 547–548.

50. The classic work on the *Tanzimat* is Roderic Davison, *Reform in the Ottoman Empire, 1856–76* (Princeton, NJ: Princeton University Press, 1963). See also his very useful essay, "*Millets* as Agents of Change in Nineteenth-Century Ottoman Empire," in Braude and Lewis (eds.), *Christians and Jews, I*, pp. 319–337.

51. A first draft prepared by the Armenian elite in Istanbul was rejected by the Sublime Porte in 1857, probably because it included Armenians outside the Ottoman Empire within its purview. See Masayuki Ueno, "The First Draft of the Armenian *Millet* Constitution," *Annals of Japan Association for Middle East Studies* 23, no. 1 (2007): 213–251.

52. For a discussion of Armenians and the *Tanzimat*, see Masayuki Ueno, "'For the Fatherland and the State': Armenians Negotiate the Tanzimat Reforms," *International Journal of Middle East Studies* 41, no. 1 (2013): 93–109.

53. For the intricacies of the Armenian Church's internal politics as well as its relationship to the *Tanzimat*, see Richard Antaramian, "In Subversive Service of the Sublime State: Armenians and Ottoman State Power, 1844–1896" (Ph.D. diss., University of Michigan, 2014).

54. *Teghekagir Gavarakan Harstaharuteants* (Constantinople, 1876); discussed at length in Antaramian, "In Subversive Service," chapter 5.

55. The 1872 report by Khrimian was published in English in *Reports on Provincial Oppressions: Official Publications of the Armenian National Patriarchate at Constantinople* (London: Gilbert and Rivington, 1877), pp. 1–8.

56. Hartmann, "The 'Loyal Nation' and Its Deputies," pp. 193–195.

57. Roderic H. Davison, "Turkish Attitudes Concerning Christian-Muslim Equality in the Nineteenth Century," *American Historical Review* 40 (1953–1954): 859; Robert Devereux, *The First Ottoman Constitutional Period: A Study of the Midhat Constitution and Parliament* (Baltimore: John Hopkins University Press, 1963), p. 223; and Fikret Adanır, "Non-Muslims in the Ottoman Army and the Ottoman Defeat in the Balkan War of 1912–1913," in Suny et al. (eds.), *A Question of Genocide*, p. 115.

58. Cited by Göçek, *Denial of Violence*, p. 88, from Abdülhamid II's memoirs. It is not clear which of the sultan's memoirs this particular citation comes from, the more authentic or the more doubtful. In either case the quotation illustrates a familiar attitude of the time.

CHAPTER THREE: Nation

1. Pieter M. Judson makes this point about nationalists operating in multilingual frontier regions of the Habsburg Empire. "Making National Space on the Habsburg Austrian Borderlands, 1880–1918," in Bartov and Weitz (eds.), *Shatterzone of Empires*, p. 127.

2. "Organic intellectuals" is a term coined by the Marxist theorist Antonio Gramsci, who distinguished between "traditional intellectuals," whom he considered to be concerned with the disinterested search for reason and truth, and "organic intellectuals," who spoke for the interests of a specific interest group (in Gramsci's view, a particular social class). "Organic intellectuals" in the usage here speaks for the interests of a specific nation or state.

3. On the issue of territorialization of Armenian nationalism, see Vahe Sahakyan, "Diasporic Identities and Diasporic Representations in Post-Genocide Armenian Diaspora" (Ph.D. diss., University of Michigan, 2015).

4. *Reports on Provincial Oppressions*, p. 44.

5. Libaridian, "The Ideology of Armenian Liberation," p. 191.

6. Astourian, "Testing World-Systems Theory, Cilicia (1830s–1890s)," pp. 431–432.

7. Libaridian, "The Ideology of Armenian Liberation," pp. 145–146.

8. Antaramian, "In Subversive Service," chapter 5, pp. 32–33.

9. Bournoutian, *Russia and the Armenians of Transcaucasia*, pp. 438–439.

10. Cited in Astourian, "Testing World-Systems Theory, Cilicia (1830s–1890s)," pp. 394–395.

11. Göçek, *Denial of Violence*, p. 75; Zekeriya M. Sertel, *Hatırladıklarım* (Istanbul: Remzi, 2000), p. 16.

12. Göçek, *Denial of Violence*, p. 76; Atay, *Batış Yılları*, pp. 5–6.

13. For a particularly telling reading of Turkish attitudes toward the *gâvur* (unbeliever) and Armenians, see Stephan Astourian's analysis of Turkish proverbs in Astourian, "Testing World-Systems Theory, Cilicia (1830s–1890s)," pp. 409–431.

14. Bournoutian, *Russia and the Armenians of Transcaucasia*, pp. 282–283.

15. Ibid., p. 286. Lazarev himself was a descendant of a prominent Armenian family in Russia.

16. Gaunt, *Massacres*, p. 46.

17. George Bournoutian, *Eastern Armenia in the Last Decades of Persian Rule, 1807–1828: A Political and Socioeconomic Study of the Khanate of Erevan on the Eve of the Russian Conquest* (Malibu, CA: Undena, 1982), pp. 61–77; and Richard G. Hovannisian, *Armenia on the Road to Independence, 1918* (Berkeley: University of California Press, 1967), pp. 13, 15.

18. Austin Jersild and Neli Melkadze, "The Dilemmas of Enlightenment in the Eastern Borderlands: The Theater and Library in Tbilisi," *Kritika* 3, no. 1 (Winter 2002): 27–49.

19. Raffi [Hagop Melik-Hagopian], "Inchov enk mkhitaroum?" *Erker zhoghovatsou*, vol. 9 (Erevan, 1964), p. 501; cited in Aslanian, "Dispersion History," p. 82.

20. Based on the translations by Alice Stone Blackwell, *Armenian Poems Rendered into English Verse* (Boston: Atlantic Printing Company, 1917).

21. Rafayel Patkanian, "Nori tari," in *Erker* (Erevan: Sovetakan Grogh Hratarakchutyun, 1980), p. 91.

22. Raffi [Hakob Melik-Haobian], *Khente: Arkatner verjin rus-trkakan paterazmits*, trans. Donald Abcarian, *The Fool: Events from the Last Russo-Turkish War (1877–78)* (Princeton, NJ: Gomidas, 2000).

23. Bournoutian, *Russia and the Armenians of Transcaucasia*, pp. 450–451.

24. Ibid., pp. 444–445.

25. On Zeytun, see Astourian, "Testing World-Systems Theory, Cilicia (1830s–1890s)," pp. 573–582.

26. For Armenian writers divisions among Armenians are treated in two ways: either ignored altogether, so that the nation becomes a homogeneous whole, or presented as an unfortunate deviance toward disunity that damaged the national cause.

Gerard Libaridian, on the other hand, distinguishes two forms of oppression of the Armenian people: by alien and incompetent Ottoman rulers and by the exploitative and self-interested Armenian upper classes, the clergy, rich merchants, and bankers. Libaridian, "The Ideology of Armenian Liberation."

27. Bournoutian, *Russia and the Armenians of Transcaucasia*, pp. 297–299.

28. Houri Berberian, "Traversing Boundaries and Selves: Iranian-Armenian Identities During the Iranian Constitutional Revolution," *Comparative Studies of South Asia, Africa and the Middle East* 25, no. 2 (2005): 289.

29. Ibid.

30. Ibid., p. 291; see also Mohamad Tavakoli-Targhi, "Refashioning Iran: Language and Culture During the Constitutional Revolution," *Iranian Studies* 23 (1990): 93.

31. Bournoutian, *Russia and the Armenians of Transcaucasia*, pp. 446–447.

32. See Ronald Grigor Suny, "Populism, Nationalism, and Marxism among Russia's Armenians," in *Looking Toward Ararat*, pp. 63–78.

33. Gerard J. Libaridian, "What Was Revolutionary about Armenian Revolutionary Parties in the Ottoman Empire?" in Suny et al. (eds.), *A Question of Genocide*, p. 101; "*Dzragir*" [Program (of the Hnchak party)], *Hnchak*, nos. 11–12 (1888), reproduced in Arsen Kitur, *Patmutyun S. D. Hnchak kusaktsutyun*, 2 vols. (Beirut, 1962), vol. I, p. 35.

34. Kévorkian, *The Armenian Genocide*, p. 18; Stepanos Sapah-Gulian, "Eritasard Turkia," *Hnchak*, no. 2 (February 10, 1901): 11.

35. Kévorkian, *The Armenian Genocide*, p. 21; H. Kh., "Eritsard Turkia ev Eritsard Hayastan Antagonizme," *Hnchak*, no. 2 (May 1, 1902): 13–14.

CHAPTER FOUR: Great Powers

1. "Manifesto of the Emperor of Russia Announcing War with Turkey," St. Petersburg, April 24, 1877, in Sir Edward Hertslet (comp. and ed.), *The Map of Europe by Treaty, Showing the Various Political and Territorial Changes Which Have Taken Place Since the General Peace of 1814, IV, 1875–1891* (London: Her Majesty's Stationery Office, 1891), pp. 2588–2589.

2. *Reports on Provincial Oppressions*, p. 44.

3. Hartmann, "The 'Loyal Nation' and Its Deputies," p. 219.

4. Ibid., p. 220.

5. Davison, "The *Millets* as Agents of Change in the Nineteenth Century Ottoman Empire," p. 329.

6. Armen Garo, *Bank Ottoman: Memoirs of Armen Garo, The Armenian Ambassador to America from the Independent Republic of Armenia*, ed. and intro. Simon Vratzian, trans. Haig T. Partizian (Detroit: Armen Topouzian, 1990), pp. 47–48. The Armenian original is Armen Garo, *Aruats Orer* (Lived Days) (Boston: Hairenik, 1948).

7. Astourian, "On the Genealogy of the Armenian-Turkish Conflict," p. 175; Arshag O. Sarkissian, *History of the Armenian Question to 1885*, Illinois Studies in the Social Sciences 22, nos. 3–4 (Urbana: University of Illinois Press, 1938), p. 58.

8. Suavi Aydın and Jelle Verheij, "Confusion in the Cauldron: Some Notes on Ethno-religious Groups, Local Powers and the Ottoman State in Diyarbekir Province, 1800–1870," in Jongerden and Verheij (eds.), *Social Relations in Ottoman Diyarbekir*, p. 48.

9. Cited in Manoug J. Somakian, *Empires in Conflict: Armenia and the Great Powers 1895–1920* (London: I. B. Tauris, 1995), p. 7. See also Brad Dennis, "The Debate on the Early 'Armenian Question' 1877–1896: Strengths, Weaknesses, Lacunae and Ways Forward," *Middle East Critique* 20, no. 3 (Fall 2011): 271–289.

10. For an overview of British policy toward the Ottoman Empire and the Armenians, see Arman J. Kirakossian, *British Diplomacy and the Armenian Question from the 1830s to 1914* (Princeton, NJ: Gomidas, 2003).

11. Dan Diner, "Between Empire and Nation State: Outline for a European Contemporary Outline for the History of the Jews, 1750–1950," in Bartov and Weitz (eds.), *Shatterzone of Empires*, pp. 64–65.

12. Fuat Dündar, *Crime of Numbers: The Role of Statistics in the Armenian Question (1878–1918)* (New Brunswick, NJ: Transaction, 2010), p. 160.

13. Ibid., pp. 12–13.

14. Ibid., p. 14.

15. *Harissa* is a meat porridge made with lamb or other meats and cracked wheat.

16. Christopher J. Walker, *Armenia, The Survival of a Nation* (London: Croom Helm, 1980; rev. 2nd ed., New York: St. Martin's, 1990), p. 117; Panossian, *The Armenians from Kings and Priests to Merchants and Commissars*, p. 172.

17. K. Tololyan, "Martyrdom as Legitimacy: Terrorism, Religion and Symbolic Appropriation in the Armenian Diaspora," in *Contemporary Research on Terrorism*, ed. Paul Wilkinson and Alasdair M. Stewart (Aberdeen: Aberdeen University Press, 1987), p. 96.

18. Dündar, *Crime of Numbers*, p. 23.

19. Ibid., p. 17.

20. Cited in Jwaideh, *The Kurdish National Movement*, p. 83.

21. Dennis, "The Debate on the Early 'Armenian Question,'" p. 273.

22. Jo Laycock, *Imagining Armenia: Orientalism, Ambiguity and Intervention* (Manchester: Manchester University Press, 2009), p. 37.

23. See Kirakossian, *British Diplomacy and the Armenian Question*, and idem (ed. and intro.), *The Armenian Massacres, 1894–1896: U.S. Media Testimony* (Detroit: Wayne State University Press, 2004).

24. Balakian, *The Burning Tigris*, p. 64.

25. George Young, *Constantinople* (New York: Barnes & Noble, 1992; originally published, 1926), p. 218; cited in Astourian, "On the Genealogy of the Armenian-Turkish Conflict," p. 190.

26. William L. Langer, *The Diplomacy of Imperialism*, 2 vols. (New York: Alfred A. Knopf, 1935), vol. I, p. 159. Langer does not ask if what Abdul Hamid "felt," "knew," and "believed" was accurate or a fantasy or self-delusion. He places most of the blame for the Armenian massacres on Armenian revolutionaries who stirred up trouble to provoke a fierce Ottoman response, which they presumed would be met with European intervention. "The [Hnchak] leaders were quite prepared to have thousands of their fellow-countrymen massacred in order to force intervention by the European powers and in order to raise from the ruins of the Ottoman Empire a new Armenian socialist state" (p. 163).

27. Hanioğlu, *A Brief History of the Ottoman Empire*, p. 128.

28. Erik J. Zürcher, *Turkey, A Modern History* (London: I. B. Tauris, 1997), p. 83.

29. Cited in Mustafa Aksakal, "'Holy War Made in Germany'? Ottoman Origins of the 1914 Jihad," *War in History* 18, no. 2 (2011): 9; Selim Deringil, *The Well-Protected Domains: Ideology and the Legitimation of Power in the Ottoman Empire, 1876–1909* (London: I. B. Tauris, 1998), p. 46.

30. Cited in Carter V. Findley, *Bureaucratic Reform in the Ottoman Empire: The Sublime Porte, 1789–1922* (Princeton, NJ: Princeton University Press, 1980), p. 221.

31. Antaramian, "In Subversive Service," chapter 3.

32. Astourian, "On the Genealogy of the Armenian-Turkish Conflict," pp. 191–192.

33. See Antaramian, "In Subversive Service," chapter 6; FO 195/1376 No. 15P, Van (29 March 1881); FO 195/1804 No. 40, Erzeroum (9 November 1893); FO 195/1688 no. 10 (4 March 1890), and decipher telegram, Erzeroum (21 June 1890).

34. Cited in Murat Özyüksel, *Osmanlı İmparatorluğu'nda Nüfuz Mücadelesi: Anadolu ve Bağdat Demiryolları* (Istanbul: Türkiye İş Bankası Kültür Yayınları, 2000), p. 100; Tefrik Komisyonu Riyaset-i Umumisi'ne, BOA [Başbakanlık Osmanlı Arşivi (Ottoman Archives, Istanbul), hereafter: BOA] /DH.TMİK. S., 1/37; see also Murat Özyüksel, *Jostling for Influence in the Ottoman Empire: The Anatolian and Baghdad Railroads* (London: I. B. Taurus, 2015).

35. M. Şükrü Hanioglu, *The Young Turks in Opposition* (Oxford: Oxford University Press, 1995), p. 142.

36. Murat Özyüksel, "Rail and Rule: Railway-Building and Railway-Politics in the Ottoman Empire," in Jörn Leonhard and Ulrike von Hirschhausen (eds.), *Comparing Empires: Encounters and Transfers in the Long Nineteenth Century* (Göttingen: Vandenhoeck and Ruprecht, 2012), pp. 116–117; see also idem, *Hicaz Demiryolu* (Istanbul: Tarih Vakfı Yurt Yayınları, 2000), pp. 65–67, and its English translation: *The*

Hejaz Railway and the Ottoman Empire: Modernity, Industrialization and Ottoman Decline (London: I. B. Taurus, 2015), pp. 82–85. Özyüksel makes the important distinction that Abdülhamid's alleged pan-Islamism was a domestic program, not an effort to unify all Muslims throughout the world. "The challenge was to prevent the virus of nationalism from infecting the non-Turkish Muslim peoples, namely Arabs, Kurds, and Albanians." Özyüksel, "Rail and Rule," p. 117.

37. The British traveler H. F. B. Lynch paints an unflattering picture of the *Hamidiye* in his *Armenia, Travels and Studies, II, The Turkish Provinces* (London, 1901; reprinted, Beirut: Khayats, 1965), pp. 4–5.

38. Joost Jongerden, "Elite Encounters of a Violent Kind: Milli İbrahim Paşa, Ziya Gökalp and Political Struggle in Diyarbekir at the Turn of the 20th Century," in Jongerden and Verheij (eds.), *Social Relations in Ottoman Diyarbekir*, pp. 61–62. For a view that emphasizes the repressive role that the *Hamidiye* played against Armenians, see Stephen Duguid, "The Politics of Unity: Hamidian Policy in Eastern Anatolia," *Middle Eastern Studies* 9, no. 2 (May 1973): 139–155.

39. Cited in Aydın and Verheij, "Confusion in the Cauldron," p. 49.

40. Klein, "State, Tribe, Dynasty, and the Contest over Diyarbekir," p. 152.

41. Cemal Kafadar, "The Question of Decline," *Harvard Middle Eastern and Islamic Review* 4, nos. 1–2 (1997–1998): 30–75.

42. Edhem Eldem, "From the Chios Massacre to the 'Unspeakable Turk': Memory, Acceptance and Denial in the Late Nineteenth Century," unpublished paper, 2013.

43. Mark Levene makes the telling point that massacres in modern times need not be motivated by nationalism but in imperial states arise at moments of instability when the traditional tolerance of difference may turn into "a much more pronouncedly aggressive state ethnic policy with particularly dire consequences for those who were perceived, correctly or incorrectly, as the protégés or proxies of Western or foreign interference." This is precisely how he explains the Ottoman massacres of Armenians in 1894–1896. "By [the Great Powers] giving to the Armenians, for instance, every incentive to see themselves as a separate nationality under Great Power protection, they in effect poured a bucket of poison into Turkish-Armenian relations, yet without any intention of coming to the rescue when the Turks predictably overreacted." *Genocide in the Age of the Nation-State, II: The Rise of the West and the Coming of Genocide* (London: I. B. Tauris, 2005), pp. 223–224, 225.

44. Roy Douglas, "Britain and the Armenian Question, 1894–7," *The Historical Journal* 19, no. 1 (March 1976): 113.

45. Odysseus, *Turkey in Europe*, p. 445.

46. Enclosed in a report from Sir Philip Currie in Constantinople to the Earl of Kimberley, FO 424/178, April 3, 1894.

47. Ibid.

48. The demonstration is known as the Kum Kapu demonstration, another name for the district.

49. Report from Sir Philip Currie in Constantinople to the Earl of Kimberley, FO 424/178, March 27, 1894. Libaridian, "What Was Revolutionary about Armenian Revolutionary Parties?" p. 87.

50. Report from British Consul H. A. Cumberbatch to Sir. A. Nicolson, FO 424/178, December 29, 1893.

51. Petition from Protestant Armenians and Gregorians of Yozgat, January 19 (31), 1894, enclosed in a report from British Consul at Ankara H. A. Cumberbatch to British Ambassador to Istanbul Sir Philip Currie, FO 424/178, February 12, 1894; report from British Consul at Ankara H. A. Cumberbatch to British Ambassador to Istanbul Sir Philip Currie, FO 424/178, March 5, 1894; report from British Consul at Ankara H. A. Cumberbatch to British Ambassador to Istanbul Sir Philip Currie, FO 424/178, April 13, 1894.

52. The report of the consuls who investigated events in Sasun has been published in *The Armenian Genocide: Documentation, I* (Munich: Institute für Armenische Fragen, 1987), pp. 64–114.

53. Letter of Sir P. Currie to the Earl of Kimberley, Great Britain, Foreign Office, Turkey, no. 1 (1895), (Part I) Correspondence Relating to the Asiatic Provinces of Turkey, Part I. Events at Sassoon, and Commission of Inquiry at Moush (London, 1895), pp. 8–10

54. Cited in Douglas, "Britain and the Armenian Question," p. 116.

55. Ibid. Armenians were held responsible for a half dozen wanton killings.

56. Ibid., pp. 116–117.

57. Ibid., p. 118.

58. Ibid., p. 125.

59. Cited in Deringil, "'The Armenian Question is Finally Closed,'" p. 349; Başbanlık Osmanlı Arşivi, Y.PRK. 32/94, 3 September 1893.

60. Douglas, "Britain and the Armenian Question," p. 121.

61. Michael Reynolds, *Shattering Empires: The Clash and Collapse of the Ottoman and Russian Empires, 1908–1918* (Cambridge: Cambridge University Press, 2011), p. 54.

62. For the full treatment of the lethal combination of domestic and international factors in the origins of genocide, see Bloxham, *The Great Game of Genocide*; on the Hamidian massacres, see ibid., pp. 46–57.

63. Dispatch of M. P. Cambon, French ambassador to Constantinople, to M. Hanotaux, minister of foreign affairs, September 30, 1895, in *The Armenian Genocide: Documentation, I*, pp. 117–118; "Rioting and Bloodshed in Constantinople," *The Times* (London), October 3, 1895, in ibid., pp. 118–119; Dispatch of M. P. Cambon

to M. Hantoux, October 2, 1895, in ibid., pp. 120–121; "Renewed Rioting in Constantinople," *The Times* (London), October 2, 1895, in ibid., pp. 121–122; Cambon to Hanotaux, October 6, 1895, in ibid., pp. 122–124; "The Constantinople Riots," *The Times* (London), October 7, 1895, in ibid., pp. 124–125.

64. A. W. Terrell, "An Interview with Sultan Abdul Hamid," *Century Magazine* (November 1897), pp. 133–138.

65. Malcolm MacColl, "The Constantinople Massacre and its Lesson," *The Contemporary Review* (November 1895), in *The Armenian Genocide: Documentation*, I, pp. 136–142.

66. James L. Barton (comp.), *"Turkish Atrocities": Statements of American Missionaries on the Destruction of Christian Communities in Ottoman Turkey, 1915–1917* (Ann Arbor, MI: Gomidas, 1998), pp. 75–76; statement of George E. White, National Archives, Washington, DC, General Records of the American Commission to Negotiate Peace, Special Reports and Studies, Record Group 256, Inquiry Document 818. This volume contains twenty-one eyewitness accounts of the Armenian massacres in 1915 collected in 1917–1918 by the Reverend James L. Barton, foreign secretary of the American Board of Commissioners for Foreign Missions, for an American presidential commission.

67. Report from the British Acting Consul at Erzurum H. A. Cumberbatch to Mr. Herbert at the British embassy in Istanbul, November 12, 1895, enclosure in no. 630.

68. Kévorkian, *The Armenian Genocide*, p. 13; Ahmed Rıza, "Atrocités contre les Chrétiens," *Mechveret*, I/11, May 15, 1896, p. 3.

69. Cited in Deringil, "'The Armenian Question is Finally Closed,'" p. 355.

70. Ibid., pp. 356–357.

71. The incident is reported on the basis of archival documents in ibid., p. 353.

72. Emrullah Akgündüz, "Some Notes on the Syriac Christians of Diyarbekir in the Late 19th Century: A Preliminary Investigation of Some Primary Sources," in Jongerden and Verheij (eds.), *Social Relations in Ottoman Diyarbekir*, pp. 217–240.

73. Even though they were defined by their distinctive religion, yet divided by the particular church to which they belonged, some Assyrian intellectuals aspired in the nineteenth century to an inclusive secular, national identity, as did many Armenians, Kurds, and Turks. Western missionaries and Orientalist scholars were fascinated by these ancient Christians and aided in the standardization of the Assyrian (Syriac) language and the spread of literacy. They promoted the idea that the Assyrians in the Ottoman Empire and Iran were the descendants of ancient Assyria, and therefore the original inhabitants of the lands where they now lived. When the Assyrian secular nationalist journal *Kukhva* appeared in 1906, this organic connection to antiquity was woven into their national myth. Sener Akturk, "Perspectives on Assyrian Nationalism," *Hemispheres* 25 (2002): 134–155.

74. Aydın and Verheij, "Confusion in the Cauldron," pp. 20–22.

75. Jelle Verheij, "Diyarbekir and the Armenian Crisis of 1895," in Jongerden and Verheij (eds.), *Social Relations in Ottoman Diyarbekir*, p. 91.

76. Ibid., pp. 111, 119–120.

77. Ibid., p. 94.

78. Gustave Meyrier, *Les massacres de Diarbekir: Correspondance diplomatique du vice-consul de France,* ed. and annot. Claire Mouradian and Michel Durand-Meyrier (Paris, 2000), p. 85; from Meyrier, cited in Deringil, "'The Armenian Question is Finally Closed,'" p. 352. Meyrier was the only foreign official in the city at the time of the 1895 massacres.

79. Verheij, "Diyarbekir and the Armenian Crisis of 1895," pp. 102–105.

80. Ibid., pp. 124–126.

81. Ibid., p. 86.

82. Joost Jongerden, "Elite Encounters of a Violent Kind: Milli İbrahim Paşa, Ziya Gökalp and Political Struggle in Diyarbekir at the Turn of the 20th Century," in Jongerden and Verheij (eds.), *Social Relations in Ottoman Diyarbekir*, pp. 73–74.

83. Ibid., p. 81. In the early twentieth century Turkish nationalists like Ziya Gökalp and Diyarbakır notables like his maternal uncle, Arif Pirinççizade, attempted to have the sultan, İbrahim Paşa, removed, even accusing him of aiding Armenian revolutionaries. Ibid., pp. 75–78.

84. David Gaunt, "Relations Between Kurds and Syriacs and Assyrians in Late Ottoman Diyarbekir," in Jongerden and Verheij (eds.), *Social Relations in Ottoman Diyarbekir*, p. 263.

85. Verheij, "Diyarbekir and the Armenian Crisis of 1895," pp. 112–117.

86. Report of British Vice Consul Fitzmaurice from Urfa to Sir Philip Currie, March 16, 1896, in *The Armenian Genocide: Documentation*, I, pp. 154–155.

87. Deringil, "'The Armenian Question is Finally Closed,'" pp. 362–363.

88. Geoff Berridge, *Gerald Fitzmaurice (1865–1939), Chief Dragoman of the British Embassy in Turkey* (Leiden: Brill, 2007), p. 27; Deringil, "'The Armenian Question is Finally Closed,'" p. 365.

89. P. Currie to Salisbury, December 13, 1895, *Parliamentary Papers*, 1896, 95 (Turkey no. 2); cited in Somakian, *Empires in Conflict*, p. 21.

90. Telegraphic report from the British Ambassador at Istanbul Sir Philip Currie to Foreign Secretary the Marquess of Salisbury, FO 424/186, February 3, 1896.

91. Telegraphic report from British Ambassador at Istanbul Sir Philip Currie to the British Foreign Minister the Marquess of Salisbury, FO 424/188, September 25, 1896; report from Consul-General Cecil G. Wood in Tabriz to Sir M. Durand, British ambassador at Tehran (?), July 16, 1896, enclosed in a report from Michael Herbert at the British embassy at Istanbul to the British Foreign Minister the Marquess

of Salisbury, FO 424/188, July 16, 1896; report from Consul-General Cecil G. Wood in Tehran to Sir M. Durand, British ambassador at Tehran (?), July 23, 1896, enclosed in a report from Michael Herbert at the British embassy at Istanbul to the British Foreign Minister the Marquess of Salisbury, FO 424/188, July 23, 1896.

92. Report on the disturbance at Marsovan, enclosed in a letter from the British Acting Consul at Ankara Raphael Fontana to the British Ambassador at Istanbul Sir Philip Currie, FO 424/184, December 4, 1895.

93. Report from the British Acting Consul at Erzurum H. A. Cumberbatch to the British Ambassador at Istanbul Sir Philip Currie, FO 424/184, December 5, 1895; "Statistics collected by the Gregorian Episcopate of Kharput, comprising that town and seventy-three villages, showing the number of persons killed, &c., and houses pillaged, &c., during the disorders of 1895," enclosed in a report from British Consul H. A. Cumberbatch in Erzurum to the British Ambassador at Istanbul Sir Philip Currie, FO 424/186, March 11, 1896.

94. Substance of a report from a "presumably trustworthy source," forwarded by the British Acting Consul at Ankara Raphael Fontana to the British Ambassador at Istanbul Sir Philip Currie, FO 424/184, December 6, 1895.

95. Report from British Ambassador at Istanbul Sir Philip Currie to the British Foreign Secretary the Marquess of Salisbury, FO 424/183, August 29, 1895.

96. Report from British Ambassador at Istanbul Sir Philip Currie to the British Foreign Secretary the Marquess of Salisbury, FO 424/183, September 6, 1895.

97. Telegraphic report from "Mr. Herbert" at the British embassy in Istanbul to the British Foreign Secretary the Marquess of Salisbury, FO 424/184, November 1, 1895.

98. Report from Tevfik Pasha to Rustem Pasha, November 13, 1895, communicated by Rustem Pasha, FO 424/184, November 14, 1895.

99. Garo, *Bank Ottoman*, pp. 205–206. See also Edhem Eldem, "26 Ağustos 1896 'Banka Vakası' ve 1896 Ermeni Olayları," in *İmparatoruğun Çöküş Döneminde Osmanlı Ermenileri: Bilimsel Sorumluluk ve Demokrasi Sorunları: 23–25 Eylül 2005*, ed. Fahri Aral (Istanbul: Bilgi Üniversitesi Yayınları, 2011).

100. Garo, *Bank Ottoman*, p. 101.

101. Ibid., p. 112. Most of the account of the bank seizure comes from *Bank Ottoman*.

102. Ibid. p. 131.

103. Ibid., pp. 133–139.

104. Göçek, *Denial of Violence*, p. 142; Mahmut Nedim Kerkük, *Hatıratım 1918* (Istanbul: Altınküre, 2002), pp. 30–32, 68.

105. Cited in Douglas, "Britain and the Armenian Question," p. 127.

106. Langer, *The Diplomacy of Imperialism*, vol. I, p. 326.

107. Garo, *Bank Ottoman*, pp. 145, 149.

108. Ardern G. Hume-Beaman, *Twenty Years in the Near East* (London: Methuen, 1898), p. 305; cited in Langer, *The Diplomacy of Imperialism*, vol. I, p. 325.

109. Kévorkian, *The Armenian Genocide*, pp. 14–15; Stepanos Sapah-Gulian, *Batashanatunnere* (Providence: Eritasard Hayastan, 1916), pp. 164–173.

110. Cited in Melson, *Revolution and Genocide*, pp. 59–60; Great Britain, Sessional Papers, c. 7894, enclosure 1 in no. 35, November 4, 1894. On Abdülhamid's involvement Selim Deringil argues that "there is substantial evidence, albeit circumstantial, that points in the direction of his benign neglect, if not actual covert support for the perpetrators of the massacres and forced conversions." He concludes, "Abdülhamid intended to cow, decimate, and humble the Armenians, but not to destroy them." Deringil, "'The Armenian Question is Finally Closed,'" pp. 351, 368. Stephan Astourian is less equivocal about Abdülhamid's responsibility for the massacres: "The geographical scope of these events, the similar pattern of the killings, the supervision of the army or its participation in the massacres, and the subsequent attitude of the Ottoman government all suggest that these events were planned and ordered by the Sultan." Astourian, "On the Genealogy of the Armenian-Turkish Conflict," p. 199.

111. Sultan Abdülhamid, *Siyasi Hatıratım* (Istanbul: Dergah Yayınları, 1987), p. 84; cited in Astourian, "On the Genealogy of the Armenian-Turkish Conflict," p. 195, n. 89. This memoir was first published in French as Ali Vahbi Bey, *Pensées et souvenirs de l'ex-sultan Abdul-Hamid* (Paris: Attinger Frères, n.d. [1910s]). They contain the thoughts of the sultan, taken down by his private secretary (some say doctor) and are dated 1893. These purported memoirs were taken down by someone close to the sultan and first published while Abdülhamid was alive. Therefore they are considered to be quite reliable, unlike other alleged memoirs of the sultan. I am grateful to Murat Özyüksel for this information.

112. Göçek, *Denial of Violence*, p. 150.

113. "Another Armenian Holocaust," *The New York Times*, September 10, 1895.

114. Aksakal, "'Holy War Made in Germany'?" pp. 9–10; Deringil, *Well-Protected Domains*, p. 114.

115. Göçek, *Denial of Violence*, pp. 67–69; Sadeddin Pasha, *Sadeddin Paşa'nın Anıları: Ermeni-Kürt Olayları, Van 1896*, ed. S. Önal (Istanbul: Remzi, 2003), pp. 20–22, 44–50.

116. Göçek, *Denial of Violence*, pp. 69–71; Sadeddin Pasha, *Sadeddin Paşa'nın Anıları*, pp. 65–67; see also Göçek, *Denial of Violence*, pp. 130–131, on Sadeddin's address to Kurds, in which he blamed them for their role in anti-Armenian violence.

117. George Hughes Hepworth, *Through Armenia on Horseback* (London: Isbister, 1898), p. 12.

118. Langer, *The Diplomacy of Imperialism*, vol. I, p. 326.

119. Unsigned article, "The Constantinople Massacre," *The Contemporary Review* (October 1896), reprinted in *The Armenian Genocide: Documentation, I*, pp. 215–221.

120. Hepworth, *Through Armenia on Horseback*, pp. 44–45.

121. Cited in Douglas, "Britain and the Armenian Question," p. 132.

122. "The policies of centralization from the Tanzimat onwards had shifted not only the relative power relations within the Ottoman Empire, but also turned them into antagonistic ones. Now the policy was to unite (the Sunni majority) and rule against the minorities. Ottoman politics had been redefined as a zero-sum game, one in which the Armenians were bound to lose." Astourian, "On the Genealogy of the Armenian-Turkish Conflict," p. 207.

123. A secret report intercepted by the military attaché of the Austrian embassy, cited in Stephan H. Astourian, "Le génocide arménien: Massacre à l'asiatique ou effet de modernité?" in *Quand tombe nuit: Origines et émergence des régime totalitaire en Europe*, ed. Stéphane Courtois (Lausanne: L'Age d'Homme, 2001), p. 71.

124. On state reform, interethnic relations, and economic developments in Abdülhamid's reign, see Findley, *Bureaucratic Reform in the Ottoman Empire*; Duguid, "The Politics of Unity"; and Quataert, *Social Disintegration and Popular Resistance in the Ottoman Empire*. Note that a pro-Islamic policy is not the same as a pan-Islamic policy aimed at uniting all Muslims under the sultan's hegemony.

125. Melson, "A Theoretical Inquiry into the Armenian Massacres," pp. 503, 509.

126. Astourian, "Le génocide arménien," p. 72.

127. For a discussion of Turkish proverbs, see ibid., p. 73.

128. Hepworth, *Through Armenia on Horseback*, p. 55.

129. Astourian, "The Silence of the Land," p. 66; translated from Ali Vahbi Bey, *Pensées et souvenirs de l'ex-sultan Abdul-Hamid*, pp. 14–15.

130. Cyrus Hamlin, "A Dangerous Movement Among the Armenians," *The Congregationalist*, December 28, 1893. Hamlin's "testimony" was reproduced as evidence blaming Armenian revolutionaries for initiating the events leading to the Sasun massacres in an unsigned article in *The New York Times*, August 23, 1895.

131. Reproduced in Greene, *The Armenian Crisis in Turkey*, pp. 167–168.

132. Odysseus, *Turkey in Europe*, p. 442.

133. Ibid., pp. 146–147.

134. Davide Rodogno, *Against Massacre: Humanitarian Interventions in the Ottoman Empire, 1815–1914* (Princeton, NJ: Princeton University Press, 2012), pp. 185–211.

135. Georges Clemenceau (foreword), *Les massacres d'Arménie: Témoignages des victimes* (Paris: Édition du Mercure de France, 1896), pp. 5–18.

136. Margaret Lavinia Anderson, "Who Still Talked about the Extermination of the Armenians?: German Talk and German Silences," in Suny et al. (eds.), *A Question*

of Genocide, pp. 199–200; M. L. Anderson, "'Down in Turkey, far away': Human Rights, the Armenian Massacres, and Orientalism in Wilhelmine Germany," *Journal of Modern History* 79, no. 1 (March 2007): 80–113.

137. Theodore Roosevelt to George Otto Trevelyan, May 13, 1905, in Elting Morison, *The Letters of Theodore Roosevelt*, 8 vols. (Cambridge, MA: Harvard University Press, 1951), vol. 4, p. 1175; James R. Holmes, *Theodore Roosevelt and World Order: Police Power in International Relations* (Washington, DC: Potomac, 2006), p. 73; Karine Walther, "Sacred Interests: U.S. Foreign Relations in the Islamicate World, 1821–1921," unpublished manuscript, pp. 406, 407.

138. Walther, "Sacred Interests," pp. 420–421.

139. Gregor Thum, "Megalomania and Angst: The Nineteenth-Century Mythicization of Germany's Eastern Borderlands," in Bartov and Weitz (eds.), *Shatterzone of Empires*, pp. 42–60.

140. Eric D. Weitz, "Germany and Young Turks: Revolutionaries into Statesmen," in Suny et al. (eds.), *A Question of Genocide*, pp. 178–179.

141. Ussher, *An American Physician in Turkey*, pp. 125–126.

CHAPTER FIVE: Revolution

1. See Ilham Khuri-Makdisi, *The Eastern Mediterranean and the Making of Global Radicalism, 1860–1914* (Berkeley: University of California Press, 2010).

2. Keith Brown, *Loyal Unto Death: Trust and Terror in Revolutionary Macedonia* (Bloomington: Indiana University Press, 2013), pp. 4–5, and Ipek Yosmaoğlu, *Blood Ties: Religion, Violence and the Politics of Nationhood in Ottoman Macedonia, 1878–1908* (Ithaca, NY: Cornell University Press, 2013).

3. For a contemporary critical, satirical view of the Armenian revolutionaries, see Ervand Otian [1869–1926], *Enger Banchuni* (Istanbul: Tparan ev Gratun Nshan-Papikian, 1911); English translation: Yervant Odian, *Comrade Panchoonie*, trans. Jack Antreassian (New York: St. Vartan, 1977).

4. Hratch Dasnabedian, *History of the Armenian Revolutionary Federation Dashnaktsutiun 1890/1924*, trans. Bryan Fleming and Vahe Habeshian (Milan: OEMME Edizioni, 1990), pp. 47–48.

5. Letter from Dr. Jewett to British Consul Longworth in Trabzon, Sivas, July 23, 1895, enclosed in a letter from British Ambassador at Istanbul Sir Philip Currie to the British Foreign Secretary the Marquess of Salisbury, FO 424/183, July 23, 1895; accessed via http://www.archivesdirect.amdigital.co.uk/default.aspx on May 2, 2012.

6. Tololyan, "Martyrdom as Legitimacy," pp. 94–95; Khachig Tololyan, "Cultural Narrative and the Motivation of the Terrorist," *Journal of Strategic Studies* 10, no. 4 (December 1987): 222–224.

7. Dasnabedian, *History of the Armenian Revolutionary Federation Dashnaktsutiun*, pp. 47–48.

8. Ibid., pp. 49–51.

9. In 1901 a small band of Armenian and Macedonian rebels clashed with Ottoman troops. Six were killed; four were captured and hanged. Ibid., pp. 59–60.

10. In this work the term "Young Turks" refers to the Ottoman oppositionists to the Hamidian regime and those who carried out and supported the revolution of 1908. Young Turks were not a single, unified party, but a movement, and various groups within the movement, like the Committee of Union and Progress and the liberal followers of Prince Sabahaddin, opposed each other.

11. Kévorkian, *The Armenian Genocide*, p. 16; "Arajin Kail," *Droshak*, no. 6/86 (June 30, 1898): 59–60.

12. Suny, *Looking Toward Ararat*, p. 93.

13. M. G. Nersisian and P. G. Saakian (eds.), *Genotsid armian v Osmanskoi imperii*, http://www.genocide.ru/lib/nersisyan/066–074.htm#71.

14. Ibid.; TsGIA Arm. SSR [Central State Archive of the Armenian SSR], f. 56, d. 338, ll. 27—28.

15. "Letter from Andranik and Kevork, Chiefs of the Insurgents Near Mush," July 1904, cited in Libaridian, "What Was Revolutionary about Armenian Revolutionary Parties?" p. 91. See also Andranig Ozanian [General Antranig], *The Battle of the Holy Apostles' Monastery*, originally recorded by L. G. Loulegian, trans. Ara Stepan Melkonian (London: Taderon, 2009).

16. For an excellent account of the plot against the sultan and its aftermath, see Toygun Altıntaş, "The Yıldız Bombing: Regicide and Revolutionary Violence in the Hamidian Era in the Ottoman Empire," unpublished paper, University of Chicago, March 2013.

17. On the development of the separate nationalisms of the peoples of the Ottoman Empire, see Fatma Müge Göçek, "The Decline of the Ottoman Empire and the Emergence of Greek, Armenian, Turkish and Arab Nationalisms," in *Social Constructions of Nationalism in the Middle East*, ed. M. Göçek (Albany: State University of New York Press, 2002), pp. 15–83.

18. Hanioğlu, *The Young Turks in Opposition*, p. 216. This occurred around 1902 at the time of the Congress of Ottoman Oppositionists in Paris. For a full treatment of Ahmed Rıza, see Erdal Kaynar, "Ahmed Rıza (1858–1930): Histoire d'un Vieux Jeune Turk" (Ph.D. diss., École des Hautes Études en Science Sociales, 2012).

19. Mim Kemal Öke, *The Armenian Question 1914–1923* (Oxford: K. Rustem & Brother, 1988), p. 63.

20. Cited in ibid., p. 64; from Uşklığil, *Kırk Yıl*, p. 508.

21. Hanioğlu, *The Young Turks in Opposition*, p. 32.

22. Ibid., p. 17.

23. Kévorkian, *The Armenian Genocide*, p. 12; Ahmed Rıza, "Chrétien, musulman et humanité," *Mechveret*, I/11, May 15, 1896, p. 3.

24. Kévorkian, *The Armenian Genocide*, p. 15; on the relations of the Turkish radical opposition and the Armenian revolutionaries, see Sapah-Gulian, *Batashanatunnere*, pp. 150–173. The Dashnaks adopted a critical attitude toward attending the Hague Peace Conference. Kévorkian, *The Armenian Genocide*, p. 17; "Kaghakakan Drama te Fars," *Droshak*, no. 4/95 (April 30, 1899): 50–51.

25. Hanioğlu, *The Young Turks in Opposition*, p. 193.

26. Ibid., p. 195.

27. Ibid., p. 197.

28. Kévorkian, *The Armenian Genocide*, pp. 21–22; H. Kh., "Eridasard Tiurkia ev Eridasard Haiastan Antagonizme."

29. Kévorkian, *The Armenian Genocide*, p. 26; P. Fesch [Sabahaddin's secretary], *Constantinople aux derniers jours d'Abdulhamid* (Paris, 1907), p. 50.

30. M. Şükrü Hanioğlu, *Preparation for a Revolution: The Young Turks, 1902–1908* (Oxford: Oxford University Press, 2001), p. 83.

31. Sabahaddin's mother was Georgian. Kévorkian, *The Armenian Genocide*, pp. 27, 819, n. 102; Hanioğlu, *Preparation for a Revolution*, pp. 88–89.

32. See, for example, Ernest Edmondson Ramsaur Jr., *The Young Turks: Prelude to the Revolution of 1908* (Princeton, NJ: Princeton University Press, 1957), and Feroz Ahmad, *The Young Turks: The Committee of Union and Progress in Turkish Politics, 1908–1914* (Oxford: Oxford University Press, 1969).

33. The two terms *İttihat* (union) and *Terakki* (progress) were used by various different committees—first by students of the Imperial Military Medical Faculty—sometimes in reverse order until the 1908 revolution, when the order was stabilized as *İttihat ve Terakki Cemiyeti* (Committee of Union and Progress, or CUP). In this work I use the most standard term, *İttihat ve Terakki Cemiyeti* (Committee of Union and Progress, or CUP), throughout, except when clarity requires otherwise.

34. Cited in Hanioğlu, *A Brief History of the Late Ottoman Empire*, p. 147; Uğur Ümit Üngör and Mehmet Polatel, *Confiscation and Destruction: The Young Turk Seizure of Armenian Property* (London: Continuum International, 2011), p. 32; Yusuf Akçura, *Üç Tarz-ı Siyaset* (Istanbul: n.p., 1909).

35. Cited in Astourian, "Modern Turkish Identity," p. 33.

36. Cited in Uriel Heyd, *Foundations of Turkish Nationalism: The Life and Teachings of Ziya Gökalp 1876–1924* (London: Luzac and Co. and Harvill, 1950), p. 128.

37. Cited in Masami Arai, *Turkish Nationalism in the Young Turk Era* (Leiden: Brill, 1992), p. 61.

38. Kévorkian, *The Armenian Genocide*, p. 31; Hanioğlu, *Preparation for a Revolution*, p. 135. This information is from the private papers of Bahaeddin Şakir to which Hanioğlu has access.

39. Kévorkian, *The Armenian Genocide*, pp. 32–35; Sapah-Gulian, *Bataskhanaturnerr*, pp. 185–186, 190–195.

40. Kévorkian, *The Armenian Genocide*, pp. 38–42; *Niuter H. H. Dashnaktsutyan Badmutyan hamar*, III (Beirut, 1985), *passim*.

41. Hanioğlu, *Preparation for a Revolution*, pp. 197, 205; Kévorkian, *The Armenian Genocide*, pp. 45–47; *Droshak*, no. 1, "Kusaktsutyunneri Hamazhoghove December 27–29, 1907" (January 1, 1908): 1–5.

42. Ozan Arslan and Cınar Ozen, "The Rebirth of the Ottoman Committee of Union and Progress in Macedonia Through the Italian Freemasonry," *Oriente Moderno* n.s., no. 24 (85), 1 (2005): 109.

43. Hanioğlu, *Preparation for a Revolution*, p. 226.

44. Hanioğlu, *A Brief History of the Late Ottoman Empire*, p. 148.

45. Bedross Der Matossian shows in great detail how the public sphere of the empire was revived in the heady months after July 1908 and contributed to the violence in Adana in 1909. "From Bloodless Revolution to Bloody Counterrevolution: The Adana Massacres of 1909," *Genocide Studies and Prevention* 6, no. 2 (Summer 2011): 152–173. See also his "Ethnic Politics in Post-Revolutionary Ottoman Empire: Armenians, Arabs, and Jews in the Second Constitutional Period (1908–1909)" (Ph.D. diss., Columbia University, 2008); and his book *Shattered Dreams of Revolution: Politics, Religion, and Ethnicity in the Ottoman Empire (1908–1909)* (Stanford, CA: Stanford University Press, 2014). On the reaction to the 1908 revolution, see Michelle Campo, *Ottoman Brothers: Muslims, Christians, and Jews in Ottoman Palestine* (Stanford, CA: Stanford University Press, 2011).

46. On Grigor [Krikor] Zohrap, see A. S. Sharurian, *Grigor Zohrapi Kianki ev Gortsutneutyan Taregrutyun* (Ejmiatsin, 1996).

47. Arkhiv vneshnoi politiki Rossii, f. 543, report by Consul Akimovich, 1 (14), March 1909; cited in Somakian, *Empires in Conflict*, p. 38.

48. Kévorkian writes, "A few statistics provide the best proof that the Young Turk Central Committee's program was indeed translated into reality. Between July 1908 and March 1910, all the valis of the Empire's twenty-nine vilayets were replaced. Ninety-three percent of the directors of regional telegraph offices, ninety-three percent of the provincial directors of education, one hundred percent of the Empire's ambassadors and ninety-four percent of its charges d'affaires were dismissed, to be replaced by men loyal to the regime." Kévorkian, *The Armenian Genocide*, p. 58; Hanioğlu, *Preparation for a Revolution*, p. 287.

49. Matthias Bjørnlund, "Adana and Beyond: Revolution and Massacre in the Ottoman Empire Seen Through Danish Eyes, 1908/9," *Haikazean Hayagitakan Handes* 30 (2010): 125.

50. Çetinkaya, *The Young Turks and the Boycott Movement*, pp. 44, 47.

51. Ibid., p. 218. Gustave Le Bon (1841–1931) was an influential French social psychologist whose principal work, *La psychologie des foules* (1895) (The Crowd: A Study of the Popular Mind), argued that when people come together in a crowd, marked by anonymity, contagion, and suggestibility, a "collective unconsciousness" takes over that makes people susceptible to the appeals of strong-willed leaders.

52. For these events, see Der Matossian, *Shattered Dreams of Revolution*, pp. 74–76.

53. Sharurian, *Grigor Zohrapi Kianki*, pp. 155–156.

54. Der Matossian, *Shattered Dreams of Revolution*, p. 8.

55. Rose Lambert, *Hadjin and the Armenian Massacres* (New York: Fleming H. Revell, 1911), p. 51.

56. *Puzantion*, no. 3592 (July 31, 1908); cited in Der Matossian, "From Bloodless Revolution to Bloody Counterrevolution," p. 153.

57. Dasnabedian, *History of the Armenian Revolutionary Federation*, p. 91. Publication of *Pro Armenia* resumed in 1912 with a new name, *Pour les Peuples d'Orient*, and then was published under its original name once again in 1914.

58. Anahide Ter Minassian, "The Role of the Armenian Community in the Foundation and Development of the Socialist Movement in the Ottoman Empire and Turkey, 1876–1923," in *Socialism and Nationalism in the Ottoman Empire, 1876–1923*, ed. Mete Tunçay and Erik J. Zürcher (London: British Academic Press, 1994), p. 140.

59. Kévorkian, *The Armenian Genocide*, p. 114; "Erkrord Heghapokhutyun," *Droshak*, no. 4/201 (April 1909): 41–45.

60. Kévorkian, *The Armenian Genocide*, p. 51; Sapah-Gulian, *Bataskhanatunnere*, pp. 232–233.

61. Kévorkian, *The Armenian Genocide*, p. 68; *Zhamanak*, no. 61 (January 6, 1909).

62. The ten Armenian deputies were Grigor Zohrap (Istanbul), an independent liberal; CUP members Hakob Babikian (Istanbul) and Bedros Halajian (Istanbul); Dashnaks Armen Garo (Erzurum), Vartkes Serengulian (Erzurum), Kegham Der Garabedian (Muş), and Vahan Papazian (Van); a Hnchak, Murad Boyadjian (Kozan); and two independents, Nazareth Daghavarian (Sivas) and Sdepan Spartalian (Izmir).

63. Among its leading members were the poet Vahan Tekeyan, Bishop Mushegh Seropian, and the activist Mihran Tamatian.

64. Garo, *Bank Ottoman*, pp. 183–184.

65. Dikran Mesrop Kaligian, *Armenian Organization and Ideology under Ottoman Rule, 1908–1914* (New Brunswick, NJ: Transaction, 2011), pp. 29–30.

66. Based on extensive reading in the memoirs of Armenian revolutionaries, Kévorkian estimates their influence on the Armenians of eastern Anatolia. Kévorkian, *The Armenian Genocide*, pp. 59–62.

67. Ibid.; see also the memoirs of the Dashnak activist Vahan Papazian (1876–1973), who served as a deputy to the Ottoman Parliament after 1908 (*Husher*, I [Boston, 1950]; II [Beirut, 1952]); and those of his fellow revolutionary, Ruben Ter Minassian, *Mémoires d'un partisan révolutionnaire arménien*, trans. Souren L. Chanath (Athens, 1994).

68. After receiving threats from the CUP, the opposition journalist Ahmet Samim was murdered by *fedayi* attached to the CUP. Göçek, *Denial of Violence*, p. 197; Refik Halit Karay, *Bir Ömür Boyunca* (Istanbul: İletişim, 1990), p. 12.

69. On the internal workings of the CUP, see Hanioğlu, *A Brief History of the Late Ottoman Empire*, pp. 153–162.

70. Hasan Kayalı, *Arabs and Young Turks: Ottomanism, Arabism, and Islamism in the Ottoman Empire, 1908–1918* (Berkeley: University of California Press, 1997), p. 15.

71. The historian Feroz Ahmad writes, "Pan-Turanism, like Pan-Islam was an expansionist ideology which suited the mood of the Young Turks, then in full retreat at the opposite front [in Europe]. . . . Turkish nationalism, centered around the Turks in Anatolia, was in the process of development in 1914. It was to emerge out of the defeats in World War I, only after Pan-Turanism and Pan-Islam had proved to be mere dreams." Ahmad, *The Young Turks*, pp. 154–155. M. Şükrü Hanioğlu underlines the depth and consistency of Turkism among the Young Turks, taking issue with those historians who argue that Turkish nationalism took hold only after the defeats in the Balkan Wars of 1912–1913. Hanioğlu, *A Brief History of the Late Ottoman Empire*, pp. 187–188, but also throughout his work. "The main task that the CUP leaders took upon themselves was the preservation of the multinational empire," Hanioğlu writes (ibid., p. 16). A particularly fruitful approach has been suggested by Y. Doğan Çetinkaya in his study of the boycott movement after 1908, who argues that even though the early twentieth century "is considered an era of rising Turkish nationalism, the era's discourse was predominantly based on Muslim identity. The main frame of reference of the nationalist movement was Islam as a distinct marker of a communal identity." Çetinkaya proposes that the nationalism of this era be defined as "Muslim/Turkish nationalism." Çetinkaya, *The Young Turks and the Boycott Movement*, p. 5.

72. The difficulty of assessing the weight of nationalism and Ottomanism among the Young Turks is reflected in the work of Nyazi Berkes, who considered three competing schools of thought among the Young Turks from 1908 to 1918: the Westernist, the Islamist, and the Turkist. Writing about the period just before World War I, Berkes argues, "When later rival parties became harbingers of anti-Ottoman nationalisms, Turkish nationalism gained some influence in the Society, but never replaced Ottomanism." Nyazi Berkes, *The Development of Secularism in Turkey* (Montreal:

McGill University Press, 1964), p. 329. The historian Hasan Kayalı also argues that an ecumenical Ottomanist program remained key to the CUP: "The Young Turks envisaged the creation of a civic-territorial, indeed revolutionary-democratic, Ottoman political community by promoting an identification with the state and country through the sultan and instituting representative government. Though they remained committed to the monarchy within the constitutional framework, they conceived of an Ottoman state and society akin to the French example in which religion and ethnicity would be supplanted by 'state-based patriotism.'" Kayalı, *Arabs and Young Turks*, p. 9.

73. Some historians have also come to this conclusion. Manoug J. Somakian writes, "The term 'Ottomanism' thus meant in most cases little more than Turkification, and it substantially alienated the interests of national minorities. The CUP was convinced that Turkification was an effective process by which the Ottoman Empire could be re-created and raised to the status at which they aimed." *Empires in Conflict*, p. 40.

74. Erik Jan Zürcher, "Ottoman Labour Battalions in World War I," in Kieser and Schaller (eds.), *Der Völkermord an den Armeniern und die Shoah*, p. 190.

75. Cited in Eric D. Weitz, "Germany and the Ottoman Borderlands: The Entwining of Imperial Aspirations, Revolution, and Ethnic Violence," in Bartov and Weitz (eds.), *Shatterzone of Empires*, p. 161.

76. Kévorkian, *The Armenian Genocide*, p. 122; letter from the French vice consul in Üsküb to Bompard, "translation of a speech attributed to Talât Bey, minister of the interior," CADN, Ambassade de Constantinople, série E/126, September 20, 1910. This statement attributed to Talat has been interpreted by some historians, among them Vahakn N. Dadrian, to be a call for ethnic cleansing and physical elimination of minorities. "The Armenian Genocide and the Pitfalls of a 'Balanced' Analysis: A Response to Ronald Grigor Suny," *Armenian Forum* 1, no. 2 (Summer 1998): 117.

77. Özok-Gündoğan, "A 'Peripheral' Approach to the 1908 Revolution in the Ottoman Empire," pp. 187–189.

78. Kévorkian, *The Armenian Genocide*, p. 69; "Enver *Paşa'nın* Gizli *Mektupları*," ed. Şukru Hanıoğlu, *Cumhuriyet*, October 9, 1989; cited in Hamid Bozarslan, "Les Courants de pensée dans l'Empire ottoman 1908–1918" (Thèse de doctorat, 2 vols., EHESS, 1992), vol. I, p. 210, n. 815.

79. Kévorkian, *The Armenian Genocide*, p. 73.

80. Adanır, "Non-Muslims in the Ottoman Army," p. 116.

81. "After the revolution," writes Bedross Der Matossian, "the growth in Adana's public sphere not only fomented political activism within formerly outlawed groups, but it also contributed to an escalation of ethnic tensions. The physical and verbal manifestations of Armenians in the public sphere in the forms of cultural and

political processions, the bearing and selling of arms in public, and theatrical presentations as well as the use of print media sent alarming vibes among the dissatisfied elements, which began to use the same medium to air their anxieties about and discontent with the newly created order." Der Matossian, "From Bloodless Revolution to Bloody Counterrevolution," p. 155.

82. Ibid., pp. 156–157.

83. Cited in ibid., p. 159. See also Aram Arkun, "Les relations arméno-turques et les massacres de Cilicie de 1909," in *L'actualité du genocide des arméniens: Actes du colloque organisé par le Comité de Défense de la Cause Arménienne à Paris-Sorbonne les 16, 17 et 18 avril 1998*, ed. Hrayr Henry Ayvazian et al. (Paris: Eidpol, 1999), p. 60.

84. Kévorkian, *The Armenian Genocide*, pp. 77–79.

85. Der Matossian, "From Bloodless Revolution to Bloody Counterrevolution," p. 160.

86. *İtidal*, no. 33, 1–2 (April 20, 1909), cited in Der Matossian, "From Bloodless Revolution to Bloody Counterrevolution," p. 163.

87. Frederick Zaccheus Ferriman Duckett (1856–1934), a writer on Greek and Turkish matters at the time, argued that it was Turks who fired on the tents. Ferriman Duckett, *The Young Turks and the Truth about the Holocaust at Adana in Asia Minor, during April 1909* (London: n.p., 1913; reprinted, Erevan: The Armenian Genocide Museum-Institute, 2009), p. 22.

88. Kévorkian, *The Armenian Genocide*, p. 92; (P.) Rigal, "Adana: Les massacres d'Adana," *Lettres d'ore, relations d'Orient* (November 1909): 199–223.

89. Ferriman Duckett assembled eyewitness accounts. *The Young Turks and the Truth about the Holocaust at Adana*, pp. 24–27.

90. Arkun, "Les relations arméno-turques et les massacres de Cilicie de 1909," pp. 62–63.

91. Lambert, *Hadjin and the Armenian Massacres*, p. 104. Ferriman Duckett calculates that 30,000 Armenians lost their lives. The government's official Enquiry Commission estimated the total deaths, non-Muslim and Muslim, at 15,000. *The Young Turks and the Truth about the Holocaust at Adana*, pp. 54–58, 93.

92. This is an allusion to the massacre of thousands of French men and women in 1282 by rebels opposed to Norman rule in Sicily. Steven Runciman, *The Sicilian Vespers* (Cambridge: Cambridge University Press, 1958). My maternal grandfather, Avedis Kesdekian, was a teenager and a tailor when he departed from Samsun on the Black Sea for the United States in 1909. His family urged him to stay, but the news of the Adana massacres convinced him that there was no future for Armenians in the Ottoman Empire. He died at the age of one hundred in the suburbs of Philadelphia. Most of his family that remained in the central Anatolian city of Yozgat were killed in the 1915 genocide.

93. Report from British Vice Consul in Mersina and Adana Major Doughty-Wyllie to Sir G. Lowther, Adana, FO 424/219, pp. 107–108, May 2, 1909; http://www .armenocide.de/armenocide/armgende.nsf/24599fab3538b532c1257794007b610b /b106cd5c40535087c12575970073cc8e!OpenDocument.

94. Cited in Duckett, *The Young Turks and the Truth about the Holocaust at Adana*, p. 89.

95. Cited in ibid., p. 127.

96. Kévorkian, *The Armenian Genocide*, p. 90; AMAE [Archives du ministère des Affaires étrangères], Correspondence politique, Turquie, n.s., vol. 283, ff. 121–123, June 16, 1909. "The real culprits of the Adana Massacres," the historian Bedross Der Matossian concludes, "escaped justice." Der Matossian, "From Bloodless Revolution to Bloody Counterrevolution," p. 173, n. 110.

97. Duckett, *The Young Turks and the Truth about the Holocaust at Adana*, pp. 95–104.

98. Kévorkian, *The Armenian Genocide*, pp. 100–101; *Azatamart*, no. 156 (July 9, 1909): 3.

99. Kévorkian, *The Armenian Genocide*, p. 109; *Azatamart*, no. 9 (July 2, 1909), records of the 104th session.

100. Kévorkian, *The Armenian Genocide*, p. 105; *Azatamart*, no. 42 (August 12, 1909): 1, 3.

101. Raymond Kévorkian argues forcefully that the Young Turks were responsible for the Adana massacres. His evidence, he says, suggests "at the very least that the committee 'provided accompaniment' for the massacres and handled the situation that resulted from them in accordance with Hamidian rules of conduct. Moreover, there are reasons for presuming that it organized them.... The thesis that the Cilician affair resulted from a spontaneous upsurge of violence is untenable. Only an order from the government that guaranteed the perpetrators impunity could have convinced the populace to plunder and kill its neighbors." *The Armenian Genocide*, p. 113. My own reading—a pogrom that occurred in a reopened public sphere in which rumors and mutual suspicions inflamed fears that led to mass killing by Muslims—is closer to Bedross Der Matossian's. This is his argument in "From Bloodless Revolution to Bloody Counterrevolution."

CHAPTER SIX: Counterrevolution

1. Kaligian, *Armenian Organization and Ideology*, p. 49.

2. Ibid., p. 44.

3. Ibid., p. 47.

4. Kévorkian, *The Armenian Genocide*, p. 173; Arsen Gidur (ed.), *Batmutiun S. D. Hnchakean Gusaktsutean*, 2 vols. (Beirut: Shirag, 1962–1963), vol. 1, pp. 323–335.

5. Cited in Joseph Heller, "Britain and the Armenian Question, 1912–1914: A Study in Realpolitik," *Middle Eastern Studies* 16, no. 1 (January 1980): 4.

6. This intervention by tsarist Russia into Kurdish affairs is explored in Reynolds, *Shattering Empires*.

7. The historian who has worked most closely on the question of Armenian lands in the late Ottoman Empire, Stephan Astourian, concludes, "What those reports suggest is a systematic policy of expropriation, abuse, and condoned violence aimed at reducing the Armenian settled peasantry to misery and emigration. The goal was to de-Armenianize the Armenian plateau." Astourian, "The Silence of the Land," p. 65. See also Raymond Kévorkian and Paul Paboudjian, *Les Arméniens dans l'Empire ottoman à la veille du génocide* (Paris: Arhis, 1992), pp. 44–45.

8. Kaligian, *Armenian Organization and Ideology*, pp. 53–65.

9. Astourian, "The Silence of the Land," p. 65; "Great Britain; Foreign Office, Confidential Print. Turkey," *Further Correspondence Respecting the Affairs of Asiatic Turkey and Arabia*, FO 424, Volume 239, Document 321, enclosure by Fitzmaurice, annexed to a report by Marling to Sir Edward Grey (Constantinople, 27 August 1913), pp. 346–47.

10. Ibid., pp. 98–101.

11. FO 424/228/90, Sir Gerard Lowther to Sir Edward Grey (Constantinople, August 18, 1911, enclosure 1, Consul McGregor to Mr. Marling (Erzurum, July 7, 1911); cited in Kaligian, *Armenian Organization and Ideology*, p. 104.

12. This shift is demonstrated in Çetinkaya, *The Young Turks and the Boycott Movement*, pp. 89–159.

13. Kévorkian, *The Armenian Genocide*, pp. 146–152, reviews the Armenian press and memoirs in this period and shows the anxieties Armenians felt because of the deterioration of the situation in eastern Anatolia.

14. Üngör and Polatel, *Confiscation and Destruction*, pp. 23–25; see pp. 26–27 for related discussions; see chapter 2, notes 38–46, for citations for Şerif's articles.

15. Göçek, *Denial of Violence*, p. 170; Ahmet Hilmi Kalaç, *Kendi Kitabım* (Istanbul (?): Yeni Matbaa, 1960), p. 86.

16. Kévorkian, *The Armenian Genocide*, pp. 126–130; Stepanos Sapah-Gulian, *Pokr-Hayki hishatakner, I, 10-Mayis-i Ogostos* (Chicago, 1917), pp. 93, 154–158, 176, 178, 195–203, 294, 296–297.

17. Hüseyin Rauf Orbay, *Yüzyılımızda bir İnsanımız: Hüseyin Rauf Orba*, ed. Cemal Kutay (Istanbul: Kazancı, 1992), vol. II, p. 77.

18. Çetinkaya, *The Young Turks and the Boycott Movement*, p. 137.

19. Ibid., p. 168; report by Heathcote Smith from Smyrna, FO 195/2458, No. 84, July 11, 1914, p. 470.

20. Çetinkaya, *The Young Turks and the Boycott Movement*, pp. 180–181; BOA/DH.İD. 108–2/30, 14 March 1914; BOA/DH.H., 70/2, 3 April 1914.

21. Kévorkian, *The Armenian Genocide*, pp. 115–116; *Adenagrutyun Azkayin Zhoghovo* [Minutes of the National Assembly] (Constantinople, 1909), records of the November 25, 1911, session, pp. 430–444.

22. Kaligian, *Armenian Organization and Ideology*, p. 86.

23. Kévorkian, *The Armenian Genocide*, pp. 131–133. Much of the information on this Dashnak-CUP cooperation comes from Stepanos Sapah-Gulian, "Ittihad-Dashnaktsakan Gaghni Hamadzainutyan Barunagutyune ev Anor Hetevanknere," *Gohag*, no. 2 (127) (January 23/February 6, 1913); and subsequent issues.

24. Kévorkian, *The Armenian Genocide*, p. 173; Gidur (ed.), *Badmutiun S. D. Hnchakean Gusaktsutean*, pp. 343–348.

25. Noradounghian is an example of an Ottoman Armenian who faithfully served the empire, both during the reign of Abdülhamid II and after. See Raymond Kévorkian, "Gabriel Noradounghian (1852–1936)," *Revue d'histoire amenienne contemporaine* 1 (1995), http://www.imprescriptible.fr/rhac/tome1/noradounghian.

26. Kaligian, *Armenian Organization and Ideology*, p. 141.

27. FO 424/233/66, Mr. Marling to Sir Edward Grey (Constantinople, September 24, 1912); cited in Kaligian, *Armenian Organization and Ideology*, p. 143; Heller, "Britain and the Armenian Question," p. 5.

28. Kévorkian, *The Armenian Genocide*, p. 135.

29. Kaligan, *Armenian Organization and Ideology*, p. 149.

30. Keith Brown, "'Wiping Out the Bulgar Race': Hatred, Duty, and the National Self-Fashioning in the Second Balkan War," in Bartov and Weitz (eds.), *Shatterzone of Empires*, pp. 300–301.

31. For a detailed study of the Ottomans in the Balkan Wars, see Edward J. Erickson, *Defeat in Detail: The Ottoman Army in the Balkans, 1912–1913* (Westport, CT: Praeger, 2003), and the illustrated history compiled by Aram Andonian, *Badkerazart Intartsak Batmutyun Balanean Baderazmin* (*Badkerazard endardzak batmutyun Balkanean baderazmin*) (Constantinople, 1912) in five volumes, translated into Turkish by Zaven Biberian as *Balkan Savaşı* (Istanbul: Aras Yayıncılık, 2002).

32. Mark Mazower, *Salonica, City of Ghosts: Christians, Muslims, and Jews, 1430–1950* (New York: Alfred A. Knopf, 2005).

33. Y. Doğan Çetinkaya, "Illustrated Atrocity: The Stigmatization of non-Muslims through Images in the Ottoman Empire during the Balkan Wars," unpublished manuscript, and idem, "Atrocity Propaganda and the Nationalization of Masses in the Ottoman Empire during the Balkan Wars (1912–1913)," unpublished manuscript, pp. 23–24.

34. Kévorkian, *The Armenian Genocide*, p. 152; *Tanin*, 1/14 November 1913; *Tasfiri Efkar*, 12/25 and 13/26 November 1913. See M. Hakan Yavuz and Isa Blumi (eds.), *War and Nationalism: The Balkan Wars, 1912–1913, and Their Sociopolitical Implications* (Salt Lake City: University of Utah Press, 2013).

35. Ömer Seyfeddin, *Butun Eserleri* (Ankara, 1970).

36. These reflections on Seyfeddin's ideas were influenced by a series of lectures on the origins of Turkish nationalism by Halil Berktay at the University of Michigan in February 2007.

37. Eyal Ginio, "Paving the Way for Ethnic Cleansing: Eastern Thrace During the Balkan Wars (1912–1913) and Their Aftermath," in Bartov and Weitz (eds.), *Shatterzone of Empires*, pp. 288–293.

38. Çetinkaya, *The Young Turks and the Boycott Movement*, p. 201; FO 195/2458, file of "Anti-Christian Boycott," (former reference 306/3080), enclosure No. 6 (account of the conversation between Rahmi Bey, governor of Smyrna, and Dr. Nazım Bey), p. 553. The acting consul-general Smith reported that (in Çetinkaya's words) "many moderate-minded Turks believed that they had to express their hatred against Greeks to prove their patriotism." Ibid., p. 202.

39. Göçek, *Denial of Violence*, pp. 188–189; Ahmet Hamdi Başar, *Türkiye'de sermaye birikimi sorununa tarihsel perspektiften bir bakış* (Ankara: Sermaye Piyasası Kurulu Yayını, 1997), vol. I, pp. 75–77.

40. Göçek, *Denial of Violence*, p. 238; Sükuti Tükel, *Tatlı ve Acı Hatıralar* (İzmir: Piyasa, 1952), pp. 4–6.

41. Göçek, *Denial of Violence*, p. 238; Hüsamettin Ertürk, *İki Devrin Perde Arkası* (Istanbul: Hilmi, 1957), pp. 120–121.

42. Göçek, *Denial of Violence*, p. 238; Arif Cemil Denker, *Sürgün Hayatlar* (Istanbul: Emre, 2005), p. 201.

43. Göçek, *Denial of Violence*, p. 244; Raif Necdet Kestelli, *Osmanlı İmparatorluğunun batışı (Ufûl): Edirne savunması* (Istanbul: Arma, 2001), pp. 77, 113.

44. Üngör, *The Making of Modern Turkey*, p. 45; letter of May 8, 1913, from Enver Pasha to his wife, cited in M. Şükrü Hanioğlu (ed.), *Kendi Mektuplarında Enver Paşa* (Istanbul: Der, 1989), p. 242. Aksakal's translation is even stronger: "My heart is bleeding.... If I could tell you all the atrocities which the enemy has committed right here at the gates of Istanbul, you would understand the sufferings of the poor Muslims farther away. But our hatred is intensifying: revenge, revenge, revenge, there is nothing else." Aksakal, *The Ottoman Road to War*, p. 38.

45. Göçek, *Denial of Violence*, p. 246; Celaleddin Orhan, *Bir Bahriyelinin Anıları: 1914–1981* (Istanbul: Kastaş, 2001), p. 37.

46. Göçek, *Denial of Violence*, p. 245; Yakup Kadri Karaosmanoğlu, *Gençlik ve edebiyat hatıraları* (Yenişehir, Ankara: Bilgi Yayınevi, 1969), p. 219.

47. Aksakal, *The Ottoman Road to War*, pp. 25–29. The popular author Ahmed Hilmi wrote: "O Turk! Anatolia is the heart and soul of our homeland. O Turk! If we continue our old ways, if we face the enemy again in slumber, unprotected, then this time the enemy's sword will come to our [homeland's] heart and soul and kill each one of us." Cited in ibid., p. 31; Özdemir [Şehbenderzade Filibeli Ahmed Hilmi], *Türk Ruhu Nasıl Yapılıyor? Her vatanperverden, Bu Eserciği Türklere Okumasını Ve*

Anlatımasını Niyaz Ederiz, İkaz-ı Millet Kütüphanesi, no. 1 (March 1913–March 1914), pp. 6–7.

48. Erik-Jan Zürcher, "Macedonians in Anatolia: The Importance of the Macedonian Roots of the Unionists for Their Policies in Anatolia after 1914," *Middle Eastern Studies* 50, no. 6 (October 2014): 960–975.

49. Sam Lévy, "Les méfaits du comité d'union et progrès, la perte de l'Albanie," *Mecheroutiette Constitutionnel Ottoman*, no. 39 (February 1913): 27; translation in Kévorkian, *The Armenian Genocide*, pp. 120–121.

50. Hanioğlu, *A Brief History of the Late Ottoman Empire*, p. 165.

51. Der Matossian, *Shattered Dreams of Revolution*, p. 3.

52. Weitz, "Germany and the Young Turks," 186–187, 191; Kaiserlich Botschafter Wangenheim to Bethmann-Hollweg, Therapia, October 20, 1913, PAAA/R14161/ A21246/Nr. 302, pp. 3–4 (of the report).

53. Zürcher, *Turkey, A Modern History*, p. 114.

54. Yeghiayan, *My Patriarchal Memoirs*, p. 28; Kaligian, *Armenian Organization and Ideology*, pp. 209–210.

55. Chris B. Rooney, "The International Significance of British Naval Missions to the Ottoman Empire, 1908–1914," *Middle Eastern Studies* 34, no. 1 (January 1998): 1–29.

56. Aksakal, *The Ottoman Road to War*, pp. 80–83.

57. Aksakal concludes that "the political ideas appearing in the publications of 1913–14 were accepted, if not wholly embraced, by that regime [those who carried out the coup of January 1913]." Aksakal, *The Ottoman Road to War*, pp. 39–40.

58. Eşref Kuşçubaşı, *The Turkish Battle at Khaybar*, ed. and trans. Philip H. Stoddard and H. Basri Danışman (Istanbul: Arba Yayınları, 1999), pp. 220–221, 249.

59. Akçam, *The Young Turks' Crime Against Humanity*, p. 83; Zafer Toprak, *Türki-ye'de Ekonomi ve Toplum (1908–1950): Milli İktisat-Milli Burjuvazi* (Istanbul: Tarih Vakfı Yurt Yayınları, 1995), pp. 107–111. See also Uğur Ümit Üngör, "'Turkey for the Turks': Demographic Engineering in Eastern Anatolia, 1914–1945," in Suny et al. (eds.), *A Question of Genocide*, p. 297; George Shirinian (ed.), *The Asia Minor Catastrophe and the Ottoman Greek Genocide: Essays on Asia Minor, Pontos, and Eastern Thrace, 1912–1923* (Bloomington, IN: The Asia Minor and Pontos Hellenic Research Center, Inc., 2012).

60. Gaunt, *Massacres*, p. 37; David McDowall, *A Modern History of the Kurds* (London: I. B. Tauris, 1996), pp. 100–101; Bergfeld to Bethmann Hollweg, June 21, 1913, in *Die armenische Frage und der Genozid an den Armeniern in der Türkei (1913–1919)*, ed. Vardges Mikaelyan (Yerevan: Institut für Geschichte der Akademie der Wissenschaften Armeniens, 2004), p. 46.

61. Yektan Turkyilmaz, "Rethinking Genocide: Violence and Victimhood in Eastern Anatolia, 1913–1915" (Ph.D. diss., Duke University, 2011), pp. 69–77.

62. Cited in Kaligian, *Armenian Organization and Ideology*, p. 184; FO 424/239/40, Sir Gerard Lowther to Sir Edward Grey, Constantinople, June 29, 1913.

63. Kaligian, *Armenian Organization and Ideology*, p. 184; FO 424/240/36, Mr. Marling to Sir Edward Grety, Constantinople, October 15, 1913.

64. Üngör, *The Making of Modern Turkey*, p. 49; BOA/DH.KMS 2–2/5–7, document 7, Diyarbakır governor to Interior Ministry, March 26, 1913.

65. Kévorkian, *The Armenian Genocide*, pp. 146–147; Archives of the Patriarchate of Constantinople (APC), Armenian Patriarchate of Jerusalem (APJ), The patriarchate's Constantinople Information Bureau (PCI), 336–337, file no. 5, letter from Patriarch Arsharuni to the Russian, British and French ambassadors, May 14, 1913.

66. Kévorkian, *The Armenian Genocide*, p. 147; APC/APJ, PCI Bureau, 338–339, file no. 17, *takrir* to the grand vizier Mahmud Şevket, May 18/31, 1913.

67. Kévorkian, *The Armenian Genocide*, pp. 148–149; APC/APJ, PCI Bureau, 344–350, the grand vizier's response to the patriarchate's *takrir*, *tesdere* of the Ministry of Justice and Religious Denominations, file no. 78, June 22, 1329 (1913).

68. Turkyilmaz, "Rethinking Genocide," p. 96; Matteos M. Eplighatian, *Kiank me Azgis Kiankin Mej: Akanatesi ev Masnaktsoghi Vkayutyunner 1903–1923* (Antilias: Tparan Katoghikosutian Hayots Metsi Tann Kilikioy, 1987), p. 73. Turkyilmaz makes the important point that "the time period between the end of the Balkan Wars and World War I was not a prelude to the Armenian Genocide or to the overall catastrophe in the region. Myriad scenarios were possible. The catastrophic outcome was only one, perhaps the least foreseeable, and its occurrence was not warranted by what happened in the aftermath of the Balkan Wars but rather by political actors' decisions after World War I broke out" (Turkyilmaz, "Rethinking Genocide," p. 114).

69. "General Consul Adamov to Ambassador in Constantinople, Giers," Erzurum, April 7, 1913, АВПР, Posol'stvo v Konstantinopole, d. 2684, pp. 36–37; Nersisian and Saakian (eds.), *Genotsid armian v Osmanskoi imperii*.

70. "Viceroy of the Caucasus to the Minister of Foreign Affairs, Sazonov," May 2, 1913, AVPR [Arkhiv vneshnoi politiki Rossii (Archive of the Foreign Policy of Russia)], Politarkhiv, d. 3461, ll. 1–4; http://www.genocide.ru/lib/nersisyan/112–137.htm; M. Nersisian and Saakian (eds.), *Genotsid armian v Osmanskoi imperii*.

71. "Ambassador in Constantinople to the Minister of Foreign Affairs, Sazonov," December 29, 1913 (January 11, 1914), AVPR, Politarkhiv, d. 3465, l. 125; Nersisian and Saakian (eds.), *Genotsid armian v Osmanskoi imperii*.

72. Kévorkian, *The Armenian Genocide*, p. 134; "Preuves et réalité," *Hnchak*, no. 3 (March 1913): 6.

73. Kévorkian, *The Armenian Genocide*, pp. 173–174; (ed.), *Batmutiun S. D. Hnchakean Gusaktsutean, I*, pp. 348–349, 364–366, 371–373. See also the official

Ottoman government brochure, *La vérité sur le mouvement révolutionnaire arménien et les mesures gouvernementales* (Constantinople, 1916).

74. Yeghiayan, *My Patriarchal Memoirs*, p. 59; Kévorkian, *The Armenian Genocide*, p. 255,

75. Kaligian, *Armenian Organization and Ideology*, p. 149.

76. Ibid., p. 187; C/61–72/Western Bureau to U.S. Central Committee, November 9, 1913.

77. This was the first instance of using this term, later shorted to *Hai Tad*. Kaligian, *Armenian Organization and Ideology*, p. 187. I

78. Kévorkian, *The Armenian Genocide*, p. 151; "Mahaber Patrank," *Droshak*, no. 4 (231) (April 1913): 49. I slightly altered the translation for grammatical purposes.

79. Kaligian, *Armenian Organization and Ideology*, pp. 187–190.

80. Ibid., p. 216.

81. Ibid., p. 235.

82. Yeghiayan, *My Patriarchal Memoirs*, p. 23.

83. Aksakal, *The Ottoman Road to War*, p. 42; Norman Rich, *Great Power Diplomacy, 1814–1914* (New York: McGraw-Hill, 1992), p. 425.

84. Roderic H. Davison, "The Armenian Crisis, 1912–1914," *American Historical Review* 53, no. 3 (April 1948): 488–490.

85. Kévorkian, *The Armenian Genocide*, p. 157; letter from B. Nubar to Galli, ADA/BNu, file 2, June 25, 1913.

86. Yeghiayan, *My Patriarchal Memoirs*, p. 24.

87. Aksakal, *The Ottoman Road to War*, p. 78.

88. André Mandelshtam (1869–1949) was the first dragoman of the Russian embassy in Istanbul, the author of a reform plan, and the author of *Le sort de l'empire ottoman* (Lausanne: Librairie Payot, 1917). In the interwar period he was highly regarded as an international jurist and a pioneer of human rights.

89. Davison, "The Armenian Crisis," p. 491. The Russian government had expansionist plans in Persia, encouraging Russians to acquire farmland and settle in their sphere of influence. Peter Holquist, "'In Accord with State Interests and the People's Wishes': The Technocratic Ideology of Imperial Russia's Resettlement Administration," *Slavic Review* 60, no. 1 (Spring 2010): 166–167.

90. Heller, "Britain and the Armenian Question," p. 17.

91. Ibid., p. 20.

92. Yegiayan, *My Patriarchal Memoirs*, p. 7

93. Ibid., pp. 4–9. Patriarch Zaven had been a pupil and friend of the former patriarch Maghakia Ormanian (1896–1908) and benefited from the older man's political and personal connections.

94. Ibid., pp. 13–18.

95. Ibid., p. 18.

96. Ibid., p. 23; Heller, "Britain and the Armenian Question," p. 18.

97. Göçek, *Denial of Violence*, p. 207; Halil Menteşe, *Osmanlı Meclisi Mebusan Reisi Halil Menteşe'nin Anıları* (Istanbul: Hürriyet, 1986), pp. 12, 175.

98. Kévorkian, *The Armenian Genocide*, p. 160; Papazian, *Husher*, II, p. 191.

99. Garo, *Bank Ottoman*, pp. 184–185.

100. Turkyilmaz, "Rethinking Genocide," p. 61; *Tasvir-i Efkâr*, no. 942 (December 16, 1913); see also *Azatamart*, no. 1381 (December 17, 1913).

101. Davison, "The Armenian Crisis," p. 504.

102. Akçam, *The Young Turks' Crime Against Humanity*, pp. 130–131.

103. Djemal Pasha, *Memoirs of a Turkish Statesman, 1913–1919* (London: Hutchinson, n.d.; New York: George H. Doran, 1922), p. 276; Cemal Paşa, *Hatırlar ve Vesikalar* (Istanbul: Vakit, n.d.), p. 502.

104. Akçam, *The Young Turks' Crime Against Humanity*, pp. 132–133.

105. Garo, *Bank Ottoman*, pp. 189–191.

106. Kévorkian, *The Armenian Genocide*, p. 171.

107. See L. C. Westenenk, "Diary Concerning the Armenian Mission," *Armenian Review* 39, 1–153 (1986): 29–89.

108. As Sir Harry Luke noted long ago, Enver "and his colleagues envisaged the three policies being pursued simultaneously and side by side, each one being emphasized in whatever place, at whatever time, it was the most appropriate policy to apply. Ottomanism continued to be the keynote of internal politics; Turkish nationalism, the keynote of relations with the Tatars of Russia, some of whom were beginning to manifest sentiments of sympathy with their cousins in Turkey in their time of trouble; Pan-Islam, that of relations with the Arabs and other non-Turkish Moslems within the Empire and of the Moslem peoples of North Africa and elsewhere outside it." Harry Luke, *The Making of Modern Turkey: From Byzantium to Angora* (London: Macmillan, 1936), p. 157.

109. Djemal Pasha, *Memories of a Turkish Statesman*, pp. 251–252; quoted in Jacob Landau, *Pan-Turkism in Turkey: A Study of Irredentism* (London: C. Hurst and Co., 1981), p. 50.

CHAPTER SEVEN: War

1. Mustafa Aksakal, "The Ottoman Empire," in *The Cambridge History of the First World War*, ed. Jay Winter (Cambridge: Cambridge University Press, 2014), p. 464.

2. Ibid., p. 468; Erik J. Zürcher estimates 325,000 directly killed in action and between 400,000 and 700,000 wounded. "The Ottoman Soldier in World War I," in idem, *The Young Turk Legacy and Nation Building: From the Ottoman Empire to Atatürk's Turkey* (London: I. B. Tauris, 2010), p. 186.

3. Ibid., p. 478.

4. Yiğit Akın, "The Ottoman Home Front during World War I: Everyday Politics, Society, and Culture" (Ph.D. diss., Ohio State University, 2011), p. 245.

5. Aksakal, "'Holy War Made in Germany?'" p. 12; Erik-Jan Zürcher, "Griechisch-orthodoxe und muslimische Flüchtlinge und Deportierte in Griechenland und der Türkei seit 1912," in *Enzyköpadie Migration in Europa Vom 17 Jahhundert bis zur Gegenwart*, ed. Klaus J. Bade et al. (Paderborn: Ferdinand Schöningh/Wilhelm Fink, 2007), pp. 623–627.

6. Grigoris Balakian, *Armenian Golgotha*, trans. Peter Balakian with Aris Sevag (New York: Alfred A. Knopf, 2009), p. 18.

7. Mustafa Aksakal writes that "the generations of pro-European reformers were eventually replaced by increasingly radical, younger leaders who believed that diplomatic history had taught a single lesson: only military power could preserve the empire." *The Ottoman Road to War*, p. 9; pp. 13–14.

8. Dündar, *Crime of Numbers*, p. 47; Hans-Lukas Kieser, *İskalanmış Barış: Doğu Vilayetleri'nde Misyonerlik Etnik Kimlik ve Devlet 1839–1938* (Istanbul: İletişim, 2005), p. 784.

9. On the removal of the Greeks from Foça, see Emre Erol, "Organised chaos as diplomatic ruse and demographic weapon: The expulsion of the Ottoman Greeks (Rum) from Foça, 1914," *Tijdschrift voor sociale en economische geschiedenis* 10, no. 4 (2013): 66–96. Erol makes the important argument that "those who were subjected to nationalist violence are more likely to participate in nationalist projects" (p. 66).

10. Matthias Bjørnlund, "The Persecution of Greeks and Armenians in Smyrna, 1914–1916: A Special Case in the Course of the Late Ottoman Genocides," in Shirinian (ed.), *The Asia Minor Catastrophe and the Ottoman Greek Genocide*, pp. 103–106. See also Taner Akçam, "The Greek Deportations and Massacres of 1913–1914: A Trial Run for the Armenian Genocide," in ibid., pp. 69–88.

11. Aksakal, *The Ottoman Road to War*, pp. 42–48.

12. Henry Morgenthau, *Ambassador Morgenthau's Story* (Detroit: Wayne State University Press, 2003), p. 34. The original publication (New York: Doubleday, Page & Co., 1918) has been followed by successive reissues, among them one published by the Gomidas Institute in Princeton, New Jersey, in 2000, with an introduction by Ara Sarafian. All references in this book are to the 2003 Wayne State University Press edition.

13. "Statement by the Turkish Ambassador (Rüstem) as Published in the Washington 'Evening Star,'" September 8, 1914, in *Papers Relating to the Foreign Relations of the United States. The Lansing Papers, 1914–1920*, 2 vols. (Washington, DC: Government Printing Office, 1939), vol. I, p. 70; Walther, "Sacred Interests," p. 483.

14. Morgenthau, *Ambassador Morgenthau's Story*, p. 222.

15. Ibid., p. 223.

16. Akçam, *The Young Turks' Crime Against Humanity*, pp. 99–100; report by Hans Humann, military attaché at the Istanbul embassy, Ernst Jaeckh Papers, Manuscript and Archival Collection, Yale University Papers, Group no. 467, Box 1, File 17, November 1, 1914.

17. Akçam, *The Young Turks' Crime Against Humanity*, pp. 100–101; coded telegram from the Ministry of Interior's General Directorate of Security to the provinces . . . , BOA/DH.ŞFR., no. 46/133, November 2, 1914; report by Hans Humann, military attaché at the Istanbul embassy, Ernst Jaeckh Papers, Manuscript and Archival Collection, Yale University Papers, Group no. 467, Box 1, File 18, November 17, 1914.

18. Akın, "The Ottoman Home Front during World War I," p. 241; Murat Bardakçı, *Talat Paşa'nın Evrak-ı Metrukesi: Sadrazam Talat Paşa'nın Özel Arşivinde Bulunan Ermeni Tehciri Belgeler ve Bazı Hususi Yazışmalar* (Istanbul: Everest Yayınları, 2008), p. 79. This is the so-called Black Book prepared for Talat Paşa with statistical material on population movements and deportations during the war. The removal of the Greeks in 1914 constituted an ethnic cleansing rather than the systematic killing that characterizes genocide. Matthias Bjørnlund sums it up best: "In 1914, the aim of the Turkification policy was not to exterminate but to expel as many Greeks from Ionia and Ottoman Thrace as possible as not only a 'security measure' but as also an extension of the policy of economic and cultural Turkification, while at the same time accommodating the *muhadjirs* who had been driven out of their homes under brutal circumstances." Bjørnlund, "The Persecution of Greeks and Armenians in Smyrna," p. 111. Akçam emphasizes the "continuity between the organized cleansing operations against the non-Muslim populations of western Anatolia—primarily the forcible expulsion of the Greek population—that began in the spring of 1914 and the cleansing of Anatolia of its Armenian population during the First World War." Akçam, "The Greek Deportations and Massacres," p. 85; idem, *The Young Turks' Crime Against Humanity*, pp. 94–96.

19. Erik-Jan Zürcher, "Greek and Turkish Refugees and Deportees 1912–1924," in *The Encyclopedia of European Migration and Minorities From the Seventeenth Century to the Present*, ed. Klaus J. Bade, Peter C. Emmer, Leo Lucassen, and Jochen Oltmer (Cambridge: Cambridge University Press, 2011).

20. Talat admitted that acts of terror and violence were carried out against the Greek population in the region: "The [departing] Greeks are leaving a great many of their possessions, except for transportable beds and such; there are instances of looting, and there have been both fights and killing." Akçam, *The Young Turks' Crime Against Humanity*, p. 84; Yusuf Hikmet Bayur, *Türk İnkılabı Tarihi, Cilt II, Kısım III* (Ankara: Türk Tarih Kurumu, 1983), p. 255. The translation here, offered by Candan Badem, differs slightly from that given by Akçam.

21. Fuad Dündar, "Pouring a People into the Desert: The 'Definitive Solution' of the Unionists to the Armenian Question," in Suny et al. (eds.), *A Question of Genocide*, p. 280. See also Emmanoul Emmanouilidis, *Ta teleftaia ete tes Othmanikes Aftokratias* (Athens, 1924).

22. Dündar, *Crime of Numbers*, pp. 78–79.

23. Aksakal, *The Ottoman Road to War*, p. 72.

24. Ibid., pp. 85, 87.

25. Murat Özyüksel, *Osmanlı-Alman İlişkilerinin Gelişim Sürecinde Anadolu ve Bağdat Demiryolları* (Istanbul: Arba, 1988), *passim*.

26. Aksakal, "The Ottoman Empire," p. 471; BOA/DH.ŞFR 43.141, August 2, 1914, Talat to the governors of Erzurum, Adana, Aydın, Bitlis, Halep, Dıyar-ı Bekır, Sıvas, Trabzon, Kastamonu, Mamuret-ül-aziz, Mosul, Van, Bolu, Çanık Kale-i Sultaniye, and Antalya.

27. Aksakal, "'Holy War Made in Germany?'" p. 13; Enver to Cavid, 24/25 Temmuz 330 [August 7–8, 1914], Archives of the Turkish general Staff [ATASE], BDH, klasör 68, yeni dosya 337, fihrist 1 and 1–1.

28. Aksakal, *The Ottoman Road to War*, p. 4; BA-MA, RM 40–457, sheet 254, Giers to St. Petersburg, August 6, 1914, no. 631; *IBZI* [*Die Internationalen Beziehungen im Zeitalter des Imperialismus*], Series I, vol. 2, no. 9, Giers to St. Petersburg, August 6, 1914, pp. 6–7; Sean McMeekin, *The Russian Origins of the First World War* (Cambridge, MA: The Belknap Press of Harvard University Press, 2011), pp. 106–107.

29. Cited in Aksakal, *The Ottoman Road to War*, p. 128; *IBZI*, Series II, vol. 6/1, no. 60, Giers to Sazonov, Urgent, August 10, 1914, pp. 40–41.

30. Aksakal, *The Ottoman Road to War*, pp. 3–4; *IZBI*, Series II, vol. 6/1, Izvvolskii to Sazonov, August 11, 1914, p, 44 and n. 2.

31. Aksakal, *The Ottoman Road to War*, p. 129; *IBZI*, Series II, vol. 6/1, no. 94, Leontiev to Danilov, August 13, 1914, Enver Pasha's Proposal for the Conclusion of a Military Alliance, pp. 64–69; ibid., Series II, vol. 6/1, no. 107, Giers [Leontiev], to Sazonov, August 15, 1914, pp. 80–81.

32. Aksakal, *The Ottoman Road to War*, p. 130.

33. Cited in ibid., p. 132; *IBZI*, Series II, vol. 6/1, no. 191, Sazonov to Goremykin, August 30, 1914, pp. 144–145; no. 295, Klemm to Giers, September 23, 1914, pp. 227–228.

34. Cited in Aksakal, *The Ottoman Road to War*, p. 134; *IZBI*, Series II, vol. 6/1, no. 182, Sazonov to Basili, August 29, 1914, pp. 137–138.

35. "If such an alliance had materialized, it would certainly have marked a diplomatic revolution; not only would it have altered the course of the First World War, as Russia could have been supplied through the Straits by its Entente partners, but it

undoubtedly would also have charted a different path for the history of the modern Middle East." Aksakal, *The Ottoman Road to War*, p. 128.

36. Aksakal ends his book with a pessimistic assumption about the prospects for Ottomanism after 1914, but the failure to create a multinational state did not necessarily mean that genocide was the only option. He writes, "one might speculate that, given the incompleteness of the nationalizing process in the Ottoman territories in 1914, the diverse peoples of the region might have managed to continue their fare within the old Ottoman framework. The radical change in leadership after January 1913, however, suggests that the time in which 'continuation' would have been an option had already passed." Ibid., p. 194.

37. Turkyilmaz, "Rethinking Genocide," p. 127.

38. Morgenthau, *Ambassador Morgenthau's Story*, pp. 85–86.

39. Ibid., p. 87.

40. Cited in Aksakal, *The Ottoman Road to War*, p. 136; ATASE, BDH Klasör 2430m Yeni Dosya 1009ö Fihrist 7, Cemil to Enver, August 3, 1914.

41. Aksakal, *The Ottoman Road to War*, p. 138; PA/AA, R, Zimmerman to Jagow [Enver Pasha to German headquarters], August 20, 1914; Wolfdieter Bihl, *Der Kaukasus-Politik der Mittelmächte*, vol. I, *Ihre Basis in der Orient Politik und ihre Aktionen, 1914–1917* (Vienna: Böhlau, 1975), p. 230.

42. Aksakal, *The Ottoman Road to War*, p. 161.

43. Ibid., pp. 168–169; PA/AA, R 1914, Besprechung mit Enver Pascha am 2 Oktober 1914, reported by Humann, and also found in BA-MA, RM 40–4, sheets 94–97.

44. Aksakal, *The Ottoman Road to War*, pp. 176–178. The Ottomans joined reluctantly, not enthusiastically, "after three months of foot-dragging, deception, and protracted negotiations with Berlin, and only after the German-Ottoman alliance came close to rupturing." Ibid., p. 193.

45. "The choice, on the Ottoman side, lay solely in the hands of the Deputy Commander-in-Chief (*Başkumandan Vekili*) Enver Paşa. . . . [His biographer wrote,] 'So much so that it would be no exaggeration to call this war Enver Paşa's war.'" M. Naim Turfan, *Rise of the Young Turks: Politics, and the Military and Ottoman Collapse* (London: I. B. Tauris, 2000), p. 363; the biographer is S. S. Aydemir, *Makedonya'dan Ortaasya'ya Enver Paşa* (Istanbul: Remzi Kitabevi, 1971–1972), p. 487.

46. Morgenthau, *Ambassador Morgenthau's Story*, p. 88.

47. Kévorkian, *The Armenian Genocide*, pp. 180–187. Kévorkian's account of the formation of the Special Organization is based on the testimonies at the trials of the Unionists held in 1919–1920 and published originally in *Takvim-ı Vekayi*.

48. Kévorkian, *The Armenian Genocide*, p. 184; testimony from the First Session of the Trial of the Unionists, April 27, 1919, at 1:50: *Takvim-ı Vekayi*, no. 3540 (May 5,

1919): 5, col 2, lines 8–14; Krieger [pseudonym of Father Grigor Gergerian], *Enggbati Haiaspanutean Vaveragrakan Patmutiune* (New York, 1980), p. 215; Sixth Session of the Trial of the Unionists, May 14, 1919, questioning of Midhat Şükrü, (pp. 91–99): *Takvim-i Vekayi*, no. 3557 (May 25, 1919): 92.

49. A useful review of the historiographical literature on *Teşkilat-i Masusa* can be found in Polat Safi, "History in the Trench: The Ottoman Special Organization—*Teşkilat-ı Masusa* Literature," *Middle Eastern Studies* 48, no. 1 (January 2012): 89–106. Regrettably, the article deals primarily with what cannot be said about the Special Organization rather than what it actually was. An early account still worth reading is Philip H. Stoddard, "The Ottoman Government and the Arabs, 1911–1918: A Preliminary Study on the Teşkilat-ı Masusa" (Ph.D. diss., Princeton University, 1963).

50. Üngör, *The Making of Modern Turkey*, p. 49; BOA/DH.SYS 23/4, document 2, Diyarbakır governor to Interior Ministry, May 1914; ibid., p. 50; BOA/DH.ŞFR 44/234, Emniyet-i Umûmiye Müdüriyeti (Ali Münif) to Diyarbakır, September 13, 1914.

51. Thomas K. Mugerditchian, *The Diyarbekir Massacres and Kurdish Atrocities* (London: Gomidas, 2013), p. 13.

52. Ibid., pp. 10–11.

53. Balakian, *Armenian Golgotha*, p. 28.

54. Ibid., p. 31.

55. Akçam, *The Young Turks' Crime Against Humanity*, p. 171; coded telegram from Van governor, Tahsin Bey, to the Interior Ministry, BOA/DH.EUM, 2 Şube, no. 1/31/1, August 25, 1915.

56. Akçam, *The Young Turks' Crime Against Humanity*, pp. 171–172; coded telegram from Mustafa Bey, governor of the province of Bitlis, to the Interior Ministry, BOA/DH.EUM, 2. Şube, no. 68/17/1, August 25/26, 1915.

57. Akçam, *The Young Turks' Crime Against Humanity*, p. 172; coded telegram from Sabit Bey, governor of the province of Mamuretü'laziz, to the Interior Ministry, October 5, 1914.

58. Jacques Derogy, *Resistance and Revenge: The Armenian Assassination of the Turkish Leaders Responsible for the 1915 Massacres and Deportations* (New Brunswick, NJ: Transaction, 1990), p. 11.

59. Yeghiayan, *My Patriarchal Memoirs*, p. 33.

60. Kachaznuni (1868–1938), who later served as the first prime minister of the independent Armenian Republic, denounced the formation of the volunteer units in a postwar pamphlet, *The Armenian Revolutionary Federation (Dashnagtzoutiun) Has Nothing To Do Anymore*, trans. Matthew A. Callender, ed. John Roy Carlson [Arthur A. Derounian] (New York: Armenian Information Service, 1955), pp. 1–2.

The pamphlet was originally a report delivered to the Bucharest Congress of the Dashnaktsutyun in April 1923 and published in Armenian in Vienna the same year by the Mkhitarian printing press. Highly critical of the policies of his former party comrades, Kachaznuni's work has been widely used in the genocide denialist literature and websites.

61. Kévorkian, *The Armenian Genocide*, p. 172; *Adenagrutyun* (minutes of the inaugural session of the National Chamber), Constantinople, record of July 4, 1914 session, pp. 15–20.

62. Kuşçubaşı, *The Turkish Battle at Khaybar*, pp. 220–221, 249.

63. Kévorkian, *The Armenian Genocide*, pp. 172–175; Gidur (ed.), *Batmutiun S. D. Hnchakean Kusaktsutean*, I, pp. 376, 380–390.

64. Kaligian, *Armenian Organization and Ideology*, pp. 220–221; C/103–30/ Vramian to Western Bureau, August 17, 1914. Details on the operation of *Teşkilat-ı Mahsusa* can be found in the memoirs of Arif Cemil [Denker], *I. Dünya Savaşında Teşkilât-ı Mahsusa* (Istanbul: Arba, 1997); published earlier as *Umumi Harpte Teşkilât-ı Mahsusa*, in installments (ninety issues) in *Vakit*, from November 2, 1933, to February 7, 1934; trans. into Armenian by V. Ishkhanian in *Harach*, November 19, 1933–April 7, 1934 (ninety-two issues). Armenian opponents of the Dashnaks have been critical of the party's relationship with the CUP. Kaligian, who is generally balanced though sympathetic to the Dashnaktsutyun, concludes, "There was no blind faith in the intentions of the CUP, but the ARF leadership may have held out hope too long for the triumph of the progressive current." Kaligian, *Armenian Organization and Ideology*, p. 228.

65. Kévorkian, *The Armenian Genocide*, p. 175; Hratch Dasnabédian, *Histoire de la Féderation révolutionaire arménienne dachnaktsoutioun, 1890–1924* (Milan: Oemme, 1988), pp. 107–108; encrypted telegram read at the sixth session of the trial of the Unionists, May 14, 1919, published in *Takvim-i Vekayi*, no. 3557 (May 25, 1919): 98. Similar proposals were made to the Assyrian clergy, who like the Dashnaks refused to incite insurrection in other states but pledged the loyalty of Ottoman Assyrians. Gaunt, *Massacres*, pp. 56–57; statement by Roupen of Sasun to the Armenian community of Moscow and narrative of Y. K. Rushdouni, in *The Treatment of the Armenians in the Ottoman Empire 1915–1916*, ed. James Bryce and Arnold Toynbee (Princeton, NJ: Gomidas, 2000; originally published, 1916), pp. 16, 94; Johannes Lepsius, *Le rapport secret du Dr. Johannes Lepsius sur les massacres d'Arménie* (Paris: Payot, 1918), pp. 200–201.

66. Üngör, *The Making of Modern Turkey*, pp. 56–57; BOA/DH.ŞFR 44/200, Talat to provinces, September 6, 1914.

67. Akcam, *From Empire to Republic*, p. 164; Cemil, *I. Dunya Savaşında Teşkilat-ı Masusa*, pp. 46–47.

68. Kévorkian, *The Armenian Genocide*, p. 176; Papazian, *Husher*, II, pp. 280–281.

69. Kévorkian, *The Armenian Genocide*, p. 176; Gabriel Lazian, *Hayastan ev Hai dte* (Cairo, 1957), pp. 175–176.

70. Kévorkian, *The Armenian Genocide*, p. 177; Simon Vratsian, "Hayutyune Rus-Tachkakan Paterazmi Handep," *Droshak*, nos. 9–12 (September–December 1914): 129–130.

71. Balakian, *Armenian Golgotha*, pp. 39–40.

72. Ibid., pp. 37–38; Yeghiayan, *My Patriarchal Memoirs*, pp. 54–55; see Simon Payaslian, "The Destruction of the Armenian Church during the Genocide," *Genocide Studies & Prevention* 1, no. 2 (Fall 2006): 149–171.

73. Hilmar Kaiser, "Historical Introduction: Max Erwin Von Scheubner-Richter and the Armenian Genocide," in Paul Leverkuehn, *A German Officer During the Armenian Genocide: A Biography of Max von Scheubner-Richter*, trans. Alasdair Lean (London: Gomidas, 2008), pp. xxxv–xxxvi.

74. Kévorkian accepts the thesis of Vahakn Dadrian that the Armenian Genocide was already part of the war plans of the CUP government. *The Armenian Genocide*, p. 179.

75. Much of the discussion of the home front and the mobilization of the Ottoman population is based on Akın, "The Ottoman Home Front during World War I." See also Mehmet Beşikci, *The Ottoman Mobilization of Manpower in the First World War Between Voluntarism and Resistance* (Leiden: Brill, 2012).

76. Akın, "The Ottoman Home Front during World War I," p. 86; Ephraim K. Jemazian, *Judgment Unto Truth: Witnessing the Armenian Genocide*, trans. Alice Haig (New Brunswick, NJ: Transaction, 1990), pp. 46–47; Jakob Kunzler, *In the Land of Blood and Tears: Experiences in Mesopotamia during the World War (1914–1918)*, ed. Ara Ghazarian (Arlington, MA: Armenian Cultural Foundation, 2007; originally published, 1921), p. 9.

77. Akın, "The Ottoman Home Front during World War I," p. 97.

78. Yeghiayan, *My Patriarchal Memoirs*, p. 38. The effects of the mobilization are reported in numerous letters and reports documented in ibid., pp. 34–44.

79. Henry H. Riggs, *Days of Tragedy in Armenia: Personal Experiences in Harpoot 1915–1917* (Ann Arbor, MI: Gomidas, 1997), p. 15.

80. *Seferberlik* became a term whose meaning stretched far beyond mobilization to connote the entire period of the war and was associated with hunger, famine, and death. Akın, "The Ottoman Home Front during World War I," pp. 222–223.

81. Aksakal, "The Ottoman Empire," p. 463.

82. Cited in Yeghiayan, *My Patriarchal Memoirs*, p. 42.

83. Aksakal, "The Ottoman Empire," pp. 467–468, 478.

84. "Transport and communications were the Achilles' heel of the Ottoman army. The empire only had 5700 kilometres of railway at its disposal—a density (when compared to the surface area of the country) which was thirty times lower than that

of France. The railways were single track and the vital railway connection with the fronts in Palestine and Mesopotamia was interrupted where it crossed the Taurus and Amanos mountain ranges, making it necessary to load and unload all trains four times." Zürcher, "Ottoman Labour Battalions in World War I," p. 1910.

85. Akın, "The Ottoman Home Front during World War I," pp. 159–179.

86. Ibid., p. 121.

87. Aksakal, "The Ottoman Empire," p. 469.

88. Zürcher, "Ottoman Labour Battalions in World War I," p. 192.

89. Jacques Rhétoré, *Les Chrétiens aux Bêtes: Souvenirs de la guerre sainte proclamée par les Turcs contre les chrétiens en 1915* (Paris: Éditions du Cerf, 2005), pp. 26–27.

90. Yeghiayan, *My Patriarchal Memoirs*, p. 45.

91. Ibid., pp. 46–48.

92. Report from the prelate of Muş, Nerses Kharakhanian, November 9, 1914, cited in ibid., p. 48.

93. Ibid., p. 49.

94. Even after the Ottomans bombarded Russian ships and bases, Foreign Minister Sazonov informed his ambassador in France, Maurice Paléologue, that "His Majesty has decided that not a man shall be withdrawn from the German front. Our first concern is to beat Germany. The defeat of Germany will necessarily involve the ruin of Turkey. We shall keep down to a minimum the forces required for defense against the Turkish fleet and army." Cited in Ozan Arslan, "A Front 'Bon Pour L'Orient': An Analysis of a Russian War Presumed Won Before It Actually Was," unpublished manuscript; M. Paléologue, *La Russie des Tsars pendant la Grande Guerre* (Paris: Librairie Plon, 1921), pp. 181–182.

95. "Russian policy was less offensive than defensive. Since its war strategy was predicated upon defeating Germany in the west, it foresaw only 'active defence' in the conflict with Turkey, and to this end it was important to keep Russian commitments to a minimum and to utilize any means available at the discretion of the military commander and viceroy of the Caucasus, Count Illarion Ivanovich Vorontsov-Dashkov." Bloxham, *The Great Game of Genocide*, p. 72.

96. Russia was primarily interested in annexing Austrian Galicia, not eastern Anatolia. Peter Holquist, "The Politics and Practice of the Russian Occupation of Armenia, 1915–February 1917," in Suny et al. (eds.), *A Question of Genocide*, p. 153.

97. McMeekin, *Russian Origins of the First World War*, p. 114; A. Bodger, "Russia and the End of the Ottoman Empire," in *The Great Powers and the End of the Ottoman Empire*, ed. Marian Kent (London: Frank Cass, 1982), p. 91.

98. Arslan emphasizes the fact that the best soldiers in the Caucasus were sent to the western front while less well-trained and equipped men were recruited for the Caucasian front. Arslan, "A Front 'Bon Pour L'Orient,'" pp. 18–20.

99. Ozan Arslan, "Les faits et les buts de guerre ottomans sur le front caucasien pendant la premiere guerre mondiale" (Ph.D. diss., Université Paul Valéry, Montpellier III, 2011), pp. 141–142; William Edward David Allen and Paul Muratoff, *Caucasian Battlefields: A History of the Wars on the Turco-Caucasian Border, 1828–1921* (Cambridge: Cambridge University Press, 1953), p. 242.

100. Arslan, "A Front 'Bon Pour L'Orient,'" p. 11.

101. *Mshak*, no. 215 (September 27, 1914): 1; cited in Turkyilmaz, "Rethinking Genocide," p. 189.

102. *Mshak*, no. 238 (October 22, 1914): 2; cited in Turkyilmaz, "Rethinking Genocide," p. 195.

103. *Horizon*, no. 234 (October 22, 1914): 1; cited in Turkyilmaz, "Rethinking Genocide," p. 247.

104. See his articles in *Mshak*, nos. 234–236 (October 17–19, 1914); and the careful treatment of Ananun's views in Turkyilmaz, "Rethinking Genocide," pp. 197–205.

105. Balakian, *Armenian Golgotha*, p. 22. The historian Yektan Turkyilmaz echoes Balakian's estimation of the effect of the organization of Armenian volunteers by the Dashnaks: "I do not address the question of why the Armenian genocide happened; but, as the party's audacious political maneuvers in joining forces with Tsarist Russia fuelled the paranoia and rage toward Armenians, I claim that the ARF's role in the escalation is undeniable." Turkyilmaz, "Rethinking Genocide," pp. 185–186.

106. Bloxham, *The Great Game of Genocide*, pp. 72–73; Arthur Beylerian (ed.), *Les Grands Puissances, l'empire ottoman et les arméniennes dans les archives français* (Paris: Panthéon Sorbonne, 1983), no. 2; Arslan, "Les faits et les buts de guerre ottomans sur le front caucasien," p. 206.

107. Arslan, "Les faits et les buts de guerre ottomans sur le front caucasien," p. 206.

108. Bloxham, *The Great Game of Genocide*, pp. 72–73; Vatche Ghazarian (ed.), *Boghos Nubar's Papers and the Armenian Question 1915–1916* (Waltham, MA: Mayreni, 1996), no. 2.

109. On the Armenian volunteer units, see Murad Karapetyan, *Haykakan Kamavorakan Khmbere Ev Azgayin Gumartaknere Kovkasyan Razmachakatum, 1914–1917 Tt.* (Erevan: HH GAA "Gitutyun" Hratarakchutyun, 1999).

110. Gaunt, "The Ottoman Treatment of the Assyrians," in Suny et al. (eds.), *A Question of Genocide*, p. 249; Minorskii to Ministry of Foreign Affairs, September 24, 1914, AVPRI Persidskii stol, f. 144, O528/b, d. 83, l. 42; cited in John Tchalenko, *Images of the Endgame* (London: I. B. Tauris, 2006), p. 186.

111. Holquist, "The Politics and Practice," p. 158; secret report from the Kutaisi provincial gendarme department to the chancellery for the viceroy of the Caucasus, May 14, 1914, SSTsSA, f. 13 [Kantseliariia namestnika na Kavkaze], op. 27s., d. 3265, ll. 89–91; ll. 17, 103, 107, 128.

112. Holquist, "The Politics and Practice," pp. 158–159; reports submitted by Russian officials over the course of November–December 1914 and January 1915 in SSTsSA f. 13 op. 27s., d. 3193.

113. Holquist, "The Politics and Practice," p. 159; M. Philips Price, *War and Revolution in Asiatic Russia* (London: George Allen & Unwin, 1918), pp. 223–224, p. 208.

114. "Thus Russian authorities in January–April 1915 faced a situation not unlike the one which the Ottoman state claimed as a justification for its reprisals against Ottoman-subject Armenians. What the Russian case demonstrates, however, is that a similar structural situation did not produce identical results." Peter Holquist, "Forms of Violence During the Russian Occupation of Ottoman Territory and in Northern Persia (Urmia and Astrabad), October 1914-December 1917," in Bartov and Weitz (eds.), *Shatterzones of Empire*, pp. 334–361. Holquist argues that Russian violence was the result of "generic institutional concerns of the military" rather than ideologically driven like the violence carried out by the Ottomans against Armenians, Assyrians, and Greeks (p. 343).

115. Eric Lohr, *Nationalizing the Russian Empire: The Campaign against Enemy Aliens during World War I* (Cambridge, MA: Harvard University Press, 2003), pp. 151–152.

116. Uğur Ümit Üngör and Eric Lohr, "Economic Nationalism, Confiscation and Genocide: A Comparison of Ottoman and Russian Economic Persecution in World War I," *Journal of Modern European History* 12, no. 4 (2014): 500–522.

117. The fundamental work on the Ottomans on the Caucasian front is the superb dissertation of Arslan, "Les faits et les buts de guerre ottomans sur le front caucasien." A classic work is Allen and Muratoff, *Caucasian Battlefields*. See also Edward J. Erickson, *Ordered to Die: A History of the Ottoman Empire in the First World War* (Westport, CT: Greenwood, 2001).

118. Kaiser, "Historical Introduction," pp. xx–xxx.

119. Akçam, *The Young Turks' Crime Against Humanity*, p. 148; coded telegram from the Interior Ministry's General Directorate of Security to the provinces of Van, Bitlis, Mamuretülaziz, Adana, Diyarbakır, and Sivas, BOA/DH.ŞFR., nr. 45/115, August 28, 1914.

120. Kévorkian, *The Armenian Genocide*, p. 340; Arif Cemil, *Umumi Harpte Teşkilât-ı Mahsusa*, in *Vakit*, November 2, 1933–February 7, 1934; *Harach*, November 19, 1933–April 7, 1934, 17.

121. Kévorkian, *The Armenian Genocide*, p. 225; AMAE, Perse, n.s., vol. 18, ff. 112 and 113.

122. Gaunt, *Massacres*, pp. 127–128; AVPRI [Arkhiv vneshnei politiki rossiiskoi imperii], I.F. 293, des. 571, dossier 420, list 5–6; AVPRI, I.F. 293, des. 571, dossier 420, list 59–61.

123. Gaunt, "The Ottoman Treatment of the Assyrians," p. 248; BOA/DF.ÍFR 46/78, Ministry of Interior to Van *vilayet*, October 26, 1914.

124. This project, writes the historian of the Assyrian Genocide, "was not simply a resettlement, since the dispersal of the Assyrians in the manner described was designed to destroy their culture, language, and traditional way of life." Gaunt, "The Ottoman Treatment of the Assyrians," p. 248; see also Surma d'Beit Mar Shimun, *Assyrian Church Customs and the Murder of Mar Shimun* (London: Faith, 1920), p. 67.

125. Gaunt, "The Ottoman Treatment of the Assyrians," p. 249; William Walker Rockwell, *The Pitiful Plight of the Assyrian Christians in Persia and Kurdistan* (New York: American Committee for Armenian and Syrian Relief, 1916), p. 64.

126. Gaunt, "The Ottoman Treatment of the Assyrians," p. 249; statement by the Reverend William A. Shedd, in Bryce and Toynbee (eds.), *The Treatment of Armenians in the Ottoman Empire*, pp. 136–140; Eugène Griselle, *Syriens et chaldéens leur martyre, leurs espérances* (Paris: Bloud et Gay, 1917), pp. 41–42.

127. Gaunt, *Massacres*, p. 135; Letter of Y. K. Rushdouni, June 7, 1915, in Bryce and Toynbee (eds.), *The Treatment of the Armenians in the Ottoman Empire*, pp. 88, 96–98. See also Akçam, *The Young Turks' Crime Against Humanity*, p. 147; coded telegram from the Interior Ministry's General Directorate of Security to the provinces of Van and Mosul, BOA/DH.ŞFR., nr. 45/242, October 11, 1914.

128. The German pastor Johannes Lepsius reported that 1,276 Armenians were killed in these 2 villages and 250 young women and girls were abducted. He estimated that the total killed in the region in November and December reached 7,000. Kévorkian, *The Armenian Genocide*, p. 220; Lepsius, *Le rapport secret du Dr. Johannes Lepsius sur les massacres d'Arménie*, p. 90.

129. Gaunt, *Massacres*, pp. 131–132; Henry Barby, *Au pays de l'épouvante: L'Arménie martyre* (Paris: A. Michel, 1917), p. 234.

130. Gaunt, "The Ottoman Treatment of the Assyrians," p. 251; Rossiiskii gosudarstvennyi voenno-istoricheskii arkhiv (The Russian State Military-Historical Archive) [RGVIA], Fund 13159, dossier 1428, list 22, testimony of Judad Abdarova, August 27, 30, 1916.

131. Arslan, "Les faits et les buts de guerre ottomans sur le front caucasien," pp. 208–209.

132. Ibid., p. 209; Akcam, *A Shameful Act*, pp. 198–199, 328.

133. Gaunt, *Massacres*, p. 103.

134. Gaunt, "The Ottoman Treatment of the Assyrians," p. 252.

135. Letter from Hans von Wangenheim, to Chancellor Bethmann Hollweg, Pera, December 30, 1914, no. 342; Johannes Lepsius (ed.), *Archives du génocide des Arméniens: recueil des documents diplomatiques allemands* (Paris: Fayard, 1986), doc.

14, pp. 68–69; available online at http://www.armenocide.net/armenocide/arm-gende.nsf/$$AllDocs/1914–12–30-DE-00.

136. Balakian, *Armenian Golgotha*, p. 49; Kévorkian, *The Armenian Genocide*, p. 211; the circular was published in Yervant Perdahdjian, *Événements et faits observés à Constantinople par le vicariat [patriarcal] (1914–1916)*, trans. R. H. Kévorkian, *Revue d'Histoire Arménienne Contemporaine 1* (1995): 250–251.

137. Yeghiayan, *My Patriarchal Memoirs*, p. 51.

138. Ibid., pp. 50–51.

139. Gaunt, *Massacres*, p. 57; statement by Roupen of Sasun to the Armenian community of Moscow, in Bryce and Toynbee (eds.), *The Treatment of the Armenians in the Ottoman Empire*, pp. 116–117; Cevdet to minister of interior, November 30/ December 1, 1914, document no. 1996, in *Askeri Tarih Belgeleri Dergisi* 34, no. 85 (October 1985).

140. See Michael Bonner, *Jihad in Islamic History: Doctrines and Practices* (Princeton, NJ: Princeton University Press, 2006; 2nd ed., 2007).

141. Kévorkian, *The Armenian Genocide*, p. 212; the text of the call for a jihad was read out at the first session of the trial of the cabinet, on June 3, 1919, and published in *Takvim-i Vekayi*, no. 3571 (June 11, 1919): 127–140.

142. Gaunt, *Massacres*, p. 62; Ulrich Gehrke, *Persien in der deutschen Orientpolitik während des ersten Weltkrieges*, 2 vols. (Stuttgart: W. Kohlhammer, 1961), vol. 1, p. 32; vol. 2, p. 22.

143. For a thorough and sensitive discussion of *cihad*, see Aksakal, "'Holy War Made in Germany'?" "Jihad had many faces. It could be a key component in forging an alliance with a non-Muslim European power such as Germany and be employed against other non-Muslim European powers at the same time. It could be an ideology hostile towards non-Muslims in the Ottoman Empire and, at other times, explicitly include non-Muslims in the Ottoman fold. Jihad could be evoked against Muslims as well as Christians. The Ottoman leadership thought of jihad instrumentally, using it whenever they thought it would benefit the interests of the state" (p. 16).

144. Morgenthau, *Ambassador Morgenthau's Story*, p. 116.

145. Ibid., p. 117.

146. While no anti-colonialist uprising ever occurred, Morgenthau ominously concluded that the German incitement of the "Mohammedan soul" stimulated "all the intense animosity toward the Christian which is the fundamental fact in his strange, emotional nature, and thus started passions aflame that afterward spent themselves in the massacres of the Armenians and other subject peoples." But rather than being primarily a matter of religious difference or conflict, according to Morgenthau, the decision to carry out an anti-Christian pogrom was a strategic choice. Ibid., pp. 118, 221–222.

147. Yervant Odian, *Accursed Years: My Exile and Return from Der Zor, 1914–1919*, trans. Ara Stepan Melkonian, intro. Krikor Beledian (London: Gomidas, 2009), p. 11.

148. Akın, "The Ottoman Home Front during World War I," p. 217.

149. On Armenian songs and memories of the war years and the Genocide, see Verjiné Svazlian, *The Armenian Genocide and Armenian Memory*, trans. Tigran Tsulikian (Erevan: Gitutyun, 2004), and idem, *The Armenian Genocide in the Memoirs and Turkish-Language Songs of the Eye-Witness Survivors*, trans. Tigran Tsulikian (Erevan: Gitutyun, 1999).

150. "Obsessed with the recent loss of the Balkan provinces, the Unionists spent considerable effort to instill the desire for revenge into every Ottoman citizen's heart. In the months preceding the First World War, 'revenge' became a central theme in public education, the military, and the press." Akın, "The Ottoman Home Front during World War I," p. 191.

151. Ibid., p. 195.

152. "While Ottoman war propaganda presented the image of a unified nation in order to ward off the threat to the very existence of the motherland, it excluded non-Muslims from this picture altogether or relegated them to marginal roles." Akın, "The Ottoman Home Front during World War I," pp. 202–203. Akın contrasts the Ottoman propaganda effort from the Russians, which included non-Russians in the story of battlefield achievements. See Karen Petrone, "Family, Masculinity, and Heroism in Russian War Posters of the First World War," in *Borderlines: Genders and Identities in War and Peace, 1870–1930*, ed. Billie Melman (London: Routledge, 1998), pp. 95–119.

153. Cited in Akın, "The Ottoman Home Front during World War I," p. 204.

154. Erickson, *Ordered to Die*, p. 53.

155. Arslan, "Les faits et les buts de guerre ottomans sur le front caucasien," pp. 175–176. Aksakal claims that 80 to 90 percent of the Third Army was destroyed at Sarıkamış, which was the "worst military disaster in Ottoman history." Aksakal, "The Ottoman Empire," p. 467. Some historians estimated that Enver's army suffered 70,000 to 90,000 casualties.

156. Erickson, *Ordered to Die*, p. 59.

157. Arslan, "A Front 'Bon Pour L'Orient,'" p. 24.

158. Morgenthau, *Ambassador Morgenthau's Story*, p. 135.

159. Ibid., p. 138.

160. Ibid., p. 158.

161. Ibid., pp. 176, 190–191.

162. Yeghiayan, *My Patriarchal Memoirs*, p. 63. The soldier died at the front soon after; Enver noted the incident in a letter to Karekin *vartapet*, the Armenian primate of Konya.

163. Kévorkian, *The Armenian Genocide*, p. 291.

164. Akın, "The Ottoman Home Front during World War I," p. 51; Arslan, "Les faits et les buts de guerre ottomans sur le front caucasien," pp. 211–212; telegram from Enver Paşa, February 25, 1915, in *Askeri Tarih Belgeleri Dergisi, Ermeni Belgeleri Özel Sayısı*, no. 85, October 1985, document no. 1999. See also Erik J. Zürcher, "The Ottoman Soldier in World War I," in his *The Young Turk Legacy*, pp. 171–173.

165. Erickson, *Ordered to Die*, p. 98; Aksakal, "The Ottoman Empire," p. 468; Ali iza Eti, *Bir Onbaşının Doğu Cephesi*, ed. Gönül Eti (Istanbul: Türkıye İş Bankası Kültür Yayınları, 2009), pp. 104, 135.

166. Raymond H. Kévorkian, "Recueil de témoignage sur l'extermination des amele tabouri ou battaillons de soldats-ouvriers arméniens de l'armée ottomane," *Revue d'histoire arménienne contemporaine* 1 (1995): 289–303; Zürcher, "Ottoman Labour Battalions in World War I," p. 192.

167. See Edward J. Erickson, "The Armenians and Ottoman Military Policy, 1915," *War in History* 15, no. 2 (2008): 141–167. A military historian, Erickson reproduces Ottoman accounts of Armenian treachery and argues that there were actual insurrections and a threat credible to the Ottomans, which influenced their decision, costly as it was, to deport Armenians. Yet, he concludes, "[i]n fact, the actual Armenian attacks on the rear of the Ottoman army and its lines of communications were isolated and sporadic, causing only minor disruptions to the war effort." He distinguishes between the minimal threat from the Armenians and the perceptions of the Ottomans of an existential danger. Viewing the "Ottoman relocation decision . . . as a military solution to a military problem," Erickson writes somewhat contradictorily in the final line of his article, "While political and ideological imperatives perhaps drove the decision equally, if not harder, these do not negate the fact that the Armenians were a great military danger." Ibid., pp. 165–167.

168. Edward J. Erickson, "Captain Larkin and the Turks: The Strategic Impact of the Operations of *HMS Doris* in Early 1915," *Middle Eastern Studies* 46, no. 1 (January 2010): 151–162. For a contemporary German diplomatic account of the events around Dörtyol, which doubts the veracity of the reports of Armenian subversion (a report that Erickson does not mention), see "From the Consul in Aleppo (Roessler) [relaying a report of Imperial Vice Consul Hoffman in Alexandretta] to the Ambassador in Extraordinary Mission in Constantinople (Wolff-Metternich)," no. 10, Aleppo, January 3, 1916; Gust (ed.), *The Armenian Genocide*, pp. 511–512.; available online at:http://www.armenocide.de/armenocide/armgende .nsf/24599fab3538b532c1257794007b610b/5021202a11fe47a8c1256d3d005371b6 !OpenDocument.

169. Translation of the telegram, along with copy of the Ottoman original, in Dündar, *Crime of Numbers*, pp. 209–210.

CHAPTER EIGHT: Removal

1. Balakian, *Armenian Golgotha*, p. 50.

2. Ibid., p. 52.

3. Akçam, *The Young Turks' Crime Against Humanity*, p. 175; A. Mil, "Umumi Harpte Teşkilat-ı Mahsusa," *Vakit*, part 98, February 10, 1934; see Kévorkian, *The Armenian Genocide*, pp. 247–249, for a possibly authentic partial reproduction of the minutes of the meeting by Sebuh Aguni, the former editor of the Istanbul newspaper *Zhamanak* (Time), himself arrested on April 24, 1915, and the author of *Milion me Hayeru Jardi Batmutyune* (Constantinople, 1921), based on materials in the patriarchal archive.

4. Kévorkian, *The Armenian Genocide*, p. 223; Cemil, *Umumi Harpte Teşkilât-ı Mahsusa*, published originally in *Vakıt*, from November 2, 1933 to February 7, 1934, and in V. Ishkhanian's Armenian translation in *Haratch*, no. 88.

5. Göçek, *Denial of Violence*, p. 217; Hüseyin Cahit Yalçın, *Tanıdıklarım* (Istanbul: Yapı Kredi Yayınları, 2001), p. 83.

6. The quotation is from the memoirs of the *vali* of Aleppo, Celal Bey, who declares that he was opposed to the deportations. Celal Bey, "Ermeni Vakay-i ve Esbab-i ve Tesiratı," *Vakit*, December 12, 1918; cited in Akçam, *The Young Turks' Crime Against Humanity*, pp. 135–136. For the dating of the relevant meetings of the CUP, see ibid., pp. 183–184.

7. Akçam, *The Young Turks' Crime Against Humanity*, p. 137. "In this tangled web of political relations . . . the argument that the CUP had decided on a policy of annihilation and was awaiting an opportune moment to put it into practice is speculative in nature." Ibid., p. 139.

8. On reports from the East, see ibid., pp. 139–148; quotation from p. 148.

9. See the account of an Armenian survivor of the labor battalions, *Crows of the Desert, The Memoirs of Levon Yotnakhparian* (Tujunga, CA: Parian Photographic Design, 2012).

10. Hilmar Kaiser, "The Baghdad Railway and the Armenian Genocide, 1915–1916: A Case Study in German Resistance and Complicity," in Hovannisian (ed.), *Remembrance and Denial*, pp. 67–112.

11. Zürcher, "Ottoman Labour Battalions in World War I," pp. 192–194; Sarafian, "The Absorption of Armenian Women and Children," in *In God's Name: Genocide and Religion in the Twentieth Century*, ed. Omer Bartov and Phyllis Mack (Oxford: Berghahn, 2001), p. 211. Both Vahakn Dadrian and Raymond Kévorkian are convinced that the disarming of Armenian soldiers and their subsequent murders were manifestations of the Ittihadist government's intention to liquidate the Armenians, while Erik Jan Zürcher is more equivocal, arguing that Enver's order to send Armenian soldiers to labor battalions made the subsequent killings easier but

was not anticipated as part of wholesale massacres. "[T]hese battalions," he writes, "were not created for the specific purpose of killing off the Armenians." Kévorkian, *The Armenian Genocide*, p. 242; Zürcher, "Ottoman Labour Battalions in World War I," p. 187.

12. Sarafian (comp.), *United States Official Documents on the Armenian Genocide, II*, p. 103; report from George Horton, American consul general, to the secretary of state, Smyrna, February 4, 1915, U.S. State Department Record Group 59, 867.00/739.

13. Kévorkian, *The Armenian Genocide*, p. 290.

14. Ibid., p. 227; Magdalena Golnazarian-Nichanian, *Les Arméniens d'Azerbaïdjan: Histoire locale et enjeux régionaux, 1828–1918* (Paris: Centre d'histoire arménienne contemporaine, 2009), p. 350.

15. Taner Akçam, *Armenien und der Völkermord* (Hamburg, 1996), p. 64; Dadrian, *The History of the Armenian Genocide*, p. 236.

16. Gaunt, "The Ottoman Treatment of the Assyrians," p. 253; Vladimir Genis, *Vitse-konsul Vvedenskii: Sluzhba v Persii i Bukharskom khanstve (1906–1920gg.)* (Moscow: Izdatel'stvo Sotsialno-politicheskaya Mysl', 2003), p. 44; Rockwell, *The Pitiful Plight of the Assyrian Christians*, p. 65; K. Matikyan, letter of March 9, 1915, in *Genotsid armian v osmanskoi imperii: Sbornik dokumentov i materialov*, ed. M. G. Nersisyan (Erevan: Izdatel'stvo Aiastan, 1982), pp. 276–277.

17. Gaunt, "The Ottoman Treatment of the Assyrians," p. 254; AVPRI, III F. 133, 1915, des. 470, dossier 49, vol. II, list 580.

18. Ibid.; Genelkurmay Başkanlığı, *Birinci Dünya Harbinde Türk Harbi Kafkas Cephesi 3üncü Ordu Harekâtı*, vol. 2:1 (Ankara: Genelkurmay Basım Evi, 1993), p. 582.

19. Gaunt, *Massacres*, p. 82; F. N. Jessup, March 17, 1915, in Bryce and Toynbee (eds.), *The Treatment of Armenians in the Ottoman Empire*, p. 153.

20. Göçek, *Denial of Violence*, p. 212; Hüseyin Cahit Yalçın, *Siyasal Anılar* (Istanbul: Türkiye İş Bankası Kültür Yayınları, 1976), p. 233.

21. Akçam, *The Young Turks' Crime Against Humanity*, p. 193; *Meclis-i Ayan Zabıt Ceridesi*, 3rd Electoral Term, Year of Assembly 5, vol. I (Ankara: TBMM Basımevi 1990), p. 123.

22. Akçam, *The Young Turks' Crime Against Humanity*, p. 195; Archives of the Armenian Patriarchate in Jerusalem, Box 21, File M, No. 492.

23. Yeghiayan, *My Patriarchal Memoirs*, p. 45; Kévorkian, *The Armenian Genocide*, pp. 431–432, gives a slightly different account of the bread poisoning incident.

24. The best account of the events in Zeytun leading up to and including the Genocide is by Aram Arkun, "Zeytun and the Commencement of the Armenian Genocide," in Suny et al. (eds.), *A Question of Genocide*, pp. 221–243.

25. Ibid., pp. 222–224.

26. Ibid., p. 227; Kiud Mkhitarian, "Truakner kayg. koghkotayen (1912–1937)," *Armenia*, November 26, 1940; Hovhannes Aharonian, "Badmutyun Zeytuni 1877–1915," in *Zeytuni batmagirk* (Buenos Aires: Zeytuni hayrenaktsakan miutyun [Montevideo, Uruguay], 1960), p. 656.

27. Arkun, "Zeytun and the Commencement of the Armenian Genocide," pp. 227–228; Aharonian, "Badmutyun Zeytuni," p. 656; Levan Norashkharhyan, *Zeytune 1914–1922 t.t. (husher)* (Erevan: Haykakan SSH Gitutyunneri Akademia Batmutyan Institut, 1984), pp. 32–33.

28. Report by Simon Agabalian, Adana, March 12, 1915, enclosed in report from Büge, German consul in Adana, to Wangenheim, German ambassador to Constantinople, Adana, PA-AA/BoKon/168; A53a, 1712, March 13, 1915; Gust (ed.), *The Armenian Genocide*, pp. 153–155.

29. See Hilmar Kaiser, *Eberhard Count Wolffskeel Von Reichenberg, Zeitoun, Mousa Dagh, Ourfa: Letters on the Armenian Genocide* (Princeton, NJ: Gomidas, 2001).

30. On April 25 seventy-one Zeytun families were sent to Konya. Sarafian (comp.), *United States Official Documents, I,* pp. 14–15; report from Jesse B. Jackson, American consul in Aleppo, to Henry Morgenthau, American ambassador to Constantinople, Aleppo, April 25, 1915, U.S. State Department Record Group 59, 867.4016/72.

31. Barton, "Turkish Atrocities," p. 145; statement of William S. Dodd, National Archives, Washington, DC, General Records of the American Commission to Negotiate Peace, Special Reports and Studies, Record Group 256, Inquiry Document 809.

32. Arnold Toynbee (ed.), *The Treatment of Armenians in the Ottoman Empire* (London, 1916), p. 397; Sarafian (comp.), *United States Official Documents, I,* pp. 24–26; statement of Reverend John E. Merrill, president of Central Turkey College, to Jesse B. Jackson, American consul in Aleppo, Aintab, June 14, 1915, enclosed in a letter from Jackson to Henry Morgenthau, American ambassador in Constantinople, Aleppo, June 16, 1915, Morgenthau Papers, 7/591–592.

33. For a more complete analysis and narrative of the Zeytun resistance and deportations, see Arkun, "Zeytun and the Commencement of the Armenian Genocide," and Kévorkian, *The Armenian Genocide*, pp. 249–250.

34. Kévorkian, *The Armenian Genocide*, pp. 234–240; Papazian, *Husher,* II, pp. 303–357; APC/APJ, PCI Bureau H 529–530, file nos. 26, 27.

35. Lynch, *Armenia, Travels and Studies, II, The Turkish Provinces*, p. 38.

36. My thanks to Anoush Suni and Akıl Arslan for this information.

37. Besides Ussher, *An American Physician in Turkey*, another memoir of the Van resistance by an American is Grace Higley Knapp, *The Mission at Van in Turkey in War Time* (Privately printed, 1916).

38. Tahsin Uzer, born in the Albanian region of Kosovo in the Balkans, later served as *vali* in Erzurum and as an important official in the Turkish Republic. On

his origins and biography, see Ryan Gingeras, *Sorrowful Shores: Violence, Ethnicity, and the End of the Ottoman Empire, 1912–1923* (Oxford: Oxford University Press, 2009), p. 35.

39. Ussher, *An American Physician in Turkey*, pp. 219–220.

40. Akçam, *The Young Turks' Crime Against Humanity*, p. 155; coded telegram from the Interior Ministry's General Directorate of Security to the provinces of Erzurum, Van, and Bitlis, BOA/DH.ŞFR., nr. 48/166, December 27, 1914.

41. Kévorkian, *The Armenian Genocide*, p. 230; memorandum from Vramian to Talat, March 1915, APC/AP, PCI Bureau, Z 58.

42. Turkyilmaz, "Rethinking Genocide," pp. 115–116; National Archives of Armenia (NAA), 227.1.416.9–10.

43. Kévorkian, *The Armenian Genocide*, p. 232; A-To [Hovhannes Ter Martirosian], *Mets depkere Vaspurakanum 1915–1917* (Erevan, 1917), pp. 150–151; Bloxham, *The Great Game of Genocide*, p. 77; Hans-Lukas Kieser, *Der verpasste Friede: Mission, Ethnie, und Staat in den Ostprovinzen der Türkei 1839–1938* (Zurich: Chronos, 2000), p. 446.

44. Gaunt, "The Ottoman Treatment of the Assyrians," pp. 255–256; Johannes Lepsius, *Deutschland und Armenien* (Potsdam: Tempelverlag, 1919), pp. xiv, 471; idem, *Les massacres d'Arménie* (Paris: Payot, 1918), p. 94; Griselle, *Syriens et chaldéens leur martyres*, p. 24.

45. Ussher, *An American Physician in Turkey*, pp. 237–238.

46. Detailed accounts based on myriad sources of the massacres around Van are given in Kévorkian, *The Armenian Genocide*, pp. 319–326. There is a large literature on the Van "Uprising" or "Resistance." Among the works that should be consulted are M. G., *La defense heroique de Van* (Geneva: Droschak, 1916); Ruben G. Sahakyan, *Haykakan Vostikanutyan Kazmakerpume ev Gortsuniutyune Vani Nahangapetutyan Srjanum (1915 Tvakani Mayisi 8 -Hulisi 17): Pastatghteri ev Niuteri Zhogovatsu* (Erevan, 2008); and Souren Aprahamian, *From Van to Detroit: Surviving the Armenian Genocide* (Ann Arbor, MI: Gomidas, 1993). Also see the collection of articles in the special issue of Armenian monthly *Hayrenik* 18, no. 7 (May 1940): 1–109. Eyewitness accounts include Onnik Mkhitarian, *Vani Herosamarte* (Sofia: Tpagr. P. Palegchian, 1930), and Kalipse Solakhyan, *Tezh Martere Vani Kaghakamijum: Masnaktsi Husherits* (Erevan: Zangak-97, 2000). An account sympathetic to the Turks can be found in Justin McCarthy, Esat Arslan, Cemalettin Taşkıran, and Ömer Turan, *The Armenian Rebellion at Van* (Salt Lake City: University of Utah Press, 2006).

47. Rafaël de Nogales, *Four Years Beneath the Crescent*, trans. Muna Lee (New York: Charles Scribner's Sons, 1926; reprinted, London: Sterndale Classics, 2003), pp. 72–97. All references are to the reprinted edition.

48. Ibid., pp. 17, 20.

49. Ibid., p. 21.

50. Ibid., pp. 56–57.

51. In modern Turkish the saying is "*baş üstüne*" or "*başım üstüne*," which can be translated as "certainly," or "with pleasure," and is similar to the Kurdish saying "*ser çavan*" or "*ser serê min*," meaning "on my eyes," or "on my head." I thank Anoush Suni and Akıl Arslan for this information.

52. De Nogales, *Four Years Beneath the Crescent*, pp. 58–60.

53. Ibid., p. 62.

54. Ibid., p. 90.

55. Ibid, p. 93. Kévorkian cites de Nogales but claims that "Cevdet had the women and children who had been rounded up by his *çetes* during their raids on the villages brought to the city, where he had them executed in full view of the besieged Armenians." *The Armenian Genocide*, p. 330. Knapp, *The Mission at Van*, mentions Cevdet's tactic of bringing Armenian villagers into the city but does not refer to their being killed (p. 22).

56. Ussher, *An American Physician in Turkey*, pp. 266–272.

57. Ibid., pp. 282–283.

58. Kévorkian, *The Armenian Genocide*, p. 333.

59. Turkyilmaz, "Rethinking Genocide," pp. 285–286. Turkyilmaz's account is based on the memoirs of a Ramkavar leader, Avedis Terzibashian, *Andranik*.

60. Ussher, *An American Physician in Turkey*, pp. 284–285.

61. Turkyilmaz, "Rethinking Genocide," pp. 292–293; Egarian, *Husher*, pp. 233–234.

62. Turkyilmaz, "Rethinking Genocide," pp. 295–300.

63. Ibid., p. 302; *Ashkhatank*, no. 24 (223) (June 13, 1915): 1.

64. Kévorkian, *The Armenian Genocide*, p. 231; encrypted telegram from the *vali* of Erzurum, Tahsin Bey, to the Ministry of Interior, May 13, 1915, APC/AP, PCI Bureau, file XLIX, M285; original in Ottoman Turkish, transcription in the Armenian alphabet and French translation.

65. Telegraphic report from the German consul in Adana (Büge) to the embassy in Constantinople, Adana, May 18, 1915; and reply by Wangenheim, May 21, 1915; PA-AA; BoKon/168; A53a, 3032; secret report from the administrator in Erzurum (Scheubner-Richter) to the ambassador in Constantinople (Wangenheim), Erzurum, May 20, 1915; PA-AA; BoKon/169; A53a, 3323; p. 01.06.1915; Gust (ed.), *The Armenian Genocide*, pp. 183, 184–185.

66. Report from the ambassador in Constantinople (Wangenheim) to the Imperial chancellor (Bethmann Hollweg), Pera, June 17, 1915; PA-AA; R14086; A 19743; pr. 24.06.1915 p.m.; Gust (ed.), *The Armenian Genocide*, pp. 210–211.

67. Hartmann, "The Central State in the Borderlands," p. 182.

68. For the genocide scholar Roger W. Smith, *Ambassador Morgenthau's Story* "is the classic, contemporary account of the first large-scale genocide of the twentieth century." Roger W. Smith, "Introduction," in Morgenthau, *Ambassador Morgenthau's Story*, p. xxv. For the Holocaust scholar Robert Jay Lifton, Morgenthau's account is a unique and remarkable source because of its view of genocide from the top. "I do not know of any other example of a critical outsider who had regular access to the highest-ranking planners and perpetrators of genocide, even as it was taking place." Ibid., p. xxi. The narrative presented by Morgenthau was considered devastating enough to the official Turkish governmental denial of genocide for Dr. Heath Lowry, at the time the director of the Institute of Turkish Studies, later the Atatürk Professor of Ottoman and Modern Turkish Studies at Princeton University, to issue a small book that attempted to undermine the authenticity and veracity of the ambassador's witness. Lowry, *The Story Behind Ambassador Morgenthau's Story*. See also the website "Tall Armenian Tale," http://www.tallarmeniantale.com/morgenthau.htm.

69. Henry Morgenthau III, "Epilogue: the Rest of the Story," in Morgenthau, *Ambassador Morgenthau's Story*, p. 296.

70. Morgenthau, *Ambassador Morgenthau's Story*, p. xxxix. Read today largely for his account of the Armenian Genocide, the book's original concern was Germany's role in the war, the intrigues of the German ambassador in Constantinople, Baron von Wangenheim, and German influence on the Young Turk leaders. Ibid., p. 10.

71. Letter to Josephine Sykes, December 27, 1913, The Papers of Henry Morgenthau, Sr., Library of Congress, Manuscript Division, Reel 6, pp. 5–6.

72. Morgenthau, *Ambassador Morgenthau's Story*, p. 10.

73. Ibid., p. 228.

74. Ethnicity and self-identity often did not coincide. Many of the most virulent Turkish nationalists were ethnically Kurds, Jews, or Azerbaijanis. Of the Young Turks Talat identified as a Turk, and, while many of his fellow party members were secular modernizers, he was relatively religious.

75. Morgenthau, *Ambassador Morgenthau's Story*, p. 14.

76. Ibid., p. 16.

77. Ibid., p. 18.

78. Ibid., p. 121.

79. Ibid., pp. 164, 191.

80. Ibid. p. 191.

81. Ibid., pp. 101, 170.

82. Ibid., pp. 192–193.

83. Ibid., p. 196.

84. Ibid., p. 43.

85. Ibid., pp. 53, 155.

86. Letter of Ambassador Henry Morgenthau in Istanbul to President Woodrow Wilson, January 11, 1915, The Papers of Henry Morgenthau, Sr., Library of Congress, Manuscript Division, Reel 7.

87. Morgenthau, *Ambassador Morgenthau's Story*, p. 135.

88. Ibid., p. 100.

89. Ibid., p. 101.

90. Ibid., p. 200.

91. Ibid.

92. Ibid., p. 201.

93. Ibid., p. 224.

94. Ibid.

95. Ibid., p. 231.

96. Ibid., p. 233.

97. Ibid., p. 229.

98. Ibid., p. 234.

99. Ibid., p. 232.

100. Ibid.

101. On April 21, 1915, *Tanin* published an article entitled "The Accomplices," detailing alleged atrocities committed by Russians against Turks on the Russian front with the supposed cooperation of Ottoman Armenians. Kévorkian, *The Armenian Genocide*, p. 335; Aram Andonian, *Chronological Notes, 1914–1916*, written in 1925, ff. 34–35, Bibliothèque Nubar, mss. 17 and 18, PJ 1–3.

102. Libaridian, "What Was Revolutionary about Armenian Revolutionary Parties?" pp. 106–107; Gidur, *Batmutiun S. D. Hnchak Gusaktustyun*, pp. 386–388.

103. Kévorkian, *The Armenian Genocide*, pp. 255–256; Yeghiayan, *My Patriarchal Memoirs*, pp. 58–59. See also H. M. Poghosyan, "Paramaz (Matteos Sargsyan)," *Patma-Banasirakan Handes* 2 (1988): 101–111.

104. Yeghiayan, *My Patriarch Memoirs*, p. 61.

105. Ibid., pp. 61–62.

106. Ibid., pp. 59–60.

107. Arslan, "Les faits et les buts de guerre ottomans sur le front caucasien," pp. 216–217; Yalçın, *Tanıdıklarım*, pp. 49–50.

108. Kévorkian, *The Armenian Genocide*, pp. 251–254; Teotig [Piuzant Bozajian], *Hushardzan Nahatak Mtavorakanutyan* (Constantinople, 1919), pp. 20–70, *passim*. For a largely exculpatory explanation of the Ottoman motivations for the arrests and the fate of those incarcerated, see Yusuf Sarınay, "What Happened on April 24, 1915? The Circular of April 24, 1915, and the Arrest of Armenian Committee Members in Istanbul," *International Journal of Turkish Studies* 14, nos. 1–2 (Fall 2008): 75–101.

109. For a first-person account of the arrests in April 1915 and his own imprisonment in September, see Odian, *Accursed Years*, pp. 14–40. Even more details of the arrest and exile of the Istanbul intellectuals can be found in Aram Andonian, *Trilogy—April 24, 1915, I. Exile, Trauma and Death: On the Road to Chankiri with Komitas Vartabed*, trans. and ed. Rita Soulahian Kyumjian (London: Gomidas, 2010).

110. Arslan, "Les faits et les buts de guerre ottomans sur le front caucasien," p. 215; telegram of the minister of interior, Talat Bey, to the Ottoman High Command, April 24, 1915, ATASE, B.D.H., no. ½, dossier 50, index 1–3.

111. Ara Sarafian (ed. and comp.), *United States Diplomacy on the Bosphorus: The Diaries of Ambassador Morgenthau, 1913–1916* (London: Taderon, 2004), pp. 215–216.

112. Akçam, *The Young Turks' Crime Against Humanity*, p. 185; coded telegrams from Interior Minister Talat to the provinces of Edirne, Erzurum, Adana, Ankara, Aydın, Bitlis, Halep (Aleppo), Hüdâvendigâr (Bursa), Diyarbakır, Sivas, Trabzon, Konya, Mamuretülaziz, and Van, and the provincial districts of Urfa, İzmit, Kütahya, Karahisar-ı Sahip, Bolu, Canik, Karesi, Kayseri, Maraş, Niğde, and Eskişehir, BOA/DH.Şfr., nr. 52/95, and BOA/DH.ŞFR., nr. 52/96–97–98, April 24, 1915.

113. Dündar, "Pouring a People into the Desert," p. 281; Dahiliye Nezareti Şifre Kalemi (BOA/DH.ŞFR), 52.93 (April 24, 1915). The telegram from the EUM to Cemal Pasha is translated and the original is reproduced in Dündar, *Crime of Numbers*, pp. 211–212.

114. Mann, *The Dark Side of Democracy*, p. 148.

115. Morgenthau, *Ambassador Morgenthau's Story*, p. 224.

116. Ibid., p. 227.

117. Ibid., p. 228.

118. Ibid., p. 233.

119. Ibid., pp. 224, 230.

120. Balakian, *Armenian Golgotha*, pp. 56–67.

121. Andonian, *Trilogy—April 24, 1915, I*, pp. 41–42.

122. Ibid., p. 101.

123. Balakian, *Armenian Golgotha*, p. 66.

124. Cited in Yeghiayan, *My Patriarchal Memoirs*, p. 64.

125. Ibid., pp. 64–65.

126. Ibid., p. 65. Italics in the original.

127. Grigoris Balakian accompanied Kelegian on his visit to Asaf. Balakian, *Armenian Golgotha*, pp. 68–82.

128. Ibid., pp. 113–114.

129. Kévorkian, *The Armenian Genocide*, p. 533.

130. Balakian, *Armenian Golgotha*, p. 105. Taner Akçam argues that on the basis of mutually corroborating Ottoman and German documents and Armenian accounts,

a detailed picture of the killing and subsequent events can be reconstructed: "Istanbul was well aware of the murders and other crimes in the provinces.... [T]he Unionist government in Istanbul was not only aware of these crimes but in the case of several well intentioned local administrators who made extraordinary personal efforts to identify and bring the murderers to justice, the state took pains to ensure that the perpetrators would go free." Akçam, *The Young Turks' Crime Against Humanity*, p. 216.

131. Yeghiayan, *My Patriarchal Memoirs*, p. 67.

132. Kévorkian, *The Armenian Genocide*, p. 291; Hilmar Kaiser, "'A Scene from the Inferno,' The Armenians of Erzurum and the Genocide, 1915–1916," in Kieser and Schaller (eds.), *Der Völkermord an den Armeniern und die Shoah*, p. 133; Aguni, *Milion me Hayeru Jardi Patmutyune*, p. 139; notes by the consul general in Constantinople (Mordtmann), Pera, April 26, 1915; PA-AA; BoKon/168; A53a, 2473; Gust (ed.), *The Armenian Genocide*, pp. 172–173.

133. "From the Administrator in Erzurum (Scheubner-Richter) to the Ambassador in Constantinople (Wangenheim)," no. 12, Erzurum, 20 May 1915; PA-AA: BoKon/169; A53a, 3323; p. 01.06.1915; Gust (ed.), *The Armenian Genocide*, pp. 184–185.

134. Kévorkian, *The Armenian Genocide*, pp. 289–317. Kévorkian has compiled the records of the deportations and massacres in 1915–1916 region by region. The interested reader can consult the text and footnotes in Kévorkian to obtain greater detail and learn about the sources he used.

CHAPTER NINE: Genocide

1. Yeghiayan, *My Patriarchal Memoirs*, p. 83.

2. Akçam, *The Young Turks' Crime Against Humanity*, pp. 171–172; Vahakn Dadrian, "Party Allegiance as a Determinant in the Turkish Military's Involvement in the World War I Armenian Genocide," *Hakirah Journal of Jewish and Ethnic Studies* 1, no. 1 (2003): 57–67.

3. Akçam, *The Young Turks' Crime Against Humanity*, p. 168; for his full discussion of these documents, see pp. 162–170.

4. For details on the operation of the Secret Organization and the responsible secretaries of the CUP, see Vahakn N. Dadrian and Taner Akçam, *Judgment at Istanbul: The Armenian Genocide Trials* (New York: Berghahn Books, 2011), pp. 137–146.

5. Report from the administrator in Erzurum (Scheubner-Richter) to the ambassador in Constantinople (Wangenheim), Erzurum, July 9, 1915; PA-AA; BoKon/169; A53a, 4354; p. 23.07.1915; Gust (ed.), *The Armenian Genocide*, p. 245.

6. Kévorkian, *The Armenian Genocide*, p. 291; report about facts to prove the culpability of Cemal by in the deportation of Armenians of Erzurum and Dercan, APC/APJ, PCI Bureau, I 775, doc. no. 14 (in English), T 347 (in French).

7. Kévorkian, *The Armenian Genocide*, p. 292.

8. Akçam, *The Young Turks' Crime Against Humanity*, p. xxiv; Bardaçı, *Talat Paşa'nın Evrak-ı Metrukesi*, p. 211.

9. Arslan, "Les faits et les buts de guerre ottomans sur le front caucasien," p. 237.

10. After Enver Paşa served as commander of the Ottoman Third Army (December 18, 1914–January 8, 1915), he was briefly replaced by Ismail Hâfız Hakkı Paşa (January 8–February 15, 1915), and then by Mahmud Kâmil Paşa (mid-March 1915–January 8, 1916). Successive commanders were Abdülkerim Paşa (acting January 8–29, 1916); Mahmud Kâmil Paşa (January 29–February 27, 1916); Abdülkerim Paşa (acting February 27–March 6, 1916); Mehmed Vehib Paşa (March 6, 1916–June 9, 1918); and Mehmed Esad Paşa (June 9–October 30, 1918). I am grateful to Ozan Arslan for this information.

11. Akçam, *The Young Turks' Crime Against Humanity*, p. 160; Genelkurmay Başkanlığı, *Arşiv Belgeleriyle Ermeni Faaliyetleri, 1914–1918*, 8 vols. (Ankara: Genelkurmay Basımevi, 2005–2007), vol. I, p. 123.

12. Kaiser, "Historical Introduction," pp. liii, lv–lvi.

13. Leverkuehn, *A German Officer During the Armenian Genocide*, pp. 25–26.

14. Arslan, "Les faits et les buts de guerre ottomans sur le front caucasien," p. 220; telegram sent by the Ottoman High Command to the Ministry of Interior, May 27, 1915, ATASE, B.D.H., no. 1/1, File 44, Dossier 155/207, Indexes 2–2 and 2–3; cited with a facsimile in Hikmet Özdemir and Yusuf Sarınay (eds.), *Türk-Ermeni İhtilafı, Belgeler* (Ankara: Türkiye Büyük Millet Meclisi Kültür Sanat ve Yayın Kurulu Yayınları, 2007), pp. 66–67; also cited in Kamuran Gürün, *The Armenian File: The Myth of Innocence Exposed* (London: K. Rustem & Bro., and Weiderfeld & Nicolson Ltd., 1985), p. 206.

15. Arslan, "Les faits et les buts de guerre ottomans sur le front caucasien," pp. 220–221; Bayur, *Türk İnkilabı Tarihi, III*, p. 37.

16. Dündar, *Crime of Numbers*, pp. 84–85; Arslan, "Les faits et les buts de guerre ottomans sur le front caucasien," p. 221; T. C. Başbankanlık Devlet Arşivleri Genel Müdürlüğü, *Osmanlı Belgelerinde Ermeniler 1915–1920* (Ankara, 1995), pp. 30–32. This collection is available online: http://www.google.de/url?sa=t&rct=j&q=&esrc=s&source=web&cd=1&ved=oCCwQFjAA&url=http%3A%2F%2Fwww.devletarsivleri.gov.tr%2Fassets%2.

17. Dündar, *Crime of Numbers*, pp. 84–85.

18. Arslan, "Les faits et les buts de guerre ottomans sur le front caucasien," p. 221; Özdemir and Sarınay (eds.), *Türk-Ermeni İhtilafı, Belgeler*, pp. 72–76, 78–81.

19. See Ara Sarafian, "The Absorption of Armenian Women and Children into Muslim Households as a Structural Component of the Armenian Genocide," in Bartov and Mack (eds.), *In God's Name*, pp. 209–221.

20. Arslan, "Les faits et les buts de guerre ottomans sur le front caucasien," p. 227; telegram of Talat Bey to the under-prefect of Deir ez-Zor, June 23, 1915, BOA/DH.ŞFR. Dossier 54, 895/19.

21. Kévorkian, *The Armenian Genocide*, p. 314; this telegram was first published in *Takvim-i Vekayi*, no. 3540 (May 5, 1919).

22. Dündar, *Crime of Numbers*, p. 114.

23. De Nogales, *Four Years Beneath the Crescent*, p. 107.

24. Ibid., p. 122. De Nogales is referring to Halil [Kut] Paşa, the uncle of Enver and a classmate at the Imperial War College of Mustafa Kemal. He was present on the Caucasian front (and in Iran) in 1915 (1st Expeditionary Corps/"Birinci Kuvve-i Seferiye") and then again in 1918 (C-in-C, Ottoman Army Group East/"Şark Orduları Grubu"). My thanks to Ozan Arslan for this information.

25. De Nogales, *Four Years Beneath the Crescent*, pp. 124, 134.

26. Ibid., pp. 99–100.

27. On the killings in Siirt, see Kévorkian, *The Armenian Genocide*, pp. 339–340.

28. De Nogales, *Four Years Beneath the Crescent*, p. 125.

29. Halil Paşa, *İttihat ve Terakki'den Cumhuriyet'e Bitmeyen Savaş* (Istanbul: Kamer, 1997; transcribed by M. Taylan Sorgun, 1972), pp. 240–241.

30. Kévorkian, *The Armenian Genocide*, p. 239; APC/APJ, PCI Bureau, Y 529–530, file no. 26, 27.

31. The principal eyewitness account of the massacres in Bitlis is Grace H. Knapp, *The Tragedy of Bitlis: Being Mainly the Narratives of Grissel M. McLaren and Myrtle O. Shane* (New York: Fleming H. Revell, 1919).

32. De Nogales, *Four Years Beneath the Crescent*, p. 133; Kévorkian, *The Armenian Genocide*, p. 343.

33. Kévorkian, *The Armenian Genocide*, pp. 346–347. The killings in Muş were witnessed and reported by a Swedish missionary, Alma Johannsen, *Ett folk i Landsflykt* (Stockholm, 1930), a version of which can be found without attribution in Toynbee (ed.), *The Treatment of the Armenians in the Ottoman Empire*, pp. 88–91.

34. Donald Bloxham, "The First World War and the Development of the Armenian Genocide," in Suny et al. (eds.), *A Question of Genocide*, p. 573; Wangenheim to Foreign Office, May 18, 1915, AAPA, Türkei 183/6.

35. Kévorkian, *The Armenian Genocide*, pp. 351–352; Aramais, *Les massacres et la lute de Mousch-Sassoun* (Geneva, 1916); Raymond Kévorkian, "The Armenian Population of Sassoun and the Demographic Consequences of the 1894 Massacres," *The Armenian Review* 47, nos. 1–2 (Spring–Summer 2001): 41–53.

36. Kévorkian, *The Armenian Genocide*, p. 353; extract from the December 5, 1918, deposition of Vehib Paşa, *Takvim-i Vekayi*, no. 3540 (May 5, 1919): 7, col. 2.

37. Kévorkian, *The Armenian Genocide*, pp. 467–475; much of the evidence for the killings in Trabzon came from the trial of the Trabzon leaders in March and April 1919.

38. Cited in Kévorkian, *The Armenian Genocide*, p. 488; U.S. National Archives, RG84, Samsun c49, c8. 1, box 5, report from Peter to Morgenthau, July 10, 1915, p. 1.

39. Kévorkian, *The Armenian Genocide*, pp. 488–489; U.S. National Archives, RG84, Samsun c49, c8. 1, box 5, report from Peter to Morgenthau, August 26, 1915, pp. 5–6.

40. Cited in the biographical article on Dr. Reşid, Hans-Lukas Kieser, "From 'Patriotism' to Mass Murder: Dr. Mehmet Reşid (1873–1919)," in Suny et al. (eds.), *A Question of Genocide*, p. 130.

41. Ibid., p. 136.

42. Üngör and Polatel, *Confiscation and Destruction*, p. 138; Mehmed Reşid, *Mülâhazât* (Istanbul, 1919), translit. in Nejdet Bilgi, *Dr. Mehmed Reshid Şahingiray'ın hayatı ve hâtıraları* (İzmir: Akademi, 1997), p. 89 n. 28; Vartkes Yeghiayan (ed.), *British Foreign Office Dossiers on Turkish War Criminals* (Pasadena, CA: AAIC, 1991), p. 151.

43. Üngör, *The Making of Modern Turkey*, p. 64; Talaat to Diyarbekir, April 6, 1915, BOA/DH.ŞFR 51/220; Reshid, *Mülâhazât*, translit. in Bilgi, *Dr. Mehmed Reshid Şahingiray'ın hayatı ve hâtıraları*, p. 112; Yeghiayan (ed.), *British Foreign Office Dossiers on Turkish War Criminals*, p. 48.

44. Sarafian (comp.), *United States Official Documents, I*, p. 19; report from Jesse B. Jackson, American consul in Aleppo, to Henry Morgenthau, American ambassador to Constantinople, Aleppo, June 5, 1915; U.S. State Department Record Group 59, 867.4016/77.

45. Üngör and Polatel, *Confiscation and Destruction*, p. 140; Reşid to Talat, April 27, 1915, quoted in Hüsamettin Yıldırım, *Rus-Türk-Ermeni Münasebetleri (1914–1918)* (Ankara: KÖK, 1990), p. 57.

46. Gaunt, *Massacres*, pp. 168–169; Ishaq Armalto, *Al-Qusara fi nakabat al-naasara* (1919), p. 141.

47. On the nature of the atrocities, see Barton, "Turkish Atrocities," p. 92; statement of Floyd O. Smith, National Archives, Washington, DC, General Records of the American Commission to Negotiate Peace, Special Reports and Studies, Record Group 256, Inquiry Document 822. A detailed account of the Genocide in Diyarbakır is available in Üngör, *The Making of Modern Turkey*, pp. 55–106.

48. Ahmet Mehmetefendioglu (ed.), *Dr. Reşid Bey'in Hatiralari, "Sürgünden Intihara"* (Istanbul: Arba, 1992), especially pp. 43–76. My thanks to Fatma Müge Göçek for translating the relevant passages.

49. Mugerditchian, *The Dyarbekir Massacres and Kurdish Atrocities*, pp. 31–33.

50. Gaunt, *Massacres*, p. 162; Yves Ternon, "Mardin 1915: Anatomie pathologique d'une destruction," *Annales du Centre d'histoire arménienne contemporaine* (2002): 88.

51. Mugerditchian, *The Dyarbekir Massacres and Kurdish Atrocities*, pp. 35–36.

52. Ibid., p. 29.

53. Ibid., p. 37.

54. Ibid., pp. 38–40. Mugerditchian's account is corroborated in the memoir of Hüseyin Demirer, *Ha Wer Delal: Emine Perixane'nin Hayatı* (Istanbul: Avesta, 2008), pp. 75–89.

55. These events are carefully reconstructed in Üngör, *The Making of Modern Turkey*, pp. 55–106, and in Kévorkian, *The Armenian Genocide*, pp. 360–362.

56. Uğur Ümit Üngör, "Introduction: The Armenian Genocide as a Complex Process," in Mugerditchian, *The Diyarbekir Massacres and Turkish Atrocities*, pp. xiii–xiv; Demirer, *Ha Wer Delal*, p. 87.

57. De Nogales, *Four Years Beneath the Crescent*, pp. 140–141.

58. Ibid., pp. 146–147.

59. Ibid., p. 139.

60. Akçam, *The Young Turks' Crime Against Humanity*, pp. 223–224; coded telegram from Interior Minister Talat to the provinces of Diyarbekir, Mamuretülaziz, and Bitlis, BOA/DH.ŞFR, no. 54/9, June 14, 1915.

61. Akçam, *The Young Turks' Crime Against Humanity*, p. 210; coded telegram from Interior Minister Talat to the province of Diyarbekir, BOA/DH.ŞFR, no. 54-A/248, August 2, 1915.

62. Telegraphic report from German vice consul in Mosul (Holstein) to the embassy in Constantinople, Mosul, PA-AA/BoKon/169; A53a, 4184, July 10, 1915; Gust (ed.), *The Armenian Genocide*, pp. 245–246.

63. Kieser, "From 'Patriotism' to Mass Murder," pp. 142–143; PA-AA/BoKon/169 (Lepsius 1919, doc. 112); note of Johannes Mordtmann, Generalkonsul in Konstantinopel: am 12/7 persönlich an Talaat bej übergeben; July 10, 1915, Walter Holstein, deutscher Vizekonsul in Mossul an die Botschaft in Konstantinopel, DE/PA-AA/BoKon 169 (cf. Lepsius 1919, doc. 110); BOA/DH.ŞFR, no. 54/406, July 12, 1915, transcribed in *Armenians in Ottoman Documents*, p. 75.

64. Akçam, *The Young Turks' Crime Against Humanity*, pp. 373–383, reviews the policies and the many telegrams from Talat dealing with deportation of Armenian Catholics and Protestants.

65. Ibid., p. 211; coded telegram from the Interior Ministry to the province of Diyarbekir, BOA/DH.ŞFR, no. 56/315, October 6, 1915.

66. Üngör and Polatel, *Confiscation and Destruction*, p. 151; Mehmed Reshid, "Günlük," in Bilgi, *Dr. Mehmed Reshid*, pp. 115–137.

67. Mehmetefendioglu (ed.), *Dr. Reşid Bey'in Hatiralari*, especially pp. 43–76.

68. Kieser, "From 'Patriotism' to Mass Murder," p. 137.

69. Arslan, "Les faits et les buts de guerre ottomans sur le front caucasien," p. 246; Mithat Şükrü Bleda, *İmparatorluğun çöküşü* (Istanbul: Remzi, 1979), p. 58.

70. Mugerditchian, *The Dyarbekir Massacres and Kurdish Atrocities,* pp. 42–43, 49–50.

71. Kieser, "From 'Patriotism' to Mass Murder," p. 144.

72. Holquist, "The Politics and Practice of the Russian Occupation of Armenia," p. 155; Boris Nol'de, "Budushchee ustroistvo Armenii: Osnovnye polozheniia," AVPRI, f. 340, op. 610 [B. E. Nol'de], d. 172; Foreign Minister Sazonov to Ambassador Benckendorff, July 7/20, 1915, in E. A. Adamov, *Razdel Aziatskoi Turtsii po sekretnym dokumentam b. ministerstva inostrannykh del* (Moscow: Litizdat, 1924), doc. 46.

73. See Holquist, "The Politics and Practice of the Russian Occupation of Armenia"; idem., "In Accord with State Interests and the People's Wishes": The Technocratic Ideology Imperial Russia's Resettlement Administration," *Slavic Review* 69, no. 1 (Spring 2010): 170–171; and idem, *Making War, Forging Revolution: Russia's Continuum of Crisis, 1914–1921* (Cambridge, MA: Harvard University Press, 2002), pp. 18–20, 33–34.

74. Cited in Holquist, "Forms of Violence," p. 349; Regional Administrator for the Dersim region Gadzhemukov to the Commander of the Caucasus Army Iudenich, March 14, 1917 (RGVIA, f. 2168 [Shtab kavkazskoi armii], p. 1, d. 274, ll. 1–3, here at 2 ob.).

75. Holquist, "The Politics and Practice of the Russian Occupation of Armenia," pp. 157–158; Sazonov to Grand Duke Nikolai Nikolaevich, June 14/27, 1916 (RGVIA, f. 2005 [*Grazhdanksoe upravlenie pri Verkhovnom Glavnokomanduiushchem*], op. 1, d. 17, ll. 1–2 ob.); reprinted in Adamov, *Razdel Aziatskoi Turtsii po sekretnym dokumentam b. ministerstva inostrannykh del,* doc. 140.

76. Holquist, "The Politics and Practice of the Russian Occupation of Armenia," p. 158.

77. Those who indict the Germans include Artem Ohandjanian, *Armenien: Der Verschwiegene Völkermord* (Vienna: Böhlau, 1989); Christoph Dinker, "German Officers and the Armenian Genocide," *The Armenian Review* 44, no. 1 (1991): 77–133; and Vahakn Dadrian, *German Responsibility in the Armenian Genocide: A Review of the Historical Evidence of German Complicity,* foreword by Roger W. Smith (Watertown: Blue Crane, 1996). The most convincing case against German responsibility or participation (except in the single case of the officer Eberhard Wolffskeel von Reichenberg in Urfa) has been made by Hilmar Kaiser; see his "Germany and the Armenian Genocide: A Review Essay," *Journal of the Society for Armenian Studies* 8 (1995): 127–142; response by Dadrian, pp. 143–150; "Germany and the Armenian Genocide, Part II: Reply to Vahakn N. Dadrian's Response," ibid., 9 (1996, 1997, 1999): 135–140; response by Dadrian, pp. 141–148; idem, "The Baghdad Railway and the Armenian Genocide," pp. 67–112; and idem, "Historical Introduction," pp. xv–cxvi. See also Donald Bloxham, "Power Politics, Prejudice, Protest and Propaganda: A Reassessment of the

German Role in the Armenian Genocide of WWI," in Kieser and Schaller (eds.), *Der Völkermord an Den Armeniern und Die Shoah*, pp. 213–244. Older, classic accounts are given in Ulrich Trumpener, *Germany and the Armenian Persecutions, 1914–1918* (Beirut: Hamazgain, 1968), and idem, *Germany and the Ottoman Empire, 1914–1918* (Princeton, NJ: Princeton University Press, 1968). A singularly interesting treatment of the question can be found in Hull, *Absolute Destruction*, pp. 263–290.

78. Notes by Mordtmann, the consul general in the German embassy in Constantinople, Pera, PA-AA/BoKon/169; A53a, July 21, 1915; Gust (ed.), *The Armenian Genocide*, pp. 262-263.

79. Weitz, "Germany and the Young Turks," pp. 193–194; "Bericht von Dr. Jäckh über Konstantinopel und Dardanellen," October 17, 1915, PAAA/R13750.

80. Ibid., p. 189; Marschall to Bethmann-Hollweg, May 13, 1911, Constantinople, PAAA/R14160/A7812/Nr. 112, 16–17.

81. "From the Ambassador in Constantinople (Wangenheim) to the Imperial Chancellor (Bettman Hollweg), no. 453, Pera, 7 July 1915"; Gust (ed.), *The Armenian Genocide*, p. 230.

82. "Memorandum. Handed by the German Embassy in Pera to the Grand Vizier on 4./17.15"; Gust (ed.), *The Armenian Genocide*, p. 231.

83. Report from German Ambassador in Constantinople (Wangenheim) to the Imperial Chancellor (Bethmann Hollweg), No. 449, Pera, July 16, 1915, PA-AA/R14086; A 22101; pr. 23.07.1915 a.m.; Gust (ed.), *The Armenian Genocide*, pp. 256–257. A month later the embassy issued its second message to the Porte with "new warnings against these acts of violence and to renounce any responsibility for the consequences that could arise from them." The embassy was particularly upset that "public opinion tends to believe that Germany in its capacity as a friend and ally of Turkey approved of these acts of violence or even instigated them." "Memorandum" [to the Sublime Porte], Pera, August 9, 1915, enclosed in a report from the German ambassador in extraordinary mission in Constantinople (Hohenlohe-Langenburg) Pera, PA-AA/R14087, August 12, 1915; Gust (ed.), *The Armenian Genocide*, pp. 302–303.

84. Report from the German ambassador on extraordinary mission in Constantinople (Hohenlohe-Langenburg) to the Imperial chancellor (Bethmann Hollweg), No. 549, Pera, September 4, 1915; PA-AA/R14087; A26474; pr. 10.09.1915 a.m.; Gust (ed.), *The Armenian Genocide*, pp. 357–358.

85. Ibid., Pera, September 25, 1915, PA-AA/R14088; A 28578; pr. 02.10.1915 a.m.; Gust (ed.), *The Armenian Genocide*, pp. 380–381.

86. Hull, *Absolute Destruction*, p. 288; Stange to Military Mission, Erzerum, August 23, 1915; Lepsius, *Deutschland und Armenien*, Doc. 149; Dadrian, *German Responsibility*, pp. 61–62.

87. Memorandum on the Measures on Behalf of the Christians in Turkey, enclosed in a letter from German MP Matthias Erzberger to Legation Councillor in

the Foreign Office Rosenberg, Berlin, March 3, 1916; PA-AA; R14090, A 05914; pr. 04.03.1916; Gust (ed.), *The Armenian Genocide*, p. 562.

88. Report from the consul in Aleppo (Rössler) to the Imperial chancellor (Bethmann Hollweg), Aleppo, December 20, 1915; PA-AA; R14089; A 00468; pr. 06.01.1916 p.m.; Gust (ed.), *The Armenian Genocide*, pp. 496–498.

89. Weitz, "Germany and the Young Turks," p. 194; Metternich to Bethmann-Hollweg, on a journey from the Dardanelles to Constantinople, December 15, 1915, PAAA/R13750/A36980/No. 722, 65.

90. Report from the German ambassador in extraordinary mission in Constantinople (Wolff-Metternich) to the Imperial chancellor (Bethmann Hollweg), Pera, December 9, 1915; PA-AA; R14089; A 36583; pr. 18.12.1915 a.m.; Gust (ed.), *The Armenian Genocide*, pp. 493–494.

91. Ibid., No. 711, Pera, December 7, 1915; PA-AA; R14089; A 36184; pr. 15.12.1915 p.m.; Gust (ed.), *The Armenian Genocide*, pp. 490–493.

92. Ibid., No. 725, Pera, December 18, 1915; PA-AA; R14089; A 37207; pr. 25.12.1915 p.m.; Gust (ed.), *The Armenian Genocide*, pp. 494–495.

93. The views in this section have been influenced by the work of Eric Weitz and Margaret Lavinia Anderson and their remarks at the international conference "Not all Quiet on the Ottoman Fronts: Neglected Perspectives on a Global War, 1914–1918," Istanbul Bilgi University, April 11, 2014. See Weitz, "Germany and the Young Turks," pp. 175–198, 367–372; Anderson, "'Who Still Talked about the Extermination of the Armenians?'" pp. 199–217, 372–379.

94. Report from the German ambassador in extraordinary mission in Constantinople (Wolff-Metternich) to the Imperial chancellor (Bethmann Hollweg), Pera, December 7, 1915; with a note from Bethmann Hollweg, December 17, 1915; PA-AA; R14089; A 36184; pr. 15.12.1915; Gust (ed.), *The Armenian Genocide*, pp. 490–493.

95. Anderson, "Who Still Talked about the Extermination of the Armenians?" p. 209; "[Memorandum] March 9, 1916, PAA, NL Stresemann Bd. 158."

96. Weitz, "Germany and the Young Turks," p. 198; Kühlmann to Bethmann-Hollweg, Pera, date unknown, 1917, PAAA/R14162/A4660.

97. Telegraphic report from the charge d'affaires at the embassy in Constantinople to the German Foreign Office (Radowitz), Constantinople, November 13, 1916; PA-AA/BoKon174; A 30700; pr. 13.11.1916 p.m.; Gust (ed.), *The Armenian Genocide*, pp. 684–685; telegraphic report from the German ambassador in extraordinary mission in Constantinople (Kuehlmann) to the Foreign Office, Pera, November 17, 1916; PA-AA/R14094; A 31174; pr. 18.11.1916 a.m.; Gust (ed.), *The Armenian Genocide*, pp. 687–688.

98. Weitz, "Germany and the Young Turks," p. 195; press guideline quoted in Hull, *Absolute Destruction*, p. 284.

99. Morgenthau, *Ambassador Morgenthau's Story*, p. 236.

100. Ibid., pp. 236–238.

101. Ibid., p. 258; the characterization of Humann is from Hull, *Absolute Destruction*, p. 271.

102. Hull, *Absolute Destruction*, p. 278; Humann marginalium (dated June 15, 1915) to a telegram of the consular deputy in Mosul of June 10, 1915, BA-MA Freiburg, RM 40, nr. 456, p. 93; cited in Dinkel, "German Officers and the Armenian Genocide," p. 113.

103. Morgenthau, *Ambassador Morgenthau's Story*, p. 240.

104. Ibid., p. 246.

105. Ibid., p. 69.

106. In Morgenthau's account, the Germans played on these Turkish fears, and for the Young Turk leaders, particularly Enver, the German alliance was the only salvation for the empire. Ibid., pp. 111–112.

107. "Seeks Funds For Starving Armenia," *Detroit Free Press*, May 21, 1916, p. E4.

108. Anderson, "'Who Still Talked about the Extermination of the Armenians?'" p. 210; *The New York Times*, September 25, 1915, p. 3, cols. 3–4, reprinted in Richard D. Kloian (ed.), *The Armenian Genocide: News Accounts from the American Press: 1915–1922* (Berkeley: Anto, 1988), p. 36.

109. Anderson, "'Who Still Talked about the Extermination of the Armenians?'" pp. 210–214.

110. PA-AA; R14089; A 00972; pr. 11.01.1916 p.m.; Gust (ed.), *The Armenian Genocide*, pp. 527–528.

111. From the secretary of state of the German Foreign Office (Jagow) to the Legation in the Hague, Berlin, November 9, 1916; PA-AA/R14094; A34247; Gust (ed.), *The Armenian Genocide*, pp. 677–678.

112. Letter written June 30/July 13, 1915; Yeghiayan, *My Patriarchal Memoirs*, pp. 86–87.

113. As Peter Holquist has shown, the Russian move was not a "cynical act [but] had a far more complicated genealogy," building "on earlier measures by the Russian government throughout the nineteenth century for humanitarian intervention on behalf of Christian peoples of the Ottoman empire, as well as its decades-long insistence, in its efforts to codify the international law of war, that there existed 'laws of humanity.'" Holquist, "The Politics and Practice of the Russian Occupation of Armenia," p. 154; see also idem, "The Origins of 'Crimes against Humanity': The Russian Empire, International Law, and the Allies' 1915 Note on the Armenian Genocide' (in preparation).

114. Martin Gilbert, *Winston S. Churchill, III: 1914–1916: The Challenge of War* (Boston: Houghton Mifflin, 1971), p. 195; and *Companion*, III, Part 2, "May 1915–December 1916" (1973), pp. 1230–1231.

115. Dündar, *Crime of Numbers*, pp. 122–123; MAZC [*Meclis-Ayan Zabit Ceridesi* (Minutes of the Ottoman Senate)], 3, 1, 1, 26, September 28, 1915, pp. 419–420; 4, October 27, 1915, pp. 433–434; 28, October 11, 1915, p. 441; 3, 2, 1, 10, December 13, 1915, pp. 133–136.

116. Bedross Der Matossian, "The Taboo within the Taboo: The Fate of 'Armenian Capital' at the End of the Ottoman Empire," *European Journal of Turkish Studies* (2011): 8; Bayur, *Türk Inkilâb Tarihi, Cilt III*, p. 48.

117. Kévorkian, *The Armenian Genocide*, p. 595; Puzant Yeghiayan (ed.), *Atanayi Hayots Patmutyun* (Antelias, 1970), pp. 342–345; on the deportations from Adana, see also Barton, "Turkish Atrocities," p. 161; statement of Harriet J. Fischer, National Archives, Washington, DC, General Records of the American Commission to Negotiate Peace, Special Reports and Studies, Record Group 256, Inquiry Document 813; Üngör and Polatel, *Confiscation and Destruction*, pp. 111–112; BOA/DH.ŞFR 53/113, Interior Ministry to Adana, Bitlis, Aleppo, Erzurum, May 25, 1915.

118. Balakian, *Armenian Golgotha*, pp. 82–85.

119. Kévorkian, *The Armenian Genocide*, pp. 362–363.

120. Balakian, *Armenian Golgotha*, p. 139.

121. Yeghiayan, *My Patriarchal Memoirs*, p. 88.

122. On the deportations and massacres in Sivas province, see Kévorkian, *The Armenian Genocide*, pp. 429–466.

123. Leslie A. Davis, *The Slaughterhouse Province: An American Diplomat's Report on the Armenian Genocide, 1915–1917*, ed. Susan K. Blair (New Rochelle, NY: Aristide D. Caratzas, 1989). See also Sarafian (comp.), *United States Official Documents on the Armenian Genocide, III*.

124. Maria Jacobsen, *Diaries of a Danish Missionary: Harpoot, 1907–1919*, trans. Kristen Vind, ed. and intro. Ara Sarafian (Princeton, NJ: Gomidas, 2001), p. 8.

125. Riggs, *Days of Tragedy in Armenia*, pp. 3–7.

126. Jacobsen, *Diaries of a Danish Missionary*, p. 47.

127. Ibid., p. 72.

128. Ibid., pp. 73–74; Riggs, *Days of Tragedy in Armenia*, pp. 123–124.

129. Riggs, *Days of Tragedy in Armenia*, p. 46.

130. Ibid., p. 47.

131. Ibid., p. 49.

132. Ibid., p. 50.

133. Ibid., p. 85.

134. Ibid., p. 133.

135. Cited in Akçam, *The Young Turks' Crime Against Humanity*, pp. 200–201; *Takvim-i Vekayi*, no. 3540 (May 5, 1919), report of the trial's first session, April 27, 1919.

136. Jacobsen, *Diaries of a Danish Missionary*, pp. 77, 83.

137. Kaiser, "The Baghdad Railway and the Armenian Genocide," p. 75.

138. Letter from German Field Marshal Liman von to the chargé d'affaires in the embassy in Constantinople (Radowitz), Panderma, PA-AA/BoKon/174; A53a, 3351; R14094; A 31505, November 12, 1916; Gust (ed.), *The Armenian Genocide*, pp. 679–682.

139. Kaiser, "The Baghdad Railway and the Armenian Genocide," pp. 82–86, 89–90, 92–93.

140. See Armin T. Wegner, *Die Austreibung des armenischen Volkes in die Wüste* (Göttingen: Wallstein Verlag, 2010), and *Armin T. Wegner e gli Armeni in Anatolia, 1915: immagini e testimonianze/Armin T. Wegner and the Armenians in Anatolia, 1915: images and testimonies* (Milan: Guerini e Associati, 1996).

141. Report from German vice consul in Alexandretta (Hoffmann) to the consul in Aleppo (Rössler), Alexandretta, November 8, 1915, included in a report from Rössler to the German ambassador in extraordinary mission in Constantinople (Wolff-Metternich), Aleppo, PA-AA/R14090; A 02889, January 3, 1916; Gust (ed.), 503-522.

142. Information from the two Arab officers recently arrived in England from Kermanshah, via the Caucasus and examined by Sir Mark Sykes, September 25, 1916, attached to a communication from Le Colonel de La Panouse ; Attaché Militaire de France à Londres, au Général Joffre, Commandant en Chef des Armées françaises, London, September 30, 1916, in *The Armenian Genocide: Documentation, I*, p. 505.

143. Report by A. Bernau, an employee of the American Vacuum Oil Company, enclosed in a report from the consul in Aleppo (Rössler) to the Imperial chancellor (Bethmann Hollweg), Aleppo, September 20, 1916; PA-AA/; R14094; A 28162; pr. 17.10.1916 p.m.; Gust (ed.), *The Armenian Genocide*, pp. 650–656.

144. Ibid.

145. Raymond Kévorkian, "L'extermination des déportés arméniens ottomans dans les camps de concentration de Syrie et Mésopotamie (1915–1916): La deuxieme phase du genocide," *Revue d'histoire arménienne contemporaine* 2 (1996): 176–177.

146. Letter of unknown authorship to the German consul in Aleppo (Rössler), Aleppo, November 11, 1915, enclosed in a report from Rössler to the Reichskanzler (Bethmann Hollweg), Aleppo, PA-AA/R14089, November 16, 1915.

147. Otian, *Accursed Years*, p. 109.

148. Ibid., pp. 126, 129.

149. Armenocide, http://www.armenocide.de/armenocide/armgende.nsf/24599 fab3538b532c1257794007b610b/0edc5b479b8e0119c125691100037709!Open Document; report by Dr. Niepage, the German assistant master of a school in Aleppo, enclosed in a letter from R. von Chelius, real privy councillor and chamberlain, to

Kaiser Wilhelm II, Karlsruhe, August 5, 1916, enclosed in a letter from the German Secret Civil Cabinet of the Emperor (Valentini) to the Imperial chancellor (Bethmann Hollweg), Command Headquarters, PA-AA/R14093, September 10, 1916.

150. Ibid.; report by a German public official from the Baghdad Railway, enclosed in a letter from R. von Chelius, real privy councillor and chamberlain, to Kaiser Wilhelm II, Karlsruhe, August 5, 1916, enclosed in a letter from the German Secret Civil Cabinet of the Emperor (Valentini) to the Imperial chancellor (Bethmann Hollweg), Command Headquarters, PA-AA/R14093, September 10, 1916.

151. Aksakal, "The Ottoman Empire," p. 476; BOA/DH.I.UM 59–1/1–38, 15 July 1915.

152. Akçam, *The Young Turks' Crime Against Humanity*, p. 35; coded telegram, from the Ministry of the Interior's Directorate-General of Security to the governors of the provinces of Edirne, Erzurum, Adana, Ankara, Aydın, Bitlis, Basra, Bağdat, Beyrut, Hicaz, Halep (Aleppo), Hüdâvendigâr (Bursa), Diyarbakır, Suriye, Sivas, Trabzon, Kastamonu, Mamüretülaziz, Mosul, Van, and Yemen, and the provincial district governors of Urfa, İzmit, İçel, Niğde, Maraş, Bolu, Canik, Çatalca, [Dyer-i] Zor, Asir, Kudûs-ü Şerif (Jerusalem), Kale-yi Sultaniye, Menteşe, Teke, Medine-i Münevvere (Medina), Eskişehir, Kütahya, and Karahisâr-ı Sâhib, BOA/DH.ŞFR., no. 54-A/51, July 20, 1915.

153. Barton, "Turkish Atrocities," pp. 195–196; statement of Mr. and Mrs. Harlow and Mr. and Mrs. Birge, National Archives, Washington, DC, General Records of the American Commission to Negotiate Peace, Special Reports and Studies, Record Group 256, Inquiry Document 816.

154. Cited in Akçam, *The Young Turks' Crime Against Humanity*, p. 203; photograph of the document, p. 205; coded telegram from Interior Minister Talat to the province of Ankara, BOA/DH.ŞFR, no. 55/290, August 29, 1915.

155. Yeghiayan, *My Patriarchal Memoirs*, p. 102.

156. Ibid., p. 75.

157. Ibid., pp. 80–81.

158. Kévorkian, *The Armenian Genocide*, pp. 455–459.

159. Ibid., pp. 610–612.

160. From the American Consulate, Aleppo, Syria, to The Honorable Henry Morgenthau, American ambassador, Constantinople, Turkey, June 28, 1915, The Henry Morgenthau, Sr., Papers, Library of Congress, Manuscript Division, Reel 7.

161. Kévorkian, *The Armenian Genocide*, p. 964; A. Sahagian, *Heroic Urfa and its Armenians* (Beirut: 1955), pp. 810–812, 858, 966; Jernazian, *Judgment unto Truth*, p. 85.

162. Enclosure, "The Armenian Riots in Urfa," in the report from the German ambassador in extraordinary mission in Constantinople (Wolff-Metternich) to the Imperial chancellor (Bethmann Hollweg) from the Imperial consul in Aleppo [Rössler]

[November 8, 16, 1915], Pera, November 29, 1915, No. 701; PA-AA; R14089; A 35268; pr. 06.12.1915 p.m.; Gust (ed.), *The Armenian Genocide*, pp. 484–487.

163. On the Urfa resistance, see Kévorkian, *The Armenian Genocide*, pp. 613–620.

164. Akçam, *A Shameful Act*, p. 200; "Halep Valisi Celal'in Anıları," *Vakit*, December 12, 1918.

165. Sarafian (comp.), *United States Official Documents, III*, pp. 27–33; report from Leslie A. Davis, American consul in Harput, to Henry Morgenthau, American ambassador in Constantinople, Harput, December 30, 1915, U.S. State Department Record Group 59, 867.4016/269.

166. On conversion of Armenians to Islam in Anatolia, see "The forced conversion to Islam of the Armenians in Anatolia," notes by the consul general in Constantinople (Mordtmann), Pera, December 21, 1915; PA-AA; BoKon/172; A53a, 7250; Gust (ed.), *The Armenian Genocide*, pp. 501–503.

167. Dündar, *Crime of Numbers*, p. 110.

168. Gust (ed.), *The Armenian Genocide*, pp. 688–691; report from the German consul general in Smyrna (Spee) to the chargé d'affaires at the embassy in Constantinople (Radowitz), Smyrna, PA-AA; R14094, November 18, 1916.

169. Dündar, *Crime of Numbers*, p. 106.

170. Riggs, *Days of Tragedy in Armenia*, pp. 103–105.

171. Ibid., pp. 110–111. See also Kévorkian, *The Armenian Genocide*, pp. 421–422.

172. Dündar, *Crime of Numbers*, p. 93.

173. Ibid., p. 92; DH.ŞFR [*Dahliye Nezareti. Mebani Emiriye ve Hapishaneler Müteferrik* (Interior Ministry/Directorate of Public Buildings and Prisons, Miscellaneous)], 50.210 (March 9, 1915).

174. Dündar, *Crime of Numbers*, p. 93; DH.ŞFR 53.222.

175. Reported in a letter from Patriarch Zaven Yeghiayan to the bishop of Bulgaria, August 25/September 7, 1915; Yeghiayan, *My Patriarchal Memoirs*, pp. 93–94.

176. Cited in Yeghiayan, *My Patriarchal Memoirs*, p. 116.

177. Ibid., pp. 118–119.

178. Balakian, *Armenian Golgotha*, p. 146.

179. Report from German engineer Bastendorff to German consul in Aleppo (Rössler), Aleppo, December 18, 1915, included in a report from Rössler to the Imperial chancellor (Bethmann Hollweg), Aleppo, PA-AA/R14090, January 3, 1916; and a separate report from the German engineer Bastendorff to Consul Rössler, Aleppo, December 18, 1915, enclosure 2, PA-AA; R14090; A 02888, in Gust (ed.), *The Armenian Genocide*, pp. 525–527.

180. Akçam, *The Young Turks' Crime Against Humanity*, brings together a plethora of Talat's telegrams indicating his direction of the Genocide and his knowledge about what was occurring in the provinces; coded telegram from Minister of Interior

Talat to the province of Halep (Aleppo), BOA/DH.ŞFR., nr. 56/4, September 14, 1915; coded telegram from the Interior Ministry's directorate-general of security to the Office of the District Governor of Teke, BOA/DH.ŞFR., nr. 58/42, November 17, 1915.

181. Kévorkian, *The Armenian Genocide*, pp. 639–644. An evocative fictionalized account of Armenians and Americans in Aleppo during the Genocide can be found in Chris Bohjalian, *The Sandcastle Girls* (New York: Random House, 2012).

182. Akçam, *A Shameful Act*, pp. 4, 167, 185; "Halep Valisi Celal'in Anıları," *Vakit*, December 12, 1918.

183. Akçam, *The Young Turks' Crime Against Humanity*, p. 280; coded telegrams from Interior Minister Talat to the provincial district of Zor, BOA/DH.ŞFR, no. 66/19, July 19, 1916; no. 66/94, July 29, 1916.

184. Akçam, *The Young Turks' Crime Against Humanity*, p. 281.

185. Kévorkian, *The Armenian Genocide*, pp. 662–670. Salih Zeki later became a founder of the Turkish Communist Party.

186. Balakian, *Armenian Golgotha*, p. 148. Consul Rössler in Aleppo "learned on 20 April [1916] from a Turkish officer on his way from Der-el-Zor, [that] the Mutesarrif of Der-el-Zor has received the order only to leave as many Armenians there as correspond to 10% of the local population, but to send the rest on to Mosul. The local population of Der-el-Zor could be perhaps 20,000." Report from the consul in Aleppo (Rössler) to the Imperial chancellor (Bethmann Hollweg), Aleppo, April 27, 1916; PA-AA; R14091; A 12911; pr. 16.05.1916 p.m.; Gust (ed.), *The Armenian Genocide*, p. 581.

187. Letter from Sister Araxia Djebedjian to Sister Beatrice Rohner, Der-el-Zor, June 22, 1916, enclosed in a report from the German consul in Aleppo (Rössler) to the Imperial chancellor (Bethmann Hollweg), Aleppo, July 29, 1916; PA-AA; R14093; A 21969; pr. 18.08.1916 p.m.; Gust (ed.), *The Armenian Genocide*, p. 611.

188. Cited in Kévorkian, *The Armenian Genocide*, p. 646; telegram from Talat to Mustafa Abdülhalik, November 18 (December 1), 1915; APC/APJ, PCI Bureau, P54, p. 7.

189. Sarafian (comp.), *United States Official Documents, I,* pp. 119–120; report from Jesse B. Jackson, American consul in Aleppo, September 3, 1916, cited in a letter from Mrs. Jesse Jackson to Henry Morgenthau, American ambassador in Constantinople, Jackson, MI, October 13, 1916; U.S. State Department Record Group 59, 867.4016/298.

190. Akçam, *The Young Turks' Crime Against Humanity*, pp. xviii–xix.

CHAPTER TEN: Orphaned Nation

1. Üngör and Polatel, *Confiscation and Destruction*, p. 78; Murat Koraltürk, "Milliyetçi bir refleks: Yer adlarının Türkleştirilmesi," *Toplumsal Tarih* 19, no. 117 (2003): 98–99.

2. Arkun, "Zeytun and the Commencement of the Armenian Genocide," p. 239.

3. Üngör and Polatel, *Confiscation and Destruction*, p. 21; BOA.DH.ŞFR 59/239, Interior Ministry to all provinces, January 6, 1916; see also the telegrams in Akçam, *The Young Turks' Crime Against Humanity*; coded telegram from the Ministry of Interior's Office of Tribal and Immigrant Settlement to the provinces . . . , and to the chairmen of the Commissions on the Liquidation of [Abandoned Property] . . . , BOA/DH.ŞFR., nr. 59/239, January 6, 1916.

4. Letter from the head of the Home for the Blind in Malatia (Ernst Jacob Christoffel) to the consul general at the German embassy in Constantinople (Mordtmann), Sıvas, PA-AA/BoKon/100, April 1, 1916.

5. Report from the German ambassador in extraordinary mission in Constantinople (Wolff-Metternich) to the Imperial chancellor (Bethmann Hollweg), Pera, January 24, 1916; PA-AA; R14089A 02530; pt. 28.01.1916 a.m.; letter from Deacon Jakob Künzler to the German consul in Aleppo (Rössler), Urfa, January 17, 1916, enclosed in a report from Rössler to the Imperial chancellor (Bethmann Hollweg), Aleppo, January 31, 1916; PA-AA; R14090; A 04546; pt. 18.02.1916 p.m.; Gust (ed.), *The Armenian Genocide*, pp. 530–531, 538–540.

6. Telegrams from Akçam, *The Young Turks' Crime Against Humanity*; coded telegram from the Ministry of Interior's General Security Directorate to the provinces of Halep (Aleppo) and Adana, BOA/DH.ŞFR., nr. 63/259, May 9, 1916; coded telegram from the Ministry of Interior's Office of Tribal and Immigrant Settlement to the province of Mamuretülaziz, BOA/DH.ŞFR., nr. 63/283, May 11, 1916; coded telegram from the Ministry of Interior's Office of Tribal and Immigrant Settlement to the provinces . . . , BOA/DH.ŞFR., nr. 63/261, May 10, 1916; coded telegram from the Ministry of Interior's General Security Directorate to the provinces of Ankara, Hüdâvendigâr (Bursa), Konya, and Adana, and to the provincial Kütahya, İzmit, Karahisâr-ı Sâhib, and Niğde, BOA/DH.ŞFR., nr. 63/294, May 14, 1916; coded telegram from the Ministry of Interior's Office of Administrative Building and Hospital Management (Mabânî-i Emîriye [idari binalar] ve Hapishâneler İdâresi) to the provinces and provincial districts . . . , BOA/DH.ŞFR., nr. 64/18, May 14, 1916.

7. Report from the British Intelligence Service, Cairo, May 20, 1916, in Beylerian (ed.), *Les Grandes Puissances*, p. 206; Gaunt, *Massacres*, pp. 69–70.

8. Report from the administrator in Erzurum (Scheubner-Richter) to the Imperial chancellor (Bethmann Hollweg), currently in Munich, December 4, 1916; PA-AA; R14094; A 33457; pt. 08.12.1916 p.m.; Gust (ed.), *The Armenian Genocide*, pp. 691–695.

9. Kévorkian, *The Armenian Genocide*, p. 701; *Ikdam*, September 25, 1917.

10. Coded telegram from the Ministry of Interior's General Directorate of Security to the provinces of Sivas, Kastamonu, and Ankara, and the provincial district of Bolu, BOA/DH.ŞFR., nr. 72/62, January 21, 1917; Kévorkian, *The Armenian*

Genocide, pp. 1082–1085; published in full in the September 25, 1917, *Ikdam*; report from the German ambassador in extraordinary mission to Constantinople (Kuehlmann) to the Reichskanzler (Bethmann Hollweg), Pera, PA-AA/R14095, February 16, 1917.

11. Report from the German ambassador in extraordinary mission to Constantinople (Kuehlmann) to the Imperial chancellor (Bethmann Hollweg), Pera, PA-AA/R14095, February 24, 1917.

12. "It is not as clear whether Talaat Pasha will carry out the plan he has occasionally mentioned to give up the anti-Armenian policy of the former Cabinet, as is often assumed . . . . Nothing has as yet become known of any concrete results, while various news from the interior lead us to presume that the persecutions are still continuing, although not as extensively." Note by Mordtmann on July 23, 1917, on a letter from the head of the Central Office of Information for Foreign Countries (Jäckh) to the German ambassador in extraordinary mission in Constantinople (Kuehlmann), PA-AA/BoKon/174, April 19, 1917; see also telegraphic report from the German ambassador in Constantinople (Bernstorff) to the Foreign Office, Constantinople, PA-AA/R14100, May 23, 1918.

13. See Ronald Grigor Suny, *The Baku Commune, 1917–1918: Class and Nationality in the Russian Revolution* (Princeton, NJ: Princeton University Press, 1972).

14. The brutality by irregular forces and civilians, Muslim and Christian, that ensued as armies advanced and retreated in the Caucasus and Persia in the years 1915–1921 has been described by foreign observers. See, for example, Price, *War and Revolution in Asiatic Russia*; Sir Harry Luke, *More Moves on an Eastern Checkerboard* (London: L. Dickson & Thompson, 1935); "Antranik," *Blackwood's Magazine* 245, no. 1248 (October 1919); Alfred Rawlinson, *Adventures in the Near East* (London: A. Melrose, 1923).

15. *Ermeni komitelerinin emelleri ve ihtilal hareketleri: Meşrutiyetten önce ve sonar* (Istanbul: Matbaa-yı Âmire, 1916).

16. I am grateful to Fatma Müge Göçek for this information.

17. Report from the ambassador in Constantinople (Bernstorff) to the Reichskanzler (Hertling), Pera, PA-AA/R14098, November 16, 1917.

18. Talat Pasha, "Posthumous Memoirs of Talat Pasha," *Current History* 15, no. 1 (October 1921): 295.

19. Report by E. Neuner, enclosed in a letter from Maximilian Pfeiffer, member of the Reichstag, to the German Foreign Office, Berlin, PA-AA/R13200, February 22, 1918.

20. Fatma Müge Göçek, "Reading Genocide: Turkish Historiography on 1915," in Suny et al. (eds.), *A Question of Genocide*, p. 48.

21. Notes by the Foreign Office, Berlin, PA-AA/R14099, March 19, 1918.

22. Report from the German consul in Trabzon (Bergfeld) to the Reichskanzler (Hertling), Trabzon, PA-AA/R14104, September 1, 1918.

23. Üngör and Polatel, *Confiscation and Destruction*, p. 48; *Osmanlı Belgelerinde Ermeniler* (Ankara: Başbakanlık Devlet Arşivleri Genel Müdürlüğü, 1995), p. 182.

24. Erik J. Zürcher, "The Ottoman Empire and the Armistice of Moudhros," in *The Young Turk Legacy*, pp. 191–193.

25. Dadrian and Akçam, *Judgment at Istanbul*, p. 19; Lord Curzon's remark, March 8, 1919, in E. L. Woodward and R. Butler (eds.), *Documents on British Foreign Policy, Third Series, vol. 4 (1919–1939)* (London: His Majesty's Stationery Office, 1952), p. 57.

26. Notes by the legation councillor in the Foreign Office (Göppert), PA-AA/R14105; A 54420, December 26, 1918; Gust (ed.), *The Armenian Genocide*, pp. 761–762; letter from Göppert in the German Foreign Office to Johannes Lepsius, PA-AA: R14106; A 18715, June 28, 1919; Gust (ed.), *The Armenian Genocide*, pp. 762–763.

27. Dadrian and Akçam, *Judgment at Istanbul*, p. 24: "Turkish sources indicate that the escape was organized and facilitated by General Bronsart von Schellendorf, the 1914–1917 chief of the Ottoman General Staff"; see Cemal Kutay, *Talat Paşa'nın Gurbet Hatıraları*, 3 vols. (Istanbul: n.p., 1981), vol. III, p. 1103; Fethi Okyar, *Üç Devirde Bir Adam* (Istanbul: Tercüman, 1980), p. 251; Galib Vardar, *İttihad ve Terakki İçinde Dönenler*, ed. S. N. Tansu (Istanbul: Inkilâp, 1960), pp. 386–388; Kapitänleutnant Baltzer, "Das romantishe Ende der drei grossen Türken der Kriegszeit: Talaat, Enver und Dschemal Pascha. Eine Erinnerung an den 1. November 1918," *Orient-Rundschau* 15, no. 11 (November 10, 1933): 120–121.

28. Dadrian and Akçam, *Judgment at Istanbul*, pp. 24–25.

29. Erik J. Zürcher, *The Unionist Factor: The Role of the Committee of Union and Progress in the Turkish National Movement, 1905-1926* (Leiden: Brill, 1984), p. 73.

30. Balakian, *Armenian Golgotha*, pp. 416–417, 421–423, 426–427. On the Turkish press after the armistice, see Dadrian and Akçam, *Judgment at Istanbul*, pp. 23–33.

31. See Lerna Ekmekcioğlu, *When History Became Destiny: The Re-Making of Armenianness in Post-Ottoman Turkey* (forthcoming).

32. Dadrian and Akçam, *Judgment at Istanbul*, p. 46.

33. Ibid., pp. 65–66; *Morning Post*, February 13, 1919; Tarık Mümtaz Göztepe, *Osmanoğullarının Son Padişahı Vahideddin Mütareke Gayyasında* (Istanbul: Sebil, 1969), [no. 120], p. 38; Osman Selim Kocahanoğlu, *İttihat-Terakki'nin Sorgulanması ve Targılanması* (Istanbul: Temel, 1998), [no. 92], pp. 39–40; Gotthard Jäschke, "Beiträge zur Geschichte des Kampfes der Türkei um Ihre Unabhängigkeit," *Die Welt des Islams* 5, no. 102, n.s. (1958): 12.

34. Dadrian and Akçam, *Judgment at Istanbul*, pp. 35–37, 57–63, 66, 251–257. The transcripts of the trials were published in *Takvim-i Vekayi*, the official gazette of the

Ottoman Parliament, and have been transcribed into modern Turkish by Hayre-
tin Aydin as part of a project sponsored by the Hamburg Institute for Social Research. Ibid., p. 6. Other newspapers published information on trials not reported in
Takvim-i Vekayi. Ibid., pp. 200–250.

35. Levon Marashlian, "Finishing the Genocide: Cleansing Turkey of Armenian
Survivors, 1920–1923," in Hovannisian (ed.), *Remembrance and Denial,* pp. 117–118;
Gabriel Noradoungian, "Antip husher: Gabriel Efendi Noradoungiani, Nakhkin
Osmanian Artakin Gortsots Nakharar," *Baikar,* June 17, 1952.

36. Dadrian and Akçam, *Judgment at Istanbul,* p. 77, n. 134; FO 371/4173, 72536,
April 21, 1919, folio 355; verdict of the trial of Yozgat, April 8, 1919, *Takvim-ı Vekayi,*
no. 3617 (August 7, 1919): 2.

37. Dadrian and Akçam, *Judgment at Istanbul,* pp. 195–197.

38. Ibid., p. 280; *Takvim-ı Vekayi,* no. 3540 (April 12, 1919): 7.

39. Dadrian and Akçam, *Judgment at Istanbul,* p. 201.

40. Zürcher, *The Unionist Factor,* p. 48; see also his articles collected in Zürcher,
The Young Turk Legacy and Nation Building.

41. Translated and cited by Erik Jan Zürcher, "Renewal and Silence: Postwar
Unionist and Kemalist Rhetoric on the Armenian Genocide," in Suny et al. (eds.), *A
Question of Genocide,* p. 312.

42. Zürcher, *The Young Turk Legacy and Nation Building,* p. 48. Zürcher takes
issue with the influential view of Bernard Lewis that characterized the modern history of Turkey in the framework of modernization theory and the inevitable move
from traditional empire to modern nation-state. Ibid., pp. 41–53.

43. Zürcher, "Renewal and Silence," p. 312; Nimet Unan (ed.), *Atatürk'ün Söylev ve
Demeçleri, II (1906–1938)* (Ankara: Türk Tarih Kurumu, 1959), p. 12. The advances
in the past two decades in the understanding and historiography of the Armenian
Genocide are evident when one compares its treatment in Zürcher, *The Unionist Factor,* in which the topic is hardly discussed and largely limited to footnotes, and in
his *The Young Turk Legacy* and his article "Renewal and Silence," where the author
demonstrates the fundamental importance of the deportations and massacres in the
story of the final years of the empire.

44. Stanley Kerr, *The Lions of Marash: Personal Experiences with American Near
East Relief, 1919–1922* (New York: State University of New York Press, 1973). For
the catalogue of the Stanley Kerr archives, curated by Bedross Der Matoosian, go to
http://www.zoryaninstitute.org/pdf/Stanley%20Kerr%20Archives%20Catalogue
.pdf.

45. Zürcher, *The Unionist Factor,* p. 130.

46. There is a large literature on the taking of Izmir and the fire; one might begin
with the memoirs of the U.S. consul in the city, George Horton, *The Blight of Asia,*

An Account of the Systematic Extermination of Christian Populations by Mohammedans and of the Culpability of Certain Great Powers; with the True Story of the Burning of Smyrna (Indianapolis: The Bobbs-Merrill Company, 1926; London: Sterndale Classics and Taderon Press, 2003); Marjorie Housepian Dobkin, *Smyrna 1922: The Destruction of a City* (New York: Harcourt Brace Jovanovich, 1971; 2nd ed., Kent, Ohio: Kent State University Press, 1988); Martin Giles, *Paradise Lost: Smyrna 1922: The Destruction of Islam's City of Tolerance* (London: Sceptre; Hodder & Stoughton, 2008); Heath Lowry, "Turkish History: On Whose Sources Will it Be Based?: A Case Study on the Burning of Izmir," *Osmanlı Araştırmalı/Journal of Ottoman Studies* 9 (1988): 1–29.

47. Letter from the German Foreign Office to Johannes Lepsius, Berlin, PA-AA; R14106; A 18715, June 28, 1919; Gust (ed.), The Armenian Genocide, pp. 762–763.

48. Armenocide, http://www.armenocide.de/armenocide/armgende.nsf/24599 fab3538b532c1257794007b610b/d21dfd2a3ea26159c12568f30059b36e!Open Document; *New York Tribune*, "Another Chapter in Germany's Confession of Turkish Guilt," PA-AA/R14106, July 27, 1919. See also Wolfgang Gust, "Magical Square: Johannes Lepsius, Germany and Armenia," trans. Vera Draack, http://www.armenocide .de/armenocide/armgende.nsf/GuidesView/MagischesViereckEn?OpenDocument.

49. This is from Tehlirian's testimony; two witnesses said that he was behind Talat the whole time. *Armenian Political Trials, Proceedings, I: The Case of Sogholmon Tehlirian*, trans. Vartkes Yeghiayan (Los Angeles: A. R. F. Varantian Gomideh, 1985), pp. 21–22, 28–31.

50. Anderson, "Who Still Talked about the Extermination of the Armenians?" pp. 215–216; Ernst Jäckh, "Talaat," *Deutsche Politik* 14 (1921): 315; and *Der Goldene Pflug: Lebenserinerung eines Weltbürgers* (Stuttgart: Deutsche Verlags-Anstalt, 1954), pp. 221–222.

51. The principal sources for the story of Tehlirian's assassination of Talat are the trial record, *Armenian Political Trials, Proceedings, I: The Case of Sogholmon Tehlirian*, first published as *Der Prozess Talaat Pascha*, intro. Armin T. Wegner (Berlin, 1921); Tessa Hofmann (ed.), *Der Völkermord an den Armeniern vor Gericht: Der Prozess Talaat Pascha* (Göttingen, 1985); Derogy, *Resistance and Revenge*; and Rolf Hosfeld, *Operation Nemesis: Die Türkei, Deutschland und der Völkermord an den Armeniern* (Kiepenheurer & Witsch, 2009).

52. *Armenian Political Trials, Proceedings, I*, pp. 74–75.

53. Ibid., p. 81.

54. Ibid., p. 77.

55. Ibid., p. 80.

56. Ibid., p. 84.

57. Ibid., pp. 87–88.

58. Letter from the former German consul in Aleppo (Walter Rössler) from Eger to Johannes Lepsius, PA-AA/NL/Rössler/Vol.. 1, Private Correspondence, April 25, 1921; Gust (ed.), *The Armenian Genocide*, pp. 764–768. Rössler was particularly disturbed by Andonian's attacks on the Germans. Draft of a statement to the German Foreign Office by the former consul in Aleppo (Rössler), PA-AA/NL/Rössler/ Vol. 2, May 30, 1921; Gust (ed.), *The Armenian Genocide*, p. 768.

59. Brief from the secretary of state of the German Foreign Office (Haniel) to the defense attorney in the criminal proceedings against Teilirian (Gordon), Berlin, PA-AA/NL/Rössler/Vol. 2, June 2, 1921: Gust (ed.), *The Armenian Genocide*, pp. 768–769. The commissar of deportations was Şükrü Kaya, later minister of internal affairs in the Turkish Republic. I am grateful to Erik-Jan Zürcher for this information.

60. *Armenian Political Trials, Proceedings, I*, p. 148.

61. Ibid., p. 149.

62. Cited in Rolf Hosfeld, "The Armenian Massacre and Its Avengers: The Ramifications of the Assassination of Talaat Pasha in Berlin," *IP—Transatlantic Edition* (Fall 2005): 61.

63. Kevork D. Bardakjian, *Hitler and the Armenian Genocide* (Cambridge, MA: Zoryan, 1985); the original source for the quotation is Louis P. Lochner, *What About Germany?* (New York: Dodd, Mead, 1942), pp. 1–4.

64. Anderson, "Who Still Talked About the Extermination of the Armenians?" p. 217.

65. Edward Minassian, *Musa Dagh* (Cold River Studio, 2007); see also http:// www.imprescriptible.fr/archives/usa/articles/Minassian_40-Years-of-Musa-Dagh .pdf

CONCLUSION

1. The term "ethnocide" is here used synonymously with "genocide," but scholars also make an important and useful distinction that ethnocide is the destruction of a culture while genocide is the physical destruction of a people. See, for example, Pierre Clastres, "De l'ethnocide," *L'homme* 14, nos. 3–4 (1974): 101–110, who wrote, "If the term genocide recalls the idea of 'race' and the will to exterminate a racial minority, the term ethnocide gestures not toward the physical destruction of people . . . but towards the destruction of their culture. Ethnocide moves then toward the destruction of their culture. Ethnocide is the systematic destruction of modes of life and of thought of different peoples. . . . To sum up, genocide murders the bodies of peoples, ethnocide kills their spirit. In either case, it is always a question of death, but of a different kind of death" (p. 102; my translation). In my definition, genocide involves both the physical and the cultural extermination of a people.

2. Raphael Lemkin, *Axis Rule in Occupied Europe: Laws of Occupation, Analysis of Government Proposals for Redress* (Washington, DC, 1944), p. 79.

3. Naimark, *Fires of Hatred*, p. 12.

4. Carol Anderson, *Eyes Off the Prize: The United Nations and the African American Struggle for Human Rights, 1944–1955* (Cambridge: Cambridge University Press, 2003), pp. 180, 228–229. Lemkin tried to assure the opponents of the convention that lynching was not genocidal since "the basic policy of the South is not to destroy the Negro but to preserve that race on a different level of existence" (p. 228).

5. In a provocative synthesis elaborating why Stalin's crimes should be considered genocides, Norman Naimark claims, "Political and social groups become 'invented' nations." The argument about whether the Ukrainian killer famine was directed against peasants or Ukrainians in this sense misses the point that these categories blended so easily with each other. At the very best, Stalin was determined to destroy their culture and traditional way of life." *Stalin's Genocides* (Princeton, NJ: Princeton University Press, 2010), p. 29. By this extension, the enclosure movement in England and slum clearance can become genocide. Ultimately, the argument becomes circular: by changing the definition to include what you want to call genocide, that phenomenon then becomes genocide.

6. Dündar, *Crime of Numbers*, p. 3; see Murat Bardakçi, *Talat Paşa'nın Evrak-ı Metrukesi* (Istanbul: Everest, 2008).

7. Dündar, *Crime of Numbers*, p. 149.

8. Ibid., p. 150.

9. Ibid., pp. 150–151.

10. Akçam, *The Young Turks' Crime Against Humanity*, p. 258; Bardakçi, *Talat Paşa'nın Evrak-ı Metrukesi*, p. 109; Bryce and Toynbee (eds.), *The Treatment of Armenians in the Ottoman Empire*, p. 646; Lepsius, *Deutschland und Armenien*, p. lxv.

11. Kévorkian, *The Armenian Genocide*, pp. 265–278.

12. Ibid., p. 693.

13. On the conceptual difference between empire and nation-state, see Ronald Grigor Suny, "The Empire Strikes Out: Imperial Russia, 'National' Identity, and Theories of Empire," in *A State of Nations: Empire and Nation-Making in the Age of Lenin and Stalin*, ed. Ronald Grigor Suny and Terry Martin (Oxford: Oxford University Press, 2001), pp. 23–66.

14. Ziya Gökalp, "Kızıl elma," translation from Graham Charles Kinloch and Raj P. Mohan, *Genocide Approaches, Case Studies, and Responses* (New York: Algora, 2005), p. 50; cited in Jongerden, "Elite Encounters of a Violent Kind," p. 80.

15. Uday Singh Mehta in Fitzpatrick (ed.), *Liberal Imperialism in Europe*, p. 261.

16. Among those who have argued for contingency and the distinctiveness of the Genocide are Michael Mann, Norman Naimark, and Ronald Grigor Suny. See Suny, "Empire and Nation: Armenians, Turks, and the End of the Ottoman Empire," *The Armenian Forum* 1, no. 2 (1998): 17–51; critical responses by Vahakn N. Dadrian, Engin Deniz Akarlı, and Selim Deringil, with a reply by Suny, pp. 131–136. A similar

argument had been made earlier by Yves Ternon in a series of works: *Les Arméniens: Histoire d'un génocide* (Paris, 1977); *La cause arménienne* (Paris, 1983); with Gérard Chalian, *The Armenians From Genocide to Resistance*, trans. Tony Berrett (London, 1983) and *Le génocide des Arméniens* (Paris, 1984); and his own *Enquête sur la négation d'un genocide* (Marseilles, 1989).

17. For a review of these debates, see Ian Kershaw, *The Nazi Dictatorship: Problems and Perspectives of Interpretation*, 3rd ed. (London, 1993), pp. 80–107; and Geoff Eley's introductory essay to his edited volume, *The "Goldhagen Effect": History, Memory, Nazism—Facing the German Past* (Ann Arbor: University of Michigan Press, 2000), pp. 1–31. Intentionalists argue that genocide was part of a master plan intended by the principal actors, while structuralists (also referred to as functionalists) contend that genocide is a product of policies, practices, opportunities, and contingent choices made by individuals within a polity. The argument in this book is closer to a structuralist argument with emphasis on the emotional environment and cognitive beliefs of the principal actors that led them to choose genocide as a practical and acceptable policy to secure the empire.

18. In constructivist international relations theory securitization is an extreme version of politicization that enables the use of extraordinary means in the name of security. See Barry Buzan, Ole Wæver, and Jaap de Wilde, *Security: A New Framework for Analysis* (Boulder, CO: Lynne Rienner, 1998), p. 25; and Michael C. Williams, "Words, Images, Enemies: Securitization and International Politics," *International Studies Quarterly* 47 (2003): 512; Barry Buzan, *People, States and Fear: An Agenda for Security Studies in the Post-Cold War Era* (Hemel Hempstead: Harvester, 1983; 2nd ed., 1991).

19. Jongerden, "Elite Encounters of a Violent Kind," p. 72.

20. Reviewing six case studies by other authors that examine ethnic violence from Northern Ireland, India, Sudan, Rwanda, Sri Lanka, and the Balkans, James D. Fearon and David D. Laitin make this point graphically: "Indeed, based on these studies, one might conjecture that a necessary condition for sustained 'ethnic violence' is the availability of thugs (in most cases young men who are ill-educated, unemployed or underemployed, and from small towns) who can be mobilized by nationalist ideologues, who themselves, university educated would shy away from killing their neighbors with machetes." James D. Fearon and David D. Laitin, "Violence and the Social Construction of Ethnic Identity," *International Organization* 54, no. 4 (Autumn 2000): 845–877, p. 869.

21. Ibid., p. 871.

22. On the variety of killers, see Mann, *The Dark Side of Democracy*, pp. 26–29, 167–173, 212–278.

23. As Jan Elster notes, "Emotions, like desires and beliefs, are intentional: they are *about* something. They differ in this respect from other visceral feelings, such as pain, drowsiness, nausea, and vertigo." He goes on to say that "[e]motions tend to be

associated with specific action tendencies. Guilt induces tendencies to make repairs, to confess, or to punish oneself. The action tendency of shame is to disappear or to hide oneself, and in extreme cases to commit suicide. The action tendency of envy is to destroy the envied object or its possessor. Anger induces a tendency to harm the person who harms one. The action tendency of hatred is to make the object of the emotion disappear from the face of the earth." Jan Elster, *Strong Feelings: Emotion, Addiction, and Human Behavior* (Cambridge, MA: MIT Press, 2000), pp. 35, 38–39.

24. The historian Lewis B. Namier writes, "One would expect people to remember the past and imagine the future. But in fact, when discoursing or writing about history, they imagine it in terms of their own experience, and when trying to gauge the future they cite supposed analogies from the past: till by a double process of repetition, they imagine the past and remember the future." "Symmetry and Repetition," in L. B. Namier, *Conflicts: Studies in Contemporary History* (London: Macmillan, 1942), pp. 69–70. My thanks to Roy Foster for this quotation.

25. The term "delusional rationality" comes from Turkyilmaz, "Rethinking Genocide," who writes, "These 'rationalities' have no basis in reason, and yet become a powerful motor for killing on a mass scale" (p. 43).

26. The argument from state security was made repeatedly by the Young Turk leaders and was reproduced in the first major collection of materials issued by the Ottoman government on the Armenian deportations, Nezareti Dahiliye, *Ermeni Komitelerinin Amal Ve Harekat-ı Ihtilaliyesi* (Istanbul: Matbaa-i Amire, 1916).

27. For interpretations of the Genocide that are compatible, though not identical, with my own analysis, see, for example, the thoughtful essay by Stepan Astourian, "The Armenian Genocide: An Interpretation," *The History Teacher* 23, no. 2 (February 1990): 111–160; Mann, *The Dark Side of Democracy*; Levene, *Genocide in the Age of the Nation State*; Valentino, *Final Solutions*; and Bloxham, *The Great Game of Genocide*.

HISTORIANS LOOK AT THE ARMENIAN GENOCIDE:
A Bibliographical Discussion

1. Zürcher, *Turkey, A Modern History*, p. 121; for a Turkish critique, see Türkkaya Ataöv, *The Andonian "Documents" Attributed to Talat Pasha Are Forgeries!* (Ankara: Sistem Ofset, 1984).

2. Vahakn N. Dadrian, "The Naim-Andonian Documents on the World War I Destruction of the Ottoman Armenians: The Anatomy of a Genocide," *International Journal of Middle East Studies* 18 (August 1986): 311–360. In my view the provenance of the Andonian documents remains suspect, and I have not used them in this study.

3. Edward Minasian, "The Forty Years of Musa Dagh: The Film That Was Denied," *Journal of Armenian Studies* 3, nos. 1–2 (1986–1987): 121–131. On the

resonance of the novel, see Yair Auron, "The Forty Days of Musa Dagh: Its Impact on Jewish Youth in Palestine and Europe," in Hovannisian (ed.), *Remembrance and Denial*, pp. 147–164.

4. Lewis Thomas and Richard Frye, *The United States and Turkey and Iran* (Cambridge, MA: Harvard University Press, 1951). Lewis Thomas taught the Ottoman historian Stanford Shaw at Princeton, who in turn supervised the doctorates of Justin McCarthy and Heath Lowry at UCLA; Armenian and other historians have consigned all three to the denialist camp.

5. Esat Uras, *Tarihte Ermeniler ve Ermeni Meselesi* (Ankara: Yeni Matbaa, 1950; later translated as *The Armenians in History and the Armenian Question* [Istanbul: Documentary Publications, 1988]). Bloxham calls this work "the canonical text of Turkish nationalist historiography on the Armenians," though it contains "systematic misrepresentations and exaggerations of Armenian revolutionary activism." *The Great Game of Genocide*, p. 213.

6. Suny, "Looking Toward Ararat," in *Looking Toward Ararat*, pp. 213–230.

7. Peter Novick, *The Holocaust in American Life* (Boston: Houghton Mifflin, 1999), pp. 128–142. "Holocaust" had been used by *The New York Times* in the 1890s for the Hamidian massacres of the Armenians, as well as the Adana massacres of 1910. Duckett Z. Ferriman, *The Young Turks and the Truth About the Holocaust at Adana in Asia Minor, During April, 1909* (London, 1913).

8. The only historical journal dealing with Armenians available in English in the 1940s and 1950s was *The Armenian Review*, founded in 1948 by the Dashnak party. Early articles in the journal that dealt with the Genocide included those by H. Saro (1948), Onnig Mekhtarian (1949), Vahan Minakhorian (1955), Navasard Deyrmenjian (1961), Vahe A. Sarafian (1959), Ruben Der Minassian (1964), James H. Tashjian (1957, 1962), and H. Kazarian (Haikazun Ghazarian) (1965).

9. Richard G. Hovannisian, *The Armenian Holocaust: A Bibliography Relating to the Deportations, Massacres, and Dispersion of the Armenian People, 1915–1923* (Cambridge, MA: National Association for Armenian Studies and Research, 1978).

10. Yves Ternon, *Les Arméniens: Histoire d'un génocide* (Paris: Éditions de Seuil, 1977); *La cause arménienne* (Paris: Éditions de Seuil, 1983); with Gérard Chalian, *The Armenians From Genocide to Resistance*, trans. Tony Berrett (London: Zed, 1983) and *Le génocide des Arméniens* (Paris: Complexe, 1984); his own *Enquête sur la négation d'un genocide* (Marseilles: Éditions Parathèses, 1989); and *Mardin 1915: anatomie pathologique d'une destruction* (Paris: Centre d'Histoire Arménienne Contemporaine, 2002).

11. Novick, *The Holocaust in American Life*, p. 192.

12. Israel W. Charny and Shamai Davidson (eds.), *The Book of the International Conference on the Holocaust and Genocide: Book One: The Conference Program and*

Crisis (Tel Aviv: Institute on the International Conference on the Holocaust and Genocide, 1983).

13. *A Crime of Silence: The Armenian Genocide, The Permanent Peoples' Tribunal* (London: Zed, 1985), p. 227.

14. The work of Leo Kuper (1908–1994) was particularly important in defining the field of comparative genocide studies: *Genocide: Its Political Use in the 20th Century* (New Haven, CT: Yale University Press, 1981), and *The Prevention of Genocide* (New Haven, CT: Yale University Press, 1985). Among the important works of the late 1980s and early 1990s were Hovannisian (ed.), *The Armenian Genocide in Perspective* (New Brunswick, NJ: Transaction, 1986); idem, *The Armenian Genocide: History, Politics, Ethics* (New York: St. Martin's, 1992); and Melson, *Revolution and Genocide.*

15. Melson, "A Theoretical Enquiry into the Armenian Massacres of 1894–1986."

16. See, for example, Shaw and Shaw, *History of the Ottoman Empire and Modern Turkey*, vol. II, pp. 315–316; and Langer, *The Diplomacy of Imperialism*: vol. I, p. 160. On a particular passage by Langer, Norman Ravitch notes that Langer's "labelling of the Armenian movement as *national-socialist* can hardly be considered a slip of the pen." "The Armenian Catastrophe: Of History, Murder & Sin," *Encounter* 57, 6 (December 1981): 76, n. 16.

17. Excellent examples include Sarkissian, *History of the Armenian Question to 1885*; Davison, *Reform in the Ottoman Empire*; Braude and Lewis (eds.), *Christians and Jews in the Ottoman Empire*; and Hanioglu, *The Young Turks in Opposition* and *Preparation for a Revolution.*

18. Dadrian, *The History of the Armenian Genocide*; see also his *Warrant for Genocide.*

19. Balakian, *The Burning Tigris.* See the review by Belinda Cooper, *The New York Times Book Review*, October 19, 2003.

20. Lewis, *The Emergence of Modern Turkey.* Over time Lewis hardened his position. In 2007 he was quoted in an article opposing U.S. recognition of the Genocide in the conservative *Washington Times*: "[T]he point that was being made was that the massacre of the Armenians in the Ottoman Empire was the same as what happened to Jews in Nazi Germany and that is a downright falsehood. What happened to the Armenians was the result of a massive Armenian armed rebellion against the Turks, which began even before war broke out, and continued on a larger scale." Bruce Fein (identified as "resident scholar with the Turkish Coalition of America), "Armenian Crime Amnesia?" *The Washington Times*, October 16, 2007.

21. Hovannisian (ed.), *The Armenian Genocide in Perspective.* For the ongoing development of Genocide scholarship, see Hovannisian (ed.), *The Armenian Genocide*, and Hovannisian (ed.), *Remembrance and Denial.*

22. Astourian, "Testing World Systems Theory, Cilicia (1830s–1890s)."

23. Kévorkian, *The Armenian Genocide*; Gust (ed.), *The Armenian Genocide*.

24. Akçam, *Armenien und der Völkermord, From Empire to Republic, A Shameful Act, The Young Turks' Crime Against Humanity*, and with Dadrian, *Judgment at Istanbul*.

25. See, for example, Fuad Dündar, *İttihat ve Terakki'nin Müslümları İskan Politikası (1913–1918)* (Istanbul: İletşim, 2001); his dissertation, "L'Ingénierie ethnique du régime jeune-turc" (Paris: EHESS, 2006); and idem, *Crime of Numbers*. Using hundreds of Turkish memoirs to establish the undeniability of the Genocide, the historical sociologist Fatma Müge Göçek produced *Denial of Violence*.

26. On the process and results of WATS, see Suny, Göçek, and Naimark (eds.), *A Question of Genocide*, and Suny, "Truth in Telling."

27. Explicit comparisons between the Armenian Genocide and the Holocaust inform two important collections: Bartov and Mack (eds.), *In God's Name*, and Kieser and Schaller (eds.), *Der Völkermord an den Armeniern und die Shoah*.

28. Donald Bloxham, "The Armenian Genocide of 1915–16: Cumulative Radicalisation and the Development of a Destruction Policy," *Past and Present*, 181 (November 2003): 141–191; idem, *The Great Game of Genocide*; and idem, *Genocide, the World Wars and the Unweaving of Europe* (London: Valentine Mitchell, 2008).

29. Bloxham, *The Great Game of Genocide*, p. 19.

30. Mann, *The Dark Side of Democracy*.

INDEX

Please note: page numbers for entries occurring in figures are followed by an f and those for entries in notes by an n.

HUMAN RIGHTS AND CRIMES AGAINST HUMANITY

Eric D. Weitz, Series Editor